VOLTAIRE

VOLTAIRE.

Dessiné et Gravé par Aug. S. Aubin d'après le Buste fait par Houdon.

VOLTAIRE

By
C. E. VULLIAMY

Écrasez l'Infâme!

KENNIKAT PRESS
Port Washington, N. Y./London

PQ
2099
V8

VOLTAIRE

First published in 1930
Reissued in 1970 by Kennikat Press
Library of Congress Catalog Card No: 76-113328
ISBN 0-8046-1004-5

Manufactured by Taylor Publishing Company   Dallas, Texas

" *Talent unique, le plus rare en un siècle classique, le plus précieux de tous, puisqu'il consiste à se représenter les êtres, non pas à travers le voile grisâtre des phrases générales, mais en eux-mêmes, tels qu'ils sont dans la nature et dans l'histoire, avec leur couleur et leur forme sensibles, avec leur saillie et leur relief individuels, avec leurs accessoires et leurs alentours dans le temps et dans l'espace, un paysan à sa charrue, un quaker dans sa congrégation, un baron allemand dans son château, des Hollandais, des Anglais, des Espagnols, des Italiens, des Français chez eux, une grande dame, une intrigante, des provinciaux, des soldats, et le reste du pêle-mêle humain, à tous les degrés de l'escalier social, chacun en racourci et dans la lumière fuyante d'un éclair.*"—TAINE, " Les Origines de la France Contemporaine."

PREFACE

WHEN Voltaire gave his patriarchal blessing to the grandson of Benjamin Franklin, he placed his hand on the boy's head with the words *God and Liberty*. The hazy deism which he professed made it difficult to know what he had in mind when he spoke of God, but there was never any doubt as to what he meant by liberty. He stood, as he stands now, for the free exercise and development of the human mind, and for the right of men to walk in the path of reason.

The influence of this extraordinary man was due not only to his printed works but also to the possession of strongly marked personal qualities. By a terrible concentration of energy and purpose, indifferently used to gratify some trivial spite or to strike a ringing blow for truth and humanity, he stamped himself in no uncertain way upon the picture of his times.

His true meaning is best revealed by the examination of his life. It is often obscured by a critical study of his writings ; and for this reason it has seemed proper to adopt a frankly biographical method. Full use has been made throughout this book of Voltaire's own letters, which are in themselves autobiographical material of the highest value, and are certainly among the most daring, the most brilliant and the most vivid letters which have ever been published. In every case, the author is responsible for the translation of these letters, and of other original texts, most of which have not previously been rendered into English. In the transcription of Voltaire's English letters, the original orthography is retained.

Every recent source of information has been drawn upon, and every important edition of Voltaire consulted, in the preparation of the present volume. No one can attempt a biography of Voltaire without being profoundly indebted to the great work of Desnoiresterres and to the critical and philosophic analyses of Lanson and of John Morley.

CONTENTS

CHAPTER I

THE TROUBLESOME YOUTH

THE old painters, when they drew the portrait of some illustrious person, used to surround him by the scenes or appliances of his calling. If he was a man of action, the accessories were few and simple. Behind the soldier you would see the cloudy battlefield with a line of threatening pikes ; while the admiral would point with a careless and shapely hand to the lively cannonadoes of his ships of war.

But when the portrait was that of a man of letters or learning, the machinery of the picture was more complex and more detailed ; you had instruments and diagrams, books, globes, apparatus of strange and bewildering appearance, classic temples, fragments of antiquity, all the curious and varied paraphernalia of science (half magical) or things purely symbolic.

It is the same with biographical portraiture. Of the soldier, we need only know that he was lucky or unlucky, triumphant or routed, in his battles ; with the sailor it is all a matter of weather-gage and broadside ; and it is unlikely that we shall be called upon, in either case, to admire subtlety or brilliance of an intellectual kind. Not so when the subject of biography is a man who has won for himself no mere victory of arms, no fugitive renown, but a lasting place in human thought and experience. His life cannot be fully expressed in simple terms of action, or even in simple terms of achievement. We cannot deal with him by a summary or categorical method. The picture, it seems, will be terribly over-crowded with a profusion of unfamiliar symbols. Delineation, however adroit, is not enough ; form and

I

feature, dress and accessories, even the visible signs of performance, cannot give us the whole meaning of the man—perhaps, indeed, they can give us only a very small part of that meaning. In his words, if they are faithfully recorded, in his letters, if they are carefully transcribed, in his gesture and movement, and in the adventures of his life, we find the real man.

It cannot now be maintained that Voltaire made any supremely important contribution to poetry or history, to science or philosophy, to art, polemics or drama. Yet it may be questioned whether any man has exercised a more prodigious influence over the trend of thought in civilised Europe. That influence was, and still is, largely personal. When we think of him, we think less of the great mass of his writings (and probably no man has ever written more) than of the fierce and copious energies which drove him so eagerly now in one direction and now in another, but which gave such a vital impulse to his teaching of humanity and justice. We are strongly attracted, or strongly repelled, by the amazing, insistent personality of this strange man. We pass, with some bewilderment, from the dull proficiency of the *Henriade*, the fine yet formal rhetoric of the tragedies, the unequal brilliance of histories, odes, fantasies, epistles, every imaginable kind of literary excursion and experiment, slight or voluminous, flippant or profound, to the scalding vehemence of the ripe Voltairean satire, in dialogue, verse and fable. We glance, in dismay, at the ninety-seven volumes of the first Baudouin edition, and with wondering respect at the labours of Bengesco. Here, God wot, is energy enough—a flood of energy, without its like in literature.

But Voltaire himself is still unaccountable. We shall

come nearer to knowing him, probably, if we try to understand the facts of his life ; and above all, if we read some of the many letters in which he is so clearly and so delightfully revealed.

The letters have the value, and often the character, of autobiography. Voltaire had no repressions. He took no pains to conceal what he felt and thought. In his letters he has drawn his own portrait with astounding vivacity and candour. And here, rather than in his books or collections, we find him most vividly and immediately presented to our minds, with all his force and fire and all his wayward pettiness, his touchy pride and fevered jealousies ; all the meanness and the greatness, the gnawing malice and flaming generosity of his extraordinary nature.

In his own statements concerning his age and the date of his birth, Voltaire was not consistent. His baptismal certificate is dated the 22nd of November, 1694, and according to this document he was born on the previous day. The assertion that he was born on the 20th of February, 1694 (though repeated by Condorcet, who should have been well informed, and once or twice affirmed by Voltaire himself), seems to have been due to a misunderstanding, to an obscure personal motive, or to a failure of memory.

His father, François Arouet, was a notary and a minor official, who, in 1696, obtained the post of receiver in the Chamber of Accounts. He possessed the estimable but inconspicuous qualities of industry and ·probity. Voltaire's mother, Marguerite Daumart, was a gentlewoman, evidently gay and attractive, who received occasionally in the bourgeois salon of the Arouets people of rank and fashion. She had borne four other children, two of whom had died in infancy. François-Marie

3

(who became Voltaire) had a brother, Armand, and a sister, Marguerite Catherine.

It seemed likely that François-Marie would not live. He was a frail and sickly child, expeditiously christened so that he might not perish in a state of natural sin. Indeed, he did die of extreme debility, eighty-four years later.

From his childhood, François-Marie showed an aptitude for letters and a striking gift of originality. At the age of three he could repeat verses learnt by heart. But his juvenile performances, however remarkable, were a proof of aptitude rather than of genius, and were not yet of a kind to make his father uneasy.

Arouet was one of those plain, sensible men who regard the practice of art or letters with a sort of dismay, and who believe that a man should seek both profit and security in the routine of an honourable profession, or even in the service of the state. Madame Arouet, who may not have agreed with this view, died when her youngest child was seven years old. The father, who was able to afford the most expensive education for young François-Marie, sent him, three years later, to the fashionable college of Louis-le-Grand. To this Jesuit college, pert little gentlemen, with little swords dangling under their skirts, came to be taught the humanities, and to learn, if they could, the principles of elegance, of good taste, and consequently of religion.

At Louis-le-Grand, young Arouet acquired that liking for aristocratic manners and aristocratic society which, in later life, made him sometimes a dupe and sometimes a mere flatterer. But he acquired something of far greater value. He was given a first-rate literary education. He was taught Latin by Thoulier and rhetoric by Father Porée—a man of high learning and

4

of delightful character. As far as François-Marie was concerned, no better, no more fitting education could have been chosen for him. His attainments were doubtless equally gratifying to his father and his masters. He acquired an extraordinary facility in the making of verses ; a facility by no means uncommon at that period, and sedulously cultivated by those with pretensions to elegance. He worked hard, won many prizes, and the good Jesuits, while admiring his exercises, were " struck by the audacity of his thoughts and the independence of his opinions."

Clearly, François-Marie was destined to become a man of letters. That was the last thing his father wished him to become : he wanted to make him a man of the law, a magistrate. Verses, tragedies, odes ; it was not by giving his thoughts to such easy trifles that a man could earn the respect of worthy people or reach the solid honours of a good appointment.

Young Arouet, for his part, cared nothing for such honours, and was painfully indifferent to the worthy people. He was a born verbalist, a born writer. From his earliest years he felt the desire to be famous and fashionable. Writing was easy, when there was no need to write for a living ; and, with an assured fortune, philosophy and poetry might become the most agreeable of pastimes. An extreme " independence of opinion " might be safely indulged, with a good chance of attracting notice, and—happy thought !—of galling the envious and pleasing the great. The boy was vain, ambitious and sensitive. He felt, no doubt, something of that inferiority which is commonly felt by those who are physically weak and at the same time deeply conscious of intellectual vigour. The assertion of that vigour becomes a prime necessity.

5

He was anxious, moreover, to assert himself in another way. He found himself placed in the higher ranks of the bourgeoisie, received and recognised with a patronising approval by persons of quality, but often reminded of his true level. He did not forget that his mother, Marguerite Daumart, had come of a noble family. It was not enough, therefore, to prove superiority of intellect ; he would prove an equal superiority of birth and breeding.

And who was better fitted to launch the young man than his god-father, the naughty old Abbé de Chateau-neuf, the friend of Ninon de Lenclos, his lips readier with a jolly trol-de-rol than with text or homily ? The Abbé took his young god-son into the society of dukes and marquises—de Sully, de la Fare, the Abbé de Chaulieu, the Abbé Courtin. (He had introduced the boy, when he was thirteen, to Ninon herself, then in her eighty-fifth year, and still charming. She was mightily pleased with young Arouet, and left him a legacy of 2,000 livres, intended for the purchase of books.) More epigrams, more verses ; *Amulius and Numitor*, the fragment of a tragedy. Old Arouet had now some cause for alarm.

In 1712, the Academy offered a prize for the best ode appropriate for the building of the choir of Notre-Dame by Louis XIV. Here was a chance. Young Arouet, who, if he was never a poet, had an amazing facility for rhyming lines, lost no time in writing an ode which began

> " The King of kings, whose mighty voice
> Has thundered in this place . . . "

And the ode was sent to the poet Jean-Baptiste Rousseau, who was pleased to say that it had " a great deal of spirit." In 1714 the prize was duly awarded, not to young Arouet but to the Abbé Dujarry.

What !—a parasite, a poet by profession, a botcher of halting verses, a man who never wrote a good line or said a good thing in his life ! Arouet, his jangling pride roused to a pitch of angry dissonance, grinned with malice. In the same year, he produced two strangely nasty pieces—*Le Bourbier* (*The Swamp*), and *L'Anti-Giton*.

As time passed, the differences of opinion between François-Marie and his father led to a more or less complete estrangement. Nor should we too hastily condemn old Arouet. François-Marie was now approaching early manhood. He had no profession. He had only written a few poor trifles, and although he talked about tragedies he had not produced anything which could possibly be regarded as a work of genius. The precocity of his childhood, so it would seem, had meant nothing at all. A plague on de Chateauneuf !— turning the boy's head—what would be the end of it ? Instead of applying himself to the law, according to his father's wishes and the proper inclination of a worthy young fellow, there he was, giddy-gadding with a rout of licentious noblemen, jesting with impudent whores, and seeking by stale blasphemies to prove himself a man of wit.

He had been sent to the Hague, to live under the wing of the Ambassador (another de Chateauneuf) ; and there he had fallen in love with the pretty daughter of a terrible scandal-mongering mother, Madame Dunoyer—a dreadful creature who published a sort of gazette of infamy called the *Quintessence*. Informed of this by the mother herself, the Ambassador furiously sent him back to Paris.

7

The love-letters of François-Marie were duly published by Madame Dunoyer, and his father shut the door in his face. Then his friends intervened, and François-Marie was placed in the office of the attorney, Monsieur Alain. Vile drudgery ! lightened only by the gay companionship of Thiériot, an airy, scatter-brain dog, but not lacking in loyalty of a doggish kind.

Louis XIV, the last fine figure of a king, died on the 1st of September, 1715. His death was followed by a general declaration of grievances and a general freedom of speech and manners. The spirit of the old monarchy seemed to have died with the king ; and the people, quickly forgetting their devotion, quickly forgetting the royal splendour and the royal victories of Louis the Great, began to reckon the cost of splendours and victories, and to ask whether they had not good reason to complain of tyranny or indifference. Madame de Maintenon sought the obscurity of a voluntary exile. In spite of the good intentions, one might almost say the liberal policy, of the Regent (the Duke of Orleans), there was a widespread sense of uneasiness, not far removed, indeed, from actual mistrust. Gossips were busy ; satires, lampoons, innuendoes and open libels had a free circulation.

François-Marie, when the king died, was in his twenty-first year. He had been removed from the notary's office through the kindly intervention of M. de Caumartin, one of his father's friends, and spent much of his time with this amiable old man at the château of Saint-Ange near Fontainebleau.

De Caumartin lived in the past. His mind was stored with memories of the old kings of France ; he would talk with joy and a winning enthusiasm of their great deeds, and in particular of those of Henry IV.

It was not long before François-Marie, always captivated
by enthusiasm, conceived the idea of writing a poem,
a long poem, a poem to be hailed as the great national
epic, with an idealised Henry IV as the hero. This
poem was to be called *La Ligue, The League* ; it is better
known to us now by its later title—*La Henriade*. But
young Arouet did not foresee the peculiar and unfortunate circumstances in which a considerable part of
his epic was to be written.

De Caumartin introduced his young friend to the
elderly and debauched society of the Temple. Here
he met the most incredibly wicked, witty and perverted
old men, whose red, shining faces glowed in the steam
of the heated room like the multiple suns of a drunkard's
vision. All of them were cynics, voluptuaries, up-
roariously mocking virtue, authority, decency and
religion. Most of them were churchmen, spending in
a life of unrestrained indulgence the huge revenues
which they drew from abbey or benefice. The Prince
de Vendôme, Prior of France, and the Abbés Chaulieu
and Debussy were chief among the presiding demons
of the assembly. To them young François-Marie
wrote letters, partly in prose and partly in doggerel
verse. De Chaulieu was " the Anacreon of the Temple,
preaching pleasure . . . singing in praise of Tokay at
the table of the gods." Debussy, the " ornament of
the Church and of love," was exhorted to return to " the
dear city where Venus holds her court." To the Prince
de Vendôme he wishes good health and good wine.

No young man could have found himself in a more
depraved, a more distinguished or a more amusing
company. It must have been a rare sight when the
old de Chaulieu, his wig all awry, sung elegant obscenities
to his own accompaniment upon the lute. There must

9

have been a dreadful charm in the gay blasphemies of Courtin, a dreadful joy when all propriety was blown away by some terrific epigram.

Here, thought Arouet, was the true freedom of men of spirit. This was how to live, how to think. Here indeed were leisure and pleasure, wit and learning, and a noble exemption from the dull duties and duller responsibilities of the mere ordinary man. Here indeed was the " table of the gods." And we cannot blame him. He was flattered, and naturally so, at being thus admitted to the naughtiest, the most exclusive and most brilliant society in Paris. The Temple suppers, however orgiastic they may have been, were no ordinary revels. Wit flowed as freely as wine, and when the wine overcame the wit and the company sank in the gross depravities of drunkenness, the classic imagery was still there— the Abbé Anacreon, the Prior Silenus. It was the company that young Arouet would have chosen for himself, and in which he found easily his appropriate place. He was neither contaminated nor led astray. He was receiving what was, for him, the properest education. In the shameless and elegant profanities of these men, loudly flouting all things holy and venerable, he found themes exactly fitted to his own taste. He could not, or would not, drink ; but he could rhyme with the best of them. Both at the Temple and at the frivolous parties of the Duchess of Maine, he discovered his natural entertainment.

The elements of a great revolution were even then clearly assembling themselves. And it is curious to observe how those who would naturally be the first victims of a revolution were so active in preparing the way for it. By nourishing a cynical philosophy, by destroying the old power and dignity of the Church, by disregarding every kind of moral obligation or restraint, and above all by the arrogant assertion of the individual and of the right to entire freedom in speech or conduct, the French nobility were busy hammering nails into the coffin of those very institutions by which alone a privileged nobility could be maintained.

Voltaire himself, in whom the principles of aristocracy and of feudalism were deeply rooted, can never have realised that he was helping to set in motion those forces which were ultimately to sweep away the whole preposterous fabric. He did not see that the superstition of aristocracy was every whit as insecure as the superstition of religious faith. Could he have been a spectator of his own apotheosis in 1791, no one could have looked on that amazing scene with greater astonishment ; and he would probably have said, that here was an instance of that grim play of determinism which compels every man, whether consciously or not, to serve the general purpose.

François-Marie had the strange confidence of the egoist. He seemed to think it unlikely that any one could be really angry with him ; he could not see that his own words might expose him to inconvenience, if not to danger. It appeared to him quite reasonable to print verses about the Regent, in which he said that " his Messaline of a daughter was no better than a whore." The wretched indecency of such a thing never came into his mind. He was surprised to find that the police, who had been watching him with some interest, took a very different view of the case.

On the 4th of May, 1716, an order from His Royal Highness banished François-Marie to Sully-sur-Loire, " where he had certain relations whose advice and example might correct his indiscretion and moderate

11

his vivacity." For such a scurrilous and mean offence, the punishment was not severe.

After his return to Saint-Ange he was visited by a police agent or spy, whose name was Beauregard. The spy knew his man, and found it easy enough to make young Arouet abuse the Regent, slander Madame de Berry, and through sheer vanity claim the authorship of some Latin verses beginning with the words *Regnante puero*—another sorry lampoon. The conversation with Beauregard took place early in May, 1717, and on the 16th day of the month François-Marie was conducted to the Bastille.

Here, although Beauregard was able to cite witnesses, François-Marie denied everything with placid effrontery. He even made the amusing, though refutable, suggestion that *Regnante puero* was written in the time of Catherine de' Medici. In later life, he never hesitated to repudiate his own work, or to ascribe it to some other writer, real or imaginary, whenever it suited his purpose to do so. He used to say, afterwards, that he had been arrested as the author of a satire (*J'ai vu*) written and circulated in 1715 by Le Brun ; a statement heedlessly repeated by many of his biographers. The report of his examination at the Bastille makes it sufficiently clear that such was not the case. François-Marie was detained for eleven months in the prison.

He was not idle. The energies of his mind, so often misled by spite or vanity, but which made him ultimately such a tremendous force, kept him incessantly occupied. His tragedy of *Oedipus*, begun some years previously, was revised and rewritten in the Bastille, and the national epic of the *League* was continued within the walls of the national prison. By way of lighter exercise, he wrote a silly poem on his adventure.

On the 10th of April, 1718, the king, who was then eight years old, sent a note to the governor of the Bastille, " on the advice of my uncle the Duke of Orleans," telling him to release François-Marie Arouet. He was, however, to be exiled to his father's country house at Châtenay by Sceaux. Exile of this kind was the ordinary sequel to imprisonment.

From Châtenay, on Good Friday, the 15th of April, 1718, he wrote a curious letter to d'Argenson, the Lieutenant of Police :

" Sir, allow me to make the first use of my liberty by writing to thank you for having procured it. I can only exhibit my gratitude by proving my conduct worthy of this favour and of your protection. I think I have profited by my misfortunes, and I venture to assure you that I am not less obliged to His Highness the Regent for my liberty than I am for my imprisonment. I have been guilty of many faults ; but I beg you, Sir, to assure His Royal Highness that I am neither so wicked nor so stupid as to have wrote against him. I have never spoke of this Prince but to admire his genius, and I would have done the same had he been any ordinary man. My respect for him has always been the more profound since I know that he hates praise fully as much as he deserves it. Although you resemble him in this, I cannot forbear from congratulating myself on having fallen into your hands, and from telling you that your merit ensures the happiness of my life.

" I am, with the highest Respect and Gratitude,
" Your most humble most obliged Servant,
AROUET."

Is this mere effrontery ? We can hardly believe in

13

the sincerity of these protestations, and yet we should
like to think that Arouet's gratitude was not wholly
affected. At the same time, we cannot suppose (as
Condorcet does) that he was set free because there
was no longer any doubt of his " innocence." The
fact that his offences were clear never prevented Voltaire
from declaring himself quite incapable of such offences,
and from assuring his victims that he had always regarded
them with the highest esteem. He never allowed himself to be troubled by so slight a thing as the apparent
contradiction between what he said and what he did.
He had all the dreadful advantages of egoism ; and it
was this which made it difficult for any honest man to
get him in a corner.

It was about this time (1718) that François-Marie
Arouet assumed publicly the name of Voltaire. Arouet
was a poor sort of name for a gentleman, and even worse
for a poet. Think of it below the title of a tragedy !
It would never do. Arouet de Voltaire, on the other
hand, looked well enough ; and was not Voltaire (or
something like it) the name of a family estate ?
Monsieur de Voltaire began to cut a figure in the world :
old Arouet grumbled over his accounts.

Oedipus was now being prepared for the stage. Permission to visit Paris for twenty-four hours was granted
on the 19th of May ; another permission, this time for
eight days, was obtained on the 11th of July ; and
another, for a whole month, is dated the 8th of
August.

The tragedy was first performed on the 18th of
November, 1718. Dismayed by the fitting austerity
of the piece, the players had demanded a love scene.
Without such a scene, they said, no play had a ghost of
a chance. Voltaire, whose taste was infinitely better

than that of the players, had been forced to include a dreary romantic episode, with characters about as true and lifelike as the gilded cupids upon a mirror.

We are now, perhaps, inclined to look upon a Voltairean tragedy as we should look upon some old piece of carefully made and admirably ingenious clock-work. It is very clever ; but we have no desire to wind it up and set it going. The literary museum is full of such pieces. They are essentially the relics of a period, of taste or fashion ; we find it a little hard to realise the excitement of those who first saw them, or to appreciate the fulsome praises which were showered upon the inventors. But to the audience of 1718 *Oedipus* represented a supreme theatrical achievement. Here, they said, was a man worthy to be compared with Racine and Corneille, if he was not positively greater than either of them. In some ways, indeed, he was quite as good as Sophocles. Barely twenty-four years old—clearly a marvellous youth.

And if we turn to the last scene of the last act, we find something like this :

THE HIGH PRIEST

Good folk, a happy calm dispels the storm ;
Behold, serene, the sun above your heads ;
Contagious fires no longer shine around ;
Your tombs, late opened, now are clos'd again ;
Death hurries hence ; the god of heav'n and earth
Makes known his goodness by the thunder's voice.
                (Here thunder is heard and lightning seen.)

JOCASTA

What flashes ! Heaven ! Where am I ? What means this ?
Barbarians ! . . .

15

THE HIGH PRIEST
It is done. The gods relent.
Laius, from death return'd, no more pursues ;
He grants to thee to live, and yet to reign ;
The blood of Oedipus hath quench'd his rage.
CHORUS
Ye gods !

That is how the machinery works at a moment of high emotional tension. To us, the lines are painfully artificial, and the whole scene appears to lack device or character. We are more interested in those lines which foreshadow the real Voltairean philosophy :

" Our priests are not what folk would vainly think ;
'Tis our Credulity makes all their Power.

. . . .

Ah wretched Virtue ! sterile, fatal word
Whose dreary rule hath govern'd hateful days."

The tragedy had a run of forty-five performances: a success almost without parallel on any European stage. Pamphlets, praising or decrying it, were quickly printed and quickly sold. Jean-Baptiste Rousseau spoke of the play with generous enthusiasm : he compared it with that of Sophocles, and " was compelled to admit that the Frenchman of twenty-four was in many respects victorious over the Greek of eighty." His Highness the Prince de Conti deigned to address a long and flattering poem to the new Racine. La Motte, the stage censor, was equally enthusiastic. Nor was the social triumph of Voltaire less gratifying than the public triumph of his work.

During the first representation of *Oedipus*, the high priest was followed on the stage by a pert, ridiculous young man bearing his train. The beautiful Marquise de Villars turned to her friends. " Who is that queer fellow, who is doing his best to ruin the whole performance ? " " That, Madam, is the author." She was amused by what seemed to her an exhibition of striking originality, and desired to make the acquaintance of so odd a creature. Thus began Voltaire's romantic friendship with Madame de Villars and with her husband, the elderly, dull but famous Marshal.

That he was deeply and desperately in love with Madame de Villars, or that he was capable of being deeply and desperately in love with any one, is highly improbable. He was never the man for a serious passion. With the one possible exception of Madame du Châtelet, it is doubtful whether he had ever a real and lasting fondness for any woman. He was, in his youth, a libertine, a gallant, but not a lover in the nobler sense of the word. He could make no sacrifice ; he could offer no tenderness, no consideration, none of those pretty displays of sentiment to which a true passion may give so high a value. Nor would he run the danger of the least interference with his personal freedom.

Madame la Maréchale de Villars had no intention of allowing Voltaire to become her lover ; not because of any scruples, but because it pleased her better to flirt with him. She gave him, none the less, a real friendship, and even a certain measure of affection. He spent many days at the great château of Villars ; and there he was always a very entertaining and a very welcome guest.

For some three years, or more, Arouet de Voltaire led the life of an elegant vagabond, passing from one great country house to another ; a flighty, a most diverting fellow, telling pretty ladies the names of the

17

stars, and showing them how to spy the planets with their opera glasses, or writing verses for them ; making little essays in natural science ; always fashionable, always in demand, and flitting easily among the most illustrious companies. After all, he was himself illustrious : had he not written the finest tragedy in the French language ? And so the great folk of Sully or Villars or Richelieu were glad enough to see the lean, lively figure of Monsieur de Voltaire, the author of *Oedipus*.

But the great national epic was now laid aside. François-Marie, though he contemplated a new tragedy, found himself curiously disinclined for work. According to him, this was due to his " unhappy passion " for Madame de Villars. It is much more likely that he was merely talking about this affair in order to have his name associated with that of the Maréchale. He was at this time, and had been for two or three years, on terms of close intimacy with Madame de Mimeure.

When he visited Paris, he found life full of vexations and troubles. There was a most unpleasing money transaction, and a scandalous brawl with Poisson of the Comédie-Française. Threats of the law on the one side and a cudgelling on the other. The gallant companies of the châteaux, and occasional retirement to some luxurious retreat, were greatly to be preferred. But never could this tempestuous man find peace. His eager mind, like a flame, was in perpetual and responsive movement, searching for all the mysteries, all the knowledge and all the experience of life. No man was more fiercely anxious to obtain happiness, and none was more incapable of securing it.

Early in 1719, he writes to Madame de Mimeure : " We cannot overcome destiny : I was confident,

Madam, that I should not quit the delightful solitude in which I find myself [at Bruel] unless to go to Sully; but the Duke and Duchess of Sully have gone to Villars, and here am I, willy-nilly, obliged to seek 'em there. They must needs run me to earth in my hermitage and pray me to go to Villars ; but they shan't make me lose my repose there. I now wear a philosopher's mantle, which I would not cast aside for anything in the world." And again, later : " It seems to me that I am not at all made for the passions. 'Tis something ridiculous in me to love, and even more so in those who would love me. So there it is : I renounce it for my life." And then, later still : " I am now at Villars : I spend my time in wandering from castle to castle. . . . Our poem [the *Henriade*] makes but little progress."

In the course of these wanderings, the tragedy of *Artémire* was composed, and it was played on the 15th of February, 1720. The triumph of *Oedipus* was not repeated. On the contrary, the tragedy fell flat. It ran for eight nights with difficulty, viewed by a rather bored audience, and was then withdrawn. And yet the Abbé Debussy had been moved to tears by a reading, and Voltaire's coterie had predicted a brilliant success.

Meanwhile, the great national poem, the *Henriade*, though not complete, was already becoming famous. Thiériot was busy circulating manuscript copies of the parts which were already finished, and as the poem grew it seemed more and more assured of a splendid reception.

In 1721 we find Voltaire drifting again from one château to another, and passing his time agreeably enough. From Villars, in June, he wrote a letter to the amiable savant Fontenelle, partly in verse and partly in prose. The ladies at Villars were spending the summer evenings in the park or in " delicious gardens," naming the stars and searching the sky for Venus or Mercury. And they had noted a curious phenomenon :

" As we spend our nights in observing the Stars, we have much neglected the Sun, to whom we only pay our respects when he has covered nigh two-thirds of his course. We have but now learned that all this morning he was of a blood red colour ; and afterwards, tho' the sky was not obscured by any cloud, he was sensibly diminished both in size and brilliance; we have only heard this news at five in the afternoon. Putting our heads out of the window, we have mistook the Sun for the Moon, so pale was he. We doubt not that you have seen the same thing at Paris."

On New Year's Day, 1722, Voltaire's father died, leaving his office to the Jansenist brother Armand, and to his younger son a comfortable income. But the management of the patrimony gave rise to increasingly bitter disputes between the brothers.

Already, at the age of twenty-seven, Voltaire was talking incessantly of his ill-health. He was in the clutches of Monsieur Vinache, a quack doctor with a fashionable clientele. According to himself, indeed, he was never well at any period of his life. Yet nothing could impair the diabolical energy of this strange invalid. The impact of his colliding personality was like the impact of some explosive force, provoking his enemies to fury and violence. He was always in movement : writing, wandering, flirting, fretting, devising new works and revising old ones, quickly repairing any cracks in the fabric of his self-esteem, and ready to spring forward on the moment to any fresh encounter.

At this time (1722) he wrote many letters to Madame

de Bernières—Madame la Présidente. She was a handsome and fashionable woman, not unduly severe, but not wholly frivolous. Voltaire was probably her lover ; but here, as in other instances, the fact is not clear and the question is of little or no importance. Being a lover seems usually to have been a matter of little or no importance to Voltaire himself. To Madame de Bernières he wrote from Villars towards the end of May, 1722 :

" I stay for seven or eight days at Villars, where I drink cider and eat rice every evening, which does me a world of good. . . . I am distress'd by the treatment they have accorded to little Livry [an actress dismissed from the Comédie]. If the like treatment were applied to other bodies, methinks few would hold their places. I am reforming my poem in much the same manner, for I am occupied in chasing the bad verses out of it. 'Tis a somewhat long operation, but I hope to finish it at Rivière-Bourdet. I congratulate you upon the dissipated life you are leading. I wish indeed that I could do the same ; but with a head and health so ridiculous, I cannot have a greater consolation than the kindness with which you have lighten'd my cure by your society in *Paris*. Be assured that I shall remember all my life the proofs which I have received of your friendship, and that I shall be ever most tenderly devoted to you."

In June, or early in July, he received a letter from the Marshal de Villars ; a friendly, bluff and cheerful letter, in which the old soldier gives the poet some good advice and the renewed assurance of a welcome at Villars.

" If you'll take my word for it," he says, " you won't

abandon yourself to Vinache, although his seductive lectures, the art of uniting the influence of the seven planets with the minerals and the seven noble parts of the body . . . are truly admirable." And then a kindly prescription : " Come you here and eat good dishes at regular hours, take but four meals a day, retire in good time, see neither pen nor paper, neither biribi nor lansquenet ; I'll allow you tric-trac. Two months of this regime are worth more than Vinache.— A thousand thanks for your news. The marquis [his son] has seen the theatre clos'd with sorrow, and has thereupon resolv'd to go back to his regiment ; my post-chaise, which will take him to Paris on Saturday, shall bring you here again on Sunday." The letter closes with a customary touch of simple pride : " We have at present a fine and numerous company, since we are twenty-two at table ; but many of them are leaving to-morrow."

It seems probable that Voltaire, in spite of his alleged " unhappy passion " for the Maréchale, was never more at his ease, never more petted or more pleasantly occupied, than when he stayed at Villars ; and he stayed there often.

A very disturbing and sordid affair took place in the summer of 1722. It will be remembered that Voltaire had been committed to the Bastille on the information of a spy named Beauregard. One day at Versailles, the spy and the poet met face to face. That was too much. Without addressing himself directly to Beauregard, the poet was heard to mutter angrily about " spies," " dishonest rogues " and so forth ; and then, turning to Le Blanc, the Minister for War, he delivered himself of an unforgivable speech : " I knew well that spies were paid, but I never knew their reward was to eat at the Minister's table." This was a foolish affront to the Minister, however richly he may have deserved it, and a public insult which Beauregard at once resolved to wipe out. A few days later, Voltaire's chair was stopped on the Pont de Sèvres, Voltaire was forced to alight, and cruelly beaten.

To beat an ordinary poet was a matter of no consequence, but to beat Voltaire was to let loose the devil at one's heels. A warrant for the arrest of Captain Beauregard was at once issued : the wretched creature fled to his regiment. He could not thus escape the poet's revenge.

Whether he was righting his own wrongs or those of another, Voltaire set about his work with a terrible fixity of purpose. He was implacable, tenacious, unswerving in pursuit. Time was of no account, money was of no account, energy was of no account : revenge was everything. The pursuit of Beauregard became " the great affair." Sometimes he conducted the pursuit in person, sometimes by means of his powerful friends. Whatever his other concerns and occupations, the " great affair " was never out of his mind for long. Beauregard was pursued relentlessly for more than a year, his protector Le Blanc was banished, and at last he was run to earth and clapped into the prison of the Châtelet. And so the sorry business came to an end ; and if Beauregard deserved the prison, it is certainly a question whether Voltaire did not deserve his beating.

In July, 1722, the poet (as he was then called) set out for the Low Countries with Madame de Rupelmonde.

This new companion was the daughter of the Marshal d'Aligre, and was the lively widow of a rich Fleming. She affected philosophy, loved good verses, cared nothing for gossip, and behaved in all respects like a woman of quality, without being a fool. It would seem that she was travelling to the Hague on her own business, and, as she was not pressed for time, she invited Voltaire to " accompany " her.

No proposal could have been more to his liking. For him, mere beauty in a woman was never enough ; but here was beauty most happily allied with spirit, fancy and understanding. His own superior conversation would be appreciated ; and what more delightful than to travel with a handsome woman who could thus flatter him so agreeably and in so many ways ? His one condition was a halt at Brussels, where he might embrace the other great poet, Jean-Baptiste Rousseau.

But the first halt was at Cambrai, where the Cardinal Dubois occupied, by no means worthily, the former episcopal chair of Fénelon. Here the travellers found " all the ambassadors and all the cooks of Europe " assembled for a grand congress. And here, after a little intrigue on Voltaire's part, *Oedipus* was played in the presence of the author, followed by the *Oedipus Travestied* of Dominique. So pleasing was the poet's reception at Cambrai, so gracious the attention of the nobility, so fine the suppers, so ingenious and varied the entertainment, that the poet and the lady stayed there for something over six weeks. On the 10th of September, Voltaire wrote to friend Thiériot : " I am actually at Cambrai, where I am infinitely better received than ever I have been in Paris. If this continues, I shall assuredly renounce my country, unless you promise to love me always."

Then to Brussels, the poet and the lady discussing ethics, philosophy and religion as the chaise jolted them along on the stony roads. Out of these conversations grew the poem of the *Epistle to Julia* (or *Urania*)—

an open attack on every kind of dogmatic faith, and a statement of truculent deism. François-Marie addresses himself to his God in these assuring terms :

" I am no Christian : 'tis to love thee more."

At Brussels came the long-desired meeting with Rousseau. The two poets embraced each other with appropriate effusions ; but, as Crouslé well observes, " sparks flew at the first encounter." In the course of a few days, the French Horace and the French Sophocles were aware of a mutual hostility. Voltaire read aloud the *Epistle to Julia*, and Rousseau was profoundly shocked. Such an attitude was not surprising on the part of a man who had written sacred odes, and who professed a warm attachment to the Catholic faith. Then Rousseau, for his part, read an *Ode to Posterity*. " It seems to me, Sir, 'twill scarce reach the address," said François-Marie. After that came the turn of the *Henriade*. It was wrong, said Rousseau, to fly out against the Holy Church and the Pope and the government in what was meant to be an epic poem ; such a poem should be written in the style of Virgil and not in that of Juvenal. Jean-Baptiste presented Arouet with his own poem, *The Judgment of Pluto*. Such offences are not readily forgiven. Horace and Sophocles parted angrily and were never reconciled.

Voltaire and Madame de Rupelmonde went on to the Hague, where arrangements were made for the publication of the *Henriade*. Here, on the 10th of October, Voltaire wrote to Madame de Bernières :

" Your letter has brought a fresh delight to the life I am leading at the Hague. Of all the pleasures in the

25

world I know of none more flattering than the assurance
of your friendship. I shall remain yet a few days at
the Hague in order to take all the necessary steps for
the printing of my poem, and I shall set forth when the
fair weather has come to an end. There is no place
more agreeable than the Hague when the sun deigns
to show himself. One sees nothing but fields, canals
and green trees : 'tis an earthly paradise from the Hague
to Amsterdam. I have gazed with respect upon this
town, which is the storehouse of the Universe. There
were more than one thousand vessels in the port. . . .
At the Hague, there is greater magnificence, and more
high society for the congress of ambassadors. I spend
my time betwixt labour and pleasure, by turns a Dutch-
man and a Frenchman. We have a detestable Opera
here ; but, against that, I see Calvinist ministers,
Armenians, Socinians, Rabbis and Anabaptists who all
speak marvellously well, and who are truly all in the
right."

That Voltaire, while openly travelling with Madame
de Rupelmonde, should have carried on a free and
friendly correspondence with another woman, whom
all the world believed to be his mistress, is a fact worth
noting.

Soon after his return to France and after he had
quitted Madame de Rupelmonde, Voltaire spent a day
at La Source with Bolingbroke.

This remarkable Englishman was a friend after the
poet's own heart.

Henry St.-John, Viscount Bolingbroke, then in his
forty-fourth year, had never allowed any scruples to
interfere either with pleasure or with ambition. Orthodoxy in any form appeared to him ridiculous, and

loyalty a mask for interest. He had been Secretary for War and a friend of Marlborough, but his known sympathy with the Jacobite cause had led to his dismissal by George I. After his disgrace, he retired to France, a country for which he felt a great affection and which he had often visited. In 1717 he formed an intimacy with the Marquise de Villette, and married her, after the death of his wife, in 1720. He acquired the property of La Source, near Orleans, rebuilt the house and laid out the grounds with admirable taste in the English manner.

His posthumous works, published by Mallet in 1754, were described by Boswell as "wild and pernicious ravings," and the author was thus pompously denounced by Johnson : "Sir, he was a scoundrel and a coward : a scoundrel for charging a blunderbuss against religion and morality ; a coward because he had not resolution to fire it off himself, but left half-a-crown to a beggarly Scotchman, to draw the trigger after his death."

Writing of a later visit to La Source, in a letter to Thiériot dated the 2nd of January, 1723, Voltaire speaks of Bolingbroke with marked enthusiasm :

"I have found in this illustrious Englishman all the erudition of his country and all the politeness of our own. I have never heard our language spoke with greater justness or vigour. This man, who has been plunged all his life in pleasures and in the affairs of State, has none the less been able to learn all, to remember all. He knows the History of the Ancient Egyptians as he knows that of England. He has Virgil as well as Milton; he loves French, English and Italian Poetry; but he loves them differently, because he discerns perfectly the different Genius of each. After the portrait which I

27

have made of Milord Bolingbroke, it would ill become me, perhaps, to tell you that both he and Madame de Villette have been infinitely pleased with my poem. In their enthusiasm and approval they place it above all the poetical works which have appeared in France ; but I know how to discount such extravagant praises."

It has been suggested that Bolingbroke had a certain influence on the opinions of Voltaire, but nothing seems more improbable. As a writer, Bolingbroke was negligible, in spite of his undoubted powers of oratory. If he thought freely, he thought vaguely, and his own views amounted to little more than a pale deism. Voltaire liked him because he was a distinguished man living in the glamour of exile ; and he liked him even more because he praised the *Henriade*.

Late in 1722, or perhaps early in 1723, came a rude shock. The government refused to allow the publication of the great national poem. The agreement with the Dutch printer had to be cancelled, the money returned to the subscribers, the pretty vignettes and fleurons laid aside. But Voltaire, who could never be turned from any of his designs, resolved to have the work secretly printed at Rouen. The printing of the poem (or rather, of the greater part of it) was accordingly supervised by that willing friend, Thiériot, and it was ready for distribution in June, 1723, under its earlier title of *The League*. From Rouen, copies of the book were ingeniously smuggled to Paris. The mystery of the publication and the exciting reputation of the author would have been enough to sell any number of copies, and the great national epic had an immediate success. *Oedipus* had been proclaimed the work of a new Sophocles ; *The League* was proclaimed the work of a new Virgil. And now the applause, loud as it was, has died away and left no echo : tragedy and epic are rarely taken from the shelves, unless to receive the kindly attentions of a duster.

In this year (1723), Piron, who thought himself, and who probably was, as good a poet as Voltaire, produced the farce of *Harlequin-Deucalion*, which contained an amusing parody of the hapless *Artémire*. Such mockery was little to the taste of the new Virgil.

Piron is said to have met Voltaire in Madame de Mimeure's apartment, where the author of *The League* was stretching his legs in front of a good fire. In reply to the boisterous greeting of Piron, the other bowed stiffly, but kept silence. Piron dragged an arm-chair to the fireside, or as near as he could get to it, and attempted a conversation. The attempt failed. There they sat ; Piron with his fat round face full of bewilderment ; Arouet haughtily silent ; both staring at the fire, or taking an occasional pinch of snuff. At last the new Virgil thrust a hand into his pocket, drew out of it a large crust, and began to eat, with a noisy movement of his lean jaws. To this surprising gesture Piron made a fitting and equally unexpected reply. From his own pocket he produced a flagon of burgundy, which he drained without pausing. " Sir," said the new Virgil drily, " I can relish a jest as well as another man ; but your jest, if it is one, is very ill timed." He explained that what he did was a matter of regime: he had lately recovered from an illness which left him with a continual hunger. " Eat, Sir," replied Piron; " you do well. For my part, I have come from Burgundy with a continual thirst, and so I drink." The other condescended to smile faintly, rose, and left the room.

In November, 1723, while a guest at the château of

Maisons, Voltaire fell sick of what was then a terrible and deadly scourge : the small-pox. In Paris, the death-rate was appalling ; no precautions availed, the plague spread rapidly, and the one chance of safety lay in flight. Probably Voltaire had carried the infection with him from Paris, for the Marquis de Maisons felt indisposed on the 4th of November, but recovered.

Writing to the Baron de Breteuil in December, Voltaire describes his illness with a profusion of medical details. He " waited for death " with tranquillity, but regretting that he had not been able to give a final polish to the *Henriade* (he contemplated another edition) and to his new tragedy of *Mariamne*, and that he was obliged so soon to say good-bye to his friends. He drank, in the course of his disorder, " two hundred pints of lemonade." But the small-pox, he said, if unattended by complications, was " a purifying of the blood agreeable to nature, which, clearing the body of its impurities, prepares it for vigorous health." On the 1st of December, he was sufficiently well to leave Maisons for Paris.

The tragedy of *Mariamne* was played at the Comédie-Française on the 6th of May, 1724. It was received by the more assertive part of the house with impatience, amusement, or even hostility. When the poor heroine raised the cup of poison to her lips, some wretched wag cried out " The queen drinks ! " and the rest of the play could not be heard for tittering and laughter. This disturbance, which naturally had the effect of damning the whole piece, may have been due to a cabal against the author, who had many enemies. The tragedy is certainly as good as *Oedipus*, if not better, and was afterwards revived with success.

In August, Voltaire was at Forges with the Duke of

Richelieu, drinking the waters, and meeting a brilliant
company. The cure was by no means to his taste.
" There is more vitriol in a single bottle of Forges water
than in a whole bottle of ink, and I don't believe that
ink is particularly good for the health." But the
company made amends. Here he met Madame de
Prie, the avowed mistress of the Duke of Burgundy.
It was always a part of his diplomacy to win the support
of women who were in positions of power, and it was
not long before he was the friend of Madame de Prie.
During his visit to Forges, he wrote the little comedy
of *The Indiscreet*; a light, easy and amusing piece of
small consequence.

Returning from the waters, he sought retirement in
the town house of Madame de Bernières in the Rue de
Beaune. He was installed in the apartment of the
marquise herself, and there he hoped to work in a friendly
solitude. He was now concerned with a more complete
edition of the *Henriade*. But he could not have come
to a place less capable of providing the quiet he so greatly
desired.

The infernal racket of the street below his windows
drove him crazy. All day and all night, so it seemed,
there was a clattering of drays, rumbling of coaches,
creaking of barrows, tramping and shouting. He wrote
in desperation to Thiériot :

" I find myself in a cruel position, truly ; for be sure
that I have no wish to quit Madame de Bernières ;
and yet 'tis impossible for me to live in her damn'd
house, which is cold as the pole in winter, stinks of dung
like a stable, and where there is more noise than in Hell
itself. . . . I don't know what this will lead to ; what
I do know is that 'tis absolutely necessary for me to

finish my poem ; for that I must find some quiet corner; and in the house of the Rue de Beaune I can do nought save write descriptions of barrows and coaches."

He worried himself into what was called a " tertian fever." Yet, in the following month, he had rented a room in the same house, to be shared with Thiériot.

The friendship of Madame de Prie was soon put to the test. In December, 1724, the Abbé Desfontaines had been arrested on a charge of sodomy and had been taken to the Châtelet. On the 25th of April in the following year he was removed to the prison of La Bicêtre. He was now in danger of a terrible death, for he had been accused of that very offence for which Deschauffours, two years later, was burnt alive.

Desfontaines was a mean scribbler, a man of conspicuously evil manners, flagrantly debauched, and, as the event proved, incapable either of loyalty or of gratitude.

Voltaire, though he scarcely knew the man, undertook his defence. Why he should have done so is not clear. The writings of Desfontaines did not entitle him to consideration as a man of letters, his character was deplorable, his friends—if he had any—were like unto himself. As the law stood, there could be no question of the legality of the arrest or of the subsequent proceedings. Voltaire must have engaged himself to defend this wretched creature on principle. If we ask ourselves what that principle could have been, we shall find it, possibly, in some way connected with the question of the right to punish ; and we are not likely to be mistaken if we see, in this case, one of the first manifestations of Voltaire's generous humanity. Certainly there was no renown to be won by undertaking such a defence in such an age.

As a result of the poet's intercession with Madame de Prie, Desfontaines was released on the 30th of May, 1725, but forbidden to come within thirty leagues of Paris. On the 7th of June, a second *lettre de cachet*, unquestionably due to the continued intercession of Voltaire, allowed him to return.

It is said that Desfontaines was occupied on a pamphlet against Voltaire while still in prison. Later, he attacked the man to whom he probably owed his life with the utmost bitterness, and there was open warfare between the two. Writing to Thiériot from England four years afterwards, Voltaire applied to the Abbé an Italian word which is quite untranslatable, and in 1735 he confessed to de Cideville that he regretted his kindness.

At the close of 1725, Voltaire appeared to be in a singularly happy position. He was thirty-one years old, with the reputation of being the first poet of the age. The king and the queen had each granted him a pension. To the young queen, Marie Leczinska, he was " her poor Voltaire," and she had cried over *Mariamne* and laughed at *The Indiscreet*. Madame de Prie had taken him under her wing ; and the French court, usually ruled by a woman, was then ruled by Madame de Prie. Villars, Richelieu, Sully and the Cardinal Dubois were to be reckoned among his friends. He talked gallantly, smiling but always observant, to the gay beauties of Fontainebleau, to amiable noblemen or dapper courtiers. He may have been feared : he was certainly petted. But he was not content. His ambitions were perpetually in advance of his achievement, his vanity was insatiable, he was always planning or desiring some new triumph;

33

every kind of enterprise found room within his capacious egoism.

And now came a series of events which, though springing from a trivial cause, were to have a profound influence upon the whole course of his life.

The Chevalier de Rohan, or Rohan-Chabot, whose only distinction seems to have been the fortuitous one of descent from a noble family, met Voltaire at the Opera. He may have been annoyed by something too self-assured in the bearing of François-Marie, who, after all, was only a poet. Of the words and scenes that followed we have different accounts, but there can be no question as to the gist of de Rohan's insult : " Ah, yes !—Monsieur Arouet—Monsieur de Voltaire—I have forgot : what do you call yourself ? " Voltaire replied smartly, that he knew at least how to honour his name. And then we have a vague story of another meeting at the Comédie-Française, of the one fingering his cane and the other his sword, and of Mademoiselle Lecouvreur, the actress, discreetly fainting.

If that was all, it was a foolish affair which a sensible man would have quickly forgotten. But there may have been a more deadly sting in the retort : another version, indeed, would make us believe that such was the case. Or perhaps de Rohan would have considered any answer an impertinence. However that may be, he decided upon a method of revenge which, disgraceful as it now seems to us, was then by no means uncommon.

Two or three days later, as Voltaire was dining with the Duke de Sully, he was told that a person in the street desired to speak to him. A carriage stood at some distance from the door. As he approached this carriage,

two men seized him by his coat and belaboured him
with cudgels. From the door of another coach, which
was drawn up not far behind the first, the brave Chevalier
de Rohan appeared, and, in his own words, " gave orders
to the workmen."

Voltaire, in a pitiable state, ran back to the company.
That he was able to do so at all, frail as he was, proves
that the cudgelling was not of the severest kind. He
claimed, with passionate vehemence, the help of his old
friend de Sully. But the duke was unmoved. The
family of the Rohans was one of the most powerful in
France, and de Sully may well have thought twice before
risking their displeasure. Pale and furious, Voltaire
left the house and hurried to the Opera, where he knew
that he would find Madame de Prie. Madame, who
was above any fear of the Rohans, listened with real
compassion. But the Duke of Burgundy, who could
have dealt harshly with the offender, regarded the affair
as a matter of little consequence. To censure a Rohan
for beating a mere poet would have been too absurd—
de Sully had seen that clearly enough, and he was right
to refrain from meddling in the sorry business.

Some of the poet's friends thought otherwise. The
poet himself certainly thought otherwise. He gave
himself blindly and fiercely to the idea of revenge. He
was no swordsman, but now he began grimly to learn
all the tricks of the rapier. According to a police report
he associated with guardsmen, with bullies, and other
bad company : he was nourishing evil designs, and
preparing for " a combat."

The Rohans were seriously alarmed. The police
were vigilant. On the 28th of March, 1726, the
minister Maurepas sent a preliminary note to Hérault,
the chief of police, advising him of the king's order for

the removal of Voltaire to the Bastille. This order did not immediately come into effect, and in the meantime Voltaire seems to have challenged de Rohan, though precisely how and when is not clear. What is certain is that during the night of the 17th of April, the police agents Haymier and Tapin arrested " Arouet de Voltaire, the famous poet," and conducted him, by order of the king, to the famous prison. On the day following the arrest, Hérault informed Maurepas of the execution of the order, and noted that the foolish and wicked young man had provided himself with pocket pistols. " The family," said Hérault, " having learnt of this, have unanimously applauded the wisdom of an order which prevents this young man from committing some folly, and spares the honest folk of whom this family is compos'd from sharing in his confusion."

Whatever the family may have thought (and they were probably glad to see the wild poet laid by the heels), the arrest was not generally popular. " I am sorry for this poor Voltaire," said Madame de Prie ; " after all, he was in the right." De Villars, in his *Memoirs*, observes with good sense and fairness that " the publick, always ready to blame, found on this occasion, and with reason, that everybody was in the wrong—Voltaire for having insulted the Chevalier de Rohan ; the Chevalier for having dared, by beating a citizen, to commit a crime deserving death ; the government for not having punished an evil deed, and for having clapped the beaten man into the Bastille in order to set at ease the assailant."

But a sour priest, whose name we do not know, was mightily pleased, and saw fit to write a letter of congratulations to Hérault :

" You have just placed in the Bastille a man I have

been wishing to see there for these fifteen years. 'Tis now some ten or twelve years since, being at Saint-Sulpice for the purpose of seeing the Abbé d'Albert, I complained to him of the business of the man in question, preaching Deism openly in the dressing-rooms of our young Noblemen ; I could have ask'd for power but for one day, I told him, so that I might have clapped this poet between four walls for the rest of his life. . . . I may be excus'd for not giving you my name . . . one may justly fear those who dare to attack even Jesus Christ, the only Son of the Almighty."

Voltaire was not treated like a common prisoner. He dined with the governor, de Launay (the father of that unfortunate man who was governor in 1789), and was allowed to see some of his friends. He wrote to Maurepas and to Hérault, complaining, not without dignity, of his situation, and asking for banishment to England.

An order for his release from the Bastille was delivered to the governor on the 2nd or 3rd of May by a police officer named Condé, who was to escort Voltaire to Calais, and there to see him safely shipped for England. The order had actually been signed on the 23rd of April.

The poet wrote in haste to Madame de Bernières for the loan of her chaise, and on the 5th he was at Calais. Within a week of that date he had arrived in England.

His friends were relieved by what appeared to them to be the end of a dangerous adventure ; but François-Marie, however willingly he may have departed, still nursed a burning resentment, and still meditated revenge on the infamous de Rohan.

CHAPTER II

ENGLISH HOSPITALITY

NOTHING is more pleasing to Englishmen than to hear their country praised by a foreigner. Such praise is, or seems to be, an impartial testimony to the merit of that country, and a grateful confirmation of the fact that it is, indeed, greatly superior to any other country in the world.

There are, no doubt, many folk in this privileged country to whom Voltaire's one virtue is his affection for England and for the English people. He had good reasons for gratitude. He was handsomely entertained, equally free to choose between gaiety and retirement, able to move about with no fear of spies, and at liberty to write without danger of interruption. But we must remember that he was an angry man when he left France. He was tingling with a sense of bitter injustice, unable to digest the ignominy to which he had been subjected, and ready enough to find in some other country the haven of all his hopes.

The exile (for so he would certainly have described himself) landed on a bright spring afternoon. When he saw the green lawns of Greenwich, the sparkling river, the shining sails of the merchantmen, the king's golden barge, the crowds of young girls in their pretty flowered calicoes, the trim young men seated upon their sleek nags, the rural sports, and all the light joy of an English holiday, he was full of a happy admiration, full of excitement ; and, hearing that " gladiators " were to be seen in town, he at once " believed himself to be among the ancient Romans."

Bolingbroke had returned to England, and was now

living either in his town house in Pall Mall or in his country house at Dawley near Uxbridge. He received his friend Voltaire with eager hospitality, and it is probable that the poet spent his first evening in Pall Mall. At any rate, he met some court ladies, who listened coldly to his enthusiastic description of Greenwich. They took tea, rattled their fans, played quadrille, read the *Gazette*, or chattered about their neighbours.

We lack the material for a continuous narrative of Voltaire's life during the three years which followed. We have to draw largely upon his own correspondence, always amusing and brilliant, but not always exact in matters of place or date. And the letters dating from this period amount, in all, to little more than fifty. It seems clear, however, that the period of the exile to England was a period of comparative tranquillity, immensely fruitful in literary work, and having a corresponding, though not a profound influence upon the teaching, writing and thinking of one who had not yet shown the peculiar force and character of his genius. It was essentially a period of retirement, the one moderately serene period in the whole of his life, marked by continued or increased energy and by healthy mental development, but not by extravagance or passion. Yet he found it impossible to adjust himself easily to this new and pleasing environment. He was obsessed, even now, by the importunate desire for revenge. Before he had been in England for many weeks, he was back again in Paris, moving furtively, and avoiding all his friends. His intention, it seems, was to meet de Rohan.

Of this curious episode we have little knowledge. After a few dark and restless days in Paris, hiding and watching, he withdrew to some country place, from which, giving no address, he wrote a remarkably interesting and profoundly melancholy letter to Thiériot :

" My dear Thiériot, I have received, though much delayed, a letter from you dated the 11th of last May. You have seen my extreme misery in *Paris*. The same Destiny follows me everywhere. If the character of the hero of my poem is as well sustain'd as that of my ill fortune, my poem will assuredly succeed better than I have. You have bestowed upon me in your letter such touching assurances of your friendship that 'tis only just I should repay you by my confidence. I'll confess, then, my dear Thiériot, that I have paid a little visit to *Paris* not long ago. Since I did not see you there, you will readily conclude that I saw no one. I sought but one man, whose poltroon instinct concealed him from me, as though he had discovered that I was upon his tracks. At length, the fear of being discover'd compelled me to fly with greater haste than I had shown in arriving. So now 'tis done, my dear Thiériot ; it looks mightily as tho' I shall never in my life see you again. I am yet quite undecided whether I shall return to *London*. I know 'tis a country where all the arts are honoured and rewarded, where there is a difference of rank, but none other save that of merit. 'Tis a country where men think freely and nobly, without being hampered by any servile fear. If I followed my inclination, 'tis there I would fix myself, with the one idea of learning how to think. But I know not whether my little fortune, sadly broke by so many journeys, my ill health, more derang'd than ever, and my desire for complete retirement, will allow me to throw myself into the hurly-burly of *Whitehall* and of *London*. I am mightily well introduc'd in that country, and people receive me with kindness enough ; but I'll not swear to you that I shall undertake this journey. There are now but two things to be accomplished in my life : the one, to risk it honourably as soon as I have the occasion to do so ; and the other, to finish it in the obscurity of a retirement suitable to my manner of thinking, to my misfortunes, and to my knowledge of mankind."

This letter, apparently written in a mood of extreme dejection, is in striking contrast to the gaiety of the first days in England. But we should never take too seriously the letters of a practised writer, in whom a sense of literary opportunity is seldom absent. When the writer is a man as full of resource, as moody, change-able and vehement as François-Marie, we may well treat him with a certain measure of reserve. To speak of the " hurly-burly of Whitehall " is all nonsense. Nothing obliged his attendance at Whitehall. In no other land could he have found greater quiet or more complete obscurity ; and even if he had not yet dis-covered the friendly shelter of Falkener's house and the green lanes of Wandsworth, he knew that he was a welcome guest at Dawley, where Bolingbroke, with a modish affectation of rusticity, drank ale with the hay-makers and Whitehall was far enough.

But there was never a man to whom the idea of obscurity could have been more intolerable. He wanted leisure and freedom, not obscurity. This poor wounded creature, seeking only to recover his honour, and then to die in some unknown retreat, is not Voltaire. Gloom and pathos are both unreal. The letter must have been written in a passing mood of dreary resent-ment, of spite and thwarted revenge ; and written with

41

the intention of producing a moving and melancholy effect. Thiériot, he knew, would show the letter to Madame de Bernières, to Sully, Villars, and all his friends—in confidence. What is more, the stealthy visit to Paris (whether he had actually sought de Rohan or not) would prove that he was a man of honour, anxious to wipe out an insult, even at the risk of his personal freedom. And it may be noted, that Voltaire made no further attempt to meet de Rohan, although, after his return to France in 1729, there would have been no difficulty in doing so.

He returned to England at the end of July, and seems to have gone soon afterwards to Falkener's house at Wandsworth.

Everard Falkener was a wealthy merchant who traded with the Levant. He was appointed ambassador to the Porte in 1735, and in 1745 was private secretary to the Duke of Cumberland. Probably Voltaire had met him some years before in Paris, and Falkener had given him an invitation. In the house at Wandsworth, with its collection of rarities, its books and pictures, and the manly, ingenuous conversation of Falkener himself, Voltaire must have been happy. He always spoke of this amiable man with affection, never forgot his kindness and geniality, and dedicated to him the tragedy of *Zaïre*. For nearly thirty years after he had left England he wrote charming letters to his friend, and Falkener's death in 1758 affected him profoundly.

Wandsworth, with its trees and fields, pleasant waterways and rural quiet, was yet within a coach-ride of the noisy town. Voltaire seems to have spent his time between the town and the riverside village, but it is probable that the greater part of his first year in England was passed at Falkener's house.

In October, he wrote to Madame de Bernières from Bolingbroke's house in London :

" 'Tis but yesterday, Madam, that I have received your letter of the 3rd of September last. Misfortunes arrive quickly, and consolations are slow enough. Your remembrance of me is a very affecting consolation. The profound solitude to which I have retir'd has not permitted me to receive it earlier. I am in London for the moment ; I profit by this moment to give myself the pleasure of writing to you, and I shall go back immediately to my retreat.

" I wish you, from the depth of my cave, a happy and tranquil existence, affairs in good order, a little circle of friends, good health, and a profound scorn for what is call'd *Vanity*. I'll forgive you for having been to the Opera with the Chevalier de Rohan, provided that you felt some little confusion.

" Enjoy yourself as much as you can in the town or in the country. Remember me sometimes among your friends, and let constancy and friendship be added to the number of your virtues. Perchance my Destiny will some day bring me near to you. Let me hope that absence will not chase me altogether from your mind, and that I may find in your heart a pity for my sufferings which, at least, may resemble affection.

" For the most part, women know only passions or idleness ; but methinks I know you well enough to hope for your friendship.

" Perhaps I shall return to London soon, and there fix myself. I have but seen it in passing. If, on my arrival there, I find a letter from you, I think I shall spend the winter happily—if, indeed, the word happiness is made for the use of a wretch like myself. 'Twas for my sister [who had recently died] to live, and for me to perish : 'tis a mistake of Destiny. I am sadly affected by her loss : you know my heart ; you know what love I had for her. I thought, truly, it would be she who would mourn me. Alas ! Madam, to the world I am more dead than she is, and perhaps to you also. Remember, at least, that you and I have liv'd together. Forget all that concerns me, save the moments when you vowed that you would always keep me in your affections. Reckon those in which I may have vexed you among the multitude of my misfortunes, and love me through generosity if you can no longer love me through inclination."

This was written at a time when Voltaire, even if he was not occupied with any literary work except the continual polishing of the *Henriade*, was applying himself to the study of English with amazing industry, and was eagerly making himself acquainted with the life and character of the English people.

His " retirement " was the occasion for new activities, and soon for new ambitions. For him, idleness and resignation were equally impossible. We see him always in motion: learning, working, devising, enquiring —never still, never at rest. And if he worked with ardour, he was not less active in recreation. In society he was quick, nervous, volatile, impatient, busy or domineering ; anxious to show his erudition and to exercise his alarming wit. He is, perhaps, the only Frenchman who never complained sincerely of the national curse of *ennui*.

He found English none too easy. He could not follow the rule by which a word spelt " handkerchief " was pronounced " ankicher." Nor could he readily grasp the proper use of stops and of capital letters, for which there were no rules at all. One of his first letters written in English, addressed to Brinsden, a wine-dealer who acted as agent for Bolingbroke, has been perversely assigned to the year 1728 by two of the French editors, but with more probability assigned to the autumn of 1726 by Ballantyne. It is sufficiently curious to merit quotation :

" Sir, i wish you good health, a quick sale of yr burgundy, much latin and greeke to one of yr children, much Law, much of cooke and littleton to the other, quiet and joy to mistress brinsden, money to all. when you'll drink yr burgundy with mr furneeze, pray tell him i'll never forget his favours. But dear john be so kind as to let me know how does my lady Bollingbroke, as to my lord i left him so well i don't doubt he is so still. but i am very uneasie about my lady. If she might have as much health as she has spirit and witt, Sure she would be the Strongest body in England. Pray dear sr write me Something of her, of my lord, and of you. direct your letter by the penny post at mr Cavalier, Belitery square by the R Exchange. i am sincerely and heartily yr most humble and most obedient rambling friend Voltaire."

This is clearly the essay of a novice hand ; but in October, though with many corrections and alterations, he was able to write to Thiériot in more passable English :

" I intend to send you two or three poems of Mr Pope, the best poet of England, and at present of all the world. I hope you are acquainted enough with the English tongue to be sensible of all the charms of his works. . . . Now . . . let me acquaint you with an account of my for ever cursed fortune. I came again into England in the latter end of July very much dissatisfied with my secret voiage into France both unsuccessful and expensive. I had about me onely some bills of exchange upon a Jew called Medina. . . . At my coming to London, I found my damned Jew was broken ; I was without a penny, sick to death of a violent aguë, a stranger, alone, helpless, in the midst of a city wherein I was known to no body. my Lord and Lady Bolingbroke were in the country : I could not make bold to see our ambassadour in so wretched a condition. I had never undergone such distress ; but I am born to run through all the misfortunes of life. In these circumstances my star, that among all its direful influences pours allways on me some kind refreshment, sent to me an English gentleman unknown to me, who forced me to receive some money that I wanted. An other London citizen [Falkener] that I had seen but once in Paris, carried me to his country house, wherein I lead an obscure and charming life, without going to London, and quite given over to the pleasures of indolence and friendshipp."

It is possible that Voltaire's position had not been really so desperate. We can hardly believe that the friend of a man as rich and as well known as Bolingbroke should have found himself without credit in London, or should have been unable to make his way to Dawley, where he was assured of a cordial welcome. Who, if he was friendless, was the gentleman who so obligingly forced him to receive money ? and when and how did he meet Falkener ? It has been suggested that the

" gentleman " was King George ; but, in that case, who drew the king's attention to this friendless exile ? Moreover, he had come to England with good recommendations, including one from Horatio Walpole, the ambassador in Paris, to the Duke of Newcastle. Ballantyne is right when he says : " Voltaire's friendship with Bolingbroke and the excellent introductions which he brought with him from France, opened up to him all the English circles of rank and intellect which he could have desired to enter." Voltaire himself, as we have seen, owned that he was " mightily well introduced " and received with kindness. Yet here was the poet speaking pathetically of being " a stranger, alone and helpless " in a city where he " was known to no body." We cannot but think it highly probable that Voltaire was at Wandsworth within a few days of his return to England.

He was extremely anxious to meet Pope, with whom he had already exchanged a few light compliments, and whose work he so warmly admired. But Pope was unequal to a French conversation ; and Voltaire, however rapidly and surely he acquired a literary knowledge of English, was still unable to talk fluently in any tongue save his own. Without any possibility of exchanging ideas, or even of understanding the ordinary polite phrases, a meeting could have been of little profit to either. In spite of this, Voltaire seems to have met Pope at the first opportunity which presented itself.

On a September evening in 1726, as Pope was returning in a coach from a visit to Bolingbroke at Dawley, the coach was overturned in crossing a stream and Pope himself was cut about the fingers with broken glass. Voltaire did not hear of this until he was at

Dawley in November. He at once wrote, in English, a fulsome but not ungraceful letter to Pope :

" SIR,—I hear this moment of your sad adventure. That water you fell in was not Hippocrene's water, otherwise it would have respected you. Indeed I am concerned beyond expression for the danger you have been in, and more for your wounds. Is it possible that those fingers which have written the *Rape of the Lock*, and the *Criticism*, which have dressed Homer so becomingly in an English coat, should have been so barbarously treated ? Let the hand of *Dennis*, or of your poetasters be cut of. Yours is sacred. I hope, Sir, you are now perfectly recovered. Really, your accident concerns me as much as all the disasters of a master ought to affect his scholar. I am sincerely, Sir, with the admiration which you deserve,
" Your most humble Servant,
" VOLTAIRE."

Voltaire's first meeting with Pope seems to have taken place, probably at the Twickenham villa, soon afterwards.

There are several unreliable accounts of this meeting. Johnson's malevolent story, borrowed from Ruffhead, bears witness to his own credulity and spite. Goldsmith, who gives an entirely different version, is equally inaccurate. According to the first, Voltaire's conversation (in English) was so grossly indecent that poor Mrs. Pope, the poet's mother, was driven from the room. Others add blasphemy to the charge, and would have us believe that Pope's visitors, rising to their feet in anger, denounced the exile as a dog, a spy and a

48

scoundrel. Pretty behaviour ! But Goldsmith, on the other hand, draws a delightful, though purely imaginary picture : Voltaire enters the room and sees a little, sad, misshapen man, whom he could not help regarding " with the utmost compassion." The little man begins to talk, he reasons upon " moral obligations," he utters " the most delicate sentiments," and compassion gives way to wonder, and then to envy.

Both accounts are palpably absurd. The Ruffhead-Johnson story is damned by internal evidence. Voltaire's grossness, according to Ruffhead, lay in the description he gave of a disorder " contracted in Italy "—a country he never visited. And if that is not enough, need we point out, as Ballantyne has done, that Voltaire considered himself a man of the world, and that he was being entertained by one for whom he had the highest respect and whose company he so greatly desired ? And we should note, that the subsequent relations between Pope and Voltaire were of the most friendly sort ; and that Pope, with his acid, vindictive humour and his morbid sensibility, would have quickly resented and quickly avenged an insult. Nor is it likely that Voltaire would have been called a dog and a spy without letting the world know of it.

Johnson's perpetuation of this foolish story is to be reckoned among the rogueries of literature, and is certainly one of the most flagrant of his many blunders. The gentle and prettily finished account of Goldsmith is unhappily neutralised by the fact that Voltaire could not possibly have understood what Pope was talking about.

The account given of this meeting by Duvernet, though unsubstantial, is at least more likely to be true. According to him, the two men were unable to converse together, and Voltaire retired to "a village" (Wandsworth), in order to study at leisure and to learn how to express himself in the English tongue.

In the spring of 1727, Voltaire met a greater man than Pope—the amazing Dean of St. Patrick's, Jonathan Swift. He may have met him at Lord Peterborough's house at Parson's Green, at Twickenham with Pope, or at Dawley with Bolingbroke. In 1728, he stayed for three months at Parson's Green in the company of Swift, who was then in his sixty-first year.

Here was a man whose humour, invention and sprightly malice were thoroughly congenial. Voltaire admired Swift greatly ; he spoke of him as " Rabelais without his nonsense," and, indeed, as superior to Rabelais. But *Gulliver*, the first part of which had appeared late in 1726, was not beyond criticism. He writes, in English, to Thiériot, dating his letter March, 1727 :

" You will find in the same pacquet the second volume of *Mr Gulliver* which by the by I don't advise you to translate. Stick to the first, the other is overstrain'd. The reader's imagination is pleased and charmingly entertain'd by the new prospects of the lands which Gulliver describes to him, but that continued series of new fangled follies, of fairy tales, palls at last upon our taste ; nothing unnatural may please long ; 'tis for this reason that commonly the second parts of romances are so insipid."

When, in the summer of 1727, Swift contemplated a visit to France, Voltaire supplied him with letters of introduction and assured him of his esteem : " I shall certainly do my best endeavours," he wrote in English,

" to serve you and to let my country know that I have the inestimable honour to be one of your friends."

It may have been at this time that Voltaire met Gay, whom he " loved vastly," and who showed him the manuscript of the *Beggar's Opera.*

The date of his visit to Congreve cannot be ascertained, but the story of the interview is well known. Congreve, who in later life affected to despise his own works, as though they had been the easy diversions of a man of fashion, was then a vain, besotted creature, protesting with a decayed elegance that he wanted to be treated as " a mere gentleman." " If you was only a mere gentleman," said Voltaire, " I would not have troubled to visit you." Congreve, who was then fifty-eight, gouty, blind and peevish, died on the 19th of January, 1729.

On the 18th of April, 1727, a curious memorandum was addressed by a police commissioner of Paris to his chief, Hérault :

" This note has the honour of informing you that I have been assured that Master Arouet de Voltaire has returned from England and has been prowling in this neighbourhood [Saint-Antoine]. I don't know whether he has come to settle his accounts for what took place outside de Sully's house, but he may be running a certain risk. As I am unaware if he has permission to return, I can say nothing more in regard to this matter, and I have thought it my duty to inform you of it."

The information, unless it was a belated rumour of Voltaire's return during the previous summer, was entirely false. On the very day on which this report was made, Voltaire, who had applied to the minister Maurepas for leave to return to Paris, wrote to him as follows :

" My Lord,
    " I have received the honour of your letter with
gratitude and with submission. The ill state of my
health and of my fortunes are the sole motives which
induce me to return to Paris. I promise, moreover,
to forget the past, to forget every one, and to remember
only your kindness.
                " I am, my Lord, with respect,
    " Your most obedient, most obliged humble Servant,
                                        " Voltaire."

Maurepas, on the 29th of July, sent him the following
dispatch :
    " I send you a permit, graciously accorded by the
King, to reside in Paris for a period of three months in
order to attend to your affairs. As the time will be
reckoned from the date of your arrival, you must take
care to advise me of it ; I doubt not that you will conduct
yourself in such a way as to remove the unfavourable
impressions which have been convey'd to His Majesty,
and that the advice which I give you is sufficiently
pertinent to receive your full attention."
    Now, we are ignorant of Voltaire's reasons in applying
for this permission, and we know that he did not avail
himself of it. There are no references to the proposed
visit in any letter of his written to his friend Thiériot
in 1727 ; but in a letter wrongly ascribed to this year
in Moland's edition of the correspondence, though
clearly dated by internal evidence, and now correctly
placed by Foulet, we have the following passage (in
English) : " I intend to make use of your advice, and
to give the publick the best edition I can of the *Henriade*
[published in March, 1728], together with my true
Essay on Poetry [end of 1727]. . . . Now I want to

know when and where I could print secretly the
Henriade ? It must be in France, in some country
town . . . but let nobody be acquainted with the
secret of my being in France. I should be exceedingly
glad, my dear Thiériot, of seeing you again, but I would
see nobody else in the world ; I would not be so much
as suspected of having set my foot in your country, nor
of having thought of it : my brother especially is the
least proper person to be trusted with such a secret,
not only on account of his indiscreet temper, but also
of the ill usage I have received from him since I am in
England." In speaking of " my true *Essay*," he refers
obliquely to a bungling French translation which had
been made by the Abbé Desfontaines, a translation which
he criticises freely in the earlier part of the same letter.
The letter is thus written definitely nearly a year after
the permit had been dispatched by Maurepas, and
Voltaire seems to be still contemplating a visit to France.
His purpose, then, apparently, was to supervise a French
edition of the *Henriade*, for the English edition had
been proscribed in France ; but what were his designs
in 1727 ?

Writing early in 1729, presumably in February, he
refers again to a projected visit. " I had, two years
ago, snatched from your court a short leave to come to
Paris for three months. If I am smoaked out this bout,
I will plead that former leave for my excuse, though it
is perhaps good for nothing."

We have thus, on all three ocasions, evidence of
Voltaire's wish to return secretly to France, not always
with a clear motive ; and yet, having obtained permission, he never made use of it. The 1727 negociations, whatever they were, may conceivably represent
a final half-hearted scheme for running down the wicked

de Rohan-Chabot. It is not easy to see in what way his health would have benefited from a visit to Paris, and he was adequately supplied with money. But this is mere conjecture.

Of his life and activities in 1727 we know very little. Early in this year he was presented at court, and he probably saw something of fashionable life in London. But there was never a man who exemplified more thoroughly his own axiom, " to work is to live," or one who discredited more thoroughly the axiom of Johnson that " no man would work unless he was obliged to." With him, living was writing. When he was not writing books, plays or poems, he was devising them in his mind, or improving those which had already emerged, or composing some of the ten thousand letters which, in the course of his industrious lifetime, he sent to his friends. It may be doubted whether any man ever wrote, with his own hand, so many words, or used words in so many ways. His energy, his life, flowed out of him in words. Expression—the swift conveyance of his thoughts from the glowing core of his brain to his ready hand ;—that was everything. The niceties of style, though he was careful to attend to them, were of less importance. Not only the ardour of the mental fight, but the less noble impulse of vanity played its part in this furious, bewildering, unceasing production. No man ever rode harder in the pursuit of fame.

One of his chief concerns in 1727 was obviously the printing of what we should now call the definitive edition of the *Henriade*—a fuller and more polished edition—in London. If it could afterwards be produced in France, so much the better : we have seen how he wrote on this subject to Thiériot in the following year. But a work in English, intended partly to advertise the forthcoming *Henriade*, was also in his mind ; and so was the tragedy of *Brutus*. In addition to this, his admirable *History of Charles XII* was written, almost wholly, during his stay in England, and he was composing, from time to time, those graceful, daring and diverting *Letters Concerning the English Nation*, or *Philosophick Letters*, which were later to be collected in the form of a book.

The first act of *Brutus*, in English prose, was written at Falkener's house, probably in 1727, and was re-cast in French verse after Voltaire's return to France. Towards the end of the year he published the puff preliminary of the *Henriade—An Essay upon the Civil Wars of France Extracted from Curious Manuscripts And also upon the Epick Poetry of the European Nations from Homer down to Milton*. In the preface to this odd performance he wrote :

" As to the present Essay, it is intended as a kind of Preface or Introduction to the *Henriade*, which is almost entirely printed, nothing being wanting but the printing of the Cuts, which I must recommend here as particular Master-Pieces of Art in their kind : 'tis the only Beauty in the Book, that I can answer for."

The essays can now only be regarded as curiosities of literature, lively and audacious, like all that he wrote, and stuffed with appropriate compliments, but with many faults and much exaggeration. The style, though it breaks down in places, is less halting than might have been supposed. There is no doubt, however, that the manuscript was carefully revised by an English reader.

It was in 1727 that Voltaire, busy collecting material for his *Charles XII*, met Sarah Jennings, Duchess of Marlborough. She was then a teasy, petulant old woman of sixty-eight, with a sharp tongue and a brusque manner. From her he obtained particulars of a conference between her famous husband (who died in 1722) and the King of Sweden. But Sarah was more interested in her own memoirs, which she was then writing. Might he see them ? " You must wait a while," said her Grace ; " for I am now mending the character of Queen Anne : I have come to love her again since these good folk have become our rulers." The untrustworthy Goldsmith gives another story, according to which Voltaire found fault with a lack of decency and restraint in the manuscript, whereupon the Duchess plucked the papers from his hands, crying out that she thought the man had sense, but discovered him to be a fool or a philosopher.

Bubb Dodington, Lord Melcombe, the wealthy and elegant patron of poets, received the exile with much kindness. It was at Dodington's country house in Dorset that he met Young, the author of *Night Thoughts* (a poem not yet written in 1727) ; and here, in all probability, he met Thompson also.

The greatest Englishman of his time, Newton, was near his death when Voltaire arrived in England. On the 31st of March, 1727, Voltaire was a witness of his funeral, and was deeply impressed by the respect shown to the memory of a man of learning. To him, Newton was one " whose equal is hardly found in a thousand years." He sought eagerly the acquaintance of Mrs Conduit, the niece of the great man, and from her he received the famous story of the falling apple. He sought also a close personal friend of Newton's, Dr Samuel Clarke.

The Doctor was a grim and godly person, dry, whimsical, an inveterate polemist, to whom the feeble repartee of " Sir, do you acknowledge that two and two make four ? " seemed weighty enough to close an argument. At the same time, it was probably Clarke who inspired Voltaire with a liking for metaphysics, and who taught him to make the first exhilarating plunge in the gulf of learned speculation.

Clarke died in 1729, not long after Voltaire's return to France.

Voltaire's own correspondence throws little light upon these activities and meetings. But on the 27th of May, 1727, he wrote one of the most interesting of his letters to Thiériot. With the exception of a few lines in French, here reproduced in italics, the letter is in English throughout :

" *My dear Thiériot, 'tis but lately that I have received, in the country place to which I have withdrawn, your charming letter of the 1st of April.* You cannot imagine with what sense of sorrow I have received the account you gave me of your sickness. I have carried my concern for you further than an ordinary friendship could allow. Remember the time when I was used to write to you that I believed you had a fever upon you whenever I had an ague. That time is come again. I was very ill in England while you suffered so much in France. An year absence added a new bitterness to my sufferings. Now I hope you are better, since I begin to revive.

" I hear that *M. Gulliver* is now translated and takes pretty much. I wish the translation could be yours : but I am afraid the Abbot [Desfontaines] has outrun you, and reaped the benefit which such a book should have procured to you.

" You must have received the two books addressed to Madame de Bernières from Calais, and conveyed by the stage coach. If you intend seriously to make a translation of some valuable book, I advise you to sit still for a month or two, to take care of your health, and to improve your English till the book of Mr Pemberton [*A View of Sir Isaac Newton's Philosophy*] comes out. This book is an easy, clear and regular explanation of Sir Isaac Newton's philosophy, which he undertakes to make palatable to the most unthinking man. It seems the man intends to write chiefly for your nation.

" If I am in England when the book shall be published, I will not fail of sending it to you with the utmost speed. If I am abroad, as I will be in all likelihood, I will order my bookseller to send you the book by the first opportunity. I fancy it will be an easy task to translate it, the language being very plain, and all the terms of philosophy being just the same in French and in English. Take care only not to be outvied in the future by any priest : be cautious in the choice of all those you will consult about your translation. I fancy the bishop of Rochester [Atterbury] is more amiable an acquaintance and a less dangerous one than the priest you speak of. But I believe you are now in Normandy, mending your health, loitering with Madame de Bernières, and talking of physick with des Alleurs. I must acquaint you, my dear, that there is an engine in England to take a clyster, which is a master-piece of art, for you may carry it in your fob and make use of it whenever and in what place you please. If ever I enjoy the pleasure of seeing you again, be sure to have a dozen of these delightful engines. Farewell, do not talk of the ' Occasional Writer.' Do not say it is not by my lord Bolingbroke ; do not say it is a wretched performance : you cannot be judge neither of the man nor of this writing. *Adieu, my very dear friend.*

" I have just wrote an English thesis for the Chevalier des Alleurs. I have addressed the letter Quai des Théatins ; if it has not been received, you must advise me of it : it must not be lost, for I have plac'd all my physick therein. Adieu, be well. Non vivere, sed valere vita. If you want to enter into a course of strict diet, begin soon and keep it long.

> To morrow I will live, the fool does say.
> To day's too late, the wise liv'd yesterday.

" I am the fool, be the wise, and farewell."

In December, 1727, Voltaire was living at the White Perruque in Maiden Lane, Covent Garden. From this address he sent a copy of his English *Essay* to Swift, with the following English letter :

" Sir,
    " You will be surprised in receiving an English essay from a French traveller. Pray forgive an admirer of you who ows to yr writings the love he bears to yr language, which has betray'd him into the rash attempt of writing in English.
    " You will see by the Advertisement that I have some designs upon you, and that I must mention you for the honour of yr country and for the improvement of mine. Do not forbid me to grace my relation with yr name. Let me indulge the satisfaction of talking of you as posterity will do.
    " In the mean time, can I make bold to interest you to make some use of yr interest in Ireland about some subscriptions for the *Henriade*, wch is almost ready and does not come out yet for want of a little help. The subscriptions will be but one guinea in hand.

" I am with the highest esteem and the utmost grati-
tude, Sir,
" Your most humble and most obedient servant,
" VOLTAIRE."

The *Henriade*, " printed on Royal Paper with large
Cuts," was published, with an English dedication to
Queen Caroline, in March, 1728—more than ten years
after the inception of the poem, and five years after the
unauthorised printing of *The League* at Rouen. It
was to be had at Messrs Woodman and Lyons in
Russell Street for three guineas. The book sold well,
its fame spread rapidly, and three printings of a cheaper
octavo edition were sold out in three weeks.

This poem, conceived in tribulation, polished, revised and elaborated again and again, banned by the
very country whose great hero it was to celebrate, and
issuing at last from a place of exile, seemed to its author
the best of all his works, and it remained always the one
for which he felt the most affection. To us, the story
of the poem is more interesting than the actual performance. But then, we have no liking for epics.
History in verse, no matter how ingenious the verse
may be, does not move us. We cannot hear the trum-
peting in the heavens, or see the angels of victory
descending upon earth. Our national emblems are
mere trade-marks ; our kings are very like ordinary
men. How many of us, now, would care to read the
Henriade ? The glory of the epic has long departed,
and all the grand figures have flown away. Only in
melodrama, perhaps, and then only in the part of the
villain, do we still find a personage whose actions fill
us with delight and astonishment. We do not doubt the
sincerity of a villain. We are not quite so sure of a hero.

But in 1728, epics were in vogue. The *Henriade* was considered "the best epick Poem of the year." The royal family headed the list of subscribers, and no one who thought himself a man of taste, or who wished others to think he was, could afford to be without a copy. Few poems have been commercially more successful ; though here, as in the case of so many later writings, the rumours which gathered about the author himself were of no small service in helping to sell his work.

Before the end of March, Voltaire was embroiled with a publisher named Prevost, who had a shop in Southampton Street, and was a well known distributor of French books in London. The quarrel and the transaction which led to it are both obscure. Prevost advertised, "by the author's privilege," a new edition of the great epic, which, he said, was "not emasculated" as the original quarto and octavo editions were, and which contained "a Criticism upon the whole Work." The advertisement appeared in the *Daily Post* of the 19th of March, and in the next day's issue Voltaire published a refutation. He had never authorised Prevost. He had given leave to "one Coderc" to print an edition for his own benefit after the original edition was exhausted. Nor was this all. Prevost, he said, had printed "six bad and insignificant low lines," to be found, it is true, in a former edition of *The League*, but not by Voltaire. In place of these bad lines, readers would find " six others a great deal bolder and stronger " in the *Henriade*.

To this, Prevost retorted that he had the author's permission, given to Coderc, to print the new edition, and Coderc's assignment of the said permission to him, Prevost. As for the bad lines and the good lines, his edition had both. The public might judge whether

61

the new printing was not fully as correct as the *editio princeps*. Voltaire replied that Coderc had been instructed to destroy all the sheets in which the six bad lines had been printed, and that if he had not done so, he would call him to account. By the end of May, Voltaire and the publisher were openly reconciled, and the six bad lines were finally expunged.

It has been suggested, not without plausibility, that the whole episode was engineered with a view to advertisement. Voltaire was certainly capable of such a manœuvre, but the quarrel seems genuine enough. Coderc was a bookseller at the Pliny Head in Little Newport Street, near Leicester Fields. He had been of service to Voltaire in the printing of the quarto edition, and it was probably in return for this obligation that the poet granted him the right to print a limited edition for his own benefit. If Coderc transferred his right to Prevost, without observing the author's conditions, he was much to be blamed. Prevost was equally to be blamed for describing the authorised edition as " castrated "—a statement altogether without meaning, and one which could have done nothing but harm to Voltaire himself. Finally, there is an English letter from Voltaire to a French refugee, Desmaizeaux, which is not always quoted in connection with this affair, but is extremely pertinent. The letter is not dated ; it must have been written, we think, not earlier than June :

" SIR,

"I hear Prevost hath a mind to bring you a second time as an evidence against me. He sais that I have told you I had given him five and twenty books for thirty guineas. I remember very well, Sr, I told you at Rainbow's coffee house that I had given him twenty subscription receipts for the *Henriade* and received thirty guineas down. But I never meant to have parted with thirty copies at three guineas each for thirty one pounds. I have agreed with him upon quite another foot, and I am not such a fool (tho a writer) to give away all my property to a bookseller. Therefore I desire you to remember that I never told you of my having made so silly a bargain."

This letter, certainly never intended for publication, throws light on the character of Prevost, whose methods, however adroit from a business point of view, were scarcely those of an honourable man.

An early consignment of the *Henriade* was forwarded to Ireland, and the following undated letter to Swift was probably written at the end of March, or early in April. It is, like his other letters to Swift, in English :

" SR,
        " I sent the other day a cargo of French dullness to mylord Lieutenant. My lady Bollingbrooke has taken upon herself to send you one copy of the *Henriade*. She is desirous to do that honour to my book, and I hope the merit of being presented to you by her hands will be a commendation to it. However, if she has not done it already, I desire you to take one out of the cargo which is now at mylord Lieutenant. . . . I have not seen Mr Pope this winter, but I have seen the third volume of the *Miscelanea*, and the more I read yr works, the more I am ashamed of mine."

Swift used his recommendation to some effect, and the *Henriade* had a ready sale in Ireland.

63

No sooner was the great national epic printed than its author was again considering how he could improve it ; he was devising " many alterations and corrections which would do good to the work."

This continual repolishing of his work was one of the most peculiar of his literary habits. If he had a particular fondness for any of his pieces, he could never leave it alone. We have seen him raging over six bad lines in the Prevost edition ; but a single line, a single word, if it struck him as awkward or questionable, had to be removed or changed. And the great majority of these corrections or improvements were made after the work had been printed. In some cases, the alterations were due to a personal reason, as, for example, the removal of de Sully's name from the *Henriade*, in revenge for de Sully's attitude in the affair of Rohan-Chabot. Yet he wrote with extraordinary speed. A tragedy was dashed off in a few weeks, sometimes in a few days. His production is almost without parallel.

It may have been that his style was impaired by this very facility and quickness, and that he was himself aware of his failure to attain the smooth elegance of La Bruyère or Montesquieu. In any case, we find with him the nervous anxiety, the teasing cares, of a man who could never leave well alone ; a man who was always pruning, patching, trimming and snipping his work, so that it might become excellent beyond all imaginable excellence. The hand which made it mighty was to make it mightier yet ; the straining and striving could never come to an end. In this, no doubt, the impulse was not altogether literary. He desired greatly to see the astonishment and to hear the applause of his fellows.

The curious literary history of the *Henriade* is

developed in several interesting letters written during the spring and summer of 1728. The first of these is presumably addressed to des Alleurs, and is undated. It is written throughout in English :

"Dear Sir,
          "I received lately two letters of yours, one directed to Lord Peterborough's and the other to Lord Bolingbroke's. . . . I have sent this morning by the packet-boat a bundle of three copies of the *Henriade*, with your direction upon it. . . . If they are left at the Custom-house at *Paris* you may claim them, and they will be delivered to you. . . . One of the books is for Thiériot, though he has utterly forgot me, and does not write one single word either in French or in English. He may get a good deal of money by printing it in France. But in case he attempts it I must at least be acquainted with his design, and I will send him many alterations and corrections which will do good to the work and more to him. . . . Though the poem is written in a language not much admired here in regard to poetry, yet three editions have been made in less than three weeks, which I assure you I attribute intirely to the lucky subject I have pitched upon, and not at all to the performance. I do not send you yet my great edition, because I am really afraid of having not copies enough to answer the calls of the subscribers. . . .
          "I heartily wish to see you and my friends, but I had rather see them in England than in France. You, who are a perfect Briton, you should cross the Channel and come to us. I assure you again that a man of your temper would not dislike a country where one obeys to the laws only and to one's whims. Reason is free here and walks her own way. Hypochondriacks es-

pecially are welcome. No manner of living appears strange. We have men who walk six miles a day for their health, feed upon roots, never taste flesh, wear a coat in winter thinner than your ladies do in the hottest days : all that is accounted a particular reason, but taxed with folly by nobody."

Early in May he wrote to Thiériot (in English) :

" As to the *Henriade*, I think you may easily get a private licence of printing it : I intend in about a fortnight to ask that licence. In the mean time you must go to M. Hérault, the *lieutenant de police*. I have already sent a copy of the *Henriade* to him, and intreated him to seize all the copies which might steal into France till I had leave from the government to publish the book. I have assured him I would never send into France anything without the consent of the ministry ; therefore it will be very proper for you to speak to him in the same manner, and to inform him that the person you speak of [Desfontaines] undertakes an edition of the *Henriade*, contrary to my honour, to my interest and to the laws. . . . Depend upon it, the man will be terrified from his undertaking. In the mean time, we will get our private licence, and in case the license is granted, I advise you to make a bargain with some notable bookseller. . . . The bookseller must make two editions ; one in quarto, for my own account, and another in octavo for your benefit. But nothing can succeed to our advantage and to my honour, unless you go to M. Hérault, and implore his assistance against the interloper."

Desfontaines, who was then translating the English

Essay, evidently had his eye on the great epic. " I know of nothing so impertinent as to go about to translate me in spight of my teeth." The Abbé had to be " terrified " at all costs.

But Thiériot declined to print the *Henriade* from the copy in his possession. Voltaire thereupon determined " to give the publick, as soon as possible, the best edition I can of the *Henriade*, together with my true *Essay on Poetry*." It was at this time that he seems to have contemplated a visit to France, as we saw above.

Towards the end of the summer, Voltaire heard that Dr Richard Towne, who lived and worked in remote Barbadoes, had some thoughts of translating the epic into English. Little is known of the ingenious Towne, except that he wrote *A Treatise of the Diseases most frequent in the West Indies, and herein more particularly of those which occur in Barbadoes*, and that he was a friend of Sir Hans Sloane. The idea of having his work translated by this lonely West Indian doctor appealed to Voltaire, and he sent him an amusing letter. The letter, which is in English, was written at Wandsworth :

" Dear Sir,
         " I received yesterday your kind and witty letter, which was sent to my lord Peterborough at the Bath. You do me the greatest honour I could ever boast of, in bestowing an Englis dress upon my French child. I receive the best reward of all my labours if you go on in the generous design of translating my undeserving work into a language which gives life and strength to all the subjects it touches. . . . I wish I could be the happy witness of your labour. I assure you, dear Sir, I am strongly tempted of coming to Barbadoes ; for as the *Henriade* wanted to be translated

by you, I want a warmer climate for my health, which grows worse and worse in England. . . . As I am talking to you about physick, I must acquaint you that doctor *Freind* is a dying for having outphisied himself : he took the other day ten ounces of herapicra at once, with some sene, and since that noble experiment he lies speechless. This must be looked upon as self-murther. . . . I hear this minute doctor *Freind* is dead, leaving behind him an ample fortune. . . ."

The precise date of Voltaire's return to France cannot be determined. He received permission to return, but not to enter Paris, early in 1729. At this time he was complaining bitterly of ill health and depression. There is some doubt as to the date of a letter which he wrote to Thiériot early in the year, nor is it certain whether, at the time of writing, he was in England or in France. In this letter he tells his friend that he hopes to be in Paris " about the fifteenth of March."

A visit to Paris would then have been unauthorised, and would have exposed him to the danger of arrest, for the official permit to return to Paris, signed by Maurepas and preserved in the archives of the Bastille, is dated the 9th of April. There follows the passage, already quoted, in which he speaks of " pleading the former leave for my excuse." The letter, begun in English, proceeds gloomily in French :

" Concerning your health, I cannot speak too emphatically ; I have known many evils ; I know by sad experience that sickness is the worst of all. Having the fever or the small-pox in passing is nought ; but to be oppress'd by langour for whole years together, to see one's appetites fading, to have still enough life to wish to enjoy it and too little strength to do so, to become useless and intolerable to one's self, to die in detail—that is what I have suffered, and what has been more bitter to me than all my other sufferings. If you are in such a state of langour, you will find no cure in medicine ; I have there sought for one in vain, and I have found it only in nature. If I am still living after all that I have endured, and after the sorrows which have poison'd the few drops of blood which remained in this frail machine, I owe it solely to regime and exercise. The air in which I live is good for nothing ; I have been very ill here ; I arrived feeble. Moreover, I am born of sickly parents who died young ; and you know, in addition to all that, the agonies of mind which have made life so cruel to me ; yet, thanks to regime and exercise, I exist—and for me that is much. . . . Believe me, there is no happiness for our bodies in this world, but in the possession of five healthy senses, or for our minds, but in the possession of a friend. I fear that the man with whom you are living [M. de Nocé] has learnt from the late Duke of Orleans to love good cheer too well : if men would but live as the poor do, there would be no need for doctors."

It is strange to find one who was so restless and so active complaining of langour. But he wrote always in the present sense of his moods ; moods changing, not only from day to day, but from hour to hour. Whatever he imagined himself to be, he was ; and it was this instability, this quick rearrangement of the whole personal complex, which made him at once so interesting and so dangerous. It seems to us not improbable that the letter was written soon after his

69

return to France, when he found himself in a state of disturbing transition : repatriated, but not wholly pardoned. This appears to be also the opinion of Lucien Foulet, whose edition of the letters of this period is the only one which has any real authority. The letter ends with the mysterious words in English : " I have nothing to say to you from the place where I am. Malaffaire does not know me : I am here upon the footing of an English traveller."

But the dating of the correspondence of this period is a matter of difficulty, and one upon which the editors are not in agreement. The same difficulty occurs frequently in the course of the correspondence : not only was Voltaire careless enough in dating his letters, when he dated them at all, but his editors have been equally careless in ignoring their natural order.

In a letter which is dated the 10th of March by Voltaire himself he says : " In all likelihood I will stay at Saint-Germain, and there I intend to arrive before the fifteenth." Where had he been previously ? On the 25th of March he was certainly at Saint-Germain, and to this place he invites friend Thiériot : " If you can forget a few days your golden palace, your feasts, and *fumum et opes strepitumque Romae*, you will find a homely frugal fare, a hard bed, a poor room ; but here is a friend who expects you."

The problem of these obscure movements is further complicated by a note dated the 1st of April, in which he says that he appeared " like a hobgoblin " to the Duke de Richelieu in Paris. The note was clearly written in Paris, whence he was returning in two hours' time to Saint-Germain. And in a letter which, though dated the 2nd of March and printed under this date by Moland, was obviously written after this flying and secret visit to Paris, and is correctly ascribed to the 2nd of April by Foulet, he says : " Before I went out of Paris I received, at M. Cavalier's house, a letter written to me by Cardinal Fleury, which was sent to London, and back from London to Paris."

What were his motives in thus entering the capital by stealth ? First, beyond a doubt, the recovery of 500 livres of the queen's pension, already promised by secretary Pallu. He was also anxious to bargain for the publication of his *Charles XII*, and to obtain a few final particulars of the king's life. Thiériot is asked to visit the Swedish ambassador, " or his secretary, or his chaplain, or his whore," and to ask any of them for certain information of which he is in need.

On the 4th of April he sent a note to friend Thiériot at 8 o'clock in the morning. He was again in Paris, and had " something of importance " to communicate. " I am leading the life of a Rosicrucian, always rambling and always concealed, but not pretending to wisdom. *Quanquam o !* "

By the middle of the month, having received permission from Maurepas, he openly installed himself in Paris, taking rooms in the Rue Traversière-Saint-Honoré (now the Rue Molière). He advised Thiériot of his new address. " 'Tis near the last houses on the left on the side of the fountain—one of the worst-looking doors."

From this address he wrote, in English, a graceful letter of acknowledgement to one of his English friends, Mrs William Clayton, a lady of the bedchamber to Princess Caroline :

" MADAM,
    " Tho I am out of London the favours yr Ladiship has honoured me with are not, nor ever will

be, out of my memory. I'll remember as long as I live that the most respectable lady who waits and is a friend of the most truly great queen in the world has vouchsafed to protect me and receive me with kindness while I was at London. I am just now arrived in Paris and I pay my respects to your Court before I see my own. I wish for the honour of Versailles and for the improvement of virtue and letters we could have some ladyes like you. You see my wishes are unbounded ; so is the respect and the gratitude I am with, Madam,
"Yr most humble obed. servant,
"VOLTAIRE."

Before any attempt to reckon the effects of the visit to England upon his mind and character, it is well to remember what Voltaire brought with him when he came to England, and then to consider the nature of his susceptibility and the characters of the men with whom he was on terms of intimate friendship. He brought with him a definite grievance against his own countrymen, and a readiness to believe in the sympathy and superiority of any other civilised people. That is commonly the attitude of those who know their own country too well. But however bright his impressions, however marked his response to a new environment, no impressions, no influence could ever lessen the sturdy independence of his mind. He had often the seeming indifference of those who are essentially mutable. He was, indeed, too sensitive, too easily moved by a passing scene or emotion, to be capable of receiving any lasting influence. Whatever was uncongenial was flung aside by his revolving egoism, as a spinning top flicks away the snippets of paper which are thrown upon it. He could not be reckoned with. He was capable of extreme generosity ; but it was not safe to count on his generosity. He was capable of real, but not profound affection. No man was less adaptive or less able to compromise with himself. In what way, then, was he changed, if changed at all, by his residence in England ?

His English friends—Pope, Swift, Bolingbroke, Dodington and Peterborough—were no ordinary men. Falkener, perhaps, was an ordinary man ; but Falkener represented, to Voltaire, the hospitality and not the genius of England. Bishop Atterbury, whom he had met previously in France, was by no means an ordinary bishop. As for the high society which he occasionally met—the Claytons, Hervey and his beautiful wife, Lyttleton, Walpole and Mrs Howard—, it provided him only with such elegant entertainment as he could have found elsewhere. Clarke, with his metaphysical talk, probably had more influence than any of the others, but Clarke's personality was never congenial.

Voltaire himself tells us that he was impressed by the freedom of speech and letters in England. Men of letters were sought after and patronised by men of rank : Pope was the friend of Bolingbroke and Swift of Peterborough. He does not seem to have realised the exceptional characters of these men, or to have known that they were regarded with abhorrence by the greater number of their shocked countrymen. The Quakers were free, fearless and high-minded : but who loved the Quakers ?

It is true that he found, in England, none of that fearful bigotry which so widely prevailed in Catholic France. A more rational, and so a happier, life was possible. Superstition, though not extinct, had been

73

robbed of its grimmest horrors by the Reformation. What is more, diversity of schism was producing tolerance :

" An *Englishman*, as one to whom liberty is natural, may go to heaven his own way . . . every one is permitted to serve God in whatever mode or fashion he thinks proper. . . . That sable mix'd kind of mortal (not to be defin'd) who is neither of the clergy nor of the laity ; in a word, the thing call'd *Abbé* in *France*, is a species quite unknown in *England*. All the clergy here are very much upon the reserve, and most of them pedants. When these are told that in *France*, young fellows famous for their dissoluteness, and raised to the highest dignities of the church by female intrigues, address the fair publickly in an amorous way, amuse themselves in writing tender love-songs, entertain their friends very splendidly every night in their own houses, and after the banquet is ended, withdraw to invoke the assistance of the Holy Ghost, and call themselves boldly the successors of the apostles, they bless God for their being Protestants. But there are shameless Hereticks, who deserve to be blown hence through the flames to old Nick, as *Rabelais* says ; and for this reason I don't trouble myself about them."

But however much he may have appreciated the institutions of England, we can hardly say that he was radically changed by his visit. The preparation of the *Henriade*, the writing of *Brutus* and the *History of Charles XII*, show no change of literary habit and no trace of a foreign influence. The *Letters Concerning the English People*, rewritten after his return to France, are occasional pieces in the true sense of the word : a set of essays upon typical Voltairean themes.

Two of our greatest men—Locke and Newton— certainly influenced him, and even influenced him profoundly; but he knew them only through their works, and to obtain those works it was not necessary to visit England.

CHAPTER III

MADAME DU CHÂTELET

AFTER his return to France, Voltaire was concerned, first of all, with repairing his fortunes. In this he was remarkably successful. He obtained the arrears of his pension ; and then, by two daring transactions in State bonds and lotteries, he became, in the course of a few weeks, a man of considerable wealth. He had all the shrewdness and quick understanding of a skilled financier. During his lifetime he secured an immense sum of money, not by his writings, but by brilliant financial diplomacy, guided by an extraordinary sense of coming developments and by a knowledge of the men with whom he was dealing.

The first year after his arrival in Paris (1729–1730) seems to have been a year of sustained labour, and a year of comparative retirement. The tragedy of *Brutus* was played on the 11th of December, 1730. It was well received on the first night, but the success was not repeated on the following nights, and the play was withdrawn.

Meanwhile the *Henriade* was in trouble again. The London edition was proscribed in France, and sheets of the book were being smuggled over as the wrapping of bales and packets. Marais, not suspecting the stratagem, had seen with malicious amusement a copy of the *Life of Bayle* wrapped in a sheet of the great epic. All the copies intended for the French subscribers were seized and destroyed at Calais. At the same time, Voltaire was devising a new and improved edition ; he was also drafting the tragedies of *Eriphyle* and *Caesar*.

On the 20th of March, 1730, Voltaire was called away

from his work to the death-bed of one of his friends, the famous actress Adrienne Lecouvreur. Five days before her death she had played the part of Jocasta in *Oedipus*, though suffering greatly ; and on the following night she had bravely and brilliantly played an even more exacting rôle in *The Florentine*. " She died," wrote Voltaire, " in my arms " ; and he repudiated with indignation the rumour that she had taken poison. The curé of Saint-Sulpice refused the right of burial in consecrated earth : it would appear, indeed, that he actually turned the funeral cortège from the gates of the cemetery. In this deplorable action he was supported by the authority of the Archbishop of Paris. At midnight, an old hackney coach, attended by two porters, conveyed the body of poor Adrienne to a piece of waste ground known by the evil name of La Grenouillère, and there it was buried. Such were the orders of Hérault, the chief of police.

Adrienne Lecouvreur, perhaps the greatest actress of her time, a woman of rare generosity, charming, gallant, never ignoble and never treacherous, neither more nor less free than any great lady of the period, was thus dishonoured by the church. Voltaire was not alone in his rage. The friends of Adrienne—and they were many—felt, with him, both fury and amazement. Here, in truth, was a sad enough example of priestly malice and of the ugly power of superstition. The episode produced one of Voltaire's most vigorous poetical satires—*The Death of Mademoiselle Lecouvreur*. It strengthened him in the grim, unending fight against the inhumanity, the corruption and the hypocrisy of something which was then called religion.

In 1731, the *History of Charles XII* was produced. The first volume was approved, the second was banned, and the whole edition confiscated. The Keeper of the Seals, in giving a reason for this procedure, alleged that the author had not treated the Elector of Saxony with proper respect. Voltaire thereupon withdrew to Rouen with his manuscript, had the book secretly printed, and conveyed to Paris by the servants of the Duke de Richelieu. He told his friends that he had gone to England, and pretended to write from Canterbury ; in Rouen he tried to pass as an English gentleman upon his travels. He lived in the house of the bookseller, Jore, a shifty and troublesome fellow, with whom he was later embroiled. Returning to Paris in the autumn, he finished the tragedies of *Eriphyle* and *Caesar*.

Eriphyle was presented, with only a moderate degree of success, on the 7th of March, 1732. It seemed as though Voltaire was never to repeat the triumph of *Oedipus*. But five months later, on the 13th of August, the fine new tragedy of *Zaïre* was a far greater triumph.

At the first hearing, the reception was doubtful. Confused voices were heard in the parterre, some applauding and others unfavourable. The actors were not inspired. Certain faults in the construction, a certain halting of the rhythm, were clear to the author, and these were accordingly mended. On the fourth night, the success of the piece was overwhelming. The actors realised the full emotional value of their lines ; the house responded warmly ; and when Voltaire showed himself in one of the boxes he received a most gratifying ovation. Having thus obtained so delightful a proof of their good taste, he felt himself reconciled once more with his own countrymen, and honoured by their frank applause. He felt his energies greater than ever before, and set about his work with an even greater degree of ardour and confidence. In a letter to Formont, written in September, he gives an account of his plans :

"What a deal of pains and pother for this bubble of vain glory ! And yet, what should we do without this chimera ? 'Tis as needful for the spirit as nourishment for the body. I mean to recast *Eriphyle* and the *Death of Caesar*—all for the sake of this *bubble*. Meanwhile, I am obliged to work at some additions which I am preparing for a Dutch edition of *Charles XII*. . . , When I have washed my hands of this ungrateful task. I shall complete the *English Letters*, which you have seen ; it will be at most a month's labour ; after that I must indeed return to the theatre, and finish, at last, with the history of the *Age of Louis XIV*."

He had also published his *Epistle to Urania*, written, it will be remembered, for that fair unbeliever, Rupelmonde ; whereupon the Archbishop of Paris made a complaint to Hérault, who so often found himself concerned with the doings of Arouet de Voltaire.

The chief of police summoned the poet, and asked him if he was truly the author of this wicked, antireligious poem. Voltaire did not hesitate to ascribe it to the Abbé Chaulieu, who had died some years previously, one of the roystering company of the Temple. No one believed this ; but the matter was dropped. Secretary Langlois declared warmly that " Voltaire ought to be locked up in a place where he could have neither pen, ink, nor paper : *a man of this humour is capable of destroying a kingdom*."

If the clergy was incensed by the *Epistle*, men of letters were equally incensed by a deliciously arrogant satire— *The Temple of Taste*. Jean-Baptiste Rousseau, in particular, was exposed to ridicule in the *Temple*; and he replied with a venomous epigram. Such warfare was then common enough among writers, and provided the age with one of its literary amusements. Writing had not yet become a purely commercial enterprise, and publishing was full of adventures and perils.

Early in 1733, the death of Madame de Fontaine-Martel deprived Voltaire of his comfortable quarters (he had been living in her house) and of " 40,000 livres spent upon his diversion." In May, he moved to the house of a flour merchant, Desmoulin, in the Rue du Long-Pont. It was a shabby house, but it gave him the privacy and convenience of rooms of his own. Here he was free to work, or to receive company, as he pleased. He found himself, so he said, " in the worst house in the worst quarter of Paris, more deafened than a sacristan by the noise of bells " ; but then—" I shall make such a twanging with my lyre that I shan't care a fig for the noise of the bells."

He was ill (but when was he not ill ?) and exceedingly busy setting up house, buying and hanging pictures, revising his plays, all the time suffering " like a damned soul." Yet even here this extraordinary man showed that he had an eye for business : he was anxious to speculate in the export of grain, and Desmoulin became his agent.

A sentimental reason may also have played a part in his choice of a dwelling ; for he was now close to the gate of Saint-Germain, which he had celebrated as a masterpiece of architecture in the *Temple of Taste.*

In the dingy rooms of the Rue du Long-Pont, with Flemish pictures on the walls, and some very doubtful Titians, he received many visitors. Among them was Madame la Marquise du Châtelet.

This remarkable woman was then twenty-seven years old. She had married du Châtelet in 1725, six months before her nineteenth birthday. Her husband was one of those men who are so obligingly insignificant that they pass through life without leaving behind them a word or an action that need be recorded. He lived in a very dilapidated château, and amused himself amiably and obscurely by planting a few trees, shooting a few duck, or riding nowhere in particular upon a bay horse. He was the least offensive and least intrusive of husbands, and never troubled himself about his wife's affairs, or indeed about any others.

Madame du Châtelet was no ordinary person. She was a generous ardent creature, anxious to enjoy in the highest degree not only the pleasures of the senses, but those of the intelligence. If she pursued her loves with intensity of purpose and a clear aim, she pursued with equal intensity of purpose the teaching of Newton or the speculation of Maupertuis. She was a fine Latinist, far advanced in mathematics, and above all in metaphysics. She learnt how to read, speak or write in English as readily as Voltaire himself. No one had a more profound acquaintance with the works of Leibnitz and Descartes. She knew Italian, could play the harpsichord and sing passably well. She was a talented amateur actress. In society, she was a gay and attractive figure, with a light, easy, or even trivial conversation. She had a liking for dainty dresses and pretty jewels. Never giving herself airs of superiority, but always ready to show enthusiasm for the topic or pastime of the moment, she would take up a hand of cards as readily as the last essay of Fontenelle. If her lover is to be believed, she spoke ill of no one. In all that she did, her warm, vital and impulsive nature was apparent. Free she may have been, but frank she certainly was, without malice in her mind or cruelty in her heart.

She was tall, of a rather masculine build ; her face was not beautiful, but abundantly charming ; her eyes large, soft and expressive. Probably she was not as alluring as we see her in the pastel of La Tour. Her portrait by the queen of cats, Madame du Deffand, is a harsh libel, without the excuse either of wit or of real observation.

Madame du Châtelet had been the mistress of de Guébriant, of Richelieu, and perhaps of others. She loved seriously, ardently, and with tenderness. When de Guébriant deserted her, she tried to kill herself. With Richelieu, long after their intrigue, she remained on terms of loyal and open friendship. It was, perhaps, this virile quality of frankness, this honesty of word and action, which made Voltaire describe her, in later years, as " a great man in skirts," and which taught him to respect her memory and " to think not at all of her womanly weakness." For him, she was always " the divine Emilie."

In the summer of 1733, Voltaire addressed to Madame du Châtelet an *Ode on Calumny*, itself containing some of the vilest and most brutal calumny ever written. He had not forgotten Rousseau's epigram, and here, for twenty-five lines, he coarsely abuses the " old rhymer."

It is pleasant to be able to contrast with such acid malevolence the kindness which he showed at this time to two obscure and penniless young writers, Lefèvbre and Linant, both of whom he lodged and fed in his own house.

The tragedy of *Adélaïde du Guesclin*, presented on the 18th of January, 1734, was a failure, and had to be withdrawn after the first calamitous performance. In a changed form, and under another name, the play was immensely successful in 1752. But the chief literary event of 1734 was the publication of the *English Letters* or *Lettres Philosophiques*, of which the English translation had already appeared, under Thiériot's supervision, in London. The sheets had been printed by Jore at Rouen some time previously ; the Keeper of the Seals, having heard something of this wicked and subversive work, sent an agent to Rouen to get hold of the books and to question the printer. Jore, advised of what was coming, was duly prepared. The ultimate publication of the *Letters* in their original form took place in circumstances which are now very obscure, but evidently without Voltaire's consent.

No sooner had the book made its appearance in Paris than the edition was seized, Voltaire's rooms in the Rue du Long-Pont were raided, and Jore was clapped into the Bastille. With picturesque barbarity, the book was publicly torn to pieces and burnt by the executioner.

To us, it seems odd enough that a work apparently so moderate in tone should have been the cause of such desperate measures. We must remember, that to advocate the unrestrained use of the reason, of the intelligence and of the critical instinct, was to oppose the inevitable, unvarying policy of the Catholic church; that a light or satirical method in dealing with the clergy of this, or indeed of any other, church was an offence of the most diabolical sort ; and that the toleration of schism, and above all of such a pernicious teaching as that of the Quakers, could not be endured by the authority of the State.

Voltaire was at Monjeu, celebrating the marriage of de Richelieu—a marriage of his own contrivance—, when he heard of what was going on in Paris. He took to his heels without delay. Such flights were not infrequent. *Lettres de cachet* flew after him ; but he was not to be unearthed. After a daring visit to the French army of the Rhine at Philipsbourg, where his friend de Richelieu had been wounded in a duel, he came to Cirey, the home of the Marquis and Marquise du Châtelet.

From that time, and for many years, Cirey became the home of Voltaire.

The château of Cirey, about four miles from Vassy on the St-Dizier road, was in the pleasing and rural country of the Marne (Champagne). From Cirey to Paris was a distance of some hundred and thirty miles—a distance which, in those days, made rapid communication impossible. Here, there would be time to rest, to open negociations, and to make peace.

Du Châtelet made no objection to an arrangement which interfered in no way with his own dull, placid amusements, and which was not by any means unusual. Besides, Voltaire had just helped him to win a long and tedious lawsuit, and had thus been of use in repairing his decayed fortune. To have the good will of a man so adroit as Monsieur de Voltaire, and moreover so illustrious, was a benefit as well as a distinction. What is more, du Châtelet felt some of that admiration which the simple-minded so readily accord to those who write books.

As for Monsieur de Voltaire himself, he began, with the greatest energy and enthusiasm, to rebuild the house and to lay out new walks and terraces. You would have thought that everything belonged to him. The quiet, ruinous place was quickly over-run with masons, gardeners, architects, furnishers, painters, and what not. Madame du Châtelet posted off to Paris, not only to calm ruffled authorities and to obtain a pardon for Voltaire, but to buy curtains, carpets, books, pictures, china, and a hundred pretty kickshaws. Voltaire described her return in a gay note to Madame de Champbonin (" pussy-cat "), one of their neighbours :

" Madame du Châtelet is here, having come back from *Paris* last evening. . . . She is surrounded by two hundred packages, which arrived here at the same time. We have beds without curtains, rooms without windows, china cabinets and no arm-chairs, charming phaetons, and no horses to draw them. Madame du Châtelet is laughing, adorable, in the midst of this disorder. She came in a sort of cart, bruised and shaken, without having slept, but in very good health. She commands me to send you a thousand compliments. We are patching up old tapestries. We are searching for curtains, we are making doors—all for your entertainment. And I vow, jesting apart, that you shall be mighty comfortable here."

Then, after a short absence from Cirey, he found the divine Emilie hard at work. " She is become an architect and a gardener," he wrote to Madame de Neuville. " She has put windows where I put doors ; she is changing the staircases into chimneys, and the chimneys into staircases ; she has had limes planted where I proposed elms ; and if I have dug an herb-garden, she has turned it into flower-beds. What's more, she has done the work of a fairy in the house. She turns rags into tapestries ; she has found the secret of furnishing Cirey with nothing."

For all that, the fairy's work seems to have been very substantial and very costly. Terraces, balustrades, gardens, required the labours of many men. Inside the house, rooms, galleries and ante-chambers were being rebuilt or added ; rooms in yellow or blue or silver. There was a continual unpacking of china images, of books, pictures, apparatus, glasses, clocks, marabouts, brackets, lacquered tables, or rolls of " Indian paper." There was a " little statue " of the Farnese Hercules, and another of Venus. The bathroom (with its new porcelain bath) had to be paved with marble and lined with tiles. Panelling, painting, papering—there was no end to it.

Divine Emilie, tireless, radiant, and her strange lover, busied themselves day and night with these new toys, these delightful creations. Yet they found time, in the midst of all this enchantment, for an occasional game of chess, for many quarrels, much perusing of plans, many philosophical debates. We may well ask what had become of the husband, or what he thought of it all. No one knew. Du Châtelet, always obliging, had sunk below the horizon.

At table, the little son of the Marquise would make his appearance. Two amusing country ladies, Madame de Champbonin and Madame de Neuville, often visited Cirey and often received gallant notes from Voltaire : Madame de Champbonin acquired a room of her own at Cirey.

Madame du Châtelet was in Paris again at the end of the year, charged with many commissions by Voltaire. Here she must needs go to midnight Mass, and hear the " carols upon the organ." She had her box at the Opera, her place at cavagnole or quadrille. But her pleasures were quickly and willingly renounced so that she might look after a sick friend—poor Madame de Richelieu, who lay in bed with a fever. Even her return to Cirey had to be postponed. And at Cirey,

Voltaire was quarrelling with the workmen, afraid of being cheated, " burdened with details," and demanding the services of an agent.

Voltaire was now in his forty-first year. If he was not one of the most esteemed or most estimable men in France, he was certainly one of the most famous. His fame, indeed, had spread far beyond his own country, and was known to the whole world of letters. It was fame of a mixed and peculiar quality. Part of it was due to the notable success of *Oedipus*, of the *Henriade*, of *Charles XII* and *Zaïre*. Part was due to the light poems and satires which then appeared so scandalous and so daring. No doubt the quarrels with Rousseau and Desfontaines helped equally to build up his variegated reputation. But his fame rested then to a large extent, as it still does, upon a more intimate basis. Voltaire had become a name associated with the idea of a singular, violent and audacious personality. Voltaire had been in prison twice. He had been exiled. He had meddled in many things, and was the hero or the villain of many escapades. His friends were powerful and so were his enemies. In the general action of the period he was playing a part by no means inconspicuous and by no means without effect. He represented, with brilliance and precision, a new habit of thought which was becoming more and more congenial. He was a symbol, a legend. In reading or hearing his name, men were reminded, not so much of books or plays as of a man ; a strange, rather shocking and terrifying man, who would pull folk along with him in spite of themselves.

His health, if we are to believe his letters, was never worse. He suffered " frequent maladies," " long and cruel maladies." His energy was never greater. That wicked grotesque, *La Pucelle—The Maid*—was being composed, and so was the tragedy of *Alzire*. The *Age of Louis XIV* was in preparation.

Physical science occupied much of his time, and he presently surrounded himself with all manner of glasses, engines, and instruments for optical or chemical research. In these matters, though he was better informed than most men of his time, he was only moderately successful. With all this, much letter-writing, many quarrels, and all the planning, devising, excitement of the new Cirey.

Early in March, 1735, he received from Hérault permission to return to Paris, on condition that he behaved properly. "The more talent you have, Sir," wrote Hérault, "the more clearly you should perceive that you have enemies and rivals. Silence them, once and for all, by conduct worthy of a wise man and of one who has already reached a certain age."

By the end of March, Voltaire was in Paris, where Madame du Châtelet awaited him. Hérault received a charming note from the "wise man," who told him that he had arrived "very ill"—otherwise he would have hastened to pay his court to the kind, fatherly and generous Hérault, that most benign chief of police. The reputation of being an invalid is sometimes a great convenience.

In May, he was at the court of Stanislas Leczinski, the ex-king of Poland, at Lunéville in Lorraine.

Stanislas was the father of the French queen. He was a gentle, bewildered man, then in his fifty-ninth year, who lived quietly with his placid mistress, Madame de Boufflers, and with a following of studious, obscure men who called themselves philosophers. He liked

88

to potter about in his grounds, devising rock-gardens or fountains or little houses.

To Voltaire, the chief attraction of the court of Luné-ville was a laboratory. Physical science was then the fashion at Lunéville ; dainty dabblers like Madame de Richelieu (now recovering from her illness) would prattle of Newtonian principles, or gaze with round eyes at the wonders of an astrolabe. From this strange court, to be associated, later, with the greatest tragedy of his own life, Voltaire wrote to Thiériot :

" My dear correspondent, here am I in a court and yet no courtier. I hope to live here like those house-hold mice, who lead a gay life, without ever making the acquaintance either of the master or of the family. I am not made for princes, even less for princesses. 'Tis well enough for Horace to say

Principibus placuisse viris non ultima laus est,

I shall never deserve that praise. There is an admir-able physician here call'd Varinge, who, from being a locksmith's apprentice, has become a worthy philosopher, thanks to nature and to the encouragement of the Duke of Lorraine. . . . There is also one Duval, the librarian, who, once a peasant, is now a man of learning, and whom the same Duke of Lorraine met one day as he was looking after his sheep and studying geography. You may well believe that these are the great ones of the world to whom I shall pay my court ; add one or two intelligent Englishmen, who ('tis said) have become human enough to speak."

A more detailed and more diverting account was given in a letter to Formont, written after Voltaire's return to Cirey :

"How now ! my good philosopher ; 'tis long enough since I have had a word with you. I have been at the court of Lorraine, but you may well doubt if I have play'd the courtier. They have there a most admirable establishment for those sciences which are but little known and less cultivated. 'Tis a great hall, furnished with all the newest machines, and especially with those which display the Newtonian system. There is near a thousand crown's worth of engines of all sorts. A simple locksmith, become philosopher, and sent to England by the late Duke of Lorraine, has made the greater number of these machines with his own hands, and shows them with much acuteness. There is nothing in *France* to be compar'd with this establishment ; and all that it has in common with *French* ways, is the neglect with which it is treated by the little court of Lorraine. 'Tis the fate of kings and courtiers to have good things to their hand, and not to perceive 'em. They are like blind men in a gallery of paintings. Go to what court you please, you'll always find *Versailles*. But I must tell you, to the honour of our court of *Versailles* and the honour of our ladies, that Madame de Richelieu has taken a course of physicks in this hall of machines ; that she has become a pretty good *Newtonian*, and that she has confounded publickly a certain Jesuit preacher who knew nought save words, and who took on himself to argue, like a vain babbler, against proof and against intelligence. He was cried down, with his rhetorick, and Madame de Richelieu was the more admir'd because she is a woman and a duchess."

Voltaire was not to occupy himself for long with these peaceful amusements. The performance of *Caesar* at the Harcourt College in August led to a quarrel with

Desfontaines ; and there was another with the fatuous Lefranc de Pompignan, whose conceit exposed him, later, to the deadly ridicule of his enemy.

With all these affairs and labours, he found time for his usual immense correspondence. Among those to whom he wrote were two old Jesuit fathers, d'Olivet and Tournemine, who had been his teachers when he was a boy at Louis-le-Grand. During his visit to England, he had written to another of these old men, Father Porée.

In these letters we find the unaffected kindness and gratitude which Voltaire could feel as truly as any other. He sought, indeed, to draw Tournemine into a long polemic upon the nature of the soul and the properties of the elusive *être pensant*. " My very dear and reverend Father," he wrote to him, " I have always loved truth, and I have always sought her in good faith." It is clear that he valued the intelligence of Father Tournemine as highly as he valued his good will and friendship. He put his questions carefully.

The good father replied with Latin verses, with some old-fashioned arguments about the divisibility of matter, and with various theological subtleties concerning the personal and the immaterial.

Voltaire answered the letter with grace and kindly sentiment. " My dear Father, the unalterable friendship with which you honour me is indeed worthy of such a heart as yours ; it will be precious to me all the days of my life. I beg you to receive the renewed assurances of my own, and to assure Father Porée, also, of the gratitude which I shall always owe him. You have both taught me to love virtue, truth and letters. Be kind enough to assure the reverend Father Brumoy of my sincere esteem. I do not know the Father Moloni or Father Rouillé of whom you speak to me ; but if

they are your friends, they must be men of merit."
Then, gently advocating the principles of Newton, he
showed that he was unconvinced, either by Tournemine's
physics or by his theology. "If ever I find some one
who can prove to me, by pure reason, the spirituality and
immortality of the soul, I shall be eternally obliged to
him."

The letter to Father d'Olivet was of a lighter kind :

"My dear Abbé, do you know that I reproach
myself, indeed, for having let slip so much of my life
without profiting from your amiable conversation ? In
all the world, you are the man to whom I owe most,
and whom I have seen the least. I vow to you, that
if ever I quit the happy retreat in which I live, it will
be to make a better use of my time. I love the sanity
of the ancients, I devour what is good among the
moderns, but I set before all the sweetness of friendship.
All this is to be found with you. Permit me, then, to
relish some part of these many excellent things in your
letters, whilst I await the moment for seeing you. What
you call my *Ariosto* [*La Pucelle*] is a folly by no means
as long as his ; *non ho pigliato tante coglionerie.* I
should have been ashamed to have devoted thirty *cantos*
to these whimsies and to these debauches of the imagination. I have but ten *cantos* in my *Maid* Joan. So that
I'm at least two-thirds wiser than *Ariosto.* These
diversions are the interludes of my work. I find that
one has time for everything if one is ready to make
use of it. My chief occupation at present is that fair
Age of Louis XIV. Pitched battles, revolutions, are
the least part of this design ; squadrons or battalions
victorious or beaten, towns captured or recaptured, are
matters of all history ; the age of Louis XIV, in war and

politicks, has no advantage over the others. . . . Take away the arts and the progress of thought in this age, and you will find nothing remarkable, nothing which ought to receive the attention of posterity. . . . Have you heard that I had *The Death of Caesar* play'd the other day at the Harcourt College—a tragedy of my own making, in which there are no women ? But it has certain verses of the sort people used to write sixty years ago. I am mighty anxious that you should see this work. It has a *Roman* ferocity. Our young ladies would think it horrible ; one could scarce recognize the authour of the tender *Zaïre*."

Bearing the same date as the above (24th of August, 1735) is a particularly happy letter written to Berger :

" Your letters add a new charm to the pleasures which I enjoy in the Solitude to which I have retir'd, far from the braying, naughty and miserable world ; far from bad poets and bad criticks. I had a thousand times rather hear from you of what is passing than be a witness of it. There is a multitude of events which weary the spectator, but which become interesting when they are well related. Your letters embellish the follies of the age. I read them to a loveable lady, worthy of respect, whose taste is universal ; your letters please her infinitely. I am well content with this little treachery towards you, so that I may engage you to write more often. If 'twas only myself read your letters, I would not pray you to favour me with one each day in the interest of my pleasure alone ; but since they are the delight of one whom all the world desires to please, your own pride should now be engaged.

" Tell me if the great musician, *Rameau*, is also

maximus in minimis, and if, from the sublimity of his grand musick, he descends with success to the simple graces of the ballet. I could wish *Newton* had made vaudevilles ; I would have esteem'd him the more. He who has but one talent cannot be a great genius ; he who has several is more to be loved. 'Tis apparently because I am the very humble Servant of those who touch at once the two extremes, that I have been etch'd by the side of M. de Fontenelle. My friend Thiériot has had himself painted with the *Henriade* in his hand. If I had a copy of this portrait, I'd have my friend and my mistress in one frame. Tell me if you see him sometimes at the *Opera*, and reproach him for his laziness in writing."

To Falkener, appointed to the embassy at Constantinople, he wrote in English :

" My dear friend, your new title will change neither my sentiments nor my expressions. My dear Falkener, friendship is full of talk, but it must be discreet. In the hurry of business you are in, remember only I talk'd to you, about seven years ago, of that very same ambassy. Remember I am the first man that did foretell the honour you enjoy. . . . If you pass through France on your way to Constantinople, I advise you I am but twenty leagues from Calais, almost in the road to Paris. The castle is called Cirey. . . . There lives a young lady called the marquise du Châtelet, whom I have taught English to, and who longs to see you."

In all these letters we have the most human, the kindliest and more generous side of Voltaire's character. His letters to the Jesuit fathers show that his war against orthodox religion was not war of an indiscriminate kind, and certainly not a war against individuals, unless individuals were cruel, offensive or treacherous.

The year 1736 is marked by the great success of the American tragedy *Alzire*, played first on the 27th of January, and then for twenty consecutive nights. There were two special court performances, one on the 21st of February and the other on the 15th of March. Even that slippery villain, Desfontaines, praised the tragedy in high terms, and professed a warm admiration for the author.

Voltaire himself did not leave Cirey to witness the triumph of his new piece. He was unwell. Madame du Châtelet sat by his bedside, reading aloud from Cicero and Pope. Thiériot was requested to send the news from Paris : " Tell me, good friend, with your wonted candour and without fear, all that folk are saying about me. Be very sure I shall make none but a good use of it, that I shall but consider how to silence evil and how to encourage good. Let me know, without scruples, my friends and my enemies, so that I may compel these latter not to hate me, and make myself worthy of the others." A few days later, in a letter to an unknown correspondent, he said that his health " had become deplorable."

On the 22nd of February, 1736, he wrote one of the liveliest of his English letters to Falkener, who was then at Constantinople :

" Now the honest, the good and plain Philosopher of *Wandsworth*, represents his king and country, and is equal to the Grand Seignior. Certainly England is the only country where commerce and virtue are to be rewarded with such an honour. . . . Had I not regulated my life after a way which makes me a kind of *solitaire*, I would fly to that nation of savage slaves, whom I hate, to see the man I love. What would my entertainment be ! and how full the overflowings of my heart, in contemplating my dear Falkener, amidst so many Infidels of all hues, smiling with his humane philosophy at the superstitious follies that reign on the one side at *Stamboul*, and on the other at *Galata* ! I would not admire, as milady Mary Worthley Montagu says

> The vizir proud, distinguished from the rest ;
> Six slaves in gay attire his bridle hold,
> His bridle rich with gems, his stirrups gold !

For, how the devil ! should I admire a slave upon a horse ? My friend Falkener I should admire !

" But I must bid adieu ! to the great town of Constantinople, and stay in my little corner of the world, in that very same castle where you were invited to come in your way to Paris. . . . Your taking an other way, was certainly a sad disappointment for me, and especially to that lady who makes use of your *Locke* and of more of your other books. Upon my word ! a French lady who reads *Newton*, *Locke*, *Addison* and *Pope*, and who retires from the bubbles and the stunning noise of Paris, to cultivate in the country the great and amiable genius she is born with, is more valuable than your Constantinople and all the *Turkish* empire !

" You will see, perhaps, a renegado, the bastard offspring of an Irishman who went to Paris, by the name of Mac-Carthy ; a busy, bold, stirring and not a scrupulous man. He had the honour, by chance, of being known to the marquise du Châtelet ; but was expelled from her house for his rogueries and impudence, before he left Paris, with two young men in debt, whom he seduced to turn musulmen. . . . I would fain know what sort of life he leads now with the followers of Mohammed. But, what concerns me much more, what I long to be informed of is, whether you are as happy as you seem to be. Have you got a little private *seraglio* ? Or are you to be married ? Are you over-stoked with business ? . . . Do you drink too much of that good Cyprus wine ? For my part, I am here too happy, though my health is ever very weak."

In March, he was himself " overstoked with business." *Louis XIV* was nearly completed. " Barche is going to print *Zaïre* ; I am correcting it. Prault is re-printing the *Henriade* ; I am correcting that also. I correct all, save myself. Do you know, that I am retouching *Adelaide*, and that she will be one of the least unseemly of my daughters ? "

And now came a truly vexatious episode. Book-seller Jore, we remember, had been clapped into the Bastille for having dared to print the *Lettres Philosophiques*. Voltaire, in his blue and silver room at Cirey, had, no doubt, ceased to trouble himself about bookseller Jore. But Jore now reminded him of his obligations in a singularly unpleasant fashion. Hérault, he said, was prepared to release him and to restore his rights, if he would tell the whole truth about the offending book ; but of course he could say nothing without the consent of M. de Voltaire. This was a pitfall, but it was one which, with all his cunning and suspicion, Voltaire did not perceive until it was too late. Moved by pity, he sent Jore a careful account of the entire transaction. Thereupon the bookseller put forward a claim for his expenses—one thousand five hundred livres.

In the sorry and sordid quarrel which followed, neither side appeared to advantage. The poet hurried to Paris. To Jore and his terrible *factum*, he replied with a *counter-factum* in which he tried to prove that he owed nothing at all. But if Jore was wrong in bullying and threatening, if he had weakly and treacherously lent himself to the enemies of Voltaire, if his terrible *factum* was full of idle and irrelevant gossip, of mere spite, Voltaire was not less in the wrong when he attempted to disclaim all liability. Matters were finally settled in consideration of the sum of five hundred livres paid, nominally, as compensation to Jore. The Jore affair, cloudy and squalid like all commercial disputes, did Voltaire an infinite amount of harm with the public, and we may suppose that the bookseller was not unassisted by the personal enemies of the poet. The *factum*, libellous as it may be, and dishonest in intention as it certainly was, is clearly the work of a practised writer, and Jore was no writer. Nor was this his only vexation, for Rousseau published, against him, a very bitter and malicious pamphlet.

A more pleasing diversion, and one which was later to have tremendous results, was the arrival of a letter, dated the 8th of August, from Frederick, the Crown Prince of Prussia.

The great Frederick was then a youth of twenty-four, with all the glowing enthusiasm of a young intelligent mind, and with a touch of diplomatic subtlety. Like the older and greater man to whom he was writing, he had a more than ordinary share of mental energy, and a more than ordinary desire to learn and appreciate both art and science. He spoke and wrote in French habitually, despising German as the language of boors.

Our divine Emilie, however proud she may have been, must have read the letter with some little uneasiness.

Here was a rival indeed (the only one she had ever cause to fear), and one to whose impulsive advances the poet could not be insensible. The favour of a wise and generous prince, such as Frederick appeared to be, a new Marcus Aurelius—the allusion was bound to come—, and the prospect of alliance with one who was clearly destined to become a great captain and a great ruler, a patron of learning and letters and one whose decisive part in history was assured, were powerful attractions for a man as ambitious, as eager for renown as Voltaire.

" Sir," wrote Frederick, " although I have not the satisfaction of knowing you personally, you are none the less known to me by your works. They are treasures of the spirit, if one may so express oneself— pieces wrought with such taste, such delicacy, such art, that their beauties appear new each time one reads them. . . . You add to the qualities of an excellent poet an infinity of various learning which, truly, hath some affinity with poetry, but which your pen has brought to it for the first time. Never before has a poet bestow'd rhythm upon metaphysickal thoughts. . . . The kindness and support which you show to all those who devote themselves to the arts and sciences make me hope that you will not exclude me from the number of those whom you find worthy of your instructions." Then came flowery praises of the *Henriade*, *Caesar*, and *Alzire*. " Corneille, the great Corneille, he who won the united admiration of his age, if he came to life again, would see with amazement, and perhaps with envy, that the Tragick Muse showers profusely upon you the favours she gave so grudgingly to him. What may we not expect from the Authour of such Masterpieces ! What new marvels are to come from the pen which has design'd *The Temple of Taste* with such spirit and with such elegance ! " He begs him to send all his works, even those which are unpublished. He will respect the confidence. " I know, unhappily, that the word of princes is a thing of small count in these days ; but I hope, none the less, that you will not concern yourself with a general prejudice, and that you will make an exception to the rule in my favour. . . . If my destiny is not kind enough to enable me to possess you, at least I may hope to see one day him whom I have admir'd so long and from so far, and to assure you with my own voice that I am, with all the esteem and consideration due to those who, following the Torch of Truth as their Guide, devote their labours to the publick weal, Sir, your affectionate friend,

"FEDERIC."

" Federic "—the very name had to be softened, hushed to please the sensitive ear of the poet.

Voltaire was not slow in answering :

" Sire, one would need to be insensible, not to be infinitely touch'd by the letter with which Your Royal Highness has deigned to honour me. My self-love has been too greatly flatter'd ; but the love of mankind, which I have ever preserved in my heart, and which, if I may dare to say it, has form'd my character, has given me a pleasure a thousand times more pure, when I see that the world has a Prince who thinks like a Man, a Prince Philosopher who will make men happy. . . . I behold, Sire, with the joy of a heart full of love for the publick good, the immense distance which you have plac'd between men who seek the truth in peace, and those who desire to make war with words which they do not understand. I see that Newton, Leibnitz, Locke, Bayle, those souls so high, so sweet and full of light, are those who feed your mind, and that you reject that other pretended nourishment, which you would find poisoned or without substance." But he is loyal to Emilie. " I should think it a good fortune indeed if I could come to pay my respects to Your Royal Highness. One goes to *Rome* to see the churches, the pictures, the ruins and the statues. A Prince such as you is far worthier of a pilgrimage; 'tis a rarity more marvellous. But affection, which holds me in the retreat where I am living, does not permit me to leave it. You think, no doubt, like Julian, that great man who was so slander'd, who said that friends ought always to be preferred to kings."

These letters were but the forerunners of an amazing correspondence. Later, with fuller experience and fewer illusions, Voltaire could speak of these effusions with cynical frankness. " He likened me to a divine man, and I likened him to Solomon. Epithets cost us nothing. Some of these follies have been printed in my collected works ; but happily they have not printed the thirtieth part of 'em."

It is probable that, in their first letters, neither was wholly insincere. Frederick's enthusiasm seems to have been real enough ; and Voltaire was flattered by the attention, and interested in the character, of this remarkable prince, who was so unlike other princes. As for the fulsome extravagance of these letters, we must remember the age in which they were written— an age of baroque influence ; ornate, florid, curly and allusive in all its forms of speech, dress, politeness, building or writing.

French verses presently made their appearance in Frederick's letters. They were not good verses, but they were ingenious, and more flattering than ever. Our " divine man " corrected their faults with gentleness, and himself wrote verses in reply. No compliment was too rich, no comparison too exalted. Frederick was the Trajan, Maecenas, Marcus Aurelius and Solomon of the North ; he was the Star of the Northern Firmament ; he was both Achilles and Homer. As for Voltaire, he was equal, if not superior, to all the writers of antiquity ; he was not the servant but the master of the Muses.

But these were diversions. More serious writings occupied his time. On the 10th of October, the new play of the *Prodigal Son* was suddenly presented to a surprised audience at the Comédie, who had assembled, as they imagined, to see the *Britannicus* of Racine. This little stratagem, forestalling any cabal, served its purpose. No one knew who had written the new comedy, and so the critics were on their guard, and the audience could enjoy the piece without apprehension. Who was it by ? Probably, said Voltaire, it is by de Gresset. Certainly not by him, Voltaire.

These disavowals, these falsehoods, became habitual. The fear of persecution may justify them. " Falsehood," he said, writing to Thiériot, " is only a vice when it does harm ; 'tis a great virtue when it does good. Be then, more virtuous than ever. We must lie like the devil ; not timidly, not once only, but with boldness and always."

The satire of the *Mondain* was written in 1736, the tragedy of *Merope* was designed, and a work on the *Philosophy of Newton* almost completed. Abbé Moussinot was charged with various commissions in

Paris, and became Voltaire's private agent. Speculations in army contracts were a source of immense profit, and Voltaire found it equally profitable to lend money, on his own terms, to noblemen who were in need of ready cash.

It is impossible, now, to retrace the many activities of this busy and vigorous mind, for ever at work, for ever scheming, battling, full of contrivance, full of ambition, and always ready to seize a new opportunity or to follow a new thought. Nor can we describe in detail all the quarrels, all the flights, evasions, trickeries and turnings of this amazing life.

" A comedy ; after a comedy, some geometry ; after geometry, the teaching of Newton ; and in the midst of all, sickness ; and with sickness, persecutions more cruel than any fever." So he writes to de Cideville in December ; but Cirey was always a paradise and Emilie the angel. Even the " persecutions " and the great quarrels were sometimes forgotten. " The vapours, which Rousseau and Desfontaines try to raise from the midst of the filth in which they rear their heads, do not reach me. Sometimes I spit upon 'em ; but 'tis without thinking on't."

Towards the end of 1736, the publication of the *Mondain*, judged by ruffled authorities " a scandalous work," exposed Voltaire to new dangers of persecutions or even of imprisonment. Another flight : this time to Holland.

He left poor Madame du Châtelet full of anxieties and fears. She employed all her resources, all the influence at her disposal, to soften the austere de Chauvelin, the Keeper of the Seals. Voltaire himself tried to throw dust in the eyes of his pursuers by pretending that he was in England. " I am off to Cambridge," he wrote to Thiériot, knowing well that his letter would be opened in the post, " to finish my little course of Newtonism." In Holland he was received with much excitement. The clumsy *incognito* of " Revol, a trader," was easily penetrated ;   at Leyden, men flocked to see him— among them, twenty gentlemen from the court of King George.   He tells Mademoiselle Quinault the actress, " divine Thalia," that " Here I am more greatly honoured than I deserve : a magistrate of Amsterdam has translated the *Death of Caesar*.   They are going to play it, and he has dedicated it to me.   I am not thus honoured in my own country."

At the end of February he came back to Cirey, but without allowing his return to be generally known.   On the 30th of March, he writes to Moussinot " from Cambridge," and in May he says, " I am still in England."

Cirey was now provided with a little theatre, and a dark room for the Newtonian experiments.   Moussinot was overloaded with commissions ;   he had to obtain quickly an infinite number of things, minutely specified, and awaited with impatience.   He had to send telescopes, walking-sticks, pocket scissors, toilet tweezers (" not the little ones of the Quai de Gesvres, but those which are sold in the Rue Saint-Honoré "), feather brushes for the ornaments, brooms for the floors, diamond buckles for shoes and garters, barometers, thermometers (" the longest are the best "), retorts, crucibles, pans for smelting, marble chimney-pieces, clocks, watches, lenses, mirrors, bedroom slippers, powder, burning-glasses, a fowling-piece, jewels and trinkets for the divine Emilie, and a thousand and one curious and varied objects.   With all this, innumerable money transactions, and more than once a work of real charity. " There is a certain Mademoiselle d'Anfreville, a lady

of quality, who has an estate of some kind near Cirey.
I scarce know her, but she is in extreme need. She
lodges near Saint-Germain-des-Prés. My good Abbé,
take a coach and find her ; tell her that I take the liberty
of lending her ten pistoles, and that, when she has need
of more, I have the honour to be at her service."

In July, a little, vivacious, gouty Courlander, Baron
Keyserling — *Caesarion-Keyserling* — arrived at " the
earthly paradise of Cirey." He came as the ambassador
of Frederick, and he brought with him the valuable and
impressive gift of Frederick's own portrait, and a bundle
of metaphysical dissertations. " We received him as
Adam and Eve received the angel ; except that he had
better cheer and a gayer entertainment."

Keyserling, boisterous, talkative, himself confused
by his own knowledge of tongues, and speaking none of
them well, saw with delight a comedy in the little theatre ;
saw fireworks on the lawn, and his master's name traced
by coloured lights : FREDERICK THE HOPE OF
THE HUMAN RACE.

The Baron took away with him a manuscript copy
of *Louis XIV*; he might have taken the *Pucelle* ; but
Madame du Châtelet was too cautious to allow it out
of her hands. He took with him, also, a happy and
vivid impression of the divine Voltaire and not less
divine Emilie, and of all the wonders of the " earthly
paradise." The little Courlander, for his part, had
fired Voltaire's imagination with an account of his royal
master. But the poet was not to be coaxed from his
paradise. " My principal misfortune," he wrote to
Frederick, " is that my ill health will doubtless prevent
me from being a witness of the good that you will do
to men, and of the grand example that you will set
before them."

Meanwhile, Frederick continued to send long letters, with gross flattery, bad verses, and borrowed thoughts upon science and philosophy. He received a copy of *Merope* with admiration. Yet the natural vigour of his intelligence prevented him from agreeing with all the Voltairean propositions, and made him assert a deism less apologetic and less vague than that of his teacher. " I have received your metaphysical chapter upon Liberty, and I must tell you, with mortification, that I am not entirely of your advice. I base my system upon a Principle which ought not to be willingly surrendered to the Facts prov'd by mere reasoning. . . . I try to know as much of God as I can, to which end the method of analogy is of no little help to me. I see . . . that a Creator should be wise and powerful. . . . Hence it follows, that the Authour of this Universe must have had a purpose in creating it."

What says our philosopher of Cirey ? He is ready for all arguments, for all occasions. " One would have thought this letter was from Mr Leibnitz, or from Mr Wolff, to one of his pupils "—but no ! it is signed *Federic :* it is one of the prodigies of the royal mind !

So life went on, for a few months, with no disturbance, no aggravation, but full of a thousand activities. In the spring of 1738, Voltaire's niece, Madame Denis, and her husband, paid a visit to Cirey. Voltaire had always a true affection for his niece (a horrid woman) who, when he was an old man, kept house for him.

Madame Denis, in a letter to friend Thiériot, gave an account of this visit. To her, Cirey was desolation, where nothing could be seen but wild mountains, and where the civilisation of Paris was far indeed. Voltaire was living, she said, in a " terrifying solitude," and it seemed impossible for him to " break his chains." He was far from well ; but Madame du Châtelet had grown plump, and was full of good humour and good health. It had to be allowed that Emilie was " a woman of much spirit, very handsome, and employing every imaginable art to seduce him." She was continually arranging little things to please him, and reading aloud passages from " the best philosophers."

The many enquiries and purchases with which Moussinot had been charged, the many experiments in the dark room, were to bear fruit in an *Essay on the Nature and Propagation of Fire*, with which Voltaire competed for the prize offered by the Academy of Sciences. This attempt, on the part of a mere amateur, was daring enough ; but he had an extraordinary gift for acquiring rapidly the essentials of any subject in which he was interested, and he knew well how to pick the brains of others.

Madame du Châtelet decided to compete also. She did not communicate this design to Voltaire, for fear of hampering or annoying him, but worked in secret. Her friend, Madame de Grafigny, tells us how this astonishing woman composed her treatise at night. She slept but one hour ; then, after plunging her face and hands in cold water, set about her work. In a letter to the savant Maupertuis, Emilie herself gives the story of this enterprise :

" I could not make any experiments, for I was working unknown to M. de Voltaire, and I could not have concealed them from him. I did not think of it until a month before the date on which the essays had to be sent in ; I had to work at night, and these matters were quite new to me. M. de Voltaire's work, which was nearly finished before I began my own, gave me ideas ;

and I was seiz'd by the desire to run the same course. I got to work without knowing whether I would send in my *Memoir*, and I said nothing of it to M. de Voltaire, because I had no wish to blush before him for an enterprise which I feared might displease him—and moreover, I opposed nearly all his ideas in my own treatise. I did not confess it to him until I saw by the *Gazette* that neither he nor I had a share in the prize."

Both failed ; yet both were honourably· mentioned and placed high on the list—Madame du Châtelet, indeed, preceded Voltaire, for she was given the sixth place, and he the seventh. Both essays contained ingenious ideas, and advanced new theories, afterwards proved to be correct. Emilie, with a view far beyond that of many learned men of her time, assumed that "rays of different colours do not give off an equal degree of heat." The prize was divided, and the first name on the list was that of Euler : a victory for the hateful Cartesian theory of whirlpools and the flaccid optimism of Leibnitz. Our Newtonians of Cirey were heretics : and who could suppose an academy favourable to heretics ?

But the heretics of Cirey were greatly discouraged. Emilie, aware that her work could not have been pleasing to the judges, had dared to hope for the honour of an *accessit*, though not for a share in the prize ; but how could the judges have failed to reward the learning and the merit of M. de Voltaire ? And M. de Voltaire, with the fine generosity of his wonder and affection, could not understand how it was that Emilie had not received one of the prizes. It was all those damned Cartesian whirlpools. " M. de Maupertuis, the greatest geometrician in Europe, has said bluntly enough that the two winning French works are pitiful things—but that must not be repeated." He was not concerned with his own work ; but that of Madame du Châtelet, " full of things which would do honour to the most learned men," should at least be printed. He wrote to Maupertuis, asking him to use his influence with the Academy. He wrote also to Réaumur and Dufay. Réaumur, a friendly and gallant man, supported the scheme, and the two papers were accordingly printed in the *Collection* of the Academy.

In July, a Dutch bookseller published, without Voltaire's consent, a part of the *Elements of Newton*, with additions by another hand. This provoked a new satire from Desfontaines, who twitted Voltaire with having, at a ripe age, abandoned poetry for science.

" M. de Voltaire hath incontestably received from nature the talent of poetry ; but is Nature so prodigal of her gifts, and is there not something incompatible between the genius of philosophy and the genius of rhyming ? The first steps which we take in any science usually flatter our self-esteem. We work with ardour, we read with industry, we write for ourselves, and conclude easily that what we have wrote for our own instruction may serve to instruct others ; such, apparently, are the motives which have induc'd M. de Voltaire to write upon *Newtonism*, and then to print what he has written."

That was enough, and more than enough. The answering satire of the *Preservative* (if satire can fitly describe such ugly cudgelling) was quickly written and printed. It was published under the name of the Chevalier de Mouhy, a literary adventurer and purveyor of gossip. At the head of the pamphlet was a cut representing Desfontaines being flogged at the prison of La Bicêtre, and there followed a letter which the author of the *Preservative* was supposed to have received from the author of the *Henriade* in reply to certain enquiries. In this letter, the whole story of Desfontaines' imprisonment, and of his release at the insistence of Voltaire, was frankly related. All this was known before, and the wretched Abbé had no character to lose ; but the vehemence and brutality of the attack staggered him. He replied, in December, with an equally brutal attack—*Voltairomania.*

It is a little strange that Voltaire should have been so much concerned with so mean an adversary, and that he should have joined his name, in the category of hatred, with that of Jean-Baptiste Rousseau. He professed, indeed, that he was not really disturbed, and that he lashed his enemies on principle. He was but " crushing the Infamous," as he would have said later. We find him writing, on the 19th of January, 1739, to Father d'Olivet :

" You must not suppose that the sweet, industrious life of Cirey, in the midst of the greatest magnificence and the best of cheer, the best of books, and, what is of more value, in the midst of affection, can be troubled for one single moment by the croaking of a wretch, who, together with the husky voice of old Rousseau, makes a concert of insults which are despised by every intelligence and detested by every heart. In punishing the Abbé Desfontaines, I seek but one thing ; to show that I have not had a greater part than you have in the *Preservative.* The authour of this pamphlet has made use of two letters known to you for a long time : the one upon Berkeley, the Bishop of Cloyne . . . and the other upon the affair of Bicêtre. One or two people have helped the authour to patch up this *Preservative*, which is a mere inventory and not a work. I have the conclusive proof in my own hands, which I would show you, if the Abbé Desfontaines, who owes me his life, and who by way of thanks has outraged me so grossly, was capable of feeling his wrong and correcting himself."

In such evasions, Voltaire himself was using methods " despised by every intelligence and detested by every heart." Here was a great man, stooping to throw stones or fling mud at a creature so base that he had neither friends nor credit. It is a sorry picture.—But what of the life at Cirey, " in the midst of affection " ?

Madame de Grafigny has left us a vivid account of the earthly paradise, where she was entertained in December, 1738. After describing the rich and complex appearance of Voltaire's rooms, she goes on to the apartment of Madame du Châtelet :

" Her chamber is panelled and painted in yellow lacquer with pale blue hangings ; an alcove of the same, hung with charming *Indian* papers. The bed is in blue moiré ; and everything is so disposed that all, even to the dog's basket, is blue and yellow : chairs, desk, brackets and writing-table. . . . There are glasses, pictures by *Paul Veronese*. . . . On one side of the alcove is a little boudoir ; one is ready to fall upon one's knees on entering it. The panelling is blue, and the ceiling is painted and lacquered by a pupil of *Martin* who has been kept here for three years. All the little panels are fill'd with pictures by *Watteau*. There are the *Five Senses*, then two of *La Fontaine's* fables, the *Kiss Return'd*, of which I have the two prints, and the *Geese of Father Philip*. Ah ! what pictures ! the frames are gilded in filigree upon the mouldings. . . . This divine boudoir has a window which opens upon a charming terrace with an admirable prospect. On the other side of the alcove is the divine wardrobe, decorated with marble, hung with gridelin, with the most delicious prints." Everything was " gay," " divine," " enchanted." And then the bathroom— so neat, so small, but so luxurious ! " Admirably carved and gilded . . . a little sopha, charming little chairs . . . brackets, porcelains, pictures . . . the ceiling is painted, the chamber is rich . . . glasses and diverting books on lacquer tables. It would seem all made for the people of Lilliput." Philosophers were never more prettily housed.

The other rooms were far from " divine." Poor Madame de Grafigny was put in a bare, draughty chamber, with cracks in the walls and with rattling windows. She says, indeed, that " all that does not belong to my lady and to Voltaire is unspeakably mean." Du Châtelet himself had no share in the " magnificence " of the paradise.

Between ten and eleven in the morning, coffee was served in Voltaire's " gallery." There was then a general conversation on literature, geometry, plays and what not. After that, Voltaire, making a bow to the company, retired to his rooms for work or experiment, and in ordinary circumstances the household did not assemble again until it was time for supper—occasionally there was a light collation at four o'clock. Supper was at nine. Here there was good cooking and good food, though not in abundance. Madame du Châtelet once wrote with extraordinary frankness to d'Argental on the subject of health and diet :

" There are some things which would surely ruin my health, such as wine, for example, and liquors of all sorts : I have renounced them from my early youth. I have a temperament of fire, and spend the mornings in drowning myself with liquids. In return, I often give way to the gluttony with which God has endowed me ; but I repair these excesses by a rigorous diet which I impose upon myself at the first signs of inconvenience, and which has always sav'd me from illness."

Voltaire was often late for supper. He had to be enticed away from his desk, and the meal was sometimes nearly over before he appeared. His table-talk was usually charming. He was gallant, witty and good-humoured. Behind his chair stood his own lackey, to whom the other servants handed plates, dishes or wine as if they were pages waiting on a king. The shadowy husband, du Châtelet, ate in silence, or fell asleep, presently withdrawing to his own cheerless apartments. It was then that the conversation became lighter and freer. The company would consist of Madame de Champbonin, the two philosophers, and any guests who might happen to be there. After supper, Madame du Châtelet would return to her work, and it was often five or seven in the morning before she went to bed, and then only for two or three hours.

When the two philosophers had need of exercise, Madame would go riding upon the mare Hirondelle, or would jingle away in her pretty calèche ; Voltaire would sling a wonderful game-bag over his shoulder, a bag fitted with all the necessary appliances, take his fowling-piece, and trudge off to the woods. Perhaps du Châtelet may have joined him. Unfortunately, we have no account of these expeditions ; it would be pleasant indeed to be able to display the author of the *Henriade* as a sportsman ; it would be interesting to know whether he who fought so manfully against the Cartesian whirlwinds had a quick eye and a steady hand with a gun.

Sometimes there were evening entertainments in the little theatre, gay performances, frolics with marionettes, Voltaire capering and laughing like a boy. Or the magic lantern would be installed, and the most comical histories—the story of wicked Desfontaines or the adventures of de Richelieu—cunningly displayed, and made a thousand times more laughable by the invention of our naughty philosopher. Or Madame du Châtelet would sing " whole operas." But these diversions were reserved for the rare occasions when visitors were present, and when Emilie and Voltaire were disposed to amuse themselves and their company.

Little tiffs, of course, were not unknown. Emilie was quick ; she had a temper. She would request him brusquely to change his coat if it was not to her liking. Voltaire would storm or sulk ; he would swiftly and gloomily retire to his room and plead the colic ; or they would both rail at each other in forcible, fluent English.

Madame de Grafigny tells her own story of the horrible scene, in which she was accused, apparently without reason, of having circulated some copies of the *Pucelle*. First she had to endure the hysterical rage of Voltaire, crying, cursing and weeping ; and then the more terrible anger of the marquise—more terrible because it was more controlled, more cruelly directed and more insulting. If Madame de Grafigny spoke the truth, all this was due to the misreading of a private letter, treacherously intercepted by her hostess. Whatever may have been the rights and wrongs of the case, the poor soul was in a most deplorable situation.

The scene began late at night ; it was continued, with alternations of violence and ferocity, until the early hours of the morning, though Voltaire seems at last to have done what he could to appease the furious Emilie. Madame de Grafigny had no money and no friends ; she could not even afford a room in the nearest village. At midday, Voltaire, whose mood and manners had then completely changed, expressed his pity and regret. Madame du Châtelet, less ready to become agreeable or to admit her own mistake, was drily polite.

At length, mere politeness gave way to humanity, and both Emilie and the repentant Voltaire were gentle and attentive. He, indeed, " made the most humble and the most pathetick excuses." He wept, seeing his poor guest ill and suffering, and repeated again and again that he was truly a wretch for having made her so unhappy.

Such is the story of Madame de Grafigny, a woman who certainly had her misfortunes, but who was indiscreet, garrulous and imaginative, and by no means without facility as a writer. It seems probable that, in her lively account of the scene with *Atys* and *Megira*, she was less concerned with mere exactness than she was with the effect of her narrative.

CHAPTER IV

THE KING AND THE POET

THIÉRIOT was one of those weak meddling men who are perpetually anxious to prove their own importance. He was busy, officious, talkative and indiscreet. It was not long before he found himself most unhappily involved in the quarrel of Voltaire and Desfontaines.

In spite of his assurance to d'Olivet, both Voltaire and Madame du Châtelet were profoundly angered by the publication of the *Voltairomania*. They had some reason to be. Voltaire, in the *Preservative*, had cited Thiériot as a witness of Desfontaines' perfidy in writing a satire against his benefactor while he was yet in the prison of the Bicêtre. Thiériot, he said, had indignantly compelled the Abbé to throw the infamous work in the fire, and this took place at de Bernières' house at Rouen. Desfontaines, or " the young advocate," as he called himself, now printed the following denial :

" M. Thiériot is a man as highly esteemed by honest men as Voltaire is detested by them. He drags about, as tho' despite himself, the shameful relicks of an ancient bond, which he has not yet had the force to break intirely. Well, M. Thiériot, who is here call'd upon as a witness, has been asked whether the facts were true ; and M. Thiériot has been obliged to say that he has no recollection of them. Here, then, we challenge Voltaire. The visit to the country, at the house of M. le Président de Bernières, took place in the holidays of 1725. If there is in existence a libel against Voltaire, printed in this year, let it be produced. If he replies, that the Abbé Desfontaines himself threw it into the fire, let him cite witnesses. For assuredly he ought not to be believed upon his word. *M. Thiériot*, says he, *obliged him to throw it into the fire*. And here is M. Thiériot, who declares the falsity of the statement. Mister Voltaire is therefore the hardiest and the most desperate of liars."

Madame du Châtelet had tried to conceal this wretched pamphlet from her friend, well knowing to what a pitch of dangerous fury it would rouse him. She had sought the advice of d'Argental, and herself wrote a clever and stinging reply to the libel. And now it appeared that Voltaire, on his side, with equal restraint and consideration, had been concealing the pamphlet from Emilie. Such restraint, on the part of a man so impetuous and so violently disturbed by any personal attack, was truly evidence of deep affection.

But what could be said for Thiériot ? What, indeed, except that fools are treacherous by nature. Thiériot had been flattered, frightened or cajoled by the Abbé. Thiériot was a gossip, a meddler, a man whose miserable self-importance blinded him to the disastrous effect of his own foolish words. His appearance in this ugly quarrel would, at least, bring him before the public ; to be thus patted on the back by a depraved and mischievous rogue like Desfontaines was, on these terms, no indignity. What he actually said, we do not know. Probably he never " declared the falsity of the statement." He may have admitted that his recollection was not clear. That was enough. He was in one of those proverbial corners from which it was impossible to escape with honour. Voltaire, with real generosity,

refused to believe in the treachery of his friend ; Madame
du Châtelet, who may have been a little jealous of
Thiériot, was in a blaze of anger.

We have an extraordinary letter, written by Thiériot
to Madame du Châtelet in reply to her furious demand
for an explanation. He is bland, evasive and pompous :

" I recognise in the letter with which you have
honour'd me your zeal for your friends, and tho' I am
thus extremely edified, I had no need of this emulation
to engage myself, as I ought to, on the side of M. de
Voltaire in the matter of this unworthy libel. . . .
When the *Preservative* appeared, I was mightily
scandalized by it, and my friendship was moved and
alarmed in the most lively fashion by seeing this libel
attributed to M. de Voltaire, of which I believe him
altogether incapable. . . . The authour of this pamphlet
had inserted therein the fragment of a letter from M. de
Voltaire to M. the Marquis Maffei, in which I was
mentioned as a witness of what took place at Rivière-
Bourdet . . . in 1724 or 1725. I have been much
questioned upon the truth of the statement, and this
was my reply: *That I remembered the meer fact, but as
for the circumstances, they were so indistinct in my mind
that I could not give any account of them.* . . . The authour
of the *Letter of an Advocate* . . . has taken advantage
of a general and very sincere reply. . . . All the information that I can give you, Madam, is that there was
some question at Rivière-Bourdet, about this time,
concerning a pamphlet against M. de Voltaire. . . .
The Abbé Desfontaines showed it to me, and I engaged
him to suppress it. As to the date and title of this
pamphlet (circumstances of the highest importance)
I protest in honour that I remember nothing of

them. . . . My sentiments will be ever the same. Constancy is in my character, as probity, independence, the love of the arts, are in my philosophy. These are my titles to the esteem with which I am regarded by all honest men, and I am more flatter'd by meriting it than by the pretended praises of the authour of this infamous libel ; a libel which deserves the most severe punishment, and at which I am the more indignant since I detest, in general, all such libels . . . as hurtful to the consideration of letters as wholesome criticism is useful to their progress.—I am, in wishing you a happy New Year, etc."

This letter could hardly deceive a woman of Emilie's fine discernment. Her own angry hand wrote quickly upon the margin a series of damning observations.

Thiériot had been pleased enough with the *Preservative* when it first appeared. He dared not mention Desfontaines openly as the author of the *Letter*. The Abbé " showed him the libel"—he could not say who had written it. The question of date was not of the highest importance : the fact itself was of the highest importance. Finally she noted, that all the circumstances which Thiériot had so conveniently forgotten were exactly recorded in his own letters, " which shall be printed, in case he forgets them again."

Thiériot lacked the courage or the decency to write to Voltaire himself. Yet Voltaire begged him to write, in the name of their old friendship :

" Why have you wrote such a dry, ill-timed letter to Madame du Châtelet ? . . . You know the height and firmness of her character ; she looks on friendship as a bond so holy that the least diplomatick shade in friend-

ship appears to her a crime. . . . Once more, tell me
that you cannot balance for one moment between
Desfontaines and your friend ; make truth glorious.
. . . Tell me frankly if you have sent the libel to the
Prince Royal [Frederick]. That is of great importance."

But Thiériot, cowed and desperate, kept silence.

" This wretch Desfontaines," cried Voltaire, " hath
now obtained what he desired ! He has stolen your
friendship from me. 'Tis the one thing I reproach
him with." And again : " I snatch a moment from
the pangs of a nephritick complaint which is still tormenting me, to tell you that my chief sorrow is to have
no news of you. Several of my friends are approaching
the Chancellor. Every one helps me, save you : I
don't even know whether you have or have not sent
this infamous libel, directed rather against you than
against me, to the Prince Royal. I calm as best I can
the unspeakable resentment of Madame du Châtelet ;
M. de Maupertuis is on my side, but we gain nothing ;
I beg of you to repair your fault."
    Then a bitter complaint to the Count d'Argental :
" How is it that the Chevalier de Mouhy, who does not
know me, busies himself as tho' he were my brother,
and Thiériot, who owes me all, keeps his arms folded
in cowardly ingratitude ? . . . He has now the insolence,
the baseness, to write and to publish a letter to Madame
du Châtelet in which he disavows his former letters ;
he has sent it to the Prince Royal ; and to justify himself, says coolly that the *Philosophick Letters* brought
him but fifty guineas, and that he did but eat up eighty
of my subscriptions [to the *Henriade*]. Is there a soul
so dirty and so despicable ? " Such a question might

well be asked. The letter to Madame du Châtelet was not actually published, but it was shown " to more than two hundred persons " ; it was exhibited, in the words of the poor fool himself, " to gentlemen of the Court."

But Voltaire, after writing to d'Argental, received at last a letter from Thiériot. It must have been another evasive and compromising document, but Voltaire was glad enough to hear from the " dirty soul," and to patch up the old friendship. He replied with dignity and fairness, more concerned for the peace of Madame du Châtelet than for his own, yet his letter was clearly that of a friend, anxious to forgive and to be assured of Thiériot's loyalty and affection.

Meanwhile, the marquise had written to Frederick. His Royal Highness must understand that Thiériot was a mere nobody, only known through the kindness of M. de Voltaire ; one who had never entered a gentle-man's house except to carry M. de Voltaire's papers or to repeat his sayings. And Frederick showed that he knew his man. Yes ! Thiériot was a pompous fool ; he had a weak head, but a heart not entirely bad. " He never has a cold, but he must tell me about it in four pages of nonsense. . . . Apart from his faults, he is a good fellow." The truth was, that Frederick, playing upon Thiériot's love of importance, had engaged him to send all that was written or said about Voltaire.

Desfontaines was now pursued with that grim, untiring determination which always characterised Voltaire's pursuit of his enemies. Even Mademoiselle Quinault, " divine Thalia " of the Comédie, was called on to assist. It was no longer a question of pamphleteer-ing ; it was a question of grinding the wretch between the great millstones of the law. But this miserable

affair did not employ the whole of his energy, as he assures
Mademoiselle Quinault in a letter written at Cirey on
the 26th of March :

" I am deeply touch'd by your kindness, Mademoiselle.
But come now ! you must understand me. You think
that the poison which my enemies are pouring over
me by the hogshead is a cold poison which congeals
my feeble spirit : no ; it fires it, and their fury gives
me animation. *Zulime* was written in the midst of the
actions they have forc'd upon me, and in spight of an
hundred letters to be wrote every week. My grief
at being set upon by those who should have defended
me has been turned to tragick sentiments, and the
advice of M. d'Argental, joined to your own, has given
me the idea of writing a moving tragedy by way of
revenge. The secret has not been divulg'd, and I
wait always for your instructions. You fear, Mademoiselle, that my mind will not be sufficiently free for
the correction of *Zulime* ! You must know that I
have been so impatient at not receiving your critickal
remarks, that I have begun another tragedy in the
interval ; four acts of it are sketch'd already. You
will be terribly surprised by the subject ; in a word, I
carry your chains ; take delight in your victory and
crush me if you will ; but know that you have won
the day from the *Bernouillis*, the *Maupertuis*, and the
greatest geometricians of Europe, who have just left
Cirey. I made verses under their very noses, and I
slipp'd on the buskin despite Abbé Nollet's machines,
which fill my gallery. Learn something concerning the
life of your slave : I am either suffering or working ;
and when I am so afflicted by my maladies that I cannot
read, I have the resource of rhyming. My moments

are all devoted to work. Is it just that such a life should be so cruelly persecuted ? You talk to me of the scribblers who write against my works. I have always ignored the hissing of these little concealed serpents, hidden below the ground. But I complain of the monsters who would attack my life, and of the magistrates who allow these horrors to go unpunished. I have never replied to a critick. But, truly, I have enough self-respect to feel that I deserve to be treated rather differently by my own countrymen. I assure you, Mademoiselle, that you console me indeed for these many annoyances ; were I given the choice of losing at once my enemies or your indulgence, I would not accept the bargain."

Voltaire had influence ; Desfontaines had little or none ; but Voltaire himself was a pestilent fellow in the eyes of Commissioner Hérault, by whom the case was eventually tried. Hérault, anxious to bring this tedious and trivial matter to an end, forced Desfontaines to sign a retraction. Accordingly, on the 4th of April, the Abbé set his hand to this peculiar statement :

" I declare that I am in no way the author of a printed libel entitled *Voltairomania*, and that I disavow it entirely, regarding as calumnious all the actions imputed to M. de Voltaire in this libel ; and that I should have thought myself dishonoured had I had the least part in these writings, feeling, as I do, all the sentiments of esteem which are due to his talents, and which the publick so justly accords him."

This declaration, false in every word, had the effect of silencing Desfontaines, though it was not wholly acceptable to Voltaire. But Hérault would go no further ; and Hérault, as Madame du Châtelet astutely perceived, had to be carefully managed. The declaration was not to be made public ; but the Chevalier de Mouhy had a copy of it sent to the *Amsterdam Gazette*, and in that journal it duly appeared.

On the 2nd of May, doubtless under indirect pressure from Hérault, Voltaire wrote and signed a declaration of his own :

" I have always disavowed the *Preservative*, and I have had no part in the collection of pieces which are in this little pamphlet, among which there are some never intended to be made publick."

We may well be appalled by the cold falsehood of these declarations (which deceived no one), by the policy which dictated them, and by the legal and social code to which they were acceptable. Even lawyers and writers, we think, might have lied more becomingly, and with a less impudent violation of the plain truth. But we have to ask whether our indignation is not based upon purely conventional notions of procedure. Matters which plain sense and common honesty can settle between them are not usually brought before a commissioner of police, and the mean quarrel of Voltaire and Desfontaines was one in which sense, honesty and truth had no part to play. A few lies more or less really made no difference. And these formal disclaimers had obvious advantages as forms of compromise. Formal apologies, extracted by legal pressure in settlement of disputes, are in any case morally condemnable and substantially false. Profoundly unedifying as it is, the affair of the *Voltairomania* and the *Preservative* is neither more shocking nor more to be condemned than many of the literary squabbles of more recent times.

Having thus disposed of the Abbé Desfontaines, Voltaire and Madame du Châtelet were free to undertake another and more difficult enterprise. The du Châtelets were poor, but they had much to gain if they could win one of those dreary family lawsuits in which great revenues are dexterously and doubtfully suspended by the law between two obstinate claimants.

Now came a windfall. A sad little infirm personage, Mark Antony du Châtelet, a cousin of the marquis, came, or was invited, to Cirey. Mark Antony was too gouty to walk and too ill to talk; he was, in fact, inconspicuously dying ; but he made over to Madame du Châtelet his rights in a small principality between Trèves and Juliers. This principality lay within the boundaries of the Prussian states. Voltaire had already (in August, 1738) offered it to Frederick. The offer had no particular attraction for that shrewd young man, and he had declined it. But the rights to the estate of Mark Antony, now vested in the marquise, might be turned to good account and might help matters generally. Voltaire and the marquise therefore set out for Brussels on this new business.

They left Cirey on the 8th of May, and after being entertained by de Seychelles at Valenciennes, reached Brussels by the end of the month. They visited a small property of du Châtelet's at some distance from the town, but returned soon afterwards and installed themselves in the Rue de la Grosse-Tour. Here they were occupied with the intricacies of the dreary lawsuit, and the not less intricate problems of metaphysics and geometry. The marquise took lessons from the mathematician Koenig, at that time the friend of Maupertuis, and wrote pathetically to that great savant of her own limitations and of the alarming superiority of Koenig's understanding.

In spite of these grave pursuits, there was time for social gaiety, and even for gaiety of a pretentious kind.

Was not that "vile Rufus," Jean-Baptiste Rousseau, the lion of Brussels ? Voltaire was not the man to abstain from a gesture of defiance. All the fashionable folk of Brussels, Duke of Aremberg and Princess de Chimay among them, were entertained by fiddlers and fireworks at the Rue de la Grosse-Tour.

The entertainment, pleasing enough for the guests, had been spoilt and saddened for Voltaire by a grim disaster. While he was busily supervising the decorations, two carpenters fell from a scaffold on the third floor and were crushed at his feet. The effect of this horrible sight, so unnerving for a man of quick sensibilities, lingered in his mind for days.

Not long after the fête, Emilie and Voltaire were the guests of the Duke of Aremberg at Engheim. Here Voltaire wrote a charming letter to Helvetius, that sprightly youth who was later to shock every one by his essay on the *Human Spirit* :

" I perceive, my dear fellow, that the verses I wrote you were so bad that *Apollo* had no mind you should receive 'em. My letter was addressed to Charleville, where you should have been, and I took care to add a little note so that the letter might reach you in whatever corner of your province you happen'd to be. You have lost nothing ; but I, for my part, have lost the idea that you had of my exactness. Indeed, my friendship is not negligent. I love you too well to be lazy where you are concerned. I await your work, my pretty *Apollo*, with a liveliness equal to your own. I was hoping to send you from Brussels my new *Dutch* edition, but I have not yet received a single copy from my booksellers. There is not one to be had in Brussels, yet I learn they are to be had in Paris. The Dutch printers, who are bungling pirates, have doubtless made many mistakes in their edition and are afraid that I may see it in time to complain of it and cry it down.   I can only find out about this in fifteen days.   I am actually, accompanied by Madame du Châtelet, at Engheim with the Duke of Aremberg, at seven leagues from Brussels.   I play much at *brelan* ; but our precious studies do not lose thereby.   We ought to make an alliance between work and pleasure ; that is your own practice, and 'tis a little mixture that I advise you to make all your life— for in truth you are born both for the one and the other.

" I confess, to my shame, that I have never read the *Utopia* of Thomas Morus ; despite which, I took on myself to give a fête in Brussels a few days ago under the name of the Ambassadour of *Utopia*.   The fête was for Madame du Châtelet, of course ; but will you believe it ?—there was no one in the town who knew what was meant by *Utopia*.   This is not the land of the *belles-lettres*.   Dutch books are prohibited, and I cannot conceive how it was that Rousseau came to choose such an asylum.   This Patriarch of Slanderers, who has long ago lost the art of slandering, and has preserv'd only its rage, is quite as unknown here as the *belles-lettres*.   I am actually in a castle where there have never been any books except those brought by Madame du Châtelet and myself ; but, by way of compensation, there are gardens more beautiful than those of Chantilly, and here one may lead that sweet and free life which is the joy of the country.   The owner of this beautiful estate is worth more than many books ; I believe we are going to play a comedy here ; at least we are reading the parts for the actors.

" I have a very different idea in my head : I have finished this *Mahomet*, of which I shew'd you the sketch.

I am desirous of knowing how a play of a kind so new and so daring will succeed with our gallant *Frenchmen*; I would have the piece acted without disclosing the authour. In whom should I confide sooner than in you ? Do you not command this friend in Paris, who owes you all, and has such a liking for verses ? Could you not send it to him ? Could he not read it to the players ? But does he read well ?—for a good enunciation and a pathetick diction make the proper frame for the picture. So, my dear friend, give me your thoughts upon all this."

From Engheim, Voltaire and the marquise returned to Brussels. The marquise, tired perhaps of lawsuits and mathematics, felt the need of diversion. Nothing would please her but a visit to Paris. Voltaire, who, as we have just seen, was anxious to get *Mahomet* in the hands of the players, was probably willing enough to go there.

They set out, with the indispensable Koenig, towards the end of August, travelling quietly and by short stages. "We are treated like village physicians, who are fetch'd in people's coaches, but allowed to return on foot."

Voltaire wrote to Madame de Champbonin from Cambrai : "If you ask me why we are going to Paris, I can only answer for myself. I am going there because I follow Emilie. But why is Emilie going ? I don't exactly know. She pretends 'tis all necessary, and I am fated to believe her as I am to follow her."

He was not wrong in believing *Mahomet* to be one of his best tragedies, yet he was always attentive to criticism. Frederick, whose own exercises in French verse were more pretentious and more laboured than ever, saw fit to raise one or two little points. It was not correct, he said, to talk of " crushing sparks " ; you might snuff or extinguish them, but you could not crush them. This profound observation had its due effect, and the lines were altered. Mademoiselle Quinault, whose criticism was of real value, and reflected the true opinion of the Comédie, objected to the horrors of the piece. To her the author replied with playful petulance :

" Adorable Thalia, I have a good substantial dish to offer you, and you ask me for whipp'd cream ! I have now re-read *Mahomet*, I have re-read *Zulime* ; this *Zulime* is truly a poor thing, and t'other is perhaps the least bad of my works. I hope the honesty with which I condemn my *African* will allow some credit to the modest opinion which I dare have of my *Prophet*. . . Decide ; I commit myself to you ; you alone shall have the manuscript. Don't on any account leave it for so much as a quarter of an hour in the hands of Minet ; he won't fail to have copies made of it and to send 'em to the country players. Know, fair Thalia, that in sending you my *Prophet*, I'll correct him prodigiously ; but I'll correct him even more when I have learn'd your opinion. You know that you are my oracle."

Zulime, played in June, was not well received ; it was revised, and played with more success, twenty-two years later.

Meanwhile, Voltaire had plunged again into the tumultuous life of Paris, realising the inconvenience, as well as the delights, of notoriety. He wrote a description of his activities to the comfortable Madame de Champbonin :

129

" My dear friend, Paris is a gulf wherein are lost that peace and composure of the soul without which our life is but a fretting tumult ! I do not live indeed ; I am carried away, drawn from myself in these whirlwinds. I come, I go ; I sup at one end of the town, to sup the next day at the other. From a meeting of three or four intimate friends, one must needs fly to the Opera, to the Comedy, to gape at curiosities like a stranger, to embrace an hundred people in one day, to make and receive an hundred protestations ; not one moment to one's self, and no time for writing, thinking, or sleeping. I am like that hero of antiquity who died beneath the flowers which people flung at him."

All this coming and going, all this excitement, the late hours and the early visitors, were too much for him. On the 1st of October he was ill, feverish. The doctors Silva and Morand were quickly in attendance, bleeding and bathing the frail body, and talking gloomily about kidneys and intestines—luckily, said Voltaire, without offending those miserable organs. But these disorders (hardly comprehensible to the doctors, for all their solemn talk and nodding heads) never lasted for long. They were of the kind we should now call temperamental—without knowing much more than Silva and Morand—, and were due to the excessive stimulation of the mind and the excessive fatigue of the body. Purging, bleeding and bathing were good enough cures, and a few days in bed the best cure of all.

After a short stay at Cirey, cold and dreary in the November days, Voltaire and Emilie returned to the Rue de la Grosse-Tour in Brussels.

At Brussels and at the Hague, the two friends were unceasingly active. There was the dreary du Châtelet lawsuit. There was a piece of cloudy finesse with Van Duren the bookseller, concerning Frederick's *Anti-Machiavelli*. There was a squabble with Piron. And always work. Always Maupertuis moving sagely in the background and throwing a little shifting light on the tangled mysteries of natural science and a most unnatural philosophy. Always plays and histories, nervous corrections and painful revisions ; and always the copious, jingling and flattering letters of Frederick, with their horrible verses and hollow sentiments.

In the midst of it all, Voltaire had time to write a gay letter in English to Falkener, still the ambassador at the Porte. With it he sent a set of his published works, probably the Amsterdam edition. Here is the truly delightful letter :

" Dear Sir, I take the liberty to send you my old follies, having no new things to present you with. I am now at Brussels with Madame du Châtelet, who hindered me, some years ago, from paying you a visit at Constantinople, and whom I shall live with in all probability the greatest part of my life, since for these ten years I have not departed from her. She is now at the trouble of a damn'd suit at law, that she persues at Brussels. We have abandoned the most agreeable retirement in the country, to bawl here in the grotto of the flemish *chicane*.

" The high Dutch baron who takes upon himself to present you with this packet of french reveries, is one of the noble *players* whom the emperor sends into Turkey to represent the majesty of the Roman empire before the Highness of the Musulman power.

" I am persuaded you are become, now a days, a perfect Turk ; you speak no doubt their language very well, and you keep, to be sure, a pretty *harem*. Yet I am afraid you want two provisions or ingredients which I think necessary *to make that nauseous draught of life go down*, I mean books and friends. Should you be happy enough to have met at Pera with men whose conversation agrees with your way of thinking ? If so, you want for nothing ; for you enjoy health, honours and fortune. Health and places I have not ; I regret the former, I am satisfied without the other. As to fortune, I enjoy a very competent one, and I have a friend besides. Thus I reckon myself happy, though I am sickly as you saw me at Wandsworth.

" I hope I shall return to Paris with Madame du Châtelet in two years time. If, about that season, you return to dear England by the way of Paris, I hope I shall have the pleasure to see your dear Excellency at her house, which is without doubt one of the finest in Paris, and situated in a position worthy of Constantinople ; for it looks upon the river ; a long tract of land interspers'd with pretty houses, is to be seen from every window. Upon my word, I would, with all that, prefer the *vista* of the sea of Marmara before that of the Seine, and I would pass some months with you at Constantinople, if I could live without that lady, whom I look upon as a great man, and as a most solid and respectable friend. She understands Newton ; she despises superstition, and in short, she makes me happy.

" Farewell, my dear friend. . . . Yours for ever ! "

Voltaire's peculiar vagueness or indifference in regard to time will be noticed in his allusion to Madame du Châtelet. He had not, as he says, lived with her for ten years, but for rather less than seven. It was actually eleven years since he had seen Falkener, and this letter proves the worth and quality of his friendship for this plain, sensible and generous Englishman.

On the 6th of June, 1740, Frederick wrote to him from Charlottenberg, announcing his father's death, and his own accession to the throne of Prussia. The letter is a remarkable one :

" My dear friend, my lot has changed, and I have assisted at the last moments of a king, at his agony, his death. In coming to the royal estate, I had assuredly no need of this lesson in order to be sickened by the vanity of human greatness.

" I was contemplating a little work on metaphysicks ; it has become a work of politicks instead. I had thought to joust with the amiable Voltaire, and now I have to fence with Machiavelli. So, my dear Voltaire, we are not masters of our fate. The whirlwind of circumstance bears us away, and we must submit to be borne away. I pray you to see, in me, only a zealous citizen, a rather doubting philosopher, but a truly faithful friend. For God's sake, write to me as a man, and with me despise all names and titles and all outward show. . . . Farewell, my dear Voltaire ; if I live, I'll see you, and this very year. Love me always, and be ever sincere with your friend."

Frederick was now twenty-eight. He spoke the truth in saying that he despised grandeur ; but he despised it, not so much by virtue of a philosophic attitude as by virtue of those harsh, inhumane or perverted qualities which made him at once so interesting and so formidable. There is something dreadful in the dry composure of this young man, turning so coolly to his duel with " Machiavelli "—

the "old mitred Machiavelli," Cardinal de Fleury, the French minister. He had little cause to love his father, but there is something dreadful, too, in this calm, supercilious view of a death-bed : merely a lesson in human vanity, and rather disgusting.

Young Frederick, however, had the essential qualities of a great statesman ; he was never hampered by scruples or unnerved by remorse or made unsteady by sentiment. He had been well hardened. He went for his mark with the deadly insensibility of a well-aimed bullet, but not with a bullet's calculable directness. He knew how to make up his mind and how to get what he wanted. And he wanted Voltaire, and had made up his mind to get him.

Frederick wanted other distinguished men, too. He wanted Maupertuis—who, with all his oddities, had courage, and with all his inordinate vanity had real learning. Here, indeed, was the beginning of the grim Prussian ideal of "culture." Potsdam (and why not ?) was to be the intellectual centre of Europe. Great men, hired or bribed, would establish a great academy at Berlin. Frederick would have big battalions, but—yes, by God !—he would have big libraries as well.

It must be admitted that France offered little reward to men who practised art, science or literature. Upon her throne sat Louis XV, weakest and most unworthy of her kings. She was governed by feeble or corrupt men or their mistresses, and oppressed by the most irksome and debased kind of religious tyranny. Frederick had a good chance. It was not long before Maupertuis took the bait—Wolff, Euler and Algarotti (the author of *Newtonism for Ladies*) had been more easily decoyed.

In view of what subsequently occurred, it is extremely

important and interesting to see in what strain Voltaire was at this time (June to September, 1740) writing to Maupertuis. Under the date of the 22nd of June we have the following letter, written from Brussels :

" Great men are my kings, Sir, but the reverse does not hold good—kings are not my great men. 'Tis very well for a head to be crown'd, but I prize only those which can think like yours, and 'tis your esteem and friendship, not the favour of sovereigns, which I would fain possess. I would place the king of Prussia alone upon a level with you, because he is of all kings the least of a king and the most of a man. He is enlightened and benevolent, full of great talents and of great virtues ; it will astonish and afflict me sensibly if he is ever false to himself. It does but remain for him to acquire geometry ; but he is a profound meta-physician, and less of a babbler than the great Volffius.

" I shall go to observe this Star of the North, if I can quit the one whose satellite I have been for ten years. I am not like the comets of Descartes which pass from vortex to vortex.

" Talking of the vortex, I have had the fourth volume of Joseph Privat de Molières, which proves the existence of God by means of a five-pound weight placed upon a mouse-trap. It seems that your colleagues, the examiners of his book, have not signified their acceptance of this strange proof ; upon which I have taken the liberty of saying :

> Now when it comes to proving God,
>   The folk of your Academy
> Give up the game without a word,
>   And prove their true sagacity.

. . . . . .

" Farewell, Sir ; I am devoted to you for ever. You know that I have always loved you, although I have admired you : sentiments which are rarely compatible."

He wrote again on the 1st of July :

" The King of Prussia tells me, Sir, that he has *acquired* you, and also Messieurs Wolff and Euler. Does that mean that you will go to Berlin, or that you will direct from Paris the academic labours of the Society which the most amiable of kings, the one most worthy of a throne and of you, desires to establish ? I pray you tell me what your ideas are, and to believe that you cannot communicate them to a man who is more your admirer and more your friend."

Again, on the 21st of July :

" So here you are, Sir, like the *Messiah* : three kings running after you. But I see well that, since you have 7,000 livres from France, and are a Frenchman, you will not abandon *Paris* for *Berlin*. Had you reason to complain of your country, you would do mighty well to accept another, and, in that case, I'd congratulate my adorable King of Prussia ; but 'tis for you to realise your own position. . . . You see me for a few days at the Hague ; I shall return presently to Brussels ; will you permit me to speak to you here of another matter which hath lain upon my heart this long while ? I am distress'd to behold you at variance with a lady who, after all, is the only one who can understand you, and whose manner of thinking deserves your friendship. You are made to love each other ; write to her (a man is always in the right when he puts himself in the wrong with a lady) ; you will re-discover her friendship, since you have always had her esteem."

The policy of these charming letters is quite clear. What was said about Frederick was palpably intended for the eyes, or ears, of that monarch ; and if Maupertuis removed to Berlin (as he did very soon) it was advisable to keep on the right side of him. There may have been something more than policy. It is doubtful whether Voltaire ever had a profound affection for Maupertuis, but he certainly did appreciate his learning and his conversation. He thought of him, rightly, as one of the best informed men of his age, and one of the men best worth knowing. Maupertuis had not yet uttered those crazy notions which exposed him so fatally, some thirteen years later, to the awful broadsides of *Dr Akakia and the Native of Saint-Malo*. The coldness towards Madame du Châtelet was probably due to her book on the *Institutions of Physics*, in which she had shown a preference for the system of Leibnitz. The book was not published until the end of the year, but Maupertuis had doubtless seen the manuscript.

In the meantime, Frederick became more insistent. He did not want to see Madame du Châtelet. Frederick had no fondness for ladies unless they were of a manly build, or slim like his drummer-boys. He could not, so he said, endure the combined brilliance of Apollo and the divine Emilie—no ordinary mortal, indeed, could endure such a blaze of genius.

The marquise offered him the house in the Rue de la Grosse-Tour. The very idea of a meeting in Brussels was too much for the exalted sensibilities of the poet and the king. Voltaire protested that he would faint for sheer joy, he would swoon away at the very sight of his Northern Star : Frederick, not to be outdone, vowed that he would die of delight.

At last, the king arranged to meet Voltaire and the marquise *incognito* at Anvers, but the quartan fever intervened, and Voltaire had to set out alone, some days later, to meet the Star of the North at Clèves.

Voltaire and Frederick met for the first time on the 11th of September, 1740, at the bare and desolate castle of Moyland or Meuse.

After such preludes, the meeting might have been a little awkward, there might have been a shade of embarrassment when Apollo and Solomon beheld each other face to face. The situation was made easier by Frederick's illness, and by the extreme simplicity, or downright discomfort, of his quarters. Voltaire found the king in a plain, cheerless room. He was lying on a small camp bed, and was shivering and sweating with his quartan fever. He wore a dressing-gown of coarse blue cloth and was covered by a tattered quilt. His retinue consisted only of a few troopers and orderlies, and he was attended by the sage Maupertuis, by the ladies' Newtonian, Algarotti, and by the gouty and garrulous Keyserling. There was also the privy councillor, Rambonet, who wore a strange magisterial perruque—one tail of it hardly falling below his shoulder, and the other stuck into his pocket.

In the evening, when the access of the fever had passed, the king rose and came down to supper.

When, some twenty years later, Voltaire wrote his brief *Memoirs* concerning Frederick, he affected to make light of this interview. He had learnt that kings were dangerous playfellows, and had found the new Marcus Aurelius capable of perfidies which ill became his borrowed character. He says nothing of how he read

Mahomet to his royal friend, of Frederick's delight, and the applause of that curious little group of soldiers and philosophers.   He does, indeed, allow that he felt drawn towards the king, who showed both grace and spirit, and who, after all, had the attractions of royalty.   In actual fact, it is clear that both men were deeply and sincerely impressed with each other.   Writing to de Cideville shortly afterwards, Voltaire thus described the meeting at Clèves :

" 'Twas there [at Clèves] that I saw one of the most loveable men in the world, a man who would be the delight of society, who would be sought everywhere, if he was not a king ; philosopher without severity, full of sweetness, charm and complaisance, forgetting that he is a king when he finds himself with his friends, and forgetting it so perfectly that he had almost made me forget it also, and I had need to jog my memory to remember that I beheld, seated upon the foot of my bed, a sovereign who had an army of an hundred thousand men.   This was indeed the moment for reading your amiable verses to him ; Madame du Châtelet, who ought to have sent them to me, has not done so.   I was mightily vexed."

He wrote to Maupertuis, almost immediately after his return to the Hague ; and the letter, though obviously politic, has a touch of enthusiasm which is not altogether unreal :

" When we parted from each other at Clèves, and you went to the right and I to the left, I thought myself at the Last Judgment, where God separates the elect from the damn'd.   To you said *Divus Federicus :* Be seated

at my right hand in the paradise of Berlin ; and to me :
Go, accursed one, to Holland.

" So here am I in this phlegmatick *hell*, far from that
divine fire which animates Frederick, Maupertuis,
Algarotti. For the love · of God, bestow on me the
charity of a few sparks in the stinking waters where I
am founder'd ! Tell me, at least, of your pleasures,
your designs. . . ."

He wrote also, with unquestionable sincerity, to his
friend the President Hénault :

" If the king of Prussia had come to Paris, Sir, he
would not have belied the charms you have discovered
in his letters. He speaks as he writes. . . . 'Tis a
miracle of nature that the son of a crowned ogre, reared
with brutes, should have found, in his wilderness, all
that delicacy and all those easy graces, which in Paris
are only possess'd by a few, and yet have made the
reputation of Paris. I think I have already said that
his ruling passions are those of being just and pleasing.
He is made for society as he is for the throne. . . .
You have reason to be surpris'd with his letters ; you
would be even more so with the *Anti-Machiavelli*. . . .
As I despise and detest the base and infamous Superstition, which dishonours so many States, so I worship
true Virtue, and I think to have found it, both in this
Prince and in his Book."

Frederick, for his part, had been fairly transported.
" I have seen this Voltaire," he wrote. " He has the
eloquence of Cicero, the sweetness of Pliny and the
wisdom of Agrippa ; in one word, he reunites the
virtues and the talents of three of the greatest men of
antiquity. His mind works without ceasing ; each

drop of ink is a shaft of wit leaping from his pen. . . . Du Châtelet is indeed happy in possessing him."

But poor Madame du Châtelet was not so sure of possessing him. She was uneasy. The dreary lawsuit, as well as the interests of Voltaire himself, required her presence in Paris, and when Voltaire was at the Hague, seeing to the printing of the *Anti-Machiavelli*, she had already left Brussels. Now, she thought, Frederick, of whose design to *acquire* the poet there could be no doubt at all, had a more open field. Every woman knows how much her influence depends upon mere proximity. What is more, the affairs of Europe were changing in a way that might prove disastrous to France. The emperor Charles VI ate a dish of mushrooms, and the mushrooms killed him. Young Frederick at once gathered an ominous mass of troops near the Silesian borders. What were his intentions? Cardinal de Fleury would have given much to know. The cardinal thought of the poet and the poet thought of the cardinal. A present of the *Anti-Machiavelli* and a letter from Voltaire drew from the cardinal a little masterpiece of diplomatic subtlety, obviously intended for Frederick's perusal.

Voltaire, when he received this letter, was actually in Berlin. He had yielded to the royal cajoleries and to his own inclination, but he did not intend to pay a long visit to the Prussian court.

In actual fact, there was little cause for Madame du Châtelet's fears. Voltaire's affection for the marquise, if it was neither profound nor exacting nor passionate, was a real affection. She could never have taxed him justly with being unfaithful to her. As he himself had said, he was no Cartesian comet. His moods and variations may have been trying enough, but they were

141

signs, not of a natural flightiness, but of the range and vigour of his mind. And the marquise was exceptionally well fitted to be his companion. The only qualities which could win his respect and admiration were intellectual qualities which resembled his own, and Madame du Châtelet possessed those qualities in a remarkable degree. A stupid woman, no matter how loving and loyal, would have driven him crazy. On the other hand, her intelligence was not insufferably acute ; it was, in truth, decently and becomingly inferior to his ; but not too inferior ; it was finely adjusted and finely responsive to his particular needs.

Voltaire had no thought of disloyalty when he set out for Potsdam. He had meant what he said when he told Frederick that he would never leave the marquise, and he would have been shocked, incredulous, or even amused, if any one had now told him that he was making her unhappy. Perhaps there are no cruelties more piercing than the unconscious cruelties of the egoist. It seemed proper enough, to him, that he should play the lion at Frederick's court, the pet of a whole royal family and the favorite of a king—and was he not, in a sense, the ambassador of France ? What prodigious importance, and what a great adventure ! How could the vainest of men resist these invitations ? He had, besides, the exquisite joy of humiliating his enemies at the French court by showing them how well he was entertained, and how highly esteemed, at the court of this great emperor.

The cost of the journey and the cost of the entertainment had been the subject of negociations between the king and the poet. In this extraordinary bargaining, Voltaire had the best of it, and Frederick agreed—not without lamentation—to settle the bill.

" His appearance for six days only," wrote the king, " will cost me five hundred and fifty crowns a day. Good payment for a fool ; the jester of a great nobleman had never such wages." And yet these two strange men could find in each other's company the rare delight of mutual appreciation without jealousy, and each had for the other a radical sentiment of true esteem.

Life at the court was pleasantly informal. Voltaire was gay and brilliant, and seldom complained of indisposition. There was much making and reading of odes, and much talking of scandal. There was dancing, gaming and feasting ; and at night, Frederick would play " two or three concertos " upon the flute. The charming Sophia Wilhelmina, Margrave of Bayreuth and sister of the king, smiled prettily at Voltaire, whose vivacious gallantry amused her.

Who would have thought of the mustering and marching of Frederick's grim troops upon the borders of Silesia ? Who would have seen, in the pale, slender young man, trilling such light ritornellos upon his flute, the dreadful power which threatened Europe ?

From the court of Remusberg, Voltaire went to Berlin, to pay his respects to the queen-mother, Prince Henry and the royal sisters ; and here he sent a note to Maupertuis : " My dear owl of a wandering philosopher, come and dine to-day at M. de Valori's, and if he is dining with M. de Beauvau, we'll eat at M. de Beauvau's. I must needs embrace my philosopher before I take leave of the amiable, singular and worthy whore who arrives presently." The person so described is none other than Frederick. Those who believe that Voltaire was always elegant should remember this note.

On the 2nd or 3rd of December, the awful little man started on his return to Brussels, cursing his German postillions, cursing the cheerless inns of Westphalia, cursing the atrocious winter roads, on which straps, wheels or axles were so easily broken. He had enjoyed himself. He had been monstrously flattered. He had been treated like a great man, and had flirted with a princess.

But what had come of the diplomatic mission? Little enough. He wrote briefly to de Fleury, telling him that Frederick had seen his letter. "He is the more sensible of your praises because he deserves them, and methinks he will continue to deserve those of all the nations of Europe. 'Tis to be wished, for their welfare, or at least for that of the greater part, that the king of France and the king of Prussia should be friends. That is your business. . . ." That is your business ! The little man in the post-chaise, jolting along the West-phalian roads, grinning and cursing, and observing all with his quick, malevolent eyes, had very different ideas in his head.

Poor Madame du Châtelet, meanwhile, was ill at Brussels. She had fretted herself into a fever of anxiety, and believed she was dying.

" I have been cruelly paid," she wrote," for all that I have done at Fontainebleau; I have brought to a happy end the most difficult affair in the world. I have ob-tained for M. de Voltaire an honourable return to his country ; I have recovered, for him, the good will of the minister ; I have open'd, for him, the road to the Academies. . . . Do you know how he rewards so much zeal and so much affection ? When he left for Berlin, he told me of it drily, knowing well it would pierce me to the heart, and he has abandoned me to a sorrow with-out example . . . the fever has got hold of me, and I hope to finish soon, like the unhappy Madame de Richelieu."

Yet the poor lady, as she soon knew, to her joy, was mistaken. The voyage to Berlin was a mere excursion of vanity—delightful escapade, if it had not been for those damned slushy roads and those boorish Westphalians, who thought you were asking for beer when you asked for a nag or a post-chaise. Even on the way back, rhyming to the plosh of the horses' feet, he had reeled off whole strings of paltry doggerel verses to Frederick, and had reminded him of his devotion to Emilie :

> "You open with a hardy hand
> The horrid gates of war ;
> While I come back to this dear land
> And her, whom I adore."

Voltaire did not return directly to Brussels. He came back by way of the Hague, where he was delayed for more than a week by frozen waterways. When, early in January, he reached the house in the Rue de la Grosse-Tour, Madame du Châtelet was more anxious for his health than for her own, but he arrived well and in lively spirits. Fears and tears were at an end, and there was no more talk of dying.

His chief concern was now the production of *Mahomet*. The tragedy had been polished again and again, and was ready for the players. Thalia Quinault had retired, the great Dufresne was away, and there was a certain risk in presenting the play to a Parisian audience. The actor-producer, La Noue, offered his theatre and his company at Lille. The offer was gladly accepted, and at Lille, accordingly, early in May, 1741, *Mahomet* was played four times with great success. Lord Chesterfield, who had met Voltaire, and happened to be in Lille soon after the performances, honoured the tragedy with his genteel though reserved approval, and was astonished to find that the clergy had taken it in such good part. He had reason to be surprised. *Mahomet* is essentially an attack upon revealed religion, and there can be no doubt as to the intention of such lines as these :

> " O, Superstition, thy exacting laws
> Rob feeling hearts of all Humanity !
>
> . . . .
>
> Promise or threaten, so the Truth be known ;
> Let them adore my God, but fear him most."

But the bourgeois society of Lille was not ill disposed towards the author. It was a society which comprised that pert, silly and vulgar woman, Madame Denis, Voltaire's niece, and her pompous husband, the war commissioner. What is more, there had been a moment of gratifying excitement during the first representation. A dispatch from the King of Prussia had been brought to the house and handed to Monsieur de Voltaire. And Monsieur de Voltaire, with his fine sense of opportunity, had read the dispatch to the audience. It gave the news of Frederick's great victory at Mollwitz. It might just as well have told them anything else : what mattered was that it came from an emperor, and was now read in the playhouse by the emperor's friend to the good citizens of Lille. Loud huzzaing and loud clapping of hands. *Mahomet* was a fine play, and no one could reasonably doubt it.

We can pass over the metaphysical brawling with de Mairan, Koenig and Maupertuis which was occasioned by Madame du Châtelet's little book on the *Institutions of Physicks*. It was not seemly for à woman to write on such matters. " Born without talent, without memory, without imagination," wrote the queen of cats, " she made herself a geometrician so as to appear above other women, not perceiving that singularity is not superiority." And yet the public had the bad taste to like her book, and to make sport of a worthy fellow like de Mairan.

There was a short visit to Cirey in June, and time to experiment with de S'Gravesande's machine for " fixing the image of the sun." Then there was a return to Brussels, and then a stay in Paris, but not yet in the vast Hotel Lambert which Madame du Châtelet had acquired some two years previously, and which Voltaire intended to make so luxurious and wonderful " if he could find the money." Back to Brussels, and back to Paris again, with occasional visits to Cirey. The dreary lawsuit was turning in du Châtelet's favour. There was less need to keep in close touch with the notaries.

Voltaire was happy, in good humour, and for a little while in security and peace. A letter written from Cirey to d'Argenson, on the 11th of January, 1742, is full of humanity and wit :

" Brother Macaire and Brother Francis are commended, Sir, to your benevolence. Brother Macaire is a little hermit who knows not his catechism, but who is good, simple and sweet, and earns a livelihood by cleaning old pictures, patching up old chairs and bedaubing windows and doors. He lives in the forest of Doulevant, one of our estates near Cirey. He passes in the district for a good religious man, seeing that he does no harm, and is useful. His hermitage is a little chapel which belongs to the Duke of Orleans ; he is desirous of obtaining a little permit to remain and be establish'd there.

" I believe there is, at Toul, a sort of Hermit-General

who makes 'em travel about like the devil of Popefiggery, and Brother Macaire has no wish to travel. Madame du Châtelet, who finds this hermit a good fellow, would be mighty pleased if he could remain in his chapel, whence he would come now and then to ply his trade at Cirey. And so, Sir, if you could give Brother Macaire a patent as Hermit of Doulevant, or a permit to rest there as best he can, Madame du Châtelet would thank you, and you would be blessed by God and by Saint Antony.

" As for Brother Francis, 'tis myself, Sir, who am even more of an hermit than Brother Macaire, and would leave my hermitage only to pay my respects to you. Here I live between study and friendship, even happier than Brother Macaire ; and had I but health, I wou'd envy no one's Destiny ; but health is not mine, and denies me even the pleasure of writing to you as often as I could wish. Instead of going to Paris, we are off, Brother Francis and Sister Emilie, to Franche-Comté, in the midst of snow and ice. One might have chosen a more agreeable time, but Madame d'Autrey is ill (we lodg'd with her in Paris). Friendship and good works know not the seasons."

He was a strange man, who could thus unite such loveable qualities of gentleness and humour with such blind fury and such biting spite. Learning, this year, that his old enemy, bookseller Jore, was in distress, he sent him a present of 300 livres : Jore, full of penitence and gratitude, felt the nobility of this revenge, and protested that he had been " seduced by monsters."

An awkward affair in the summer of 1742 seemed likely to undo all Madame du Châtelet's good offices with the ministers, if not to put Voltaire once again in danger of the Bastille. By some means, we cannot say how, a foolish letter from Voltaire to his " adorable king " Frederick was being handed about in Paris. Voltaire denied the letter, but it was clearly his, and he admitted as much to Frederick himself. Frederick was inclined to believe that a clerk in the post office at Brussels had made a copy of the letter and sent it to the French government. For reasons among which may be reckoned the delicate political situation, nothing was done ; but the affair was none the less regrettable, and the more so as it occurred shortly before the first performance of *Mahomet* in Paris.

Mahomet was played before a very distinguished audience at the Comédie on the 19th of August, 1742. The buzzing of Piron and Desfontaines among the devout, and even in the very ears of de Fleury, had prepared every one for a new scandal. Nor were the Jansenists idle. It was pointed out by a doctor of the Sorbonne that Mahomet and Jesus-Christ were both names of three syllables—whence it was clear enough that the tragedy was a blasphemous attack upon the Christian church. The ministers of Lille had not been so perspicacious. But in such cases, learning, of course, settles the matter. It is true enough, buzzed Piron and Desfontaines ; this indecent thing ought never to be performed. Yet, in spite of these cabals, *Mahomet* was received with a great outburst of enthusiasm. It was played three times ; and then the noise on both sides had become so angry and shrill, there was such a fear of grave disturbances, that the author, not without a whisper from de Fleury, was prevailed upon to withdraw his piece.

Voltaire left Paris with bitter resentment. The Jansenists, he thought, had wrecked his play : by God !

he would dedicate *Mahomet* to the Pope. And this is
what the devilish man actually did, as we shall see.

There were three days of revelry at Rheims with M.
de Pouilli, then Brussels, and then a short visit by
Voltaire to Frederick at Aix-la-Chapelle. Frederick
did all in his power to entice the poet to Berlin ; but
Voltaire was unshakably loyal to the marquise. He had
written about Frederick and Madame du Châtelet in
one of his delightful letters to Falkener not long before :

" You will hear of the new victory of my good friend
the King of *Prussia*, who wrote so well against Machiavel,
and acted immediately like the heroes of Machiavel.
He fiddles and fights as well as any man in christendom.
He routs the *Austrian* forces, and loves but very little
your King, his dear neighbour of *Hanover*. . . . He
would retain me at his court, and live with me in one
of his country houses, just with the same freedom and
the same goodness of manners you did at Wandsworth.
But he could not prevail against the marquise du
Châtelet. My only reason for being in France, is that
I am her friend."

The death of Cardinal de Fleury on the 29th of
January, 1743, a man never well disposed towards
Voltaire, but too clever and too old to be openly hostile,
left vacant a place in the Academy. Voltaire desired
this place for himself, and the brilliant success of *Merope*
on the 20th of February gave him no small encouragement.

Never had a piece been received with such a tumult
of applause, and never before had the people shouted
so loudly and so persistently for the author. And
never—if that is possible—had the critics been more

completely in the wrong. Even Thalia Quinault, and friendly d'Argental had predicted failure. And here was the entire house, singing and shouting, clapping and stamping, and Voltaire blushing (which really does seem incredible) and kissing the hand of Madame de Luxembourg, or, according to his own account, being kissed by Madame de Villars.

But a mere theatrical success could not open the doors of the Academy. Easier for the rich to enter heaven than for a blasphemer to take his place among those forty righteous men. The Bishop of Mirepoix, Boyer, and the minister, Maurepas, excluded him. The Bishop of Bayeux took de Fleury's chair. Voltaire was to return a little later, when men were less righteous, or more reasonable, but now he was checked. Nor was this the only blow, for the tragedy of *Julius Caesar* was prohibited at the Comédie after the last rehearsal.

The poet, with bitter words of despair and hatred— words excusable enough, we may think—stormed out of Paris, and took up residence in the great ruinous palace of the King of Prussia at the Hague. Madame du Châtelet was left in Paris, and left again to all the tortures of uncertainty. All that she could do, poor soul, was to get the ban removed from *Julius Caesar* ; and all that she could hope for was to join Voltaire later at Brussels. What she feared, and feared with reason, was that he would now hurry to Berlin on the first opportunity. This was precisely what he intended to do.

And now we see him turning to fresh activities. It may be said delicately that he undertook a political mission, or bluntly that he became a spy.

It had come into the minds of de Richelieu and of Madame de Chateauroux, the king's mistress, that his intimacy with Frederick might very well be of service to the state. The king himself had approved of the design, Voltaire had eagerly agreed, and matters had been arranged by d'Argenson, the Minister for War, and Amelot, the Minister for Foreign Affairs. Voltaire observes brutally in his *Memoirs* that Madame du Châtelet would have raised " a horrible outcry " if she had not been told of what was going on ; and it was decided, in order " to appease her," that all documents should pass through her hands. We read this, as we read only too many of his words, with a sensation of profound contempt. It is not pleasant, either, to find him bargaining for an army forage contract as one of his conditions, and begging a military decoration for his nephew La Houlière.

Frederick was busy reviewing his troops, and Voltaire had to wait for a while at the Hague. His time was not wasted.

The ruinous embassy at the Hague was the residence of the Prussian envoy, Count Podewils. The Count was a pretty young man, loved by the wife of one of the Dutch ministers. He was thus able to obtain from his mistress confidential documents of the highest importance, which he obligingly passed on to Voltaire, and which Voltaire passed on to his friends. Nor was this all. The movements of Dutch troops and generals could be reported, the embassy gossip could be retailed, and young Podewils was ready enough to communicate the dispatches of his royal master. History is made by these little acts of courtesy.

While Voltaire was thus busily and happily engaged in his new profession, Frederick did his best to prevent his return to Paris. Voltaire had written some stinging verses on Boyer, the Bishop of Mirepoix, and sent them in one of his letters to Frederick, and Frederick now had these verses conveyed secretly and by devious ways to the Bishop.

But Frederick knew nothing of Voltaire's political mission. It was all very well for the outraged Boyer to complain, as he did, to the court. The court replied that all this was according to plan—the poet wished it to be understood that his quarrel with Boyer was one of his reasons for leaving France. Thus, without meaning it, the infamous Frederick was playing the game of the man who was being sent to spy upon him. Voltaire was informed of this, and although he professed indignation, his sense of importance must have been most agreeably flattered. On the 30th of August, 1743, the poet arrived in Berlin for the second time.

The six weeks which followed were full of excitement. Frederick was more cordial than ever ; he did not " smell the spy " until the spy was on the point of taking his departure. There was a gay exchange of madrigals with Princess Ulrica, the sprightly girl who afterwards became queen of Sweden. A whole fortnight was spent in the marble salons and lacquered boudoirs of that delicious margrave, Sophia-Wilhelmina of Bayreuth. Life was light and joyous ; it was a round of gallant festivals, alternating with moments of delightful intimacy, when Voltaire could talk with his " adorable king," or gaze romantically, with Sophia-Wilhelmina, across the shadowy gardens of the Bayreuth *Hermitage*.

Yet he had still an eye for the tall battalions of the Potsdam guard. The diplomat was not asleep this time, and Frederick was discreetly sounded. But Frederick was the last man in the world who could be called a fool ; and Frederick was cautious, if not mistrustful. In diplomacy, he was more than a match for the poet. He thought of Louis XV as every intelligent man must have thought of that selfish imbecile, but he spoke of him " with respectful esteem." Amelot had to be content with a few scraps of information, and with one long and remarkable dispatch from Charlottenburg :

" To-day, after a dinner full of gaiety and compliments, the King of *Prussia* came to my room; he told me that he had been mighty glad to seek the French envoy yesterday, alone of all the ministers, not only to mark his consideration, but to vex those who were made uneasy by this preference. . . .

" Sire, said I, great kings know nothing of revenge : all must give way to the interests of the State ; you know whether 'tis not in the interest of Your Majesty and of *France* to be for ever united.

" The King of *Prussia* then said: How can I believe that *France* really has the intention of allying herself with me ? I know that your ambassadour at Maintz has made insinuations against me, and that peace with the Queen of *Hungary*, the re-establishment of the Emperour and reparations at my expense have all been proposed.

" I'll wager, said I, that such an accusation is a mere *Austrian* trick, of a sort too common with them. Did they not slander you in this fashion last May ? Did they not have it said in *Holland* that you had proposed to the Queen of *Hungary* to join her against *France* ?

" I swear to you, said he, but with lowered eyes, that nothing is more false. What should I have to gain thereby ? Such a lie destroys itself.

" Then, Sire, why not openly unite yourself with *France* and the Emperour against the common enemy, who hates you and slanders you both equally ? What other *ally* should you have, but *France* ?

" You are right, he replied. . . . But I can only
act openly when I am assur'd of the support of the
Empire. . . . If the Queen of *Hungary* is desirous of
taking back *Silesia*, she will force me to take *Bohemia*
from her. I am not in the least afraid of *Russia* : the
Czarina is eternally devoted to me since the last
conspiracy fomented by Botta and the *English*. I
advise her to send young Ivan and his mother to
Siberia, as well as my brother-in-law, with whom I
have always been displeas'd, and who has always been
ruled by the *Austrians*.

" The King would have continued, but he was
inform'd his *Musick* was ready. . . ."

Such, in substance, was the dispatch of Charlottenburg,
and such the alleged conversation of the king. Even
so, with some assistance, perhaps, from the diplomat's
easy pen, it was a guarded conversation. The question
of a French alliance was left in the air, and Frederick's
designs in regard to Hungary and Silesia were already
clear enough. Frederick and Voltaire parted, early
in October, with all the effusions and tender reproaches
of an elderly coquette and a young lover ; but each
had seen, and seen clearly, the snake in the grass.

CHAPTER V

DEATH OF THE MARQUISE

VOLTAIRE was now approaching his forty-ninth year. He was one of the best known and one of the most hated men in France. He had not yet produced those rollicking masterpieces of irony which have given him such a great name among writers, but he was known as the author of many fine tragedies, of the great national epic and other poems, of histories and philosophical works. He was known, too, by the vigour and variety of his correspondence. If he had not been so offensive personally, so combative and so arrogant, he might even then have been acknowledged as one of the grandest writers of his age.

He had the reputation also of being a man of affairs, a busy negociator, ambitious, and not too nice in matters of strategy. He may have had less power than men gave him credit for, but he had power enough to raise a multitude of enemies. We must remember that he was naturally defiant. He had started in life with a bitter sense of social and physical inferiority, and a clear perception of his own immense intellectual vigour. He had been treated with cruelty and stupidity by noblemen, by courtiers, pedants, ministers and men of letters. He had been insulted publicly by rogues. Even if he had won the favour of dukes and princes, he knew the cost of that favour, and he knew how little it was to be depended upon. Before blaming what may appear to be outrageous vanity, we should plainly understand the effect of early humiliations and of unpardonable affronts upon a sensitive and abnormally vigorous mind. He was determined, at any cost, to justify himself and to prove his importance. A very great man, perhaps, would have been content to leave the fools laughing and to ignore the black inventions of envy, hatred and malice : but here was one who saw in these, not merely a personal affront, but so many hideous forms of the Infamous, which had to be fought unceasingly and fought to the death.

Desnoiresterres, that industrious biographer, is certainly wrong in saying that Voltaire had now forgotten his marquise. True, he had only written to her once or twice during his travels in Germany, but she had never been driven from his mind. When he was on the way home, in October, he wrote to Maupertuis : " I might thus, in my pacifick sphere, enjoy fully the goodness of the king of Prussia, but you know that a greater sovereign, named Madame du Châtelet, calls me back to Paris." Yet he had allowed her again to suffer bitterly in his absence, and she had written pathetic and despairing letters to their mutual friend, the good d'Argental.

"It is impossible," she said, " to love more tenderly or to be more unhappy." Why had he spent so many days at Bayreuth ? " He sends me at last four lines on the road . . . without giving me the reasons for his stay at Bayreuth, nor for his silence ; without telling me about his return, or his new visit to Berlin." But once again, when they met at Brussels, all was forgiven and all forgotten in the joy of being together.

After a little travelling to and fro, Voltaire and the marquise returned to their beloved Cirey. " At Cirey in felicity," he said. The diplomat had not yet been rewarded for his work at the Hague and Berlin, but the minister Amelot was about to fall, and the diplomat had to wait for a while. What did it matter ? Never before had Cirey been so truly a paradise, never before had geometry been so divine, chemistry so alluring. Here indeed was happiness, delightful seclusion, and the quiet pleasures of country life and country gossip. And here Voltaire could lie comfortably in bed, engaged upon new works of every conceivable kind. It is probable that he was never so happy or so tranquil as he was during the five weeks that he now spent at Cirey.

In the early autumn, Voltaire and Madame du Châtelet were in Paris, and soon after the beginning of the new year (1745) Voltaire was at Versailles, busily preparing his opera-ballet of the *Princess of Navarre*.

This *Princess* was a mere court piece, which Voltaire affected to despise, written for the marriage festivities of the Dauphin. It was played in the great Salle de Ménage at Versailles on the 25th of February, before a brilliant concourse of royalty and nobility. Louis, who was capable of appreciating a ballet, liked the piece ; he was discreetly reminded of Voltaire's great services to literature and the state, and he rewarded him by the post of Historiographer to the King.

The poet could now be seen in the gardens of Versailles, trundled about in a little carriage drawn by the King's footmen. Heaven knows with what distaste or jealousy or amusement this peculiar sight was observed by the courtiers. Voltaire himself knew well enough that he owed his new dignity (and he would have chosen some other word for it), not to a true recognition of his achievement, but to a " mere farce," a command performance, and the good disposition of his friends, Madame de Pompadour, d'Argenson and de Richelieu. It was nothing more than a good disposition on the part of Madame de Pompadour ; she was too wise to associate herself closely with a man who was so liable to compromise his patrons. And Voltaire was the last man who was likely to keep his balance among the shifting intrigues of a court. As the friend of Madame de Pompadour, he was already threatened with the enmity of the small though influential group which had formed itself round the queen. Such groups are formed, not through sympathy with abandoned queens, but as oppositions to the favourite, pivoting on their natural centre. The poet was no longer the queen's " poor Voltaire," and Marie Leczinska, now a disillusioned woman of middle-age, pale, devout and cold, had little liking for the author of the *English Letters* and *Mahomet*.—Voltaire, as the lacqueys trundled him along the trim drives of Versailles, must have felt that his court reputation was hardly more solid than the elegant shell of the *calèche à bras* in which he was riding.

The bloody and glorious battle of Fontenoy, so happily restoring the moral of the army and the confidence of the nation (shaken rudely enough at Dettingen), was duly sung by the new historiographer. The poet was apparently in favour at court, and it seemed to be a proper occasion for making ridiculous advances to the Vatican.

Having actually won a couple of holy medals from the Pope, Voltaire proceeded to offer him the dedication of *Mahomet*. And the good Pope, with " greetings and apostolic blessings to his dear son," accepted the dedication. He was, so he said, exceedingly well pleased with the play, and with the beautiful *Ode* on Fontenoy, as well as with the pretty verses which M. de Voltaire had been kind enough to write for his own portrait.

The Pope was not deceived. He was a subtle, courteous and amiable old man, who, from his saintly eminence, could afford to smile indulgently and without

159

malice upon the vanities and policies of the world. He
was a scholar ; Voltaire's genius delighted him ; his
impudence amused him ; and he was clever enough
to play at the same game of compliments with dignity
and grace. As for the less dignified poet, it pleased
him to think of himself as " a Popish dog, much addicted
to His Holiness, and like to be saved by his power."

By the autumn, Voltaire and Madame du Châtelet
were at the court of Fontainebleau : he as the royal
historian, and she as a lady-in-waiting to the queen.
Here he conceived the idea of writing a history of the
recent campaigns, and among those whom he invited
to help him was Falkener, now private secretary to the
Duke of Cumberland. He did not know, when he
first wrote, that the Falkener who was now attached to
His Grace was the same Falkener, his old friend, who
had been appointed to the embassy at Pera. He wrote
to him with delight, in English more cordial than
accurate :

" My dear and honourable friend, how could I guess
your musulman person had shifted *Galata* for *Flanders*,
and had passed from the *seraglio* to the Closet of the
Duke of Cumberland ? . . . Had I thought it was my
dear sir Everard who was secretary to the great prince,
I had certainly taken a journey to *Flanders*. My duty
is to visit the place where your nation gave such noble
proofs of her steady courage. An historian ought to
look on and view the theatre, in order to dispose the
scenery of the work. . . . But what greater reason,
what better motive than my friendship for you ? "

The king's triumphant return to Versailles in
November was celebrated by another court piece,

The Temple of Glory. In this new piece, a flimsy allegory represented Louis as the noble Trajan ; but Louis, perhaps a little embarrassed by such flattery, viewed the *Temple* with chilly indifference. A new diversion was contemplated—a mere musical trifle, the *Fêtes de Ramire*, adapted, scored and prepared for the stage by the " citizen of Geneva," Jean-Jacques Rousseau. It was thus, in December 1745, that these two great men were brought into correspondence for the first time.

A more important business occupied Voltaire seriously in the following year. The death of President Bouhier on the 17th of March again left a place vacant in the Academy. Surely the king's historiographer, the singer of Fontenoy, might aspire to that place ? Had not the Pope given his blessing to the tragedy of *Mahomet* ? He had several direct claims upon the royal patronage ; what is more, he had the support of the royal favourite, splendid Pompadour, to whom he had already addressed some rather warm and hardy odes. Even the ass Mirepoix would hardly dare to oppose him. But the Jesuits had to be soothed, and for this purpose he wrote and published a curious profession of orthodoxy and innocence, a curious appreciation of the learning, piety and noble works of the Order of Jesus, addressed to old Father de la Tour, the principal of the college of Louis-le-Grand, and one of the mild instructors of his youth. He speaks of a scribbler who would injure him (was he thinking of the poet Roy, of Desfontaines or the " vile Rufus " ?) :

" The authour of the libel may set my name as often as he pleases in the immense and forgotten volume of his calumnies. . . . I will answer him as the great

161

Corneille did on a like occasion : *I submit my writings to the Judgement of the Church.* . . . I will do more indeed : I will declare to him and to those who resemble him, that if I have ever printed one page which could offend even the sacristan of their village, I am ready to tear it up before his very eyes ; that I wish to live and die tranquilly in the bosom of the Catholick, Roman and Apostolick Church, without attacking any man, without maintaining the slightest opinion which could offend any man ; I hate everything which can trouble society in the least degree. 'Tis these sentiments, known to the *King*, which have won me his kindness. Overwhelm'd by his favours, attach'd to his royal person, charg'd to write of the great and glorious things he has done for his country, solely occupied by this work, I shall endeavour, in accomplishing it, to put into practice the lessons I have learned in your respectable *Establishment* ; and if the rules of eloquence which I was there taught should be effac'd from my *memory* the character of a good citizen shall never be effac'd from my *heart*."

In following a chosen policy, a man need not be wholly insincere. Voltaire had a lively affection for his old masters, and he was always ready to admit how much he owed them. Here, at least, he spoke the truth. But these declarations were not enough : he called upon all his friends to assist him, to make ready the way for his advance and victory. He was elected on the 25th of April, 1746.

He was not allowed to enjoy his triumph in peace. His enemies buzzed about him more angrily than ever before. On the very eve of his election, the poet Roy, who thought himself good enough for the Academy, had revived and revised a brutal satire on the early misfortunes of Arouet, and had it circulated among the booksellers of Paris.

Now, in addition to Roy's *Poetick Triumph*, came a whole swarm of stinging though obscure pamphlets. Voltaire turned upon his mean tormentors with a wasteful and disproportionate fury. He pursued them all— hawkers, booksellers and writers. He set the law in motion. Houses were entered, papers were seized, men were flung into prison. With particular energy he pursued a wretched fiddler, Travenol, who played at the Opera. We need not follow these drab affairs ; it is enough to note that the anxieties of legal procedure and the uncertainty of legal judgments, seemed to him even more abominable than the offences they were supposed to correct. On future occasions, he was less ready to call in the police.

It is more pleasing to record his friendship with two needy young men, whose names are well known to students of French literature : Vauvenargues and Marmontel.

Poor Vauvenargues, a frail, unhappy man, was only thirty-one years old in 1746, and he died in the following year. He was a gentle, thoughtful soul, and a very graceful and skilled writer. No man was less fitted for the exercise of arms, yet Vauvenargues had been a captain in the king's regiment, and had fought at the siege of Prague in 1741. His health was irremediably broken in the campaign.

Marmontel, in 1746 a lad of twenty-three, has given a delightful picture of a conversation between Voltaire and his friend Vauvenargues : " Never did any one bring to a discussion more spirit, good will and sweetness of temper, and what charmed me even more was, on the one side, the respect of Vauvenargues for the genius of Voltaire, and on the other, Voltaire's tender veneration for the merit of Vauvenargues : each, without flattery or vain adulation or weak complaisance, seemed honoured by a freedom of thought which never troubled the harmony and agreement of their mutual ideas."

As for Marmontel, he was a country boy with a real aptitude for letters, though he was never a great writer. Voltaire had met him in the rooms of his friend Vauvenargues, and assisted him for many years with his money and influence.

Gentle Vauvenargues and penniless Marmontel—the one owed to Voltaire the happiest moments of a life that was nearly over, and the other owed him support and generous encouragement in a career that had scarcely begun.

On the 22nd of December, 1746, " Sieur Arouet de Voltaire, Historiographer of France and one of the forty of the French Academy," became a Gentleman in Ordinary to the King. It looked as though *le Sieur de Voltaire* might reckon upon a continuance of royal favours.

But the wretched man was never long out of trouble. After a visit, with Madame du Châtelet, to the Duchess of Maine at Anet, where the farce of *Boursouffle* was played by a company of noble amateurs, Voltaire and the marquise returned to the court at Fontainebleau. Here, one evening, there was high play at the queen's tables. Madame du Châtelet, a hardy gambler, had, or seemed to have, the most extraordinary ill luck. She lost 400 louis. It was all that she had in her purse— indeed, it was all the ready money that she had been able to get together. On the following evening, she played with 200 louis borrowed from, or given by, the poor historiographer. She lost them.

A real gambler is always encouraged by losses ; and

in spite of a few timid observations by Voltaire, a lacquey
was quickly sent to the steward, Monsieur de la Croix.
The steward as quickly borrowed another 200, and the
amiable Mademoiselle du Thil, a former lady companion,
added to this respectable sum a further 180 louis.
Returning to the game with her usual vivacity, the
marquise lost, not only her new provision, but a great
deal more besides, pledged upon credit. At this,
Voltaire, who was never a man of the world, could no
longer contain himself. He said angrily to the marquise:
" You might have perceived, Madam, that you was
playing with rogues." This, or something like it, he
said in English ; but the rash words were overheard
and understood by some of the gamesters. There was
nothing for it, now, but immediate flight.

For six weeks, or more, Voltaire remained in hiding
at Sceaux, protected by his charming old friend, the
Duchess of Maine. The shutters of his room were
closed all day, and he worked—writing, always writing
—by the light of candles. Then the storm died down,
Madame du Châtelet settled her debts, and came to
Sceaux to liberate the poet. But the stay at Sceaux was
now cheerily prolonged : there was a round of balls,
operas, concerts—and those delightful theatricals
in which Madame du Châtelet played with such
brilliance.

And then the new Gentleman in Ordinary found himself again in trouble. He had occasion to thank
Madame de Pompadour for some little service, and
sent her a gallant madrigal, with which she, for her
part, was pleased enough. But the queen's party was
highly scandalised. The queen's ladies, flocking to
the king, pointed out the indelicacy of the offence.
The king, readily moved as he was by the persuasion

of soft voices, agreed to banish Voltaire from the court. Madame de Pompadour, who had no time to intervene, heard of this with surprise, and no doubt with amusement. Whatever may have been the nature, term or intention of this banishment, Voltaire never returned to the court of France.

After a stay at Cirey, made gay with more theatricals, more comedies, proverbs and farces (divine Emilie the very life and soul of these various diversions), Voltaire and the marquise accepted the hospitality of King Stanislas at the court of Lunéville. Here they established themselves early in 1748.

We have already seen something of this remarkable court, with its faded elegance, its amiable affectation of learning and philosophy. In this court without politics, a king without ambition and a mistress without rivals led an easy, lazy, but very agreeable existence. There was nothing to do but to entertain or to be entertained, and the only administration was the free and casual administration of pure benevolence. King Stanislas, with his gentle ways and gentle raillery, was beloved by the people of Lorraine. Madame de Boufflers, too easy, perhaps, in more ways than one, had the rare merit of equability and the rare virtue of good nature.

No guests could have been more welcome at Lunéville. Stanislas, like old de Villars in earlier years, had a fatherly fondness for the poet, and a fatherly concern for his ill health. Madame de Boufflers was attracted by the liveliness and the many accomplishments of the marquise. We hear little, now, of the " hall of machines," the laboratory, but a great deal about plays and other diversions. On the 25th of February, Voltaire wrote to one of his " guardian angels," the Countess d'Argental :

" My pretended exile would be agreeable enough here, were I not so far from my dear angels. It is, truly, a delicious abode ; 'tis an enchanted castle, whose master does the honours of it. Madame du Châtelet has been able to play *Issé* three times in a very elegant theatre, and *Issé* has been mighty well received. The king's company has played *Merope* for me. Would you believe it, Madam ?—the good folk all cried just as they did in Paris. And I, who speak to you—I quite forgot myself, and cried like the others. We go every day to a kiosque, or from a palace to a cabin ; and everywhere, feasting and freedom. I believe that Madame du Châtelet would spend her life here ; but for my part, I prefer the close life and the charms of friendship to any festivals, and have a great desire to return to *your* court."

It was at Lunéville that Madame du Châtelet met Saint-Lambert, an officer in the ducal guards of Lorraine, a poet, and a charming though cynical and selfish young man. He became, some years later, the lover of Madame d'Houdetot, the woman who inspired Jean-Jacques Rousseau with such an ecstatic passion. Before long, Emilie's acquaintance with Saint-Lambert became an intimacy which was to have deplorable and fatal results.

We need not blame Madame du Châtelet too hastily. She was now forty-two years old, but still impetuous and passionate. For nearly fourteen years she had given Voltaire the full warmth of her affection, she had cared for him, nursed him, worked with him in a delicious community of taste and learning, and fought for his interest and security against the formidable intrigues of statesmen and courtiers. She gave him, still, her friendship and admiration. Voltaire, if he had not taken all this, in the way of men, as a matter of course, if he had been always loyal at heart and grateful in thought, had treated her too often with a lack of understanding, and even with the appearance of gross neglect. He was fretful, impatient, exacting. He was a sick man, with all the querulous demands and all the teasing moods of a sick man. He was absorbed by the immense energies of production.

Madame du Châtelet turned to her new lover, not for understanding or friendship, but for emotional excitement. What is more, Voltaire himself always pretended to despise chastity, and to regard a woman's fidelity as nothing more than a mere matter of convenience. The licence of the age not only encouraged gallantry, and gallantry of the most promiscuous kind, but made of it a mark of breeding and a social habit. And so, when we see the poor marquise placing her love letters—letters with pink and blue edges—in Madame de Bouffler's harp, where Saint-Lambert took them and deposited his own, we should feel, if neither pity nor benevolence, at least no heartless or senseless indignation.

Voltaire was in Paris at the end of August, to see the performance of his new play *Semiramis*. At that time, the stage itself was crowded with a part of the fashionable audience, foes or partisans of the author, and the actors were frequently hindered by interference of the most direct and objectionable kind. What with bulky properties and a multitude of people, there was so little room on the stage when *Semiramis* was played that even the shade of Ninus was hardly able to make his appearance : the usher, so we are told, had to cry more than once " Make way, gentlemen, if you please ; make way for the ghost ! "

The tragedy was not entirely successful, although Voltaire's faction was powerful enough to hold the enemy in check. On the second night, having borrowed a cloak, a huge wig, a hat with lowered brims, and a pair of spectacles, the author betook himself to a coffee-house, and there listened, with horrible alternations of pride, anger and anxiety, to the mixed opinions of the critics.

He learnt, soon afterwards, that the Italian players were busy with a parody.

Here was a piece of wicked malice, not to be endured. The angry man wrote to the ministers ; he wrote to every one. He prayed, bullied, swore and bargained. He addressed himself to Madame de Pompadour, to the queen. He did not appeal in vain. " Madame de Pompadour," he wrote to d'Argental, " has done more than the queen. She has told me that the infamy will certainly not be performed." And yet, Madame de Pompadour was even then protecting, with almost filial piety, ·the aged Crébillon, whose shaky reading of *Catiline* had so greatly pleased, not only the grand lady herself, but also the king.

The tragedy of *Semiramis* was played at Fontainebleau, with approval, on the 24th of October : the parody was forbidden.

The court of Stanislas moved, at times, from Lunéville to Nancy or Commercy. It was at Commercy that Voltaire discovered, in the most conclusive and dramatic fashion, the weakness of the marquise. Of what actually occurred we know only from the gossiping record of a secretary, as much valet as secretary, and such records can have only a relative importance.

No doubt, the scene of discovery was painful enough, grotesque, violent, humiliating. But Voltaire, in a little time, had resigned himself. He was too vital or too volatile to be depressed for long by any imaginable circumstance, or to feel for long the influence of a single emotion. And he was now, let us remember, fifty-three years old. He made his peace, not only with the still divine Emilie, but also with her new lover. He is supposed to have said to Saint-Lambert : " My child, I have forgot all, and 'tis I alone who was in the wrong. You are at the happy age when men have and give delight ; enjoy these moments, which are all too brief ; an old, sick fellow such as I am, has nothing more to do with pleasure."

Then came a more staggering blow, and one which exposed the unhappy marquise to all the dark terrors of apprehension.

The two friends—for they were still friends—went to Cirey late in December. Here the marquise busied herself with her translation of the *Principles* of Newton, and with a graceful and learned commentary upon this great work. " The preface to her *Newton*," said Voltaire, " is a masterpiece." Once again, life at Cirey was quiet, studious, even happy. The neighbourly fireside purring of Madame de Champbonin, the peace of a calm winter countryside, the well-being which is felt in bright, familiar rooms, the grateful seclusion after so many noisy days of adventure, anxiety and peril— all this must have given them a sense of delightful security and repose. But soon Madame du Châtelet feared that all was not well, and then knew that she was pregnant.

Saint-Lambert was called to Cirey. There were conferences in which, if we are correctly informed, ribaldry was not absent. Du Châtelet, that obliging simpleton, was duped, cajoled, and forced to play his part in a hideous comedy. We are glad to think that our account of this comedy does not come from a trustworthy source, though credited by Desnoiresterres.

There is little in the correspondence which indicates Voltaire's state of mind at this period. In an English letter to Falkener, written at the end of March, 1749, he says : " I have been disturbed these two months and kept from writing my history, which I hope will be the work of the historiografer of the honest man, rather than that of the historiografer to a king." He was naturally disturbed, but this disturbance was by no means wholly due to the condition of Madame du Châtelet.

Voltaire wished to be considered the one great tragic poet of the age. Nothing short of an undisputed pre-eminence, an acknowledged pre-eminence, could satisfy him. The wild hysterical vehemence with which he insisted upon his own superiority and deprecated the work of his rivals was due to a morbid weakness of character (but not an exceptional weakness) which we have already tried to explain. It was never more strongly, more regrettably in evidence than at this time, when old Crébillon's *Catiline* was being warmly applauded, not only by the parterre, but by the great Montesquieu. To Voltaire's alert vanity, such praises were intolerable. That Crébillon was a man of eighty, that his tragedy was a good one, made no difference. Any successful dramatist was a natural enemy, any good play a personal affront. His fury was not lessened when old Crébillon, nobly protected by Madame de Pompadour, became the royal censor of plays. To have his own work judged by a dotard who owed his position, not to merit, but to the unaccountable caprice of a woman, was a thought which drove him crazy. He would write a *Catiline* of his own, immeasurably superior to anything Crébillon had ever thought of. What is more, he would confront the *Electra* of Crébillon with an *Orestes*. How could the poor creature think of writing or judging tragedies at his time of life ? He should long ago have slipped quietly into his prepared tomb.

Meanwhile, on the 16th of June, Voltaire produced a new comedy, *Nanine*, based clearly on the *Pamela* of Richardson. It was interesting to part of the audience, though boring to another, and no one thought it a good comedy.

Voltaire returned to Lunéville from Paris before the short run of *Nanine* had come to an end. With Madame du Châtelet, he spent a few days at Cirey, and then settled again, with her, at the court of Stanislas.

Madame du Châtelet was now trying to chase away the terrors of her mind by work and excitement, by steady occupation or feverish activity. She had grim apprehensions of her approaching death. Childbirth at her age was an occurrence which no woman could anticipate without alarm. The poor lady put her affairs in order and wrote letters which, if she died, were to be sent to her friends. She had complained of the coldness, the indifference of Saint-Lambert ; but now she was tender and resigned. We cannot pretend to judge Saint-Lambert, though he has never been described as an amiable character : he appears to have been selfish, callous perhaps, though not brutal ; we know that he was deeply affected by Madame du Châtelet's fate. There is in existence an infinitely pathetic letter of the marquise to Saint-Lambert in which she reproaches him with not telling her of his plans.

" When I am with you, I can endure my state with patience, often without perceiving it ; but when I lose you, all seems dark. . . . Do not leave me in this uncertainty ; my suffering and lack of courage would frighten me if I believed in presentiments."

Voltaire, who had no presentiments, took matters lightly, or at least appeared to do so. Writing to Madame d'Argental in July, he said : " Madame du Châtelet, who sends you her compliments, counts on being deliver'd here of a fine boy, and I, of a tragedy ; but methinks her child will be sturdier than mine." And in writing to Frederick soon afterwards, he promised to undertake the journey to Potsdam " as soon as Madame du Châtelet has recovered from her confinement."

On the night of the 4th of September, Madame du Châtelet was delivered. Voltaire, either believing sincerely that all danger was past, or affecting gaiety in order to keep up his courage, treated the matter in a jocular spirit. He wrote to d'Argental, telling him the news :

" Madame du Châtelet, while scribbling at her *Newton* to-night, felt a little uneasy ; she call'd her chambermaid, who was just in time to receive a little lady and pop her into the cradle. The mother put her papers in order, got back into bed again ; and both are now sleeping like a pair of dormice as I write to you. —I shall not be so easily delivered of my *Catiline*. Five days at least will be needed, so that I may forget the work, and take it up again with a fresh eye."

He wrote in the same style to his friend the Abbé de Voisenon :

" My dear Abbé *Greluchon* is to know that Madame du Châtelet, being this very night at her desk, according to her praiseworthy custom, said : But I feel something ! This something was a little lady who straightway came into the world. They plac'd her upon a *quarto* which happen'd to be there, and the mother went to bed. I who, during the last days of her confinement, knew not what to do with myself, set about making a child by myself ; I was brought to bed in eight days of *Catiline*. 'Tis a jest of Nature's, who would have me do, in one week, what Crébillon was thirty years a-doing. I marvel at Madame du Châtelet's delivery, and am horrified at my own."

And the same stories, the same pleasantries were repeated to the Marquis d'Argenson :

" Madame du Châtelet informs you, Sir, that being this night at her desk and scribbling some *Newtonian* affairs, she felt a little trouble. This little trouble was a young lady who straightway appeared. They put her upon a book of geometry *in-quarto*. The mother has gone to bed, because 'tis proper to go to bed ; and if she don't sleep, she will write to you. She has but brought into the world a little lady who has nothing to say ; but for my part, I must needs make a *Cicero*, a *Caesar* ; and 'tis more difficult to make these fellows talk than it is to make a child, especially when one has no mind to affront ancient *Rome* for a second time in the French theatre."—The last allusion is to Crébillon's tragedy, which Voltaire frequently called " an insult to ancient Rome."

For a time things looked well. Voltaire and Stanislas

could make their obstetrical jokes with a light heart ; and Saint-Lambert, who was then at the court of Lorraine, could feel that he had done no great harm after all. Poor Madame du Châtelet, though fatigued, was able to smile and talk, and was already asking for her Newtonian papers. The child was put out to nurse. Du Châtelet himself was there—the inoffensive, gentle and silly man, who had been so wickedly fooled, and who was now to be the witness of a tragedy for which he believed, perhaps, that he was mainly responsible.

Four days after her delivery, Madame du Châtelet fell sick of a fever. The king's physician, Reynault, called in two doctors from Nancy. What could they do but look wise, or sad, or puzzled ?

A gloomy company, with tears not far from their eyes, gathered in Madame du Châtelet's room. The marquise, no longer thinking about Newton, was tended with care by loyal Mademoiselle du Thil, who had come to Lunéville to wait upon her former mistress. Reynault and his two colleagues devised a palliative, a febrifuge, heaven knows what, and the sick woman, on the second day of the fever, seemed more tranquil, inclined to sleep. The company went to supper with Madame de Boufflers. No jokes now ; the shadow had fallen upon the court, upon the good Stanislas and amiable de Boufflers, so gay and so hopeful only two nights before. Who remained with the dying woman ? Not du Châtelet, not Voltaire, but Saint-Lambert, Longchamp the secretary, and Mademoiselle du Thil.

Soon after the others had left her, Madame du Châtelet died, presumably while sleeping under the influence of a soothing drug. " We were so troubled that none of us thought of sending for curé or Jesuit or sacrament. She had none of the terrors of death : 'twas we alone who felt them."

The sorrows of those who are quick and volatile are not less intense, less cruel and penetrating, because they are short-lived ; nor is a grief less bitter because it may find relief in a spoken extravagance or in some wild gesture which, taken in itself, has little dignity. In whatever way Voltaire may have spoken or behaved on this occasion (and we must again hesitate before relying on the memory and veracity of a babbler such as Longchamp), his grief was profoundly real, and was literally overwhelming. His own letters are sufficient proof. We are less ready to think of him furiously accusing Saint-Lambert of having killed his friend, or miserably striking his head against the wall, than of good King Stanislas coming to the stricken man and comforting him with his own tears.

There is nothing more tragic in any correspondence than the change from his previous gaiety and relief to the cry of despair in Voltaire's letter to d'Argental, written a few hours after Madame du Châtelet's death :

" Ah ! my dear friend, I have only you in the world. What a crushing blow ! I have told you about the happiest, the most singular confinement : a terrible death has followed it ! And to crown my sorrows, I am oblig'd to remain for another day in this abominable Lunéville which has been the cause of her death. I am going to Cirey with M. du Châtelet ; thence I shall come back to weep in your arms for the rest of my unhappy life. Watch over Madame d'Argental for us. Write to me at Cirey by Vassy. Have pity on me, dear and worthy friend. Write to me at Cirey : that is the one consolation for which I can hope."

In the same hour of bitter grief he wrote to Madame du Deffand—surely the most disagreeable and the most unfeeling of women. Voltaire did not often correspond with her at that time, and it is strange to find him writing to her, of all people, on this deplorable occasion :

" Madam, I have but now witness'd the death of one who was my friend for twenty years, one who loved you truly, and who spoke to me, two days before this melancholy death, of the pleasure she would have in seeing you in Paris on the occasion of her first visit. I had begg'd President Hénault to tell you of a confinement which appeared so singular and so happy ; there was much intended for you in my letter ; Madame du Châtelet had charged me to write to you, and I thought to fulfil my duty in writing to President Hénault. This unhappy little girl, of whom she was brought to bed, and who has caused her mother's death, did not sufficiently interest me. Alas ! Madam ; we had made of this event a matter of pleasantry ; and it was in this unseemly style I had wrote by her order to her friends. If anything could add to the horrors of my present state, it would be the fact of having treated with mirth an adventure whose consequences will poison the rest of my miserable life. I wrote you nothing when she was delivered, and now I have to tell you of her death. 'Tis to the sensibility of your heart that I turn in my despair. They are taking me to Cirey with M. du Châtelet. Thence I shall return to Paris, without knowing what will become of me, and hoping soon to rejoin her. Allow me, as soon as I am arriv'd, to have the sad consolation of talking to you about her, and of bewailing, at your feet, a woman who, with all her weakness, had a spirit worthy of our respect."

Such a letter to such a woman ! It was Madame du Deffand who had written so cruelly, so falsely and with such biting malice about the unhappy Emilie. It was she—the queen of cats—who had sneered at what she chose to regard as poor Emilie's pretensions, at her supposed vanity and meanness, and even at her poverty. And now, as though to add one more touch to the tragic-grotesque of this horrible drama, here is Voltaire addressing himself to the " sensibility of her heart," and ready to " weep at her feet." His own imagination could scarcely have conceived a more sinister refinement of irony.

He wrote next day to d'Argenson, and three days later to the Abbé de Voisenon :

" My dear Abbé, my dear *friend*, what have I wrote to you ! What untimely joy, what direful consequence ! What a complication of disasters, which, if 'tis possible, render my state even more dreadful. . . . I am not quitting M. du Châtelet, I am going to Cirey with him. I must needs go, and accomplish this sad duty. And so I shall see again the place adorn'd by friendship, where I hoped to die in the arms of your friend ! "

Madame du Châtelet was buried in the new parish church of Lunéville with all the honours, pomp and ceremony that could be provided by the contrivance of Stanislas and the resources of his court. Voltaire was

overwhelmed by his grief. Good Stanislas took him
to La Malgrange, and did what he could to comfort
him, until the unhappy man decided to go to Cirey.

It would seem that Voltaire and du Châtelet arrived at
Cirey on the 16th or 17th of September. Those must
have been strange, melancholy days : Voltaire distracted,
first by the poignancy of his memories, and then by his
desire to collect his property and settle his affairs with
du Châtelet ; du Châtelet himself rapidly fading, as
far as we are concerned, into his final complete obscurity,
with no word, no action to mark his passing ; Madame
de Champbonin gently weeping, gently murmuring, and
yet with a little cheerfulness breaking through ; and
each, no doubt, aware of the painful and peculiar
embarrassment of the situation.

The letters which Voltaire wrote at this period are of
extraordinary interest.   It is certainly wrong to suppose,
with Desnoiresterres, that Madame du Châtelet was
lightly loved and briefly regretted.   The unreflecting
mind is too ready to believe that a satirist is devoid of
feeling, happily immune from the sorrows of mankind,
incapable of sentiment, and even more so of the profound emotions.   The very qualities of a satirist are
those of a quick, nervous, acutely perceiving nature,
and imply a more than common degree of sensibility.
Lanson, though he is not much concerned with the
emotional aspect of Voltaire, is right in saying that
" He mourned sincerely the poor faithless woman,
whom he had loved with a steady affection."

We cannot doubt this if we read his letters with understanding.   He did not possess the orderly, controlled
mind which he so much admired ; he had no repression,
no reserve ; he had no spiritual privacy ; and whatever
he felt or thought or desired was rapidly and vehemently

expressed in words or writing. He could not contain himself. And this very impulsiveness, untimely and distressing as it often was, made him, in a sense, the most truthful of men. In all that affected him deeply he was incapable of the least concealment. With all his power, he was a strangely unguarded man, never more pitiably mistaken than when he imagined himself able to perceive the thoughts of others and to hide his own. The following letters, written to intimate friends, are among the most remarkable in his entire correspondence.

To d'Argental, from Cirey, on the 21st of September :

" Adorable friend, I know not for how many days we shall yet remain in this house which friendship had embellish'd, and which has become for me an object of horror. 'Tis a sad duty I fulfil, and many sad things have I seen. I shall find no consolation but with you. You have wrote me letters which, in bringing tears to my eyes, have brought relief to my heart. I will start in three or four days, if my wretched health allows me to.

" I am like to die in this house ; an old friend of this unhappy lady weeps here with me ; and here I must do my duty by the son and the husband. There can be nothing more dreadful than what I have seen for the past three months, now finish'd by death. My state is appalling ; you will understand the bitterness of it, and your dear sympathies will make it less."

In a letter written to the same friend two days later, he speaks of Cirey with a changed attitude : it is no more " an object of horror." He contemplates residence in Madame du Châtelet's Paris house in the Rue Traversière.

"I will even admit that a house where she has lived, though it may fill me with anguish, is not wholly distressing to me. I do not fear my affliction ; I fly not from what speaks to me of her. I love Cirey ; I could not endure Lunéville, where I lost her in a manner more dreadful than you can imagine ; but the places she has adorn'd are dear to me. 'Tis not that I have lost a mistress ; I have lost a part of myself, a soul for whom my own was made, a friend of twenty years. . . . The tenderest father loves not otherwise his only daughter. I love to find everywhere some thought of her ; I love to talk with her husband, her son. Sorrows are never alike, and you see how mine are fashioned."

Ten days later, he was on the road to Paris, travelling by short stages.

"Here I am at Châlons," he wrote to d'Argental ; "I shall spend two or three days at Rheims with M. de Pouilly. 'Tis a mind like your own, and a true philosophick spirit ; 'tis the only society which can give me a little consolation, and in some measure take your place, if that is possible. I have but now been reading again the prodigious number of metaphysical notes which Madame du Châtelet had got together with such patience and perspicacity as astound me. With all that, how could she weep at our little tragedies ? 'Twas the genius of Leibnitz with sensibility added. Ah ! dear friend, who can measure this loss ? "

At Rheims, he could turn his attention to his work, and a fair copy of *Catiline* was prepared. He had found an excellent copyist—M. Tinois, who was no mere hack, but a ready rhymer. Tinois ventured to address

a little ode to Monsieur de Voltaire on the subject of
Catiline ; an ode discreetly flattering, of course. What
an admirable copyist ! said Monsieur de Voltaire : how
astonishing that the fellow should have so much taste !

On the 12th of October, he wrote to Madame de
Bocage :

" I am come to Paris, Madam. The excess of my
sorrow and of my ill health does not prevent me from
telling you how sensible I am of your kindness. A
noble spirit such as yours must indeed regret such a
woman as Madame du Châtelet. Like you, she was
the glory of her sex in France. She was in philosophy
what you are in elegant letters ; and this same lady,
who had translated and explain'd *Newton* (who had
done, that is, what three or four men in France might
have been ask'd to accomplish) cultivated without
ceasing, by the perusal of works of taste, that sublime
spirit which nature had given her. Alas ! Madam, it
was but four days previously that I had re-read your
tragedy with her. We read together your *Milton*, with
the English. You would have regretted her even more,
had you been a witness of this reading. . . . After her
death, four indifferent verses in her praise were being
distributed. Folk who have neither taste nor sensibility have attributed them to me. They must indeed
be unworthy of friendship, and have trivial minds,
who could believe that, in my dreadful condition, I
could have taken the wretched liberty of making verses
for her ; but what is frightful, and deserving punishment, is that a monster named *Roy* has wrote verses
against her memory."

There can be no possibility of mistaking either the

tenour or the sincerity of these letters. Nor is there less sincerity and less pathos in Voltaire's eulogies of the poor marquise.

He must indeed be devoid of understanding, who cannot see in this correspondence a bitter suffering both of heart and mind. It will be noticed, in the letters which follow, how Voltaire exaggerates the period of his alliance with Madame du Châtelet—twenty years, even twenty-five years. In reality, it was a period of about fifteen years, and this curious inaccuracy in the matter of dates and times will be observed frequently by any one who reads the correspondence. We shall take passages from three letters, written about the middle of October, from Paris. The first is to d'Arnaud :

"Dear child—a woman who has translated and explained *Newton*, and who has made a translation of *Virgil*, without the least hint in her conversation that she had accomplish'd these prodigies ; a woman who never said an ill thing of any one, and never spoke a falsehood ; a friend brave and sollicitous in friendship ; in one word, a very great man, known only to ordinary women by her diamonds, her cavagnole—you will not prevent me from mourning her all my life. I am far indeed from going to *Prussia* ; I can scarce leave the house."

The second is to the Chevalier de Jaucourt :

"My dear Sir, I arriv'd in Paris some days ago. I have found here the signs of your remembrance and of the goodness of your heart ; you must surely be of the number of those who lament this unique lady . . .

whose character was even superior to her genius. She never forsook a friend ; I have never heard her speak uncharitably. I have lived with her for twenty years in the same house. Never have I heard a lie pass her lips. I hope you will presently see her *Newton*. She has done what should have been undertook by the Academy of Sciences. Whoever can think will honour her memory, and I shall spend my life mourning her."

The next is to Frederick, to whom the loss of Madame du Châtelet must have been extremely gratifying :

" I have lost a friend of twenty-five years, a great man whose one fault was being a woman, and whom all Paris honours and regrets. Perhaps she did not receive full justice while she was alive, and you, perhaps, have not judg'd of her as you would have if she had had the honour of being known to Your Majesty. . . . The state in which I have been for the last month scarce allows me to hope that I shall see you again."

Voltaire was now established in the Rue Traversière, with his niece, that bouncing and pretentious woman, Madame Denis, keeping house for him. Cheered by his friends, d'Argental, young Marmontel, de Choiseul and the Abbé Chauvelin, he turned again to the normal concerns of his life. *Catiline* was read to the circle; *Orestes* made his appearance. Presently he was in full career. He had to prove his superiority, his plain, avowed superiority, to Crébillon, that maundering old playwright. He could even think of Potsdam again, for he was, as Lanson very truly observes, " ill cured of courts." On the 10th of November he told Frederick that he would visit him during the summer, " if he was still alive." He busied himself with the practical, rather sordid question of the settlement of his accounts, amounting to 5,000 livres, with du Châtelet. His tremendous, undiscriminating energies were soon actively employed in a hundred ways.

But the marquise was never forgotten. Those who saw the old man at Ferney, five-and-twenty years later, were shown, with respect and reverence, her portrait hanging upon the wall of the salon—that pleasing, youthful portrait by La Tour, in which the divine Emilie, richly and trimly dressed, looks at us with a kind of arch thoughtfulness, her books, papers and globe at her side.

We know nothing of the fate of that unfortunate little daughter who, by coming into the world, so tragically ended her mother's life. Madame du Châtelet's son was guillotined in 1794. As for Saint-Lambert, his wretched intrigue gave him a certain prestige in the world of fashion. He became a friend of the Encyclopaedists, and wrote poems which were considered in their time, and by Voltaire himself, to be very good poems.

Voltaire's tragedy of *Orestes* was first played on the 12th of January, 1750. It had been written as a counterblast to the *Electra* of Crébillon, and with the avowed purpose of vexing and defeating a rival. Such a purpose was no commendation. Crébillon, as the royal censor, had passed *Orestes* without any demands, and had returned the manuscript with a simple and dignified little speech : " Sir, I have been content with the success of *Electra* ; I hope the brother will do you as much honour as the sister has done me." Knowing in what circumstances and with what aim the tragedy had been composed, the public was not prepared to give it a cordial reception. Ancient Crébillon, a placid, courteous and worthy old man, had many friends. Voltaire, in accordance with his custom, had organised a formidable body of supporters who, with noisy approbation, were to cry down the others and prove the merit of *Orestes.* He did more. At the first performance, watching with equal anxiety the progress of the play and the behaviour of his partisans, he sprang up suddenly in his box and shouted, with a crazy gesture : " Courage, ye brave Athenians—'tis Sophocles ! " That was bad enough, but worse was to follow.

One night, while the brave Athenians were dutifully clapping, he saw a little man with a muff. The little man was clearly not of the Athenian party : there he stood, the nasty provoking creature! with both hands in his wretched muff : a silent insult. " Who are *you*, sir ! " cried the furious poet.—" Rousseau."—Disastrous name ! " *What* Rousseau ? " Not Jean-Baptiste or Jean-Jacques, this man with a muff, but some obscure person, known only as *dramatic author.* But he answered Voltaire, as he deserved to be answered, tartly enough. The foolish and humiliating scene ended by Voltaire's hurried retirement, not without angry words and angry glances from all parts of the theatre.

More and more occupied with the stage, Voltaire patronised young Lekain, who was to become a great actor, and fitted up a private theatre in his own house. Here, following a successful performance of *Mahomet*, the new *Catiline* was produced before a fashionable and carefully chosen audience. For this production, de Richelieu obtained from the Comédie the very scenery and properties which had been used in Crébillon's play. The new *Catiline* was acclaimed with fervour ; Voltaire was in transports of delight ; and the memory of Cicero (so he said) was avenged.

This pleasing though private triumph was followed soon by another. *Alzire* was performed by noble amateurs at Versailles, with Madame de Pompadour playing the chief part. The first performance was on the 28th of February, and it was repeated on the 2nd of March. On the latter occasion, Voltaire was present. He had the satisfaction of seeing *Alzire* splendidly played by Madame de Pompadour, more beautiful than ever, and the less obvious satisfaction of hearing the king declare " it was astonishing that the author of *Alzire* was the same who had written *Orestes*."

It was now that a new enemy, and one by no means contemptible, made his appearance. Fréron, at that time (1750) a young man of thirty-one, was a journalist with ability superior to that of the ordinary kind. He was a critic, also, of no ordinary kind ; for he was not wholly devoid of judgment, and could himself write in a style which was vigorous, elegant and well directed. He was led into the way of journalism by Desfontaines, and soon acquired the methods of that amiable master. In his periodical *Letters* he attacked Voltaire with acidulous humour. To attack Voltaire was a sure way of becoming known, for the great man, by crying out, invariably drew attention to his assailant.

But Fréron was hateful to Voltaire for more than one reason. Fréron had written a Fontenoy ode which had been compared, in a way not wholly pleasing, with that of the royal historiographer. And Fréron had been recommended as a correspondent to Frederick. Voltaire, by sending a villainous portrait of Fréron to Potsdam,

187

had easily quashed the recommendation ; but the mischief was done. Twice, in March 1750, Voltaire wrote to Berrier, Lieutenant-General of Police, begging his protection against the libels of Fréron and his associate, La Porte.

" It is deplorable, that, at my age, surrounded by a numerous family of magistrates and officers, and myself an officer of the king's household, I should be exposed continually to the insolence of these paper-smudgers. One is not allowed to speak for oneself. I do but ask of you, Sir, and I beg you in the name of all honest men, to have the goodness to order Fréron to have a word with you, and to command him to be more circumspect. He lives in the house of a distiller, Rue de Seine. You, Sir, may put an end to this scandal with one word."

Persecuted, or believing himself to be so, surrounded by vexations, feeling the indifference or hostility of the public, out of favour at court, and with no companion to share his life and his troubles, Voltaire now turned readily and hopefully towards Frederick. At Potsdam, with Solomon of the North and his charming family, he would be praised and petted and treated as a great man, a great poet, historian, philosopher. He would escape from the silly importunities of his pretended friends, the chatter of Mignot Denis, and the wickedness of the pamphleteers and journalists. He would escape, too, from the expense and worry of costly entertainment. Once more he would be avenged on the cruel injustice of his countrymen ; he would be the prime favourite of a powerful king. Who could hesitate between Louis and Frederick ? He would have but one regret— separation from his " dear angels," the Count and Countess d'Argental.

In April, the young poet Baculard d'Arnaud had left Paris to join the group of illustrious or singular men who were assembling at Berlin. He had gone with Voltaire's blessing, with verses and letters for his patron, and Voltaire was now making ready to follow his lead.

"Here," wrote Frederick in his most insinuating manner, "is a little community raising altars to the *invisible god* ; but have a care, for *hereticks* will certainly raise altars to *Baal*, if our *God* does not show himself soon. I will say no more."

The god was quite willing to move to his new quarters, but money had to be advanced. "I have set up house, as they say in Paris, and live like a philosopher with family and friends. . . . In spite of that, 'tis impossible for me to incur any expenses out of the ordinary : first, because it has cost me a great deal to establish my little household ; secondly, because the affairs of Madame du Châtelet, involv'd with my own, have cost me even more. . . . I cannot procure a good travelling coach, nor start with the conveniences necessary for an invalid, nor provide for my household during my absence, etc., with less than 4,000 crowns from *Germany*." It was to be a loan, of course, payable on the liquidation of certain properties. Frederick sent flattering verses, and a bill of change.

Voltaire was now able to arrange quickly for his departure. On the 18th of June, with his coach and conveniences, he set out on the road to Berlin. On the 26th of June he wrote to d'Argental from Compiègne :

"Why am I here ? why am I going yet further ? why have I quitted you, my dear angels ? You are not my guardians, for here am I deliver'd to the demon of journeys—*video meliora, proboque, deteriora sequor.*"

But when, on the 10th of July, he reached Potsdam, there were no more regrets, and all was new, delightful, exciting.

" Here I am, at last, in Potsdam," he wrote to Madame Denis. " Under the late king, it was the place of *Pharasmanus* ; a mere parade-ground with no garden at all ; the only musick, the march of the *Guard* regiment ; the only spectacles, reviews ; and the *Army List* instead of a library. To-day, it is the palace of *Augustus*, of legions and men of spirit, of pleasure and glory, of magnificence and taste, etc."

Even the dear angels must hear of it, and he wrote to d'Argental :

" Behold me here, in this place, once so barbarous, to-day as much grac'd by the arts as dignified by glory. An hundred and fifty thousand victorious troops, no procurers, comedy, philosophy, poetry, a hero both philosopher and poet, grandeur and graces, grenadiers and Muses, trumpets and fiddles, Platonick festivals, society and liberty ! Who would believe it ? Yet 'tis all true ; and all that is not more precious to me than our little suppers."

With rising enthusiasm, he wrote, some days later, to de Thibouville:

" What would you that I should do ? To find all the charms of society in a king who has won five battles; to be surrounded by *drums*, and yet to hear the lyre of *Apollo*; to enjoy delicious conversation, at four hundred leagues from Paris ; to spend one's days, partly in celebrations, partly in the delights of a tranquil and busy life, sometimes with *Frederick the Great*, sometimes with *Maupertuis*—all that takes the mind from mere *tragedies*."

And so, for many days, letters were filled with accounts of carnivals, banquets, plays, operas, balls, gaiety, and the rare pleasures of intercourse with a brilliant, unique society of wits and scholars, genially patronised (or so it seemed) by the wonderful king. The god was on his appointed throne ; no talk of heretics or Baal. Here was distraction, and the appearance, at least, of happiness.

But the two most remarkable and most disagreeable men in Europe could not live long together in harmony.

CHAPTER VI

FREDERICK THE GREAT

THE fame of a soldier looks uncommonly as if
it depends more upon luck than anything else.
It certainly does not depend upon qualities of a moral
or intellectual kind, although the most noteworthy
performances of soldiers are not infrequently the clever
apologies which they compose in times of peace or
retirement. Men who have been termed great because
of their military achievements might equally well have
been termed fortunate, brave, obstinate, or simply
well-disciplined.

Frederick was more than a mere commander. He
played with ease and proficiency upon one of the most
difficult of wind instruments—the flute, or *flauto traverso*.
He wrote copiously, with vigour if not with elegance.
He desired to surround himself with men of learning,
and to establish in Berlin a famous academy of letters,
philosophy and science. Such a desire may have sprung
from a ruler's vanity, but it was not the vanity of the
ordinary ruler, who would have thought far more of
surrounding himself with guns and grenadiers. The
nature of his mind was harsh, cold and cynical ; his
conduct was often that of a cruel buffoon, and his policy
evasive and treacherous. Yet it would be incorrect
to say that he had no sense of public responsibility.
He had an austere and formal concept of his duty to
the State, which, however grey and cheerless it may
have been, served him well enough, and served the
State well enough, as a substitute for principles of a more
generous and humane origin. Frederick wished to
build up a strong, secure and " respectable " Prussia,

without unnecessary hesitation in the choice of means and methods. He wished, also, to govern justly ; not so much because a just government would be good for the " damned race " of his Prussians, but rather because it would mark him as a man of intelligence and a ruler of distinguished character, and because he saw it to be a thing clearly desirable for its own sake. Here, in the skill and firmness of his later administration, and not in the noisy victories of Mollwitz or Rossbach, he could base a claim to greatness. If he had not been a king, Frederick might have been known only as an eccentric man with ability in music, a few scraps of learning and philosophy, an ugly wit, and extremely disagreeable manners.

In 1750, he had chosen, for his familiars, a number of curiously assorted men.

There was Algarotti, the ladies' Newtonian, a sly, courtly, amusing fellow, who, like Fontenelle, made science an elegant pastime. In 1736 Algarotti had stayed at Cirey with Émilie and Voltaire, and had shared, or guided, the studies of the two philosophers. Algarotti was a fop and a poetaster, discreetly frivolous, always amiable, with all the subtlety and charm of a true Venetian. He had need of subtlety in that little group, where jealousy was never asleep and spite was quick to take revenge. He was born in the same year as Frederick, and in 1750 he was thirty-eight.

By way of contrast to this graceful Italian, there was La Mettrie—a man who might well have figured in the *Midnight Conversation* of Hogarth. La Mettrie was an atheist physician, a roystering, jovial, noisy creature, perfectly unrestrained in speech and manners, treating all serious respectable things with a rude, hilarious mockery. Not lacking wit or invention, he

had written the *Man-machine*, and two or three clever
satires. It was usual enough, at Frederick's intimate
supper-parties, to see this Hogarthian figure, with loose
cravat, unbuttoned waistcoat, a napkin tied round his
bald shining head—perruque flung on the floor. No
one could match La Mettrie in bold extravagance of
talk, or in the licence, vigour and crudity of his jesting.
He was entirely without shame or reserve, unseemly
and slovenly, greedy and drunken, but liked by Frederick
for his profuse, energetic humour. In his profession,
he was by no means unlearned. He had translated
the *Aphrodisiacus* and had written a *Treatise upon the
Vertigo*.

D'Argens, another favourite, was very different from
La Mettrie. He was a polished man of letters, weak
and vain, the hero of many comic adventures, with a
rare gift of conversation. Frederick made him one
of his chamberlains, and treated him with cordial
familiarity.

Of the fiery Chasot, a cavalry major, little need be
said. Chasot, like his royal patron, had a passion for
the flute. He practised upon this instrument so often,
and with such obstinacy and powerful blowing, that his
neighbours wished him at the devil. He served in the
Bayreuth regiment, but spent much of his time at the
court.

Darget, the king's reader, and Professor Maupertuis,
the head of the Berlin Academy, figured less frequently
at the supper-parties.

It is odd that the official representative of France,
at this court where Frenchmen were so much in evidence,
should have been an Irish refugee. Lord Tyrconnel,
a great, raw Irishman, bluff, cynical, an epicure of the
brutish kind, appeared to Voltaire as " a worthy English-

man," with a " sharp and caustic tongue," and " something frank, which is peculiarly English, and which men of his profession so often lack." What was Tyrconnel's profession ? Heaven knows ; and heaven knows why Voltaire should have considered him a worthy man, or found in him an assemblage of English virtues. It may have been with an ironical intention that Frederick, at whose court France was thus represented by an Irishman, sent as his envoy to the French court a Scottish Jacobite, George Keith. At the time of Voltaire's arrival, George Keith and his brother were both in residence at Potsdam.

In this group of imported favourites, we find only one German who was on the same footing of intimacy. The Baron Pollnitz, an elderly courtier, supple and insincere, could amuse Frederick by his gossip, and could bear Frederick's unpardonable insults. He was anything but worthy ; but worthiness was not a quality which Frederick insisted upon in his companions.

Voltaire might have imagined himself in a French court, had it not been for the grim battalions, the ordered regularity of the king's life, and the general heaviness of style which marks the Teutonic affectation of gaiety and elegance. The inner circle of the court was formed almost entirely of his own countrymen : d'Argens, Maupertuis, Chasot, Baculard d'Arnaud, La Mettrie, Darget—and now Voltaire himself had joined the group. Frederick set the fashion, and Frederick talked and wrote in French. Everything was done, or attempted, in the French manner. " I'll admit the Prussian *tragedies* are no better than ours ; but you would be put to it to celebrate Madam the Dauphine's confinement by a spectacle as noble and as gallant as the one being got ready at *Berlin*." So Voltaire wrote to d'Argental ; and he spoke with delight of the " unspeakable goodness of the victor of *Silesia*, who bears the whole burden of a king from five in the morning till dinner-time, who gives all the rest of the day to elegant letters, who condescends to work with me for three hours together, who submits his great genius to the critick, and who, at supper, is the most amiable of men, the charm and bond of the whole society."

In August, Frederick conferred the rank of chamberlain upon Voltaire, and gave him a golden chain to wear round his neck, a golden key to dangle over his waistcoat, and a pension of 20,000 francs. He offered to Madame Denis a pension of 4,000 for life if she would come to Berlin and keep house for her uncle. Madame Denis preferred to be mistress of the house in the Rue Traversière.

Voltaire's proper and appointed work at Potsdam was the correction of Frederick's verse and prose. On this subject he wrote to d'Argental :

" He has more imagination than I, but I have more method. I profit by the confidence he has in me by telling him the truth more boldly than I would tell it to Marmontel, to d'Arnaud, or to my niece. He does not send me to the mines because I criticize his verses ; he thanks me, he corrects them, and always with improvement. He has wrote some which are admirable. His prose equals his verse, at least ; but here he goes too quickly. There were some good courtiers who told him that all was perfect ; but what is perfect, is that he believes me rather than his flatterers—he loves, he perceives the truth. We must not say *Caesar est supra grammaticam*. Caesar wrote as he fought. Frederick plays upon the flute like *Blavet* ; why should he not write like our best authours ?   This occupation is worth more than gaming or hunting.   His *History of Bran-denburg* will be a master-piece when he has revised it with care ; but has a king the time for such cares ? a king who, alone, governs a vast monarchy ?—aye ; 'tis this confounds me ; I am in a perpetual surprize.   And you must know, moreover, that he is the best of men— or I am the most foolish.   Philosophy has made his character even more perfect.   He has corrected himself, as he corrects his works."

This, in view of what is to follow, is curious reading. He has more imagination than I !   His *Brandenburg* will be a masterpiece !   What did he mean ?   Voltaire's attitude had changed considerably when, a few months later, he spoke both of prose and of verse as " the King of Prussia's dirty linen."   At the same time, it is just to remember that, when he wrote his short *Memoirs* at Les Délices in 1759, he said : " I gave him all my reasons in writing, and thus compos'd a manual of rhetorick and poetry for his use ; he made good use of it, and his genius served him even better than my lessons."

So, for a time, life was gay enough, and full of promise. There were torchlight tournaments, with quadrilles of Romans, Greeks, Carthaginians and Persians, led by four royal princes.   There were splendid fireworks, grand operas.   A little theatre, built under the direction of Voltaire himself, was fitted up in the apartments of the Princess Amelia, and here *Catiline or Rome Sav'd* was performed, with Voltaire in the part of Cicero. Then came a period of tranquillity in the agreeable retreat of Sans-Souci, Frederick's baroque pleasure-house at Potsdam, and Voltaire was able to work quietly on his *Age of Louis XIV*. Many of his most delightful letters were now written for Madame Denis, and to her he sent the following account of his life in October :

" Here we are in the Potsdam retreat ; the tumult of fêtes has ended, and my spirit is not a little reliev'd. I am not sorry to find myself with a king who has neither court nor council. It is true that Potsdam is inhabited by the moustachios and bearskins of grenadiers ; but, thank God, I see nothing of them. I work quietly in my apartment, to the sound of the drum. I have withdrawn from the king's dinners : there are too many generals and princes. I cannot accustom myself to be always on a ceremonial footing with the king, and to talk in publick. I sup with him, in a smaller company. The supper is shorter, gayer and more natural. I would die of grief and indigestion at the end of three months, if I had to dine every day publickly with a king."

About a month later, he wrote, also to Madame Denis, one of the happiest and gayest of his letters :

" So, my dear child, they know already in Paris that we have played at Potsdam the *Death of Caesar*, that Prince *Henry* is a good actor, has an accent, and is mighty amiable, and that we are enjoying ourselves here ? All that is true ; . . . but . . . the supper-parties of the king are delicious ; we talk reason, wit, science ; liberty reigns ; he is the soul of it all ; no ill humour, no clouds—at least, no storms. My life is free, industrious ;   but . . . but . . . operas, comedies, tourneys, suppers at *Sans-Souci*, exercizing of the army, concerts, studies, readings ; but . . . but . . . the city of Berlin, grand, far more spacious than Paris, palace, theatres, affable queens, charming princesses, stately and handsome ladies-in-waiting, Madame Tyrconnel's house always full, and often too much so ; . . . but . . . but, my dear child, the season grows plaguey cold.

" I am in the humour for buts, and I will say : But it is impossible that I should start before the 15th of December. You cannot doubt that I am burning with anxiety to see you, to embrace you, to speak to you. My mad wish to see Italy does not approach the sentiments which call me to you ; but, my child, allow me yet a month ; beg this grace for me from M. d'Argental : for I say always to the King of Prussia that, although I am his chamberlain, I belong none the less to you and to M. d'Argental. But is it true that our *Isaac* d'Argens has gone to shut himself up at Monaco with his wife, who is a great *virtuoso* ? Therein is a grain of madness or a large dose of philosophy. He would do well to come here to join our colony.

" Maupertuis is a little unhing'd just now ; he takes my measure severely with his quadrant. They say there's a shade of jealousy in his problems. There is here, by way of compensation, a fellow who is too gay by far : 'tis La Mettrie. His ideas are like fireworks: all squibs and rockets. This hullabaloo is amusing for a quarter of an hour, but mortally wearisome at last. Without knowing it, he has just had a wicked book printed at Potsdam, in which he proscribes virtue and remorse, sings in praise of vice, invites the reader to every dissipation—and all without evil designs. In this book there are a thousand bright flashes, and not half a page of reason ; lightnings in darkness. Sensible folk have took on themselves to point out to him the enormity of his teaching. He has been quite astonished;

he knew not what he had written ; to-morrow he would write the contrary, if he was ask'd to.   God forbid that I should make him my physician !—he would give me a blue sublimate in place of rhubarb, very innocently, and would then die of laughing.   This odd physician is one of the king's readers ; and the best of it is, he is now reading to him the *History of the Church*.   There are hundreds of pages, and there are certain passages where the king and his reader are like to choke with merriment.

" Farewell, my dear child.   They wish to play *Rome Sav'd* in Paris ? but . . . but . . . Farewell ; I embrace you with all my heart."

Voltaire had no intention of returning to Paris.   He was having it all his own way.   He had a quarrel with Baculard d'Arnaud, and Baculard was quickly dismissed by Frederick.   The tragedy of *Zaïre* was being rehearsed by royal amateurs.

He had all the delight of being a courtier, with none of the apprehensions or duties of the ordinary life at court.   He had ample leisure for his own work.   He was exchanging gay letters with the Margrave of Bayreuth. Frederick was more than amiable ; the suppers were glorious ; even the flute could be endured cheerfully. The world was good enough, and Potsdam the best place in the world, and Frederick the best of kings and kindest of men.

On the 5th of January, 1751, *Zaïre* was played at Potsdam, and " brother Voltaire " wrote an account of it to " sister Guillemette," the margrave.   " Prince Henry surpassed himself.   The Prince Royal spoke his words very clearly.   Prince Ferdinand modulated his voice.   The Princess Amelia had sensibility, and the Queen-Mother was enchanted."   And there is a note

on the same performance in a letter to Madame Denis:
" The Princess Amelia was Zaïre, and I was the good
Lusignan. Our princess plays Hermione much better
—it is, moreover, a better part. Madame Tyrconnel
acquitted herself well enough as Andromache. There
are not many actresses with such fine eyes."

Then came the dreadful affair of the Jew Hirsch,
and the black storm of Frederick's displeasure.

The affair of the Jew is so involved, so complicated by
ingenious lying, that we can do no more than give its
bare outline.—During the wars, the *Steuer* or State
Bank of Saxony had issued a large series of notes which
had rapidly depreciated in the foreign exchanges. By
the treaty of Dresden, in 1745, Frederick had stipulated
that these notes, if presented at the *Steuer* by his own
subjects, were to be honoured at their full value. As
a result of this, depreciated notes were bought up in
Holland and other places, and then cashed at the *Steuer*.
In 1748 the importation of the notes was prohibited,
but the practice continued.

A speculation in these depreciated notes had an
irresistible attraction for Voltaire, and he did not consider the treachery, danger and dishonesty of such a
proceeding. Having learnt that the notes could be
bought in Dresden at 35 per cent. below par, he commissioned the Jew Hirsch to acquire them in large
quantities. As a guarantee, he gave the Jew certain
letters of change, and received from him, as surety on
his part, a number of trinkets and diamonds. In settling
accounts, the two conspirators fell out, and each roundly
accused the other of being a rogue. Hirsch, indeed,
accused Voltaire of having tampered with the agreement
after it was signed—a charge which was not proved, and

was probably without foundation. But the shameful business was taken before the judges, before the Chancellor himself ; and although Voltaire won the case, he appeared hardly less blameable than the Jew.

No more suppers, no more delightful studies, no more dallying and flattery. It was all very well to pass it off as a joke, as he did in a letter to charming Wilhelmina the margrave :

" Brother Voltaire is doing penance ; he has had a devil of a business with a Jew, and according to the law of the *Old Testament* he must pay for having been robbed ; and what is more, a pretty hubbub has come of it, which, divided in three or four parts, would provide matter for a comedy as pleasant as the manifesto of the *Czarina*, who calls *Europe* to witness that M. *Gross* was not invited to supper."

The margrave, uneasy, wrote to her brother Frederick, and received a thundering reply :

" You have asked me about this business of Voltaire with a Jew. 'Tis the affair of a knave trying to deceive a pick-pocket. . . . Voltaire . . . has behaved like a madman. I am waiting until the affair is settled before I chastise him, and before seeing whether, at the age of fifty-six, one can make him, if not reasonable, at any rate less of a rogue."

On the 24th of February, the angry king (and he was justly angry) sent a crushing, unanswerable letter to the poet :

" I was pleased enough to receive you as my guest ; I esteemed your genius, your talents, your learning, and I had reason to think that a man of your age, tired of brawling with authours and exposing himself to the tempest, had come here for refuge in a quiet haven ; but, first of all you exacted from me, in the most singular manner, that I should not engage Fréron to act as my correspondent. I had the weakness or the complaisance to give way to you here, although it was not for you to decide whom I should choose for my service. You had some little grievances against d'Arnaud ; a generous man would have forgiven him ; a vindictive man pursues the objects of his hatred. In short, although d'Arnaud had done nothing against me, it was for your sake that he was dismissed. You have been to the *Russian* minister, talking to him about matters in which you had no right to meddle, and it was thought I had ordered you to do so. You have meddled with the affairs of Madame de Bentinck, which were certainly no concern of yours. You have had the most disgraceful affair in the world with a Jew. You have behaved outrageously in the town. The affair of the Saxon notes is so well known in Saxony that I have received the most serious complaints from that State. For my part, I had kept peace in my house until your arrival ; and I warn you, that if you have a passion for scheming and plotting, you are come to the wrong place. I love men who are gentle and peaceable, whose conduct does not display the violent passions of tragedy : if you can resolve yourself to live as a philosopher, I shall be pleased to see you ; but if you abandon yourself to the impetuous fury of your passions, and fall foul of every one, you will not please me at all by coming here, and you may as well stay in Berlin."

To this letter Voltaire replied submissively, and with becoming airs of desolation and repentance. Frederick was appeased, but he wrote back in a style which was plain, manly, and very much to the point :

" If you wish to come here, you are free to do so. I hear nothing of any lawsuit, not even of yours. Since you have gained it, I congratulate you, and I am truly glad that the affair is ended. I hope you'll have no further quarrels, either with the *Old* or the *New Testament* : such imbroglios tarnish honour, and, even with the talents of the rarest genius in *France*, you will not wipe out the stains with which conduct of this sort must eventually besmirch your reputation. A book-seller *Gosse* [Jore ?], an opera fiddler, a jeweller Jew— sure, these are names which ought not in any circum-stances to be found associated with yours. I am writing this letter with the rough good sense of a *German*, who says what he thinks without using equivocal terms or sweetening phrases which disfigure the truth : 'tis for you to profit thereby."

Voltaire was back at Sans-Souci in March, and life went on, for a while, very much as it had before the shocking business of the notes, the Jew and the diamonds.
" Potsdam is more than ever a mixture of Sparta and Athens," he wrote to d'Argental. " Every day we have reviews and verses. We have Maupertuis and Algarotti. We work, and then sup gaily with a king who is a rare good companion. All that would be charming ;—but health ? Ah ! 'tis health, 'tis you that I miss, dear angel ! . . . My gentleman sets out every day, doubt-less, at four o'clock ; my gentleman goes to the play, and brings with him to supper his placid joy and equable humour ; and I, such as I was, such as I am, holding my belly with both hands, and then my pen ; suffering,

working, supping, hoping for a morrow less tormented by the stomach-ache, and always deceived by the morrow. I tell you again : without these aches, without your absence, this land would be my paradise."

Voltaire's ill health, partly the result of a sedentary life, partly of his natural debility and a tightly strung nervous organisation, was constantly mentioned in his letters. Writing to his niece, Madame de Fontaine, in August, 1751, he spoke of it with unsparing frankness :

" As for me, after having tried hot water and cold water and every sort of good and bad regime, after having passed through the hands of cooks and quacks and doctors, after having been ill at Berlin last winter, I have took to supping, dining, and even breakfasting : they say that I am better, that I look younger. I know very well 'tis nothing of the kind ; but I have lived quietly for nigh six months together with my king, eating like a devil, and taking, as he does, a little powder'd rhubarb once every two days."

He was not the only one at Sans-Souci who had reason to complain of ill health. La Mettrie, with all his quips and jollity, Tyrconnel, with all his rude bluster, were both mortally sick. It was La Mettrie who brought to Voltaire the celebrated story of the orange-skin :

" This La Mettrie is a man of no consequence, who talks on familiar terms with the king, after his reading. He speaks to me with entire candour : he swears that, when he was talking with the king a few days ago, about my pretended favour and the little jealousies it excites, the king answered him : ' I shall need him for one more year, at the most : one squeezes the orange, and throws away the skin.' "

Was this true, or a stroke of malice on the part of La Mettrie ? Probably it was true. La Mettrie had no ambitions, and Voltaire was fond of him. The poor doctor, jolly and careless as he seemed to be, had a desperate longing to see France again, and Voltaire had interceded for him with de Richelieu—apparently without success. The doctor was an undesirable.

La Mettrie died on the 11th of November, 1751. He had been summoned to attend Lord Tyrconnel, whose condition was deplorable, but who was eating, jesting and cursing like a Potsdam philosopher. He found Tyrconnel, with his lady and a large company, about to dine. La Mettrie joined the company. " He ate and drank, laughed and talked more than all the guests. When he was full to the very chin, they brought in a pie made of an eagle disguised as a pheasant, which had been sent from the North, well stuff'd with rancid fat, minced pork and ginger. Our good fellow ate the whole pie, and died next day in Lord Tyrconnel's house, attended by two physicians, of whom he had made rare sport. Here is a great epoch in the history of gluttons." So Voltaire described this edifying death to his niece.

There was a great dispute as to whether La Mettrie had died " like a Christian or like a doctor." He had begged Lord Tyrconnel that he might be buried in his garden. " The king had himself exactly informed of the manner in which he had died, whether he had observ'd all the Catholick forms, whether he had received any benefit from them : at last it was made clear that this *gourmand* had died a philosopher : *I am mighty glad of that*, said the king to us, *for the repose of his soul.* We fell a-laughing, and he also."

Thus, in the manner of the Potsdam epicures,

Frederick and his ribald crew made a mockery of the death of a boon companion. Yet Frederick wrote the elegy of this poor buffoon, and himself read it before the Academy of Berlin. The madness of La Mettrie, said Voltaire, must have been catching ; but a man who commands a hundred and fifty thousand men can do as he pleases.

Late in October, a very unpleasant young man of twenty-four had come to Berlin. His name was Laurent Angliviel de la Beaumelle. In 1747 he had entered the service of Baron de Gram at Copenhagen as tutor to his son. At Copenhagen, he had started a periodical —the *Danish Spectator* or *Modern Aspasia*—and in 1750, to his own astonishment, he was appointed to the chair of French Literature in the University. During the last year of his residence at Copenhagen (1751), this bumptious young man published a book which he called *My Thoughts* or *What would they say of it ?* In this book, after the manner of young men, he touched upon all things under the sun, and touched upon them with the beautiful assurance of immaturity. Voltaire, hearing that La Beaumelle had arrived, asked civilly for a copy of *My Thoughts*. La Beaumelle hesitated, as well he might.

On page seventy of this precious book there was the following passage : " If we read through all ancient and modern history, we shall find no instance of a *Prince* who gave a pension of seven thousand crowns to a man of letters, simply as a man of letters. There have been greater poets than *Voltaire* ; there have been none so well paid, for taste sets no limit to its rewards. The *King of Prussia* heaps benefits upon men of talents, for precisely the same reasons which induce a little *German* prince to heap benefits upon a dwarf or buffoon." What would they say of it ?

The book was sent to Voltaire, who kept it for three days, and then returned it to the author with the corner of page seventy carefully turned down.

La Beaumelle, if he knew his man, had now cause for alarm ; but that did not prevent him from visiting Voltaire and appearing quite at his ease. Voltaire criticised *My Thoughts*, justly, though with a certain harshness, and then turned to the offending page. What was the meaning of it ?

The meaning of it, said the bumptious young author, was clear enough, surely. It meant that Voltaire was handsomely pensioned, as a man of his eminence deserved to be : the King of Prussia, unlike the little German princes who would have taken delight in buffoons, chose for his companions men of learning and genius. The sense was clear enough.

Perhaps it was, said Voltaire with one of his malicious grins ; but would it be so easy to persuade d'Argens, Professor Maupertuis, Baron Pollnitz and the Count Algarotti ? And Frederick himself had read the passage, and was very angry. Who showed it to him ? cried the bumptious one, forgetting himself : you promised to respect my confidence ! It was Darget, the king's reader. So the uneasy author, perhaps regretting his *Thoughts*, ran to Darget, and then ran to Maupertuis.

War between Voltaire and La Beaumelle was now declared, and each waited for the opportunity to strike a telling blow. That opportunity presented itself to La Beaumelle in the publication of *Louis XIV*.

In March, 1752, Voltaire sent some copies of *Louis*

XIV, and probably of other books, to his friend Falkener, to whom he wrote in English :

" My dear and beneficent friend, I send to you, by the way of Hamburgh, two enormous bales of the scribbling trade. I direct them to our envoy at Hamburgh, who will dispatch them to you, and put my wares to sea, instead of throwing them into the fire ; which might be the case in France or at Rome.

" My dear friend, I have recourse to your free and generous soul. Some French good patriots, who have read the book, raise a noble clamour against me, for having praised Marlborough and Eugène ; and some good churchmen damn me for having turned a little into ridicule our *jansénisme* and *molinisme*.

" If our prejudiced people are fools, booksellers and printers or book-jobbers are rogues. I am like to be damned in France, and cheated by the Dutch ; the old German honesty is gone."

Falkener was to arrange for the sale of some of the copies, and to give others to his friends: " Burn the book, in case you should yawn in reading it ; but do not forget your old friend, who will be attached to you till the day of his doom."

But while La Beaumelle was preparing his attack on *Louis XIV*, a more serious quarrel began. This quarrel, which is in itself one of the most curious episodes in the history of literature, was the outcome of a growing enmity between Voltaire and Maupertuis.

The causes of that enmity are not obscure. In every distinguished man, Voltaire saw a possible rival. Maupertuis, however vain or eccentric he may have been, was a man of extraordinary achievement, of wide learning and of striking character. Few men of his day had a more profound knowledge of the natural sciences, and fewer still had the courage, as he had, to lead scientific expeditions in search of the North Pole or to brave the dangers and annoyances of life in the tropics. In 1752 he was fifty-four: suffering in health, irritable, morbidly vain, giving himself strange airs and wearing strange clothes, attracting a good deal of notice, and highly esteemed by Frederick. That was enough to make Voltaire dislike him, in spite of his old friendship; but dislike ripened quickly to a blazing hatred.

Maupertuis, though he had been Voltaire's friend for many years, had made it clear to the poet that he had no business to meddle in matters of science, in physics or in mathematics. His attitude to Voltaire had always been a trifle patronising. Maupertuis—whose portrait shows him gravely and firmly patting and flattening the North Pole with his plump hand—was a great leader of human progress, and Voltaire was just an amusing fellow, whose plays and histories were good enough, but whose physics were only those of an amateur. So, too, when he taught the divine Emilie or smiled condescendingly over her work, his attitude was always that of a master, and he had no willingness to admit her genius. And when Emilie favoured the Leibnitzian Koenig, Maupertuis took no pains to conceal his coldness and displeasure.

There is no doubt that Voltaire was jealous of his countryman's renown at Potsdam, and was eagerly watching for some weakness, some gesture of unguarded vanity, which would give him a chance of opening fire. It was Koenig who provided the chance.

Maupertuis hated Koenig, who had once addressed him as " my poor friend,"—" but my poor friend, you must remember. . . ." Yet they had formerly been friends ; and Koenig, a plain good-natured Swiss, had a great admiration for the attainments of Maupertuis.

But Koenig disagreed with the Professor on the subject of the *least quantity of action* (an early form of our quantum theory) and its effects upon *hard or elastic bodies*. This principle, which had the immense advantage of being reconcilable with the idea of a Supreme Being, for reasons which are not altogether plain, was published in 1749 in the *History of the Academy*. It was opposed by Koenig, who had previously shown his manuscript to the Professor, in the *Nova Acta Eruditorum* of March, 1751. In this reply, a letter from Leibnitz was quoted, showing that Leibnitz himself had already examined the *principle of action*.

Upon this, Maupertuis, crazy with a rage in which there were evident symptoms of mental disorder, declared that the alleged letter of Leibnitz was a forgery or invention. He convened a tribunal of his academicians, who confirmed this dreadful accusation, and stated, on the authority of Euler, that no such letter could ever have been written by Leibnitz. This decision was made known on the 13th of April, 1752.

Soon parties were engaged on both sides, the papers were full of skits and libels, and the pamphleteers were busy.

Voltaire did not immediately enter the field. He watched events with a prudence more ominous for Maupertuis than his usual sudden attack. On the 23rd of May, he wrote to Madame Denis:

" This world is an huge Temple of Discord—our Berlin *Academy* is a chapel given over entirely to the protection of this *Goddess*. Maupertuis has just committed a little act of tyranny there which is unworthy of a philosopher. By his personal authority, he has denounced as a forger, in convocation, one of the Academy's members—Koenig, a great geometrician, librarian to the Princess of *Orange*, and Professor in Publick Law at the Hague. This Koenig is a man of merit, who is quite incapable of being a forger. I lived for near two years with him in the house of Madame du Châtelet. . . . He is not the man to suffer such an affront.

" I am not yet fully inform'd of the details of this newly begun War. I do not leave Potsdam. Maupertuis is in Berlin, sick through too much drinking of brandy . . . but he deals me a good many glov'd blows, and I am afraid he may do me even more harm than he has done to Koenig. A false account, a timely word, circulated, whisper'd in the king's ear, and which sticks in his memory, is a weapon against which there is often no shield. D'Argens has not done so ill to seek the shores of the Mediterranean; I should do even better to seek those of the Seine."

Koenig, who could produce no original, stoutly maintained that his transcription from Leibnitz was from an authentic copy, and late in September he published his *Appeal to the Publick*, a formidable denunciation of Maupertuis, of his Academy, and of his procedure. A few days before the issue of this *Appeal*, Voltaire had opened his campaign with a little pamphlet entitled *The Reply of an Academician of Berlin to an Academician of Paris*, a short but horribly concise account of the Koenig affair. Although the *Reply* was merely a statement of the case against the Academy and the President, its concentration, its grim, condensed energy, left no doubt as to the author.

The reputation of Maupertuis was in grave danger, and Koenig, if not completely vindicated, was able to take up a more aggressive posture. He had secured, on his side, the most redoubtable pen in Europe, and had reason to feel encouragement. Voltaire was now greatly occupied with the controversy, and he was presently given an opening which enabled him to crush Maupertuis beneath an overwhelming satire. On the 1st of October, he wrote to Madame Denis :

" I send you bravely Koenig's *Appeal to the Publick*. You will read the history of the proceedings with interest. The work is extremely well compos'd : innocence and reason are victorious. *Paris* will think as *Germany* and *Holland*. Maupertuis is here look'd on as a ridiculous tyrant ; but I fear lest his atrocious behaviour should have tragick results.

" He has conducted himself in this affair as a man more skilled in intrigue than in geometry ; he has secretly irritated the *King of Prussia* against Koenig, and has cunningly availed himself of his authority to cause a search for the original letters of Leibnitz in a place where he knew well they could not be found ; by this unworthy manoeuvre he has involved the King in his own schemes. Would you believe, that the King, instead of feeling anger, as he should, at being thus deceived and compromised, hath taken the part of this tyrant philosopher with zeal ? He will not even read Koenig's reply. No one can open his eyes when he has determined to shut them. Once calumny has entered the mind of a king, 'tis like the gout in a bishop—there's no shifting it.

" Maupertuis, in the midst of these quarrels, has gone quite mad. You will remember that he was chained up at Montpellier, some twenty years ago, in one of these fits. His malady has fallen upon him with violence. He has just printed a book in which he pretends that the existence of God can only be prov'd by an algebraick *formula* ; that any man can predict the future if he does but exalt his soul ; that we should go to *Patagonia* and dissect the heads of giants if we would discover the nature of the human understanding. The whole book is in this style. He has read it to his Berlin ladies, who find it admirable."

Here was the opening. Maupertuis had played into the hands of his enemy in a manner which filled the enemy with fierce delight and with unfeigned amazement. *Quem Deus vult perdere*—never had there been such a case in point ; never had a man chosen so well the method and moment of his own destruction.

The President, broken in health, agitated by the bitterness and violence of the quarrel, drinking many glasses of brandy, and thinking that the time had come for a splendid revelation of his genius, composed and printed an extraordinary volume of *Letters*. It was even as Voltaire had said, and worse. The soul was to be discovered through experiments on the large and living heads of Patagonians ; people were to be smeared with resin so that they might live for ever ; a shaft was to be driven to the centre of the earth, for the advancement of learning ; one of the pyramids was to be blown up, in order that the Academy might know precisely what was beneath it ; a town was to be built, in which every one was to speak Latin, by which means the use and knowledge of that tongue would be prodigiously extended ; criminals were to be dissected alive, in hope of observing the elusive operations of the soul

—and so forth. To attack all this—the disordered ramblings of a man who was more than a little mad—was easy enough. It was a perfect opportunity. Into this enormous gap in the enemy's line Voltaire could pour the whole of his forces, and he did not hesitate to do so.

But Frederick, in the meantime, had come to the assistance of his tottering President and the sadly maligned Academy. Frederick himself wrote and circulated *The Letter of an Academician of Berlin*, a pamphlet with the royal arms on the title, in which he defended the virtuous Maupertuis and his colleagues, and attacked the wicked men who spoke against them. From the most wicked of these men there came a cry of anger and amazement:

" Here is a thing unknown indeed," he wrote to Madame Denis; " a thing which will not be copied; 'tis unique. The *King of Prussia*, without having read one word of Koenig's reply, without hearing, without consulting any one, has just printed a pamphlet against Koenig, against me, against all those who have wished to prove the innocence of this professor who was so cruelly condemned. He treats all his partisans as jealous, foolish or dishonest men. . . . The German scribblers, who could not believe that a king who has won battles could be the authour of such a work, have spoke of it freely as the essay of a schoolboy who knows nothing at all of the matter. But the pamphlet has been reprinted in Berlin, with the Prussian eagle, a crown and a sceptre below the title. The crown, eagle and sceptre are very much surpriz'd to find themselves in such a place. Every one shrugs his shoulders, lowers his eyes, and dares say nothing. . . . And what is most rare in this cruel and absurd business, is that the king has no liking at all for Maupertuis, in whose favour he employs his pen and his sceptre. *Plato* thought to die of grief at not being ask'd to certain little suppers when I was present, and the King has told us an hundred times that the savage vanity of this *Plato* makes him unsociable. . . . But this is only but a part of what has happen'd. Unfortunately, I find myself writing too, and on the other side. I have no sceptre, but I have a pen; and in some way, I know not how, I have cut this pen in such a fashion as to make ridiculous this *Plato*, with his giants, his predictions and dissections, and his impertinent quarrel with Koenig. The raillery is innocent ; but I knew not then that I was aiming a shot at the king's fancy. 'Tis an unlucky business. I have provok'd self-love and despotick power, two very dangerous things. . . . As for myself, I am sorely afflicted and very ill, and to crown all, I sup with the king. 'Tis the banquet of *Damocles*."

Voltaire's " innocent raillery " was the famous *Diatribe of Doctor Akakia, Physician to the Pope*. In order to publish this, he deceived Frederick. He obtained leave to print certain articles on religious questions, including the *Defence of Lord Bolingbroke*, and then, by virtue of this leave, he published the awful *Diatribe*.

Doctor Akakia is perhaps the cruellest and most diverting satire in the world. It is, however, an occasional piece, and the force of the satire cannot be relished without an understanding of the quarrels and controversies which produced it. The outline of those controversies has been presented to the reader; and we need not examine the written follies of poor

Maupertuis. But before we laugh at the furious fun of the *Diatribe*, we should remember, once again, that Maupertuis was not a contemptible man, that he had been one of the great discoverers of his age, that he was now sick, mentally disordered, and in a state more proper to excite pity than malice or ridicule. His deplorable action in the affair of Koenig was due to the injured pride of a man who was half crazy ; and the unlucky *Letters* (which he himself admitted to be "without order") were vagaries of a kind which a generous public would have quickly forgotten. We do not judge great men by the products of their decay or dotage. Maupertuis, if not a great man, was one of extraordinary accomplishment, and in more than one respect superior to his terrible enemy.

The methods of *Doctor Akakia* are direct and devastating. The *Letters*, he says, cannot really be the work of the grave President ; they are written by some impudent young fellow, who, stealing the name of an illustrious man, has tried to sell his own extravagances. "This great man [Maupertuis], so incapable of charlatanism, would never have given to the publick letters which are not address'd to any one, and would certainly never have fallen into certain little errours which are only pardonable in a youth." After an absurd *Decree of the Inquisition of Rome*, and a more absurd *Judgement of the Professors of the College of Sapience*, the wicked author proceeds to *An Examination of the Letters of a Young Authour disguis'd under the Name of a President*. In this *Examination* occur the following passages of ferocious gaiety :

"We pass over several things which would fatigue the patience of the reader and the intelligence of Milord the Inquisitor; but we think he would be mighty surprised to learn that the young student is positively anxious to dissect the heads of giants twelve feet high, and of hairy men with tails, so as to get to the bottom of the human understanding ; that with dreams and opium he regulates the soul ; that he creates eels big with other eels by means of fine flour, and fish with grains of wheat. We take this occasion for diverting Milord the Inquisitor.

" But Milord the Inquisitor will laugh no more when he shall see that every one may become a prophet; for the authour finds no more difficulty in seeing the future than in seeing the past. He vows that the reasons in favour of judicial astrology are as strong as the reasons against it. In short, he assures us that our perceptions of the past, of the present and of the future do but differ in the degree of the soul's activity. . . . We judge unanimously that his brain is prodigiously exalted, and that he will presently utter prophecies. We know not yet whether he will make big or little prophecies, but we are mightily afraid that he may be a prophet of evil, since, in his treatise on Happiness, he speaks only of affliction: he says, in particular, that all fools are unhappy. We present to all such our condolences ; but, if his exalted soul has seen the future, has she not beheld there something a little ridiculous ?

" He should also be assur'd that it will be difficult for him to make, as he pretends, a *hole* reaching to the very middle of the earth (wherein, it would seem, he desires to hide himself for shame at having put forward such things). To make this *hole*, we should have to dig up at least three or four hundred leagues of the country, which might perhaps disturb the system of the *balance* of Europe.

" In conclusion, we pray Doctor *Akakia* to prescribe
him some cooling drink; we exhort him to study in
some university, and to be modest."

After this comes the uproarious mockery of the
Memorable Séance—three pages of the purest devilment.

An extraordinary general meeting of learned men is
convened at the Academy. Here the President, with
all his apparatus and chosen examples, demonstrates
the new discoveries. For example :

" In the first place, two physicians produced each
one a sick man smeared with resinous wax, and two
surgeons pricked the legs and arms of these sick men
with long needles; whereupon the patients, who before
were scarce able to move, began to cry and run about
with all their strength ; and the *Secretary* noted this
in the register. . . . Then all the workmen of the
town presented themselves, for the purpose of quickly
making a hole to reach the very centre of the earth,
according to the special orders of the *President*. Even
so far reach'd his vision ; but as the operation would
have been somewhat lengthy, it was reserved for
another time ; and the *Perpetual Secretary* arrang'd
a meeting between the workmen and the builders of
the tower of *Babel*.

" After that, the *President* ordered the preparation
of a vessel for the dissection of giants and of hairy
men with long tails in the *Southern* parts of the globe:
he declared that he would himself undertake the
voyage, and would go to breathe his native air; upon
which the whole assembly clapped their hands. . . .
The *President*, having toss'd off a glass of *rogum*, prov'd
to the assembly that it was as easy for the soul to see
the future as to see the past; and then he lick'd his

lips with his tongue, roll'd his head about, and prophesied. We do not relate the prophecy, which will be found entire in the *Almanack* of the Academy.

"The sitting was concluded by a very eloquent discourse spoken by the *Perpetual Secretary* : *'Tis only an Erasmus*, said he, *who could worthily sing your praises*; whereupon he raised the *monad* of the *President* to the very clouds, or at least to the very foggs. He set him boldly by the side of *Cyrano de Bergerac*. They made him a throne of bladders, and he set out next day for the *Moon*, where *Astolphus* (so it is said) found what the *President* had lost."

The publication of the *Diatribe* was not merely resented by Frederick ; it made him furiously angry, and there was nothing unreasonable in his anger. He had been tricked by Voltaire, who had now crushed with ridicule the President of the Academy, whose crazy *Letters* had received Frederick's approbation. Desnoiresterres is probably right in refusing to believe the story about Voltaire and Frederick reading the satire together with explosions of merry laughter. Voltaire, seeing the gathering clouds, denied the work, and was promptly confounded by a signed statement from the printer.

"Your effrontery," wrote Frederick, " astounds me, after what you have done, which is clear as daylight. . . . Do not imagine that you will make us believe black is white. When one cannot see, 'tis because one has no mind to see; but if you persist in this affair, I will have everything printed; and folk will see that, if your work merits the erection of statues to honour you, your conduct is deserving of chains."

All the unsold copies of the *Diatribe* were seized and

220

publicly burnt in the open squares of Berlin on Christmas Eve. A particularly large pile was fired in the neighbourhood of the Taubenstrass, where Voltaire was lodging with M. de Francheville.

But Doctor Akakia had done his work. The burning of the book to ashes could not extinguish the impression which it had made, nor could the gift of the ashes to Maupertuis (a pretty gesture on the part of Frederick) heal the injured vanity of the President. It has been said that Maupertuis was literally killed by this dreadful squib and the other little writings of Akakia which were to follow it. He died at Bâle in 1759, completely broken in health and mind.

That any written satire could have such effects may well seem strange to a phlegmatic race whose cool heads and level humours protect them so mercifully against the darts of malice. But with Frenchmen of the eighteenth century it was very different. Satire is a peculiar gift of the Latin peoples, and a peculiar danger to their excitable nerves. We have seen how easily a play could be damned in eighteenth-century Paris by a little touch of wit at the right moment. Men were actually ruined by pamphlets, and ministers could be laughed out of office. Rousseau was driven crazy by persecution of this kind.

At the same time, it should be remembered that Maupertuis had been in ill health for a long while before the publication of the *Diatribe*. He had more than once shown signs of madness, and he was overstrained and overworked. This, however, does not exempt Voltaire from a serious charge ; for, if he did not hasten the death of Maupertuis, he was pursuing and tormenting a man who was already sick and discouraged, and who was unable to defend himself.

Shortly before the burning of Doctor Akakia, La Beaumelle had launched his attack on Voltaire. He published an unauthorised edition of *Louis XIV*, " augmented " by his own notes and comments. La Beaumelle had acquired, by questionable means, some questionable letters of Madame de Maintenon. In his " notes," he endeavoured to prove certain errors in Voltaire's history, and at the same time attacked Voltaire personally, as well as the members of the Potsdam circle. Voltaire sent a letter to Roques, an ecclesiastical councillor of Hesse-Homberg and a friend of La Beaumelle, and complained of the outrage.

The letter is of interest from more than one point of view. After stating his case against La Beaumelle, and accusing Maupertuis of having incited the young man to write against him, he says :

" I now find myself constrained to endure, at the same time, two most unhappy quarrels. I have to fight, both against Maupertuis, who seeks my destruction, and against La Beaumelle, whom he has employed to insult me. The life of a man of letters is a continual warfare, sometimes of a stealthy kind, and sometimes full of noise, as it is between princes; but we have an advantage which kings have not: between them, force is the arbiter, and with us 'tis reason. The publick is an incorruptible judge who, in time, makes known his irrevocable decrees. The publick will say whether I am wrong in taking the part of M. Koenig, cruelly oppressed as he is, and in refuting the lies with which La Beaumelle, incited by the oppressor of Koenig and of myself, has filled the *Age of Louis XIV*.

" La Beaumelle has told you, Sir, that he *will pursue me to Hell itself*. He is free to go there; and, in order to merit this retirement, he tells you that he will print, at the end of *Louis XIV*, a lawsuit in which I was engaged, nearly three years ago, with a Jew, and which I won. I am ready to furnish him with all the papers, and he can bind them together, with the *Peace of Nimègue*, that of *Riswick*, and the *War of Succession* ; nothing would contribute more to the advance of the sciences."

Here is a charge against Maupertuis; and one which is altogether unfounded. It is true that Maupertuis was a gossip, and that he was jealous of Voltaire. But we know of nothing which leads us to suppose that he was planning Voltaire's destruction. The lawsuit with Hirsch the Jew had taken place less than two years previously, and not " nearly three years ago."

Frederick had now seen enough, and more than enough, of the dealings and trickeries of the great man. His patience was at an end. Frederick himself was capable of trickery, but he was not capable of mean evasions. His own faults were of a more manly character. His own mind was more disciplined; at least he knew how to restrain himself and how to act with decency, whatever his thoughts or designs. Probably he was less angered by Voltaire's audacity than he was by his cowering denials and foolish deceit. It was clear that Voltaire could not remain in Berlin for much longer, but the king and poet could still cajole each other with something of the old spirit and playfulness.

On New Year's Day, 1753, Voltaire handed back to the king his key, his cross and golden chain, and the last quarterly payment of his pension. Upon the envelope which contained these relics of favour he had written some touching verses, in which he likened himself to a sorrowing lover who returns the portrait of his mistress. Frederick sent them all back again, with a coquettish note, inviting Voltaire to supper, and promising that all should be well.

Was he really anxious to forget and forgive, and to allow Voltaire another chance? Or was he afraid of him? Frederick's hundred and fifty thousand men could not defend him against the attacks of Doctor Akakia, or some other formidable personage.

It was Voltaire himself who decided to go.

" Sire," he wrote to Frederick, " urged by the tears and solicitations of my family, I find myself oblig'd to lay at your feet my destiny, and the benefits and distinctions with which you have honoured me. My sorrow equals my resignation. . . . I have lost all: there does but remain with me the memory of happy days spent in your retreat at Potsdam. I shall find any other solitude unhappy enough, doubtless. It is hard, moreover, to set forth at this season, oppress'd by sickness; but 'tis harder still to leave you. Believe me, 'tis the one grief I can feel at the present time."

Then, seeking for a more definite excuse, he pleaded ill health, and said that he had been ordered to take the waters at Plombières.

Yet, early in March (1753), Frederick was still on good terms with his poet; he could joke with him about the " grace of Beelzebub," and sent him quinquina when he had a cold. On the 16th of March, the tune had changed: Voltaire was told that he might leave when he pleased, that excuses were not necessary, that he was to return—finally—the golden key and the cross, and a book of " poesies " by Frederick himself.

Voltaire came to Potsdam on the 18th of March, and was installed, for the last time, in his old quarters at

Sans-Souci. The following afternoon, he spent two hours with the king in his private apartment.

Frederick was affable, amusing, ready to make jokes at the expense of poor Maupertuis, responding, as so often before, to the lively sallies or quick fancy of the poet. Voltaire (so it might have seemed) was never in higher favour. For six days he remained at Potsdam, petted and courted by Frederick, but always reminding the king of his wretched health, of his impatient " family," and of the necessity for a course of the waters at Plombières—he was, in fact, making arrangements for his departure.

On the morning of the 26th Frederick was on the parade-ground when he was told that Monsieur de Voltaire awaited his arders.

" So, Monsieur de Voltaire, you have really made up your mind to leave us ? "

" Sire, urgent business affairs, and above all the state of my health, oblige me to."

" Then, Sir, I wish you a good journey."

And Frederick turned back to the stiff lines of his grenadiers.

Thus parted those two extraordinary men, who, in spite of their devilish humours, their hideous grimacing and treacherous designs, their grim coquetry and affectation, had always a fondness for each other. However indecently and heartily each might abuse the other behind his back (which is how we generally abuse each other), however fierce their mutual explosions of anger, there came, sooner or later, the desire to be reconciled. No one could amuse Frederick as Voltaire could amuse him; no one interested Voltaire more profoundly than Frederick, or possessed a mental complexion which more nearly resembled his own. For a while their intercourse was broken, and those brusque words on the parade-ground were the last they ever spoke to each other. But, in little more than a year's time, they began to exchange letters again, and the correspondence was maintained for some four-and-twenty years, ending only with Voltaire's death in 1778.

Voltaire, travelling like a great gentleman, with roomy coach and heavy baggage, reached Leipsic the day after his departure from Potsdam. Here he wrote some more bitter and brilliant additions to the *Diatribe*, and had them printed.

Was there no end to this infernal malice ? Doctor Akakia wrote a *Treaty of Peace between Monsieur the President and Monsieur the Professor*; and when poor Maupertuis, trembling with fear and anger, sent a note to the author and threatened him with " the most complete vengeance," the note itself was printed at the head of yet another page of savage jollity. " Since the late M. de *Pourceaugnac*, who wanted to draw his sword upon the doctors, there has never been such a naughty patient. Doctor *Akakia*, dreadfully frighten'd, had recourse to the University of Leipsic." And then came *The Letter of Dr Akakia to the Native of Saint-Malo*.

From Leipsic, Voltaire proceeded to Gotha, where he spent rather more than a month with the Duke and Duchess of Saxe-Gotha, handsomely entertained and making merry with a brave company. On the 26th of May he arrived at Cassel, intending to go thence to Strasburg. But now he learnt that Baron Pollnitz, the emissary of Frederick, was lying in wait for him. He was being pursued.

The reason for this was clear enough. In one of his innumerable packages, Voltaire had stowed away Frederick's book of *poesies*—a book which Frederick

was naturally anxious to get back at the earliest possible
moment. Such royal *poesies*, in the hands of Dr Akakia,
might be put to heaven knew what abominable usage.
It was a terrifying thought. And Voltaire had no
sooner reached the *Golden Lion* at Frankfort than he
found himself arrested by the Baron Freytag, acting
under instructions of the most explicit kind from
Potsdam.

Now the package—" the great package "—with
Frederick's book of verses, and also, so it was alleged,
the chamberlain's golden key, the cross and the chain,
was at Leipsic or Hamburg.

Very well, said Freytag; Monsieur de Voltaire would
be under arrest until these things had been duly handed
over, and above all the precious book : " Das Buch,
welches hauptsächlich mit retour kommen soll, ist
bennant *Oeuvres de Poésie* "—" The book, the return
of which is of the highest importance, is entitled *Oeuvres
de Poésie.*"

Voltaire, whose retention of the book and the golden
trinkets is unaccountable, and can hardly have been
due, as Macaulay has suggested, to negligence, wrote
at once for the " great package," and Freytag promised
him his liberty as soon as the precious things were
handed over. Meanwhile he was under close arrest.
He could not leave the inn. At most, he could walk
in the garden with secretary Collini. Days passed,
and still they waited for that accursed package. This
arrest, this outrage (for so it was), became more than
irksome; it was terrifying. Thoughts of imprisonment, even of death, came into the raging mind
and the anxious heart of Monsieur de Voltaire. It
was all very well to rant and bluster at Freytag or
Councillor Schmidt: these grave, dutiful Germans had

their orders, and they would carry them out with no
deviation, no softening of rigour. After all, what was
this runaway Frenchman doing with the *poesies* of the
king, their master? It was a solemn business.

And still the days passed, and there was no package,
and all the town began to talk, and there were curious
visitors at the *Golden Lion*. Among these visitors who
should come but the rascally Dutch bookseller, one of
the " bungling pirates," Van Duren! It was too much.
Voltaire, his nerves all on edge, rushed upon the pirate
and slapped him in the face. Van Duren did not at
once perceive that he was greatly honoured. " Sir,
sir! " cried the anxious Collini; " you have been slapped
by the most famous man in Europe."

Letters, entreaties were sent in all directions. The
Emperor of Germany was petitioned. Madame Denis
hurried from Strasburg to the rescue of her imprisoned
uncle; her dying uncle, if he was to be taken at his own
word; and Madame Denis was likewise placed under
arrest. Baron Freytag and Councillor Schmidt, with
their guards posted at the *Golden Lion*, waited for the
package.

All this may be grotesque, but it has a more serious
aspect. It was an act of lawless tyranny. Voltaire
was imprisoned, without any charge, in a free town;
a practice contrary, even then, to the first principles of
justice. He was not accused of stealing the book and
the miserable trinkets, but only of having them in his
possession. For five weeks, Voltaire, his niece and his
secretary, were kept under arrest in a German inn, in
a free town of Germany, by order of the King of Prussia.
Even if we discount the exaggerations and lamentations
of Voltaire himself, the most unrestrained, most passionate of men, we are right if we consider Frederick's

action as wholly indefensible, and truly astonishing in one who was supposed to combine the wisdom of Solomon with the clemency of Marcus Aurelius. The arrest of Madame Denis, whether due to the fine devotion of Schmidt and Freytag or to an order from Potsdam, was even less excusable ; and the whole wretched affair is deplorable from every point of view.

Even after the arrival of the package and the surrender of the book and the trinkets, there were further delays. Voltaire, desperate, eluded his guards, and, with Collini, attempted flight. They were arrested at the barrier, subjected to the coarse affronts of the populace, and taken to the house of Councillor Schmidt, who was a shop-keeper. Here, all their belongings were sequestered, and when Voltaire asked for the return of his snuff-box, he was told brutally that " everything would be locked up, according to custom." Crazy with fear and anger, the miserable man saw an open door and rushed out of it: he was pursued by Frau Schmidt and her servants. After scenes of the most humiliating kind, with Voltaire feigning sickness, he was taken to the *Buck's Horn* inn with Collini, and there guarded by soldiers. In the meantime, Madame Denis had been rudely treated at the *Golden Lion*, and was now sent to rejoin her uncle.

Voltaire had reached Frankfort on the 31st of May ; the package arrived on the 18th of June; and it was not until the 7th of July that he was allowed to go. The culmination of this atrocity was the presentation of an enormous bill for the costs of his detention at the *Golden Lion* and the *Buck's Horn*.

We are willing to believe that the treatment of Voltaire at Frankfort was due to the mere boorishness of Freytag and his lieutenant, to the dull obstinacy of the official mind, and to the zeal of service. Such treatment was probably never a part of Frederick's intention, although he signified his approval of what Freytag had done. However that may be, Frederick's behaviour is not to be excused. Its atrocity can be, at most, a little mitigated by the fact that he had often been duped by Voltaire, and that he had no reason to believe that the *poesies* had been taken away inadvertently. Neither Collini nor Voltaire himself has explained how it was that the book and the chamberlain's badges came to be packed with Voltaire's belongings. And it may be noted, that Voltaire was in no doubt as to the precise packet in which they were to be found. He knew where they were, and he knew that he had no right to them. He could hardly have forgotten that he had been expressly commanded by Frederick to return them before he left Potsdam.

It may have given some satisfaction to Maupertuis to behold the inventor of Akakia thus humiliated and tortured; for we may doubt the assurance of Frederick that Maupertuis was the most forgiving of men.

CHAPTER VII

FIGHTING THE INFAMOUS

NOW, at the age of sixty, Voltaire began to show that peculiar force and brilliance which place him, as a writer, in a category which is altogether his own. And if *Akakia* marks the beginning of the true Voltairean style, the Frankfort affair marks the end of the Voltairean illusions.

Although, on formal occasions, Voltaire would still sign himself "Gentleman in Ordinary to the King," he was cured of any longing for the favours or honours of a court. His thoughts were turned now to ambitions of a different and more rational kind. He had considerable wealth. He was able to think, as one of his age might fittingly think, of comfortable retirement. He desired to live, in his own words, "obscure and tranquil." So he might desire ; but how could a man so famous be obscure ? and how could one with such diabolical energy ever be tranquil ?

From the time of his departure from Frankfort in July, 1753, to the time of the acquisition of Les Délices in March, 1755, he was a wanderer, moving from one place to another in accordance with opportunity or caprice. He was virtually, though not officially, exiled from Paris. The king was opposed to his return, and Madame de Pompadour had become indifferent.

After a stay of a few weeks at Mainz, he was the guest of the Palatine Elector, Charles Theodore, at Mannheim; and a little later, he was in Strasburg. Here he was occupied in writing the *Annals of the Empire*, and a new tragedy, *The Chinese Orphan*. Early in 1754, he was at Colmar. Then he stayed with Dom

231

Calmet and his monks in the Abbey of Senones for about three weeks; and thence he sought the fine company and the healing waters of Plombières. In November, he was at Lyon, where he met "sister Guillemette," the margrave, and her husband, who had previously paid him a surprise visit during his stay at Colmar. Wilhelmina, so it appears, was anxious to make peace between her brother Frederick and her "brother" Voltaire; but Frederick had written a stiff, dignified letter, in which he complained that Voltaire had broken his word by pestering Maupertuis after he had left Potsdam.

The more Voltaire wandered, the stronger became his desire to settle peaceably in a house of his own— a house, naturally, with a theatre, and gardens, and accommodation for many visitors.

To find such a house was not easy. The craziest fancies passed through his mind. Pennsylvania was talked of; a land of promise in a new world. In a new world there might be room for a new prophet: he would go to Pennsylvania. More sensible and more serious thoughts prevailed, and Switzerland was chosen. He arrived in Geneva on the 12th of December, 1754.

In Geneva he was the guest of the councillor Francis Tronchin, the head of one of the most distinguished families in that town. Voltaire had previously made the acquaintance of the banker, Robert Tronchin, at Lyon; and he was soon to know intimately the celebrated physician, Theodore. Not long after his arrival, Voltaire, Madame Denis, and the secretary Collini, were housed in the vast, cold, draughty and sombre castle of Prangins, lent by the proprietor, who was a friend of the Tronchin family. This was anything but comfortable. The strident, quavering voice of his master summoned Collini at every moment: Make up the fire! Shut the window! My fur cloak! My cap!—With satisfaction might Collini write: " We are going to leave this castle."

First, a house was rented at Monrion, between Lausanne and the lake; and then the property of Saint-Jean, near Geneva, was purchased, to be known and made famous under the new name of Les Délices.

Again, as at Cirey (but with what a different companion!), Voltaire had the delight, the annoyance, the incessant cares, of arranging a house and grounds to his liking. " We are occupied, Madame Denis and myself, in making boxes for our friends and our chickens. We have ordered coaches and barrows; we plant onions and orange-trees, carrots and tulips; we are short of everything—but Carthage must be founded. My territory is scarce larger than the bull's hide given to fugitive Dido."

Here, of course, a theatre was built; and here, to the grave displeasure of Geneva ministers and their following, comedies and tragedies were played, and the great Lekain made his appearance. But these tormenting pleasures could not occupy him exclusively. Jean-Jacques Rousseau, the " citizen of Geneva," was beginning to make a stir; and a quarrel with Jean-Jacques was clearly inevitable.

Rousseau, who believed sincerely that Voltaire would approve of his teaching, sent a copy of his *Origin of Inequality* to Les Délices. Upon this, Voltaire wrote him a long letter, which, in a somewhat altered form, he printed incongruously in the first edition of the *Chinese Orphan*. The letter was a declaration of war:

" Sir, I have received your new book against the human race, and thank you for it. You may give pleasure to men, to whom you show the truth, but you will not correct them. We cannot choose colours too strong for painting the horrors of human society, from which our ignorance and weakness promise so many consolations. No one has ever employed so much wit in trying to make brutes of us; in reading your book, one has a mind to start running on all fours."

To this, Rousseau answered with dignity: " I have every reason to thank you, Sir. In sending you the outline of my sad thoughts, I never believed I was making you a gift worthy of your merit, but I meant to acquit myself of a duty, and to render you the homage that we all owe to you, as to a Chief. Sensible, moreover, of the honour you do my country, I share the gratitude of my compatriots; and I hope it will be greatly increas'd, when they have profited by the instructions you can give them." He proceeds with a short review of his ideas, cool, measured and extremely graceful, and showing in every line the most profound respect.

Voltaire's poem upon the Lisbon earthquake (1st of November, 1755), a bitter and splendid satire against optimism, was a challenge to Rousseau's doctrine of providence. Clearly, the two men could never be in agreement, and a fierce explosion of hatred was only a matter of time.

If Rousseau was at last provoked to violence by the attacks of Voltaire, he was never the aggressor. We have no wish to compare Jean-Jacques with the author of *Candide*, for no two men could have been more unfitted for each other; but it may be allowed that Jean-Jacques had fine qualities of courtesy and restraint which made him, in more than one way, superior to Voltaire.

We turn gladly from the unhappy quarrel with Rousseau to Voltaire's collaboration with Diderot and d'Alembert in the work of the *Encyclopaedia*. Here indeed was a labour after his own heart. The *Encyclopaedia* was far more than a mere compendium of knowledge, such as industry alone might compile. It was a great engine of war directed against the Infamous. In a manner by no means equivocal, the articles of the *Encyclopaedia* attacked the bases of superstition, proclaimed the emancipation of the human mind, pointed the way to the attainment of real knowledge, and proved, or sought to prove, that men could never be happy while they were ignorant, irrational or prejudiced.

No other book or collection of books had so great an effect upon the movement of the age. Proscribed or censored, furtively sold or furtively imported, the work played its part in bringing about the final destruction of the old order. To those who planned the *Encyclopaedia*, religion appeared to be a source of discord, misery and injustice. The civil authority, ruled or encouraged by the leaders of religion, was not less corrupt than the church herself, and not less deserving of unqualified censure. If, then, it was religion which had brought society to such a pass, religion must be abolished.

Nor was this view unaccountable in the France of the eighteenth century. At no other period had religion decayed to such a foul compost of horrors and persecutions. At no other period had there been a clergy more cynical, more vicious, more addicted to every kind of chicanery and indulgence. At no other period, and in no other country, had justice been so corrupted, or the law so open to contempt. And at no other period had wealth, learning and comfort

been distributed with a more shocking inequality.
All this, said Voltaire and the Encyclopaedists, was
due to the prevalence of the Infamous. At the foot
of their letters, they wrote the mystic abbreviation
of their countersign—"écr. l'inf."—"écrasons l'infâme":
" crush the Infamous ! "

What did they mean, precisely, by this term ? They
meant, partly, the dominance of what was then called
the Christian church ; but they meant a great deal
more. The dragon of the Infamous represented, in
a visible and vulnerable form, all the cruel, unworthy
and oppressive elements in the social order. Most
of those elements, they said, were developed from
ignorance and superstition, and many of them from
the cowardice which is a natural weakness of autocratic
government. The term comprehended, also, those
tendencies which we now understand by the single
word reaction. The Encyclopaedists were therefore
among the leaders of the great intellectual revolution
of the eighteenth century, a revolution in which the
solvent agencies of ridicule and scepticism played a
decisive part. In the mind of Voltaire himself, the
Infamous had a more extended personal meaning; it
covered everything with which he was in disagreement,
and could be applied without hesitation to his enemies.

In December, 1756, Voltaire's fury was aroused by
an ugly decree of the Infamous. Admiral Byng,
whose fleet had been scattered by the French off Majorca,
was tried by a court martial and sentenced to death.

No one doubts that Byng was offered up by a
frightened ministry to a clamorous rabble. The
English had been defeated, but this grim sentence would
prove the energy of the national character, and would
have a cheering effect upon the services.

With noble generosity, Voltaire took up the defence of the Admiral. He had met Byng (at that time a young naval officer) during his visit to England. He wrote to de Richelieu, who had been the French commander at Majorca:

" An Englishman came to see me the other day, and lamented the fate of his friend Admiral *Byng*. I told him you had done me the honour of telling me that this sailor had by no means misconducted himself, and that he had done all he could. He replied, that one word from you would justify him; that you had made *Blakeney's* fortune by the esteem with which you had publicly honoured him; and that, if I would transcribe the favourable words you wrote to me concerning *Byng*, he would send them to England. I beg your permission to do so; I cannot, in duty bound, undertake anything without your consent."

De Richelieu, with equal generosity, replied :

" Sir, I am profoundly moved by the affair of Admiral *Byng*: let me assure you that all I have seen and heard of him is entirely to his honour. After having done all that could be reasonably expected of him, he ought not to be blamed for having suffered a defeat. When two generals dispute the victory, altho' equally men of honour, it is obvious that one of the two must be defeated; and there is nothing against M. *Byng* except that he was beat. His conduct was altogether that of a skilful seaman, and worthy of being justly admir'd. . . . I am convinced (and 'tis the general opinion) that if the English had obstinately continu'd the fight, their entire fleet would have been destroyed. There could be no more signal act of injustice than what is now actually contemplated against Admiral *Byng*."

A copy of this letter was at once forwarded by Voltaire to Byng, with the following note:

" Sir, tho' I am almost unknown to you, I think it my duty to send you a copy of the letter I have just received from the Marshal de Richelieu; honour, equity and humanity command me to place it in your hands. This testimony, so unexpected and so noble, from one of the most sincere and most generous of my compatriots leads me to presume that your judges will render you the same justice."

De Richelieu's letter actually gained four voices in favour of pardon, but the majority of the judges voted for death, and Byng was shot upon the quarter-deck of the *Monarque* on the 14th of March, 1757. He entrusted his executor with the conveyance of his warmest gratitude to Voltaire and to the Marshal— " so generous a soldier."

Less serious concerns now occupied a great part of Voltaire's time. The furnishing and arrangement of Les Délices continued to be the source of many pleasures and many anxieties for whole months on end. " I am become a gardener, a vine-dresser and a workman. I must needs do in a small way what the King of Poland [Stanislas] has done in the grand style; I must plant, uproot, and build houses for rats, while he dreams of palaces. I hate the towns, I can only live in the country, and, since I am old and feeble, I can only live in my own house." The " pretty nudities " of Natoire and Boucher were to be copied

" to cheer his age "; everything was done to make the house gay and comfortable.

But all the time, Voltaire was busy with his pen. It may be doubted whether he ever passed a day in which he did not write many pages, whether of some new work, or some careful revision, or of notes and letters. The *History of Russia under Peter the Great* was now contemplated, and Voltaire was engaged in a long correspondence with Schouvaloff, the chamberlain of the Empress Elizabeth. *Candide*, the work which, at the present day, is unquestionably the best known of all his writings, was probably begun during his visit to the Elector at Mannheim in July, 1758. He was also employed on the congenial labours of the *Encyclopaedia*, corresponding chiefly with d'Alembert, who had visited him in 1756, but writing on occasion to Diderot. In August he spent a part of his time in a new property, a house in the Rue du Grand-Chêne at Lausanne.

It was at Lausanne that he was visited by Gibbon, then a youth of twenty-one, in August, 1758.

Gibbon was freely admitted to Voltaire's private theatricals, and saw the great man himself play in *Zaïre*, *Alzire*, *Zulime* and the *Prodigal Son*. " His declamation," he said, " was founded upon the pomp and cadence of the old theatre, and display'd rather an enthusiasm for poetry than a feeling for the natural sentiments. My ardour, which was quickly remark'd, rarely failed of procuring me a ticket. The habit of this amusement strengthened my taste for the French theatre, and that taste has perhaps weakened my idolatry for the gigantick genius of *Shakspear*, impress'd upon us from childhood as the first duty of an *Englishman*. The spirit and philosophy of *Voltaire*, his table and theatre, sensibly contribute to the refinement of Lausanne and the improvement of manners."

Another visitor of this period was the Italian poet, Bettinelli, who has left us a lively account of his interview, and one which is worthy of partial transcription:

"When I arrived at Les Délices, he was in his garden; I went up to him and told him who I was. 'What!' cried he, 'an Italian, a Jesuit, a Bettinelli!—'tis too much honour for my cabin. I am but a peasant, as you see,' he added, showing me his stick, which had a little mattock at one end and a pruning-knife at the other; 'with these tools I sow my wheat, grain by grain, like my salad; but my crop is more abundant than the one I sow in my books for the good of humanity.' His grotesque and singular figure made upon me an impression for which I was not prepared. Beneath a cap of black velvet, which came down to his very eyes, could be seen a huge perruque, which covered three-quarters of his face, and made his nose and chin even more pointed than they are in his portraits. His body was wrapp'd in a cloak from head to foot; his glance and his smile were full of expression. . . . The conversation often turned upon the King of *Prussia*. He had just been told that, after losing a battle, he had beaten the Duke de Deux-Ponts, raised the siege of Neiss and of Leipsick, and put to flight the Austrians in Bohemia. 'Is it possible!' cried Voltaire. 'This man astounds me always; I am sorry I have quarrelled with him.' In this prince, he admired the quick movements of Caesar, but his admiration ended always with an epigram against Caesar. He had a monkey which he call'd *Luc*, and it pleased him often to give this name to the King of *Prussia*. One day, I expressed my surprise at this. ' Do you not see,' he replied, ' that my monkey bites every one ? '—and he fell a-laughing."

This offensive nickname of *Luc* (which, to a French eye, is a wicked anagram) was often enough applied to Frederick in speech and letters; but his correspondence with Frederick, verses, badinage and all, was briskly renewed by the end of 1759. The two men had been drawn together, in the April of that year, probably for the first time and certainly for the last time, by the mutual experience of a real emotion: their sorrow at the death of the margrave, Wilhelmina.

In the winter of 1758, Voltaire acquired the domain of Ferney. This domain comprised, then, a large house, a ruinous church, and a rather dilapidated hamlet. He acquired, at the same time, the deeds of Tournay, another decayed estate, which allowed him to call himself the Count of Tournay, a title of which he occasionally made use.

Ferney is about five miles to the north of Geneva, below the Jura slopes, in the little province of Gex, and on French territory. Voltaire was now the owner of four properties, four citadels or places of retreat: two at Lausanne and two near Geneva. By the acquisition of Ferney, he had a footing in two countries, France and Switzerland: a matter of sound strategy rather than of mere ostentation.

At Ferney he spent the greater part of the last twenty years of his life. Here, cultivating his garden, playing, jesting, quarrelling, and always fighting the Infamous, he became the great Voltaire, the man who shocked, surprised or delighted the whole of civilised Europe.

He secured at Ferney, not the peace which he pretended to seek, but at least immunity from serious persecution. On the one side of his frontiers he could defy the sour Calvinists of Geneva; on the other, he could hurl thunders at the Jesuits of France. At Ferney he had a sheltered house for the winter; at Les Délices, a pleasant summer residence; at Lausanne, the charming little theatre of Monrepos. But Ferney became his real home; and it was here, as we shall see, that he entered upon his last astonishing phase of the *seigneur de village* or Patriarch.

Voltaire was now sixty-five. And at this age, the age at which most men suffer a decent eclipse or potter placidly within a narrow circle of domestic enjoyments, be began to flame out in the supreme display of his powers. He was like one of those astonishing rockets, which crack and flash with the greatest violence and brilliance towards the end of their long flight, scattering in all directions a hundred bright stars. And as children cry with fear or delight while the rocket pours out its energy in this wholly unexpected fashion, so men were moved to fear or delight, to applause or anger, by the ascending and flashing energies of this extraordinary man.

The expense of maintaining his estates was no small matter, and, rich as he was, Voltaire's revenues were heavily taxed.

" I know well that I am ruining myself," he wrote to the banker, Tronchin. " But it was absolutely necessary that I should be the master of Tournay and Ferney, because it will happen infallibly, in thirty or forty years from now, that the priests of Baal will desire to have me burned like *Antoine* or *Servet*, and I must be prepared to hang 'em from the battlements of my castles. I have a great love for countries which are free, but I love even more to be master in my own house. . . . I have wished, for once in my life, to show how, in the present age, one is able to feed an hundred and fifty souls with nothing at all. For one month, I was quite penniless, and in spite of that I was buying land, for I love land more than money. My miracle is a mighty pretty one, but we must not enlarge upon miracles, or they are discredited. I ask you, therefore, for five hundred louis to set up my credit again. And I would reckon this very credit as a prodigy. I was born poor enough. All my life I have plied a beggar's trade, that of scribbling upon paper, that of Jean-Jacques Rousseau. And yet, here I am with two castles, two delicious houses, a revenue of seventy thousand livres, two hundred thousand livres of ready money, and a few scraps of royal bounty, which I don't trouble to compute."

With such affluence, and so much of comfort and security, Voltaire could afford to laugh at the spite or petty persecution of bigots.

On the 2nd of March, 1759, *Candide* was denounced by the Venerable Company of Geneva, and was publicly burnt by the executioner. Voltaire retorted by circulating a number of irreligious pamphlets in the town—a minor skirmish with the Infamous.

Between the author of *Candide* and the ministers of Geneva there could never be any question of truce. The ministers and the council of Geneva had forbidden plays and theatres. They had been outraged by the article on Geneva in the *Encyclopaedia*, written by d'Alembert, and frankly Voltairean. In this article, the ministers themselves had been accused of Socinian leanings, and the establishment of a Genevese theatre was strongly recommended. Jean-Jacques, like a good citizen, had taken the side of the ministers, and had written, in reply to d'Alembert, his famous and provoking *Letter upon Spectacles.* And so, Jean-Jacques and the Venerable Company, and all the black gowns of Geneva, became a part of the Infamous.

In August, 1759, Voltaire heard of the death of Maupertuis. "What say you of Maupertuis?" he wrote to d'Alembert; "dead between two Capucins. He had been sick for a long while of a surfeit of vanity; but I never thought him either a hypocrite or an imbecile." Voltaire could feel no charity, no generosity towards the dead man; and he had some reason to reproach himself for having added so much to the bitterness of his last years. This ugly pursuit of Maupertuis, not ceasing with his death, marks an almost incredible persistence of malice. In a letter to Frederick, Voltaire spoke of this death with a flippancy so outrageous, and accused Maupertuis of such baseness, that Frederick answered with furious indignation. It is true that his answer was mostly in doggerel verse; it was none the less effective. He compared the poet to a "vile raven" croaking with hideous joy at sight of carrion, and finished by conjuring him to think of his honour and of the "blackness of his incorrigible heart."

To these just reproaches, Voltaire replied with a violent counter-attack. First, he tried to justify his accusations, and then he rounded briskly upon Frederick. It may be doubted whether any great king has ever been attacked with such vigour in a letter sent to him personally.

" You have done me harm enough. You have embroiled me for ever with the King of France; you have caused me to lose my pension and appointments; at Frankfort, you treated villainously both myself and an innocent woman, who was dragg'd in the mire and put in a prison; and finally, in honouring me with your letters, you poison the sweetness and consolation of this intercourse by bitter reproaches. Is it possible 'tis you who treat me thus, when I was solely occupied for three years, though without success, in trying to serve you, with no other aim save to follow my own way of thinking ?

" The greatest evil which has come of your works, is that they have allowed all the enemies of philosophy in Europe to say : Philosophers cannot live in peace and cannot live together. Here is a king who does not believe in Jesus Christ; he summons to his court a man who thinks likewise, and he abuses him; there is no humanity in these pretended philosophers, and God makes them punish each other.

" That is what they say, that is what they publish on all sides; and so, while fanaticks are united, philosophers are unhappily scatter'd. And whilst they accuse me, at the court of Versailles and elsewhere, of having encouraged you to write against the Christian religion, 'tis you who reproach me, and add this triumph to the insults of the fanaticks ! This makes me hate the world with good reason; I am happily retir'd from it in my solitary domains. I shall bless the day when, dying, I need suffer no more, and above all need suffer no more from you; but I shall then wish you a happiness which your state makes difficult, and which philosophy alone can procure for you amid the storms of your life, if your fate allows you to cultivate exclusively and continually those principles of wisdom which you have; worthy principles, but all dried up by the passions inseparable from a high imagination, and partly, too, by irritability and by vexing circumstances which pour their poison upon your spirit; and also by the unhappy delight which you have always taken in seeking to humiliate other men, to gall them in speech and writing; a pleasure unworthy of you, and the more so as you are raised above them by your rank and by your exceptional gifts."

Having thrust home, on both sides, with telling effect, Voltaire and Frederick renewed their correspondence with perfect amiability.

We cannot follow at length the various quarrels in which the author of *Candide* was engaged during his first years at Ferney. Even before he took up residence in the castle, he had declared war upon the curé of Moens, who was a pestilent rogue. Then came the quarrel with the President de Brosses, that cultured and accomplished man, over a few bundles of wood; and then a true victory over the Infamous—the restitution to its rightful owners of some land seized by the Jesuits of Ornex.

An attack of a lighter kind was directed against the most ridiculous and most conceited of French poets, the Marquis Lefranc de Pompignan.

Lefranc was a writer of tragedies, verses, religious poems, and rhyming translations. He had some facility, a little skill, and an infinite amount of assurance. He was a pompous, affected creature, whose fatuity exposed him to the deadly aim of satire. On the 10th of March, 1760, he was elected to the Academy. His oration to the members was a foolish, aggressive piece of bombast, full of petulant commonplace and manifestly directed against the new philosophy. The President, in his reply, compared Lefranc to Moses, and his brother, the Bishop of Puy, to Aaron.

It was not long before the unhappy Lefranc heard in his ears Voltaire's diabolical laughter. Ah, ah ! Moses Lefranc de Pompignan ! Consider, my good Moses; is it wise to cry down the age when one's own works do it so little credit ? Or is it wise, when you are admitted to a society of men of letters, to talk so noisily and so rudely about men of letters, and thus to insult both the company and the public ? Have a care, my good Moses !

Lefranc de Pompignan, still buoyant with a huge inflation of vanity, sustained for a while these dreadful attacks. *Whens*, *Ifs*, *Buts*, and *Whys* followed each other in rapid succession. Madame Lefranc was driven half crazy with anger. But Moses, rushing blindly and sublimely to his fate, published a *Memoir to the King*, a memoir in which he ascended to incredible heights of pretentious glory. The most wicked inventions of Voltaire himself could hardly keep pace with the enormous folly of Lefranc.

" All the court," said Moses, " saw in what fashion Their Majesties gave me a welcome. Let the *Universe* know also, that Their Majesties have taken notice of my *Work*, not as a novelty of little consequence or of passing value, but as a production not unworthy of the particular Attention of *Sovereigns*." And he went even further. Speaking of his visit to the court, and of his return to his native place, he said: " I was receiv'd at *Montauban* with honours so *extraordinary*, that the memory of them will be long preserv'd in the Town and in the rest of the Province." The memory of poor

Moses is indeed preserved; but not in the way he desired.

As Maupertuis had exposed himself by his *Letters*, so Lefranc exposed himself by this grotesque vanity. Voltaire, who could hardly believe his eyes, fell on his prey with savage delight. " My doctor," he said to Marmontel, " has ordered me a course of Pompignan every morning by way of exercise." The journey of Lefranc to visit the king, and his reception at Fontaine-bleau, were told of in a little masterpiece of concentrated irony:

" At Cahors I found my picture in *acqua-tinto* hang-ing in the ale-house, and beneath it were five little verses with a pretty allusion to the stars, among which I was seated. . . . When I reached Orleans, I found that the canons already knew by heart the most remarkable passages in my discourse. I pursued my journey to Fontainebleau, and the next day I went to the King's levee, accompanied by M. Fréron, whom I had expressly commanded. As soon as the King perceiv'd us, he addressed himself graciously to each. ' Monsieur le Marquis,' said His Majesty, ' I know that you have as great a reputation at Pompignan as your grandfather the *Professor* had formerly at Cahors. Have you not with you that fine sermon of your composing which has made so much noise ? ' I then presented copies to the King, the Queen, and His Grace the Dauphin. The King had the finest parts read aloud to him . . . joy overspread every countenance; the whole company looked at me with eyes half clos'd, raising gently the corners of the mouth towards the cheeks, which is the pathologick indication of delight. ' Faith ' said His Grace the Dauphin; ' we have but one man in France who can write in such a style—'tis Monsieur le Marquis de Pompignan.' "

This deadly prose was followed by even more deadly verse, by a satire *Upon Vanity*, and then came the *News from Montauban*. Even the puffy pride of Lefranc was pricked at last, and the wretched man collapsed. The final blow was presumably unintentional. Lefranc's tragedy of *Dido* was followed at the Comédie by the *Fool Punish'd* of Pont-de-Veyle. The parterre was in ecstasies of mirth; and although on the second night the comedy of Pont-de-Veyle was replaced by another, the change merely emphasised the irony of the sequence. Moses Lefranc de Pompignan found himself pursued everywhere by cruel reminders of the Voltairean attack, and particularly by lines from the poem on *Vanity*, such as

> " Unhappy the wight, above all, in this age,
> Who thinks if he's odd he's a great personage.
>
> .   .   .   .
>
> And sure, I am *something*, says Master Lefranc."

Moses de Pompignan was extinguished. He retired to his castle at Montauban, wrote no more, or wrote discreetly, and never again dared show his face at the Academy or approach the king.

It was at this time that Voltaire began to build, of all things, a new church at Ferney. The old church was in bad repair, it was ugly, uncomfortable, ill designed for service.

His motives were not altogether pious. The fantasy of building a church was one which appealed to his ironical humour, and the church, as it stood (or crumbled) obscured his view. Parts of the old church were to be moved and used in the new building; the tall wooden cross which stood above the cemetery was to be taken away. (There is no authority for the legend that Voltaire, in ordering the removal of the cross, had said " Take away that gibbet.") And so was built " the one church in the universe dedicated to God himself," and over its doorway men could read that famous incription: DEO EREXIT VOLTAIRE.

Hearing that the grand-niece of Corneille was destitute, and that she was a gentle, charming and modest young woman, Voltaire adopted her. Mademoiselle Corneille became a member of the Ferney household, and she was cared for in the most exemplary fashion. Voltaire himself taught her the art of writing. She wrote little notes to him, and he corrected them ; she read the great authors of his choice, and then gave him an account of her reading. Mademoiselle Corneille was eighteen years old when she arrived at Ferney in the winter of 1760. Her sweetness of temper, her natural gaiety and quaint humour gained the affection of every one in the house; and this vicarious paternity must have been particularly grateful to her benefactor. Voltaire, indeed, came to think of Mademoiselle Corneille as he might have thought of a child of his own. And it should be noted, that she was encouraged to fulfil all the duties of a Christian, to attend church, and to pay heed to the counsels of her spiritual advisers.

The righteous, of course, were scandalised. A pretty house indeed! they said, and a pretty teacher for a young respectable girl ! Mademoiselle Corneille, said the viper Fréron, had fallen into good hands. But Fréron was crushed by dreadful *Anecdotes*, and wished he had not spoken so hastily.

Never had Voltaire's activity been more surprising.

His name was legion. He watched over the lives and welfare of the people of Gex with unceasing vigilance. The affairs of his estate received, in all their details, his close attention. He was always quarrelling with two or three persistent adversaries. He was always entertaining friends or visitors. Plays were frequently performed in his theatre at Tournay. In 1760 he produced, in addition to a mass of lesser works, the comedy of the *Scotchwoman* (against Fréron) and the fine tragedy of *Tancred*. And yet he was never well. Sometimes he would spend the whole morning in bed, waving desperately his thin arms, complaining to worthy Tronchin, calling with fevered impatience for soothing drinks or comforting appliances.

All the time, he was profoundly concerned with fighting the Infamous, and with the preparation of that great engine of war, the *Encyclopaedia*. " How goes the *Encyclopaedick Dictionary*? " he wrote to d'Alembert. " Is it to be disfigured and debased by vile concessions to fanaticks? or are we really bold enough to tell the dangerous truth? " And the furious voice cries to young Damilaville: " Rush, all of you, upon the *inf.* . . . What concerns me is the propagation of the faith, of truth, the advance of philosophy, and the trampling down of the *inf.* . . ." Soon he was engaged in grim battle, no mere polemic or war of words, with the Infamous in a terrible form.

The affair of Calas, which we are about to describe, gave him an eminence in the popular mind far above that which he could have attained by writing or precept alone, and set him in the first rank of the great humanitarians. Let us examine, first of all, the simple facts of the tragedy.

Jean Calas, a worthy and highly respected man, lived in Toulouse. He was a Protestant. He carried on a considerable trade in various Indian stuffs, and had a small shop and warehouse in the Rue des Filatiers. His family, in 1761, consisted of three sons, two daughters, and his wife.

The eldest of the sons, Mark Antony Calas, was then twenty-eight years old. He was a sturdy but melancholy young man, suffering bitterly from thwarted ambitions. The idea of becoming, like his father, a humble cloth-merchant, had no attraction for him. He had studied the law, and, as he had an easy manner and facile speech, there seemed every reason to suppose that he would make a good advocate. But before he could practice, it was necessary for him to obtain a certificate of orthodoxy, of loyalty to the Catholic faith. This was usually accorded as a matter of form, but when young Calas applied for it he was told that he was not eligible. Here, then, was an obstacle which he could never surmount, for Mark Antony refused to become a member of the Holy Church, or to " perform any act of Catholicity." What was he to do? He would not take a subaltern position in his father's business, but had less objection to being on the footing of a partner. It seems that he actually made this proposal, and that Jean Calas was unable to give his consent. Mark Antony, proud, sensitive, and with a notion of his own value, felt that his life was a failure. He found a gloomy relief in private theatricals, declaiming with infinite fervour and pathos the sad lines of *Polyeucte*, or reciting the monologues of Hamlet. At other times he would seek the distraction of billiards in the public saloons.

And here it is important to note, that Mark Antony, desperate as he was, never considered the possibility of changing his professed religion; a thing which he might have done easily enough, and which his younger brother, Louis, had done already.

On the fatal evening of the 13th of October, 1761, the Calas family sat down to supper with a young friend, Gaubert Lavaysse, who had looked in for an hour or so.

The party consisted of Jean Calas, his wife, Mark Antony, the second son, Pierre, and the visitor, Lavaysse. They were attended by the maid, Jeanne Viguière.

While they were eating their dessert, Mark Antony rose from the table. There must have been something strange or ominous in his manner, for the maid, looking at him, asked whether he was cold. "No," said he; "on the contrary, I am burning." And he left the room.

At nine o'clock, M. Lavaysse took his leave, and went down the stairs with young Pierre Calas. They observed with surprise that the door of the shop was open. Pierre had a candle in his hand, and they went into the shop to see if all was in order. And there they saw, hanging from a calico roller, the dead body of Mark Antony. The grey cloth coat which he had been wearing, and his nankin waistcoat, were neatly folded upon the counter.

News of the suicide ran quickly round the town, and soon the house was filled with curious neighbours, with police officers and magistrates. Among the magistrates was that ferocious imbecile, David de Beaudrigue.

Suddenly, from the confused murmur of many voices, there came a loud accusing cry: "Mark Antony has been strangled by his Huguenot parents, for fear he should turn Catholic!"

No accusation could have been more absurd, but none has ever had more terrible results. There is no thrill so pleasing to the vulgar mind (the penny-paper mind of the present day) as the excitement of a tragedy. What is more, the Huguenots of Toulouse were a despised or hated minority; and thus, to the mere sadistic passions of the mob, there were added passions of an even more hideous nature. Without any charge, without the least pretence of any legal formality, de Beaudrigue had the entire household, including Lavaysse and the servant Jeanne Viguière, conveyed to the town prison.

While the wretched family were thus imprisoned, the body of the suicide was buried with extraordinary pomp and ostentation by the Catholics of Toulouse. After witnessing this impressive funeral, clearly the funeral of a martyr, no reasonable man—no Catholic, at any rate—could doubt that Mark Antony had been foully murdered by his parents. In the vulgar mind, Calas was condemned already.

Having tormented their prisoners for more than four weeks with questions and depositions, the magistrates of Toulouse duly made known their decree: Calas, his wife and son, were to be subjected to the torture; Lavaysse and the servant were to be " presented " to the torture, and then to undergo a fresh interrogation.

An appeal was lodged by the prisoners, and the case was taken before the parliament of Toulouse. The sentence on Lavaysse and Jeanne Viguière (a sentence which the magistrates had no legal right to impose) was revoked, and the court proceeded with a formal trial of the accused. On the 9th of March, 1762, after hearing witnesses who had witnessed nothing, but who were fervently religious and determined to prove, at any cost, the guilt of Calas, the court gave judgment.

Of the thirteen judges who had tried the case, seven voted for the death of Calas, three for torture only, two for a further examination of the circumstances, and one for acquittal. A majority of seven was not enough to carry the sentence; a casting vote was given to the councillor Bojal, and he joined the seven men who voted for death.

The details of the sentence were now promulgated: Jean Calas was to undergo the question ordinary and extraordinary; wearing a shirt only, he was to be taken in a cart from the prison to the cathedral, and there, before the great doors, on his knees and with a wax taper in his hand, he was to beg in all humility for the pardon of God, of the king and of the state; he was then to be taken to the Place Saint-George, where, on a scaffold in view of all, the executioner would break his arms, legs, thighs and loins; after that, he would be tied to the wheel, his face towards the sky, living, if it pleased God, " in pain and repentance of his crimes "; and finally, the dead body would be flung into a fire, and the ashes scattered to the wind.—As for the son, Pierre, he was to be banished in perpetuity. Madame Calas, Lavaysse and the servant were to be released.

Here we may well pause in horrified bewilderment. We may ask ourselves, what complicity of wickedness, of crude fanatism, brought about this terrible drama. How could such a thing have been possible ? For the honour of humanity, we would find, if we could, some kind of extenuation, some alleviating circumstance. We can find none. When the facts of the case were examined, a year or so later, it was proved that there was no evidence against Calas. We would gladly believe that the judges had some reason for supposing their verdict justified; for, if that was not so, these seven men were little better than seven devils or seven imbeciles. And yet, the most impartial research has failed to show us even the shadow of a reason.

Jean Calas was handed over to the executioner on the 10th of March. He made no complaint, accused no one, protested only his perfect innocence. First came the torture of the question, then the penance. Two Jesuit fathers attended him. Stretched on the cross, his bones crushed by every stroke of the bar, he never cried out, never ceased, when questioned, to declare himself an innocent man. At last, when the poor dying creature was tied to the wheel, de Beaudrigue, in a frenzy of cruel impatience, shouted in his ear : " Wretch ! behold the fire which is to consume thee ! —speak the truth ! " But Calas could say no more; he could only turn his head in weariness and pain. Then came the fire, and the tragedy was over.

When he first heard of this, Voltaire could not believe that the parliament of Toulouse had condemned and cruelly murdered an innocent man. But, as the truth became clear, he hesitated no longer. With all his energy, and all the influence at his disposal, he sought to prove the innocence of Calas; and at once offered his protection to the widow and her family. On the 29th of March, soon after he had received the news of the affair, he wrote to d'Alembert. After telling him of the death of Mark Antony Calas, he went on :

" The city of Toulouse, greatly exceeding Geneva in folly and fanatism, made a martyr of this young man. No one thought of finding out whether he had hung, himself, which is highly probable. They buried him with pomp in the cathedral; some of the parliament assisted with bare feet at the ceremony; the new saint was invok'd; after which, the criminal court broke the father on the wheel by a majority of eight votes against five. This judgment was the more Christian, since there was no evidence against the accused. . . . All our heretickal cantons are crying aloud, all say that we are a nation as barbarous as we are trivial; able to break men, but not able to fight, and passing from *Saint Bartholomew* to the *Comick Opera*. We are become the horror and scorn of Europe."

Then he pressed for exact information on all matters connected with the trial and execution of Calas. De Richelieu advised him not to meddle in the affair; Calas, he said, was guilty.

But the two brothers of Mark Antony, first young Donat and then the fugitive Pierre, had found refuge near Geneva. If the judges were right, Pierre had been an accomplice in the murder of his brother. He had been confined in a monastery at Toulouse, and forced to change his religion, but had succeeded in escaping. Voltaire, at first on his guard, spoke often to the young man; he employed respectable persons to watch him, to observe his conduct, to see what company he chose. Before long, he was convinced, by the talk and behaviour of the two brothers, that there could be no doubt whatever as to the innocence of Calas and his family. In April (when still undecided) he had written to a lady whose name is not preserved:

" It is true, Mademoiselle, that, in a reply to M. de Chazelles, I demanded information concerning the horrible adventure of *Calas*, whose son [Donat] has excited my sympathies as well as my curiosity. I have sent to M. de Chazelles an account of the clamours and sentiments of all the strangers who come to see me; but I could not have spoke to him of my opinion upon this cruel business, for I have none. I have only seen the statements in favour of *Calas*, and that is not enough to justify me in taking a part. I have sought to be inform'd in the quality of an historian. An event so appalling as that of an entire family accused of a parricide committed through religious fervour; a father dying upon the wheel for having strangled his son with his own hands, upon the mere suspicion that the son wanted to quit the opinions of *John Calvin*; a brother fiercely charg'd with having helped to strangle his brother; the mother accused; a young advocate [Lavaysse] suspected of having served as hangman in this unheard-of execution; this event, I say, belongs essentially to the history of the human spirit and to the vast portrayal of our follies and furies, of which I have already given the outline. . . . However things may turn out, I persist in hoping that the parliament of Toulouse will condescend to make publick the trial of *Calas*, as that of *Damiens* was publish'd. . . . These two trials concern the human race, and if aught can check the rage of fanatism among men, it will be the making known and the *proving* of the murder and sacrilege which brought *Calas* to the wheel, and which left the whole family a prey to the most dreadful suspicions. Such is my sentiment."

He was right. The affair of Calas has a place in the dark histories of cruelty and persecution, in the " vast portrayal " of human activities. He was yet in some doubt as to the nature of the tragedy, so clearly a tragedy from any point of view; but he was not far from conviction. In May, he wrote to d'Argental:

" The Marshal de Richelieu has wrote me a long letter upon the Calas family, but he knows no more than I do. The parliament of Toulouse, which now sees what a shocking blunder it has made, is preventing the truth from being known. It has always had the idea that the whole Calas family, assisted by their friends, hanged young Calas to prevent him from turning Catholick. With this idea, they had the father broke on the wheel, hoping that the poor fellow, who was sixty-nine years of age, would confess everything. The poor fellow, instead of confessing, called upon God to witness his innocence. The judges, who had him broke upon simple conjecture, having absolutely no juridical proofs, but persisting in their opinion, con- demned to banishment one of the sons of Calas, who was suspected of helping to strangle his brother; they had him taken to one of the city gates by the executioner, with a cord round his neck, and then made him return by another gate, clapp'd him in a monastery, and forc'd him to change his religion. All that is so illegal, and the spirit of faction is so clearly perceiv'd in this horrible occurrence, foreigners are so incensed, that 'tis inconceivable the Lord Chancellor will not have this extraordinary decree properly examined. If ever there has been need to know the truth, it is, methinks, on such an occasion."

On the 11th of June, when the widow Calas was in Paris, trying to obtain justice, he wrote two letters, one to d'Argental, and the other to the great advocate, Elie de Beaumont.

" Divine angels, I throw myself at your feet, and at those of the Count de Choiseul. The widow Calas is in Paris, with the design of claiming justice; would

she dare this if her husband was guilty? She is of
the ancient house of Montesquieu (the Montesquieus
are a family of Languedoc); she has sentiments worthy
of her birth, and superior to her dreadful misfortune. . . .
I have sent her a little paper which will be her passport
to your house. . . . My dear angels, this good work
is worthy of your heart."

And to Elie de Beaumont:

" Sir, I commend to you the most unhappy of women,
whose demand is the most just in the world. Tell
me at once, I beg you, what steps can be taken; I charge
myself with repayment. . . . This affair, in which
I take the liveliest interest, is so extraordinary that it
calls for extraordinary measures. You may be sure
that the parliament of Toulouse will not provide us with
the means of attacking it; it has forbidden the communication of the documents, or even the report of
the arrest, to any person whatsoever. Only great
influence can obtain from My Lord the *Chancellor*,
or from the *King*, an order to dispatch copies of the
registers. We are seeking this influence: the voice
of a troubled, anxious publick will surely obtain it.
To know on which side is the most horrible fanatism,
is a matter which concerns the *State*. I doubt not that
such an enterprise will appear to you mighty important;
I beg you to speak of it to the magistrates or juriconsults
of your acquaintance, and so to contrive matters that
'tis spoke of to the *Chancellor*."

It was Voltaire himself who had persuaded Madame
Calas to seek justice. He paid the expenses of her
journey and of her residence in Paris, and he engaged
without hesitation the two greatest advocates of the time:
Elie de Beaumont and Loyseau de Mauléon. He
himself stirred public opinion by a pamphlet on *The*

History of Elizabeth Canning and the Calas Family, and
by an immense number of letters, as well as by that
tremendous personal influence which, in a hundred
subtle ways, he could now exercise.

Of his letters actually addressed to Madame Calas,
not many have been preserved. One is of doubtful
date, but was probably written in 1763, when the
papers relating to the trial had been sent to Paris by
order of the Privy Council:

" Madam, all those who have the happiness to serve
you in so just a cause have reason equally to congratulate
themselves. You know I have never doubted the
issue of your litigation. It seems to me that the King's
Council are engag'd to give you entire satisfaction by
forcing the judges of *Toulouse* to send the procedure
and motives of the arrest. You may now enjoy your
repose; I send you, and the young ladies your daughters,
the most tender and sincere compliments. You have
deported yourself like a worthy mother, a worthy wife;
the people should praise you as much as they should
abhor the judgement of *Toulouse*. Meanwhile, be
consoled in knowing that the whole of *Europe* does
justice to the memory of your husband; you are a grand
example to the world. I shall ever be, with the sentiments which are due to you, Madam, yours, etc."

He had tried, though apparently in vain, to win the
support of Madame de Pompadour. But there was
no need to invoke the aid of courtiers and favourites.
The conscience of the entire nation was deeply moved,
and the proof of the guilt or innocence of Calas became
a national concern.

We may here anticipate the end of the long drama.

On the 9th of March, 1765, forty judges, assembled in council, unanimously revoked the sentence of the court of Toulouse. The innocence of Jean Calas, and the ghastly incompetence or more ghastly fanatism of his judges, were proved conclusively. Madame Calas and her daughters were received by the queen, and the family were indemnified by the royal bounty: 12,000 francs for the widow, 6,000 for each of her daughters, 3,000 for Pierre Calas, 3,000 for the servant, Jeanne Viguière, and 6,000 towards the travelling, residential and legal expenses. No action was taken against the magistrates of Toulouse, but David de Beaudrigue, deprived of his office in February, 1765, died a raging lunatic.

Long before the Calas affair was ended, Voltaire was busy with another.

Peter Paul Sirven, living with his family at Castres in Languedoc, was a land surveyor and estate agent. He had three daughters; the eldest married to a shopkeeper, the two others living at home with their father and mother. All were Protestants. The second daughter, Elizabeth, was a poor, frail, half-witted creature, presumably a mental defective with strongly marked sexual proclivities, and their frequent corollary —hallucinations. In March, 1760, Elizabeth wandered away from home. Sirven was informed by the Bishop of Castres that his daughter had professed an ardent desire to become a Catholic, and to be admitted to the convent of the Black Ladies. Actually, she had done nothing of the kind. She had been influenced by the sister of the bishop, to whom a wandering half-witted girl seemed to offer reasonable chances of conversion, and to be a proper and easy subject for the attentions of the church. Elizabeth entered the convent, and was driven half mad by the austerities of a religious life. In about seven months' time, having greatly disturbed the Black Ladies by fits, visions and convulsions, the girl was sent back to her parents. Apparently she had not been converted after all. On the 15th or 16th of December, Elizabeth disappeared for the second time. Nothing more was heard of her until, on the 3rd of January, her dead body was found floating in a well at St-Alby, near Castres.

In this unpleasant story there are certain features which grimly resemble those of the Calas affair. At this very time, the Calas family were in chains at Toulouse, and to the heated mind of the local magistrate it was clear that the Huguenots of Languedoc were killing their children to prevent their conversion to the holy church. A writ was issued for the arrest of Sirven, his wife, and their two daughters.

Hearing of this, ill prepared as they were, the terrified family decided upon immediate flight. After many weeks of alternate hiding and travelling, destitute and wholly dependent upon the charity of strangers, exposed to all the miseries and dangers of a winter in the mountains, the unhappy Sirven reached Lausanne. Here he was joined, two months later, by his wife and his daughters. The Sirvens were now deprived of all their property; Sirven and his wife were convicted, in their absence, of parricide. Sirven was to be broken alive, and his wife hanged. The daughters were convicted as accomplices, and were condemned, first to witness the execution of their parents, and then to be banished. And as the Sirvens could not be hung in person, they were hung in effigy.

Sirven managed to earn a living in Geneva, while

his wife and children were charitably maintained by the republic of Berne at Lausanne. Before they had been long in Switzerland, the four Sirvens were presented to Voltaire at Ferney. At once he undertook their defence.

As in the affair of Toulouse, he set about this new battle with tremendous energy and courage, and employed for the Sirvens, as for Madame Calas, the great lawyer, Elie de Beaumont.

He was now defending an obscure family in a case which, though tragic enough, lacked the awful horror of the Calas affair, and would never have been known to the world if he had not taken it up with such magnificent zeal. For no less than nine years he fought for the Sirvens against the dark powers of the Infamous. In 1769, Sirven was again condemned; in 1771, an appeal was heard before the parliament of Toulouse. This was the very parliament which had sent Calas to his fearful death, but even parliaments learn their lessons; a new spirit was moving, and the Sirvens were acquitted.

We have summarised in a few words the course and result of a long defence, and one which required extraordinary tenacity of purpose and a truly noble devotion. In 1771, let it be remembered, Voltaire was in his seventy-eighth year. And it cannot be said that, when once he had set the defence in motion, he left matters to take their course. Nor can it be said that he was bound to win, with truth, reason and justice on his side. The passions of cruel, foolish and ignorant men, particularly when they believe themselves religious, know little of reason, care little for truth; nor is there any oppression more dreadful to endure, more blindly unscrupulous, than the oppression of men who see the weakening of their power and credit.

In the defence of the Sirvens we have a noble instance of the courage and loyalty of a single man. The Sirven affair was not, like that of Calas, a matter which became of national importance. There was no overwhelming tragedy. There was no great popular movement in favour of the accused. It was not felt that the honour of the whole nation was concerned here, as it was in the other case. For these very reasons, the defence was the more difficult, and required a greater degree of resolution. Yet the issue, in both cases, was precisely the same. Innocent people had been condemned without evidence. The mere barbarity of the sentences, hideous as it was, ought not to obscure this prime issue. All the appalling details of the death of Calas were authorised by the law and cordially approved by the church ; the ultimate horror was not here, but in the fact that Calas had been condemned without justice. Voltaire himself always laid stress on this point. He was protesting, not so much against methods of torture and execution, as against the enormity of the whole procedure. If the Infamous was to kill men judicially, without proving any crime, how could France be admitted to the community of civilised peoples? That was the question. And with all his intense compassion for the suffering of the victims, it was as the defender of principles rather than as the defender of persons that Voltaire fought with all his energy against the Infamous. To write a *Henriade* is less admirable than to fight the battle of humanity and justice and civilisation.

In 1770, he undertook another desperate defence— that of Montbailly and his wife, falsely accused, like the others, of parricide. Montbailly was executed; but Voltaire obtained the reversal of the sentence and saved the wife, to whom the council of Arras made full reparation.

CHAPTER VIII

THE PATRIARCH

THOSE who visited the old man at Ferney came away with a sense of bewilderment. This terrible old man, so dry, fragile and withered in appearance, amazed them by his abounding energy, his tricks, alertness and vehemence. And yet he was always ill, always dying. He was crushed, so he said, by his "fourscore years and fourscore maladies." In the morning he would be dejected, peevish, full of querulous complaints and wearisome demands; but the arrival of a visitor quickly brought him back to life. The best perruque was trimmed, the best coat brushed, and the old man would meet his guest with all the grace and gaiety in the world. He would show proudly the house, the garden, his books and pictures: a Venus by Veronese, a Flora by Guido, and above all, La Tour's fine pastel of Madame du Châtelet. He would argue, joke, bluster, laugh, declaim, with shrill voice and quick gestures. His conversation, not always of the most elevated kind, was invariably amusing. From every civilised country, men of learning or distinction came to see him. He could entertain them on a scale that was almost princely. After a play in his own theatre, the table was laid for sixty or even eighty persons. There were always twelve horses in the stables, and always a multitude of servants busy in the house and gardens. In 1768, after a drastic reform of his budget, the expenses of Ferney could not be less than 40,000 livres a year.

We have a pleasant account of a visit to Ferney, written by the Prince de Ligne in 1763.

" I was eight days in his house, and I wish I could remember all the sublime, gay, simple and loveable things which illustrated his character; but truly that is impossible. I laughed and I admired. I was continually intoxicated. Even in his errors, his faulty knowledge, his whims, his lack of taste for the fine arts, his follies and pretentions, all that he was and all that he could not be, all was charming, new, provoking and unforeseen. . . . He wore grey shoes, iron-grey stockings, a large dimity waistcoat reaching to his knees, a big, trailing perruque and a little cap of black velvet. On Sunday, he would sometimes put on a fine broidered coat, all of a piece, vest and breeches of the same sort, but the vest with great flaps galooned in gold after the *Burgundian* style, with huge sleeves and lace extending to the tips of his fingers; for *thus*, said he, one has a noble appearance. M. de Voltaire was good-humour'd with all his neighbours, and made them laugh. He embellished all that he saw and all that he heard. He questioned an officer of my regiment, whose answers he thought sublime. ' What is your religion, sir ? ' he demanded.—' My parents reared me in the *Catholick* persuasion.'—' A splendid reply! ' said M. de Voltaire; ' he don't say that he *belongs* to it ! ' All this might seem ridiculous to relate, and likely to make him absurd; but one should see him, animated by his fine, lively fancies, bestowing freely his wit, his gay sallies, upon every one; dispos'd to see and believe in what is good and beautiful, abounding in sound sense, and causing it to abound in others; relating all to what he writes and what he thinks; awakening speech and thought in those capable of either; giving help to all the unfortunate, building for poor families and a good fellow in his own; a good fellow in his village, a good fellow and a

great man at once—an union without which no one is
ever completely either the one or the other: for genius
gives a wider scope to goodness, and goodness makes
genius more humane."

After the suppression of the Jesuits in 1762, Voltaire
received into his house a gentle, friendless man, Father
Adam. This amiable Father, with his neat, thin figure,
his black clothes and air of sad propriety, became a
familiar of the household. He did not mind the little
jokes of his patron, which, in his case, were always of
a kindly sort. He would smile rather mournfully, place
the tips of his long fingers together, and shake his head.
In his heart, he believed that Voltaire might be converted.
He prayed, with fervent desire, for this conversion.
Boswell, who saw him at Ferney in 1764, describes him
as " a lively old man with white hair," and tells us how
Voltaire spoke of him as " a broken soldier of the Company of Jesus." Father Adam, moving softly and
unobtrusively in the background, and still asserting,
with pathetic dignity, his right to wear a hat indoors,
was always treated with kindness and respect. Indeed,
he took his place in the family picture. We see him,
in conversation pieces, with Doctor Tronchin, Madame
Denis and the pretty maid, standing by Voltaire's bed
or taking tea in the drawing-room.

In fine weather, Voltaire spent much of his time walking in his park or up and down his long avenues, or
round his gardens. He had a little lawn, with a lime
tree in the middle of it, which was called his " study."
When he passed through the hedge into the " study,"
it was understood that no one was to disturb him.

He was fond of receiving visitors in the garden, and
of showing them his trees, plants and flowers. In the

midst of conversation, he would dart suddenly upon some lurking parasite or hidden weed, with a quickness of eye and motion remarkable enough in the case of an old man who declared that he was blind, infirm, and dying.

After dinner, he used to go for a drive in his coach, and after supper he would retire to his room and work. He slept only for four or five hours, and was in the habit of writing at all hours of the night. He had a contrivance for holding several candles at the head of his bed, and if he woke at any time, and felt disposed to work, he summoned the secretary, Wagnière, by rapping upon the floor. Much of his writing was done while he lay in bed, either at night or in the late hours of the morning. He seldom rose before noon.

It is interesting to compare the impressions of a graceful humbug like the Prince de Ligne with those of two other visitors, different both in race and character: that vain, ridiculous, invaluable creature, James Boswell; and the Middlesex patriot, John Wilkes.

Boswell, whose happiness in being able to force himself upon the attention of a great man was only equalled by his pleasure in writing about him afterwards, could not leave Geneva without paying his respects to Monsieur de Voltaire. He had taken care to provide himself with a letter of introduction from " a Swiss Colonel at the Hague." On the 28th of December, 1764, he presented this letter at Ferney. He had the satisfaction of being received by " two or three footmen," but Voltaire was unwell, and not in the best humour. It is quite conceivable that Boswell annoyed him. He " sat erect upon his chair and simpered when he spoke." But then, says Boswell, " he was not in spirits, nor I either."

With the awful tenacity of a journalist, Boswell decided, the very next day, to write to Madame Denis and to beg for another interview. " I was in the finest humour," said the complacent fellow to his friend William Temple, " and my letter was full of wit." So he came back, and was even allowed to spend the night at Ferney. There seems to have been no other company, and in the evening the old man and the young visitor (he was twenty-five) settled down to a long talk.

They must have been oddly contrasted: the old man, shrill and vehement; the young visitor, with his round, serious face, dreadful pertinacity, slow northern voice and foolish questions. " I placed myself by him. I touched the keys in unison with his imagination. I wish you had heard the Music. . . . When he talked our language he was animated with the Soul of a Briton. He had bold flights. He had humour. . . . He swore bloodily as was the fashion when he was in England. . . . At last we came upon Religion. Then did he rage." A great bible was opened on the table between them. " And if ever two mortal men disputed with vehemence we did. . . . For a certain portion of time there was a fair opposition between *Voltaire* and *Boswell*." But not for long. " The daring bursts of his Ridicule confounded my understanding. . . . He went too far. His aged frame trembled beneath him." The old man was growing tired and desperate; and still the solemn youth, with dreadful composure and dreary persistence, poured out one question after another. " But must we not believe, Sir, in the Master of the Universe ? " Well might the aged frame tremble. At last, using a trick which he often employed, Voltaire shammed a faint. He fell back in his chair and closed his eyes. Boswell, who had no intention, either of

retiring or of calling help, sat and watched him. And
when the old man hopefully opened his eyes again,
the solemn youth was still there.

A more placid conversation was clearly desirable.
Just as well to admit the Master of the Universe, and
have a little peace. " He exprest his veneration—his
love—of the Supreme Being, and his entire resignation
to the will of Him who is All-wise."

And what of immortality ? said James Boswell.
" He says it may be; but he knows nothing of it." And
the next morning, the old man was careful not to show
himself until his guest had gone; but he sent him a
little note, in which he spoke lightly of " that pretty
thing call'd Soul," and admitted that, for his part, he
was " but a very ignorant fellow."

The visit of John Wilkes took place a little later
(in 1765), and he wrote a manly, simple account of his
impressions:

" I have been with Voltaire at Ferney, and was
charmed with the reception he gave me, and still more
with the fine sense and exquisite wit of his conversation.
I think he is the most universal genius, the most amiable
as well as the wittiest of our species. He is a divine
old man, born for the advancement of true philosophy
and the polite arts, and to free mankind from the
gloomy terrors of superstition. . . . He has done
more to persuade the practice of a general toleration,
of humanity and benevolence, than the greatest philosopher of antiquity. His conduct in the affair of the
family of Calas is more meritorious than the whole lives
of most saints. He is exactly well-bred, and in conversation possesses a fund of gaiety and humour which
would be admir'd in a young man, and he joins to it

those immense stores of literature only to be acquir'd by age. . . . He lives in the noblest, gayest style of a *French* nobleman, receiving all strangers, giving plays in his own theatre, and you have the entire command of his house, equipages, horses, etc. He is adored by all the inhabitants and vassals of his extensive domains, and with reason, for he hath been the creator of everything useful, beautiful, or valuable in the whole Tract near him, which before was a rude Wilderness. . . . He has built little towns and villages, established several manufactures, and peopled the country with a happy race of mortals who are daily blessing their Benefactor."

Of these "little towns and villages" we shall have occasion to speak presently. The picture of John Wilkes, highly coloured as it is by the enthusiasm of a liberal mind, is true in substance. The *seigneur de village* was building good farms and houses on his estates, and was filling them with quiet, industrious people who found life hard enough in Geneva.

During the last fifteen years of his life, Voltaire published more than three hundred miscellaneous writings, and although many of these are fragments or trifles, such prolixity is truly amazing. He wrote or dictated in this time more than five thousand letters. He carried on a most delightful correspondence with his old friend, Madame du Deffand, and he began, in 1765, to exchange letters with the Empress Catherine of Russia.

His admiration for this great ruler may be compared with his earlier admiration for Frederick. Catherine was a new Star of the North. Her liberality and courage, the tolerance of her administration, her industry and vigilance, delighted him. "Your Imperial

Majesty," he said, " has found a road to glory unknown
to all other sovereigns." He wrote for her, as he had
written for Frederick, adulatory verses. " Sir," she
said, " my head is as hard as my name is inharmonious;
I will answer your delicious verses in clumsy prose.
I have never wrote verses, but I admire none the less
those of others." Nor would she allow that she was
the Star of the North—a mere *aurora borealis*, a
flickering occasional radiance, perhaps, but no star !

With Madame du Deffand he could exchange ideas
and compliments with entire freedom. These two old
people were extremely well fitted for mutual entertainment, and perhaps for the truest friendship of which
either was capable. They were united by rare gifts
of wit, gaiety and malice, and by those mutual memories
of a past age which are so dear to survivors. They
were both secure, both independent; they could think
and write as they pleased:

" I can never allow you," he said, " to tell me that
the more one thinks, the more unhappy one is. That
is true of those who think ill; I don't mean those who
think ill of their neighbours, which is often extremely
amusing; I mean those who think all awry: they are
doubtless to be pitied, because they have a sickness of
the mind, and to be sick is always a sad condition. But
you, whose mind has the best health in the world,
consider, if you please, what you owe to nature. Is
it nothing to be rid of those unhappy prejudices which
fetter the greater part of mankind, and women in
particular ? . . . I would console you, too, by telling
you that I think your situation very superior to my
own. I find myself in the very middle of Europe.
Every traveller comes to see me. I have to hold my

own with Germans, English, Italians, and even Frenchmen, whom I shall never see again; while you see only
those who are dear to you."

He wrote to her of his thoughts, his plan of life, his
views and actions, with entire candour. In no other
letters, not even those written to the d'Argentals or
young Damilaville, did he speak so frankly. It is
ridiculous to suppose that he was never sincere,
ridiculous to see in his courteous phrases only the
amusement of a shallow mind. He never took the
trouble of writing long and frequent letters except
for those he admired, or loved, or hated. He wrote
to Madame du Deffand as to a congenial spirit; and
even if we can excuse Mr. Lytton Strachey for talking
of these two singular old people as " a monkey and a
cat " (and we agree that Madame du Deffand was a
cat), we must remember that monkey and cat were
fond of each other. Take, for instance, the intimate
revelation of the following letter, written early in 1766:

" There are those who envy me this rocky retreat,
who would have pity neither on my age nor on the
maladies which oppress me, and who would persecute
me beyond the tomb; but I am fully reassured by your
letter, and you must have seen, by my last one, with
what confidence I open my heart to you. This heart
is full of you, and is continually sensible of your merit,
your well-being; it loves your candour and imagination,
and will be attached to you as long as it beats in my
feeble body. . . .
" I have nothing in common with our modern
philosophers, except their horror of intolerant fanatism;
a horror which is very reasonable, and with which we

ought to inspire the human race, for the surety of princes, the peace of States, and the welfare of individuals.

" That is why I have associated myself with men of merit, who, perhaps, are too inflexible in their way of thinking, little inclined to conform to the usage of the world, seeking rather to instruct than to please, wishing rather to be heard than to listen to others—but who atone for these faults by immense learning and by great virtues.

" Yet be persuaded, Madam, that of all friendships, yours is the most dear to me. I cannot, without extreme bitterness, see myself in the necessity of dying without having spent a few days chatting with you; it would have been my dearest consolation. Your letters supply it: I hear you speak as I read your words. . . . I love you, Madam, because I love the truth: in one word, I'm in despair at not being able to pass a few days with you before I return this wretched machine to the four elements."

Yet, in spite of these complaints of the feebleness of age and the weight of maladies, Voltaire was never more furiously active with his pen. He made a practice (as we have often seen already) of denying the authorship of his works, or even of imputing them to other writers. He had, or believed he had, some excuse for this procedure. He adopted it so that he might avoid persecution. The heavier the fire from his guns, the more anxious he was to conceal their position, and to move audaciously from one emplacement to another. This was all a part of the campaign against the Infamous. He did not want to be hampered by the problems of defence at a time when all his energies were directing this awful bombardment.

It was a part of his policy, therefore, to deny the authorship of one of the most famous of all his works, the *Dictionnaire Philosophique Portatif*, or *Portable Philosophick Dictionary*, which had first appeared furtively in 1764.

In this work, he had chosen a form ideally suitable for the conveyance of his views, and capable, at any time, of enlargement. Under chosen headings he could string together a series of devastating and brilliant essays on church, religion, history, ethics, fables, and all that he desired to attack or defend, from Abraham and anthropophagi to tyranny and tolerance, from dreams, miracles and idolatry to the Chinese and Japanese catechisms and the falsity of human virtues. In later editions he added much to his original work, and his editors have added even more. But the original book presented, in a very concise and very convenient form, the whole essence of the Voltairean doctrines. It was, according to the righteous Bonnet, " the most detestable of all the books of this pestilent writer." Nor was it long before the righteous council of Geneva had it burnt publicly by the executioner—probably the best possible method of advertising a new book.

The *Philosophick Dictionary* played a part, as we shall presently see, in the grim tragedy of La Barre; a tragedy not less appalling than the affair of Calas. It caused more anger, more delight and more astonishment than any book of the same period; more, even, than the *Social Contract* or the *Emile* of Jean-Jacques Rousseau. It was, in the eyes of the orthodox, a dreadful book, a book stinking of infidelity, full of a subtle corrupting poison. Catholic or Calvinist, priest or minister, all men of good principles were profoundly shocked. Voltaire, of course, was quite as much surprised as any one else. How could people suppose him capable of such a thing ? Poor old dying man—why could they not leave him alone ?

" God preserve me, dear brother," he wrote to Damilaville, " from having the least part in the *Portable Philosophick Dictionary* ! I have read some of it; it smells horribly of the faggot. But since you are curious about these works of impiety, so that you can refute 'em, I'll search for a few copies and send them to you on the first occasion." Sending a few copies meant, of course, the circulation of the book in Paris. A little later he wrote to d'Alembert:

" I have heard speak of this abominable little *Dictionary* ; 'tis the work of Satan. . . . Be sure that, if I can get hold of it, you shall have a supply." And again: " This collection is by several hands, as you will have easily perceived. I know not by what madness people insist in believing me the authour of it. The greatest service you can render me is to affirm sturdily, upon your share in *Paradise*, that I have no part in this work of *Hell*, which, moreover, is very ill printed, and full of ridiculous faults. . . . I suppose there are but few copies of this atrocious *alphabet* in Paris, and those not in dangerous hands; but, if there should be the least danger, I beg you to advise me of it, so that I may disavow the work, with my usual candour and innocence."

As the clamour grew more intense, with louder and longer echoes, echoes heard only too clearly at Fontainebleau and Versailles, so the denials became more vehement, and the origins of the book were described with more convincing detail.

" Dear brother," he wrote again to Damilaville, " the tempest growls on all sides against the *Portatif*.

What barbarity to accuse me of writing a book stuff'd with quotations from St Jerome, Ambrose, Clement of Alexandria, Tertullian, Origen. . . . The book is *known* to be by one named Dubut, a little Dutch theological apprentice."

Then came a more subtle, though rather contradictory statement to d'Argental: " They ascribe the *Portatif* to me, because it actually contains certain articles which I formerly intended for the *Encyclopaedia*, as *Love*, *Self-Love*, *Socratick Love*, etc.; but 'tis proved that the rest is none of mine. . . . In one word, I have no part in this edition, I have never sent the book to any one. . . . The King is too just and too good to condemn me on the word of frivolous backbiters." And finally, also in a letter to d'Argental: " I beg you to observe the *certain truth* that the *Portatif* is by several hands; and 'tis of no small advantage to the establishment of the reign of reason, that several persons, among whom there are actually Clergymen, have contributed to this work. Certain councillors of Geneva have seen absolute proof of this with their own eyes."

But all these fictions, cowardly and futile as they well may seem, had no effect, unless to remove any doubt as to the author of the *Dictionary*.

In October, 1765, the possession of this book was cited in the evidence against a young man who was condemned to death for sacrilege and blasphemy—the unhappy La Barre.

On the night of the 8th of August, 1765, a crucifix on the Pont-Neuf at Abbeville, and another in the cemetery of St Catherine, had been mutilated. This hateful outrage angered even those who were least religious, and the whole town was concerned in finding and punishing the culprits.

Before long, suspicion pointed to a group of silly young gentlemen, La Barre, his friend Gaillard d'Etallonde, Moisnel, and two others. It was known that La Barre, d'Etallonde and Moisnel had insulted a religious procession by not removing their hats. On the 24th of August, a warrant of arrest was issued against all three. D'Etallonde had already taken to flight: La Barre and Moisnel were brought before the magistrates.

It was proved that all the accused had been guilty of singing profane songs, reciting blasphemies, making a mock of saints and sacraments, reading such forbidden books as the *Nun in the Nightgown*, the *Doorkeeper of the Chartreuse*, the *Gallantries of Theresa*—and the *Philosophick Dictionary*.

And while the case was being heard, priests were grimly chanting in the town, and people were going in procession to the outraged crucifix in dark fervours of atonement. Already the Bishop of Amiens had prayed that the offenders might be made " worthy of their last agonies in this world "—a prayer which could have but one aim and one meaning.

In this atmosphere of terror, Moisnel, who was a delicate boy of seventeen or eighteen (fifteen, according to Voltaire), broke down. He told all that he knew, inculpated La Barre, and stated that d'Etallonde had mutilated the crucifix on the Pont-Neuf. After a trial conducted, so it would seem, with little regard for correct procedure, sentence was given on the 28th of February, 1766. Gaillard d'Etallonde and La Barre were condemned to do penance before the main door of the church of St. Wolfram, then to have their tongues cut out, and then to be beheaded in the square of Abbeville, after which their heads and bodies were to be consumed in a great fire. Sentence in the other cases was withheld, and the accused were allowed the right of appeal. It has been said, that the judges reckoned upon a royal pardon, and wished only to make a terrifying example of La Barre. However that may have been, Louis XV was inflexible. Let the youth suffer, he said, for his abominable wickedness. We must remember that the queen of Louis XV was an extremely pious woman.

La Barre, brave and careless, was taken to the scaffold on the 1st of July. As a final grace, his tongue was not cut out, and the poor boy was able to jest with the executioner. " What ! " said he, as they cut off the long hair over his neck; " would you make a chorister of me ? " The square of Abbeville was full of people, elegant ladies among them, and when the executioner struck off the head with one clean blow, there was a loud clapping of hands. The body was thrown into the fire, and with it, in accordance with the sentence, the *Portable Philosophick Dictionary*.

Voltaire, when he heard of the execution, was filled with terror. He felt himself concerned personally in the death of La Barre; it was like a dreadful challenge on the part of the Infamous. " You know," he cried to d'Argental, " that, of the twenty-five judges, only fifteen voted for death. But when more than one third of the voters incline towards clemency, the other two thirds are indeed cruel. On what does the life of men depend ! If the law was clear, all the judges should be of the same opinion; but even if that is not so, even if there is no law at all, should five additional votes be enough to destroy, in the most horrible torments, a young man whose only crime is foolishness ? What more could they have done if he had killed his father ? "

What was more, he said, there was no legal penalty for such an offence as that of La Barre and d'Etallonde: it was left to the wisdom or fantasy of the judge. And two days later, he cried out even more bitterly:

" The atrocity of this event fills me with rage and horror. I repent indeed of having ruined myself in building houses and doing good on the borders of a land where, in cold blood and before going to dine, people commit abominations which would revolt a parcel of drunken savages. And yet 'tis a people so gentle, gay, and light ! Anthropophagous *Harlequins* ! let me hear no more of you. Go from the stake to the masquerade, from the Grève to the Opéra Comique; break Calas, hang Sirven, burn five poor young gentlemen who, as my angels say, ought to have been confin'd for six months at Saint-Lazare—I would not breathe the same air as you do. . . . What ! the crazy whim of five old fools is enough to inflict tortures which would have made Busiris tremble ! "

And then, the intolerable thought of being associated, through the little *Dictionary*, with the awful sentence ! Was there not, here, an implication too dreadful for words ? Might it not be said, that here was one whose books corrupted young men, and brought them to a death of shame and agony ? Nor was this all. In the library of the unhappy La Barre they had found the *Pucelle*, and the *Epistle to Urania*, a folly of his own youth. Again, with desperation, but without relieving his own mind or convincing others, he denied the terrible *Dictionary*. On the 19th of August he wrote to de Richelieu:

"You know the earth is covered with oaks and reeds: you are the oak, and I am an old reed all bent by storms. I will admit fairly that the tempest which has destroy'd this young fool, La Barre, has bowed my head. . . . I must tell you a singular thing. They have pretended to assert, in the evidence against La Barre, that he made genuflections before the *Philosophick Dictionary*;—*he never had this book*. In the report of the proceedings it is said that he and one of his comrades went on their knees before *The Doorkeeper of the Chartreuse* and Piron's *Ode to Priapus;* they recited the *Litanies of the Bum;* they indulg'd in the pranks of young pages—there was not one of the whole band capable of reading a work of Philosophy. . . . I am interested in this *Philosophick Dictionary* which has been most falsely imputed to me. I am so little the authour, that the article *Messiah*, which may be found entire in the *Encyclopaedick Dictionary*, is by a Protestant minister, a man of wealth and condition, whose manuscript, wrote by his own hand, is in my possession. There are several other articles whose authours are known, and, in one word, no one can ever convict me of being the authour of this work."

And so Voltaire, miserable and frightened as he certainly was, lied to his friends, and lied in vain. La Barre "never had the book." He was not capable of reading such a book. In any case he, Voltaire, had nothing to do with it. But he says nothing, it will be observed, of the burning at Abbeville.

La Barre was dead; but something might still be done for young d'Etallonde. He entered the service of the King of Prussia, and Voltaire, moved by generosity in which, perhaps, his conscience played a part, did all that he could to recommend the young man to Frederick's attention. He wrote several letters to d'Etallonde himself, and had the satisfaction of seeing him make good progress. " Serve the *philosophick King*," he told him, " and detest for ever the most detestable of superstitions."

Meanwhile, Ferney was prospering. Farmers, artisans and clockmakers were living there in clean new houses, and the craftsmen of Ferney were producing silk stockings of beautiful texture and little watches with fine cases of gold or enamel.

The *seigneur* Voltaire was ruining himself, so he said, in the building of these new farms and factories and houses; but he was taking a pardonable delight in the industry and well-being of his vassals. Let Rousseau, that odious fellow, say what he pleased: here, in these neat houses and busy people, were pictures of true philosophy.

It was all pretty enough, but the *seigneur* had no intention of losing on his village industries; clocks, watches and stockings had to be sold, and he was always bringing them persistently to the notice of his friends. In all that he did, he acted with a bewildering complexity of motive: much of this, unquestionably, was pure benevolence, and much was mere commercial enterprise. Again, the idea of founding a *colony*, a colony ruled by philosophic principles, had a peculiar fascination for him. He had, in fact, a scheme for a settlement of Encyclopaedists at Clèves, on the territory of the King of Prussia. Frederick would have granted the land, but Diderot and d'Alembert were not so anxious to leave Paris.

There remained the satisfaction of presiding over

the lives and prosperity of his industrious workers at Ferney. He planted trees where no trees had been before, he built villages and planned his fields, he bought the newest kinds of machinery and employed the most capable teachers. By working in a little field of his own, he set the example. He desired to see round him, not only a happy and industrious people, but a people who would turn to him with seemly gratitude as their master and benefactor. So, as the coach with its blue lining and silver stars rumbled down the long avenue at Ferney, the labourers could look up and cry, " There he goes—the good *seigneur*, the kind *seigneur*; God bless him ! "

His pride in the industries of Ferney was not wholly of the vainglorious kind. He took a real delight in the advancement of his people. " To my thinking," he wrote, " there is nothing prettier than a large rustick mansion, through whose great doorways you may see, going and coming, wagons laden with all the spoils of the fields. . . . On the one side are fifty handsome cows with their calves, the horses and oxen are on the other; their fodder falls in the racks from huge granaries; in the midst are the barns where the grain is crushed; and you know that all the animals, each one lodg'd in his proper place in this great building, understand mighty well that the fodder and oats which it contains belong to them by right."

For some years the colony was prosperous enough. The watches were sold to royal customers, they were sent to Versailles, to St Petersburg, to Constantinople, to Morocco (which Voltaire called " the heart of Africa "); the silk stockings were patronised by the ladies of Paris. But after the fall of the friendly minister de Choiseul at the end of 1770, and the weakening of Voltaire's credit, the trade of Ferney declined.

In 1772, Voltaire wrote sadly to Madame du Deffand: " I had thought to see my colony destroy'd. As soon as one tries to do good, one is sure to find enemies. . . . Write prose or verse, or build houses, 'tis all one; you will certainly be pursued by envy. There is but one means of escaping this harpy; it is, never to write anything save one's epitaph, to build only one's tomb, and to get inside it as quickly as one can. . . . When I tell you, Madam, that I have builded a little town which is pretty enough; that is mighty ridiculous, but 'tis very true. This town has even carried on a considerable trade, but, if they go on cheating me, all must perish."

In speaking of the fall of de Choiseul, we have moved some way in advance of the period we now have to consider—the years immediately following the tragedy of La Barre.

Affecting not to hear the sombre growling of Rousseau, the Patriarch busied himself with works of every conceivable kind. And Rousseau had reason for growling. In spite of Jean-Jacques and the Calvinist opposition, a theatre had been set up in Geneva. This theatre, after some months of precarious existence, was burnt down. Even if it was not intentionally fired, no efforts were made to save the building, and people, when they heard it was " only the theatre," emptied their buckets in the gutter and went home again.

In a cruel grotesque poem upon the *Civil War of Geneva*, Voltaire not only attacked Rousseau with indecent fury, but accused him of having planned the destruction of the theatre.

The baiting of Rousseau was never a very serious occupation. He was a " madman," a quarrelsome dog who had lost all his friends (which was only too true), a silly fellow who could not leave any one alone.

The Patriarch had other concerns. His literary performance was almost incredible. In 1767 and 1768 he published more than fifty various writings, including the play of the *Scythians*, the *Examination of Lord Bolingbroke*, the *Defence of my Uncle*, the well known stories of the *Princess of Babylon*, *The Simpleton*, *Charlot*, and the *Man with Forty Crowns*, the splendid dialogues of the *Count de Boulainvilliers*, the *Singularities of Nature*, *Brother Pediculoso*, the *Pyrrhonism of History*, and the comical *A.B.C.* And all the time he was managing his estates, carrying on an immense correspondence, receiving endless visits, and often entertaining in the grand manner. On the occasion of his own particular festival (the 4th of October) in 1767, a high mass followed by a Te Deum was performed in the new church at Ferney, in the presence of a whole regiment of troops and all the notables of Gex. After that came a theatrical performance in his own house; then a mock-heroic apotheosis of the Patriarch, a grand supper and a ball.

We need not speak of the perfidy of young La Harpe, who stole the manuscript of the *War of Geneva* and the *Memoirs*, or of his expulsion, together with his accomplice, that detestable creature Madame Denis. Both were eventually pardoned. We have to describe two shocking affairs, which do little credit to the Patriarch.

In April, 1768, he decided to receive the Easter Communion in the church at Ferney. He obtained a casual absolution from a monk who had dined with him, and on Easter Sunday he dressed with unusual care. No doubt he attired himself " *in the Burgundian manner,*" with his galooned waistcoat. This occurred in the absence of Madame Denis, and Voltaire requested the secretary, Wagnière, to accompany him. " I have a mind," he said, " to preach a little to these rascals who will persist in stealing." He walked to the church, preceded by a " superb " offering of *pain bénit*, and accompanied by two armed gamekeepers. After receiving the sacraments, he turned suddenly at the chancel rail and began to deliver an address to the bewildered congregation. " Natural law is the most ancient—" and he proceeded, if Wagnière is correct, with " lively, eloquent and pathetic reproaches " on the subject of pilfering. When this had gone on for a few moments, the priest, with a gesture of petulance and dismay, went back to the altar and continued the office. The extraordinary preacher concluded his discourse with a few flattering words addressed to the curé and returned to his place.

One of the most curious results of this escapade was the reception of the news at Versailles. Poor Marie Leczinska, like other women with bad husbands, had become profoundly religious, and she heard with magnanimity and satisfaction that Voltaire had mended his ways and returned to the true faith. The king, too, openly made known his entire approval.

Not so the Bishop of Annecy, Monseigneur Biort. The Bishop, who knew Voltaire, and knew all the circumstances of this abominable farce, wrote to the Patriarch with dignified restraint, with charity and hopefulness, but with a stern note of warning:

" They tell me, Sir, that you have received the Easter Communion. Many persons have been little edified by this, because they imagine 'tis only one more comedy for the publick, in which you would again make sport of what is most sacred in our religion. As for me,

Sir, I think more charitably; I cannot persuade myself
that M. de Voltaire, the great man of our age, who,
by the force of pure reason and the principles of a
sublime philosophy, has declared himself above all
mere pride, all the weaknesses and prejudices of humanity, could have been capable of betraying and
dissembling his sentiments by an act of hypocrisy
which in itself would suffice to tarnish all his renown,
and to debase him in the sight of all thinking men.
I must believe that all your actions are marked by
sincerity. . . . If, on the day of your Communion,
you had been observ'd, not preaching to the people
in the church about theft and pilfering, but proving
to them, like another Theodosius, by your sighs, your
tears and lamentation, the purity of your faith, the
sincerity of your repentance, and the disavowal of all
the unedifying principles which they might suspect
in the past by your manner of speaking and acting,
then no one could possibly have regarded as equivocal
your apparent manifestation of religion. . . . But,
whatever may be said of the past (which I must leave
to the Great Surveyor of hearts and consciences), the
quality of the tree will be judg'd by the fruits; and I
hope that, by your future works, you will leave no
room for doubting the probity and sincerity of what
you have already done. . . . A wearied body, already
bowed beneath the weight of years, warns you that you
approach the term which all the famous men who have
preceded you have reach'd at last—men who are now
almost forgotten. In allowing themselves to be dazzled
by the false light of a frivolous and fugitive glory,
most of them lost sight of those immortal gifts and
glories, far worthier to have been the objects of their
hope and striving. Please Heaven that you, wiser

and more prudent than they, will concern yourself only in the pursuit of that sovereign good which alone can fill the emptiness of a heart that finds nothing here wherewith to be content ! "

" This letter," said the Patriarch in reply, " causes me much satisfaction, but some surprise. How can you reproach me for having fulfilled the duties of which every master should give the example upon his own territory, which no Christian should dispense with, and which I have fulfilled so often ? 'Tis not enough to save his vassals from the horrors of poverty, to encourage their marriages, to contribute, as well as he can, to their temporal happiness—he should enlighten them; and it would be strange indeed if the Lord of the Manor did not perform, in the church which he himself builded, what all other pretended *converts* have perform'd in their own way in their own temples."

The Patriarch would have been well advised, either to have chosen some better ground for argument or to have kept silence. The Bishop was a man of energy and character; he had on his side the formidable union of eloquence and faith, the impulse of duty and conviction, against which no sophistry can long prevail. In this peculiar correspondence, Voltaire was clearly defeated. His poor impertinences broke down miserably before the close and well directed fire of the Bishop:

" I could not but be highly surprised that, in affecting not to understand what was clear enough in my letter, you should have supposed me ready to congratulate you upon a Communion of *policy*, with which *Protestants* have not been less scandaliz'd than *Catholicks*. . . . I have been horrified more than any other man; and, if you were less enlightened, less instructed, I should think it my duty to tell you . . . that, in view of the publick scandal, whether of the writings which are ascribed to you, or of the abstention from almost any act of religion for many years, a Communion . . . required on your part preparatory and signal repentance.

" Without being as learned as you gratuitously suppose me to be, I am learned enough to know that the conduct of a Lord of the Manor who has himself accompanied by armed guards in the very church, and who takes upon himself to harangue the people during the celebration of the Holy Mass, far from being authourized by the usages and the laws of *France*, is, on the contrary, proscribed by the wise ordinances of the Christian kings, who have always made a distinction, both in place and time, between what belongs to the ministry of the Clergy and what belongs to the exercize of the common Law—which you would hand over to the Lords of the Manor."

The Patriarch was not yet crushed. He replied with a long letter, weak in argument, but having passages of considerable eloquence:

" My Lord, your second letter astonishes me even more than the first. I know not what false reports have drawn upon me such bitterness on your part. . . . Literary trifles have nothing to do with the duties of a citizen and a Christian; elegant letters are a mere amusement. Benevolence, a piety solid and without superstition, the love of one's neighbour and resignation to God, should be the chief concerns of every man who can think seriously. I try, as best I can, to fulfill all these obligations in my retreat, which becomes every day more profound. But since my weakness gives little support to these efforts, I would prostrate myself once more, with you, before the *Divine Providence*, knowing that we bring before *God* but three things which can have no part in his Immensity—our littleness, our faults and our repentance."

The Bishop had the last word: "You know the works which are attributed to you; you know what is thought of you in every part of Europe; you know that nearly all the unbelievers of our age boast of having you for their Chief, and of having derived from your books the principles of their irreligion. . . . If these are calumnies, as you pretend, you must vindicate yourself, undeceive the very publick which now believes them. It is not difficult for one who is a true Christian in heart and spirit to show what he is; he would not think himself permitted to betray his profession by the amusements which you call *literary trifles*. . . . I will leave you, Sir, to judge what it is proper for you to do."

Voltaire could make no direct answer. He had taken up a series of positions which he could not defend against the plain reasoning of the Bishop; he was like a bad chess-player, whose game is lost from the opening. And soon he was to hear of something which made him furious.

The Bishop sent a copy of the correspondence to the King. There could no longer be any doubt, at Versailles, as to the nature of the wicked Patriarch's conversion. The King replied, through his minister

La Vrillière, that the Bishop had done well in exhorting M. de Voltaire to mind his own business, and that M. de Voltaire would be informed that he was not to behave disgracefully in church. The Bishop, though he could have wished for more drastic measures, now printed a neat little duodecimo pamphlet, in which he gave the text of the letters and La Vrillière's reply. It was all very well for the Patriarch to resort, as he so often did, to crazy abuse, to call the Bishop a " fanatical idiot " or the " son of a miserable mason," " a fool," " a monster," and so forth; he was checked, and check-mated, by the Bishop's move.

And now comes another shocking episode, which, together with the one just described, must be taken into account if we would properly understand Voltaire's attitude towards the church, and, above all, the nature of the so-called " recantations " which he made not long before his death.

In Holy Week, 1769, Voltaire summoned to his bedside a Capucin monk, slipped a bright new crown piece into his hand, and demanded absolution. Upon this, the poor father was seized with a violent trembling, protested that he had many people waiting for him in the church, and hurried out of the room, promising to return within three days. Obviously, he had no intention of returning at all.

Voltaire kept to his bed, simulating a fever, and sending his doctor each morning to the curé, with an account of his deplorable condition. Then, as the curé showed little readiness to attend him, he threatened the unhappy man with a report to the Parliament of Geneva, in which he would be indicted with refusing to administer the sacraments to a dying Christian. The curé, seeing himself between the devil and the bishop, fell into a sad state of physical and mental disorder, tortured alternately by colic and conscience. But there was no help for it. On the 1st of April (and what day could have been more grimly appropriate ?) the last act of this atrocious farce was played at Ferney. The Capucin father, timidly proffering a confession of faith, prepared according to the rules, and only waiting for a signature, was bullied by the awful Patriarch into the granting of absolution. The sacraments were administered by the curé, and the lawyer Raffo, called in for the purpose, duly and formally recorded the proceedings.

No sooner were the priests, the lawyer and the attendants out of the room; than the dying man sprang lightly from his bed. " I had some trouble with those fellows," he said to Wagnière, with one of his diabolical grins; " but 'tis all very amusing and very profitable. Let us take a turn in the garden."

In this mixture of policy, buffoonery and sheer devilment, a leading motive was that of revenge on the Bishop of Annecy. Voltaire, while receiving the sacrament, had most impudently " pardoned those who wrote calumnies against him and sent them to the king," and called upon Raffo to witness the declaration. Other motives were less personal. By pretending to observe the rituals of the church and to encourage others to observe them he was disconcerting his enemies by a sudden change of front. It was not so easy to attack a man who, no matter for what reason and in what circumstances, had done precisely what the church required of him. To call him blasphemer and hypocrite was to invite a terrible counter-charge—the charge of intolerance, bigotry and persecution. After all, might he not have been sincere ? By doing what he had done, he placed the righteous in a strange dilemma, and mischievously surrounded himself by a screen of impenetrable cunning. He made no mystery of the affair in writing to his friends. It is enough to quote the following passages from letters to d'Argental:

" My dear angels are all in a fluster about a certain little breakfast [his communion] before a notary; but if they knew that all was done upon the advice of a lawyer who knows the province; if they knew what a fanatical rogue I am dealing with, and in what an awkward position I was placed, they would confess that I did mighty well. One cannot give a greater proof of one's contempt for these farces than by playing them oneself."

And again: " With regard to the *breakfast*, I tell you once more, it was indispensable. I needed a shield to ward off the mortal blows which were aimed at me. . . . By *communicating*, I set a good example to my own tenants and to all my neighbours. . . . The king wishes us to fulfill the duties of a Christian: not only do I acquit myself of my duties, but I send my Catholick servants regularly to the *church*, and my Protestant servants regularly to the *temple*; I engage a schoolmaster to teach the catechism to the children. I have the *History of the Church* and the *Sermons* of Massillon read publicly to me at my meals. I will have no truck with the Imposter of *Annecy*, and I'll drag him openly before the Parliament of Dijon, if he has the audacity to take one step against the laws of the State."

There can be no question of the intention here; nor are we more edified when we see him, in 1770, under letters patent duly granted by the General at Rome,

becoming a father of the Capucin order. A pretty
father ! Well might he sign himself, as he often did,
" *Brother Voltaire, unworthy Capucin.*" But there was
no denying the authorisation, and the Bishop of Annecy
might say what he pleased.

We may turn now from these disgraceful adventures
to more congenial aspects of the Patriarch.

During the later years of his residence at Ferney,
much time was devoted to the vindication of young
d'Etallonde, and the revision of the sentence on Lally,
who had been executed for his failure to hold Pondi-
cherry for the French. In the case of d'Etallonde,
he does not appear to have been successful, though he
never slackened his efforts; but Lally was rehabilitated,
fifteen years after the promulgation of the sentence,
and only a few days before the death of his defender.
Much time, also, was devoted to the protection of the
people of Gex, by preserving them from the depredations
of the Farmers General.

And all the while, this extraordinary Patriarch was
capering, if he spoke the truth, on the very edge of the
tomb. There is hardly a letter in which he does not
complain of his maladies, and hardly one which is not
signed with some melancholy reminder, such as " the
sick old man," " the poor old invalid," " *Le Vieux
Malade de Ferney.*" Doctor Burney, who saw him
in 1770, said: " It is not easy to conceive it possible
for life to subsist in a form so nearly composed of mere
skin and bone as that of M. de Voltaire. He complained of decrepitude, and said, he supposed I was
curious to form an idea of the figure of one walking
after death." And Doctor John Moore, the ingenious
author of *Zeluco,* expressed himself in the same style:
" The first idea which has presented itself to all who

have attempted a description of his person, is that of a skeleton."

Yet we should observe, that in the whole of this long life of bewildering, incessant activity, of intense mental effort, there was never a period of real illness, apart from the attack of small-pox at Maisons in 1723, when Voltaire was in his twenty-ninth year. Nor was that vigorous mind ever quelled, until the very hour of death. His visitors at Ferney were always in amazement. Some of them were terrified by the alarming, the unaccountable vivacity, the fury and vehemence of this fragile creature. Was he possessed of a devil ? How could there be life enough in that poor little body, which looked so dry and brittle, to give to the eyes their piercing brilliance, or to fill the mind with so many inventions ?

Two late views of the Patriarch, by two observers essentially unlike each other, may be compared with advantage. The first of these is Madame Suard, a young and handsome woman, who, if a trifle vapid, was no fool. She was at Ferney in 1775, and although her posture is that of a devotee, her very devotion made her greedy of opportunity and gave her the desire to observe and record with the fullest possible detail. From the long accounts which she wrote to her husband, and which she intended only for his perusal, we take the following passages:

" I have at last reached the goal of my journey and my desires: I have seen M. de Voltaire. . . . Ah ! how greatly was I astonished when, instead of the decrepit figure I thought to see, I beheld this countenance full of fire and expression; when, instead of an old bent man, I saw one who was upright, noble and elevated, tho' free, with a carriage firm and even sprightly, and with a tone, a politeness which, like his genius, are uniquely his own ! . . . He spoke much of M. Turgot. 'He has three terrible enemies,' he said: 'financiers, rogues, and the gout.' I told him that one might oppose to them his virtues, his courage, and the esteem of the Publick. 'But, Madam, they tell me you are one of our enemies.' 'Come, Sir ! you will not believe what is wrote to you, but perhaps you will believe me. I am not the enemy of any one. I honour the virtues and the learning of M. Turgot ; but I recognize in M. Necker, also, great virtues and great learning, which I honour equally. . . .' As I pronounced these words in a serious, emphatick tone, M. de Voltaire seem'd to fear he had offended me. 'Come, Madam,' said he with a benevolent air; 'compose yourself. God will bless you, for you know how to love your friends. I am by no means the enemy of M. Necker, but you will forgive me if I prefer M. Turgot. Let's say no more of it.' "

A few days later, Madame Suard wrote one of the most intimate and most engaging accounts of the Patriarch which have been preserved. She had risen early, and was admitted to the bedroom of the great man :

" I sat down by the side of his bed, which is extremely simple and of the most perfect neatness. He was sitting up, straight and steady, like a youth of twenty years; he had a pretty waistcoat of white satin, a nightcap tied on with a very becoming ribbon. He has no other writing table by the side of this bed, where he is continually at work, but a chess table. I was struck

by the order of his cabinet: 'tis not like *yours*, with books
all over the place and great piles of paper; all is arrang'd;
and he knows so well the places where his books are
kept, that, when he wished to consult a *memoir* on the
suit of M. de Guines, which we were talking of at the
moment—' Wagnière,' said he to his secretary, ' my
good Wagnière, prithee take this memoir from the
third shelf on the left '—and there it actually was.
There was a vast quantity of pens upon his writing
table. I begged him to allow me to take one, which
I would guard as the most precious of relicks; and he
himself aided me in finding one with which he had
written the most. He has by the side of his bed the
portrait of Madame du Châtelet, whom he remembers
with the truest affection. But within his bed-hangings
are the two engravings of the Calas family. I still
remember the one which represents the wife and children
of this victim of Fanatism embracing their father at
the moment when he is being led away to the torture.
. . . I reproached M. de Voltaire for having placed
it so that it was always before his eyes. ' Ah, Madam !
for eleven years I was occupied continually with that
unhappy family and the family of Sirven; and in all
that time, Madam, I reproached myself, as for a crime,
whenever I found that I was smiling.' "

On the occasion of another visit, she found that the
Patriarch had dressed himself up to receive her. He
had put on his best perruque and a magnificent dressing-
gown. " See ! " cried Madame de Luchet as he came
out of his room; " is he not fine ? And you, Madam,
are the object of this coquetry."

" M. de Voltaire smiled with benevolence, and with
a sort of charming confusion at being catch'd in this

little folly. His smile, so full of grace, reminded me of the statue by *Pigalle*, which has preserved some of its character. I told him I had made haste to view the statue and had kiss'd it. ' And it kiss'd you back again, did it not ? ' cried M. de Voltaire."

Madame Suard observed, as others did, that Voltaire was not always treated with kindness and understanding by his niece, and by those who lived with him. We know, indeed, that Mignot Denis was a hard, stupid, mercenary woman, who regarded her uncle merely as a source of distinction or profit. Her actions after his death are sufficient proof of her aims and character. Nor was Tronchin, the great Theodore, as good a friend as he might have been.

" I observe with pain that the persons around him, and even his niece, have none of those little indulgences to which his age and feebleness properly entitle him. He is often looked upon as a teasy child; as if, at eighty years of age, he might not be expected, after entertaining a company for three hours together, to feel the need of rest—and is it not a very real need ? They are scarce ever willing to believe that he suffers; it seems as tho' no one wishes to pity him. This air of unconcern, which struck me very much to-day, has angered me and touched me to the very heart."

From this attitude of sentimental devotion, marked by real sensibility and real insight, we turn to the impressions of Madame de Genlis; a woman of strict morals, rigid orthodoxy, and a less impulsive nature. She disliked Voltaire, and went to see him through mere curiosity, determined to preserve a stately balance and to show, if there was need to, her disapproval of his teachings. She was accompanied by Mr Ott, a German painter who was returning from Italy.

On their way to the house, they looked with pious horror at Voltaire's church, and the dreadful inscription above the door. Admitted to the antechamber of Ferney, Mr Ott was not slow to perceive a picture hanging in a dark corner. "Correggio !" he cried, with joy if not with discernment. And it was indeed, according to Mr Ott and Madame de Genlis, "a fine original painting of Correggio." Then, with Madame de Genlis maintaining "all the tranquillity of her deportment," they were introduced to the great man. Mr Ott, his head all in a whirl of excitement, produced from his pocket some miniature copies which he had made in Rome, and eagerly handed them to Monsieur de Voltaire. Among them was a picture of the Virgin and Child. Monsieur de Voltaire permitted himself to utter "several impieties," while Madame de Genlis turned away, "extremely shocked," to Monsieur de Voltaire's niece.

Things were no better at dinner. "M. de Voltaire was anything but amiable: he seemed to be always quarrelling with his people, shouting at the top of his voice, with such force that I trembled involuntarily several times; the dining room is very resonant, and his thundering tones rang out in the most terrifying manner. They had warned me of this fashion of his, which is so unseemly before strangers, and one perceives at once 'tis a habit, for his people appeared to be not in the least surprized or troubled." After dinner, they drove out in the *berline* to look at the village of Ferney, and here, at least, was something which Madame de Genlis could admire without injury to her conscience.

"He took us into the village to view the houses he

has built and the benevolent institutions he has promoted. Here he is greater than in his books, for one sees everywhere a thoughtful goodness, and one can scarce believe that the same hand which has wrote such impiety, such wickedness and falsehood, could have made such wise, noble and useful things. He shows his village to all visitors, but with a becoming air; he talks of it simply and frankly; he explains what he has done, but without the least kind of boastfulness."

She gives a vivid picture of the Patriarch himself— a picture full of detail and character, but differing in more than one respect from the inspired portrait of Madame Suard:

" All the portraits and all the *bustos* of M. de Voltaire are of an exact likeness, but no artist has properly represented his eyes: I expected to see them brilliant and full of fire; they are, indeed, the most animated I have seen, but they have, at the same time, something tender and an inexpressible sweetness; the soul of *Zaïre* is all in these eyes; the extreme *malice* of his laugh and smile changes at once this charming expression. He is much bent, and his *Gothick* manner of attiring himself makes him appear even older. He has a sepulchral voice, which gives a singular tone to what he says, the more so as he is in the habit of speaking with excessive loudness, tho' he is not at all deaf. When there is no question of his enemies or of religion, his conversation is simple and natural, with no pretention, and consequently (with such a genius as his) perfectly delightful. It seemed to me that he would not allow any one, upon any subject, to hold an opinion contrary to his own; as soon as he is contradicted, his tone becomes sharp and piercing; he has certainly forgot much of the polite usage which

he ought to possess, and nothing is more easily understood: since he has been in this place, he is only visited
by those who intoxicate him with their praises, his
decisions are oracles, all his neighbours are at his feet;
he hears of nothing save of the admiration which he
inspires, and the most ridiculous exaggerations of this
kind appear to him as ordinary compliments."

CHAPTER IX

THE tragedy of *Irène* had been accepted by the players of the Comédie in January, 1778, and the rehearsal of this work seemed to Voltaire a favourable occasion for a visit to Paris.

Louis XV had died in 1774, and Louis XVI and his young queen Marie Antoinette were seated upon the precarious throne of France. But the court, fatally adhering to orthodoxy of the most rigorous kind, was not well disposed towards the Patriarch.

A dimly apprehended knowledge of insecurity may even then have stiffened the enmity of Versailles against those who were leading the intellectual revolution. Then, as in other countries at other times, any attack directed against the church could not fail to strike at the principles of monarchy. It is only necessary to add to these considerations the natural hostility which is always excited by men of greatly superior intelligence, in order to understand the attitude of Louis and his courtiers. The queen, it is true, did not conform to this attitude. She, with her dislike of stuffy decorums, and with all the vivacious curiosity of a young woman, would gladly have met Monsieur de Voltaire and listened to his amusing talk. But Louis, dull, saintly man, fumbling with his poor hobbies and blundering amiably among his bewildered ministers, could not hear of Monsieur de Voltaire without exasperation.

Lekain was to have played in *Irène*; but Lekain, with the petulance and caprice of a great actor, suddenly declined. However excusable mere petulance may be in the irresponsible constitution of an artist, ingratitude is less easily defended, and Lekain, who had been discovered by Voltaire and who owed so much to the friendship of his patron, was acting here in a way which distressed even his fellow players. Voltaire, who might well have been enraged, behaved with dignity and circumspection. He wrote to Lekain expressing his willingness to abide by his decision, yet still hoping that he would play a part in the tragedy. It seemed more than ever desirable to visit Paris.

Voltaire had not set foot in Paris for twenty-eight years—not since the day on which he started for Potsdam. He had a great longing to return, to see his " dear angels," and feel himself in the full tide of intellectual life. He was not formally exiled. The avowed displeasure and insulting coldness of Louis XV, and the solid front of his enemies at Versailles, had deterred him from running the risk of danger or disgrace. Now, so it seemed, he had less to fear. Yet, even while he was contemplating the journey, he felt himself broken in health, and more likely to embark upon " the little voyage of eternity." He had been working with feverish anxiety upon the tragedies of *Irène* and *Agathocles*; he was excited by all the delights and all the terrors of his project. An old man of eighty-four, feeling himself near the end of a long and strenuous life, might well hesitate before facing the discomfort, the perils of a journey at the dreariest season of the year. But his mind was made up (Mignot Denis had no wish to deter him), and on the 4th of February he left Ferney.

Six days later, his travelling coach, heated by a portable stove, reached the barriers of Paris. The customs men asked if there was anything to be declared.

" Faith, gentlemen," said the Patriarch, " I think there is nothing contraband here except myself." Wagnière stepped out of the coach, and one of the guards, having a clearer view of who was inside it, turned with excitement to his comrade: " By the Lord ! 'tis Monsieur de Voltaire." Already the face and form of this great man were familiar to the people of Paris, as the face and form of—let us say —Mr. Bernard Shaw are familiar to the Londoners of the present time. Guards and revenue officers, withdrawing with respect and many comical salutes, begged Monsieur to continue his journey.

It was about half-past three in the afternoon. Voltaire, gay and smiling, rattled away in the merriest manner, so great his joy at seeing once more the busy streets of Paris. He was to stay in the very house in the Rue de Beaune where, in his youth, he had lived with Madame de Bernières, and which now belonged to his friend the Marquis de Villette.

After a cursory glance at his new quarters, he hurried off, walking briskly, to see d'Argental. The " angels " were living not far away, on the Quai d'Orsay.

Nothing could have been more touching than the meeting between these two affectionate old men, these lifelong friends who had been separated now for so many years. At first there was only weeping, embracing, a few halting words, a joyous confusion. Then came the news. Lekain was dead. He had died only two days previously, not long after he had played in a successful revival of *Adélaïde du Guesclin*. That was bad news for Voltaire; he had lost, not only a man of whom he was extremely fond, but the actor he had most desired to see in *Irène*. He did not think of Lekain's ungracious refusal, or of the strange letter he had received from him not long before leaving Ferney. And the loss was more than personal: Lekain at the Comédie held the same position that Garrick held at Drury Lane; he was by far the most brilliant and most versatile actor of his period.

But no grief could endure for long amid the happy influences that now surrounded him, and Voltaire was soon talking gaily with his visitors. These visitors, indeed, gave him little peace. They came every day to the Rue de Beaune, and were received in the salon by Madame Denis, fat, pretentious and affable, and the young Marquise de Villette—*Belle et Bonne*.

" Monsieur de Voltaire," said Linguet, " has quitted the woods of Ferney which he has sung, the houses of Ferney which he has ′built, the quiet of Ferney with which he was so well content, for the mud, the noise and the incense of Paris."

All day long the amazing old man, in nightcap and flowered dressing-gown, received the friendly multitudes. He was radiant. He had the elaborate courtesy and studied graces of an earlier period; he spoke with happy allusions, a nimbleness of mind and memory, a kindness which touched the heart, a humour which charmed the imagination. All that was good and lovable, all that was gay and pleasing in this versatile nature, had free play. He seemed to have a renewed youth, a gift of energy rarely seen in so old a man. But, standing a little apart, grim Theodore Tronchin, now installed in Paris—grim Doctor Theodore watched him with professional curiosity. This cannot last for long, thought the Doctor; he is spending his capital instead of living upon his income; and how interesting—yes ! how extremely interesting it will be to observe in what manner he greets the last visitor—death.

The court must have learnt of this popular and social demonstration with a sort of uneasiness. M. de Voltaire was clearly overshadowing every other man in Paris—in France—perhaps in Europe. It was not at all agreeable to see such honours accorded openly to an infidel, and one who had spoken so rudely and roughly about the church and the government of the land. Had he not called his own countrymen *Welches*, barbarians, savages ? Why, then, was all Paris hastening to see this detestable creature ? " Monsieur de Voltaire ? " said the king with affected carelessness: " Monsieur de Voltaire ?—ah yes !—he is in Paris, I believe; though not with my approval." But the French populace, so flighty and wayward, has always loved a hero, has always been ready enough to flow with a blind violence of enthusiasm towards a great man, especially towards a man of singular personality, and above all towards a man who has cleverly abused them.

What is more, the shadow of coming changes was already felt by the people; and those who were observant could see it beginning to spread over the whole face of society. Already Versailles was left to its own dreary devices of self-destruction, and even the genius of Turgot had been unable to restore credit. It was not for nothing that people in the street pressed forward to see " the defender of Calas." In their eyes, Calas represented the people themselves; people who were now preparing their own defence, and to whom Voltaire had become a symbol of justice and toleration.

Among the visitors in the Rue de Beaune was the Commissioner from America, that grave and venerable man, Doctor Benjamin Franklin. He came with his grandson, for whom he asked " a blessing." The boy knelt reverently, and Voltaire, placing his hands on the bowed head, spoke those memorable words: *God and Liberty*. Those words were spoken in English, with a fervour and simplicity so touching that all those who were in the room were profoundly moved.

There were visitors of a less welcome sort. Before he had been many days in Paris, Voltaire received a letter from the Abbé Gaultier. The Abbé, who was a Jesuit, and had been the curé of Saint-Marc in the diocese of Rouen for twenty years, seems to have been a worthy and charitable man. His letter, a little grim at first glance, had evidently been dictated by a kindly spirit:

" Sir, there are many persons who admire you, and I desire with all my heart to be of their number; if you consent, I may have that privilege; it does but depend on you. . . . Although I am the most unworthy of all ministers, I will say nothing unworthy of my ministry and nothing which could be unpleasing to you. And if I dare not flatter myself that you will bestow such happiness upon me, I shall none the less remember you in the Holy Sacrifice of the Mass, and I shall pray the just and merciful God, with all the fervour of which I am capable, for the welfare of your immortal soul, which is perhaps soon to be judg'd for all its actions. Forgive me, Sir, if I take a liberty in writing to you: my intention is to render you the greatest of all services; I may do so with the help of Him, who chooses the weakest to confound those who are most mighty."

Voltaire was not wrong in forming his opinion of the writer:

"Your letter, Sir, appears to me that of an honest man. . . . I am eighty-four years old; I must soon appear before God, Maker of all the Worlds. If you have something to tell me, I shall think it a duty and an honour to receive your visit."

On receiving this answer, Gaultier at once proceeded to the Rue de Beaune.

It is necessary here to remind ourselves that Voltaire was a man of policy. He had no wish to be troubled by the church, and he had no wish to embitter the last days of his life by a violent controversy. He wanted to be left in peace; and to leave others in peace. And there was another reason for his willingness to see the Abbé. He had often expressed the fear that his body might be buried, like that of poor Adrienne Lecouvreur, in waste ground, without the decency of ceremonial and the honour of a tomb. This fear, a little odd in one so philosophic, became more intense as he grew older. And the one way to avoid this ignominy was to die as a Christian. In considering his last dealings with the clergy, these motives have to be taken into account; nor must we forget the ugly farce of the Easter Communions, in which he showed to what length he was prepared to go in matters of strategical conformity.

The Abbé Gaultier was received in a manner almost cordial, and listened to with patience. When he had proved that he came on his own initiative, and not as the result of any move on the part of the Archbishop or of the curé of the parish (Saint-Sulpice), Voltaire appeared to be deeply touched.

"And what did you think of the Abbé, Sir?" asked Wagnière when the visitor had gone. "He is a good-natur'd old imbecile," replied the grinning Patriarch.

On the day following this interview with Gaultier there came to the Rue de Beaune a visitor of a more congenial kind—indeed, none could have been more congenial—old Madame du Deffand.

By the end of the month, the strain of all this excitement, as Tronchin had anticipated, began to take effect. On the 25th there was a violent spitting of blood, followed by a state of extreme lassitude. A very experienced young woman was called in to nurse the sick man, to see that the doctor's instructions were carried out, and to shut the door in the face of importunate visitors. On the 2nd of March, Voltaire, lying extenuated upon his bed, received the Abbé Gaultier and told him that he desired to make his confession. Wagnière's comic anxiety that his master should not "dishonour" himself was somewhat out of place, and when he was questioned as to the cause of his agitation he "could find no answer." Voltaire and Gaultier were left alone in the room, and in a little while Voltaire called for paper, pen and ink.

What had taken place between the two men? We cannot say; we have only the evidence of the strange document to which Voltaire now set his hand, and that document is not an orthodox confession of faith. Such as it is, it should be read with attention, for it is on the evidence of this alleged "recantation," and on this alone, that we are asked to believe in the sincerity of Voltaire's repentance and the intensity of his desire to be received again into the church.

"I, the undersigned, declare that, having suffered from a spitting of blood for four months, at the age of eighty-four years, and having been unable to drag myself to the church, and the curé of Saint-Sulpice having willingly added to his good works that of sending to me the Abbé Gaultier, priest, I have confess'd to him, and that, if God will dispose of me, I die in the Catholick religion in which I was born, hoping the Divine Mercy will deign to pardon all my faults, and that if ever I have scandalized the church I seek the pardon of the church and of God.—Signed VOLTAIRE, the second of March, 1778, in the house of Monsieur le Marquis de Villette."

Now, Gaultier knew well enough that this was not a retraction, or a confession of faith, in accordance with the forms of the church: and if he dictated it, as he is supposed to have done, he could only have regarded it as a preliminary measure. When the Abbé Mignot (Voltaire's nephew) and de Villeveille were called into the room, Gaultier was therefore expressing himself truly in saying " Here is a little declaration which has no great meaning." It was, moreover, written entirely by the hand of Voltaire.

Only two days before, the Patriarch had signed his true profession; a statement in which it seems to us that the whole character of the old man is nobly revealed:

" I die adoring God, loving my friends, not hating my enemies, and detesting superstition."

There can be no reason for refusing to believe that Voltaire was perfectly sincere when he wrote those words, conforming as they do to the essential ideas of his philosophy, if not to his invariable practice. There was never the slightest doubt as to what he understood by superstition.

On the other hand, there are many reasons, as we have tried to show, for believing that the Gaultier document was merely a declaration of policy. Nor can it be urged that, when he saw Gaultier, the fear of imminent death was upon him. It seems far otherwise, for he was then recovering from his collapse, and the fact that he wrote the document with his own hand proves the degree of recovery. When he was afterwards reproached or taunted by his friends for having made so great a concession to the church, he replied airily that he had done so in order " to get a little peace." That was not a full explanation, because, as we have seen, he was anxious to secure a decent burial, but it probably explains his attitude towards the clergy of Paris. Observe, there was no question of receiving the sacraments ; and there could have been no such question without the preliminaries of true confession and absolution. Clearly, neither confession nor absolution had taken place. And if any doubt existed, that doubt was finally removed by the last efforts of the church to obtain a death-bed confession, and by the action of the Archbishop of Paris in refusing to allow the rites of Christian burial. This refusal was only justified on the ground that Voltaire was not, at the time of his death, a member of the Catholic church.

The whole position was admirably summarised by Madame du Deffand in a letter to Horace Walpole. Walpole had been told of the alleged retraction, and took it for a sign of weakness. Madame du Deffand corrected him with some asperity:

" You have a great and good intelligence, but it does not always preserve you from certain errours of judgement; I know this by experience, and I see it now in the case of Voltaire. You do not properly judge the motives of his behaviour. He would be mightily vexed if any one thought he had changed his way of thinking; and all that he has done, has been done for the sake of *decorum*, and in order that he might be left in *peace*." And if any one had a right to know, Madame du Deffand certainly had that right.

Soon after the interview with Gaultier, Voltaire's health improved greatly; he was able to see his friends again, and to take a hand in preparing *Irène* for the stage. But he was still kept in bed, and when, on the 10th of March, the players assembled in the salon of Monsieur de Villette for a full rehearsal, Tronchin would not allow him to see them. Perhaps that was just as well, for the Patriarch treated the actors, even the great Vestris, with little regard for their feelings. No ! no ! Madam, he would cry; you are too calm; it will never do ! And then, raising his voice and waving his lean arms, the old man would stamp and rant, run here and there, now explaining and now declaiming, until they all expected to see him fall dead.

Irène was first played on the 14th of March. No first night had ever caused so much excitement, and seldom before had such a great and brilliant concourse filled the theatre. For the first time since his return to Paris, the court showed a friendly disposition towards Voltaire. There, in the royal box, was the queen, Marie Antoinette, the Duke and Duchess of Bourbon and the Count of Artois. And as the play went on, it was observed that the queen took a pencil and quickly wrote down the lines which pleased her.

The king stayed at home. He, indeed, showed no friendly disposition; there he sat in his palace, all dumb and cloudy like a man foredoomed. Perhaps he had made a stiff yet gentle remonstrance as he saw the young queen, in all the superb abundance of her beauty and all the bravery of dress and jewels, set out for the theatre. He had certainly refused to allow the reception of Monsieur de Voltaire at Versailles. How could he approve of a man whose teachings were so subversive and so disloyal ?

After the third act, a messenger hurried from the Comédie to the Rue de Beaune. The play was going very well; it was, indeed, already a triumph. Other messengers followed after the third and fourth acts. And when the last act was over, and the sound of tumultuous applause rose in the theatre, Monsieur Dupuits forced a passage through the crowd and ran to congratulate the author. Other friends made their way to the bedside, and the old man, smiling and delighted, asked them innumerable questions. Which lines, which sentiments had been the most applauded ? Those, to be sure, in which he was clearly attacking the clergy. Ah ! that was good: people would know what to think when they heard those ridiculous stories about his confession. *Irène* was not only a triumph; it was an affirmation of principle.

Monday, the 30th of March, was probably the happiest, and certainly the most triumphant, day of his life. It was the day of apotheosis. Voltaire seemed to have cheated the grave as he had cheated the church; he was weak, it is true, and more than ever like a skeleton; but Tronchin was more hopeful, and told him that he might safely venture to leave the house.

In the evening, the sixth representation of *Irène* was to take place at the Comédie. Voltaire had decided to be present, and before going to the theatre he would attend the special meeting of the Academy.

It was quickly known that Monsieur de Voltaire would drive in his coach from the Rue de Beaune to the Academy, and as the day was fine, though cold, the streets were soon filled with masses of excitable, happy and curious people. The coachman had no small difficulty in making his way through the cheering multitudes. In the courtyard of the Louvre there were at least two thousand people, all shouting *Vive Monsieur de Voltaire !* and clapping their hands.

To many of those who thus applauded, the old man in the coach was the author of *Candide* and the *Philosophick Dictionary* ; to others, he was the great dramatist who, for nearly half a century, had kept alive the great traditions of the French theatre; but to most of them, and perhaps to those who cheered loudest, he was the brave defender of the Calas family, of the Sirvens and La Barre.

The Academy, departing from its ordinary customs (a thing most unusual with academies), paid him extraordinary honours. All the members attended him in the great hall: " an honour never before accorded to any of its members, or even to foreign princes." The clerical members were absent—and was not that, in itself, an honour ? Voltaire was given the chair of the director, and was unanimously elected to his office, although such election was generally decided by lot. D'Alembert then proceeded to read to the assembly his *Elegy upon Despréaux*, in which he placed the author of *Merope* and the *Henriade* by the side of Boileau and Racine, and finally compared the style and character of the three great masters of French verse—Despréaux, Racine and Voltaire. He finished the discourse by a series of ingenious comparisons in which, however, there may seem to our modern taste an element of absurdity. " In conclusion," he said, " may we not add, in seeking among the masterpieces of the fine arts for an object serving us for a comparison between these three great writers, that the style of Despréaux, firm, correct and nervous, is well represented by the fine statue of the *Gladiator*; that of Racine, also correct, but softer and more rounded, by the *Venus de Medicis*; and that of Voltaire, supple, easy and ever noble, by the *Apollo Belvedere*?"

As for Voltaire, his eyes moist with delight and gratitude, he found it no easy matter to maintain the austere calm which was proper in such a man and in such a place. All the members rose and followed him to the outer hall—another unprecedented mark of distinction—and he entered his coach again to drive to the Comédie.

By this time, the crowds in the streets had become denser, and their enthusiasm had risen to an even higher pitch. Boys climbed upon the cornices of buildings, upon pillars and boundary stones, and every place from which they could get a view. People were even clambering upon the roofs of the houses, and seeking perilous perches on ladders and scaffolds. Persons of all ranks and ages took part in this ovation. Shouting and pushing with all the others, the powder knocked out of their wigs, and hats knocked awry on their heads, young noblemen waved their tasselled canes and cried loudly *Vive Voltaire!*

At the door of the theatre, it was necessary to protect the old man from the friendly violence of the crowd. No sooner had the coach come to a standstill than people climbed on the wheels, on the box, on every part that offered a footing or a holding, pushing their hands inside, to feel, if they could not see, Monsieur de Voltaire himself. Some one seized the hand of the Marquise de Villette, who was in the coach, and kissed it reverently, believing it to be the hand of the Patriarch.

With difficulty, Voltaire reached the vestibule. Women ran up, in a frenzy of excitement, to see the great man, to pull little tufts of fur out of his cloak (the gift of royal Catherine), to look closely at the old face, not diabolical now, but radiant with a simple joy, and perhaps a little frightened.

When it was known in the theatre that he had entered the box of the King's Gentlemen, and was hiding himself behind Madame Denis and *Belle et Bonne*, there was no stilling the uproar. The parterre claimed him. And when he appeared in the front of the box, between his niece and the marquise, the uproar was even greater. A new cry arose: The crown ! the crown !

On this, the actor Brizard entered the box and placed on the Patriarch's head, on the huge perruque with its grey bows, a wreath of laurel. " Ah ! " cried the old man; " you will make me die with all this glory!" And he took the wreath from his head and placed it in the fair hands of *Belle et Bonne*. New clamours, new insistence. The marquise tried in vain, all blushing and smiling, to put the crown back on the head of the delightfully obstinate Monsieur de Voltaire. This pretty play was ended by the Prince de Beauvau, who took the wreath and planted it respectfully but firmly on the grey perruque, while the cheering house gave token of its approval.

With the whole theatre full of the dust stirred by moving feet, full of cries and excitement, people kneeling, standing, crowding and talking together, fashionable ladies going down to the pit to have a better view, all the players ranged before the curtain, all the corridors blocked, it seemed as though the play could never begin. And when at last it did begin, no one paid the least attention to it. Voltaire, perhaps, had come to see the play, but all the people had come to see Voltaire. No one looked at the players, no one listened to the lines; but never was a play more furiously applauded.

When the curtain fell at the end of the last act, it did but mark the beginning of a loud and long ovation. It was impossible for any one to leave the theatre, nor did any one seem anxious to go.

Then the curtain rose again upon a most surprising scene.

One of the players, Mademoiselle La Chassaigne, had remembered how, six years before, there had been a little private apotheosis of Voltaire at Mademoiselle Clairon's rooms in the Rue du Bac. The bust of the poet had been saluted by a chosen company of friends, and verses had been recited in his honour. Was not this the occasion for a grander apotheosis, and one of a more public kind ? That was a fine idea, said the players; and by thus rendering homage to Voltaire they would express their own gratitude to the man who had done so much for them, and whose name had become one of the chief glories of the Comédie.

The bust of Voltaire was already standing in the foyer. Some burly fellows took the bust, pedestal and all, and set it down in the centre of the stage. It was a happy improvisation. The whole cast, with palms and garlands in their hands, ranged themselves in a semicircle round the bust; while behind them were the shifters and carpenters, all the humble folk of the theatre, who had assisted in the representation. When all this had been arranged (and it was only the work of a few moments), the curtain was hauled up, and the spectacle was greeted with sounds of indescribable enthusiasm.

In all the history of the theatre we have no record of a scene more extraordinary, more happily conceived, more touching.

First Brizard, still in the monk's dress in which he had played the part of *Léonce*, placed his wreath upon the bust. Then, amid a clamour of voices and the sounding of all the drums and trumpets in the orchestra, the other players followed his example. And as the bust could not support so many crowns, they were slung gaily over the bayonets of the stage guard, who improvised a triumphal arch.

Once more the old man had hidden away, but now he was called for by such a thunder of voices that he was obliged to show himself. There he stood, tears running from his eyes. It was all too much for him. And now Madame Vestris, advancing to the front of the stage with a paper in her hand, read aloud some verses which had just been composed, on the instant, by the Marquis de Saint-Marc. The verses were not good, but everything was good on that night of glory; the fine voice of Madame Vestris made them seem admirable indeed; and soon a hundred copies, industriously made (goodness knows by whom) were circulated among the audience.

After this, the curtain was lowered, and then raised again for a performance of Voltaire's comedy of *Nanine*. The bust had not been taken away, and there it stood in the middle of the stage while the actors played round it—another happy effect of improvisation which must have been exceedingly striking. Before the end of the play, it was seen that the Count of Artois, who had been at the Opera with the queen, was in his box. He arrived just in time to send the captain of his guards to Voltaire, with a message of royal congratulation.

319

The last scenes of this amazing night are well described by Grimm, a man not readily transported by enthusiasm, who was himself a witness of what took place:

" The moment when M. de Voltaire left the theatre seemed even more touching than that of his arrival; he looked as if broken beneath the weight of his years and of the laurels heaped upon his head. He appeared extremely moved; his eyes were still sparkling in the pallor of his countenance; but it seemed to us as tho' he was kept alive only by the sentiment of his *glory*. All the women stood waiting for him, both in the corridors and upon the staircase; they bore him along, as it were, in their arms, and 'tis thus he arrived at the steps of his coach. He was kept back, as long as possible, at the doors of the Comédie. The people cried out: *Torches, torches ! Let us have a good look at him !* Once he was in his coach, the crowd pressed all around him; people got up on the step and clung to the doors of the coach in order to kiss his hands. Some of the common people began to shout: *'Tis he who wrote Oedipus, Merope, Zaïre; 'tis he who has sung of our good king, etc.* They begged the coachman to walk his horses, so that they might follow him, and a great number of persons accompanied him thus, crying out *Vive Voltaire !* as far as the Pont-Royal."

Among those who thus followed the coach there must have been many who, fifteen years later, followed, with acclamations of another kind, the grim carriages which took so many of those who had been among that gay audience to their death on a bloody scaffold. In those days, men thought again of Voltaire and again honoured him, not as the man who " had written *Merope* and sung of our good king, etc.," but as the man who had fought the Infamous and avenged the memory of Calas and Sirven.

When he found himself back in the Rue de Beaune, the old man gave way to a flood of tears. So much happiness, so much glory and excitement in one day was too much for his endurance. Yet he was able, the next day, to see a multitude of friends and to busy himself with the ordinary concerns of his life.

It is probable that he had now made up his mind to return to Ferney; but Madame Denis, that vain and selfish woman, would hear of no such thing. Why should they go back to the desolate Jura slopes, when they might so well stay among the delights of Paris ?

Madame Denis, the niece of the great man, was giving herself prodigious airs; she was meeting the aristocracy, and playing a part which (in her own view) suited her to perfection. She had no affection for her uncle, as we have said already, and although we will not suppose that she desired his death, she could certainly anticipate that death without misgivings. By the terms of Voltaire's will, Madame Denis was the " universal inheritor "—or, as we should now say, the residuary legatee—and as there were only a few special legacies, practically the whole of the estate became her own.

It was certainly in accordance with her suggestion that Voltaire began to look for a house in Paris. On the 27th of April he acquired a mansion belonging to M. de Villarceaux, to be leased for life in his name and that of Madame Denis, but he did not live to occupy his new residence.

In the meantime, recovered from his fatigue, he seemed surprisingly well. He went about freely, and wherever he went, he was still the hero of the people.

" He is followed in the streets by the common folk,"
wrote Madame du Deffand to Walpole, " who call him
l'homme aux Calas. 'Tis only the court which abstains
from enthusiasm. He is eighty-four years old, and
in truth I believe he is immortal; he rejoices in all his
senses, not one of which is weakened; 'tis a very singular
creature, and one who is indeed very superiour to others."

There can be little doubt that, if he had not left
Ferney, he might have lived for many more years.
As it was, the strain, the varying excitements of his life
in Paris could have but one result. He was, in
Tronchin's phrase, " living upon his capital," and before
long the capital was exhausted.

Exactly one week after the apotheosis at the Comédie,
Voltaire was the recipient of a new and peculiar honour.
He was invited by the Freemasons of Paris to a meeting
at the lodge of the Nine Sisters. Here, without preliminaries, he was made a brother of the order. Only
those who are themselves Masons can be aware of the
scope and value of this tremendous privilege. We
can only repeat reverently how the " brethren of the
columns of Euterpe, Terpsichore and Erato " executed
" the first part of the third symphony for grand orchestra
by Guenin " ; how brother Chic led the second fiddles;
how the newly elected brother Voltaire " after having
received the signs, words and touchings," was placed
in the Orient (whatever that may mean); and how a
brother of the column of Melpomene placed on the
head of brother Voltaire a crown of laurels, which he
quickly removed. After that, the Venerable Lalande
tied round the waist of brother Voltaire the apron of
brother Helvetius, given to the lodge by the widow of
that illustrious man, and brother Voltaire kissed the
apron before receiving it. When he was presented

with a pair of woman's gloves, as ritual prescribed, he handed them to brother Marquis de Villette, saying prettily: " As these are the signs of a tender, honest and deserved affection, I beg you to give them to *Belle et Bonne.*"

There followed a series of congratulatory and flattering speeches, while brother Monet, painter to the king, was stealthily employed with his pencil and drew a clever likeness of the Patriarch. Then the orchestra renewed the symphony and the brethren moved into the banqueting hall. After the toasts had been drunk, brother Voltaire asked permission to retire; he was escorted to the door by the greater number of the brethren, and there he was awaited by the usual cheering crowd.

Having dined at home, he showed himself to the people, as a king might have done, on the balcony of the house, between the Count d'Argental and M. de Thibouville. Indeed, there were many who spoke now, some with affection and some with irony, of *le roi Voltaire*—King Voltaire.

The day of the Nine Sisters was concluded by a visit to the house of Madame de Montesson, the secretly married wife of the Duke of Orleans. Of all the royal princes, d'Orleans was the only one with a real taste for letters, philosophy and the drama. He was delighted to receive the man of whom all Paris was now talking, and the warm sincerity of his welcome may have atoned in some measure for the official attitude of the court.

The last great literary work in which Voltaire was concerned was the new dictionary of the Academy. He had been for a long while persuaded of the need for this dictionary, and on the 7th of May he presented to the Academy a comprehensive plan for the work, which, after discussion, was finally approved.

For more than a week he applied himself with all his energy, with an unlicensed degree of energy, to the preliminaries of this formidable undertaking. He stimulated or refreshed himself by drinking innumerable cups of coffee; but he was now drawing too largely upon his capital, and nature could allow no further advances. The renal disease from which he had been suffering for a considerable time began to gain ground, and there were ugly signs of inflammation and of functional derangement. At the same time, a senile disorder of the prostate became only too apparent, and soon Tronchin was shaking his professional head, and again wondering, in his cool and cruel fashion, how this curious patient would meet his death.

But he was not dead yet; he was, on the contrary, extraordinarily active, and still enjoying his days of triumph and his minor apotheoses.

One evening he had gone to see *Alzire* played. He had gone incognito—as though he could escape recognition !—and was in the box of Madame Hébert. He had determined to be good and quiet, but he had never in his life been able to watch a play without forgetting himself and letting loose some ejaculation of anger, contempt, or approval. At the end of the fourth act he betrayed his presence. Delighted by the fine acting of Larive, he sprang up with gleaming eyes and cried out: " Admirable ! " Every one in the theatre turned towards the box, and M. de Voltaire was acclaimed with frenzied enthusiasm. All through the entr'acte it was one continuous demonstration of joy, and when the curtain rose for the fifth act, and

Madame Vestris tried to carry on the performance, she could not make herself heard.

Voltaire, who could not make himself heard any better, thanked the audience by his gestures; and with other gestures pleaded for silence. The play started again, but the people could not restrain their excitement, and soon the clapping and calling were as loud as ever. No matter: the act proceeded, and we are assured that it had a prodigious effect, and was never played more magnificently or seen with greater appreciation. And as he was about to leave the theatre, Voltaire was respectfully accosted by " an officer in the regiment of the Orleans Infantry," who handed him a copy of four impromptu verses. The verses compared the author of *Alzire* to the sun in the firmament, and the people in the pit to a company of worshipping Incas: a compliment to which the author quickly and happily replied by a parody of two of his own lines.

Another emotional scene took place at a meeting of the Academy of Sciences. Voltaire was not a member of that Academy, and he attended the meeting as a guest, but he could not prevent it from being known that he intended to be present, and the hall was filled with pretty, excited women, elegant young men, writers, philosophers and critics.

The fellows of the Academy insisted on Voltaire taking his place among them. Here he met the " foreign associate," Benjamin Franklin, and again the two old men fell into each other's arms, while the whole assembly cheered and stamped and shouted in a long delirium of hero-worship.

D'Alembert proceeded to read the elegy of a deceased member, written by Condorcet, who was himself unable to attend the meeting. Ingenious allusions to Voltaire were cleverly interpolated, and these allusions were not lost upon the responsive audience.

The occasion was not a happy one for poor M. Macquer, who now had to read his paper on *How to make out of imperfectly ripen'd Grapes a Wine quite free from any Trace of Sourness.* It may have been a very excellent and interesting paper, but the people in the hall were not disposed to listen with the full attention it properly deserved. They had not come in order to learn what to do with imperfectly ripened grapes. Nor were they more disposed to hear two more dull elegies by Condorcet.

We need not suppose that the homage of the Academy of Sciences was of a purely fortuitous description, and a mere reflection of the popular mood. It was the Academy which had printed Voltaire's *Essay on Fire*, and which had approved of his work on *The Principles of Newton.* Voltaire, if he was never more than a distinguished amateur in the sciences, was a man of recognised scientific ability; and we may note that he had been elected a fellow of our own Royal Society in 1743.

At the beginning of May, Voltaire was rapidly declining, and by the middle of the month it was clear that he had not much longer to live. At last the grand energies were failing and the busy mind was dark and troubled. He was unable to attend a meeting of the Academy on the 11th, though he was still occupied with the plan of the dictionary and still able to discuss matters with his friends. He kept his brain stimulated by incessant draughts of coffee, and he dulled the pains of his body, as best he could, by doses of laudanum. After the 18th he seems to have been too unwell for sustained intellectual work. His last verses, gay and full of spirit, were written on the 16th for the old Abbé L'Attaignant, one of the ancient revellers of the Temple. There are two short undated notes, written, as Bauchot so pathetically observes, " in a trembling hand," which were sent to Doctor Tronchin, probably about the 24th or 25th.

" Your old patient has the fever. The legs of his glorious body are much swollen and covered with red patches. This morning, he wished to transport himself to the Temple of Aesculapius; he could not do so."

And the later of the two:

" The patient of the Rue de Beaune has suffered all night, and still suffers, from a violent convulsive cough. He has spat blood three times. He begs pardon for giving so much trouble over a mere carcase."

To this note there was fastened by two wafers a dirty playing card, on which he had written:

" *Non cecedit. Panem mitto. Non in solo pane vivit homo, sed in omni verbo quod oritur ex ore Tronchin.*"

Last of all, dated the 26th of May, and gloriously concluding his immense and vigorous correspondence, is a note written in his own hand to the Count de Lally. The verdict of the parliament which had condemned Lally's father to death had just been rescinded, and Voltaire was thus assured of a final victory over the Infamous. No news could have been more grateful to him.

" The dying man," he wrote, " comes back to life on hearing this great news; he tenderly embraces M. de Lally; he sees that the king is the defender of justice; he will die content."

When he spoke of " coming back to life," he spoke truly. He had been lying in bed for many days, with hardly a word, hardly a movement. The news of Lally's vindication, the triumph of his last and not least glorious cause, filled him with a noble, invigorating joy.

Not content with writing his note to Lally, he had a little placard written out and pinned to his bed-curtain: " On the 16th of May, the juridical murder committed by Pasquier on the person of Lally has been avenged by the King's Council." Now, indeed, might the weary soldier die content, with a sound of victory in his ears.

We have no wish to pry with unwholesome curiosity into the circumstances of his death. Nor is it possible to depend with complete reliance upon any account of these circumstances. The enemies of the old man would have us believe that he faced death with a hideous terror, with agony unspeakable and with a dreadful violence of word and action. Such an end would have allowed the church to point a warning moral, and to exhibit the last moments of the mocker with a grim satisfaction. There were many churchmen to whom that satisfaction would have given the most acute pleasure. On the other hand, his friends, and those who were actually present (with the exception of Tronchin, who was unaccountably spiteful) would have us believe the exact opposite. One thing, at least, is abundantly clear: there was no final " recantation," no ceremony of penitence, and no acceptance of the Catholic discipline. Gaultier, who presented himself almost daily in the Rue de Beaune, had been refused admittance, and when, on the day of Voltaire's death, the 30th of May, he arrived with de Tersac, the curé of Saint-Sulpice, he was not successful in obtaining any addition to the " profession of faith " which he had secured in March. We are inclined to believe, after the most complete investigation which is now possible, that Voltaire died peacefully. In this, we agree with Desnoiresterres; and we do not see how it could have been otherwise. Aft · the flicker of animation on the 26th, Voltaire had s ık almost to the level of unconsciousness. His :ail body was exhausted; his mind and senses were mercifully numbed by copious doses of laudanum.

The story of the last efforts of the church, represented by Gaultier and de Tersac, is well known, and may be taken as authentic in substance. It should be noted, in La Harpe's account, that there was some difficulty in making Voltaire understand that these men desired to see him, and that, when he knew they were waiting outside the door, he murmured faintly but inconsequently: " Assure them of my respects."

De Tersac, a loud, arrogant, stupid man, entirely without gentleness or decorum, approached the bedside with a sort of desperate importunity: " Monsieur de Voltaire, you have reached the end of your life; do you acknowledge the divinity of Jesus Christ ? " At this, Voltaire, turning wearily towards him, replied: " *Leave me to die in peace.*"

Various accounts add other words, and describe various gestures; but these words—" Leave me to die in peace "—are cited independently, and there seems good reason to believe they were actually spoken.

" Ah ! " said de Tersac, with a movement of exasperation: " you see, he has lost his senses." And the two priests left the room.

This interview took place between seven and eight o'clock in the evening, and at eleven o'clock Voltaire died.

No account which can bear the test of close examination has any details to add to the above. The horrible particulars which are given in such documents as the anonymous *Enquiry* published for the first time in 1908 by Lachèvre are entirely unconvincing, and in nearly every case the documents provide internal evidence both of prejudice and of falsity.

Was there, in those last moments, a struggle between pride and fear? We cannot say, and there can be little interest in knowing. The Marquise de Villette, *Belle et Bonne*, who seldom left the sick man's room, and was present at the moment of his death, told Lady Morgan that he died placidly. "To the very last moment," she said, "everything showed the goodness and benevolence of his character, everything bespoke tranquillity, peace and resignation, except the little movement of impatience which he exhibited towards the curé of Saint-Sulpice, when he begged him to retire, and said, *Leave me to die in peace.*"

The Archbishop of Paris, to the shame and scandal of those (and they were the most numerous) who believed Voltaire the greatest man in France, refused burial in consecrated ground. This refusal must have been known in some way, or at least anticipated, almost immediately after Voltaire's death, for the body was hastily embalmed during the night and conveyed in a travelling coach the next day to the Abbey of Scellières. Here, through the offices of the Abbé Mignot, it was buried with the rites of the church. The heart of Voltaire was placed in a casket and given to the Marquis de Villette.

In 1791, when so many castles of the Infamous had been taken by storm, with the king a prisoner in the Tuileries and the Bastille an empty shell, the body of Voltaire was brought back to Paris for a new triumph.

A decree of the National Assembly, dated the 8th of May, 1791, ordered the removal of the body from the Abbey of Scellières to the parish church of Romilly. On the 30th of May, there was another decree:

"The National Assembly, having listened to the report of the Committee of the Constitution, decrees that Marie-François Arouet de Voltaire is worthy to receive the honours accorded to great men; and that, in consequence, his ashes are to be transferred from the church of Romilly to that of Saint-Geneviève in Paris."

Charron, the master of the pageant, went to Romilly to escort the body to Paris; and in Paris, meanwhile, the Marquis de Villette and *Belle et Bonne*, the friends of Voltaire, were to make ready for his reception. At ten o'clock on the evening of the 10th of July, the funeral convoy reached Paris. On the following day, the body was taken in state to the Panthéon.

The king and queen, poor souls, after the inglorious flight to Varennes, and now guarded by an angry populace, must have heard of this new triumph with bitterness and dismay. Louis had refused to meet Voltaire; and now Louis was a king without a crown, a king with powerless hands; while Voltaire, a dead man, was moving with royal honours to his resting-place. If anything could have made yet more dreadful the dreadful loneliness of that poor king, it was the tribute now paid to the man he so cordially detested.

On the evening of the 10th the body of Voltaire had been received in Paris by the municipal officials, and placed upon "a carriage of antique form." Accompanied by deputations from the National Guard and from the patriot clubs, the carriage had been driven to the ruins of the Bastille. Here, a platform had been prepared on the emplacement of the very tower in which young Arouet had been imprisoned in 1717. The tower was a pile of blackened stones, and grass was already growing over the tumbled masonry of the prison. As the coffin was placed on the platform, surely the most symbolic of all halting-places, a silence fell upon the people. Looking upon a great heap of the old stones of the Bastille, men could read a new, inspiring device, engraved in large letters on the face of a block:

" Receive, in this place where Despotism enchained thee, Voltaire, the Honours of thy Fatherland."

The morning of Monday, the 11th of July, 1791, had been showery, and there had been some thought of postponing the ceremony of the Panthéon; but it seemed better not to disappoint the people, and especially the good citizens of Varennes who had escorted the fugitive king to Paris, and who were anxious to witness the triumph of the Citizen Voltaire. At two o'clock in the afternoon the procession started from the Bastille.

First came a cavalry detachment with trumpets, and then the cannoneers, the sappers and drummers, and a whole battalion of children—the young cadets of the National Guard. Then followed a company of students and patriot deputies with their gay banners. After these came the grim legion of the Halle, ferocious, haggard men carrying pike or musket, marching under their ominous device:

" Great gods, exterminate throughout our land
Those who with pleasure spill the blood of men."

Next came large medallion portraits of Voltaire, Jean-Jacques Rousseau, Mirabeau and Désilles, grouped round the bust of Mirabeau presented by citizen Palloy to the commune of Argenteuil. With these marched the men of Varennes, and the provincial comrades of Nancy and Arras. Workmen who had been engaged in the demolition of the Bastille carried the chains, irons and cannon-balls taken from the wrecked prison. Then came the citizens of the Faubourg Saint-Antoine, with their great model of the Bastille, accompanied by an Amazon, dressed in the uniform of the National Guard, who had taken part in the storming of the fortress. These terrible citizens carried pikes with caps of liberty stuck upon them. Behind the electors of 1789 and 1790, the members of the Jacobin club and the Swiss Guardsmen, came a golden statue of Voltaire, crowned by laurels, and carried by sturdy fellows dressed " in the antique manner." Round the statue were pyramids bearing medallions with the titles of his books. Academicians and men of letters walked on either side of a golden casket which held the seventy volumes of the collected works, given by Beauharnais. They were followed by choirs and bands of music, by young painters and poets, municipal officers and more guardsmen.

The funeral car bearing the sarcophagus which held the body of Voltaire was drawn by twelve magnificent grey horses, four abreast, led by men attired as ancient Greeks or Romans. Two of these horses, we are told, had been provided by the queen, Marie Antoinette.

Unhappy queen ! Did the king know of this gift from the royal stables ? did he acquiesce in this forlorn and touching gesture of regard ? The whole ceremony, if we accept the word of Grégoire, was designed less to honour Voltaire than to express contempt for religion; and if that was so, it is hard to believe that Louis, that saintly person, could have agreed to such a strange mark of royal favour.

Above the sarcophagus was a bier on which reposed a marble effigy of Voltaire (the masterpiece of Houdon) with a broken lyre by his side, and the figure of Renown bending over him. Upon the sarcophagus itself was the inscription:

He avenged Calas, La Barre, Sirven and Montbailly.
Poet, historian, philosopher, he has trained the human mind to lofty flights, and has prepared us for Freedom.

The wheels of the funeral car were of massive bronze. " Those are fine wheels, citizen," said one in the crowd. " Aye, citizen," replied his fellow; " they are crushing fanatism."

The car was followed by a deputation from the National Assembly, members of the law courts, and the high municipal officers of Paris, with Mayor Bailly at their head—the Mayor bowing politely, and seeming to acknowledge the great bursts of applause. After these came the battalion of veterans, and another squadron of cavalry.

First, the cortège halted at the Opera. The bust of Voltaire had been placed in front of the building, surrounded by garlands; and here the actors placed a wreath on the bust, while the pupils of the Academy of Music chanted a hymn.

Then the procession passed the long front of the Tuileries. The people of the royal household were crowding at the windows; but the shutters were closed over one of these windows, and behind the shutters, looking out through the narrow slits, were the king and queen. It must have been a cruel moment for those two unhappy prisoners, guarded in their own palace, and watching the triumphal progress of democracy and reason. What thoughts were in the mind of the queen as she saw her two grey horses ? What thoughts were in the poor, stupid head of the king as he listened to the roaring of the multitude ? Many there were, no doubt, who glanced up at the shuttered window with fierce hatred or with galling contempt, for there was little compassion now in the hearts of the people. That piteous flight to Varennes, a last act of misery and weakness, had destroyed, once and for all, every lingering trace of loyalty and every spark of affection. There is no mercy for a king who runs away.

So the procession moved across the Pont-Royal and halted again before the house in the Rue de Beaune, the house of the Marquis de Villette. In front of the façade, four tall poplar trees were planted, with long festoons of oak-leaves twined about them. On the front of the house was this inscription:

His Spirit roams the World, his Heart is here.

A great company of young girls in white, with crowns of roses on their heads and blue sashes round their waists, charmingly represented the new tricolour. And there, standing with the Marquis and Marquise de Villette, were the ladies of the Calas family.

A woman in the crowd, looking up and reading the inscription, asked what it could mean. " Why," said her neighbour, " do you not know ? His heart—'tis Madame de Villette."

When the catafalque had been drawn up at the appointed place, the Marquise, Voltaire's beloved *Belle et Bonne*, placed a wreath on the head of the effigy;

and then, taking by the hand her little daughter, she appeared to dedicate the child " to reason, philosophy and liberty."

The choirs now sang hymns of triumph; *Belle et Bonne* and the daughters of Madame Calas took their place behind the funeral car; and the procession moved on again.

There was another halt outside the Comédie, another scene of triumph, with Rameau's chorus from *Samson*:

> " People, awake and break thy chains,
> For Liberty is calling.
> Proud people, thou art born for her ;
> People, awake and break thy chains ! "

At ten o'clock in the evening the procession reached the Panthéon, and there the coffin was lowered reverently into its appointed place.

. . . . .

Such were the honours paid by his country to that extraordinary man, who, for half a century, had been the most remarkable figure in Europe.

If we try to measure his influence or to understand the secret of his power, we have to consider him in relation to the ideas and necessities of his period. He was not, like Rousseau, a constructive thinker. He was no prophet. He was not the preacher of a new creed, but the affirmer of the tremendous principles of common sense. In his concept of the human advance, mysticism had no part to play. He was in fixed opposition to the sentimental, the negative and the imaginary. As we understand the meaning of the terms, he was neither a poet nor an artist. It is important to remember that he had no appreciation of music and that he hated Shakespeare. He attacked religion, not only because it was a source of persecution and depravity, but also because it represented elements of the human mind which he was totally incapable of understanding. His own particular god was a mere abstraction, a philosophic necessity, entirely without form or effective influence. If he had known of such a thing as the first law of thermodynamics, it would probably have taken the place of God altogether. It is more than likely that he called himself a deist only to strike at the Christian church from a position of advantage, or only to avoid the charge of idiocy implied by the term atheist. Nor was he in the strict sense of the word a social revolutionary. He believed it was only necessary to infuse the body social with a strong dose of rationalism in order to restore it to perfect health. The idea of a completely reorganised body never occurred to him. It was, perhaps, by virtue of his bourgeois foundation that he never wavered in his attachment to the principles of aristocracy and monarchy. Those principles appeared to him compatible with a generous and free social order, and even as an essential part of it.

But, if he was no revolutionary, he was certainly a reformer. He was appalled by the unholy alliance between the church and the secular power. He was appalled by the foul horrors of bigotry and persecution, by the waste of war and the misery of civil discord. He had reason to be. In his day, superstition was powerful, obstructive and cruel. The full weight of oppression is never more blindly and brutally applied than when the governed mass beneath it shows the first unequivocal sign of revolt. Nor was he alone in protesting against the Infamous. The French

Catholicism of the eighteenth century was a thing which no just man could look upon without shame and anger. There were some who viewed religious persecution with despairing laughter, and others who, like Voltaire, were stirred to magnificent fury.

He did not represent the general intellectual advance of the eighteenth century, but he represented, in an overwhelming degree, a certain aspect of that advance. His power as a social and intellectual force was due to his prodigious concentration upon a limited group of problems, not to any wide comprehension of social development. He had nothing to say on questions of education, government or finance. As far as we can judge, he knew nothing, or next to nothing, of the real condition of the people; and yet, for many years before the end of his life, an alarming number of the French people were starving to death.

A man is great, not in spite of his limitations, but because of them; because of his particular and exclusive adaptation for a given purpose. We do not say that Samuel Johnson was not a great man because he asked whether Bach was a piper; nor do we say that Voltaire was not a great man because he thought Shakespeare no better than a village clown.

If Voltaire is neither a great poet nor a great playwright, he is absolutely unapproachable in the field of satire. If there is little depth in his philosophy, he is without a rival in the sparkling brilliance of a forcible, keen dialectic. He is a master of literary form, a writer of extraordinary vigour, fluency and resource. But no analysis of a literary kind is able to reveal his immense influence upon the men of his age or to explain the wild anger of those who opposed him.

To a large extent, his influence was personal. In

a subtle yet penetrating fashion the living man impressed himself upon the minds of his period, adored by some, execrated by others, but to none indifferent.

His noble intolerance of folly, hypocrisy and superstition forced men to declare themselves either for him or against him. He saw that the one hope of society was the enlightened mind and the enlightened conscience. His opinions were not unfamilar, but no one else had expressed them with such uncompromising vehemence, or defended them with such overpowering logic. Other men had written with greater elegance, like Montesquieu, or with sounder learning, like Diderot; none had the prestige, the fire and ascendancy of Arouet de Voltaire.

In teaching men to escape from the horrors of religious intolerance, there is always the danger of leading them towards the colder horrors of rationalism, and so towards intolerance of another kind. Voltaire himself is occasionally an example of that danger. He does not see that mere rationalism is not good enough to satisfy the complex needs of humanity.

We have to remember, that a dreary materialism appeared the only means of countering the hateful tyranny of the church. To-day, with science pointing to a new concept of materialism and religion, we may be inclined to judge that view too harshly. We may even fall into the error of supposing that Voltaire has no significance for the present age. To fall into that error would be to confuse method with intention or parable with principle. Voltaire was a great man; not only because he wrote *Candide*, the *Philosophick Dictionary*, and the *Essay on Manners*, but also because he fought so gloriously for tolerance, justice, and the freedom of the human mind. No changed estimate of Voltaire as a writer need change our estimate of

Voltaire as an intellectual force; nor, until society has improved so prodigiously that it ceases to resemble society as we know it, need we imagine that we have no longer anything to learn from the vigour of his example. At present, we seem far enough from that state of happy superiority. Remember Frederick's appeal, not in mockery, to the shade of his friend:

" Divine Voltaire—*ora pro nobis.*"

THE END

INDEX

he closes the door to any more exploratory investigation of particular dramatic structures.

Nor could he have conceived the matter otherwise. Bradley, it will be remembered, followed his chapter on "The Substance of Shakespearean Tragedy" with another chapter called "Construction in Shakespeare's Tragedies." The very division of topics is significant. For the fact that his two chapters separate the "substance" from the "construction" of the tragedies is no mere matter of convenience of treatment. It is the indication of a failure to transcend the obdurate dichotomy of philosophical "content" and technical "form." Bradley can give no account of happenings in drama which allow the unfolding of the "substance" to be seen as constituting the dramatic form itself.

A still later shift of critical interest brought into prominence anthropological theories, whose model for tragedy is a version of ritual, "a mimesis of sacrifice" in Frye's phrase:[17] the sacrificial death of the scapegoat king brings about reintegration within community as once the land's fertility was renewed by the death of the god, or as primal Oedipal guilt is incurred and expiated by the band of brothers (in the Freudian version).[18] Ritual origins (themselves highly speculative)[19] tend to take us as far from particular forms as theological, moral, or metaphysical axioms. Fergusson, however, while he leans heavily upon the Cambridge school of anthropology, and (to good effect) upon Kenneth Burke's conception of symbolic action, does promisingly offer an analysis of structure. In *The Idea of a Theater* he presents an analysis of *Hamlet* in which he has the play consist of prologue, agons, climax with peripety and recognition, pathos, sparagmos, and

[17] Northrop Frye, *The Anatomy of Criticism* (Princeton: Princeton Univ. Press, 1957), p. 214.

[18] *Totem and Taboo* (London: Routledge and Kegan Paul, 1960).

[19] They are refreshingly challenged by William Arrowsmith, "The Criticism of Greek Tragedy," *Tulane Drama Review*, III (1959), pp. 31-67.

11

epiphany.[20] However it appears that his interest in these parts is subservient to an overriding thematic concern. His main search is for what he calls the "master analogue," which organizes all the play's actions—its "rituals and improvizations" —into a meaningful pattern. In the case of *Hamlet* this is, he says, the attempt to find and destroy the hidden impostume of Denmark, and it is this which, in his interpretation of the play, gives it tragic meaning in terms of the mythic quest for the welfare of a city. To this theme his differentiation of the play into parts stands in no necessary connection; it is adventitious; and its correlation with the acts is either imperfect or fortuitous. Moreover it will be noticed that some of these terms are Aristotelian and strictly structural ("peripety and recognition"); some are borrowed from rhetoric (prologue, climax); some are structural in the narrower local sense, which is properly a matter of texture rather than structure (agons); some are taken from the anthropological descriptions of ritual (sparagmos), while "epiphany" is quasi-theological. Fergusson's chapter on *Oedipus* is admirable, and his general conception of tragedy as an "ordered succession of modes of suffering" is one with which one is happy to concur: "tragic rhythm," he says, "analyses human action serially into successive modes, as a crystal analyses a white beam of light spatially into the colored bands of the spectrum."[21] Nevertheless his book as a whole fails to live up to the expectations it arouses of a thoroughgoing treatment of dynamic structure. That which is ostensibly structural in his analysis is fatally flawed by eclecticism, by overriding thematic concerns, and by an inadequate account of the nature of the dramatic instrument upon which Shakespeare played, a point to which I shall presently return.

[20] Francis Fergusson, *The Idea of a Theater* (Princeton: Princeton Univ. Press, 1968). The discussion of *Hamlet* is on pp. 98-142.
[21] Ibid., pp. 31, 32.

Of the accounts of tragedy given by those "accustomed to think archetypally about literature"[22] Northrop Frye's is undoubtedly the most brilliant and influential. No student of tragedy can fail to have been indebted to it at some point in his thinking. Yet Frye's archetypes are also too steeply abstracted to help us as much as we might have expected at the level of the concrete articulated individual drama. Seeing "the archetypal human tragedy in the story of Adam," Frye finds that

Adam, then, is in a heroic human situation; he is on top of the wheel of fortune, with the destiny of the gods almost within his reach. He forfeits that destiny in a way which suggests moral responsibility to some and a conspiracy of fate to others. What he does is to exchange a fortune of unlimited freedom for the fate involved in the consequences of the act of exchange, just as, for a man who deliberately jumps off a precipice, the law of gravitation acts as fate for the brief remainder of his life. . . . The discovery or *anagnorisis* which comes at the end of the tragic plot is not simply the knowledge by the hero of what has happened to him . . . but the recognition of the determined shape of the life he has created for himself, with an implicit comparison with the uncreated potential life he has forsaken. . . . Tragedy seems to move up to an *Augenblick* or crucial moment from which point the road to what might have been and the road to what will be can be simultaneously seen. Seen by the audience, that is: it cannot be seen by the hero if he is in a state of hybris, for in that case the crucial moment is for him a moment of dizziness, when the wheel of fortune begins its inevitable cyclical movement downward.[23]

[22] See also Maud Bodkin, *Archetypal Patterns in Poetry* (New York: Vintage, 1958), and John Holloway, *The Story of the Night* (Lincoln, Nebr., Univ. of Nebraska Press, 1963).

[23] Frye, *Anatomy of Criticism*, pp. 206-223, passim.

Though Frye's account does contain an idea of tragic progress, it is insufficiently developed; truncated, indeed, in the formula—"the tragedy of Adam . . . resolves, like all other tragedies, in the manifestation of natural law"—which is then subjected to that dazzling Catharine-wheel classificatory system of archetypal "displacements" which makes of the *Anatomy* so heady (and ultimately vexatious) a brew.

What one might characterize as an existential view of tragedy (not necessarily that of declared existentialists in any formal philosophical sense) has yielded notable insights in recent years. Such views identify the tragic fable of resistance, and adversity, dread with a primary rhythm of existence, a "tragic sense of life," a "tragic qualm" before the recognition of inevitable pain, fear, limitation, and evil in life itself. Richard Sewall quotes Unamuno's anecdote about Solon: "Why do you weep for the death of your son," Solon is asked, "when it avails nothing?" "I weep," Solon replies, "precisely because it avails nothing."[24] Sewall's own rhythm (which he does not himself formularize) of ordeal, protest, and compassion is a case in point. So is Fergusson's purpose-passion-perception, which he adapted from Kenneth Burke; and so is Susanne Langer's rhythm of growth, efflorescence, decline, which, translated into the personalist terms of tragic drama, becomes self-assertion, self-discovery, self-exhaustion. "As comedy presents the vital rhythm of self-preservation," she says, "tragedy exhibits that of self-consummation."[25] These latter views all bring us profitably closer than their predecessors to what we must surely feel as the immediate expressive impulse which gives rise to tragic drama; they veer around a center of feeling rather than a center of discursive thought, and this is to their advantage, and to the advantage of our

[24] Richard B. Sewall, *The Vision of Tragedy* (New Haven: Yale Univ. Press, 1959), p. 6.

[25] Susanne Langer, *Feeling and Form* (New York: Charles Scribner's Sons, 1953), p. 351.

response to tragedy. Nevertheless we still require a *tertium quid* to carry us from the axioms of tragic theory to the richly varied phenomenon itself: the expressive forms the dramatists have constructed. As I have suggested, that *tertium quid* is to be sought where it is so often overlooked: in the differentiation of parts through which forms are articulated. And so we come back to Aristotle, his remarks upon *Mythos*, or "plot," and his insistence upon form as "the first principle . . . and soul of a tragedy."[26]

The principles of plot-construction to which Bradley referred were those which had indeed originated with the rediscoverers of Aristotle in the fifteenth and sixteenth centuries but had ossified into external and mechanical rules since the decline of the neoclassical critical tradition. They pertain to the narrative process of complication and unraveling, or the tying and untying of the knot of intrigue, and are to be found preserved in amber in the nineteenth century's arid if convenient formulae of the "well-made play" and in the encyclopedias and textbooks on the subject.[27] Bradley's account of the specifically Shakespearean features of this well-known physiognomy is valuable and perceptive, but he fails to break its dominance over his thinking; and this shortcoming was perceived by Maynard Mack in a packed and fruitful short essay entitled "The Jacobean Shakespeare." Mack indicates his admiration for Bradley's pioneering attempt to revitalize the humanist analysis of plot in application to Shakespearean tragedy, and himself most notably extends the boundaries of the inquiry. He presents his conception of

[26] See Gerald F. Else, *Aristotle's Poetics: The Argument* (Cambridge, Mass.: Harvard Univ. Press, 1957), pp. 262, 263 on Aristotle's understanding of "an action."

[27] Alex Preminger's *Encyclopedia of Poetry and Poetics* (Princeton: Princeton Univ. Press, 1965) gives under the entry "plot" the following elements: exposition, initiating action, rising action, crisis, falling action, and denouement (p. 622).

15

another kind of construction in Shakespeare's tragedies than the one he [Bradley] designates, more inward, more difficult to define, but not less significant. This other structure is not, like his, generated entirely by the interplay of plot and character. Nor is it, on the other hand, though it is fashionable nowadays to suppose so, ultimately a verbal matter. . . . Some of its elements arise from the playwright's visualizing imagination, the consciousness of groupings, gestures, entrances, exits. Others may even be prior to language, in the sense that they appear to belong to a paradigm of tragic "form" that was consciously or unconsciously part of Shakespeare's inheritance and intuition as he worked.[28]

The tragic protagonist, Mack says, passes through a cycle of psychic change, signaled by the journey of self-discovery always to be found in the center of a Shakespearean tragedy. This cycle takes him through a phase in which he becomes "the antithesis of himself" and brings him to a final phase of recovery, in which his powers and sanity are restored, but in a form undreamt of at the beginning. Mack is hesitant about the third stage and careful to disclaim both Burke's notion of *mathema*—illumination—and the Christian notion of redemption or regeneration. His archetype of the tragic hero is the prophetess Cassandra, whose madness was both punishment and insight, "doomed to know, by a consciousness that moves to measures outside our normal space and time; and doomed never to be believed, because those to whom she speaks can hear only the opposing voice." The first phase of tragedy, he explains, consists of a presentation of the two voices; the hyperbolic and the accommodating, the heroic and the choric, in the shape of the protagonist and his foil. It is from this dialogue of self and soul, as he calls it, that the whole drama takes its rise. Then, in the second stage, he locates conflict,

[28] "The Jacobean Shakespeare," *Stratford upon Avon Studies: Jacobean Theatre*, ed. Brown and Harris (London: Edward Arnold, 1960), I, 12, and passim.

crisis, and falling action; the journey of the protagonist into himself and the process whereby he becomes "his own antithesis." For the third phase is reserved the Hegelian "recovery" —"in some cases, perhaps, even a species of synthesis." Though Mack's is the most stimulating account of the structure of Shakespearean tragedy that I have encountered, rich in insight and in directions for inquiry, it does not (nor could it, of course, in the space available) provide us with an analytical method sufficiently discriminated to discern the intricate dynamics of progression in Shakespearean dramas. One reason for this is Mack's adoption (following Bradley) of the triadic scheme. It must be evident that Mack's second phase is far too swollen with important and crucial matters. His triad has too big a belly. And any dramaturgy, let alone the expansive and episodic representation of the Elizabethans, would find it difficult to weld such a quantity of dramatic material as Mack describes into a close-knit triple structure. Mack's stumbling block is the circumstance that Shakespearean tragedy is in fact a quinquepartite structure. It is of course possible to digest a fivefold division into a triune pattern. Most of the theories mentioned above do so in fact, whether Christian, Hegelian, or existential. But in analysis, such a compression of a quinquepartite into a tripartite structure inevitably introduces a degree of distortion, ignores certain remarkably interesting features both in individual plays and by way of cross-reference, and leaves a great deal that is either confusing or obscure to interpretation.

The argument of this book is that the structure of a Shakespearean tragedy is to be apprehended as an unfolding five-phased sequence, continuous, accumulative, and consummatory, rather than as a simple up-down movement, or even a more complex thesis-antithesis-synthesis. Much of consequence for the accuracy of our responses follows. My studies of the plays will attempt to show how Shakespeare, inheriting a five-act model, learned to use and to understand its potentialities in the way that a poet who inherits, shall we say, the form of the sonnet, learns during a lifetime of use to render expressive in the highest degree its various possibilities of articulation. The result is that "other kind of construction in Shakespeare's tragedies than the one he [Bradley] designates, more inward, more difficult to define, but not less significant." I believe it is of the utmost importance to call attention to the five-phase structure, not only because the historical evidence that Shakespeare in fact thus ordered his conceptions seems incontrovertible but because, as I shall hope to show, a great deal of the sheer beauty and intricacy and seemingly infinite variety of Shakespeare's inventions are otherwise lost to view. Study of the plays in terms of their fivefold structure enables us to give clearer definition to Mack's formula of the tragic progress, and makes further useful distinctions possible.

The history and theory of the five-act structure has been exhaustively studied by T. W. Baldwin in a monumental and indispensable work.[29] But Shakespearean criticism has made remarkably little of his findings. Though the wild untutored genius has long vanished from our imagination, it is perhaps not sufficiently realized that Shakespeare inherited, through the dramatic theory and criticism of his time, not only a convention of dramatic form but also with it a highly developed rationale. For the Renaissance tradition, in the form of prefatory analysis and commentary in both the school editions and the English versions of Terence, constituted the literary critical training of every grammar-school child in Europe during the fifteenth and sixteenth centuries. The historical evidence Baldwin adduces for the dissemination of these commentaries, not only in the centers of learning but in the grammar schools of Europe, places almost beyond dispute the supposition that this tradition was very much a conscious part of Shakespeare's intuition as he worked. And scrambled and infinitely layered

[29] T. W. Baldwin, *William Shakespeare's Five-Act Structure* (Urbana, Ill.: Illinois Univ. Press, 1947).

as this continental tradition was, it provided more than a casual stimulus. To the dramatist of genius it was the springboard to structural insights of the highest order.

The Italian and German humanists were familiar with the three terms protasis, epitasis and catastrophe from Donatus' account of the plays of Terence. But they also knew Horace's five-act rule and Terence's and Seneca's own five-act practice. Their problem too, therefore, was to adjust a theoretical tripartite to an actual quinquepartite division. They were concerned with the practical matter of editing the printed texts of Terence from manuscripts which were divided not into acts, but into scenes (unnamed and unnumbered) in accordance with character grouping. As editors they were required to determine what part of the plot should go into each act. Many of them also ardently desired to be able to compose plays upon the classical model, and therefore their interest extended to the question of the principles upon which the classical drama had been constructed. They drifted far enough from strictly structural relations in their various attempts both to elucidate the texts and reconcile their authorities, but in their conglomerating, infinitely conservative, and eclectic fashion, they gradually evolved a complete theory of structure, which was then applied to Terence, Plautus, in due course Sophocles, and in time, to the learned and vernacular dramas of the late sixteenth century.

What to the end they had difficulty deciding was whether the epitasis was to be regarded as a crisis and turning point in the middle of Act III, or as the entire middle between beginning and end, whose climax of emotional intensity might be anywhere within it or later—in the catastrophe. In other words their problem was to find a home for the notion of an ascending scale of intensity, a crescendo rising to a climax, as well as for the notion of a central crux or turning point, which implies an up-down movement. By the mid-sixteenth century the rediscovery of Aristotle made confusion worse confounded.

His remarks on the "quantitative" parts of tragedy (Part 10 of the *Poetics*) attracted most attention in the context of the editorial problem with which the humanist critics were preoccupied. And these were radically misunderstood. For when Aristotle mentions the parts—prologue, episode, exode, and chorus, divided into parode and stasimon—he does not indicate the order in which these anatomical parts are to occur. Nor was it clear to the first Latin commentators in the mid-sixteenth century whether "episode"—"all that comes between two whole choric songs"[30]—was to be regarded as everything between the first chorus after the prologue and the last before the exode, or as each of the parts between each of the choric odes. The former interpretation yielded a triple structure with a middle section, as Ascham put it in 1570, "the hiest and hotest and full of greatest trobles";[31] the latter could be made to correlate with the familiar fivefold system of prologue-protasis, three episodes, and exode-catastrophe. Thus the problem of reconciling a tripartite with a quinquepartite conception was simply reactivated by the reentry into the field of *The Poetics*. And that this is a problem which has not yet found a solution the pervasive confusion between the terms "crisis" and "climax" in most discussions of drama shows.

Clearly, any shift from one decision to the other has considerable consequences both for the composition and for the interpretation of a structural sequence. For if Act III constitutes the "climax" then clearly all that follows must be anticlimax; if all that leads up to the climax is tension, then what follows is relaxation of tension, saved from being felt as such by the artist's skill in introducing new material. This was essentially Bradley's view. But if what we have over and above the desis-lysis (complication and unraveling) of plot is a stage-by-

---

[30] *The Poetics*, ed. Ingram Bywater (Oxford: The Clarendon Press, 1947), p. 48.

[31] "The Scolemaster," *English Works of Roger Ascham*, ed. W. A. Wright (Cambridge: Cambridge Univ. Press, 1904), p. 284.

stage advance, a pressing steadily to an issue, a crescendo of intensity of some kind, then clearly the climax will not be other than the catastrophe itself (a perception which common speech confirms), and what occurs in Act III, if it is a crux or turning point in terms of the plot, is a further stage in the continuing process of unfolding or discovery in terms of the tragic progress. Failure to make this distinction, and the related failure to distinguish between plot-crisis and the committing of the fatal error, which may or may not coincide with it, has led to endless errors of the kind which springs from a misconception of the functions of parts of a complex structure. In the following account of Shakespeare's five acts I shall propose new names for the old parts both in order to avoid the incomprehensibility and the codified or ossified effect of the old names (where they exist: protasis, epitasis, catastasis, for instance) and in order to give some indication of the nature of each expository phase.

The axis of development in the Shakespearean sequence of events is the tragic hero, through whom all that was potential in the beginning is actualized by the end. He may be conceived as a prism whose facets are turned successively toward the light by the moving plot, of whose dynamic structure he is a constituent part. The process begins with the establishment of his specific and unique gift, power, or virtue, which, by its very nature renders him vulnerable, in his circumstances, to the dangers which it impels him to risk. His decisions expose him to great suffering as victim of opposing forces, or of aspects of his own nature. A fatal error committed by him in the course of this struggle issues in an ironic reversal of his situation in which he is intensely perturbed and greatly afflicted and becomes, in Mack's phrase, "the antithesis of himself." As a consequence of this phase of disaster he comes to repudiate or renounce in some radical way his former values, his former self or his world, which he sees now in terms of a darkened vision. At some variable point on this downward progress is born and expressed a counterknowledge, that of error and its cost, and of the goodness of that which is lost. These tensions are resolved in the final passion and death, in which he in some way discovers, identifies, bears witness to or affirms the authenticity of the human value his experience in the play has realized.

All the stages, of course, not only the first, are "expository" in the sense that each discloses further and further reaches or implications of the fall of the tragic hero from fortune to misfortune. They are not separate numerical narrative units related by addition, but serial phases in the sequence of a tragic discovery which develops as from an embryo, with each phase giving rise to what follows and implied by what precedes.

However, that Act or Phase I contains the primary exposition no one will dispute. I propose to call it the "predicament" of the play, in order to exploit both the logical and the psychological connotations of the word. It presents, that is to say, both the peril or evil that can be predicated generally of the protagonist's circumstances, and that aspect of himself which causes them to constitute for him a test situation, a plight. That the tragic action comes to an end with the catastrophe in Act v is self-evident, and the traditional name as good as any. Again, no one will deny that in Act III we regularly find the greatest turbulence, a crisis in the hero's fortunes, and a turning point. I propose the Aristotelian peripeteia for Act III, and define it as the articulation of the total reversal of the hero's initial status and situation: King Lear destitute upon the heath; the disclosure of Macbeth's guilt in the eyes of all at the banquet; Romeo, killer of Tybalt, banished from Verona; Antony in flight from Actium; Coriolanus banished from Rome; and Hamlet, would-be avenger of his father's murder become the killer of Polonius.

It is, as it always has been, Acts II and IV that require most elucidation. If in terms of subtlety and variety of effect these acts can only be accounted for by personal genius, in terms of mode they can be ascribed to the popular nature of Shakespeare's theatre and to the entire Christian coloring and temper of the Elizabethan imagination. Act or Phase II condenses the whole homiletic morality tradition, in which forces of good and evil engaged in conflict for the soul of the hero. In Shakespeare's drama these forces are now internalized; they have become components of the protagonist's personality, part of the very structure of the self.[32] These forces are, as Bradley puts it, "whatever [acts] in the human spirit, whether good or evil, whether personal passion or impersonal principle; doubts, desires, scruples, ideas—whatever can animate, shake, possess, and drive a man's soul."[33]

The challenge of Act I presents the protagonist with—it now emerges—the conditions of an impossible choice—impossible because it bifurcates the man. Whichever of his alternatives he chooses will seem to him deeply wrong, to involve him in great guilt, to constitute the greatest conceivable danger to the structure of his life, to require him to place in jeopardy the goals and values to which he most passionately aspires. His encounter with these circumstances constitutes what Sewall has called "the agony of dilemma,"[34] which is characteristic of tragic suffering: every decision presents itself as costing no less than everything. It is thus his deepest allegiance, his inmost being, which is tested by his circumstances and hammered out, so to speak, upon the anvil of successive events. It is in Phase II that the terms of the conflict are made clear, the nature of the dilemma established. It is here that we are enabled to perceive by what he is tempted and by what held back; what is involved and invested, for him, in circumstances which, for another, might not present a problem at all. Thus Brutus in the orchard speech; Hamlet, spectator of the player's per-

[32] N. Rabkin, *Shakespeare and the Common Understanding* (New York: Macmillan, 1967), has some excellent observations which confirm this point, p. 244ff.

[33] Bradley, *Shakespearean Tragedy*, p. 25.

[34] Sewall, *Vision of Tragedy*, p. 19.

formance and in anguish about the nature of his own; Macbeth struggling with prohibition; Lear at bay between his daughters; Antony torn between Rome and Egypt; Coriolanus forcing himself to don the napless vesture of humility and exhibit his wounds in the marketplace. The heroic qualities, the distinctive courage, or energy, the pitch and intensity of his specific aspiration—all the attributes which mark him out from his fellows as the one for whom choices will be portentous— have been indicated in the predicament. Act II frames the impossible choice as it presents itself to him. It renders comprehensible the psychomachia in which the protagonist is, or will be, engaged. "Psychomachia," therefore, is the term I have chosen for this phase.

Act IV is no less indebted to the specifically Christian origins of Shakespeare's theatre and to his own Christian culture. Act IV characteristically contains scenes of pathos or comedy or both, which Bradley, tied to the triad, observed but notably failed to explain in terms of a dynamic of structure. He found the pathos and the comedy to be mere devices, though marvelously effective, for overcoming the lull or pause after the excitements of the crisis and before the counteraction is sufficiently developed to bring about the catastrophe. The effect of Act IV as an integral part of the tragic unfolding is extremely complex, as I shall hope to show in subsequent chapters. For the moment, suffice it to note that both the pathos and the humor are essentially products of a Christian sensibility; both rooted in a profoundly ambivalent attitude to "humankindness" in which compassion for vulnerability and *contemptus mundi* inextricably merge.

In Phase IV the subsuming category of responses is irony. Irony is, of course, tragedy's regular accomplice, its own principle being inherent in the reversal of expectation which is the formal cause of tragedy. But Shakespeare develops highly specialized ways of placing the irony inherent in the tragic event, and the pathos of suffering itself, in perspectives not available (for instance) to Sophoclean tragedy. Shakespeare reveals a more complex tragic self through the unfolding of the tragic event and so glosses his tragic experience with a more sustained and differentiated irony in which both the cosmic despair of the protagonist and the pathos of the helpless victims of disaster are distanced and diminished by the fool's wisdom of common man or clown.

To understand the phase of tragic experience upon which these perspectives are thus brought to bear we must return to the crisis of Act III. The peripeteia reverses the protagonist's status and situation; it characteristically gives rise to and is accompanied by horrified recognitions. The protagonist may undergo physical suffering at this stage, but more vital is the suffering produced by the recognitions—the sense of self-violation and of inestimable loss. Then in Act IV the tragic hero, whose inner perturbation, whose inner overthrow reached a stage of disintegrating violence in Act III (Lear's madness, Othello's frenzy, Coriolanus' fury, Hamlet's distraction, Macbeth's panic at the appearance of Banquo's ghost), renounces or repudiates his previous world of values. The torment of Act III (the dismemberment or sparagmos, if you will) has issued in a deliberate truncation of the self, as if the pain were so great that the limb must now be amputated. The self has been invaded, shattered. The struggle has been won by the forces of evil, or the antagonist, or whatever in himself was opposed and contrary to the hero's aspiration. He has lost his ascendancy, he is far indeed from that which he might, or should, or could have become. He has achieved the reverse of what he desired. That is one reason why there is so often a reminiscence or return in Act IV to the circumstances of the beginning. The protagonist's darkened vision in Act IV (Othello's defamation of Desdemona in the brothel scene, or Coriolanus' repudiation of Rome; Lear's invective against love and justice; Hamlet's complex rejection of reason in "How all occasions"; Macbeth's dedication to murder) is a nadir, but it is now viewed from

25

outside the hero, measured by norms and criteria derived from the viewpoint of common humanity. A certain symmetry is established with the temptation phase, for this is the outcome of the choice then made. While the scenes of pathos—the murder of Lady Macduff and her son; Desdemona's willow-song, Ophelia's madness, Lear's recognition of Cordelia—poignantly measure distance traveled from a central nexus of common happiness, the irony of a graveyard scene, or of the Carioli servants or of an Emilia, superimposes upon the absolute extremities of tragic experience the modifying, distancing, mitigating effect of a common man's evaluations. The richly paradoxical effect is that of a preservation both of the world's sanity and of the distinctive heroic stature.

In the end all is lost. The worst of the possibilities inherent in the initial situation has been pressed to its ultimate issue. But from this wreckage that tragedy portrays, this climax of "the terrible, the pitiful and the shameful" in which tragedy culminates, as Camerarius held,[35] some value is finally fully revealed and recognized, and therefore survives. It is the function of the tragic hero to mediate that survival. This he does through the manner of his dying, whereby he in some way exhibits and affirms that in which he has had faith, that which defined his inmost being or with which he has identified himself, despite his rejection of it or his previous failure to recognize it. It is to the goodness of a specific good and the badness of a specific evil that he bears witness in his death: the former realized in imagination, in re-cognition, as value; the latter in the irrevocable outcome of events, as cost.

These five phases thus articulate and order the traditional components of tragedy: the fall of a protagonist at some high point on Fortune's wheel, as Frye put it, his intense suffering, his hard-won knowledge, and his death; in Aristotle's terms, reversal of fortune and recognition. One necessary element

[35] Baldwin, *Shakespeare's Five-Act Structure*, p. 202.

requires further comment. This is the fatal error, the act which disjoints the entire frame of things and, as it appears in the outcome, seals the protagonist's doom. It is fatal, this act, in that it constitutes a point of no return. It is a deed from which there is no going back like the killing of Tybalt, the murder of Duncan or Caesar or Desdemona, or the flight from Actium. But comprehended under the neutral Aristotelian term "error" will be found, in Shakespeare's tragedies, a variety of most finely discriminated fatal acts ranging from the most criminal (in *Macbeth*), to the least (in *Coriolanus*). I choose the Aristotelian term (which appears to evade moral implications) for the reason that there is no other which covers the whole Shakespearean range, and in order to stress the dramatic function all these acts have in common, however differently they would be judged in, shall we say, a celestial court of justice. Moreover, as Aristotle saw, what a man chooses to do and what he avoids doing is the fundamental basis of character, and it is the passage of character to self-discovery, "through an eventful life to full individuation" (in Auerbach's phrase),[36] and not a providential distribution of rewards and penalties, that constitutes the axis of development in Shakespearean tragedy. I place the emphasis therefore upon the act of erroneous choice, rather than, though not necessarily in exclusion of, Pauline sin or Bradleyan flaw, the use of which terms invites a moralistic view of the development of events.

In most of the tragedies the fatal error takes place in Act III, brings about the peripeteia, and is accompanied by anagnorisis, as Aristotle indeed prescribed. Of this kind is the killing of Tybalt, the assassination of Caesar, Antony's flight from Actium, Hamlet's killing of Polonius instead of Claudius. But such is not always the case. While Act III always contains the

---

[36] E. Auerbach, *Mimesis*, trans. Willard Trask (Princeton: Princeton Univ. Press, 1953), p. 15.

overthrow of the protagonist, the great reversal, and perturbations or afflictions of disintegrating violence, it is extremely important to note that the fatal error does not always in fact fall at this point of the play. The consequences of this mobility of the fatal error are dramatically momentous. In *Othello*, for instance, the fatal error (the murder of Desdemona) is delayed to the very catastrophe; and the knowledge when it comes at the very end of the play has a peculiarly traumatic and horrifying force. A similarly retarding effect is to be found in *Coriolanus* where the fatal error (it will be argued presently) is the return to Carioli in Act v.

In *Macbeth*, on the other hand, and even more in *Lear* the fatal error, with its accompanying recognitions, is advanced to the second or even the first act. Time is thus gained for an immense extension or expansion of consciousness in the protagonist. *Lear* exhibits the possibilities of this dimension of internality to a degree unequalled in any drama. Lear is himself fully responsible for the initial precipitating act, and it is this early placing of the fatal error which provides him (and Macbeth and Titus) with the inalienable dramatic asset of a past—a memory which thrusts its intolerable burden into every moment of the dramatic present. The shifting of the fatal error is one of the sources of the variety, the freedom, and the range of Shakespeare's great tragedies, and a reason why the plays, though perfectly consistent in observing the five-act differentiation of the tragic phases, never impress us as in the slightest degree mechanical applications of a formula.

It is important to notice that the very mobility of the tragic error makes evident that it is not necessarily the "cause" of the tragedy. In Shakespearean tragedy, grounded in Christian chronicle, the protagonist's life is in process; his existence unfolds before us. Options are open, possibilities manifold. The protagonist plays out his life as we watch. And the sifting and winnowing of choice, the development of his tragic recognition, is coextensive with the whole of the action. As he recognizes himself and the course of his life from beyond the gulf of things not to be undone, the Aristotelian pity and terror produced in an audience by the enactment of a predetermined, even preaccomplished, destiny deepen into what can be distinguished as compassion and awe. In the end life is lost, but we see that it has been played for the highest of human stakes; and we are left with a sense of unique and distinctive human transcendence.

Tragedy indeed needs no "causes" beyond those inherent in the finitude of man's existence, his liability to error of every conceivable kind, and his mortality. Tragedy's formal cause is simply a cruel reversal of expectation, the more poignant by virtue of whatever guilt, of whatever degree and kind, has been incurred by the protagonist, paradoxical victim-agent of his doom, in the course of the development. Unlike theodicy, or its modern stepchild, psychiatry, tragedy does not deal with guilt by means of a calculus of condemnation, or the apologetics of poetic justice; for guilt is an inescapable concomitant of tragic existence. The equation between "cause" and moral culpability, so pervasive in the criticism, is a didactic fallacy the remote and original authors of which are the comforters of Job. Their descendants are to be found at all times, requiring great tragedy to be an awful warning whereas it is born to be a permanent stronghold against the easy retributive answers with which the popular moralist seeks to exorcise terror.

Considered therefore in terms of the mechanics of plot, the progress of a Shakespearean tragedy consists of the exposition, the complication of intrigue and/or peril, the knot of crisis and the turning point, the counteraction, and the denouement. With structure in this sense of plot-construction I shall not, or only very occasionally or marginally, be concerned in the following pages. My concern will be with the exploration of that rich array of forms which Shakespeare fashioned, exploiting the exigencies of plot, for the articulation of the tragic progress as he distinctively conceived it. Considered in terms of the tragic progress of the protagonist, the development proceeds through the phases of challenge, temptation or dilemma, disintegration, and despair to the final recognition in which all that was hidden is revealed, and self and destiny fully and finally confronted. Considered in terms of the dramatic action through which this progress is projected, the tragedies sequentially exhibit predicament, psychomachia, peripeteia, perspectives of irony and pathos, and catastrophe.

My study takes the view that the structure of Shakespearean tragedy as it gradually and unceasingly emerges and develops is itself an instrument of imaginative inquiry, creative and exploratory, whereby the dramatist orders and comprehends his perceptions; and that the discovery of the principles at work in that structure can illuminate at all levels a tragic art which, for complexity, power, and suggestiveness of effect, has never been matched.

CHAPTER II

ROMEO AND JULIET

Shakespeare places his young lovers in peril from a double source in the predicament of *Romeo and Juliet*. The play opens with the chatter of the Capulet servants echoing their masters' feud. The family enmity is the matter at issue; but it is a perennial libidinous humanity, sexual and belligerent, that we recognize in their idle bawdry:

> SAMPSON. 'Tis all one, I will show myself a tyrant:
> when I have fought with the men I will be cruel
> with the maids; I will cut off their heads.
> GREGORY. The heads of the maids?
> SAMPSON. Ay, the heads of the maids, or their
> maidenheads; take it in what sense thou wilt.
>
> (I.i.23-28)

While the comic-braggart style of these exchanges and of the subsequent thumb-biting denies seriousness and consequentiality to these petty swashbucklers, yet we are to perceive that the impulses touched off in Sampson and Gregory are the irrational constants of lust and anger, and that therefore what follows is endowed with a certain inevitability despite the fortuitous circumstances. Here in this street scene is an image of the precarious, potentially explosive human reality in which the protagonists' lives are set. In *Julius Caesar* and *Coriolanus* the street erupts in the mob violence of the death of Cinna and the lynching of Coriolanus. In *Romeo and Juliet* the violence is less terrifying because it is channeled into the conventional form of the feud: it is not therefore utterly anarchic. But the idle brawl escalates, and the masters find themselves in full-scale collision as a result of this chance encounter.

31

It is not possible to be oblivious of the degree to which the plot of *Romeo and Juliet* stresses sheer chance. The accidental meeting of Romeo and Benvolio with Capulet's messenger bearing the invitations to the ball, the mischance of the encounter between Romeo and Tybalt at a most unpropitious moment, the outbreak of the plague which quarantines Friar John, the meeting of Romeo and Paris at the Capulet tomb, and the ill-luck of the delay in Juliet's awakening from the effects of the drug are the cardinal instances. Shakespeare, so far from mitigating the effect of unfortunate coincidence, is evidently concerned to draw our attention to it—to the presence of uncontrollable forces which frustrate all human plannings and arouse a fearful and rebellious sense of unintelligible contingency. The plot of *Romeo and Juliet* is the plotting of the lovers and Friar Lawrence and father Capulet, all of whom are outplotted with what seems so malicious a consistency as to tempt us to give it a name and a persona. This is just what Mercutio does in his Queen Mab speech, where considerable artistry is lavished upon the characterization of the intractable and mischievous "other" which thwarts the will of mortals. No more than impish at first, Queen Mab by the end of the speech enters into subversive alliance with the anarchic appetites of her victims. So too the bad luck that dogs the lovers is interwoven with the bad habits of ingrown pride in the Capulets and the Montagues, whose conventionalized aggressions mask a violent and tyrannous will. Significantly, the first chance meeting between the lovers is shadowed by the menacing hostility of Tybalt.

These twin familiar sources of calamity in human affairs— ill-will and ill-luck—coalesce in Shakespeare's later most comprehensive account of the evil in experience. Folly brings about great calamity in its ignorance of the true nature of things; but knaves are fools too, in their blindness to their own true interests. It is the radical unknowability of the phenomenal world that determines both; and it is the radical unknowability of the phenomenal world that causes the good man's deepest consternation. Here the protagonists do not concern themselves with the larger issues. They know all they need to know; they are assured of certain certainties, and this protects them from the perception of the darker possibilities that can present themselves to human anxiety in the face of vicissitude. *Lear* is the play in which Shakespeare explores the darkest of these possibilities, presents the anguish of a mind under the threat of chaos, hovering above a void. In the earlier play the question of a cosmic malice takes a milder and more contingent form. These lovers had bad luck, we are to feel; another couple might do better.

The turns of fortune, however, do obstinately present themselves in alliance with folly, with failure to penetrate appearances, with blindness to the real state of things. The theme which will receive its greatest virtuosity and depth of treatment in *Hamlet* is present throughout, from the arrival of Capulet's illiterate messenger in i.ii, carrying the invitation which precipitates the entire subsequent action, to the tragic mistakings of the tomb scenes. "I pray you," the messenger inquires of Romeo, "can you read any thing you see?" "Ay," replies Romeo, "if I know the letters and the language." In the familiar manner of Elizabethan stagecraft, the fool's patter, ostensibly drawing a jest from the discrepancy in wisdom between the learned and the ignorant, actually serves as an ironic commentary upon all human ignorance in knowledge, on all that men do not knowing what they do. And if the company of fools is one Shakespearean means of dramatizing the wry discrepancies of human understanding, the arras, drawn by the Nurse to reveal what is nevertheless still concealed, is another, providing, wherever it occurs, profound and various images of unawareness.[1]

---

[1] Bertrand Evans, "The Brevity of Friar Lawrence," *PMLA*, lxv (Sept. 1950), has an interesting study of *Romeo and Juliet* in which he traces the patterns of unawareness which culminate in the universal

The twin components of calamity fall apart at the end. We feel as separate the bad luck of the timing that brings about the lovers' deaths and the ill-will that brought about the family feud, in a way that we do not in the equivalent case of Cordelia's death. The reason for this difference in effect is that the alliance between ill-will and ill-luck is mediated neither by a consciously adopted villainy in any of the characters, nor by a deep division of the self in the tragic protagonist. What takes the place of these is Romeo's conviction that he is dogged by an external and inimical power; his self-awareness is of a man doomed. The Senecan formula of enormous fate-defying passion still, at this stage, conditions Shakespeare's conception of his tragic hero. The misgiving, the sense of an implacable and omnipotent force by which they are harried, which is shared by the lovers and becomes increasingly specific and increasingly urgent as their passion grows in intensity and their anxiety in time-riddenness, is their own imaginative creation. Fate is the all-powerful enemy and time is on fate's side, as they read their experience. As they press on to grasp and possess their happiness, they do not reflect upon themselves nor upon others. They do not look within. Nor is ill-will accorded the diabolic power it has in the great tragedies; it never invades experience, nor undermines the possibilities of existence to the same degree. In this early tragedy Shakespeare fails to actualize to the full the possibilities inherent in the initial situation. It is as a consequence of this that the vision of human harm conveyed by it is less deep, less complex, less comprehensive, less profoundly imprinted upon the consciousness of the characters, less, in the last analysis, cogent than in the later master works.

Romeo and Juliet is more tragic than the *Mirror*, or Brooke's story, or *Gorboduc*, because it embodies the distinctive tragic

bewilderment at the mouth of the tomb in Act v, when the bodies of Paris, Romeo, and Juliet (bleeding though three days dead), are discovered.

movement of spirit. It is less tragic than the major tragedies, not because it is different in kind—a "tragedy of chance" rather than a "tragedy of character,"—but because the possibilities of the medium are not yet fully exploited, perhaps not yet fully understood. Its parts are less finely coordinated, less rigorously pressed to a final issue, less integrally related. To understand the potentialities of a medium is indeed no less than a lifetime's task.

What is involved in the forming of tragic "character," in tragic becoming, is what *Romeo and Juliet* is about. Though didacticism will always offer us a *Romeo and Juliet moralisée* (with the "meaning" of the play a Verona regenerated by sacrifice), or such neo-Christian indictments of romantic passion as that of Gervinus[2] in the nineteenth century or of De Rougemont[3] in the twentieth, it is worth remembering the words of a great writer of our own day, who has deeply pondered upon the mysteries of human experience and of human destiny: "Very much happens in the world; and as we cannot wish that it might rather have peacefully remained unhappened, we may not curse the passions which are its instrument; for without passion and guilt nothing could proceed."[4] True, there are doctrinal statements concerning Providence in the play itself. The chorus, the Friar in his capacity as purveyor of religious instruction, and the Prince at the end all moralize the woeful story into the means found by heaven

---

[2] "In him [Romeo] a hidden fire burns with a dangerous flame; his slight forebodings are fulfilled, not because a blind chance causes them to be realised, but because his fatal propensity urges him to rash deeds; . . . We cannot accuse fate. . . . It is Romeo's tumultuous nature alone which exercises justice upon itself" (*Commentaries*, London: Smith, Elder, 1903, p. 223).

[3] See *Passion and Society* (London: Faber, 1940). De Rougemont sees in the Liebestod myth "a passion sprung from dark nature . . . in search of the coercion which shall intensify it. . . . Death is the one kind of marriage that Eros was ever able to wish for" (p. 17).

[4] Thomas Mann, *Joseph and His Brothers*, trans. H. T. Lowe-Porter (London: Secker and Warburg, 1934), I, 276.

to punish and to reconcile. And indeed there remains something of an unbridged gap between the new tragic form and these traces of the older providential conception. If we wish to follow the new configuration, to perceive the shape of the emergent pattern, our clues are to be sought not in doctrinal statements but in the disposing of that which is exhibited. The characters who initiate and suffer the events undergo a drastic reversal of intention and expectation, in the process of which they choose, reflect upon, and discover themselves.

Since the protagonists in *Romeo and Juliet* do not look deeply within, we can only fully comprehend the progress of the tragic hero toward his own self-definition—that which gives form to the tragic experience—because we have the whole Shakespearean opus before us. With the perfected model in mind we can return to *Romeo and Juliet*, perceive its presence there, and assess the relative awkwardness of its embodiment at this stage of Shakespeare's dramatic career. For it is not until *Richard II* that Shakespeare learns to articulate the expression of the inner life in a way that enables him to achieve the freer and richer explorations of mind of the later tragedies. And it is the later lovers, Othello and Antony, who experience the ultimate anguish of tragic knowledge which accompanies irrevocable error fully discovered. Romeo, killing himself in the belief that Juliet is dead, dies in blessed ignorance of his mistake. Nevertheless, examination of the management of the immensely complex task of articulation will show us a rudimentary, yet impressively complete, finely sketched, though not fully mastered, Shakespearean tragedy.

What we first of all discover is the particular personal distinction or power of the tragic hero, which sets him apart from his fellows and sets him goals other than theirs, which he pursues with an energy greater than theirs. The nature of his bond with the life of his fellows and his own aspiration set up contrary claims upon him. Thus he is confronted with necessities of choice, which try him and test him; he is placed in a dilemma both horns of which impale him. The fatal error which he commits as a consequence of his choice totally reverses his situation and causes him to experience the pain of knowing himself now to be poles apart from the object of his desire. At the same time the goodness and desirability of this object is realized by him with a progressive vigor and vividness, so that when he despairs of its attainment it is with a full knowledge of the measure of that which he has lost. His death is the final issue of his choice, wherein he realizes its cost and affirms the inalienable value of what is lost. It is this discovery of value that constitutes the coming into being of complete individuality. And it is this process of self-definition through adversity, passion, and choice that we perceive emerging from the half-romantic, half-didactic tale Shakespeare found in his sources.

What the play tells us of Romeo in Act I is that he is a young man of honor, high spirits, and amorous melancholy, at once one among his companions and yet set apart from them by his predilection for the imaginative life, his readiness to be fired by a high and wayward passion. He is indeed, when the play opens, already aflame with his adoration for Rosaline, who is also a Capulet. And the eclipsing of Rosaline by the sun of Juliet is the play's first crucial event.

To Rosaline Romeo was the devoted and hopeless servant of love, and it is this fixed and static Petrarchian role that he allows to be put to the test of realities when he agrees to the comparison with other beauties. His first anticipatory speech of misgiving and premonition marks, it is perhaps not fanciful to see, his sense of undreamt-of risks attendant upon the abandonment of the safe, if doleful, standardization of the Petrarchian libretto:

> . . . my mind misgives
> Some consequence, yet hanging in the stars,
> Shall bitterly begin his fearful date
> With this night's revels, and expire the term

Of a despised life closed in my breast
By some vile forfeit of untimely death:
But He, that hath the steerage of my course
Direct my sail!

(I.iv.106-113)

The ball scene enacts his entry upon an experience fraught
in the highest degree with the potentiality for discovery, exploration, development; and his explanation, "O, she doth
teach the torches to burn bright!" wonderfully registers the
excitement of this awareness of discovery. If love is, as has
been said, the longing to make another I one's own in order
to discover oneself there and to lose oneself,[5] it is certainly
something of this feeling that is expressed in the pilgrim sonnet
—the rapt and joyous *pas-de-deux* which is their discovery of
each other.

ROMEO. If I profane with my unworthiest hand
    This holy shrine, the gentle sin is this,
    My lips, two blushing pilgrims, ready stand
    To smooth that rough touch with a tender kiss.
JULIET. Good pilgrim, you do wrong your hand too much,
    Which mannerly devotion shows in this;
    For saints have hands that pilgrims' hands do touch,
    And palm to palm is holy palmers' kiss.
ROMEO. Have not saints lips, and holy palmers too?
JULIET. Ay, pilgrim, lips that they must use in prayer.
ROMEO. O, then, dear saint, let lips do what hands do;
    They pray, grant thou, lest faith turn to despair.
JULIET. Saints do not move, though grant for prayers' sake.
ROMEO. Then move not, while my prayer's effect I take.

(I.v.96-110)

The sonnet form of the passage frames the meeting and
enacts the reciprocity of their recognition. Its particular ex-

[5] P. Philippe de la Sainte Trinité, quoted by M. C. D'Arcy, *The
Mind and Heart of Love* (London: Faber, 1945), p. 335.

pressiveness derives from the daring interplay of its terms. That which in terms of Christian caritas can be no more than metaphorical is made to function as literal affirmation in terms of romantic eros. Thus what is profanity to the one is epiphany to the other. The polarity of the two loves, antithetical, opposed to each other, challenging each other, historically and psychologically interwoven, intensifies the climactic moment. The moves in the language game are themselves the devices which establish intensity of feeling.[6] And if here it is felt to be a little too stylized, a little too explicitly displayed, a bravura passage, it is so no doubt by implicit comparison with later no less artful but apparently effortlessly naturalistic renderings of the tension and intensity of romantic passion, such as Othello's "Where either I must live, or bear no life, / The fountain, from the which my current runs," or Antony's "Then must thou needs find out new heaven, new earth," or Cleopatra's "Eternity was in our lips and eyes, / Bliss in our brows' bent. . . ."

The dramaturgy of multiple reflection brings each of the characters into a relationship of contrast with the lovers, some later in the play, but most already in Act I. Romeo is flanked by the inimitable Mercutio, who regards love as a foolishness that men invent to torment themselves with when they would be better employed wenching—"a great natural, that runs lolling up and down to hide his bauble in a hole." Juliet, on

[6] M. M. Mahood, *Shakespeare's Word-Play* (London: Methuen, 1957), finds the kissing sonnet "social persiflage" to disguise their real feelings. It seems improbable that they should want to disguise their real feelings when they are, in effect, alone in the midst of the festive crowd. More profitable for dramatic criticism than the Empsonian ambiguities this critic is able to discover (she finds the Friar's "O, so light a foot. . . ." in II.v.16ff., for instance, susceptible of four different and incompatible interpretations) is the notion of "word-play" developed by W. Nowottny: the heightening devices of style, syntax, and metaphor, which are designed to lend credence to the speaker's claim to intensity of emotion. See *The Language Poets Use* (London: Athlone Press, 1962).

the other hand, is flanked by the Nurse, the epitome of the earthy, the base, the material, and the utterly unimaginative. As naturalist as Mercutio, though of infinitely less wit, she is one of Shakespeare's finest creations in the mode of contrast between high and low, heroic and base, rare and common; between dignity and comedy. And in this mode she is the apogee of that view of love as simply either sex or match-making which is the bedrock contrast to the lovers' vision. To them, love is an enlightenment of the human condition perfectly fulfilling all needs of flesh and spirit, absolutely self-justifying. Friar Lawrence, standing in paternal relationship to Romeo, with all his own resigned tolerance for youth, regards his doting as a regrettable carnality; while Juliet's father's sole concern is the very proper one, in a dutiful and affectionate paterfamilias, of prudential matchmaking.

What then is clearly established in Act I is that Romeo and Juliet, and they alone, are possessed of a light incomprehensible to the rest of Verona's citizens to whom love is irrelevant. Their possession of the light is suggested by the light imagery throughout the play, but it is to be noted that this imagery itself undergoes progression. At first light is an hyperbole for the powers of sensuous delight:

> Two of the fairest stars in all the heaven,
> Having some business, do entreat her eyes
> To twinkle in their spheres till they return.
> What if her eyes were there, they in her head?
> The brightness of her cheek would shame those stars
> As daylight doth a lamp; her eyes in heaven
> Would through the airy region stream so bright
> That birds would sing and think it were not night.
>
> (ii.ii.15-22)

In the course of the play there is a development from the light which is a grace of appearance to the light which is a gift of insight; from a metaphor for beauty to a metaphor for knowledge. Even in "O she doth teach the torches to burn bright," there is a suggestion of the platonic, while the "feasting presence full of light" is a ghostly symposium. And that this final light shines in the darkness of the tomb is a symbolic rendering of the very essence of tragic discovery. So Romeo and Juliet are the light-bearers, to whom the contrasting others, unrecognizing, unknowing, acting out their natures, bring harm.

It is worth noticing that the two marginal figures, Rosaline and Paris, are, at least in retrospect, the subtlest reflectors of all. Less clearly modeled, further in the middle distance of the play, attenuated shadows out of courtly love, chaste and devoted respectively, it is their kind of fixity which is cast like a snake's skin by the eruption into tragic existence of Romeo and Juliet.

The introduction of a prologue-chorus at the beginning of Act II is a mark of an as yet imperfect mastery of dramatic craft. In later tragedies Shakespeare will have no need for a chorus to tell us how the development will be shaped in subsequent phases of the action. Dramatic speech itself will directly exhibit what is here recounted:

> Now Romeo is beloved, and loves again,
> Alike bewitched by the charm of looks . . .
> Being held a foe, he may not have access
> To breathe such vows as lovers use to swear;
> And she as much in love, her means much less
> To meet her new-beloved any where:
> But passion lends them power, time means, to meet,
> Tempering extremities with extreme sweet.
>
> (Chorus. 5-15)

What immediately follows this summary of events so far and indication of the evident difficulties ahead is the orchard scene. Romeo's predicament has already been indicated in his being one among his companions and yet set apart from them. The orchard scene may be taken as emblematic of this relationship. The whole scene, without the artificial break at line 45, runs right through from Mercutio's irrepressible mock "conjuring" of Romeo by the outdated Rosaline (By her high forehead and her scarlet lip, / By her fine foot, straight leg, and quivering thigh, / And the demesnes that there adjacent lie II.i.18-20) to the balcony dialogue between the lovers. Thus is dramatized Romeo's separation from his fellows as he leaps the garden wall and hides from them; and his consciousness of what irreducibly separates them is indicated by his observation upon Mercutio's salacious merriment on the subject of medlars and pop'rin pears. The ribald jesting, in which he joins with a will when he "is sociable," belongs now to a different realm—the realm of those "that never felt a wound." And this division between realms is the burden of Juliet's balcony monologue. What has been suggested by Romeo's relation to his friends is the great divide between habitual, conventional conformity—the grooves of Mercutio's wit are well worn however high spirited the *élan* of his particular performance—and imaginative immediacy, the fully realized subjective pain of the wound. It is a sharp awareness of this very collision that Juliet expresses in her " 'Tis but thy name that is my enemy":

> O, be some other name!
> What's in a name? that which we call a rose
> By any other name would smell as sweet;
> So Romeo would, were he not Romeo call'd,
> Retain that dear perfection which he owes
> Without that title.

> (II.ii.42-47)

While the intrigue is skilfully managed, the whole of Act II is devoted to exhibiting the setting apart of the lovers in the Veronese milieu. Even the Nurse and the Friar, who help the lovers, do so uncomprehendingly, in no way understanding the nature of their feelings. The Nurse derives an earthy and vicarious glee from her role as go-between. The Friar, who chides Romeo for inconstancy, for the rapidity with which he has changed the object of his affections, expresses throughout the gravest reservations regarding violent delights and intensities of deliciousness. And his agreement to the marriage is for ends quite external to it. The cross purposes between the lovers and their spiritual father are brought to a fine point of irony in the matter of the marriage ceremony itself, where it is patently clear that the Friar's anxiety to have them married as soon as may be ("you shall not stay alone / Till holy church incorporate two in one") is not in the very least for the same reasons as theirs.

The Friar fears the lovers' destruction from their very first abandonment, in his view, to unbridled passion, rash impetuosity, and headstrong will. His words at their marriage are richly prophetic:

These violent delights have violent ends
And in their triumph die, like fire and powder,
Which as they kiss consume.

(II.vi.9-11)

But as Dowden long ago perceived,[7] it is simply in character, perfectly natural and appropriate to the persona, for the Friar to preach to Romeo upon the disastrous consequences of unbridled passion. It would have been a dereliction of his evident Christian duty not to do so. It is similarly sound Christian tradition beautifully adapted to the style of reflection of a gentle hermit-apothecary which ascribes to the beneficent paradoxes of Providence the evil presence of poison in the good herbs of the earth, and canker death to the evil presence of rude will in man:

---

[7] Edward Dowden, *Shakespeare: His Mind and Art* (London: Kegan Paul, 1906), p. 121.

O, mickle is the powerful grace that lies
In herbs, plants, stones, and their true qualities:
For naught so vile that on earth doth live
But to the earth some special good doth give;
Nor aught so good but, strain'd from that fair use,
Revolts from true birth, stumbling on abuse,
Virtue itself turns vice, being misapplied,
And vice sometime's by action dignified
Within the infant rind of this weak flower
Poison hath residence and medicine power. . . .
Two such opposed kings encamp them still
In man as well as herbs, grace and rude will;
And where the worser is predominant,
Full soon the canker death eats up that plant.

(II.iii.15-30)

The Friar's "grace and rude will" speech has a comprehensive, generalizing, and reverberating quality—the generalizing and reverberating quality of Christian doctrine that will necessarily identify the "greater power than we can contradict" with Providence. How much more ironic is it then that the Friar's enactment of his Christian view, his own benevolent, would-be "providential," and truly Christian interference in the course of events in fact helps to precipitate the catastrophe as much as anything in the play. His drug is, in the outcome, as lethal as that dispensed to Romeo by his dusty and down-at-heel Mantuan counterpart, a fact which should help to preclude a "providential" reading of the play.

What is dramatized in Act II is the cross purposes which mark Romeo's relations with all who surround him in Verona —his father confessor and his fellows. Cross purposes characterize the witty exchanges between Romeo and Mercutio ("Why, is this not better now than groaning for love?"), and, more importantly, though again in deliberately contrived comic vein, between the Nurse and Juliet when the former withholds the information she was commissioned to bring back, to the utter exasperation of the latter's patience.

Once again we may perceive the apprentice hand. Few indeed would wish to be deprived of the picture of the Nurse stalking indignantly off stage with the plaintive Peter at her heels, but it is evident that the ebullience of the comedy is in excess of the requirements of the main development. It is dissipating rather than concentrating in its effect, and all but overlays our perception of the import of the play at this point—the battle between opposing principles, or opposing aspects of the protagonist's personality, in terms of which Romeo's temptation is conceived.

For in Act II the extremities are defined: on the one hand the claims, codes, and comradely conventions of Verona (the comic world on the whole, though it includes the long-established enmity between the feuding families); and on the other the imperious demands of an authentic passion: the overriding need to realize and to consummate the larger possibilities of human existence suggested by a high imagination of love. Juliet's sense of the irrelevance of the mere agreed name to the sweet immediate scent of the rose bears directly upon this opposition, upon the nature of the conflict and the choice the drama will present the tragic hero as making. It is precisely the opposition which he fails, in the event, to surmount.

It is in Act III that Romeo's failure to surmount the opposition, which constitutes his fatal error, is powerfully exhibited. Once again the streets are restive, tense; mad blood is stirring, and heads are as full of quarrels as an egg is of meat. Romeo, aglow from his marriage ceremony, a vessel of goodwill, happens upon the truculent Mercutio and the irate Tybalt, his kinsman of an hour, precisely at the moment when Mercutio's contemptuous dismissal of him—"Alas, poor Romeo, he is already dead! stabbed with a white wench's black eye . . . is he a man to encounter Tybalt?"—has become true in a sense undreamt of by Mercutio. The good-will and the joy with which he is filled become the cause of the death of his friend and of his own "calm, dishonour-able, vile submission" as he then himself interprets his be-havior. Thus the conventional code of honor vanquishes the goodwill and Romeo, alone of the participants, suffers the anguish of knowing that "what might have been" has been supplanted by "what must now be,"[8] and of enacting the fatal transformation of the one into the other. His despairing cry, "Oh, I am fortune's fool," poignantly expresses his sense of a baffled, degrading impotence, a loss of the autonomy of a self-determining being. Given the circumstances—the com-panionship of young hotheads acting in ignorant and conven-tional truculence—given his own character as young man of honor, then what happens as a result of Mercutio's death un-der his arm is completely intelligible. But it is important to perceive that Romeo's challenge of Tybalt is not merely an instance, as in the stock moralizing interpretation, of a rash-ness which fatally flaws his character and brings about his doom. If this were so, then the consequences in the play, though certainly possible, would be considerably less moving. The play would be morally exemplary but without tragic sig-nificance. Romeo would be too simply to blame, as indeed he has often been held to be, and the great tragic error too simply moralized. And in point of dramatic fact Romeo's action in challenging Tybalt is precisely not rash, though it puts him into great danger. On the contrary, it is an action first avoided, then deliberately undertaken. It is a choice, and it is entirely expected of him by his society's code.

What Shakespeare's craft has achieved here is a finely turned peripeteia in which the protagonist is responsible for his ac-tions, though he is not accountable for the circumstances in

---

[8] The formula is Northrop Frye's; see *The Anatomy of Criticism* (Princeton: Princeton Univ. Press, 1957), p. 213.

which he must act. He is the paradoxical victim-agent of tragedy, whose actions recoil ironically upon his own head, so
that his entire situation is reversed, and the knowledge that
springs from the reversal (Aristotle's anagnorisis) is of the
fullest kind. If "O, I am fortune's fool" richly expresses his
frustration and sense of helplessness in the face of the forces
that are ranged against him, it is not only the uncalled-for,
unchosen, outrageous event which he blames. The epithet also
points to his own dilemma of opposing loyalties—his own acceptance of the code of honor, and his own momentary repudiation, in its terms, of his love: "O sweet Juliet, thy beauty has
made me effeminate." Thus the psychomachia developed in
Act II: the conflict between the autonomous dictates of an
imaginative passion and the socially sanctified codes of conventional behavior here reaches its tragic crisis. Romeo fails
to abide by the former, fails to obey at all costs the command
of his deepest and most inward experience, and so feels himself the plaything of fortune. His banishment represents not
only the deprivation of his love but the indignity of slavery
to circumstances. In the Friar's cell this dual aspect of his
suffering is effectively dramatized in the collapse of all composure, and in the intensity of his despair at the thought of
banishment:

> 'Tis torture, and not mercy: heaven is here,
> Where Juliet lives; and every cat and dog
> And little mouse, every unworthy thing,
> Live here in heaven and may look on her;
> But Romeo may not: more validity,
> More honourable state, more courtship lives
> In carrion flies than Romeo: they may seize
> On the white wonder of dear Juliet's hand
> And steal immortal blessing from her lips,
> Who, even in pure and vestal modesty,
> Still blush, as thinking their own kisses sin;

But Romeo may not; he is banished:
This may flies do, when I from this must fly:
They are free men, but I am banished:
And sayst thou yet that exile is not death?

(III.iii.29-43)

Lear's cry, "Why should a dog, a horse, a rat have life," immeasurably deepened by the graver context and the incomparably richer diapason of the later play, is faintly anticipated. Certainly, in terms of a morality of Stoic *apatheia*, to which the Friar's Christian strictures upon self-control, manliness, and temperance are akin, Romeo's transports here are a regrettable lapse, an outburst of immature extravagance. But I believe we should learn to see them as fully expressive—to Shakespeare's capacity at this stage—of the poignance and complexity of his anguish, an anguish which is composed of loss and grief, of humiliation, self-reproach, and exacerbated tenderness.

In Juliet's reception of the news, in her distracted wordplay, can also be construed the sense of a loss of the other which is a loss of the self:

What devil art thou that dost torment me thus?
This torture should be roar'd in dismal hell.
Hath Romeo slain himself? Say thou but "I,"
And that bare vowel "I" shall poison more
Than the death-darting eye of cockatrice:
I am not I, if there be such an "I";
Or those eyes shut that make thee answer "I."
If he be slain say "I"; or if not, "no":
Brief sounds determine of my weal or woe.

(III.ii.43-51)

The word games with which Shakespeare renders intensities of feeling become in time subtler, less patently contrived, yet there is no reason to suppose that it is inability to render naturalistic speech which leads him to this particular artifice.

Indeed the naturalness, the monosyllabic simplicity of the lovers' exchanges are a noteworthy feature of this play.[9] Their idiom is a refinement of common speech which captures its very essence: "But to be frank, and give it thee again"; "My bounty is as boundless as the sea"; "I would I were thy bird"; "Dry sorrow drinks our blood"; "I am content, so thou wilt have it so"; "I have forgot why I did call thee back." It is by the artifice of rhetoric in this early play that Shakespeare marks the unusual complexities and intensities which chequer their relationship. That both the Friar and the Nurse concur in reducing the misery of the lovers to terms of weeping and blubbering merely dramatizes the gulf of noncomprehension which separates them.

Juliet's anguish indeed parallels Romeo's. In her too is precipitated a conflict of loyalties by her cousin's death at the hand of the man she loves; but where Romeo yielded to the demands of convention, she reacts to the Nurse's "shame come to Romeo!" with the passionate: "Blister'd be thy tongue / For such a wish!" And with the assertion, moving in its youthful harshness, of love's devouring exclusiveness, its ruthless priorities:

"Tybalt is dead, and Romeo—banished!"
That "banished," that one word "banished,"
Hath slain ten thousand Tybalts. Tybalt's death
Was woe enough, if it had ended there:
Or, if sour woe delights in fellowship
And needly will be rank'd with other griefs,
Why follow'd not, when she said "Tybalt's dead,"
Thy father, or thy mother, nay, or both,
Which modern lamentation might have moved?
(III.ii.112-120)

[9] H. Levin, "Form and Formality in *Romeo and Juliet*," *Shakespeare Quarterly*, XI (Winter 1960), has a number of valuable observations upon the play's insistence on stylized polarity at every level of language and action, against which the monosyllabic mutuality of the lovers stands out.

For Juliet, who is not the agent of events, the peripeteia, the reversal of her situation, the conversion of all good into its opposite, is articulated by the modulation of the great speech of delighted anticipation, "Gallop apace," into the violent series of realizations culminating in "I'll to my wedding bed; / And death, not Romeo, take my maidenhead!" in iii.ii. It is with great skill that Shakespeare tightens at this point the knot of errors, the perturbations and dangers classically a feature of the crisis phase of tragedy, with the antedating of the betrothal to Paris. For it is in response to this precipitating factor that Juliet's ordeal is significantly extended. Thus she is brought to face both her father's fury, his total repudiation of her in which the hidden Veronese violence bursts forth— "hang, beg, starve, die in the street"—and the nurse's repudiation of all that she believed understood between herself and her confidante:

> I think it best you married with the county.
> O, he's a lovely gentleman;
> Romeo's a dishclout to him: an eagle, madam,
> Hath not so green, so quick, so fair an eye
> As Paris hath. Beshrew my very heart,
> I think you are happy in this second match,
> For it excels your first: or if it did not,
> Your first is dead, or 'twere as good he were
> As living here and you no use of him.
>
> (iii.v.218-226)

Where in the first case she pleads:

> Is there no pity sitting in the clouds,
> That sees into the bottom of my grief?
> O, sweet my mother, cast me not away!
>
> (iii.v.197-199)

in the second she accuses:

Ancient damnation! O most wicked fiend!
Is it more sin to wish me thus forsworn,
Or to dispraise my lord with that same tongue
Which she hath praised him with above compare
So many thousand times? Go, counselor;
Thou and my bosom henceforth shall be twain.
I'll to the friar to know his remedy:
If all else fail, myself have power to die.

(III.v.234-241)

In both she is driven to an uncompromising knowledge of her aloneness, of her isolation, and of the cost of this love, which is not less than everything.

Act III does not end, however, without the parting scene in III.v., which, with the effect of counterpoint—of counter-knowledge—sends a shaft of light into the darkness, the disintegration, and the defeat of Act III, and solves for Shakespeare the extremely difficult problem posed by having two protagonists. The chiastic formality, the mock-rhetorical reversals and substitutions of the lovers' parting aubade, suggest not merely the reciprocity of their experience but also the perspective of life, of jocund day, in which to view Romeo's playful-serious "Come, death, and welcome!"

JULIET. Wilt thou be gone? it is not yet near day:
It was the nightingale, and not the lark,
That pierced the fearful hollow of thine ear;
Nightly she sings on yond pomegranate tree:
Believe me, love, it was the nightingale.
ROMEO. It was the lark, the herald of the morn,
No nightingale: look, love, what envious streaks
Do lace the severing clouds in yonder east:
Night's candles are burnt out, and jocund day
Stands tiptoe on the misty mountain tops:
I must be gone and live, or stay and die.

JULIET. Yond light is not daylight, I know it, I:
  It is some meteor that the sun exhales,
  To be to thee this night a torchbearer,
  And light thee on thy way to Mantua:
  Therefore stay yet; thou need'st not to be gone.
ROMEO. Let me be ta'en, let me be put to death;
  I am content, so thou wilt have it so.

(III.v.1-18)

In it is affirmed and exhibited the love which is "an inter-inanimation of two souls." Not, as De Rougemont claimed, "the passion that wants darkness and triumphs in a transfiguring Death" but the passion that strives towards fullness of life. There is no naked sword between these lovers. Theirs is not a desire to die to the world but a most energetic desire to live in it, to survive crises and to have "all these woes serve / For sweet discourses in our time to come." It is of a piece with the brief episode of the dream in Act v and serves a similar function. Johnson wondered why Shakespeare gave Romeo a mood of involuntary cheerfulness immediately before his reception of Balthazar's news:[10]

I dreamt my lady came and found me dead . . .
And breathed such life with kisses in my lips
That I revived, and was an emperor.

(v.i.6-9)

Apart from the obvious pathos of the dramatic irony, the lines effectively underline the contrast between his experience of a bondage of dread and his deepest intuition of a state of liberation and sovereignty.

It is the presence of this counterknowledge that gives tragic

[10] Horace Howard Furness, ed., *Variorum*, new ed. (New York: Dover Publications, 1963), p. 258.

poignance to Juliet's leave-taking from the world in her poison speech. The Nurse's betrayal has undermined her confidence in every seeming friend, so that to the fear naturally attending the taking of the drug is added a terrible suspicion of the Friar's motives. The poison speech is masterly in its rendering of horror enacted in imagination; the source of its great strength lies in the imaginative pressing to an issue of her knowledge that "my dismal scene I needs must act alone." It is not of death or of being dead that she is afraid; she is afraid, of course, of a miscarriage of the plan. But her terror is for that moment when she may find herself imprisoned and alone with the appalling dead. What her imagination projects is an image of the ultimate aloneness, the maximum distance which can be traveled by a human being from the sustaining and comforting presence of his kind. That she is ready for this is the measure both of the absolute value their love possesses for her and of her fidelity to this perception. It is a great fourth-act scene in which desperation and affirmation combine and intensify each other.

The equivalent phase in the case of the main protagonist is to be found at the start of Act v, and is abbreviated in proportion as it is delayed, no doubt on account of the need to present the experience of two protagonists. Romeo's dream of empire is immediately followed by Balthazar's news and by the decision "then I defy you, stars!" His self-control contrasts with his self-abandonment in the Friar's cell when told of his banishment, but, by a paradox which is only apparent, is the measure of his loss of all hope. His darkened vision of the world which he now repudiates is given a remarkable "objective correlative" in the episode of the meager apothecary. The vivid realistic detail of the passage makes it a perfect counterpart to that of the earlier pastoral hermit-apothecary, whose beneficence now seems therefore to belong to a world of romantic dreams.

> Meager were his looks,
> Sharp misery had worn him to the bones:
> And in his needy shop a tortoise hung,
> An alligator stuff'd and other skins
> Of ill-shaped fishes; and about his shelves
> A beggarly account of empty boxes,
> Green earthen pots, bladders and musty seeds,
> Remnants of packthread, and old cakes of roses,
> Were thinly scatter'd to make up a show.
>
> (v.i.40-48)

Romeo construes his commerce with this caitiff wretch as an emblem of the world's transactions:

> There is thy gold, worse poison to men's souls
> Doing more murder in this loathsome world
> Than these poor compounds that thou mayst not sell. . . .
>
> (v.i.80-83)

The point to be noted is again a dual one: the motif of corrupting gold has not been sufficiently integrated into the play's conceptual material to make the observation resound as it should. It therefore strikes us as an arbitrary, unjustified generality. But the impulse obscurely working, directing the shaping of the material, is akin to that at work in the vastly more subtle and sophisticated rendering of the darkened vision of tragic despair in the fourth acts of subsequent plays.

It is indeed in the handling of his fourth acts that the individuality of Shakespeare's tragedy is most clearly to be perceived. As Bradley observed:

> In this section of a tragedy Shakespeare often appeals to an emotion different from any of those excited in the first half of the play, and so provides novelty and generally also relief. As a rule this new emotion is pathetic; and the pathos is not terrible or lacerating, but, even if painful, is accompanied by the sense of beauty and by an outflow of admira-

tion or affection, which come with an inexpressible sweetness after the tension of the crisis and the first counter-stroke.
. . . Sometimes, again, in this section of a tragedy we find
humorous or semi-humorous passages.[11]

"Novelty, "relief," "relaxation of tension" are Bradley's explanation for this recurrent feature of Shakespeare's art, but
it will be the purpose of this and subsequent chapters to show
that they are less than adequate. Bradley's analysis of construction is tied to the notion of plot-management which he
derived from the long tradition of neoclassical theorizing upon
the mechanics of dramatic narration. It is for this reason that
his observations do not take us below the immediate surface
effect upon audience sensibility, do not penetrate to the inner
life of the whole dramatic sequence, nor fasten upon a functional principle which will enable us to perceive the formal
integrity of the immensely complex relatedness of parts which
tragic structure produces at this penultimate stage of its progress. Tentatively then, and with no more elaborate and advanced a model than *Romeo and Juliet* in mind, we may
establish the principle that the stage of tragic progress which
is marked by some form of despair in the hero, some sense of
his maximum distance from his goal, is accompanied also by
scenes productive of irony and pathos. We are to step back
from the events and view them from a distance, a distance
provided by some common human experience or plain man's
point of view. This radical shift in perspective from the subjective to the objective juxtaposes the individuality of the tragic
hero—the self in its process of anguished or obsessive self-reali-
zation, in Auerbach's phrase, its "differentiation into full individuality"[12]—with a general or universal worldly wisdom.
At the same time some simply moving episode close to a universal norm of human happiness or human harm enables us
to measure the extent of the hero's loss. The complex act of

[11] *Shakespearean Tragedy*, p. 57.   [12] *Mimesis*, p. 15.

assessment and of measurement thus initiated channels the twin responses of pity and terror which flow towards the play's catastrophe.

The following pages will have much to say concerning the increasing virtuosity, skill, and sensitivity with which Shakespeare manipulates, interweaves, combines, and plays off against each other these gamuts of feeling and of evaluation. Suffice it for the moment to suggest that it is this structural principle which serves to explain the strange interlude of the musicians and the foolish Peter. It is indeed prime evidence in the argument concerning the tentative emergence of Shakespearean form in *Romeo and Juliet*. As it stands it is not convincing, however symbolic we wish to make its "discords" and its "silver sounds." Shakespeare will learn so to integrate his fool's patter with the deepest concerns of the play that the reverberations of meaning will seem practically infinite. To claim that this is the case here would indeed be special pleading. What is indubitable however, is that they are *there*, the musicians, with their carefully contrived wordplay, at a moment when no one would have expected them and when there seems little point in their elaborate comic artifice. What inchoate artist's impulse put them there can only be inferred from the consummately meaningful ironies later derived from their analogues and equivalents in the great tragedies.

The management of the pathos in *Romeo and Juliet*, though not by any means negligible, is subject to a similar reservation. In iv.v. the Nurse potters about before the arras which hides the inert body of Juliet, calling to a slugabed bride, as she believes, to arouse her for her wedding: Nor when it is drawn is the truth disclosed to the participants in the drama, so that the bride-death, though simulated, is the occasion for the genuine pathos which is preceded by Capulet's joy, as he bustles about the kitchen, that "this same wayward girl is so reclaim'd." His subsequent grief, upon the discovery of Juliet's body, is simply and movingly expressed:

> O child! O child! my soul, and not my child!
> Dead art thou! alack! my child is dead;
> And with my child my joys are buried.
>
> (iv.v.62-64)

From the wreckage that tragedy depicts, something of the spirit survives to effect our reconcilement with the pity and terror we have experienced. The scene of the lovers' death dramatizes that survival. Their love has involved them in misfortune, guilt, loss, sorrow, and betrayal, but it has survived—survived even Mercutio's death, and Tybalt's. It is affirmed by Romeo:

> For here lies Juliet, and her beauty makes
> This vault a feasting presence full of light
>
> (v.iii.85-86)

and enacted with the most direct simplicity by Juliet:

> O churl! drunk all, and left no friendly drop
> To help me after? I will kiss thy lips;
> Haply some poison yet doth hang on them,
> To make me die with a restorative.
>
> (v.iii.163-166)

It is not true to the facts of the play to say that they are married only in death, for their marriage is consummated before Romeo leaves for Mantua. What one can say is that marriage forms their view of their relations with each other from the very first balcony scene, so that death itself is robbed of its sting, is even made welcome, under this figure. This is the effect of the conjugal and erotic imagery of their final scene. The Elizabethan pun contains manifold possibilities and Juliet's "This is thy sheath; there rest, and let me die" is without doubt a metaphorical sexual act. But it is an act undertaken because she is in love with Romeo, not because she is in love with death. Nor is their death a sacrifice of love, as certain of the Christianizing critics would have it.[13] Their death is an assertion of freedom and of fidelity; hence an affirmation of the reality, vitality, and value of the experience which has animated them. Nor do we reconcile ourselves to their deaths because they have become immortal in literature, whereas "they would have become old and worldly in time."[14] We reconcile ourselves to the compassion and fear their story arouses because we have witnessed one complete cadence of the human spirit, enacted to the full, rendered entirely intelligible in its distinctive human value. What reconciles us is not what could possibly reconcile us in life. Only achieved art can so order and satisfy our appetencies, our perceptions, and our insights. Shakespeare's dramatic reticence in the context of boldly erotic imagery gives the scene the suggestiveness of an analogue: we glimpse something of the resources of tenderness, desire, and gaiety, freedom and self-possession, which lie in the power of an idealized sexual relation to discover.

For the lovers, all losses are restored and sorrows end. The observers have been made sensible both of the magnitude of the loss and the grandeur of the possibilities. It is precisely with such a sense of lost possibilities that a romance tragedy will leave us, and it is to this tragic end that every significant change in the old story of Brooke, every departure from the fatal Senecan and the providential tragic formulae, can be seen to have been conducive.

[13] Notably John Vyvyan, *Shakespeare and the Rose of Love* (London: Chatto, 1960); Irving Ribner, "Then I Denie You Starres," *The English Renaissance Drama*, ed. J. W. Bennett, O. Cargill, V. Hall (London: Peter Owen, 1961), and John Lawlor, *Early Shakespeare* (London: Chatto, 1961).

[14] Mahood, *Shakespeare's Word-Play*, p. 25.

CHAPTER III

RICHARD II

Beyond the woeful or happy outcome brought about by the catastrophe Elizabethan dramatic theory did not distinguish between the structure of tragedy and comedy;[1] neither were the dramatic practitioners possessed of a theory of genre which would enable them to distinguish with any rigor between tragedy and history. Polonius' familiar puzzlement is not only his own but the age's failure to achieve radical definitions. Thus the "chronicle" plays of the period, which deal with the fall of princes, great changes of fortune, tyrannical intrigues, and Machiavellian betrayals, based upon no clear generic principle of either tragedy or history, based, indeed, at best upon a *de casibus* interpretation of events indifferent to the distinction, present a bewildering medley of hybrids, a spectrum of mixed or intermediate tints.[2] And whether any given instance is an example of "tragicall historie" or historical tragedy or of English Seneca requires a more systematic philosopher than Polonius to determine. Both *Richard III* and *Richard II*, though integral parts of their respective historical tetralogies, are called "tragedies" in the Folio and in the Quartos upon which it was based.

Shakespeare, therefore, found few clear conceptions of genre ready to hand. Nor did he possess a theory of tragic character. He invented as he went along; and as he proceeds from the histories to the tragedies, his exploratory, creative deployment of his art discovers and establishes the distinctions that he

[1] See T. W. Baldwin, *Shakespeare's Five-Act Structure* (Urbana, Ill.: Illinois Univ. Press, 1947), passim.

[2] See V. K. Whitaker, *The Mirror up to Nature* (San Marino, Calif.: Huntington Library, 1965), for useful discussion of the tragic and chronicle history structures; also J. V. Cunningham, *Woe or Wonder* (Denver, Colo.: A. Swallow, 1951).

59

needs. The chief distinction between history and tragedy rests in the restructuring the narrative undergoes in order to bring out the protagonist's personal responsibility for events and his personal response to them. It is his distinctive aspiration, will, or purpose that becomes salient.[3] In the history plays the protagonists are exhibited as struggling for freedom to initiate events. Even that artist in villainy, Richard III, has not fully escaped from the destined role of a scourge of God. If they are made vivid, it is by a degree of idiosyncrasy in their response to their destined roles, but they are nevertheless governed by an overall ironic process of history. If we may imagine them as figures in bas-relief compared to the sculptures in the round of the tragedies, they may also thus be compared with the tapestry figures of pure chronicle. But in *Richard II* the providentialist view of events which dominated Shakespeare's historical sources gives way to a rival concern.[4] In *Richard II* Shakespeare's tragic idea takes the form of a development in the dimension of character that is decisive for future directions.

The play's overt conflict is between the strong and successful Bolingbroke and the vain and vacillating Richard; and looked at from the point of view of the management of events, the play is well made, Richard's decline and Bolingbroke's rise crisscrossing effectively in the center. But the simple fall-rise pattern does not exhaust the potentialities of the dramatic material as Shakespeare presents it. The play

---

[3] Cf. "the traditional link between the epic poem and the drama is the historic drama . . . in the epic poem a preannounced fate gradually adjusts and employs the will and the events as its instruments, whilst the drama, on the other hand, places fate and will in opposition to each other, and is then most perfect, when the victory of fate is obtained in consequence of imperfections in the opposing will, so as to leave a final impression that the fate itself is but a higher and more intelligent Will." S. T. Coleridge, *Shakespearean Criticism*, ed. T. M. Raysor (London: J. M. Dent, 1960), I, 128-129.

[4] I am indebted for this view of the relation between the historical tetralogies and the Tudor providentialist myth to work done by David Frey during the preparation of a doctoral dissertation.

is not contained without remainder, so to speak, within the historical pattern. The remainder inheres in the characterization of Richard, in which the play's distinction lies. It is this study of the complex figure of the tragic hero that exerts pressure upon the shape of the play, so that from within the episodic chronicle form we perceive the emergence of what we can recognize, in the light of our knowledge of the later tragedies proper, as the distinctively tragic structure. The play does not exhibit the consummate articulation of phases of the great tragedies. The first two acts are episodic and the study of tragic character does not really get under way until the peripeteia of Act III. And when it does it is almost, though not quite, independent of the content of Acts I and II. But the play does possess a movement which approximates to that of the great tragedies. Coleridge's remark concerning Richard's "continually increasing energy of thought, and as constantly diminishing power of acting"[5] takes on an added significance when to Coleridge's psychological interest in character portrayal is added an interest in the structure of tragedy that directs us to search for the principle informing this movement.

As Act I proceeds we perceive, through the considered juxtaposition of scenes, the predicament in which Richard is placed. The act is composed primarily of two scenes of elaborate formal challenge between rival claimants for justice. At three points, however, the façade of highly ceremonial assertion and counterassertion between Bolingbroke and Mowbray is rent to provide a glimpse of the historical actualities that lie behind these rituals. The inserted dialogue (I.ii.) between Gaunt and the Duchess of Gloucester points to the hidden and ambiguous source of all the trouble: the murder of Woodstock; the final scene of the act indicates, possibly, the real import both of Richard's fear of Bolingbroke (his courtship of the common people) and of Bolingbroke's challenge of Richard. (Though Holinshed, and Bolingbroke himself, in

[5] Coleridge, *Shakespearean Criticism*, p. 136.

2 Henry IV [III.i.72-74] deny the imputation of forethought: "Though then, Heaven knows, I had no such intent, / But that necessity so bow'd the state, / That I and greatness were compell'd to kiss".) And the dialogue between Richard and Gaunt after the sentence of banishment makes clear the nature of the political arrangement that has taken place behind the scenes to make the present solution feasible. To Gaunt's lament for his son's exile Richard replies:

> Thy son is banish'd upon good advice,
> Whereto thy tongue a party-verdict gave:
> Why at our justice seem'st thou then to lour?
>
> (I.iii.233-235)

And Gaunt's reply admits his complicity:

> Things sweet to taste prove in digestion sour.
> You urg'd me as a judge, but I had rather
> You would have bid me argue like a father.
> O, had it been a stranger, not my child,
> To smooth his fault I should have been more mild.
> A partial slander sought I to avoid,
> And in the sentence my own life destroy'd.
> Alas, I look'd when some of you should say
> I was too strict to make mine own away;
> But you gave leave to my unwilling tongue
> Against my will to do myself this wrong.
>
> (I.iii.236-246)

What is presented then is the tangential relationship between the dramatized conflict of wills and the complex reality of history, where political morality or amorality is still further complicated by the blood relationship between the various contenders for power. Feudal rituals mask the ulterior political realities of collusion and guilt. In the predicament thus presented, power and justice are divided and disjoined. And it is in these circumstances that the King must play his allotted role. Richard must rule, in his circumstances, either by what the Elizabethans, following Machiavelli, called *virtù*, or by that older dial of princes called virtue. He must govern by either power or justice, since the breach between them already exists.

When we ask what is wrong with Richard's interruption of the lists, an act for which he has been richly and variously scolded by his severer critics, we are forced to the conclusion that it represents no more, but also no less, than simple political expediency, in circumstances which leave little other alternative.[6] Later in the play we are given a parallel scene in which we watch Bolingbroke, at the height of his power and success, encountering a similar situation. And the comparison is instructive.

Once again the question at issue is Gloucester's death. Bagot is now the chief witness and Aumerle the accused, as Mowbray was accused by Bolingbroke in Act 1. Once again the situation shapes itself in terms of the challenges and counter-challenges of honor, with the civil dissension inherent in the situation made manifest by the successive involvement on one side or the other of Fitzwater, Surrey, and Percy. The question, by an evident irony, circles back to the original contender, Mowbray, and we are only prevented from finding ourselves, so to speak, back at base, by Mowbray's death meanwhile in exile. But what is significant is that Bolingbroke, too, can do no more than shelve the whole matter, leaving the contenders under gage, "Till we assign you to your days of trial." The intransigeance of the original ugly fact is a perpetual stumbling block to the house of Edward's sons, those "seven vials of his sacred blood" which has been shed. Thus the ulti-

---

[6] Wilbur Sanders, *The Dramatist and the Received Idea* (Cambridge: Cambridge Univ. Press, 1968), sturdily anti-orthodox in the matter of the dominance in the histories of the Tudor ideology of providence, concurs in finding the import of Richard's action in the supervention of "policy" upon an elaborate and suspect formality. Shakespeare wanted, he says, to establish right from the start "the moral impenetrability of the political order" (p. 160).

mate source of evil in this play and those which follow it (in the chronology of history, not by date of composition) is clearly identifiable. It is Woodstock's murder—a crime which sets up the chain reaction of violence and counterviolence, of guilt and the incurring of guilt, that scourges England through half-a-dozen reigns. But if Woodstock's death is the ultimate cause of these events, it is nevertheless not what is dramatized in *Richard II*. The play leaves this original act of Cain in impenetrable obscurity; but it presents Richard, at the outset, in precarious command of a dangerous and complex situation. He cannot place his dubious position at hazard upon the outcome of the duel, and he certainly cannot circumvent the challengers without the behind-the-scenes political arrangements we observe.[7] This is Richard's predicament; and what the first two acts are engaged to exhibit is his disastrous incapacity to establish his ascendancy.

Richard's handling of the difficult situation presented in Act I is, I have suggested, not unmarked by a shrewd political acumen. But it is marred by levity. His speech to the combatants, in the high vein of prophetic patriotism which is struck again and again, and with the utmost seriousness, throughout the play, has impressive dignity:

> For that our kingdom's earth should not be soil'd
> With that dear blood which it hath fostered;
> And for our eyes do hate the dire aspect
> Of civil wounds plough'd up with neighbours' sword,
> And for we think the eagle-winged pride
> Of sky-aspiring and ambitious thoughts,
> With rival-hating envy, set on you
> To wake our peace, which in our country's cradle
> Draws the sweet infant breath of gentle sleep. . . .
>
> (I.iii.125-133)

[7] A completely contrary view of the cessation of the trial by combat is taken by Hardin Craig, *An Interpretation of Shakespeare* (New York: Dryden Press, 1949).

But behind the regal bearing and the regal gesture is revealed Richard's dismal lack of that inalienable personal power which a later age would come to call charisma, and which alone could carry him through. He has not that in his face which either Mowbray or Bolingbroke would feign call master. And this is made manifest by their refusal, insolent in Bolingbroke's case, conciliatory in Mowbray's, to obey him, notwithstanding the brave show of "lions make leopards tame" or "we were not born to sue, but to command." The dramatic conduct of the first scenes throws into relief the "high pitch of the contender's resolution," rather than any high pitch of the King's. And though divinity hedges him (Gaunt will raise no hand against the Lord's anointed despite the appeal of his widowed sister-in-law) we are left with the overriding impression of a precariousness in his exercise of authority. The main source of this impression lies in the frivolity of Richard's attitude to Gaunt. The first note of this frivolity is heard in the flippant "pluck'd four away" with which Richard announces his commutation of Bolingbroke's sentence, and the scarcely veiled effrontery of "Why, uncle, thou hast many years to live." It is the note, or the major chord, upon which Act I closes:

> Now put it, God, in the physician's mind
> To help him to his grave immediately!
> The lining of his coffers shall make coats
> To deck our soldiers for these Irish wars.
> Come, gentlemen, let's all go visit him,
> Pray God we may make haste and come too late!
>
> (I.iv.59-64)

This is the mainspring of the development in Act II. For if in Act I was revealed Richard's lack of *virtù*—he plays neither lion nor fox with sufficient conviction—in Act II, against the powerful remonstrance of the dying Gaunt, is revealed his lack of virtue. And much is to be learned from the way in which this lack of virtue is in fact revealed. As we have seen, Act II is the phase of tragedy which presents the tempting or testing of the protagonist in terms of personal decisions which have to be made. Richard's "Can sick men play so nicely with their names?" and "A lunatic lean-witted fool, presuming on an ague's privilege," contrasting with the passion of Gaunt's "Landlord of England art thou now, not king," represent not merely a callous indifference to mortal illness, but a deliberate refusal to entertain the seriousness of the issues. Thus it is Richard's flippancy, exhibited in the deathbed confrontation with Gaunt, that indicates the nature of his "temptation." The difficulty is that the king's frivolity is exhibited only in the passage with Gaunt and made only by implication to bear the whole brunt of the indictment against him. It is by narrative hearsay that we are informed of Richard's unstaid youth, light vanity, the thousand flatterers which sit within his crown, the throne's bankruptcy, the shame of the leasing out of English land, and the burdensome exactions and taxes under which groan commons and nobles alike—charges which are made to account for the defection of Willoughby, Ross, and Worcester. But these defects and abuses are given no self-reflection or reverberation or internalization in Richard's mind, nor are they mediated by some powerful private motivation with which he must engage. Marlowe did better with his Edward in this respect.

Whether this summary fashion is due, as Rossiter thought,[8] to Shakespeare's leaning too heavily (by allusion) upon *Woodstock* is less to the purpose than the perception that in the encounter between uncle and nephew is encapsulated the morality content of the older play. There Richard's three uncles exhort him to virtue, and Tresilian, Bushy, and Green to vice; the familiar form of the medieval debate constitutes the whole structural frame of *Woodstock*. It is noteworthy that in *Richard II* this psychomachia is reduced to one stage

[8] A. P. Rossiter, *Woodstock* (London: Chatto, 1946), pp. 47-53, 226-229.

of a process, in keeping with the new kind of structure and the new kind of tragic issue toward which Shakespeare is evidently feeling his way. But the treatment suffers from too radical an abridgement. The effect is of a dramatic thinness, or flatness, or absence of relatedness. The discontinuity, the gaps, so to speak, between given, fixed aspects or attributes of character (regality, levity) are not only too great but also too empty of reflection to allow that play of inference which alone constitutes psychological density and creates our sense of character. Shakespeare overcomes this dramatic thinness in an impressively skillful manner through his presentation of the role of York. But this is still in the earlier episodic mode, not capable of the effects of integration later achieved.

York, upon Bolingbroke's return, becomes a vessel of ambivalence, swaying between fealty and justice, dynastic legitimacy and virtue. This is the conflict which Richard's frivolity imposes upon his subjects; it is also a continuation of the conflict implicit in the play's predicament. For as Bolingbroke presents his case to York it becomes abundantly clear that whichever principle York chooses he must do violence to another no less imperative.

> Will you permit that I shall stand condemn'd
> A wandering vagabond, my rights and royalties
> Pluck'd from my arms perforce, and given away
> To upstart unthrifts? Wherefore was I born?
> If that my cousin king be King in England,
> It must be granted I am Duke of Lancaster.
> You have a son, Aumerle, my noble cousin;
> Had you first died, and he been thus trod down,
> He should have found his uncle Gaunt a father,
> To rouse his wrongs and chase them to the bay.
>
> (II.iii.118-127)

The dichotomization of values is complete, and York mirrors the conflict which is externalized, in the plot, in the struggle between the two contenders for the crown. But he does not mirror a dilemma within the soul of the protagonist, as, for instance, does Enobarbus; he merely substitutes for it. Maynard Mack has spoken of "umbrella" speeches or episodes, those mirrors of analogy in the mature Shakespearean drama "under which more than one consciousness shelters." These are screens, he says, citing Lear's Fool, Poor Tom, Enobarbus, and the sleepwalking Lady Macbeth, on which "Shakespeare flashes, as it were, readings from the psychic life of the protagonist."[9] York is incipiently such a figure, but it is not until the end of the play, as I shall presently show, that the readings flashed onto the screen he provides are from the psychic life of Richard himself.

In Act II we watch the actualization of Gaunt's prophecy: the callous indifference of Richard to his death, the seizing of Bolingbroke's inheritance, the defection of Willoughby, Ross, and Worcester, and the mournful forebodings of the Queen. It is the expropriation of Bolingbroke, of course, that makes possible his return as claimant for simple justice. But the fatality of this act, which in fact precipitates Richard's downfall, is obscured by the secondary issues, so that its effect is dissipated in a catalogue of political abuses of which the expropriation of Bolingbroke appears to be only one. We are thus catapulted straight into the peripeteia of Act III—the unkinging of the King—with no transition other than the episodic reference to the Irish expedition by Bushy, Green, and Bagot. These scapegoat figures, caterpillars of the commonwealth, serve the ends of historical apologetic for the sweet English rose, but they usurp attention that should be concentrated upon the figure of the tragic hero. What Shakespeare, it seems, has not mastered in this play is the foregrounding of the fatal choice—the act, portentous in the inescapability of its consequences, fully expressive of the protagonist's nature (though it may be unpremeditated) which

[9] *Jacobean Theatre* (London: Edward Arnold, 1960), pp. 24, 26.

precipitates both disaster and the recognitions that constitute the emergence of tragic consciousness in one who is, paradoxically, both agent and victim of his fate.

Because Shakespeare has thus failed to bring out and make salient the tragic error, Act III appears to set off, so far as the character of Richard is concerned, in a completely new direction. The effect of discontinuity, of too sudden a shift of focus, is the result of an insufficient anchoring of present responses in purposes, feelings, desires, intentions previously entertained. By the time Shakespeare comes to write *Lear*, in which so much that is implicit in *Richard II* is developed, and *Macbeth*, in which so much that is implicit in *Richard III* is developed, he will know how to exploit a tragic error committed at the outset of the events. Richard's tragic life begins, in effect, only in Act III itself; unlike Lear and Macbeth, he is not yet possessed of that great tragic asset, a past—is not yet haunted and hounded by the memory of that which is done. It is precisely, indeed, toward a realization of the nature of his temporal existence that he is made to struggle in Act III. And it is this which gives one the sense of being in the very forge and workshop of Shakespeare's art. For it is the "inside of the event" that we are given throughout these central perturbations in Act III, the very process of Richard's discovery of self. Those critics who complain of "self-dramatization" overlook the fact that for a character to have a self to dramatize is one of the more remarkable achievements of European literature. The question is important enough to warrant a moment's digression.

In *Richard III* Shakespeare had achieved a density of characterization by the essentially simple device of impersonation, which was his inheritance from the Devil-vice figure of the moralities. Richard not only acts the villain; he delights in the exercise of his skill as an enactor of villainy. He is both actor and *régisseur* of his own part, and the fascination of the performance hinges upon the very ambiguity of the notion of playacting, interchangeably illusion and reality. All reference in Shakespeare to playacting, direct or implicit, has this effect, creating a metatheatre in which levels of representation interact. The same principle accounts for the density of Falstaff. And in the multiplication of possibilities of interplay between the projection, the performance, the assessment, and the awareness of a role lies the inimitable impression of exuberance and zest which mark both characters, each in his own mode. The moment, however, we are tempted or invited to probe behind a public role to a private reality, to press beyond the imitation of a histrionic toward the imitation of an historic mode of existence, we find that such characters become dynamic in a totally new way. A principle of growth, of modification, of real human development is introduced into figures which, whatever their versatility, are tied to the irreducible fixity of Crookback or Fatbelly. Falstaff as comic character cannot truly survive the sense of self which is beyond the sense of role. Hence the notorious fracture, so to speak, of the whole conception, in *2 Henry IV*. In Richard, on the other hand (since by a paradox of terminology, it is the tragedies which explore the "historic," or inward, as opposed to the "histrionic," or outward, mode of existence) we perceive, in his soliloquy after the dream, the very point of emergence of a new possibility: a dialogue of self and soul.

> Give me another horse, bind up my wounds:
> Have mercy Jesu! Soft, I did but dream.
> O coward conscience! how dost thou afflict me?
> The lights burn blue. It is now dead midnight.
> Cold fearful drops stand on my trembling flesh.
> What do I fear? myself? There's none else by,
> Richard loves Richard; that is, I am I.
> Is there a murderer here? No; yes, I am:
> Then fly. What from myself? Great reason why?

Lest I revenge. What, myself upon myself?
Alack, I love myself. Wherefore? For any good
That I myself have done unto myself?
O no! Alas, I rather hate myself
For hateful deeds committed by myself.
I am a villain: yet I lie, I am not.
Fool, of thyself speak well: fool, do not flatter.
My conscience hath a thousand several tongues,
And every tongue brings in a several tale,
And every tale condemns me for a villain;
Perjury, in the high'st degree,
Murder, stern murder, in the dir'st degree;
All several sins, all us'd in each degree,
Throng to the bar, crying all, Guilty! Guilty!
I shall despair. There is no creature loves me;
And if I die no soul shall pity me.
Nay, wherefore should they? Since that I myself,
Find in myself no pity to myself?

(v.iii.178-204)

It is rudimentary, though powerful; it is the merest sketch—too little and too late. But it is of the highest significance. And it is the germ which will develop through subsequent plays, adding to dramatic character an entire inner dimension of tragic self-discovery.

It is thus not further evidence of Richard's failure as a king that we are invited to perceive throughout Act III. His failure as a king has been sufficiently established, as has Bolingbroke's cool confidence and masterly practicality. We are invited to perceive, stage by stage, through the direct disclosure of monologue and through inferences that the detail of the language enables us to make, a total curve of experience. The emotions that constitute that experience—shattered confidence, the sense of inadequacy, impotence, humiliation, grief—find

cumulative expression throughout Richard's speeches in Acts
III and IV and culminating expression in the speech at Pomfret. And their delineation of emerging self-awareness and the
struggle for self-possession is masterly. We have been mis-
directed to find in these speeches the luxuriatings in misery
of a "poet *manqué*, who loved words more dearly than his
Kingdom,"[10] or a dilettante sentimentalist, "morbid, vacillating, impotently reflective and emotional,"[11] "whose tragedy
expresses itself in terms that clearly point to the weakness
[acute self-consciousness] that has been, in part, its cause."[12]
These speeches are properly to be construed not as educing
the cause of his fall before the onslaught of Bolingbroke, but
as the consequences of that fall, suffered, known, experienced,
and reflected in the mind. Self-dramatization (Eliot's notorious stricture upon Othello) is the very medium of the art
of tragedy, the method whereby it articulates its progress. It
is as fallacious to regard it as an idiosyncrasy which demands
particularistic psychological explanation as to construe the
sculptured immobility of the discus-thrower as an indication
of his curious inability to throw a discus. How shall we become aware of a character's thoughts save by his utterance of
them, of a character's emotions save by his expression of them,
of a character's possession of self save by his manifestation of a
consciousness of self, or of a character's tragic identity save by
his tragic agon, his pressing to the limit the experience of
adversity in existence. The tragic hero is locked in struggle
with himself, like Jacob with the angel.

As Moulton perceived, this fall of Richard is constructed on
Shakespeare's favorite plan: "its force is measured, not by

[10] R. D. Altick, "Symphonic Imagery in *Richard II*," *PMLA*, LXII
(June 1947), 364.

[11] L. Schücking, *Character Problems in Shakespeare's Plays* (Gloucester, Mass.: P. Smith, 1959).

[12] D. A. Traversi, *Shakespeare from Richard II to Henry V* (Stanford, Calif.: Stanford Univ. Press, 1957).

suddenness or violence, but by protraction and the perception of distinct stages."[13] Aristotle's anagnorisis—the transformation of ignorance into knowledge through recognition of identity—provides the paradigm for all such transmutations in tragedy. What distinguishes the Shakespearean kind is the richness, depth, inwardness, and range of awareness which the expressive, self-revelatory, self-exploratory speech of the hero enables him to articulate. In Greek drama what is recognized is identity. In Shakespearean drama what is recognized is self. Characteristically the self-exploration is given substance and definition by the terms of the psychomachia set forth in Act II. And though this, as we have seen, is less than sufficiently "done" in this play, nevertheless particular analysis of the self-exploration of Richard shows that the observation holds good here too.

Richard's vacillations are a function basically of that failure to summon up the maximum resources of the will, that lack of self-confidence, which characterizes men who are weaker than the opponents they encounter. But the substance of his vacillations consists of desperate recurrent attempts to achieve or fix an image of himself with which he can live should his native role slip from his grasp.

When we first encounter Richard upon his return from Ireland, weeping for joy to stand upon his kingdom once again, the speech is in direct emotional continuation of his address to the combatants in Act I, in which he adjured them to protect the peace "which in our country's cradle / Draws the sweet infant breath of gentle sleep" (I.iii.132).

[13] Moulton, *Shakespeare as Dramatic Artist* (Oxford: The Clarendon Press, 1893), p. 119. The reference is to *Richard III*, but the point is equally applicable to *Richard II*. Henry James, in the preface to *The Princess Cassamassima*, expresses a similar perception of this aesthetic law: "A character is interesting as it comes out, and by a process and development of that emergence—just as a procession is effective by the way it unrolls, turning to a mere mob if all of it passes at once."

Dear earth, I do salute thee with my hand
Though rebels wound thee with their horses' hoofs.
As a long-parted mother with her child
Plays fondly with her tears and smiles in meeting,
So weeping, smiling, greet I thee, my earth,
And do thee favours with my royal hands;
Feed not thy sovereign's foe, my gentle earth,
Nor with thy sweets comfort his ravenous sense,
But let thy spiders that suck up thy venom
And heavy-gaited toads lie in their way,
Doing annoyance to the treacherous feet,
Which with usurping steps do trample thee. . . .

(III.ii.6-17)

These speeches are in marked contrast with the historically oriented nationalism of Gaunt's prophecy:

This royal throne of kings, this scept'red isle . . .
This happy breed of men, this little world . . .
This blessed plot, this earth, this realm, this
  England,
This nurse, this teeming womb of royal kings,
Fear'd by their breed, and famous by their
  birth,
Renowned for their deeds as far from home,
For Christian service and true chivalry,
As is the sepulchre in stubborn Jewry
Of the world's ransom, blessed Mary's son;
This land of such dear souls, this dear dear land,
Dear for her reputation through the world,
Is now leas'd out—I die pronouncing it—
Like to a tenement or pelting farm.

(II.i.40-60)

Richard, unlike Gaunt, is invoking an ancient, sacramental magic. It is prenational, a-historical; it is the sacred, animistic bond between king and land—the *corpus mysticum* which includes and transcends both political kingdom and physical earth, as kingship includes and transcends both the king's eternal "body politic" and his personal, natural self.[14] From this he draws the strength of his asserted belief that "Not all the water in the rough rude sea / Can wash the balm off from an anointed king." He is also invoking a lover's relationship, caressing, tender, maternal, erotic. His personifications persistently link rebellion with suggestions of sexual violation—a rape of the land:

> And when they from thy bosom pluck a flower,
> Guard it, I pray thee, with a lurking adder,
> Whose double tongue may with a mortal touch
> Throw death upon thy sovereign's enemies.
>
> (III.ii.19-22)

Gaunt's patriotism, on the other hand, takes the form of a national pride in the virtues and achievements of an historical nation-state, its martial valor, its renown abroad, its strength and independence. It is noteworthy that his rhetoric consistently distinguishes between "land" and "state"—indeed in the famous lines, "This blessed plot, this earth, this realm, this England, / This nurse, this teeming womb of royal kings" (II.i.50-51), he makes perceptible transition from the merely native to the consciously national. That Gaunt's patriotism is anachronistic, far more Elizabethan than feudal, is less to the purpose than the perception that Richard, by contrast, is drawing upon constitutional and legal doctrine and quasi-erotic sentiment to supply the strength and confidence which "worldly men" derive from the exercise of political arts. Richard's identification of himself with his kingship and with the land he is part of and possesses constitutes the inherited

---

[14] E. H. Kantorowicz, *The King's Two Bodies* (Princeton: Princeton Univ. Press, 1957) shows the relevance of the doctrine of the king's "two bodies" to *Richard II*.

and as yet untried conception of himself to which he retreats at the first crisis. It is this that circumstances will test, undermine, and finally shatter; and in the ruin of which, in the catastrophe, he will find independent individual dignity.

While Carlisle and Aumerle make their plea for the practical energies of *virtù*, Fortune and Scroop, playing the torturer by small and small, announce first the defection of the Welshmen, then the general insurrection in favor of Bolingbroke, then the execution of Bushy, Green, and the Earl of Wiltshire. Richard's reactions consist of a series of violent fluctuations between dread of worse to come and renewed hope for the power of the king's name, or the power of his uncle York. These fluctuations come to rest in a stoical attempt to withstand the tidings of calamity by reducing its significance to mere worldly loss, which can be endured with a virtuous fortitude:

> The worst is worldly loss thou canst unfold.
> Say, is my kingdom lost? Why, 'twas my care,
> And what loss is it to be rid of care?
> Strives Bolingbroke to be as great as we?
> Greater he shall not be. If he serve God,
> We'll serve Him too, and be his fellow so.
> Revolt our subjects? that we cannot mend;
> They break their faith to God as well as us.
> Cry woe, destruction, ruin, and decay—
> The worst is death, and death will have his day.
>
> (III.ii.94-103)

But the culmination of the whole series of reactions, finely discriminated from this speech of rehearsal, is the great elegy with which Richard greets the blow of the news of his friends' death. Indeed it is this blow and its accompanying emotional perturbation (immediately following his carefully constructed stoicism) that transforms the protective pose of Christian fortitude into a great lament upon the theme of vanity. He believed his friends treacherous, and discovers their loyalty in the same breath as he discovers their death. The irony is pointed up by Scroop's equivocation: "Peace have they made with him indeed, my lord" (iii.ii.128). From the multiplicity of meaning radiating outward from the small word "peace" Richard's meditation upon death takes its rise. Peace of body, of mind, of conscience, the illusory peace of life—"as if this flesh which walls about our life were brass impregnable"—the peace of the grave in the hollow ground are its grand themes.

> Let's talk of graves, of worms, and epitaphs,
> Make dust our paper, and with rainy eyes
> Write sorrow on the bosom of the earth.
> Let's choose executors and talk of wills.
> And yet not so—for what can we bequeath
> Save our deposed bodies to the ground?
> Our lands, our lives, and all, are Bollingbroke's,
> And nothing can we call our own but death;
> And that small model of the barren earth
> Which serves as paste and cover to our bones.
> For God's sake let us sit upon the ground
> And tell sad stories of the death of kings:
> How some have been depos'd, some vain in war,
> Some haunted by the ghosts they have deposed,
> Some poisoned by their wives, some sleeping kill'd,
> All murthered—for within the hollow crown
> That rounds the mortal temples of a king
> Keeps Death his court, and there his antic sits,
> Scoffing his state and grinning at his pomp,
> Allowing him a breath, a little scene,
> To monarchize, be fear'd, and kill with looks;
> Infusing him with self and vain conceit,
> As if this flesh which walls about our life
> Were brass impregnable; and humour'd thus,
> Comes at the last, and with a little pin

Bores through his castle wall, and farewell king!
Cover your heads, and mock not flesh and blood
With solemn reverence; throw away respect,
Tradition, form, and ceremonious duty;
For you have but mistook me all this while.
I live with bread like you, feel want,
Taste grief, need friends—subjected thus,
How can you say to me, I am a king?

(III.ii.145-177)

His own deprivation, his own mortification, is the prelude
to the melancholy procession of monarchs from the *Mirror for
Magistrates* in all the poignant specificity of their individual
deaths. But he is one of them, and the idea of the common
destiny of all eathly kings is salient. The thought reaches its
climax in the figure of King Death keeping his court within
the hollow crown that rounds the mortal temples of a king;
the metaphor articulates illusion, juxtaposing king and mock-
king, king of flesh and king of shadows, in a flash of meaning
Lear will later expand. Richard's self-awareness emerges from
this dialectic of king and subject with the double puns upon
"Crown" (symbol of sovereignty and mere skull) and "subjected" (made a subject and thrown down) focusing his
realization of the relationship between the illusory name of
king and the real nature of man, subject to elementary needs
and sorrows. The very pronouns articulate the progress of this
arduous shift of perspective. The speech begins with the
generalizing and representative royal plural: "Let's sit," "Let's
choose," "What can we bequeath," proceeds through the immensely distanced "allowing him," "infusing him," to the
"me" and the "I" and the "you" of a fully exposed personal
existence in the final lines.

Richard's lament yields to the scarcely concealed contempt
with which the practical Carlisle urges him, "My lord, wise
men ne'er sit and wail their woes," and to Aumerle's encour-

agement to him to remember York's force. His insight gives way to the older habitual posture. He rejects his recent outburst as an "ague fit of fear" and brashly looks forward to the winning of his own as an easy task. But the final blow is decisive. Richard's "sweet way to despair" is sweet not only because it suggests to him the consolations of an indulgence in the grief which is now all that is his own, but also because it is, in terms of a medieval *contemptus mundi*, a kind of hope. The "Kingly woe" which he resolves to obey is endued with connotations of a piety—the piety of the kingdom within—which has the power to make folly the wisdom of the world. The perspective is one which makes Bolingbroke's rise to power, crowned by vanity and haunted by guilt, a grimly ironic comment upon Carlisle's "wise men."

To call Richard's behavior here vacillation is of course to classify it correctly for practical purposes. For dramatic purposes, however, what is important is what we are enabled to infer of the nature of his ordeal and the inner strategies it gives rise to. The peripeteia which reverses his status and his situation, which makes him no king, produces self-awareness of the acutest and most poignant kind. And it would seem to be crass indeed to interpret the highly original if still somewhat stilted rendering of this self-awareness as "Richard's fatal weakness." It is often done. "He cannot bring himself to live in a world of hard actuality; the universe to him is real only as it is presented in packages of fine words"; "Aumerle tries almost roughly to recall him from his weaving of sweet, melancholy sounds . . . but he rouses himself only momentarily and then relapses into a complacent enjoyment of the sound of his own tongue."[15] A juster analysis will surely perceive the subtlety with which the personal struggle is rendered. As he watches his power dwindle and knows himself without the innate capacity to rule, it is precisely "the hard ac-

---

[15] Altick, "Symphonic Imagery," pp. 349-350.

tuality" of his situation that he perceives. And in his probing
of this actuality he conceives the possibility of an alternative
"address to the world" which represents another kind of
sovereignty. Both impose claims upon his imagination, and
each frustrates the other. "What shall the King do?" is the
question that torments him. And "What shall the King do?"
in circumstances in which the King's power to initiate action
is lost becomes the far more radical and searching question,
"What shall the King be?"

The constitutive principle throughout Act III is that of rapid
alternation, and with each thrust and counterthrust further
resources of language are brought into play. Richard's appearance upon the walls of Flint castle has the imposing dignity of royal spectacle. As York points out:

> Yet looks he like a king. Behold, his eye,
> As bright as is the eagle's, lightens forth
> Controlling majesty; alack, alack for woe
> That any harm should stain so fair a show!
> (III.iii.68-71)

And his address to Northumberland takes the cue with magnificent aplomb:

> We are amazed, and thus long have we stood
> To watch the fearful bending of thy knee,
> Because we thought ourselves thy lawful king:
> And if we be, how dare thy joints forget
> To pay their awful duty to our presence?
> (III.iii.72-76)

In his speech the themes of legitimate descent, divine protection, the ravages of war to come are recapitulated and
climaxed by one of the most moving of the recurrent image
clusters:

But ere the crown he looks for live in peace,
Ten thousand bloody crowns of mothers' sons
Shall ill become the flower of England's face,
Change the complexion of her maid-pale peace
To scarlet indignation and bedew
Her pastures' grass with faithful English blood.

(III.iii.95-100)

The speech is in direct counterpoint to Bolingbroke's preceding threat:

If not, I'll use the advantage of my power
And lay the summer's dust with showers of blood
Rain'd from the wounds of slaughtered Englishmen—
The which, how far off from the mind of Bolingbroke
It is such crimson tempest should bedrench
The fresh green lap of fair King Richard's land. . . .

(III.iii.42-47)

It should not be lost upon the sensitive ear that Richard's version of the rape of the land has the advantage in resonance, seriousness, and poetic power. The metaphor which is slighting in "the fresh green lap of fair King Richard's land" recurs in "the flower of England's face," but with an access of personal dignity in the change of bodily reference; and then is almost completely personified in "the complexion of her maid-pale peace," so that the England which will be drenched by the rain of blood is presented as the object of Richard's personal love and as a lovely object of contemplative pity. The imagery in this play is still more "poetic" than "dramatic," but an instance of the specifically poetic medium taking on a dramatic dimension is the way in which the imagery of earth, flesh, peace, blood, and growth[16] is also used to discriminate between contrasting martial and tender modes of being. The

---

[16] Altick has an excellent exposition of the correlations between these systems of images.

gamut of expression thus provided constitutes the characteriz-
ing, or dramatizing, function of the imagery, and so enters
into the dynamic of the play.

Richard's wholeheartedness, his role as his land's lover, gives
way to bitterness at the thought of what his situation forces
him to do. For this reason he overstates his accession to
Bolingbroke's demands:

> Northumberland, say thus the King returns:
> His noble cousin is right welcome hither,
> And all the number of his fair demands
> Shall be accomplish'd without contradiction;
> With all the gracious utterance that thou hast
> Speak to his gentle hearing kind commends.
>
> (III.iii.121-126)

and at once plays with a repudiation of what he feels to be
intolerably debasing:

> We do debase ourselves, cousin, do we not,
> To look so poorly, and to speak so fair?
> Shall we call back Northumberland and send
> Defiance to the traitor, and so die?
>
> (III.iii.127-130)

The wild desire for an heroic death ("to send defiance to the
traitor, and so die"), checked by Aumerle's prudence, then
issues in Richard's passionate insight into the tragic discrepancy between the king's two bodies, between himself and his
role, between the man that he is and the king that he ought
to be.

> O that I were as great
> As is my grief, or lesser than my name!
> Or that I could forget what I have been!
> Or not remember what I must be now!
> Swell'st thou, proud heart? I'll give thee scope to beat,
> Since foes have scope to beat both thee and me.
>
> (III.iii.136-141)

The previous speech, which ended with the cry, "Subjected thus, / How can you say to me, I am a king?" registered his shocked realization of impotence, generated by the perception that such impotence in the face of death is the lot of common humanity. Here Richard exhibits a further stage in his awareness of himself as separate from the role history has cast upon him. The immediate result is the renunciation speech, which is flattened out of all significance if it is seen as merely another ecstasy of self-pity. The speech registers in fact a complex triple movement of feeling:

What must the King do now? Must he submit?
The King shall do it. Must he be depos'd?
The King shall be contented. Must he lose
The name of king? a God's name, let it go.
I'll give my jewels for a set of beads;
My gorgeous palace for a hermitage;
My gay apparel for an almsman's gown;
My figur'd goblets for a dish of wood;
My scepter for a palmer's walking staff;
My subjects for a pair of carved saints,
And my large kingdom for a little grave,
A little little grave, an obscure grave;
Or I'll be buried in the King's highway,
Some way of common trade, where subjects' feet
May hourly trample on their sovereign's head;
For on my heart they tread now whilst I live:
And buried once, why not upon my head?
Aumerle, thou weep'st (my tender-hearted cousin!),
We'll make foul weather with despised tears;
Our sighs and they shall lodge the summer corn,
And make some pretty match with shedding tears?
Or shall we play the wantons with our woes,
As thus, to drop them still upon one place,
Till they have fretted us a pair of graves

Within the earth, and, therein laid—there lies
Two kinsmen digg'd their graves with weeping eyes!
Would not this ill do well? Well, well, I see
I talk but idly, and you laugh at me.
Most mighty prince, my Lord Northumberland,
What says King Bolingbroke? Will his Majesty
Give Richard leave to live till Richard die?

(III.iii.143-173)

The detailed, almost ritualistic specification with which he itemizes the idea of renunciation of the world suggests the intensity with which he is attempting to make a virtue of his necessity. The culminating item, however, "And my large kingdom for a little grave," initiates a collapse of this high aim. It is marvelously dramatic. The would-be saint at this point collapses into the would-be martyr, and the self-pity which overcomes him is the surest sign of an unchastened self-love, an unreadiness for and even rejection of the idea of renunciation. In the third stage of the speech this access of self-pity itself gives way to something else as the king becomes aware of Aumerle's evident emotion. His address to Aumerle, faithful king's man to the end, is indeed what it is invariably taken to be—a sentimental excursion. But it should not, I believe, be glossed exclusively to the King's disadvantage. On the contrary, if it is the verbal equivalent of the embrace of a man's arm around a friend's shoulder, it suggests the sustaining power of a gesture of sympathy, and it is in fact bracing in its effect, enabling Richard to return to the cruelty of fact: "What says King Bolingbroke? Will his Majesty / Give Richard leave to live till Richard die?" (III.iii.172-173). Once again pronouns chart the spiritual progress. The royal "we" of the opening speech gave place to the titular third person used of himself at the start of the renunciation speech ("What must the King do now?"); this in turn gave way to the first person of the renunciation itself, as king was deposed into person. "Richard," royal and baptismal name, designates the now ironic identification of person and king, the two aspects of himself seen, so to speak, from without. But the descent to the base court of the deposed sun-king is rendered by the unreserved and unmitigated first person singular.

The descent to the base court marks the completion of the tragic reversal. Power has in fact passed from Richard to Bolingbroke and from now on Richard is no longer controller or initiator of events, but merely the object of Bolingbroke's designs. Though this transfer of power is not formalized until the abdication scene, it has in fact occurred; and Richard's role in Act IV is subtly different from all that has preceded it. In Act IV Richard is the victim of Bolingbroke's inexorable progress, and his protest takes the form of the inverted coronation-rite. His newly sharpened awareness of self now becomes a bitter sense of self-betrayal and consequent self-disgust. We are given our bearings upon this phase of Richard's progress by his increasing recourse to sarcasm, the only weapon of revenge, the only violence, of a weak man:

Alack, why am I sent for to a king
Before I have shook off the regal thoughts
Wherewith I reign'd? I hardly yet have learn'd
To insinuate, flatter, bow, and bend my knee.
(IV.i.162-165)

The one power he still has over Bolingbroke is the power to force him to be the witness of his violation of royalty, to force him to take responsibility, full human responsibility, for the *lèse majesté* which he sees as a replica of the ultimate sacrilege:

Though some of you, with Pilate, wash your hands,
Showing an outward pity—yet you Pilates
Have here deliver'd me to my sour cross,
And water cannot wash away your sin
(IV.i.239-242)

85

Had he retired in dignified silence from the stage of history, as many of his critics apparently would have wished him to do, it would certainly have been more comfortable for the new king than the woeful pageant that we have. But the abdication scene, in which Richard stage-manages the exchange of the crown and the ritual unkinging of himself, provides the context in which the mirror episode acquires its reverberating significance.

In the mirror Richard seeks to solve the mystery of identity, of who and what he is. Truth and vanity, face and mask, self and role, substance and shadow—these dichotomies are all contained in the grand symbol of the mirror. Comparison with *Richard III* is instructive. For where Richard III watched his crooked shadow in the sun, understanding what he was in that outward figure, Richard II peruses his image in the glass, "That it may show me what a face I have / Since it is bankrupt of his majesty" (iv.i.266-267). For his bafflement concerning his name and his nature has just received its most moving, passionate expression:

> Alack the heavy day,
> That I have worn so many winters out,
> And know not now what name to call myself!
> O that I were a mockery king of snow,
> Standing before the sun of Bolingbroke,
> To melt myself away in water drops!
>
> (iv.i.257-262)

The disintegrating experience of a total breach between name and self is matched by the powerful snow-king metaphor of disintegration. The bitterness is wonderfully expressed by the transference of the sun metaphor to Bolingbroke and the transference of Bolingbroke's cold qualities to himself. Throughout the play, indeed, the orchestration of the sensuous contraries expressive of Richard's fluctuating states of mind— hot and cold, sweet and sour, pale and red, high and low, solid and melting (or brittle or liquid), harsh and tuneful—is entirely admirable.

In the shattering of the mirror is the symbol shattered, and Bolingbroke's acid comment, "The shadow of your sorrow has destroy'd the shadow of your face," extracts a yet further significance from the episode. Richard responds to the truth of Bolingbroke's pragmatism with a countertruth in which resides the grandest irony of all, did Bolingbroke but know it—the irony of the inner reality of anguish and guilt of which the pomp and power of kingship's outer action is but the shadow:

> 'Tis very true, my grief lies all within,
> And these external manners of laments
> Are merely shadows to the unseen grief
> That swells with silence in the tortur'd soul.
> There lies the substance. . . .
>
> (IV.i.295-299)

The sequence of scenes which runs from III.iv to v.i is of absorbing interest from the point of view taken in these pages, that is to say from the point of view of the discovery of Shakespeare's tragic form. The act division reflects the fall-rise plot construction: the garden scene, coming immediately after the surrender at Flint castle, provides a suitable comment upon Richard's government of his kingdom, and therefore signals the change of regime which is to follow. Act IV initiates the rise to supreme power of Bolingbroke and begins therefore with his examination of Bagot and the renewed confrontation between the rival barons, echoing Act I. Act IV ends with Richard's abdication and the plans for Bolingbroke's coronation, leaving for Act v the final moves in the transfer of power: Richard's incarceration in the Tower, the queen's exile to France, Aumerle's conspiracy, which presents Bolingbroke with his first treason (foreshadowing things to come), and the death of Richard. Act division therefore faithfully reflects the construction of the play in terms of the overthrow of Richard's legitimate monarchy and the usurpation of Bolingbroke. But an eye trained by Shakespeare's later practice perceives at once that both iii.iv, the gardener scene, and v.i, the leave-taking scene between Richard and his weeping queen, in fact contain the sort of material that was to become, in the later tragedies, Shakespeare's characteristic fourth phase. This is the phase in which the tragic experience is rendered by some form of despair or repudiation of his world on the part of the protagonist, and modified by bearings taken from a vantage point outside and beyond the hero. It is the phase in which the great fall is wryly domesticated, and lit, so to speak, by transverse beams of pathos and irony. Both the pathos and the irony are methods for presenting the heroic image refracted in the medium provided by the viewpoint of simple, often anonymous, common folk.

In *Richard II* these resources are not deployed to the full as they will be later, where they are wonderfully juxtaposed and counterpointed so as to make the richest harmonic effects possible. Here they remain discrete and relatively unimpressive. The Gardener, effectively elegiac, is too explicitly allegorical for his comment upon "what men do, not knowing what they do" to have the maximum impact of dramatic irony. Later Shakespeare will transpose the key of such comment into the inspired fool's wisdom of gnomic gravediggers, or the earthy wisdom of an Emilia, while the contrapuntal darkened vision of Richard, "A king of beasts, indeed—if aught but beasts, / I had been still a happy king of men" (v.i.35-36), becomes "the wren goes to 't" and "a dog's obeyed in office" of Lear. In *Richard II* the content of the darkened vision has not been so objectively grounded in the very action of the play; nor has it the coordinated, accumulated reverberation of Lear's black apocalypse. In *Richard II* the ceremony and policy which veil human savagery are not rent entirely asunder as they are in *Lear*. Evil is fully accounted for in terms of political expediency, political error, political opportunism. Faces and fortunes are shattered, but the protagonists are not cut to the very brains. In *Lear* evil bursts all bounds and creates a vertiginous abyss. Nevertheless in Richard's somewhat decorative "lamentable tale," with which even "the senseless brands will sympathize" (v.i.40-50), is the germ of "I should e'en die with pity to see another thus"; and in his "I am sworn brother, sweet, / To grim necessity" is foreshadowed "I am bound upon a wheel of fire, that mine own tears / Do scald like molten lead."

In neither Richard's case nor Lear's is the hero's tragedy complete at this stage. The inexorable process that forces a man to face the worst the fates hold in store for him comes after he has entertained a delusive hope of accommodation with what he takes, in his ignorance, to be the worst. This total knowledge of the worst constitutes the tragic catastrophe. It is, in a sense, Aristotle's anagnorisis taken to its furthest limit and unfolded in its fullest relatedness to what has gone before. In the final turn of the tragedy the Shakespearean tragic hero offers us more than a repentant acknowledgment of his own share of responsibility for the events. He may do this. But he does very much more than this. He bears witness to his own personal self-definition, to some distinctive form of human integrity, some inalienable individual perception of value of which his life is the gauge. The prison scenes at Pomfret perfectly illustrate the process.

The first part of the soliloquy, in which Richard sets his brain and his soul to breed thoughts, provides striking confirmation of what we have already discovered to have been dramatized in the play: Richard's oscillation between "the better sort" of thought and the worse; between the conflicting impulses which have constituted his struggle to achieve and maintain either virtue or *virtù*, the inner or the outer kingdom:

> The better sort,
> As thoughts of things divine, are intermix'd
> With scruples, and do set the word itself
> Against the word,
> As thus: "Come, little ones"; And then again,
> "It is as hard to come as for a camel
> To thread the postern of a small needle's eye."
> Thoughts tending to ambition, they do plot
> Unlikely wonders: how these vain weak nails
> May tear a passage thorough the flinty ribs
> Of this hard world, my ragged prison walls;
> And for they cannot, die in their own pride.
> Thoughts tending to content flatter themselves
> That they are not the first of fortune's slaves,
> Nor shall not be the last—like silly beggars
> Who, sitting in the stocks, refuge their shame,
> That many have and others must sit there;
> And in this thought they find a kind of ease,
> Bearing their own misfortunes on the back
> Of such as have before endur'd the like.

(v.v.11-30)

Thoughts of things divine are undermined by his doubts of his capacity for them. Thoughts of grand defiance die in their own impotent pride. The elaborate figure in which the brain is female to the soul is Shakespeare's way of rendering what is actually the first passage of formal introspection in the play. The result of Richard's thus turning his eyes inward is the detachment with which he views his own attempts at resignation. These are thoughts which merely "flatter," which seek "a kind of ease" by the attempt to mitigate pain through dissipation in the thought of others' misfortunes. But in no thought can he find rest. These reflections bring him back to the great theme of role versus self, and to the ultimate nothing that awaits all men:

Thus play I in one person many people,
And none contented. Sometimes am I king,
Then treasons make me wish myself a beggar,
And so I am. Then crushing penury
Persuades me I was better when a king;
Then am I king'd again, and by and by
Think that I am unking'd by Bolingbroke,
And straight am nothing. But what e'er I be,
Nor I, nor any man that but man is,
With nothing shall be pleas'd, till he be eas'd
With being nothing.

$$(v.v.31-41)^{17}$$

"What, in ill thoughts again?" an Edgar might well have said; and indeed the transition to the idea of discord in the soul is implicit in the speech even before the music symbolizes it. The music, whose broken time apparently breaks into his train of thought, in reality focuses it. The idea of time broken, musically and metaphorically, in the music of men's lives, has the clearest relevance to his preoccupation with his own mismanagement of opportunities. And with the music, Richard's musing summary of his progress of the soul takes on a new urgency and energy of analysis:

How sour sweet music is
When time is broke, and no proportion kept!
So is it in the music of men's lives.
And here have I the daintiness of ear
To check time broke in a disordered string;
But for the concord of my state and time,
Had not an ear to hear my true time broke:
I wasted time, and now doth time waste me;
For now hath time made me his numb'ring clock; . . .

[17] A. Kernan, in a perceptive recent essay, has noted the relevance of the theatre trope to Richard's "passage into tragic existence"; "The Henriad: Shakespeare's Major History Plays," *Yale Review* (Autumn 1969).

But my time
Runs posting on in Bolingbroke's proud joy,
While I stand fooling here, his Jack of the clock.

(v.v.42-60)

It may not be without relevance to note that Marvell, whose *Horatian Ode* is in many ways a mid-century reincarnation of the drama of Richard II, uses the image of the Jack-of-the-clock in his "The first Anniversary of Cromwell's Return from Ireland" for the merely hereditary kings who are not masters of time and men's minds:

Thus (Image-like) an useless time they tell,
And with vain scepter, strike the hourly Bell;
No more contribute to the state of Things,
Than wooden Heads unto the Viols strings.

(ll.41-44)

The image has a Machiavellian resonance. In his letter to Soderini, "On Fortune and the Times," Machiavelli expounds the doctrine that a man may hope to master Fortune—the concatenation of forces which the Prince faces—by *virtù* properly understood and practiced:

and therefore the cautious man, when it is time to turn adventurous, does not know how to do it, hence he is ruined; ... For my part I consider that it is better to be adventurous than cautious, because fortune is a woman, and if you wish to keep her under it is necessary to beat and ill use her; and it is seen that she allows herself to be mastered by the adventurous rather than those who go to work more coldly.[18]

The point I wish to emphasize is one that is not usually stressed: the latter half of Richard's monologue is very definitely in the direction of the world. Richard may be a wiser and better man at the end of the play than he was at the be-

[18] *The Prince*, chap. 24.

ginning, though much of what he learns the great common-places of all times teach. But struggle as he may towards resignation or renunciation, the unregenerate bent and drag of his nature is toward his lost royalty, and no divine thoughts have succeeded in sweetening the sour taste of deposition, the bitter realization of what he has lost and of what he has allowed himself to become.

What happens between the entrance of the groom and the end needs for its full understanding the "reflector" scenes between York and Aumerle which immediately precede Pomfret, and to which I have previously referred. York has been throughout the very image of a divided spirit. He remonstrates with Richard in his brother's and his nephew's defense, yet he sharply reproves Northumberland for want of reverence to the King at Flint Castle. He is torn between kinsmen, between loyalty and justice:

> Th' one is my sovereign, whom both my oath
> And duty bids defend; th' other again
> Is my kinsman, whom the King hath wrong'd,
> Whom conscience and my kindred bids to right.
>
> (II.ii.112-115)

He can choose no path which will annul the contrary alternative. While he is the spokesman of compassion for Richard in his description of the well-graced royal actor leaving the stage,

> . . . men's eyes
> Did scowl on Richard. No man cried "God save him!"
> No joyful tongue gave him his welcome home,
> But dust was thrown upon his sacred head. . . .
>
> (v.ii.27-30)

the description prefaces his assertion that "To Bolingbroke are we sworn subjects now." The revelation of Aumerle's conspiracy in favor of the deposed but after all still legitimate king produces an extremity of reaction in York that has puz-

zled commentators. I believe it fruitful to see the York episode as dramatically functional, as preliminary to Richard's
death to which it points by contrast. For what is enacted in
the conspiracy scene is the total breakdown of the man, his
complete loss of inner coherence, the disintegration of his
identity as man and father. He is so eroded by his inner warfare with inescapable treason that he can deliver his own son
to the sword. The violence of his outburst in the teeth of the
impassioned voice of nature in his wife's pleading is evidence
of the breakdown. If the whole episode is a replica in little of
the fate of the kingdom delivered over to civil strife, and an
anticipation of Henry IV's problem with his wayward son,
York's part in it at least is the immediate prelude to the recovery of self-possession by the dispossessed king. For this is
the final outcome of the catastrophe.

The encounter with the groom and the story of the horse
recall Richard to himself and renew his fighting spirit and
his power of self-assertion. The defiant reflex of the will is
produced by the combination of the simple affection and
loyalty of the groom, which makes a "brooch in this all-hating
world," and the defection of roan Barbary—potent chivalric
symbol of martial valour, and, proudly carrying Bolingbroke,
exquisitely fitting symbol of the King's eclipse:

> So proud that Bolingbroke was on his back!
> That jade hath eat bread from my royal hand;
> This hand hath made him proud with clapping him.
> Would he not stumble? Would he not fall down,
> Since pride must have a fall, and break the neck
> Of that proud man that did usurp his back?
> Forgiveness, horse! Why do I rail on thee,
> Since thou, created to be aw'd by man,
> Wast born to bear? I was not made a horse,
> And yet I bear a burden like an ass,
> Spurr'd, gall'd, and tir'd by jauncing Bolingbroke.
>
> (v.v.84-94)

"I was not made a horse"—it is an unexpected turn, therefore splendidly expressive: "The devil take Henry of Lancaster, and thee! / Patience is stale, and I am weary of it." Richard, dispossessed of crown, queen, kingdom, hereditary role, and even the lordly creature that bore him on its back, reduced to something as near as the impure tragedy of the histories will get to unaccommodated man, finds in himself undreamt-of resources of willed defiance and sells his life dearly, in kingly fashion. It is the simplest kind of catharsis, a restoration of a lost heroic value. But it enables Exton to salute the sovereign that he kills with "As full of valour as of royal blood." King Richard is eclipsed, but the fact, or the dream, or the image of truly royal prowess, finally redemptive of folly and vanity, survives.

CHAPTER IV

JULIUS CAESAR

The central problem that any theory of tragic structure must solve in *Julius Caesar* is that of the identity of the tragic hero. The titular hero—great general and supreme consul—who falls from a point of high eminence and exhibits remarkable magnanimities, appears to possess the requisite properties, but fails to fulfil a unifying function: his death in the middle of the play splits it into two. Indeed it has been claimed that the play is a composite structure consisting of Caesar's tragedy in the first part and "Antony's Revenge" in the second. Of the two remaining candidates to the title, Cassius would have to be inflated to truly Machiavellian dimensions in order to serve the purpose, while Brutus, a central character throughout the play, and recipient of more dramatic attention than any of his fellows, has all too often been found wanting on moral grounds.

Moral grounds, however, provide no solution. In this Roman world of Shakespeare, there are neither saints nor villains. An inclusive category of radical moral limitation takes the place of a metaphysic of good and evil such as constitutes an organizing principle in *Othello* through the symbolic opposition between black and white. In all the Roman plays which are derived from Plutarch "evil" is limited to the inherent limitation of human knowledge. Ill-will as a positive, even demonic, force is absent. It is indeed with an astonishing consistency that Shakespeare presents his Roman world. Thus in *Julius Caesar* the catastrophe comes about not on account of vice, or depravity, or knavery, but simply through errors of judgment. And the tragic hero cannot simply be identified as the noblest Roman of them all for no such pre-eminence unambiguously presents itself.

Julius Caesar is composed upon a more complex system of symmetries than *Richard II*. Its four main characters are interlocked by a series of multiple contrasts and parallels. Brutus' rise in Caesar's fall; Brutus' fall is Caesar's rise again in the person of Octavius. Cassius is Brutus' henchman as Antony is Caesar's. At the same time Cassius is to Caesar, in point of temperamental oppugnance, as Antony is to Brutus. Again, at the beginning of that part of the action which culminates in the death of Caesar, Cassius is the initiator of the seduction of Brutus; at the beginning of that part of the action which culminates in the death of Brutus, Antony is the initiator of the avenging of Caesar. Portia's heroically "manly" self-inflicted wound is a final spur to Brutus' resolution; Calpurnia's "womanly" fears for Caesar's safety are manipulated by Decius to a similar end. These marked symmetries are what have tempted commentators to seek a thematic key to the design in some unifying moral antithesis. Public duty versus private affection, reason versus passion, calculation versus naïvety, practical expediency versus idealistic principle have all been proposed at one time or another. In Brutus, for example, public duty may be said to predominate over private affection (but does it?); in Cassius private affection (or disaffection) over public duty. In Caesar these two claims conflict so that he vacillates fatally on the morning of the Ides of March; in Antony they appear to coincide. Again, Caesar is (but is he?) notably uncalculating. Brutus calculates, but naïvely. Antony, though impulsive, calculates to very good purpose. Cassius, calculator by nature, fatally miscalculates in the event. Passion and reason, expediency and principle seem to change places under our very eyes. The categories all apply to some degree and illuminate episodes or facets of the play; but none completely. No character will quite fit in without remainder, so to speak, and the concepts that aided our understanding themselves shift and intertwine and crisscross until they begin to take on the character of a "ballet of bloodless categories." For instance: "Both [Brutus and Cassius] are great men who put country before self. . . . Yet in both selflessness is intertwined with a self-destructive vanity. . . . Both sapient men, Caesar and Brutus alike sacrifice wisdom to egoism. Both generous men, . . . [both] are alike unable to relax a self-destructive moral rigidity."[1] Debate abounds, distinctions proliferate, and the end is a decision either to justify or to condemn in terms of an extraliterary political position—imperial or liberal, republican or antirepublican, democratic or authoritarian; or it is a counsel of despair, like that of a recent proposal to regard *Julius Caesar* as "a problem play," which so orders events as to "place us in doubt of our moral bearings."[2] Such a conclusion, I believe, is quite beside the point. For the symmetries of *Julius Caesar* are no more than the formal expression of the play's universe of ethical relativism, its overall ironic balance, its sense of radical human limitation. The chequerboard logic of moralistic analyses, tempting as it is, ignores the dramatic principle of development and therefore can give no adequate account either of the play's structure or of the progress of the tragic protagonist.

It is Brutus' career in the play that follows the characteristic Shakespearean trajectory. It is he, and he alone, who is exhibited responding to Cassius' challenge, experiencing acute personal dilemma, committing a fatal error of choice which, in the outcome, reverses his every expectation and results in his defeat and death. His inner responses to these suc-

[1] N. Rabkin, *Shakespeare and the Common Understanding* (New York: Macmillan, 1967), p. 112.

[2] E. Schanzer, *The Problem Plays of Shakespeare* (London: Routledge & Kegan Paul, 1963), p. 5. Schanzer's earlier piece on *Julius Caesar*, "The Tragedy of Shakespeare's Brutus," *ELH*, xxii (March 1955), contains a juster estimate of the play as "the first of the poet's tragedies in what we have come to think of as the peculiarly Shakespearean kind" (p. 76). Schanzer's interesting attempt, in the latter work (pp. 57-63), to provide a definition of "the peculiarly Shakespearean kind" of tragedy might well have been more fruitfully pursued had the author not been deflected by his "problem play" thesis.

cessive stages of tragedy, the recognitions to which they give rise, are not uttered with the amplitude and resonance of the later tragedies, and it is this which must make him seem comparatively unsatisfactory as tragic hero. Nevertheless he represents an extremely important and interesting stage in Shakespeare's progress as tragic dramatist. The development of the interior monologue in *Richard II* made that play a far richer exploration of the inner life; but in *Julius Caesar* the tragic phases are more finely discriminated and more adequately represented in dramatic event and encounter. *Julius Caesar* stands, so to speak, at the threshold of the great tragedies, in which the external ironies of event and the internal resonance of recognition are unremittingly dovetailed and interlocked.

The predicament presented in Act I is the danger posed to the Roman republic by Caesar's rise to supreme power; and, of course, the consequent danger to Caesar himself. These complementary dangers define the initial circumstances, while that which renders the protagonists vulnerable in these circumstances, that which causes them to engage fatally with events, is their ambition. Each desires to be more than he is. Each sees in the historical moment a challenge to himself to extend the bounds of his personal domain, to possess a larger being, to realize in himself the idea of the nobility of Rome. Brutus aspires to be a second Junius Brutus: "Brutus had rather be a villager / Than to repute himself a son of Rome / Under these hard conditions as this time / Is like to lay upon us"; Cassius aspires to be as free as Caesar: "had as lief not be, as live to be / In awe of such a thing as I myself"; Caesar aspires to be dictator, king, Northern star, soaring "above the view of men"; Antony, in his turn, to be avenger and arbiter, unleasher of the dogs of war, who by violence and bloodshed will repay violence and bloodshed. They all aspire to the grand scale of history, to transcendence of limitation, to superhumanity. But the conspiracy demands of Brutus the rigorous repression of an inner self of sentiments and affections; it exposes Caesar in all his mortal vulnerability; it places Cassius, who initiates the conspiracy against Caesar to demonstrate that "Romans now / Have thews and limbs like to their ancestors," under a yoke and sufferance more irksome than Caesar's; and it makes Antony the leader of a triumvirate as cynically venal as Caesar was inflexibly "constant." The course of the play reveals the concomitants of the transcendent ambitions: the frustration to which they are bound by virtue of the very flesh and blood they aspire to transcend.

This ironic dialectic is conveyed throughout both by recurring situations and by figurative recurrence. Attempts to know, the rationalistic procedures in which all the characters are intensively engaged: the reading of omens, the interpretation of phenomena, the calculating, or miscalculating, of effects—these constitute throughout the root mode of the play's dramaturgy. The soothsayer's warning to Caesar in i.ii and the mysterious and menacing portents in i.iii are sufficient to suggest the irony of all the purposes and aspirations, the calculations of reason, prudence, and foresight that are destined, as the audience knows, to be frustrated. But a variety of other ways of subtly and insistently stressing human limitation are developed in the course of the play. Caesar's lofty dismissal of the soothsayer's warning, "He is a dreamer; let us leave him: pass," is cunningly juxtaposed with Caesar's own fundamentally creatural bondage to the "sterile curse" upon his marriage. Caesar's reading of Cassius' character is confidently rebutted by Antony: "Fear him not, Caesar, he's not dangerous; / He is a noble Roman, and well-given" (i.ii.193-194). Casca's account of the prodigies is followed by Cicero's sober caveat, "But men may construe things after their fashion, / Clean from the purpose of the things themselves" (i.iii.34-35), and this in turn by Cassius' own sturdy defiance of augury, and his harangue to the anxious Casca in which he puts, indeed, his own convenient construction upon the portents:

You are dull, Casca, and those sparks of life
That should be in a Roman you do want,
Or else you use not. You look pale, and gaze,
And put on fear, and cast yourself in wonder,
To see the strange impatience of the heavens;
But if you would consider the true cause. . . .
Now could I, Casca, name to thee a man
Most like this dreadful night,
That thunders, lightens, opens graves, and roars
As doth the lion in the Capitol;
A man no mightier than thyself or me
In personal action, yet prodigious grown
And fearful, as these strange eruptions are.

(1.iii.57-78)

The tribune's harangue to the populace, "You blocks, you stones, you worse than senseless things!" initiates the ironic dialectic of the play through the images of blood and stone, which recur in metaphor and metonymy throughout.[3] Flavius, berating the populace for disloyalty to Pompey, appeals to its emotions, its sentiments. To cull out a holiday for Caesar, who comes in triumph over Pompey's blood, is an outrage to human feeling. It is a speech that will be remembered with an accumulation of irony later: "You are not wood, you are not stones, but men" (III.ii.150). In Antony's oration the same sentimental emotion is aroused, but now for Caesar's blood. The governors, the choice and master spirits of the age, use (and despise) the sentiments of the governed, being masters of sentiment by virtue of patrician status and stoic discipline. It is to the condition of stone, we perceive, that their *ataraxia* aspires—to be unmoved, unshaken by motion, unassailable,

---

[3] I am indebted for this insight to H. Fisch, "*Julius Caesar* and the Bleeding Statue," ed. M. Z. Kaddari, Bar Ilan Studies in Humanities and Social Science, vol. II (Jerusalem: Kiryath Sefer, 1969), who convincingly argues that the bleeding statue provides the "dominant image" which critics have failed to find in *Julius Caesar*.

invulnerable; and this condition of stone is rendered monu-
mentally magnificent by their historical ambition. The play is
liberally adorned with Roman statuary, the "images" which
translate mere men, "flesh and blood, and apprehensive," into
a marmoreal permanence. And it is not by chance that these
marbles preside over the moments of critical decision or reversal. Cassius chafes to envisage Caesar as the Colossus which
diminishes creeping grave-destined men to pettiness. Cassius'
messages are fixed to the statue of Junius Brutus; Caesar dies
at the base of Pompey's statue; the crowd acclaims Brutus'
speech in the forum with "Give him a statue with his ancestors." But in Calpurnia's dream Caesar's statue bleeds. It is
of the essence of Shakespeare's presentation of Brutus that he
posits a "spirit of Caesar" against which he sees himself contending in order to ward off the thought of the living Caesar
who "must bleed for it." The "spirit" of the play is statuesque;
but the play is, as has frequently been pointed out, both
actually and verbally blood-drenched.[4] Thus the system of
imagery supports and reinforces the dramatic irony of events.

The sounding of Brutus by Cassius in i.ii establishes Brutus'
predicament by confronting him with his challenge. How
Brutus will respond to the challenge, whether he will take it
up, or evade it, what he risks and what is at stake for him,
becomes the chief source of dramatic interest. Cassius places
him in a situation in which he must choose, and his choice is
crucial, hazardous, momentous. Brutus has been abstracted of
late, his friend complains; he has not evinced that show of
love which the latter was wont to enjoy. Brutus offers an
apologetic explanation: his eyes have been turned inward
lately; he has been at war with himself and has forgotten the
shows of love to other men. The colloquy continues, move by
move, a contest of intimation and inference in which Cassius'
procedure is circumspect and skillful. He too, it seems, has that

[4] Particularly L. Kirschbaum, "Shakespeare's Stage Blood," *PMLA*,
LXIV (June 1949).

within which passes show: thoughts of great value, worthy cogitations. And then: "Tell me, good Brutus, can you see your face?" Brutus' reply is logically naïve, revealing to the audience, however, far more than it says, and giving Cassius his next opportunity:

BRUTUS. No, Cassius; for the eye sees not itself
But by reflection by some other things.
CASSIUS. 'Tis just:
And it is very much lamented, Brutus,
That you have no such mirrors as will turn
Your hidden worthiness into your eye,
That you might see your shadow. I have heard,
Where many of the best respect in Rome,
Except immortal Caesar, speaking of Brutus,
And groaning underneath this age's yoke,
Have wish'd that noble Brutus had his eyes.
BRUTUS. Into what danger would you lead me, Cassius,
That you would have me seek into myself
For that which is not in me?
CASSIUS. Therefore, good Brutus, be prepar'd to hear;
And since you know you cannot see yourself
So well as by reflection, I, your glass,
Will modestly discover to yourself
That of yourself which you yet know not of.

(I.ii.51-69)

To the audience is revealed a Brutus subtly at variance with the image Cassius' mirror is meant to show. "Do you fear it?" Cassius asks, as the populace, off-stage, "choose Caesar for their king"; "Then must I think you would not have it so." And to this Brutus replies:

I would not, Cassius, yet I love him well.
But wherefore do you hold me here so long?
What is it that you would impart to me?
If it be aught toward the general good,

Set honour in one eye and death i' the other,
And I will look on both indifferently;
For let the gods so speed me, as I love
The name of honour more than I fear death.

(I.ii.81-88)

The conflict of claims he himself defines as constituting his
difficulty is between "general good" and personal friendship.
Then the almost inadvertent, insidious transposition of the
terms of that conflict—"Set honour in one eye and death i' the
other"—allows us to perceive the very mechanism of Brutus'
thought. The personal claim is evaded, is instantaneously translated into the defensive assertion of an ideal honor. Cassius
drives his advantage home:

Well, honour is the subject of my story.
I cannot tell what you and other men
Think of this life, but for my single self,
I had as lief not be as live to be
In awe of such a thing as I myself.

(I.ii.91-95)

Honor, in Cassius' story, is thus pitched against the unbearable sense of an inferior or underling status which all his peers
must feel should Casear, "such a thing as I myself . . . get the
start of the majestic world / And bear the palm alone."
Cassius' exacerbated pride, his claim to absolute equality, presents itself under the guise of the stirring aspiration to be a
free arbiter of his country's history.

Men at some time are masters of their fates:
The fault, dear Brutus, is not in our stars,
But in ourselves, that we are underlings.

(I.ii.137-139)

This is Cassius' fame, as it was Lucius Brutus':

O! you and I have heard our fathers say,
There was a Brutus once that would have brook'd
Th' eternal devil to keep his state in Rome
As easily as a king.

(1.ii.156-159)

Brutus' reply to the challenge is decisive yet reserved, non-committal and yet pregnant with intimations of a favorable response:

That you do love me, I am nothing jealous;
What you would work me to, I have some aim:
How I have thought of this and of these times,
I shall recount hereafter; For this present,
I would not, so with love I might entreat you
Be any further mov'd. What you have said
I will consider; what you have to say
I will with patience hear, and find a time
Both meet to hear and answer such high things.
Till then, my noble friend, chew upon this:
Brutus had rather be a villager
Than to repute himself a son of Rome
Under these hard conditions as this time
Is like to lay upon us.

(1.ii.160-173)

Caesar's comments upon Cassius as he enters with his train at this point also invoke a name which must be lived up to, and therefore functions as a reflector of the same issue:

Would he were fatter! But I fear him not:
Yet if my name were liable to fear,
I do not know the man I should avoid
So soon as that spare Cassius.

$\cdot \quad \cdot \quad \cdot \quad \cdot \quad \cdot \quad \cdot \quad \cdot$

I rather tell thee what is to be fear'd
Than what I fear, for always I am Caesar.

(1.ii.195-198; 208-209)

105

Ironically, the name of Caesar, the superhuman public image of fearlessness, closes Caesar's mind to his personal, intuitive (and sound) perceptions concerning Cassius. And the discrepancy between name and mere mortal nature is immediately underlined. He is deaf in the ear that is turned to hear his companion's views and must call Antony to his right side. That Caesar betrays no consciousness of the discrepancy between his physical infirmities and the "name" he wills to embody produces still further reflective ironies. For to the audience his frailties are clearly enough exposed. And the capital Cassius makes out of his mere mortal liability to fever and cramps in swimming and Casca's sour account of the refusal of the crown drive home the point. Particularistic psychological explanations for Caesar's thrasonical brags,[5] or moralistic readings of an exorbitant personal vanity, blur the effect which the management of the predicament suggests is intended. It is a universal myopia of which Caesar is the chief exemplar and representative.

Act I closes with the question of Cassius' understanding of Brutus. His soliloquy reviews the progress made in the enlisting of Brutus on the conspirators' side, and plans future steps:

> Well, Brutus, thou art noble; yet, I see,
> Thy honourable mettle may be wrought
> From that it is dispos'd: therefore 'tis meet
> That noble minds keep ever with their likes;
> For who so firm that cannot be seduc'd?

[5] J.I.M. Stewart, *Character and Motive in Shakespeare* (London: Longmans Green, 1950), has an extremely persuasive statement of this view. H. S. Wilson, *On the Design of Shakespearean Tragedy* (Toronto: Univ. of Toronto Press, 1957), finds Caesar "vain to the point of infatuation," but appears to renege upon the point when he sees Caesar's character as "part of Shakespeare's reading of the tragic pattern of history, a pattern in which no man, however great, is entirely self-sufficient" (p. 91).

Caesar doth bear me hard; but he loves Brutus:
If I were Brutus now and he were Cassius,
He should not humour me. I will this night,
In several hands, in at his windows throw,
As if they came from several citizens,
Writings all tending to the great opinion
That Rome holds of his name; wherein obscurely
Caesar's ambition shall be glanced at.
And after this let Caesar seat him sure;
For we will shake him, or worse days endure.

(I.ii.313-327)

This speech has been variously interpreted. It is open indeed to two quite contrary interpretations on account of its syntactical ambiguity: the failure to specify the identity of "he" (in line 320). Which of the alternatives we choose crucially affects our entire reading of the play. If "he" refers to Brutus, the speech becomes a cynically sardonic comment in the vein of an Iago; if to Caesar, it is a practical and judicious assessment of the chances of Brutus' joining the conspiracy. The first reading makes "noble" derogatorily ironic—Brutus is burdened with too tender a conscience to countenance being easily rid of a political opponent. Cassius' reference would then be to Brutus' hesitations and scruples about joining the conspiracy, and also possibly to his finicky disapprobation of Casca's "blunt" style (in the immediately preceding scene). But, Cassius is jeeringly confident, these scruples can be overcome by skillful manipulation. Therefore Brutus had better, if he wishes to preserve his precious integrity, keep company with other "noble" spirits, i.e., others of similar tender-mindedness, for who indeed (again *con ironia*) among mortal creatures is so firm as to be proof against seduction. On the other hand, Cassius' own relations with Caesar are not marked by any excess of affection. Nor is Cassius one to go in for such softness at all. Therefore there would be no danger if their situations were reversed; no danger that is, of his (Brutus') humoring, cajoling, softening Cassius. The second part of the speech then outlines Cassius' strategy for influencing the "noble" Brutus from the true disposition of his nature. This reading yields a quasi-demonic Cassius hardly to be reconciled with the character of that name who appears in Acts IV and V, or, for that matter, with the Cassius who has just used the term "noble" in a perfectly serious fashion to his fellow conspirator Casca:[6]

> Now know you, Casca, I have mov'd already
> Some certain of the noblest-minded Romans
> To undergo with me an enterprise
> Of honourable-dangerous consequence. . . .
>
> (I.ii.121-124)

What is presupposed by this reading is a Christian rather than a stoic context for the attributes and values called "noble," which are then, allegedly, mocked and derided by Cassius. This, however, would make Shakespeare guilty of anachronism of a kind he was in fact particularly careful to avoid. His Romans nowhere betray an awareness of an ethic that entered the world after their lifetime. Nowhere are there expressed (though to the reader there may be suggested) the spiritualities of the fleshly heart to counter the spirituality of stoic *contemptus mundi* so finely expressed later by Cassius:

---

[6] D. A. Traversi, *The Roman Plays* (London: Hollis and Parker, 1963), reluctant to forgo an "ambiguity," skates over the issue in a forced and therefore confused attempt to have it both ways: "Brutus, Cassius says, is noble and so undisposed to enter into unworthy relationships, but this same 'nobility' to which he has so persistently made appeal, now appears to him as a sign of weakness. . . . The observation amounts finally to a confession of political cynicism. . . . It is typical of Cassius that appealing self-consciously to the love and friendship which his nature genuinely craves, he should yet pride himself on having seen through these attachments as illusions" (pp. 29-30).

I know where I will wear this dagger then;
Cassius from bondage will deliver Cassius:
Therein, ye gods, you make the weak most strong;
Therein, ye gods, you tyrants do defeat:
Nor stony tower, nor walls of beaten brass,
No airless dungeon, nor strong links of iron,
Can be retentive to the strength of spirit;
But life, being weary of these worldly bars,
Never lacks power to dismiss itself.
If I know this, know all the world besides,
That tyranny that I do bear
Can shake off at pleasure.

(i.iii.89-100)

It is therefore in a literal, Roman, and nonironic sense that "noble" must be taken: patriotic, self-denying, fearlessly rational, freedom-loving, disinterested, and fired by republican ideals. But, Cassius is saying, even honorable mettle (as opposed to the "base mettle" of the sentimental plebeans) may be wrought from its disposition by all kinds of influencing factors, chief among them being personal affections and private relationships, such as the love between Caesar and Brutus. Brutus had better then consort with men of republican ilk. Since on the other hand Caesar does not love Cassius, if the positions of Brutus and Cassius were reversed there would be no danger of his (Caesar's) influencing him (Cassius) out of the straight way of republican duty. He (Cassius) will therefore work toward the strengthening of Brutus' republican will by reference, through the letters, to Rome's expectations of him and to Caesar's ambitions.

That Brutus is, precisely in this sense, noble, is the point; and it is one horn of the dilemma that is presented in Act II. Brutus is distinguished from his fellows not only by his conspicuous nobility, but by the compassionate, sentimental, and affectionate nature which is revealed in the Portia and Lucius scenes—the heart of flesh for which his philosophy provides no real justification. Roman stoicism builds no value upon the irrational sentiments: it grounds its rational pride upon the capacity to rise superior to the creatural weaknesses. Fear, pity, sorrow, compassion must be repressed with an iron hand. Pain must be of no consequence. Portia is as dear to him as (significantly) the ruddy drops that visit his sad heart, but where great issues such as the freedom of Rome are concerned neither can make the slightest claim. It is no wonder that his state of man suffers the nature of an insurrection when no less than the blood of Caesar is the question at issue. The grounds of Brutus' psychomachia, exhibited in II.i, are thus made clear.

What is remarkable is the way in which the orchard speech contrives to suggest both the nature of his dilemma and the limitations of his self-knowledge.

> It must be by his death: and for my part,
> I know no personal cause to spurn at him,
> But for the general. He would be crown'd:
> How that might change his nature, there's the question.
> It is the bright day that brings forth the adder;
> And that craves wary walking. Crown him! that!
> And then, I grant, we put a sting in him,
> That at his will he may do danger with.
>
> (II.i.10-17)

Though the argument is hardly sufficiently developed to provide a republican manifesto, nevertheless the predicament of the play has sufficiently stressed the danger to republican Rome that Caesar represents to justify its preemptive logic. But the rationale which follows grounds the argument upon more general principles:

> The abuse of greatness is when it disjoins
> Remorse from power; and, to speak truth of Caesar,

I have not known when his affections sway'd
More than his reason.

(II.i.18-21)

It is this that reveals Brutus' confusion—a confusion which he
is incapable of mastering intellectually and which therefore
expresses itself in the experience of tension and conflict, a
nameless dread and the phantasms of anxiety of the following speech. For it is not simply a conflict of self-denial between personal friendship and "the general good" that troubles
Brutus. He talks not of himself but of Caesar, and thus blinds
himself to the nature of the contrary claims which struggle
for his assent. The parallel construction of the syntax makes
us construe "remorse" (in the Elizabethan sense of pity or
mercy) as one of the affections which never swayed with
Caesar more than his reason. But this is evidently absurd, because it is, Brutus says, the *abuse* of greatness to disjoin pity
from power, to become, that is, a ruthless despot; and Brutus
is here defending Caesar, in the court of his thoughts, against
the argument that absolute power will change his present
nature, which has given no grounds for trepidation. The il-
logicality of this self-contradiction forces us to construe the
sentence chiastically, so that "remorse" becomes an aspect of
reason; reason makes Caesar merciful, that is to say, where a
lesser man's affections, i.e., ambitious irrational passions, would
drive him on to the pursuit of a remorseless and despotic
power. Whether pity and mercy come under the category of
reason or of the affections would seem then to be the question
to which nothing in this speech provides an answer. And it
is upon this unanswered question that Brutus' whole enterprise founders.

What we must infer, I believe, is that Brutus genuinely
does not know how to classify "remorse." While he feels pity,
in the guise of his friendship for Caesar, as an affection, he
can only intellectually assimilate it, Stoic philosopher that he

is, as a strictly rational value. It is this rationality that is conveyed by the overtly rationalized argument with which he overcomes his reluctance to strike at Caesar. His rationalization is the bulwark he constructs against subversive instinctive pity.

> So Caesar may:
> Then, lest he may, prevent. And, since the quarrel
> Will bear no color for the thing he is,
> Fashion it thus; that what he is, augmented,
> Would run to these and these extremities;
> And therefore think him as a serpent's egg
> Which, hatch'd, would, as his kind, grow mischievous,
> And kill him in the shell.
>
> (II.i.27-34)

The Stoic Brutus, who cannot admit emotion, affection, or impulse as guarantors of value, thus determinedly suppresses the personal claim. That violence is done to his nature, however, is indicated by his reflex of shame, as of something inconsonant with an ideal self, which the monstrous visage of conspiracy induces in him; and by the abiding sadness, the sleeplessness, which are the objects of Portia's concern.

Nevertheless he accepts the necessity for "smiles and affability"; his "sick offence" he knows only by its effects. On the face of it he is resolute. But what his behavior exhibits is the deadly course of rationalization which his decision, for him, entails. His repudiation of the need for an oath is an evident overreaction to the imputation of the least possibility of irresolution:

> . . . and what other oath
> Than honesty to honesty engag'd,
> That this shall be, or we will fall for it?
> Swear priests and cowards and men cautelous,
> Old feeble carrions and such suffering souls

That welcome wrongs; unto bad causes swear
Such creatures as men doubt; but do not stain
The even virtue of our enterprise,
Nor the insuppressive mettle of our spirits,
To think that or our cause or our performance
Did need an oath; when every drop of blood
That every Roman bears, and nobly bears,
Is guilty of a several bastardy
If he do break the smallest particle
Of any promise that hath pass'd from him.
                              (ii.i.126-140)

And the envisaging of the assassination as a sacrifice is his
triumphant solution to the problem of Caesar's blood, a mental
evasion of the heart's knowledge. The idea of his grand device arises out of his argument against the killing of Antony;
and it reveals him in all his pitable, unrecognized folly:

Our course will seem too bloody, Caius Cassius,
To cut the head off and then hack the limbs,
Like wrath in death and envy afterwards;
For Antony is but a limb of Caesar.
Let us be sacrificers, but not butchers, Caius.
We all stand up against the spirit of Caesar;
And in the spirit of men there is no blood:
O! that we then could come by Caesar's spirit,
And not dismember Caesar. But, alas!
Caesar must bleed for it. And, gentle friends,
Let's kill him boldly, but not wrathfully;
Let's carve him as a dish fit for the gods,
Not hew him as a carcass fit for hounds:
And let our hearts, as subtle masters do,
Stir up their servants to an act of rage,
And after seem to chide 'em. This shall make
Our purpose necessary, and not envious;
Which so appearing to the common eyes,

We shall be call'd purgers, not murderers.
And for Mark Antony, think not of him;
For he can do no more than Caesar's arm
When Caesar's head is off.

(ɪɪ.i.162-183)

The pattern of the irony is beautifully designed: for it is a grave error of political reasoning that causes Brutus to clinch the matter of Antony's reprieve; and it is surely a self-projection which causes him to make it:

If he love Caesar, all that he can do
Is to himself, take thought and die for Caesar:
And that were much he should; for he is given
To sports, to wildness, and much company.

(ɪɪ.i.186-189)

Caesar in Act ɪɪ is also "tented." He is loftily superior to portent: "And Caesar shall go forth." Nevertheless, confident of his own unchallengeable firmness of will, he yields to Calpurnia's persuasions, only to be swayed again by Decius' shrewdly flattering interpretation of Calpurnia's dream, and his shrewdly calculated insinuation concerning the effect of Caesar's absence from the Senate, when someone will say, "Break up the Senate till another time, / When Caesar's wife shall meet with better dreams." The doublings back and forth are doubly barbed with irony; for they have been preceded by Decius' sneering boast:

I can o'ersway him; . . .
. . . when I tell him he hates flatterers,
He says he does, being then most flattered.

(ɪɪ.i.203; 207-208)

Whether strength or weakness or the ironic weakness of strength will prevail, whether some chance will intervene to save Caesar or the conspirators win the day—that is the question which keeps the quasi-suspense—a suspense which is virtual, not actual, because of the overall dramatic irony—at high pitch till the climax of the assassination. The audience, knowing what neither Caesar nor the conspirators know, views these conditions of suspense as from a distance. As they drink the wine of friendship together the audience is aware of betrayal from the point of view both of betrayer and betrayed. Every risk, every averted danger is thus dually registered with an irony positively Olympian in its inclusiveness. The near-salvation of Calpurnia's dream is followed by Artemidorous' warning schedule, and that in turn by Decius' interruption with Trebonius' suit. Caesar's magnanimity delivers him into their hands; but again discovery appears imminent. Popilius Lena's greeting throws the tense Cassius into despair; Popilius Lena smiles and is unchanged. Brutus sees that their fears are groundless. Metellus Cimber's suit for his brother sketches the irony to breaking point. As the conspirators join in the plea, Caesar's self-image of authority, his model of perfect justice, constancy, and dispassion, is assailed at the very high point of its full disclosure:

> The skies are painted with unnumb'red sparks,
> They are all fire and every one doth shine,
> But there's but one in all doth hold his place:
> So in the world; 'tis furnish'd well with men,
> And men are flesh and blood, and apprehensive;
> Yet in the number I do know but one
> That unassailable holds on his rank,
> Unshaked of motion: and that I am he. . . .
>
> (III.i.63-70)

So Caesar falls from his Olympus; and the fierce elation of the bathing of the assassins' hands in Caesar's blood modulates, with the arrival of Antony, into the blood-stained handshaking that signals Brutus' undoing. The two scenes are bloodily emphasized; while Antony's imagery of the hunt exposes this sacrifice, as Brutus wills it to appear, for the hacking, mangling slaughter that it is.[7] Both Caesar's body and the body politic are dismembered, for the blood spreads out and out like a plague from their body to their hands, to the imagination of the mob, to the innocent Cinna, and finally to the names pricked by the faction-ridden triumvirate.

In the immediate aftermath of the assassination Brutus' self-righteous self-delusion is complete. It is perhaps one of the play's chief ironies that, in the high elation of this savage killing, Brutus the rational is at peace with himself, aware of no schism, no gap, no impossibility in logic or in nature in the proposition that he loved Caesar when he struck him. But the audience perceives that Brutus' self-identification with the role of sacrificer of his best friend for the good of Rome has obliterated entirely the personal self. It is to this that Caesar's "Et tu Brute" draws poignant attention. Because he is thus so wrapped in proof, so unassailably confident of his own right reason, of his ability to convince a very son of Caesar that what has been witnessed is not a "savage spectacle" but a "lofty scene," he is blind and deaf to the reality of his situation, and so assents, against the cannier advice of Cassius, to Antony's request for a funeral oration, insisting, magnanimously, upon Antony's speaking "all the good he can devise of Caesar."

In Antony, now rising to dominance, the relation between heart and head is diametrically opposite. He plays his immediate part to perfection, deceiving the conspirators easily enough with a disarming frankness about his situation and an equally disarming candor about his feelings:

> Gentlemen all, alas! what shall I say?
> My credit now stands on such slippery ground,
> That one of two bad ways you must conceit me,
> Either a coward or a flatterer.   (III.i.190-193)

---

[7] This point is ably emphasized by Brents Stirling, *Unity in Shakespearean Tragedy* (New York: Columbia Univ. Press, 1956), pp. 40-54.

Shrewd as he is, he dissimulates his feelings not a whit; he hides nothing (save his intentions), and the role of avenger which he takes prophetically upon himself over the butchered corpse of Caesar is the full expression of a sensuous, passionate, and reckless nature:[8]

> O! pardon me, thou bleeding piece of earth,
> That I am meek and gentle with these butchers;
> Thou art the ruins of the noblest man
> That ever lived in the tide of times.
> Woe to the hand that shed this costly blood!
> Over thy wounds now do I prophesy,
> Which like dumb mouths do ope their ruby lips,
> To beg the voice and utterance of my tongue,
> A curse shall light upon the limbs of men;
> Domestic fury and fierce civil strife
> Shall cumber all the parts of Italy;
>
> .   .   .   .
>
> And Caesar's spirit, ranging for revenge,
> With Ate by his side come hot from hell,
> Shall in these confines with a monarch's voice
> Cry "Havoc!" and let slip the dogs of war;
> That this foul deed shall smell above the earth
> With carrion men, groaning for burial.
>
> (III.i.254-264; 270-275)

In the forum speech too he plays his part to perfection, *eiron* to Brutus' *alazon*, every move shrewdly calculated, every appeal perfectly timed. His pretended humility and resignation mask the working up of pity and indignation. He is the arch-

---

[8] R. G. Moulton, *Shakespeare as a Dramatic Artist* (Oxford, 1893), whose early analysis of *Julius Caesar* is still one of the most valuable accounts, notes: "In the whole Shakespearean Drama there is nowhere such a swift swinging round of a dramatic action as is here marked by this sudden up-springing of the suppressed individuality in Antony's character . . . hitherto so colourless that he has been spared by the conspirators as a mere limb of Caesar" (p. 198).

demagogue, using every persuasive trick of insinuation and suggestion to discredit his opponent; wielding his props—the mangled mantle, the body itself, and his trump card, the will —with exquisite craft; touching every available chord of moral sentiment; master of the rhythms of crescendo and delay. More, and chiefly, he creates a persona with whom his audience can identify; his calculated candor is a brave front not quite concealing the manly feelings he struggles to control. It is to this creation of a man behind the mask that they respond: "Poor soul! his eyes are red as fire with weeping." We watch the plebs fall into the carefully prepared trap:

> I come not, friends, to steal away your hearts:
> I am no orator, as Brutus is;
> But, as you know me all, a plain blunt man
> That love my friend; and that they know full well
> That gave me public leave to speak of him.
> For I have neither wit, nor words, nor worth,
> Action, nor utterance, nor the power of speech
> To stir men's blood: I only speak right on;
> I tell you that which you yourselves do know,
> Show you sweet Caesar's wounds, poor poor dumb
>   mouths,
> And bid them speak for me: but were I Brutus,
> And Brutus Antony, there were an Antony
> Would ruffle up your spirits, and put a tongue
> In every wound of Caesar, that should move
> The stones of Rome to rise and mutiny.
>
> (III.ii.223-237)

Yet the speech, in the play, achieves more than the immediate end of its oratory. For the persona that he creates is not altogether a fiction. His appeals to sentiment, to the affections, to personal pain—"He was my friend, faithful and just to me"; "I remember / The first time Caesar ever put it on"—exploits these emotions. Yet what he exploits is there to be exploited.

The contrast with Brutus' speech could not be greater, and indeed the pair of speeches are a dramatic, as well as a forensic, tour de force. In each case the style is the man, and the projection of personality through contrasted devices of rhetoric is so consummately skillful, demonstrates so unerring a linguistic insight, as to make one yield to a fantasy of regret for the treatise *De Poetica* that Shakespeare never wrote. For Brutus' laconic, euphuistic elegance is the rational abstract of a self-defence, its lofty concepts of slavery and freedom drained of all flesh-and-blood actuality by the deliberate patterning of the balanced schemata:[9]

> Had you rather Caesar were living, and die all
> slaves, than that Caesar were dead, to live all
> free men? As Caesar loved me, I weep for
> him; as he was fortunate, I rejoice at it; as
> he was valiant, I honor him; but, as he was
> ambitious, I slew him. There is tears for his
> love; joy for his fortune; honor for his
> valour; and death for his ambition. Who is
> here so base, that would be a bondman? If
> any, speak; for him I have offended. Who is
> here so rude, that would not be a Roman?
> If any, speak, for him have I offended. Who
> is here so vile, that will not love his country?
> If any, speak; for him have I offended.
>
> (III.ii.25-38)

It is by the symmetrical design of this figured logic that the play audience is bewitched. It is not by chance that the older rhetoric distinguished the devices of Brutus' oration as "figures of sound"; for that his argument should sound right is, for Brutus, the guarantee of its being right. It is an ecstasy of rationalization in which "truth" and "beauty" are interchange-

---

[9] R. Zandvoort, "Brutus' Forum Speech in *Julius Caesar,*" *RES,* XVI (Jan. 1940), has a detailed rhetorical analysis of the speech.

able because neither refers to anything outside the verbal design. Whereas the devices of rhetoric in which Antony catches the conscience of the plebs are those which the schools called "figures of sense": ironia, prosopopeia, and the tropes; figures which move and excite the imagination, animate the senses and the sentiments and arouse emotion by making even the inanimate dumb mouths of Caesar's wounds express it.

Brutus does not get "a statue with his ancestors" as the Second Plebeian demands. His "honour" and his reason are eroded and swept away by the deadly flood of Antony's rhetoric. In the overthrow of Brutus' chiseled prose by this fluent emotionalism it is perhaps not fanciful to find metaphorically enacted the defeat of the marble heart by a flesh-and-blood humanity.

The three scenes of Act III articulate the play's peripeteia: the reversal of the entire situation, and of the expectations of all concerned in it. The overthrow of Caesar leaves Brutus caught up in a blind hubris which parodies Caesar's own. But the mob violence unleashed by Antony sets the populace against him and ends in the lynching of Cinna in the street, for his name's sake, as Peace, Freedom, and Liberty dissolve in anarchy. It is a masterly reversal, in which the planned and the unplanned mesh, and intention recoils, with the consummation of the fatal act itself, ironically upon these actors' heads.

They themselves, however, have no awareness of that recoil. No recognition, no insight of any kind mars their elation. They are actors indeed, but they do not understand the script they act. A daring *trompe-l'oeil*, in which Shakespeare obliterates for a moment his representational frame and calls attention to the historical reality beyond the play, marks the irony of their ignorance:[10]

---

[10] An interesting discussion of "overstepped frames" is to be found in R. M. Adams, *Strains of Discord* (Ithaca: Cornell Univ. Press, 1958), chap. 4.

Stoop then and wash. How many ages hence
Shall this our lofty scene be acted over,
In states unborn and accents yet unknown!
(III.i.111-113)

The irony is indeed emphatic, but there is no inner concomitant. It is significant of Shakespeare's avoidance of recognitions in *Julius Caesar* that Brutus leaves the forum before Antony's speech, which he does not hear, and is in fact simply absent from the scene until the painful encounter with Cassius in Act IV on the eve of the civil war.

Act IV opens with the proscription of the triumvirs. There is no idealization of the antirepublicans. They are factious, openly cynical, and brutally callous. If ambition for office is presented as magnanimous in the first part of the play, it is stripped of all nobility now. Here is the very stuff of the disillusion which Lear will express with relentless force. But here there is no enormous despair, no repudiation in anguish of the exposed truth. Yet the main part of Act IV, the quarrel scene, articulates the moment proper to this phase, and in a manner which is particularly illuminating.

The quarrel scene has been universally admired. Coleridge "knew no part of Shakespeare that more impressed on [him] the belief of his genius being superhuman."[11] Yet it has also been felt to be episodic and extraneous to the action. What gives it its power, and made Coleridge say that Shakespeare seems here to be creating rather than representing character, is the revelation we receive from it, through superbly individualized speech and behavior, of the inner experience of both participants. Masks are off, and the two men stand revealed in hitherto unknown aspects of their natures. Here there is no public persona, no third person self-designation. The pronouns used are the I's and you's of the most direct confrontation. Here there is no elaborate rhetoric, and no carefully cal-

[11] *Shakespearean Criticism*, ed. T. M. Raysor, p. 16.

culated moves in a strategy of manipulation. Here all is blunt accusation, and stuttering, indignant incredulity. The cut and thrust of the dialogue springs not from the thinking mind intent upon the mastery of issues and the taking of decisions, but from the spontaneous flow of impulse rooted in the emotional nature. The scene gains tremendous impact from the contrast with the testing dialogue between Brutus and Cassius in Act I; but its main force arises from its position here in the fourth act, at the juncture of events between the reversals of Act III, the rise of Antony and Octavius, and the battle of Phillippi. The quarrel scene, admirable beyond praise for its verisimilitude, so far from being superfluous or tangential, articulates a major phase of the tragic process. As MacCallum noted, it lays bare the significance of the story "in its tragic pathos and its tragic irony."[12]

Its moving quality it derives from its intimacy, its domestication of the ruin already enacted upon the larger scale in the Roman polity. In the quarrel scene collapse and disintegration erode personal relations, and friends and lovers, fellow patriots, fellow conspirators fall to bickering, to taunts and recriminations which provide their own rueful comment upon human frailty and the diminishing of the grand purpose. It is the subtlest irony of all that Brutus, friend and lover of Caesar, so confident of overcoming the natural man in him, now breaks out into this bitter scolding. The fact that the scene is twice related to the news of Portia's death is further revealing of its import, for through most of the scene the real truth of his feelings is still concealed. His angry frustration proves (as Cassius understands) to have been itself a mask for the grief and sorrow forbidden expression. The charge of feeling so unnaturally repressed thus finds relief, legitimized by the bribery issue which Brutus' virtue can permit him to take up. But the irony embraces Cassius no less. For the man so iras-

[12] M. W. MacCallum, *Shakespeare's Roman Plays and their Background* (London: Macmillan, 1935), p. 526.

cibly sensitive to the imputation of inferior status believed to accrue to him from the mere fact of another's authority, the man who felt himself belittled and degraded by Caesar's power, is here slighted, insulted, and despised by one whom he himself has controlled, though also venerated. "Love" is restored between them; "love" is the shaky bridge they build over the chasm that has yawned, but it is a chasm which for a moment has revealed the hollowness at the heart of each. The poet with his message "love and be friends" is impatiently derided. Who and what they each are has been painfully divulged: each has perceived the other's feet of clay. More than this, each, in these naked moments of passion and conciliation, has perceived his own.

Brutus' exchange with Lucius immediately follows the quarrel scene and precedes the appearance of the Ghost. The whole sequence bears the unmistakable stamp of the Shakespearean fourth act. In point of naturalistic verisimilitude nothing could present more appropriately the emotional ebb and flow (high tension, anger, and scorn, followed by reconciliation and a lapse of energy) than this sudden solicitude for the tired boy. But the dramatic effect embraces more than a momentary relaxation of tension. The scene is usually glossed as providing a softer view of Brutus preparatory to a rehabilitation toward the end of the play; but the significance of the scene, I would suggest, lies deeper than this. The boy Lucius provides a legitimate, because indirect, outlet for the whole weight and burden of distress under which, we thus perceive, Brutus labors. Brutus' gentleness to the boy is expressive of far more than lies in the immediate foreground of consciousness. In its very superfluity, in terms of plot and action, its effect of tangentiality, it suggests the pressure of tenderness, of protectiveness, which has all along been so sternly repressed. All the unacknowledged griefs—Caesar's death, Portia's death, Cassius' defection—all these, I believe we are invited to perceive, lie behind the obscure impulse which issues in Brutus' "if I do live, I will be good to thee," and in his brief reflection over the sleeping young musician:

> O murderous slumber!
> Lay'st thou thy leaden mace upon my boy,
> That plays thee music? Gentle knave, good night;
> I will not do thee so much wrong to wake thee.
>
> (IV.iii.266-269)

Though it is no more than the flicker of suggestion, we catch the accent of a nostalgia for a peace to be found only in the grave.

There is no ironic fool's perspective in *Julius Caesar* and it is a significant omission. Brutus utters no desperate condemnation of the world which a moderating common man's view might measure for us. For Brutus has to the end, as has been remarked, no insight into his own inner life. The inner self which we are allowed to infer is never fully confronted or reflected upon. To what extent this is, in the fullest sense, "intentional" is impossible to determine. Whether the discretion of these scenes represents an artistry perfectly adapted to express this Roman stoic's character as consciously conceived, permanently sealed off from the humilities of self-knowledge, or whether what we witness is the limitation of an art only later to develop to full capacity is a question analysis cannot by its nature answer. The example of *Richard II* does suggest, however, that Shakespeare is practicing deliberate restraint.

So does the very significant prelude to the "well-made parting" between Brutus and Cassius. When Cassius asks Brutus what he is "determined to do" should they lose the battle, Brutus replies:

> Even by the rule of that philosophy
> By which I did blame Cato for the death
> Which he did give himself; I know not how,
> But I do find it cowardly and vile

For fear of what might fall, so to prevent
The time of life, arming myself with patience
To stay the providence of some high powers
That govern us below.

(v.i.100-107)

"That philosophy" can only be Brutus' personal interpretation of Stoicism,[13] since it led him to condemn Cato's suicide. And the sequel is surprising. No wonder Brutus himself "knows not how" to justify his finding cowardly and vile what a Christian would certainly condemn as ungodly despair. A Hamlet's "readiness" however, toward which Brutus fumbles, remains incipient; and Cassius' astonished response, "Then, if we lose this battle, / You are contented to be led in triumph / Through the streets of Rome?" (v.i.107-109), brings about a *volte face* reminiscent of a similar evasion of issues in Act I:

Then must I think you would not have it so?
I would not, Cassius, yet I love him well

.   .   .   .

Set honour in one eye and death i' th' other. . . .

(I.ii.81-86)

Here the mental habit is the same:

No, Cassius, no; think not, thou noble Roman,
That ever Brutus will go bound to Rome;
He bears too great a mind.

(v.i.110-112)

What is indubitable at all events is that where later in the great tragedies the darkened vision of the protagonist in Act IV is given with prodigious fullness and force, here we have no more and no other than a dumb malaise; and this applies even

---

[13] I am indebted to Hannah Kalach, a student of mine, for drawing my attention to the significance of this speech.

to the appearance of the Ghost. For whether the Ghost—Brutus' "evil spirit"—is to be taken as symptom of his weakness and his melancholy, or merely as another omen from Plutarch's account, it provides no self-revealing or significant response, no turning inward of a reflective eye.

So too the events of the catastrophe which follows, and which finally frustrates the intentions held at the beginning of the play, produces little enough reappraisal in the defeated protagonists. The "flyting" of the generals and the stoic suicides are all conventional. Cassius' epicurean disdain for omens is indeed chastened into a belief that the ravens and kites bode no good to the republican cause. But the ironic mistakings of the end are the external ironies of event only. There is no awareness of metaphor, of a consonance between spirit and flesh, in Cassius' "My sight was ever thick" such as reverberates from Gloucester's "I stumbled when I saw." Titinius' "Alas, thou has misconstrued everything" cuts deeper, but it is no more than a matter of fact that Cassius registers in his "Caesar, thou art reveng'd, / Even with the sword that kill'd thee." Brutus too: "O Julius Caesar! thou art mighty yet: / Thy spirit walks abroad, and turns our swords / In our own proper entrails" simply registers with sadness the vicissitudes of fortune and the world. The tides in the affairs of men have defeated them, and Brutus realizes in his death a true Stoic's resolute will to take the honorable way out in defeat: "Caesar, now be still: / I kill'd not thee with half so good a will." But to the last, though tragic recognition is invited by the structure of the play—is implicit or present, so to speak, in solution—it is never precipitated in any utterance of Brutus. Nowhere does he express a realization of a supreme value, which, through violation and loss, is now fully known. It is an immense delusion (untroubled by any reflection concerning his own treacherous role) that he expresses in "yet in all my life / I found no man but he was true to me." That Antony is indeed "true" to him after his death is an irony beyond his ken, as is the fact that the well-proportioned nature Antony praises is a polite fiction that the unbroken texture of irony in the entire drama has insidiously contraverted.

In *Julius Caesar* the articulation of Shakespeare's tragic form reaches a new high point of development. But it is a form empty as yet of its substance—the profound exploration of the inner life of consciousness that is the achievement of the tragedies which follow.

CHAPTER V

HAMLET

Our art must impart to the event its brutal freshness, its ambiguity, its unforeseeability, . . . restore to time its flow, to the world its rich and threatening opacity, and to man his long patience. . . . Let every character be a trap, let the reader be caught in it and let him be tossed from one consciousness to another as from one absolute and irremediable universe into another similarly absolute; let him be uncertain of the very uncertainty of the heroes, disturbed by their disturbance, flooded with their present, docile beneath the weight of their future, invested with their perceptions and feelings as by high insurmountable cliffs.[1]

Sartre's directive to the writer of 1947 has an astonishing applicability to the most famous of all Shakespeare's tragedies, almost as if *Hamlet* were the paradigm from which Sartre derived his observations. Certainly no character in drama has produced more powerful an impression of spontaneity, of lifelike unpredictability, than Hamlet. T. S. Eliot abandoned the enterprise of interpretation altogether, judged the play "an artistic failure," and diagnosed its cause as Hamlet's "domination by an emotion which is inexpressible, because it is in excess of the facts as they appear," and this because Shakespeare was under some mysterious "compulsion to attempt to express the inexpressibly horrible."[2] Whatever problems can or cannot be solved by an appeal to a dramatist's entirely hypothetical psychology, it might be observed that "the facts as they appear"—a faithless mother, a murdered father, a usurped inheritance, a venal and hypocritical court

[1] Jean Paul Sartre, *What is Literature?* trans. Bernard Frechtman (London: Methuen, 1950), p. 167.
[2] T. S. Eliot, *Collected Essays* (London: Faber, 1932), pp. 145-146.

society—could provide, for spirits less fastidious than T. S. Eliot's, sufficient grounds for a quite considerable measure of dismay. It must be conceded, however, that *Hamlet* does give provocation to critics in despair to take flight into the ineffable. For the very virtuosity of the performance leaves perilous gaps in the presentation. The play pursues its unfolding progress leapfrog fashion, careless of transition: point A links with point B, point B with point C, but the link between A and C seems suddenly to have disappeared. Powers of inference are thus strained to the utmost, while the prodigal eloquence and the prodigious stylistic versatility which mark Hamlet's speech generate a thematic overopulence which dies, as Claudius would say, in its own too much. Add to this circumstance the boldly experimental character of the dramaturgy, with its several plays within plays, and it is no wonder that we have more Hamlets at our beck than faculty psychology has categories to put them in, imagination to give them shape, or time to act them in. A great many of these Hamlets are self-portraits of the critics; all of them portray something of the form and pressure of the times in which they were written.[3] They constitute in themselves a fascinating chapter in the history of literary criticism. But a great many of them are illegitimate offspring of that science, having come into the world as answers to one of the most misconceived and misleading questions ever generated by criticism's protean discipline. The question is one with which we are all most intimately familiar: why does Hamlet delay the carrying out of his revenge?

The common-sense answer, "No delay, no play," is less

[3] S. Cooperman's recent existentialist among the philistines, for instance, a classic antihero, bitter, despairing, nauseated, and incommunicado, to whom action in a corrupt and parasitic world is as absurd a mockery as inaction; "Shakespeare's Anti-Hero: Hamlet and the Underground Man," *Shakespeare Studies*, I (1965). It is evidently the *zeitgeist* more than the play which decides whether Hamlet is a justified critic or an unjustified malcontent.

simple-minded than it appears. There are only two alternatives open to a dramatist who wishes to use a revenge story as the basis for the development of a full-scale tragic action—an action which shall have sufficient magnitude to contain the reversals and recognitions required for tragic realization. Either the act of revenge must be accomplished very early in the story and *followed* by complications of some kind—remorse, perhaps, or the discovery of a mistaken identity, or the discovery of an unfortunate identity, the close relationship, shall we say, of the murdered man to the revenger's lover; or the tragic development must arise out of difficulties and complications *preceding* the accomplishment of the revenge. No third possibility is logically available. Both the source story of *Hamlet*, and the revenge-play tradition already obtaining in Shakespeare's theatre, provided for the latter alternative. Hamlet does not delay his revenge because he has emotional problems; he has emotional problems because he, necessarily, "delays"—watches, awaits his opportunity, and evades his adversaries' plots and speculations concerning himself. As revenger he is in ambush, in a state of suspense. While he thus fences with the King, awaiting his moment, his inner life is divulged to us. It is this inner life, this mesh of thoughts and feelings, wrought up to the highest pitch of excitement and denied the outlet of action, which Shakespeare has exhibited.

The bewilderment, therefore, to which his fluctuations of mood, his reversals of feeling, his own sense of guilt, his reflections and introspections have given rise is misplaced. The question that has dominated the criticism of *Hamlet* has turned into a pseudoproblem what is in fact the basic *donnée* of the play; and though it has produced psychoanalytical excursions as brilliant and plausible as Ernest Jones's[4] it is ultimately as fruitless and unprofitable as an inquiry into

[4] *Hamlet and Oedipus* (New York: Doubleday, 1949).

the causes in nature that breed hard hearts would be to the criticism of *King Lear*.

Shakespeare has overcome the exigencies of his fable, but he has employed means so subtly suggestive, so chameleon-shifting, and so elliptical, as to tantalize the mind with a sense of a multiplicity not quite brought under the aspect of unity. Nevertheless—it will be the purpose of the following pages to argue—when we begin to make out the structure of the tragic experience in *Hamlet*, aided by our acquaintance with Shakespeare's regular practice, we begin to perceive the nature, and the ambitious reach, of the conception which has seemed at times to have outrun the control of the shaping power of imagination. Without the other tragedies to aid us, without a knowledge of what he had already accomplished and what he was yet to accomplish, we would possibly be unable to make any such "intentional" statements: we would have no reliable source from which to draw our insights into what he could be supposed to have "intended." But we do possess this great reservoir of evidence; and *Hamlet* is no less interesting from the point of view of Shakespeare's developing workmanship than it is as a character study or a fabric of themes. And its date in the chronology (it is the first of the great tragedies) allows it to serve as excellent test and touchstone of the structural hypothesis that has been outlined in a previous chapter.

The first council scene presents with calculated precision, power, and dispatch the nature of the predicament in which the protagonist finds himself; but there is an overture upon the battlements that is significantly placed. Barnardo is nervous, as jumpy as a cat; and Francisco sick at heart. Apprehension, unrest, fear, every man's existential anxiety has been aroused by the mystery of the visitant from beyond the grave. Rumors of danger threatening the kingdom play their part. Horatio's initial skepticism gives way to anxious recollections of the omens in Rome that heralded Caesar's assassination. The dread figure flies upon the crowing of the cock, and this suggests to Marcellus another historical analogy. Marcellus' fear and dread seek resolution in a simple man's Christian faith in the Gospel's good tidings. But the enigma remains. Whether the Ghost bodes ill or not, its appearance, verified empirically by Horatio himself, marks the boundary of knowledge, the limit beyond which human reason cannot penetrate. The anxious speculations of men trying to read the omens, torn between fear of dread events and hope that all may yet be well, prefigures the entire action.

In the first council scene speculation takes mundane forms, probing motives, intentions, purposes. The solitary black-cloaked figure—the observed of all observers—exposes the pomp and circumstance of court display for the imposture that it is. Hamlet's immediate predicament is the court world, the decorum which has decreed the propriety of "one auspicious and one dropping eye" to mark the dual occasion of mourning and marriage. He, black-robed among its golden splendors, is the one false note. Yet obviously he cannot simply call the King's bluff, expose the hypocrisy of the faces "contracted in one brow of woe," for power is with the King and his own role in the court is defined first and foremost by the fact of his dispossession. The King has popped in between the election and his hopes. What his first speech allows us to infer is the nature of the man whose irritable remonstrance to his mother is triggered by the fatal little word "seems." "Why seems it so particular with thee?"

It is the exasperation of a nature to whom integrity—the absolute consonance of deed, word, and feeling—is of extreme importance. In this he is like Cordelia in her turn, a hater of large claims. But the trouble here is not that his mother is exhibiting too much emotion, but too little. His own disclaimer, in response to her "seems," therefore takes the form, "You, apparently, feel nothing whatever; do not for that reason imagine that I am putting on a mere show of emotion; I truly feel what I show myself to be feeling." His situation places him in an inexorably false position in which he must either dissimulate his own feelings or seem to overexhibit them. He cannot speak his mind openly, while criticism that is merely implied bears interpretation as the expression of the envy of the usurped. The riddling pun in "I am too much i' th' sun," for example, does just this, while it exactly reflects the tension of his situation and its cause. The King's response to this predicament of Hamlet is totally beside the mark. For Hamlet is not a child and surely does not need to be told that all flesh is grass. The suave diplomacy with which the King makes a bid for his stepson's acquiescence (" 'tis a loving and a fair reply") must be transparent to Hamlet, but the bland pieties of his sermon on resignation can only exacerbate Hamlet's sense of alienation and irritation. What indeed is he to do? How is he to accommodate to this world of outward show and inward hollowness when every word he utters is either misinterpreted by others or compromising in his own eyes? If this is the situation which we are invited to take in, I believe we are enabled to perceive the effect of the first soliloquy without the usual recourse to depth psychology, though the peculiar intensity of filial and family emotional relationships was not, we may assume, a matter which had escaped Shakespeare's observations of human nature.

His diatribe against his mother discloses the reason for his previous tense irritability. What he could not say in public he expresses in private with the full resonance of the revulsion and horror which her remarriage has produced in him. Hamlet has three good reasons for feeling this marriage to be in the highest degree unnatural. It is too soon, incomprehensible to him regarding the object of his mother's affections, and within the prohibited degree of relationship. It casts doubt upon the very idea of women's fidelity—so long exhibited, positively flaunted, by his mother: in the event, worth less than two months. What he is to make of it he does not know. He knows only that it is not nor can it come to good; while the bitter climactic "to post / With such dexterity to incestuous sheets!" particularizes his sense of the calculated expediency which he begins to perceive here and everywhere in the unweeded garden.

That "self-slaughter" should be already uppermost in Hamlet's mind has caused concern to a multitude of commentators. Yet the desire for death is not an uncommon response to the shock of grief and loss—of both parents, in effect, be it noted, and of the one in circumstances that cause acute shame. Hamlet is indeed, in all possible senses, too much in the "son," suffering a double, even treble distress. He must redefine his entire situation. He must redefine himself. That the concomitant of this burden, this challenge, is an initial intense desire to escape, to disappear, not to be, must occasion surprise only in the most unimaginative of readers or spectators. The remarkable resemblance between Hamlet's chain of metaphors and Richard II's upon a somewhat analogous occasion of bitter shame, loss, and dispossession has not, in the innumerable discussions, generally been noticed. Richard says

> O that I were a mockery King of snow,
> Standing before the sun of Bolingbroke,
> To melt myself away in water drops!
> (IV.i.260-262)

I would therefore be inclined to return to the older reading of the soliloquy's first line: "O that this too too solid flesh would melt." Dover Wilson's "sullied" derives from, and commits us to, an hypothesis from depth psychology which postulates a neurotic puritanism as the source of Hamlet's melancholy,[5] whereas "solid" suggests no more (but also no less) than the

[5] Dover Wilson, *What Happens in Hamlet*, 3rd ed. (Cambridge: Cambridge Univ. Press, 1951), p. 40.

intense frustration engendered by circumstances which even the most easygoing libertine might be forgiven for finding corrosive.

It is precisely in these circumstances, when his most basic expectations and assumptions regarding the person closest to him and longest known by him are in disarray, that Hamlet is called to hear the Ghost's disclosure. Only to Hamlet, the perceptive spirit, is the special intelligence vouchsafed; and it is demanding, challenging, and testing in the highest degree. Hamlet must avenge his father; restore the purity of the royal bed of Denmark; forbear to "taint his mind"; and forbear to contrive ought against his mother. And he must keep silent, for he is powerless. Remembering Essex, we should not have needed Jan Kott to come from Poland to inform us of the importance of that aspect of his predicament.[6]

The predicament arises not merely from the fact that he is confronted with mystery, that "his world is preeminently in the interrogative mood," as Mack puts it, "reverberating with questions, anguished, meditative, alarmed."[7] Indeed, his first response to the Ghost is elation, the paradoxical elation resulting from a restoration of confidence in his own intuitions, however dire, and therefore in himself. But upon second thoughts (hence the tables upon which he will inscribe the revealed truth that a man may smile and smile and be a villain) the Ghost's revelation puts Hamlet into the most acute and searching of dilemmas. If he believes the Ghost, he must believe in the vicious falsehood of virtually all about him; if the Ghost's revelation is a figment of his own imagination what shall he believe of himself? That such a possibility occurs to him is suggested in several ways. The context of contemporary doubt and speculation concerning the nature

[6] *Shakespeare Our Contemporary* (London: Methuen, 1965).
[7] "The World of *Hamlet*," *Yale Review* (June 1952), p. 504. See also H. Levin, *The Question of Hamlet* (Oxford: The Clarendon Press, 1959).

and reliability of ghosts is everywhere deftly touched in.[8] The Ghost itself is evidently Catholic, in purgatory as a result of departing this life "unhousel'd, disappointed, unaneled." But Hamlet is a student at Lutheran Wittenberg, where the doctrine of the devil's cunning in producing apparitions to ensnare men's souls must have been energetically promulgated. Horatio, it will be remembered, warns Hamlet of just such a possibility: "What if it tempt you toward the flood my lord . . . ?" (I.iv.69-74); and the wild grotesqueries of the cellarage scene suggest the presence of this possibility in Hamlet's own mind even while he is ostensibly brimful of resolute belief. His later reference to "imaginations as foul / As Vulcan's stithy" shows the clarity of his recognition of the issue. What indeed is the truth about ghosts? What can Hamlet, fool of nature, be sure of? It is precisely because of his "prophetic soul" (Elizabethan doctrines of damnation were very sophisticated) that there can present itself to his mind the possibility of a devilish apparition, exploiting his weakness and his melancholy in order to abuse him of his reason and damn him.

In such circumstances no decision can be simple. Every consideration and reconsideration is multilayered, clogged and fogged at every turn by doubt as to the true nature of the issues. The mind is shadowed and shackled in its relations with reality: beset by doubt, baffled by ambiguity. His situation is thus the obverse of Orestes'. To Orestes, the divinity of the command laid upon him was unquestionable, its execution an impossible violation of his human nature. To Hamlet, the command is not impossible of performance, not unthinkable. On the contrary, he would sweep to his revenge with wings as swift as meditation or the thoughts of love; but the divinity of the command is very much in question. "Oh, all you host of Heaven! Oh Earth: What else? / And shall I

[8] See Dover Wilson, *What Happens in Hamlet*, chap. 3. See also Robert H. West, "King Hamlet's Ambiguous Ghost," *PMLA*, LXX (Dec. 1955).

couple Hell?" This radical uncertainty sets up a chain re-action of further uncertainties which the management of the action does everything to sustain and reinforce.

Speculation, interrogation, spying into, finding out, testing, probing, observing, and discovering constitute the mode of action of the entire play. It is of the essence of the play's dramaturgy that the uncertainties are felt sometimes by Ham-let, sometimes by the audience that is watching Hamlet, some-times by the stage audience that is watching Hamlet, some-times by all the watchers at once. These procedures and modes of action not only form the mainspring of major scenes (the nunnery scene, the play scene, the closet scene, the burial scene) and the subject of many of Hamlet's reflections; they also constitute the link which binds the subplot into the main action, and define the nature of the intrigue: the masked con-test in which Hamlet and Claudius engage. Both are in dis-guise, both dissimulating. From Act II onward the overt ac-tion of more than half the play is taken up, in revenge-play style, with Hamlet's attempts to expose the evildoer, while the evildoer parries with his own attempts to penetrate the secret of his adversary's antic mask. Act III brings the Chinese mime of fencers in the dark to its issue in a double trap: Polonius and Claudius behind the arras; and the mousetrap in which Hamlet will catch the conscience of the King. Ophelia is cross-examined about her suitor and told to mask her affec-tions by a father who characteristically dispatches Reynaldo to spy upon his son, and acquires information by most politic indirections; the indirections employed by Rosencrantz and Guildenstern in a similar mission are perhaps more clumsy but no less politic. The outer action consists of a plethora of eaves-droppings. The inner action is in subtle counterpoint, consist-ing of Hamlet's speculations and discoveries about the nature of appearances, the guises and disguises of evil, the dubieties of motive, the vicious moles of nature, the inscrutability of the phenomenal world; about the proper grounds, right relations,

137

and true values of things; about the discrepancy between seeming and being which makes it possible for a man to smile and smile and be a villain.

Hamlet accepts the obligation laid upon him without question, even, as we have seen, with an initial elation. Yet it is to be noticed that it is in no limited sense that he takes the obligation. Not less than the world is out of joint. And the rebound in self-deprecation or self-doubt of that elation and of that large reach of mind which is Hamlet's tragic distinction, is indicated before the scene is over: "O cursed spite, / That ever I was born to set it right!" *Hamlet* is the tragedy in which Shakespeare studied his protagonist's response, under suspense, to an awesome command. In order to obey the imperative, he, being what he is, must give to the performance inner assent. This in itself internalizes the entire drama, and opens up new reaches of the internal landscape of the mind, untrodden in either *Richard II* or *Julius Caesar*. Thus that notable feature of the other Shakespearean tragedies: the self-definition of the protagonist which is precipitated by the challenging, opposing, or frustrating of his goals as a tragic by-product of adversity, is here in the first instance a necessary preliminary and ground to all other questions and all other quests.

It is, however, not only the internalization of the drama that accounts for the realism of the character of Hamlet. Hamlet is not only himself lifelike; he is the cause of lifelike responses in others. We respond to him as we do to people, not to the constructs of character typology, however keenly generalized, however much enlivened by naturalistic touches done from observation. The answer to the question asked more than a hundred years ago, "Why is there such unanimity as to his being a man, and at the same time such diversity as to what sort of a man he is?"[9] is to be sought where Auerbach,

[9] Henry Norman Hudson, *Introduction to Hamlet* (Boston, 1870), quoted in *Variorum*, ii, 178.

the great historian of realism in Western literature,[10] indeed sought it: in the wealth of stylistic levels—verse, prose; high, low; serious, antic—which are distinguished, mingled, and juxtaposed in Hamlet's speech. Shakespeare has deployed a remarkable range of styles before; but never with so lavish a prodigality, virtuosity, and resourcefulness; nor with so many transitions so abruptly elliptical. It is this which arouses the infinite quantity of speculation that marks the *Hamlet* commentaries. The "realism" of *Hamlet* is the consequence of suppression, of discontinuity; and it is in direct proportion to the demand for mental activity, for guesswork, for interpretation and inference which is provoked by omissions in the presented object. Whatever is felt as left out, incomplete, unresolved, "open," the mind will be irresistibly tempted to fill in. For that which suggests what is yet concealed draws the beholder into the activity of creation. The formal cause of *Hamlet's* "realism" is thus ellipsis, stylistic and structural. And one of the chief sources of ellipsis—its dramatic "motivation"[11] —is the antic disposition, the brilliant device whereby, as Bridges puts it, "Shakespeare so gingerly put his sanity in doubt without the while confounding his reason."[12]

The antic disposition is introduced as early as I.v, when Hamlet dissembles with wild and whirling words the emotional tumult the Ghost has provoked in him. It will be remembered that the shock of grief and loss drove Hieronimo melancholy mad too, a circumstance which greatly extended the dimensions of that archaic personality. Shakespeare found the antic disposition in his sources, but the use he puts it to is unparalleled in any of them. In the plot of the *Hamlet* story it is the cover and the mask behind which Hamlet stalks or

[10] *Mimesis*, chap. 13.

[11] In the sense established by R. Jakobson, who contends that literary history must recognize the literary device as its only concern; all else, psychology, ideology, etc., is "motivation of the device." See V. Erlich, *Russian Formalism* (The Hague: Mouton, 1955), p. 57.

[12] Quoted by Dover Wilson, *What Happens in Hamlet*, p. 220.

evades his dangerous adversary. It proves indeed the most impenetrable of disguises. While it serves for cover, it allows him to play out his fluctuating moods and to express in derisive satire his criticism of all about him. But what is most important to perceive is that it provides Hamlet with two distinct stylistic personalities, and Shakespeare with practically infinite resources for playing one of them off against the other. The traditional melancholy, acute and paralyzing, or settled and ingrown, marks both and unifies them. Nevertheless they are separate, and what tantalizes the mind is the frequent impossibility of deciding which is which.

For the antic disposition is alternately simulated and dissimulated, exploited and exhibited; it is real and feigned at once. Both bait of falsehood and carp of truth, it is playacting which is an artifice of deception and a means of self-expression at one and the same time. It therefore serves to mediate an extremely fluid and dynamic effect. Hamlet, we are invited to perceive, is in a state of mental and emotional hyperactivity which is in direct proportion to the moratorium upon action. During his interim, as antic, he allows his own histrionic fancy free play. But a change of tone may at any moment betray the existence of an inner self aware of the role that is being played. The fishmonger dialogue with Polonius, which ends with "You cannot, sir, take from me any thing that I will more willingly part withal; except my life, except my life, except my life," is a case in point. The device is an extension and sophistication of the distinction between inner and outer, public and private self, which is suggested in both *Richard II* and *Julius Caesar* in their different ways; for here, who is to say which is "inner" and which is "outer"? The two selves are constantly juxtaposed in a series of ironic reversals of each other. Public and private, or displayed and concealed, constantly interchange. From the point of view of the public self, or the desired self-image, that which is concealed is absurd or contemptible, weak or wretched; from the point of view of the private self, that which is displayed is affected, bombastic, compromising, and sham. Hamlet shifts his point of view with every shift of role, so that one view of the self is constantly being undercut or subverted by the other. Thus the antic disposition multiplies the possible modes of self-projection—self-expression, self-deception, self-exposure, self-reproach. Opportunities for counterpoint, for ironic perspective, for reflection and self-reflection become practically unlimited.

The idea no doubt had its origin in the spectrum of opportunities the Elizabethan stage offered for the actor to come forward and involve the spectator in a kind of conspiracy of inner knowledge, or to recede and take part, as actor, in the events on the stage. But compare Iago, who plays as many parts and remains unchanging in his fixity of malice. He impersonates the characters of bluff soldier, sympathetic friend, or tavern roisterer, and reveals his true self to the audience in soliloquy. Hamlet impersonates no one. It is himself he seeks, aspects of himself that he ceaselessly rehearses, trying them out, as it were, to see if they will fit, if they will still the inner voice that craves for that obscure certainty, that peace which is to be found only when cognition and emotion, in accord, issue in definitive action. The antic disposition makes Hamlet three dimensional: he considers the role of revenger that is laid upon him; acts the antic; and seeks himself. Role, self, and masks are dazzlingly interwoven. It is not too much to say that this was as momentous a discovery for dramatic representation as Aeschylus' introduction of the second actor in fifth-century Athens, and that it made current an expressive device for the representation of the complex play of consciousness that has bewitched the European imagination ever since. Hamlet is therefore the progenitor of a large fictional family. The familiar complex characters of the twentieth century spring to mind—Stephen Dedalus, Swann, Herzog—who are at once public and private, containing their own inner and outer theatres of awareness and their own shifting consciousness of selves in interplay.

The nature of the psychomachia undergone by this complex character is established in Act II. The hypocrisies of power now appear much worse, or at least more widespread, comprehensive, and universal than the Hamlet of Act I, however shaken by his mother's behavior, had envisaged. "For my uncle is King of Denmark, and those, that would make mows at him while my father lived, give twenty, forty, an hundred ducats a-piece, for his picture in little" (II.ii.384-388). Then the world appeared to him an unweeded garden; now all that he sees is the skin and film over an ulcerous place, a mask over the pit. Corruption and imposture are in all who surround him. And Hamlet's struggle with this knowledge is vertiginous, for he knows (none better) that there is nothing either good or bad but thinking makes it so. Hamlet's melancholy, his depression, his disenchantment, his rejection of humanist optimism concerning the goodly frame and its inhabitants, his sense of the quintessence of dust, of physical decomposition, of the rarity of honesty, are the responses of a reflective mind to a real state of things, and at the same time essentially self-expressive. Hamlet's bad dreams originate in the prison that is Denmark, but they reveal to him the prison that is the self. In the meantime, in this period of necessary suspense, all action takes the form of rehearsal; he must imagine himself taking a course. It is in this way that Shakespeare restores the element of choice to a situation that has ostensibly deprived his protagonist of alternatives. Hamlet's options exist in the play of mind; the projection in imagination of alternative courses of action. The dramatist's task is to exhibit these choices, these imaginative explorations; and this he does through the extraordinarily suggestive and subtle device of the play-within-the-play. In Act II this theatrical tour de force is initiated with the arrival of the players, the welcome Hamlet affords them, and the performance of a favorite speech.

In the episode of the players Hamlet becomes the spectator at a play which has an intimate relevance to the choice and enactment of his own destiny. Thus to the antic disposition— Hamlet's own playing of a part—Shakespeare adds yet another perspectivist device: Hamlet the actor becomes audience to another's act. The spectrum of the theatrical now includes the hypocrites and impostors of the court, the amateur of theatre whose own acting is a matter of anguished self-preservation and self-discovery, and the professional player. And the result is a brilliantly inventive and subtle dramatization of Hamlet's dilemma.

What Hamlet welcomes in the fictions of the theatre he tells us himself: the players are at least honest impersonators.

> He that plays the King shall be welcome; his Majesty shall have tribute of me: the adventurous Knight shall use his foil and target; the lover shall not sigh gratis; the humourous man shall end his part in peace; the Clown shall make those laugh whose lungs are tickle o' th' sere; and the lady shall say her mind freely, or the blank verse shall halt for 't. (ii.ii.336-343)

Hamlet's irony suggests that he regards dramatic presentation in a very sophisticated manner; the stage is where we allow free rein to wish-fulfillment, while retaining an awareness of the discrepancies between the illusion of the stage and the obdurate frustrating reality of the world outside it. But what is played out in the speech Hamlet requests is not a comedy romance of knights, clowns, and lovers, but the violent killing of Priam, king of Troy, by Pyrrhus. Many have held that the speech is meant to remind a procrastinating Hamlet of the murder of his father—as if he could be supposed to have needed reminding. But the circumstances of his father's murder—the crafty poisoning of a sleeping man in an orchard—are in the highest degree remote from the circumstances of warfare and epic struggle. It is therefore, we must infer, himself that Hamlet wishes to find reflected in the description; or rather the violent, passionate, and heroic role he desires to play, and believes he ought to play. The relief of violent action, then, is what the speech vicariously offers him. It is for this reason that he requested it. He too is a hidden adversary, as was Pyrrhus in the wooden horse, and he too is bent upon vengeance, for a killed father and a stolen queen. Yet, it will be noticed, the sympathies of the speech are with the fallen Trojan, and the momentous deed is set in a vast perspective of all history, strumpet Fortune, and (hopefully) the piteous gods themselves. That in the player's account there is a moment of paralyzed inaction, in which "as a painted tyrant, Pyrrhus stood," further frames and distances the final onslaught. "And like a neutral to his will and matter, / Did nothing" receives the lingering emphasis of enjambment and pause.

The player episode can be seen to be "a screen upon which Shakespeare flashes readings from the psychic life of the protagonist,"[18] and complex readings they are indeed. The player, mirroring, at Hamlet's request, the scene in Troy, mirrors also Hamlet's mind. As we linger upon the implications of the situation, we are led to ever-deepening inferences concerning the protagonist's experience.

The player's magniloquence presents Pyrrhus' deed as grandly, if cruelly, heroic; it is part of the epic matter of Troy. But its archaic rhetoric, its Ercles' vein, is distinguished from that of the play which frames it. It is "poetical," in a mode older than that of Hamlet's contemporary speech. Polonius' comment "This is too long" draws attention to this,

---

[18] The phrase is Mack's, from "The Jacobean Shakespeare"; it is used there, however, with reference to other characters and situations (p. 24).

but Hamlet is contemptuous of Polonius' dramatic criticism. To him Polonius' comment is crass—"he's for a jig or a tale of bawdry, or he sleeps." Polonius' aside precipitates a rich awareness. A stage illusion has been broken by the interruption of a pair of dramatic critics, and this shift of attention signals a shift of mood, while Hamlet's scorn provocatively emphasizes the intense degree of interest the speech had for him. We are compelled to infer the nature of the interest, and to imagine the shift of mood.

That dramatic criticism of the speeches from Polonius' day to ours has been able to find them bombastic is a reflection of their status for Hamlet as well. He could, we are enabled in a flash to perceive, look as foolish as they seem to do, should he behave in Claudius' polished court in similar archaic fashion. Moreover it needs no more than such a break in the emotional continuity for Priam, the victim of the killing, to take imaginative precedence over Pyrrhus, the avenger. This would in turn account for Hamlet's anxiety to "come to Hecuba," as if now to test the behavior of his own widowed mother against that of "the woefullest wretch that ever lived to make a mirror of,"[14] prototype of maternal woe and queenly suffering. Thus Polonius' remark and Hamlet's reply trigger our perception of the peculiar difficulties of a self-conscious mind, a mind simultaneously aware of many issues, faced with the undertaking to act "heroically," with simplistic, single-minded violence. Through this play-within-the-play, which is repeated (for Claudius' benefit) in the Mousetrap, Shakespeare is enabled to portray the subtlest transactions of the imagination without recourse to an involved expository analysis, which, were it within his scope (or Hamlet's), would have been neither expressive nor dramatic.

The immediate effect of the players' rendering of Hecuba's plight is the arousing of intense compassion, so much so that the

[14] Quoted by H. Levin, *The Question of Hamlet* (Oxford: The Clarendon Press, 1959), p. 145.

very actor is reduced to tears. What has been enacted therefore in this episode is a transition from violent punitive action to intense grief-stricken suffering—far more "real" in the fiction than anything he has witnessed in the court of Denmark. I believe that this directly cathartic, almost kinetic effect of the twin speeches to be of great significance. It is to the cathartic aspect of the speech that the following soliloquy refers, rather than to any direct analogy with Gertrude or Claudius or the elder Hamlet. What the two speeches have reflected is the co-presence in Hamlet of the punitive (and heroic) impulse toward determining and definitive action, and that countermovement of the spirit, that inhibiting impulse to indeterminate and infinite reflection, to contemplative absorption of the impact of experience which is the mark of the nature to whom meanings bulk larger and possess a more imperious appeal than acts. Shakespeare makes a great deal of drama out of the basic conflicting modes of human response which are variously called masculine and feminine, martial and tender, assertive and receptive.

Moreover, contemplating his obligatory deed, thus diminished, thus vitiated, in the immense historical perspective of the fall of Troy, of the alternating deaths of Trojan and Greek, he knows it to be meaningless and ultimately unavailing. Had he been able to kill the King in some immediate surge of passion, obviously no problem and no dilemma would have arisen. But it is in cold blood that Hamlet must accomplish his revenge, sustaining a pitch of emotion over a long period. And as the Player-King's "dozen or fifteen lines" later tell us:

> What to ourselves in passion we propose,
> The passion ending, doth the purpose lose.
> The violence of either grief or joy,
> Their own enactures with themselves destroy. . . .
>
> (III.ii.206-209)

Thus the means he takes to keep emotion at fever pitch rebound like a boomerang. The fantasy itself—the imaginative enactment—exhausts the motive power of emotion and leaves him all the more a prey to his sense of the futility of his Herculean task. For it must be remembered that he had never, from the first moment of the Ghost's revelation, taken a limited, strictly avenging, eye-for-an-eye view of the killing of the King. It is as restorer of purity to the Augean stables of Denmark that he has hubristically seen himself.

The great soliloquy that follows the player episode gives the crowning touch to this remarkable projection of subjective experience. It renders completely perspicuous the nature of Hamlet's impossible choice. For if his task can present itself to his imagination as meaningless and unavailing, it also presents itself as a demand in the highest degree obligatory and compelling.

> Oh what a rogue and peasant slave am I!
> Is it not monstrous that this player here,
> But in a fiction, in a dream of passion,
> Could force his soul so to his whole conceit,
> That from her working, all his visage wann'd;
> Tears in his eyes, distraction in 's aspect,
> A broken voice, and his whole function suiting
> With forms to his conceit? and all for nothing!
> For Hecuba?
> What's Hecuba to him, or he to Hecuba,
> That he should weep for her? What would he do
> Had he the motive and the cue for passion
> That I have? He would drown the stage with tears,
> And cleave the general ear with horrid speech,
> Make mad the guilty and appal the free,
> Confound the ignorant, and amaze indeed
> The very faculty of eyes and ears.

147

Yet I,
A dull and muddy-mettled rascal, peak,
Like John-a-dreams, unpregnant of my cause,
And can say nothing; no, not for a King,
Upon whose property and most dear life
A damn'd defeat was made. Am I a coward?
Who calls me villain? breaks my pate across?
Plucks off my beard, and blows it in my face?
Tweaks me by the nose? gives me the lie i' the throat,
As deep as to the lungs? Who does me this?
Ha! 'swounds, I should take it; for it cannot be
But I am pigeon-liver'd, and lack gall
To make oppression bitter; or eere this
I should have fatted all the region kites
With this slave's offal; bloody, bawdy villain!
Remorseless, treacherous, lecherous, kindless villain!
O, vengeance!
Why, what an ass am I! This is most brave,
That I, the son of a dear murder'd,
Prompted to my revenge by heaven and hell,
Must, like a whore, unpack my heart with words,
And fall a-cursing, like a very drab,
A scullion!

(ii.ii.586-626)

It is with a species of panic terror that Hamlet now regards himself, perceiving his own failure of feeling by comparison with the player's emotion, and able to conceive of no reason for this but the basest cowardice, with the idea of which he punitively lashes himself. In bitter self-hatred he blames himself for this indulgence in fantasies of action, and reflections about meanings, ends, and consequences, when he should have fatted all the region's kites with this slave's offal. The violence of the language is a measure of his horrified self-mistrust before the abyss which has opened at his feet. That he may be wrong in his assessment, that there may in actual fact be no real reason for this anguished self-reproach is not to the purpose. Suspense and delay are working upon him like a poison. And he has watched the player positively produce—experience— passion for the remote and fictitious Hecuba, when he, the son of a dear father murdered, prompted to his revenge by heaven and hell, can find in his heart at this moment no grain, so to speak, of the precious commodity. What he fails to understand is his situation: emotion cannot be maintained at high pitch over long periods. But when he sees the player excelling in the art which suits the action to the word and the word to the action, which forces the whole soul to its own conceit, he lashes himself into a frenzy of verbal violence in the desperate attempt to induce the absent passion. Then, acutely self-aware, he catches himself in the meretricious act, and turns upon his own self-lacerating expressions of outrage and indignation as themselves fraudulent, whorish, and sham, cheap verbal counterfeits that usurp the deeds which are the only true counters of feeling.

Nowhere in drama are the involutions of self-awareness, of self-criticism which redoubles upon itself, rendered more impressively. The whole episode, players and soliloquy together, creates an inimitable impression of recession in depth, teasing the mind out of thought, as Hamlet's mind is teased, with the suggestion of layer upon layer of the undisclosed, the ulterior. In the visual arts this is exactly the effect obtained from the juxtaposition of planes of representation and the obtrusion of one upon another, the equivalent of the varieties of the play-within-a-play in drama. Whether or not the episode originated in an actual plague-year tour of the Lord Chamberlain's men in the provinces—a circumstance which would provide yet another piquant overstepped frame: the real strolling players playing fictional strolling players bringing real news from the metropolis to their fictional audience—Shakespeare's hall of mirrors is the true forerunner of Pirandello's and of

Weiss's later variant. The real people of Pirandello's *Six Characters* find themselves falsified by the actors' representation of them; yet they crave the one art, the theatre, which will denote them truly. Conversely the lunatic actors of *Marat-Sade* divulge the grotesque and wretched truth of themselves through, and despite, the revolutionaries' roles which they play to Sade's direction, and which they then in grim reality become, as the elegant asylum audience learns to its cost.

In Hamlet's case it is, in the first instance, not in terms of not doing, but of not saying, that he measures himself against the player and finds himself wanting. It is the art of saying, of expression, of making truth manifest in words (or in deeds) which he craves—the art which will denote him truly. By the end of the speech he regains control; and it is with courage that he addresses himself again to the task, determining to give it and himself certainty of meaning and to make that meaning manifest to all: "The play's the thing / Wherein I'll catch the conscience of the king." When we next see Hamlet he is in the throes of emotional reaction; the elation of that temporary resolution has given way to depression, while the ceaselessly active mind advances further matter for reflection.

In the volume of commentary upon the most famous of all soliloquies, one salient fact is often overlooked: that it occurs at the outset of Act III, the act which contains the *processus turbarum* of the tragedy and brings the action to a turning point. Contrivance, conspiracy, concealment, and dissimulation reach their crisis in the sequence that runs from the nunnery scene through the play scene to the killing of Polonius behind the arras. This sequence articulates the peripeteia—the complete reversal of Hamlet's situation. He who was Denmark's honored prince (and is still, after all, heir apparent) becomes in the eyes of all an overt menace to the kingdom, and this fact is exploited by Claudius, who seizes the opportunity to rid himself of his dangerous nephew. The inner progress of Hamlet through this chapter of perturbations is the progress toward a great frustration: a blind alley where both knowledge and freedom are totally confounded, and all planning brought to nought.

It is as a point upon this inner progress that the third soliloquy can most profitably be viewed. A general impression of the speech as expressing again that disaffection with life with which the play opened raises no problems. The Ghost's revelation, the duplicity of Rozencrantz and Guildenstern, Ophelia's pitiable helplessness to sustain him in his growing suspicion of all who surround him in Claudius' court, his own experience of suspense and uncertainty are sufficient to account for a melancholy acute enough to make life wearisome and the sleep of death appealing. Moreover, the strongly ethical bent of Hamlet's nature expresses itself naturally in the questioning of values and the weighing of options which form the speech's content. Its catalogue of adversities has often enough been noticed to have little relevance to Hamlet's specific situation, but an outgoing of sympathy, a partisanship with humankind is, as Sewall has noted, a characteristic consequence of the tragic hero's own distress.[15] Again, while the speech appears to backtrack upon Hamlet's immediately preceding decision to stage the Mousetrap and catch the conscience of the King, the opposition between active and passive modes of response links it with its predecessor in a quite specific way. Endurance, suffering in the mind, the absorption of adversity, corresponds to Hecuba; the taking of arms against a sea of troubles and by opposing ending them, to Pyrrhus.

The critical problem arises from the perception that the speech apparently confuses two issues. Since we know what Hamlet's obligatory task is, we cannot but register the possibility that the taking of arms and the "enterprises of great pitch and moment" refer to the killing of Claudius, though the logic of the syntax makes them refer to the self-slaughter

[15] R. B. Sewall, *The Vision of Tragedy* (New Haven: Yale Univ. Press, 1959), p. 29.

which is the subject of the whole disquisition. And conversely, because self-slaughter is the ostensible subject of the whole disquisition, we cannot read the speech simply as a case of conscience in the matter of revenge—Christian conscience producing impediments to the action dictated by the code of revenge and the secular sanctions and motivations of honor. Whether Hamlet is talking of his revenge or of his desire for death, or of both, one substituting for the other as mask for truth (or truth for mask) therefore becomes the problem that this speech poses. It is customary again to invoke depth psychology and the strategies of rationalization for a solution to this crux. But the dramatic critic, I would suggest, should anchor his interpretations in drama's method of progression by thrust and counterthrust rather than in the causal axioms of psychology. The speech is a reaction from the determination which ended the "rogue and peasant slave" soliloquy. It is not a cause of this reaction that we should attempt to uncover— such reactions are a fact of emotional life, and causes for melancholy he has in plenty—but the effects it functions to produce: the further disclosures and discoveries which it proffers us.

In the Quarto of 1603 the speech precedes the previous scene of the players, as indeed does the whole of the nunnery scene, and it is occasioned very plausibly. It evidently represents Hamlet's reflections upon the content of the book Polonius notices him reading as he sets his trap for Ophelia in order to discover the cause of the prince's distemper. In the First Quarto the speech is purely a reflection upon suicide by the grief-stricken, melancholy-mad Hamlet (much madder in the First Quarto than in the later versions), in which neither the lines "Whether 'tis nobler in the mind to suffer" nor "And enterprises of great pitch and moment" appear. There is thus no possibility of reference to the matter of revenge at all. "Conscience" makes cowards of us all in the First Quarto too, but it is, significantly, the "hope" not the dread of something after death which "pusles the braine, and doth confound the sence, / Which makes us rather beare those evilles we have, / Than flie to others that we know not of."[16] If in the debate upon the provenance of the Bad Quarto we take the side of those who see it as a preliminary (mutilated) draft of the play as we have it from the Second Quarto and Folio, rather than as a garbled copy or a shorthand record of a performance of the longer and better version, I believe we can throw considerable (if speculative) light upon the "To be" speech, and suggest the direction in which it is to be taken. For it was surely the keen shaping sense of an assured artistry that exchanged the First Quarto equivalent of Act II for the brilliant and subtle and technically extremely original dramatization of the player scene, with its dynamic projection of a finely conceived dilemma, and reserved the nunnery scene (which has no bearing upon the main revenge action) for the confusions and perturbations of Act III.[17] The "To be" speech, transferred along with the nunnery scene, is now no simple dialogue of self and soul upon the question of suicide but a much more complex reflection. The speech articulates Hamlet's heartsick realization of what is involved in the act of choice: its insuperable difficulties and the price to be paid by him who would be elector of himself. This is exactly the import and the effect of the two interpolations:

> Whether 'tis nobler in the mind to suffer
> The slings and arrows of outrageous fortune,
> Or to take arms against a sea of troubles,
> And by opposing end them?

and

> And enterprises of great pitch and moment
> With this regard their currents turn awry
> And lose the name of action.

[16] See *Variorum*, II, 56-57.
[17] For an eloquent defense of the transposition see *The Edinburgh Review* (1845) in *Variorum*, II, 20-21.

The complexity which is thus added to the cruder figure of the First Quarto complicates, of course, the critic's exegetical task. So radically ambiguous in import has the speech become, while at the same time so readily detachable, so generalized and therefore applicable to a host of occasions for melancholy reflections upon adversity, that Lamb's despair is understandable indeed: "I confess myself," he says, "utterly unable to appreciate that celebrated speech . . . or to tell whether it be good, bad or indifferent; it has been so handled and pawed about by declamatory boys and men, and torn so inhumanly from its living place and principle of continuity in the play, till it has become to me a perfect dead member."[18]

Nevertheless it has a "living place and principle of continuity": its position in Act III. It is this positioning that can direct the emphasis to fall upon the bafflement that the speech expresses rather than upon the sense of a dilemma which it also (however obscurely) suggests. Choice of action, Hamlet is saying, depends upon knowledge that is simply not available to the human mind. Hamlet's very syntax enacts the inextricable entanglement of cognition with volition, the "puzzling" of the "will." The bare, unmodified infinitive—"to be"— suggests a hovering upon the brink of an act. Yet the following lines introduce a question of preliminary knowledge—or judgment—of what is noble. What Hamlet is recognizing as the conscience which makes him a coward and causes action to lose its name subsumes and transcends the conflict of philosophy with religion,[19] or of duty with desire. Hamlet's pale cast of thought is precisely what it says it is—that mental ac-

---

[18] *Variorum*, I, 205.

[19] For the ambiguity of the speech, its hovering between the Christian and the Stoic ethic, see A. Sachs, "To be or not to be: Christianity versus Stoicism," *Scripta Hierosolymitana*, vol. XIX (Jerusalem: The Magnus Press, 1967). In the same volume is an account of "Hamlet and the Players" by A. Shalvi which argues for the "reminder" effect of the two speeches.

tivity which counters every option with its opposite, every consideration with its contrary; which takes in aspects and calculates consequences; which is stilled only by and in action, but which makes every choice of action seemingly impossible. From this cul-de-sac he sees no escape. His thought moves in clogged and wearisome circles, for he cannot know the answer to the question that he asks. Neither instinct nor ratiocination can endow value with certainty, and therefore freedom and virtue themselves are a snare and a delusion. Hamlet expresses the depth of his dismay at this discovery, which is, at some time, every thinking being's discovery. That it is so is the secret of the speech's immense popularity.

It is to further and more searing recognitions of the limitations of mind that the whole of the third act is directed. For the third act presents, with an unparalleled wealth of resource, the confounding of knowledge with knowledge and the futility of passion and action.

I take the subdued and abstracted "Nymph, in thy orisons / Be all my sins remember'd" (iii.i.89-90) as Johnson did, to be "grave and solemn,"[20] and not accusatory and sarcastic. Hamlet has hardly yet emerged from the intense preoccupation of the soliloquy. But from the moment he is jerked to attention by the gauche little importunity of Ophelia's return of his gifts to the end of his tirade, the scene becomes a powerful image of the inscrutability of appearances. The fact that the audience is informed of the "espials" of Polonius and the King while Hamlet is not permits the nunnery scene to dramatize the impenetrability and duplicity of appearance in the most direct and unequivocal mode of dramatic irony—that which obtains when the audience is in possession of more information than either the protagonist or the watchers behind the arras. All parties to the scene are on the watch. The audience watches the two spies watching Hamlet, speculating upon his motives and behavior; the audience watches Hamlet prob-

[20] *Variorum*, I, 215.

ing the genuineness of Ophelia's feelings, and announcing his own with wildly contradictory declarations, the degree of the sincerity of which it has no means of knowing; and the audience watches Ophelia utterly bewildered by all she sees and hears, and hiding in her heart the knowledge of her own role as decoy. The ellipses of Hamlet's speech force the audience to its own speculations, chief among them the question whether Hamlet knows or discovers the presence of Polonius and the King. Few can fail to have been beguiled at some time by Dover Wilson's proposal of a lost stage direction at II.ii.162, which would allow Hamlet, reading on his book, to enter in time to overhear "I'll loose my daughter to him"; or for that matter by the older stage tradition which makes Polonius betray his presence by an inadvertent movement.[21] But it should be noted that we actually need no further explanation for Hamlet's sudden "Where's your father?" than the fact that he has not recently been permitted her presence unchaperoned, if at all. And his apparent change of mood at that point in the scene might well be attributed to recollected angry resentment at Polonius' interference in his affairs. Indeed, this would seem to be born out by the diatribe on calumny—he being calumniated and exposed by his courtship of Ophelia to the insulting aspersions of such as Polonius.

[21] I count myself gratefully among the many who were betwitched (and am on record to this effect in a published article of some years ago), but have since come to believe that a rendering of the scene based upon the pun (at any of several possible points) and Hamlet's previous overhearing of Polonius, require a sleight-of-hand ingenuity which must be beyond the capacity of acting to convey. Powerful recent support for this view is to be found in the closely reasoned and admirably concise argument of H. Jenkins against the invocation of either pun or earlier entrance. "I suspect," he concludes, that "when the nunnery, at whatever stage, becomes a brothel, it becomes a red herring"; and he points out that "what the play requires is not that Hamlet shall know but that we shall know, that the King is there to hear"; "Hamlet and Ophelia," Annual Shakespeare Lecture of the British Academy, *Proceedings,* XLIX (London: Oxford Univ. Press, 1963), pp. 144 and 146.

I am inclined to believe that the deeper dramatic purport of the scene is obscured if Hamlet is made or becomes aware of Polonius at any point in the scene. For if Hamlet knows that Polonius is behind the arras, then he knows that Ophelia is lying when she tells him her father is at home—knows, therefore, that she is deceiving him. Whereas it is precisely his total inability to know her, or for that matter himself, that the scene, in this theatrically simpler view, would allow us to perceive as the center of his anguish. He is tormented precisely by doubts, not by confirmations. And how indeed should he know what Ophelia is? Is she loving and faithful to him despite parental authority? Or compliant to the latter and therefore false to him? What has she been told about him? Is he not testing her with his hyperbolic declaration: "I am very proud, revengeful, ambitious; with more offenses at my back than I have thoughts to put them in, imagination to give them shape, or time to act them in?" His mother has predisposed him to believe in women's perfidy, has produced in him a revulsion from sex and the stratagems of sex; he was unable to draw Ophelia's face by his perusal; she has refused his letters and denied him access; now she returns his gifts. What form of devious double-dealing shall he expect? He is wary, defensive. Yet he did love her once and is enraged by the thought of the father's meddling. It is surely an extremity of ambivalence that is expressed in the violent paradoxes of "If thou dost marry, I'll give thee this plague for thy dowry. Be thou as chaste as ice, as pure as snow, thou shalt not escape calumny. Get thee to a nunnery, go: farewell. Or, if thou wilt needs marry, marry a fool; for wise men know well enough what monsters you make of them" (III.i.135-139).

It is not absolutely necessary to take "those that are married already, all but one, shall live; the rest shall keep as they are" as an overt threat to the King behind the arras, for Hamlet could be thus obliquely discharging his bosom of the perilous stuff, which is, after all, the root cause of all his agitations;

157

and doing so in a semi-aside to the *audience*, who will then wonder what the King will make of it. The scene culminates in the tirade against false faces and the ape-like antics of a lying world, generalized by the "you," which takes the place of the previous intimate "thou": "God has given you one face, and you make yourselves another; you jig, you amble, and you lisp, and nickname God's creatures, and make your wantonness your ignorance" (iii.i.149-153). This is the familiar Renaissance complaint against cosmetics, against appearance and masked intention. But his final "Get thee to a nunnery" implies again sufficient tenderness for Ophelia to wish her preserved from corruption. The scene in its ambivalence and consternation accumulates a powerful charge of disgust with all the grotesque iniquities of the world as well as those of women.

In the play scene Hamlet stages his grand exposure of these iniquities. And it is in this sequence that his intention, the triumphant revealing of reality behind appearances, the peeling of the skin of hypocrisy from the onion of truth, will be at once achieved and frustrated in the play's central reversal. Hamlet's instructions to the players reflect his sense of his own aim and aspiration: ". . . for in the very torrent, tempest, and, as I may say, the whirlwind of passion, you must acquire and beget a temperance that may give it smoothness. Oh, it offends me to the soul, to hear a robustious periwig-pated fellow tear a passion to tatters, to very rags, to split the ears of the groundlings" (iii.ii.6-13). Passion is the powerhouse of the soul, the generator of all deeds. But control of passion is above all requisite for any effective expression or action. Without such temperance a man is no more than passion's slave. His encomium to Horatio directly expresses his desire for that stoic impassivity in the face of fortune's buffets and rewards that he admires in his friend in the degree that he has found it wanting in himself.

It is thus mastery of passion and of circumstance that

Hamlet enacts in the play scene. *Régisseur* prince, as Fergusson has called him,[22] with his fiction of the players he holds the mirror up to nature; he will reveal the inner truth of the guilty creatures sitting at the play. He will expose their real faces. The fiction will reflect their truth, making the mask drop from them. The assumed role of the Player King will expose the assumed virtue of the hypocrite King. Not only the King's conscience will be caught, but also the Queen's. Hence his interpolated jibes: "No, good mother, here's metal more attractive"; "look you, how cheerfully my mother looks"; "O, but she'll keep her word," "Wormwood, wormwood." In order to wound his mother he makes Ophelia her proxy, treating her like a harlot, with deliberate and brutal sexual contempt, forcing their dialogue of innuendos to bear the worst constructions. Meantime he masks his own truth with his riddling talk of ambition, crammed capons, and the chameleon's dish (knowing how easily motives of thwarted ambition will be imputed to him), and introduces a puzzling hidden threat into the already enigmatic situation for the benefit of the court, which hears him announce that Lucianus is nephew to the King.

The audience, again watching the watcher being watched, is drawn into the tissue of guesswork, speculation, and inference out of which the scene is made. All are in the dark—the court audience ignorant, Hamlet in suspense; and Hamlet's sore distraction has never seemed more open and palpable to his fellows.

Since the dumb show draws no response, the audience itself is put into the same suspense. I believe Shakespeare's stagecraft here to be both more crude and more profound than Dover Wilson's marvel of ingenuity, which takes more subtlety to follow than any audience can be assumed to have possessed.[23] An Elizabethan audience, or perhaps any other, is

---

[22] *The Idea of a Theater* (Princeton: Princeton Univ. Press, 1968).
[23] Dover Wilson, *What Happens in Hamlet*, chap. 5. See instead

likely to be undisturbed by the King's apparent inconsistency of response. It will not have supposed for a moment that an accomplished courtier would give himself away at the first hint of danger, more particularly as the essence of his quandary is his ignorance of what, or how much, Hamlet knows. It is after all a war of nerves between him and Hamlet; if his nerves are strong enough for a great deal but no more, so much the more plausible the entire episode.

The King breaks down; Hamlet has triumphed. He has made the galled jade wince and the truth unkennel itself. It is his text that the players, the court, the King, and the Queen all play. He is master of reality, making his will prevail, no fool of fortune. His elation is unbounded; and superbly expressed in the scene with Horatio which follows the Mousetrap, and in the cloud scene with Polonius, where he fools those who would fool him, articulating through the metaphors of recorders' stops and cloud-shapes his own inscrutable willful mastery. But his will, now at the top of its bent, has its crucial tests before it.

In the prayer scene and the closet scene his devices are overthrown. His mastery is confounded by the inherent liability of human reason to jump to conclusions, to fail to distinguish seeming from being. He, of all people, is trapped in the fatal deceptive maze of appearances that is the phenomenal world. Never perhaps has the mind's finitude been better dramatized than in the prayer scene and in the closet scene. Another motto of the Player King is marvelously fulfilled in the nexus of ironies which constitutes the play's peripeteia: "Our thoughts are ours, their ends none of our own." In the sequence of events following Hamlet's elation at the success of the Mousetrap, and culminating in the death of Polonius, all things are the opposite of what they seem, and action achieves

---

J. L. Styan, *Shakespeare's Stage-Craft* (Cambridge: Cambridge Univ. Press, 1967).

the reverse of what was intended. Here in the play's peripeteia
is enacted Hamlet's fatal error, his fatal misjudgment, which
constitutes the crisis of the action, and is the directly precipitating cause of his own death, seven other deaths, and Ophelia's
madness.

When the opportunity for his revenge offers itself and is
not taken, the reason is given with the greatest explicitness:

> Now might I do it pat, now he is praying;
> And now I'll do't; and so he goes to Heaven;
> And so am I revenged. That would be scann'd:
> A villain kills my father; and for that,
> I, his sole son, do this same villain send
> To heaven.
> Oh, this is hire and salary, not revenge.
> He took my father grossly, full of bread,
> With all his crimes broad blown, as flush as May;
> And how his audit stands who knows save heaven:
> But in our circumstance and course of thought
> 'Tis heavy with him; and am I then revenged,
> To take him in the purging of his soul,
> When he is fit and season'd for his passage?
> No.
> Up, sword, and know thou a more horrid hent;
> When he is drunk asleep, or in his rage,
> Or in the incestuous pleasure of his bed,
> At gaming, swearing, or about some act
> That has no relish of salvation in't;
> Then trip him, that his heels may kick at heaven,
> And that his soul may be as damn'd and black
> As hell, whereto it goes.

(III.iii.73-95)

Hamlet spares the King at prayer not because the King is
a suppliant and helpless figure; nor, certainly, because "Vengeance is mine, saith the Lord"; nor merely out of an excessive

and savage vindictiveness. Hamlet spares the King in his moment of prayer out of his need not merely for good reasons for action but for the best reasons; for total consonance between deed and retribution. Less than an absolute justice will not denote him truly, will not gain the assent of his inmost soul. Nothing less than the fittingness of punishment to crime can assuage the pain of his constant knowledge, so recently confirmed, of the lying, smiling humbug of the King's evil. Only so can he justify himself in his own eyes. Only a manifestation of divine justice in its perfection can express and appease his abhorrence and set his spirit at rest. But the elder Hamlet's spirit did not demand this of him. Nor is it demanded of any man. He plays providence, and the distinction that marked him out as tragic hero—the high demand for absolute truth shining forth in appearances—becomes corrupted in that moment of hubris by the taint of a fatal aestheticism. He becomes the artist caught in the love of his own devices, and sacrifices the deed—the end—which is the moral imperative of his situation, upon the altar of the aesthetically satisfying means.

That it is appearances that deceive him is of the essence of the irony. For the King in fact is not in a state of grace at all, and Hamlet's reasoning is based on false premises, false appearances, both when he believes the praying King to be purging his soul, and so spares him, and when he believes Polonius to be the spying King, and so kills him. The Jacobean avenger is in the nature of things a complex figure—judge and executioner, victim and culprit at once; mediating between divinely absolute and humanly contingent justice. Vendice too is hoist with his own petard in an access of overweening pride in his accomplishments as artist of revenge. The *Revenger's Tragedy* followed *Hamlet*, and throws into bold relief what was implicit in the earlier play where Hamlet's hubris represents a far subtler and more daring conception of this perfectionism. The symbolic action in which he exhibits it—the staging of the Mousetrap and its aftermath—indicates the presence of one of Shakespeare's major preoccupations: the power of the artist's will to master reality is a theme that takes many forms in many plays, and receives its final wry exorcism when Prospero—*régisseur* magician—drowns his book at the end of the *Tempest*.

Hamlet's production, at all events, is a failure. What Hamlet does do is as fatally erroneous as what he does not do; the premeditated action that he does not take is as fraught with evil consequences as the unpremeditated action that he does take. The good that he would do he does not, and the evil that he would not do he does. He exemplifies, without knowing it, the condition Claudius, ahead of him, knows so well:

> O limed soul, that struggling to be free,
> Art more engaged!

> (III.iii.68-69)

The avenger, the thunderbearer, who could drink hot blood in the fierce joy of his resolution and his certain knowledge of the King's guilt, not only fails to dispatch the evildoer, but instead murders an innocent man. Now he bears not only a tainted mind but a bloodstained hand; is involved irrevocably in the evil he fought; and has never been further from his task, or more infirm of purpose.

In the closet scene, where Hamlet is intent upon moving his mother to see, as in a glass, the inmost part of her, to see as he sees and so to admit the enormity of what she has done, a further ironic reversal of expectation is brought about. For he is as mistaken about Gertrude as he was mistaken about Ophelia. She is not, on any evidence that the text provides, the murderer of her husband, nor a party to the murder. Her comment on the protesting lady revealed no more, it seems, than a worldly self-possession. It is Hamlet's delusion that is manifested in the closet scene. "Look here, upon this picture, and on this," he demands. How could you leave to feed on

this fair mountain and batten on this moor? Have you eyes?
Can you not *see* a paddock, a bat, a gib? What I believe should
now be realized to the full is that, in very truth, she cannot
see. Nor could the audience, who has seen what she has seen:
a suave and polished courtier, of plausive manner and smiling
mien. To Hamlet it is by now self-evident that this is a satyr,
a mildewed ear, a king of shreds and patches, but he is in
this deluded. It is not self-evident at all. There is no mark of
Cain upon the murderer's forehead. There is no art by which
we can find the mind's construction in the face.

It is to be remarked how insistently Hamlet throws the
emphasis of his castigation upon what he sees as an error of
judgment qua judgment:

> You cannot call it love, for at your age
> The hey-day in the blood is tame, it's humble,
> And waits upon the judgment; and what judgment
> Would step from this to this? Sense sure you have,
> Else could you not have motion; but sure, that sense
> Is apoplex'd, for madness would not err,
> Nor sense to ecstasy was ne'er so thrall'd
> But it reserved some quantity of choice,
> To serve in such a difference. What devil was't
> That thus hath cozen'd you at hoodman-blind?
>
> (iii.iv.68-77)

The wheel has come full circle, and opaque and inscrutable
appearances seem now to be transparent to Hamlet. But they
are not, as his own recent blindness ironically underlines. The
closet scene with its arras, its images, and its apparition, is a
Shakespearean equivalent of the Platonic parable of the cave.
Shadow and substance, image, conception, apparition, illusion,
play a baffling blindman's buff. Never was Donne's "Poor
soul, in this thy flesh what doest thou know?" better illustrated; nor dramatic irony denser than in Gertrude's answer to
Hamlet's "Do you see nothing there?": "Nothing at all; yet

all that is I see." In these great central scenes of the play Hamlet's downfall enacts the epistemological anxiety of the age. Montaigne's dictum that the plague of man is the presumption of knowledge and Donne's scorn of the "Pedantery, / Of being taught by sense, and fantasie," here acquire an unexampled resonance.

Hamlet's own recognition of fallibility emerges at the close of the closet scene. By the time he has (mistakenly) spared the King, and mistakenly killed Polonius; by the time, chastened by the Ghost, he has acknowledged his blunted purposes and has found it in his heart to ask his mother to "assume a virtue, if you have it not," it has become clear, with the brutal clarity of irony, that it is indeed only in the counterfeit presentment of the playhouse, or in the mind of God, that the word can be made flesh or truth transparent in appearance. "Forgive me this my virtue" is his striking expression of a new humility. "Assume a virtue, if you have it not" is a very minimal demand for the arrogant and accusatory young man of the first act who announced that he knew not "seems."

The death of Polonius, hated and despised as he was, calls forth in Hamlet an awareness of a common tragic destiny. And this common tragic destiny he sees under the aspect of a providence at work behind the appearances of chance:

> . . . heaven hath pleased it so,
> To punish me with this, and this with me,
> That I must be their scourge and minister.
> (III.iv.173-175)

Nevertheless, in what can be interpreted as a reflex of pride, of self-assertive rebellion against that shared destiny, that shared instrumentality, he later in the same scene grimly rejoices at the prospect of counterintrigue, and concludes with the deliberate obscenity of "I'll lug the guts into the neighbor room," whereby he would make his victim, if he could, a distant and indifferent object.

Since both the Folio and the Quartos are silent upon the matter of act division after ii.ii, the delimitation of Act iv has remained a vexed question. Johnson found "this modern division into Acts" (at iv.i of the accepted text) "not very happy, for the pause is made at a time when there is more continuity of action than in almost any other of the scenes."[24] This is at the point immediately after the closet scene, when the Queen is conveying to Claudius the substance of her conclusions that Hamlet is "mad as the sea and wind." The murder of Polonius is discovered, and Rosencrantz and Guildenstern are dispatched to find Hamlet, who confuses his interlocutors with riddling remarks about the location of Polonius—"in heaven," or possibly "i' the other place," but at all events where "he will stay till ye come." The three short scenes possess an obvious continuity. There would seem to be no reason whatever, in view of the fluidity and continuity of Elizabethan stage practice, to have the act division at that point. Several nineteenth-century commentators concurred with Johnson's opinion that the act division should logically be made at iv.iv, where Fortinbras enters upon his expedition and Hamlet is on his way to England. This scene was cut in the Folio with the approval of several later critics. Lloyd, for instance, says, "Beautiful as the soliloquy in this scene is, I am disposed to think that the excision of it may have been deliberate—as unnecessary, prolonging the action, and, it may be, exhibiting the weakness of Hamlet too crudely."[25]

Upon principles derived from the study of Shakespeare's usual practice in the matter of the management of the fourth act, itself developing impressively in skill and subtlety, I believe it possible to perceive and to reconstruct the sequence in such a way as to yield a characteristic and consequential fourth act. There need be little argument concerning the extension of Act iii to what is at present iv.iii. This would bring the third act—the culmination of the *processus turbarum*, the re-

[24] *Variorum*, i, 311.   [25] *Variorum*, i, 323.

versal of the hero's situation, the disintegration and collapse
of his high aims—to a natural close with the rounding-off of
the Polonius debacle within the palace of Elsinore. Act IV, "the
preparation for the remedy" as the Terentian doctrine had it,
must bring Fortinbras into the scope of the play's action, fetch
Laertes from Paris upon his sister's death, and begin to en-
gineer the counteraction and hence the catastrophe. In addition to this already weighty task, the old plot demanded that
Hamlet be got to sea and back, and that Rosencrantz and
Guildenstern be dispatched. Part of the problem Shakespeare
solved expeditiously enough, though with inevitable loss of
pace and immediacy, by means of the dramatized narration in
Hamlet's letter to Horatio and his later retrospective account
of the sea voyage. But the sheer difficulty of managing the
narrative threads of intrigue, counterintrigue and subintrigue
remained formidable. The present act division produces an
effect of dislocation and crowding; and a further consequence
of the division as we have it is the equally crowded catastrophe
of Act V, which is made to contain the gravedigger's comic
material (normally found in Shakespeare's fourth acts), Hamlet's leap into the grave, the plotting of Claudius and Laertes,
and the complicated duel itself.

Suppose however, that, as has been suggested, Act IV were
to begin at IV.iv with Fortinbras, it would then be possible to
see the fourth phase as running right through to include the
present v.i. (the gravediggers and the burial). This would
leave, it is true, a shorter Act V, but one in which the whole
momentum of the action would be directed to the issue of the
duel, with Osric, Character of an Affected Courtier, absurd
relic of the painted court, functioning far more effectively than
he does at present in an act that is so full of directions as to
become obscure in its import. The great virtue of this shift,
however, would be to restore Act IV to a form that is recogniz-
ably Shakespearean, exhibiting a characteristic control of design, the effect of that sure shaping power which alone can

achieve the intelligible spacing and articulating of complex dramatic material.

What we would then have is a fourth act in which the protagonist is brought to the nadir of his tragic progress with the familiar Shakespearean modifying and measuring effects of pathos and irony playing upon him, while the important contrast between the three avenging sons is brought into effective prominence.[26] The act would then, in its complex strategy (though not of course in its content) resemble the fourth act of *Lear*, in which despair, pathos, irony, tragic "reunions," and the comparison between the three victims of adversity—Edgar, Gloucester, and Lear—are all constitutive of the total effect. The act would be consonant with what both the anticipations of previous plays and the developments of later ones leads us to infer as the living principle of Shakespeare's management of his fourth act; and this being so it would allow us to perceive and interpret the episodes with greater confidence. And "How all occasions" need no longer disturb us as unnecessarily prolonging the action, or as showing too crudely the "weakness of Hamlet."

It does indeed represent Hamlet's abdication from what has become the intolerable burden of thought. One continuity is worth noticing. "About, my brain!" (II.ii.627) expressed a determination to enlist thought in the service of action. The "pale cast of thought" (III.i.85) registered his awareness of

[26] A common view taken in the matter of the three avenging sons is that Fortinbras represents an Aristotelean mean or ideal (of honor, virtue, or action), while Hamlet represents defect and Laertes excess. My own view is that the two reflectors of Hamlet serve precisely to bring out the specifically tragic-heroic quality of the protagonist's experience by comparison with their own more commonplace existences. Fortinbras' revenge is a publicly sanctioned matter of armies and alliances (of the kind that is denied Hamlet by virtue of his circumstances); Laertes', a plunge into the abyss of deception and treachery. Only for Hamlet, who treads the tightrope of the task that is public duty and private burden at once, is his revenge the agent of a tragic self-discovery.

thought's power to paralyze action. Now in "My thoughts be bloody, or be nothing worth!" Hamlet is willing to subdue thought entirely to blood, to absorb himself in his role of avenger. It is a signal defeat, which we should not, I believe, regard with equanimity. Contemporary experience tells us much about the dangerous violence that can spring from defeated idealistic aspirations, or be released by them. What Hamlet was born (as tragic hero) to discover and to accept is precisely that all occasions do inform against us if we are possessed, and to the degree that we are possessed, of "large discourse"; that the anguish of looking before and after is the price to be paid for the capability and godlike reason which must not fust in us unused. That his own possession of this faculty is at this point subverted and confounded is to be discerned in the very illogic of his soliloquy. In compunction and self-blame he affirms the value of and the need for Fortinbras' uncalculating enterprise, and disparages the "thought" that hinders him, though he is unable to decide whether he thinks too little ("bestial oblivion") or too much ("some craven scruple of thinking too precisely on the event"). If in his despair of solutions he rejects the calculations of the understanding as more perfidious than the oracles, what he enlists as motive and ground for action is now no more than the puff of ambition, the blazon of honor. And in the same breath as he names the ambition of the delicate and tender prince "divine," he exposes its object for what it is—worthless and negligible, an eggshell, a plot that is not tomb enough and continent to hide the slain. Drowning, he clutches at the straw of "greatness," a factitious magnanimity. Man of conscience, of scruples, of considerations and distinctions, he envies Fortinbras his uninhibited sweep of action as he envied the player his uninhibited sweep of expression, as he envied Horatio his power to suffer nothing in suffering all—envied him his freedom from the imperious inner voice which demands integrity, its own inalienably true expression, in acts as in words. Hamlet's problem, the problem of being what he is not, or not being what he is, is here resolved by denial, by a repudiation of his "ordeal of consciousness"; and it is upon this repudiation that Claudius' antiphonal persuasion of Laertes to action —an action which will make him the impulsive tool of Claudius' machinations—throws an ironically revealing and melancholy light:

> KING. Laertes, was your father dear to you?
> Or are you like the painting of a sorrow,
> A face without a heart?
> LAERTES. Why ask you this?
> KING. Not that I think you did not love your father,
> But that I know love is begun by time:
> And that I see, in passages of proof,
> Time qualifies the spark and fire of it;
> There lives within the very flame of love
> A kind of wick or snuff that will abate it;
> And nothing is at a like goodness still,
> For goodness, growing to a plurisy,
> Dies in his own too-much; that we would do
> We should do when we would; for this "would" changes,
> And hath abatements and delays as many,
> As there are tongues, are hands, are accidents;
> And then this "should" is like a spendthrift's sigh,
> That hurts by easing. But to the quick o' the ulcer:
> Hamlet comes back; what would you undertake,
> To show yourself your father's son in deed,
> More than in words?

$$(\text{IV.vii.108-127})$$

Nothing could bring out with greater force the melancholy perception that the whole play has dramatized. Action traps the actor in the labyrinth of concealed evil: inaction in the toils of time and the lapse of passion.

What in the meantime becomes of human well-being it is

the function of Ophelia's madness to reveal. The pathos of the figure, exposed to the pitying gaze of the onlookers, withdrawn into the depths of her lunatic solitude, so alone that she can express, in her Valentine song, the most recessed and hidden of a young girl's fears and wishes, expresses powerfully the frailty of human existence, the irreparable losses it can sustain, the wreckage and flotsam that action, passion, and guilt leave in their wake. "Lord, we know what we are, but know not what we may be" is the leitmotif of the scenes, once more a study in concealments, but deeper and darker than that of the first act because what is concealed now on the stage, while it is revealed to the audience, is not a crime alone, but the sick soul of the Queen and the limed soul of the King, heavy with remorse of conscience. The songs and flowers of Ophelia are the mirrors in which each painfully and obliquely sees his own loss. "Thought and affliction, passion, hell itself, / She turns to favor and to prettiness," Laertes says. Ophelia's shattered fragments, a madness unfeigned, unglossed, and unmitigated as no other in Shakespeare, and her death, represent the play's antithesis of human well-being, its maximum of human loss; and they provide the occasion for the graveyard scene, which articulates with an unmatched density of invention Hamlet's realization of absolute mortal finitude.

The great traditional theme of *memento mori* is given a prologue before Hamlet's entrance in the fool's logic of the gravediggers, whose digging occupation is a reminder of the way of all fallen flesh since Adam. The Second Clown's worldly wisdom, "Will you ha' the truth on 't? If this had not been a gentlewoman, she should have been buried out o' Christian burial," reminds us of the specific fall—the turpitude in high places—that has been Hamlet's inheritance. The gravedigger's way with a syllogism is not Hamlet's, yet the issue of Hamlet's capability and godlike reason has scarcely proved happier, as the melancholy circumstances remind us. "Is she to be

buried in Christian burial that wilfully seeks her own salvation?" "If I drown myself wittingly it argues an act. . . ."
"Wilfully," "wittingly"—the words plunge in their trajectory
to the heart of Hamlet's matter. That he will still, when he
enters with Horatio, be unwitting of the grave's tenant to be is
no small part of the irony. The mingling of comic and tragic
modes in this encounter between prince and peasant is particularly effective because the perspective of common humanity which modifies and measures the spectator's response, and
the protagonist's own extremity of desolation are here focused
in one scene, and rendered by the gallows-wit duet between
the gravedigger and his interlocutor. The protagonist himself,
therefore, becomes the ironic vehicle for this most grimly
comprehensive and ironic vision of the enigma and the paradox of existence.

The center of the scene is the familiar material of meditation in contempt of the world. But Hamlet's satirical *ubi sunt*
—"Where be his quiddits now"—is transposed into quite another key by the revelation of the skull's identity. For a skull,
most impersonal, most anonymous of all human relics, to have
a name, and one which is bound up with Hamlet's childhood
memories, brings into his reflections, with an inescapable, vivid
immediacy, the whole impact of the vanished past—his own
as well as the dark backward and abysm of time which is
everyman's habitat. Death here is not eloquent, just, and
mighty, but a stinking skull at which Hamlet's gorge rises.
The base uses to which return the avatars of wit ("a fellow
of infinite jest, of most excellent fancy") and of will ("that
earth, which kept the world in awe") are obtrusively evident
to him, agonizingly present to his senses and his imagination.

Nor does he seek the consolations of philosophy, of the
grander verities. On the contrary, and despite Horatio's dis-
couragement, he insists on tracing the noble dust of Alex-
ander till he finds it stopping a bunghole. The poignance of
his realization is thrown at once into relief and into perspec-

tive by the gravedigger's casual familiarity with the facts of his gruesome trade: "your water is a sore decayer of your whoreson dead body." Hamlet faces the facts of death, the deliquescent, the repulsive, the abhorrent outcome of a long day's dying that no paint can disguise for long. By comparison with this thanatopsis Hamlet's first invocation of death, "O! that this too too solid flesh would melt, / Thaw and resolve itself into a dew," appears remote from reality: the yearning real enough, but the terms academic, as academic indeed as the attempt to resolve the riddles of passion and action—whether to suffer or to act, whether to live and endure or to make one's quietus with a bare bodkin—by ratiocination. Nor was it in direct contemplation of physical death that the "To be" soliloquy was spoken at all. Then death was conceived to be desirable, were it not for the dread of dreams— a sleep, a consummation devoutly to be wished, an end to griefs and burdens. That speech was the speech of a man who still struggled, despite his depression of spirit, against the admission of his own radical impotence to master his destiny; not of a man to whom the very idea of a destiny, his own or imperious Caesar's, is grotesque; not of a man mortified in the flesh by the knowledge of his nothingness.

But this stark humility is offset and modified by yet another shock, another revelation of an identity. Hamlet is precipitated out of his contemplation by the shock of the discovery that it is Ophelia who is to be buried with such "maimed rites." Her withdrawal from him in life is now to be sealed by the finality of the grave. And, still hidden, he hears himself traduced in Laertes' rhapsody of words, and is compelled to respond.

The double shock produces in him a revulsion of spirit, a new energy, an upsurge of passionate self-assertion. He leaps into the grave with a declaration of his royal identity. "This is I, Hamlet the Dane" announces that he dares, in the teeth of his adversary's ranting threats, to become who he is. The emotional sequence is almost exactly reproduced by Webster in

173

The Duchess of Malfi in the second prison scene. The dramatization there is cruder, more explicit, as is the nature of the
Duchess's ordeal; but "I am Duchess of Malfi still" registers no
less movingly the reflex of proud defiance, the dignity of self-
election. And his own rant to Laertes, in all its irascible
spontaneity, reveals the deepest and most enduring preoccupations of the self he has striven throughout to realize. "What
wilt thou do for her?" It is a theme upon which he will fight
until his eyelids do no longer wag:

> 'Swounds, show me what thou'lt do;
> Woo't weep? woo't fight? woo't fast? woo't tear thyself?
> Woo't drink up eisel? eat a crocodile?
> I'll do't. Dost thou come here to whine?
> To outface me with leaping in her grave?
> Be buried quick with her, and so will I:
> And, if thou prate of mountains, let them throw
> Millions of acres on us, till our ground,
> Singeing his pate against the burning zone,
> Make Ossa like a wart! Nay, and thou'lt mouth,
> I'll rant as well as thou.

> (v.i.296-306)

Suffering, doing, saying. What action will suit the word, what
word the action? What rhetoric but carries with it its own
evasions and falsifications, becoming spurious in the very
utterance?

Hamlet affirms at the end of the play "a divinity that shapes
our ends, / Rough-hew them how we will," as the reality behind the shows and appearances of things. Of all Shakespeare's
tragic heroes, he is the only one for whom a specifically Christian insight is the burden of his painfully acquired wisdom.
Of the nominal Christians, Romeo is clearly in need of considerable religious instruction before he will qualify as Christian
in any but a technical sense. Richard II's long dialogue with
martyrdom ends with heroic, not saintly, self-assertion. Othel-

lo's Christianity is a *donnée* of the play, and of Othello's idea of himself; he repudiates it in a spasm of pagan savagery and he employs its imagery to articulate his sense of the enormity of his own most appalling deed; but its doctrines are never the subject of his cogitations, its truths never matter for reflection. For Macbeth the question is in abeyance, and this is one way in which the dreadful limbo in which he lives is defined. But for Hamlet Christian doctrine is an assumption and an ambience, the frame of his awareness, the implicit substance of his speculations, and the basis of his ethical sensibility. The observation that the code of revenge is anti-Christian is not to the purpose, for the Christian cultures accommodated, or at least failed to displace, the code of revenge for many centuries both before and after *Hamlet*.

It is to my mind a curiously perverse understanding that continues to claim, in the words of a distinguished recent commentator, that "Hamlet, though nominally a Christian, yet in moments of sharpest crises . . . turns to the consolations of Stoicism."[27] He is speaking of Hamlet's defiance of augury: "If it be now, 'tis not to come; if it be not to come, it will be now; if it be not now, yet it will come; the readiness is all." True, it is a Senecan topos, but it is worth noticing that Hamlet is speaking in a moment not of sharp crisis but of calm decision; that he is, with a new kind of self-possession, calming the anxieties concerning premonitions of the stoical Horatio. This in itself makes its dramatic point. Moreover the evangelical affirmation that precedes the defiance of augury— "there's a special providence in the fall of a sparrow"—could hardly be more opposed to the Senecan-stoic view of the cosmos. These assertions in defiance of augury have a finality

[27] H. Weisinger, *The Agony and the Triumph* (Ann Arbor, Mich.: Michigan State Univ. Press, 1964), p. 106. But see for a contrary view, confirmatory of my own, Fredson Bowers, "The Moment of Final Suspense in *Hamlet,*" *Shakespeare 1564-1964* (Providence: Brown Univ. Press, 1964).

and a poise that is in marked contrast to the "interrogative mood" that has characterized Hamlet's idiom throughout: "What's Hecuba to him or he to Hecuba, / That he should weep for her?" "What is a man, / If his chief good and market of his time / Be but to sleep and feed?" "Did these bones cost no more the breeding, but to play at loggats with 'em?" Hamlet's realization of the folly of that self-assumption of wit whereby a man would be the artist of his own salvation, or another's, or another's damnation, has issued in fact in that most basic of mature Christian virtues: the patience, the self-control which waits upon the fullness of time in release both from anxiety and haste, passion and compulsion; which recognizes limitation with an objectivity that precludes panic.

The composure is dramatized to good effect in the encounter with Osric. Styles of response have been throughout the very stuff of Hamlet's judgments. He has expressed himself through his responses to them—his mother's, Claudius', the players', Horatio's, Polonius', Laertes'. What we know most deeply of Hamlet we know through his reactions to the styles of these others. Now the ridiculous Osric provides the occasion for a Hamlet in complete command of himself. Moreover, the parody of Osric's affectation serves to exhibit his self-possession, in marked contrast to the towering passion with which he responded to Laertes' bravery, in the court context in which we first became aware of its absence. The humor is of the kind that is the surest sign of stresses resolved in a play of intelligence. And it is shot through with sentences, such as "to know a man well, were to know himself" (v.ii.143-144), which strikes us as the very essence of a wisdom the entire sequence of events has distilled. Nevertheless, to find the final outcome of Hamlet's experience in this attainment of humility would be to do less than justice to the fine tragic balance of the catastrophe.

Hamlet kills his man, and one evil "canker of our nature" is destroyed in the full flush of its crimes. But not before it has destroyed him too, and his house, and seven other lives. What we are required to perceive at the close of the play, what the play strikes as its final note, is the enduring value of authentic individual existence; of the true record of what a man has made of himself and his circumstances. When Hamlet says "a man's life is no more than to say 'One,'" he also says "the interim is mine." And that the bearing of a wounded name should supremely matter is what we learn from Hamlet's plea to Horatio to absent him from felicity awhile, in order that the truth of the story should be made known. It is the final expression, at the very edge of silence, of a faith in the value of a life's integrity. Shakespeare has no tragedy which articulates an idea more magnanimous than this.

CHAPTER VI

OTHELLO

The greatest single source of confusion in the analysis of Othello's tragic role has been the mislocation of his tragic distinction. If it is taken for granted, as it so often is, that Othello's great love is the source of this distinction, a distorting factor is introduced into our vision of the love itself, of its place in the tragic economy, and of the whole progress and tenor of the tragic action. It is upon this issue of Othello the lover that criticism of the play has split into two contending schools. The one has given us an ideal lover, if anything too noble, too trusting, and at heart incorruptible. The other offers us a windbag, a posturer, an egotistical self-deceiver, an immature romantic in love not with a real woman but with his idealized fantasy of a woman, in reality a person of sensual and vindictive nature whose overriding need is to think well of himself, a braggart soldier, incapable of dealing with the challenges of peace and mature personal relationships; in short a balloon of self-esteem which can be exploded at a prick. The Bradleyan citadel, first stormed by F. R. Leavis (upon a hint from T. S. Eliot) in his famous essay,[1] though gallantly defended since by Helen Gardner, J. Holloway, and, more recently, Harold Jenkins,[2] has been increasingly undermined by a devoted little band of detractors. They give us a portrait, painted with verve, *schadenfreude*, and clinical acumen, of an anti-Bradleyan antihero, in whom the mask of

[1] "Diabolical Intellect and the Noble Hero," *The Common Pursuit* (London: Chatto, 1952). The hint from Eliot is in the well-known "Shakespeare and the Stoicism of Seneca" (1927).

[2] In, for instance: H. Gardner, "The Noble Moor," *Proceedings of the British Academy*, no. 41 (1955); J. Holloway, *The Story of the Night* (Lincoln, Nebr.: Univ. of Nebraska Press, 1963); H. Jenkins, "The Catastrophe in Shakespearean Tragedy," Inaugural Lecture, 1967 (Edinburgh: Edinburgh Univ. Press, 1969).

romantic idealism is stripped to reveal features dear to the mid-twentieth-century *zeitgeist*: emotional inversion, sexual repression, infantile regression. Both simplistic views—that it is Othello's too noble and beautiful, or brutally egoistic love for Desdemona that exposes him to the machinations of Iago and the sufferings of tragedy—derive from certain assumptions about the moral purpose of tragedy. A need for poetic justice formed the older "common sense" as well: the good Rymer's possession of that healthy faculty caused him to recoil with horror and aversion from this sorry tale of the murder of the poor harmless wretch Desdemona. Didacticism is always with us, and the disappearance of the tragedy with the bathwater has always seemed a minor casualty whenever the interests of mental hygiene were felt to be at stake. Bradley is undeniably sentimental about Othello; but Leavis is just as undeniably prim. Today winds blow from an opposite quarter. But the danger of "envenoming and souring our spirits" by turning *Othello* (as Jan Kott has recently done) into a proof text of the thesis that "once again Shakespeare's hatred of nature forecasts that of Swift. Nature is depraved, above all in its reproductive function"[3] is perhaps greater than any menace to manners or morals envisaged by either Rymer or Leavis. It would therefore seem to be important once again to ask, with Thomas Rymer, though with three centuries' more experience of the meaning and functioning of literary forms, "What can remain with the Audience to carry home with them from this sort of Poetry, for their use and edification?"[4] If therefore the terms of the analysis are shifted so that the consideration of Othello as tragic protagonist is conducted not through polemical definitions and counterdefinitions of an alleged nobility, nor in terms of a moral balance sheet of praise and blame, but through observation of the dynamics of the tragic progres-

[3] *Shakespeare Our Contemporary* (London: Methuen, 1965), p. 97.
[4] T. Rymer, "A Short View of Tragedy" (1693), in *The Critical Works of T. Rymer*, ed. Curt A. Zimanski (New Haven: Yale Univ. Press, 1956), p. 164.

sion, it becomes possible to give an account of the play which places in the center of attention its particular form of tragic self-discovery, and the particularly interesting variant of Shakespeare's customary structure used to articulate it.

The play begins, in fact, not with Othello but with Iago. It is this which from the outset of the play, from its very first situations, makes the origin of evil clear, explicit, and unequivocal. Iago, who holds Othello in his hate, is presented as manipulator, intriguer, mischief-maker, calumniator, mocker, deceiver, liar, envier, poisoner of men's minds, disturber of peaceful sleep. Figure of duplicity, and of deliberate hypocrisy, by the end of the act he is also subtle cynic who perverts good doctrine in the age-old fashion of the Devil quoting scripture. There seems little to be gained by "naturalizing" Iago or "motivating" him, that is, providing naturalistic reasons for what is a device patently displayed. The display is open and palpable in the addresses—pseudosoliloquies—to the audience, which exhibit Iago's impersonations to the full:

> That Cassio loves her, I do well believe it;
> That she loves him, 'tis apt and of great credit:
> The Moor, howbe't that I endure him not,
> Is of a constant, noble, loving nature;
> And I dare think, he'll prove to Desdemona
> A most dear husband: now I do love her too,
> Not out of absolute lust (though peradventure
> I stand accountant for as great a sin,)
> But partly led to diet my revenge,
> For that I do suspect the lustful Moor
> Hath leap'd into my seat, the thought whereof
> Doth like a poisonous mineral gnaw my inwards,
> And nothing can, or shall content my soul,
> Till I am even with him, wife, for wife:
> Or failing so, yet that I put the Moor,
> At least, into a jealousy so strong,
> That judgment cannot cure; which thing to do,

If this poor trash of Venice, whom I trash
For his quick hunting, stand the putting on,
I'll have our Michael Cassio on the hip,
Abuse him to the Moor, in the right garb
(For I fear Cassio with my night-cap too),
Make the Moor thank me, love me, and reward me,
For making him egregiously an ass,
And practicing upon his peace and quiet,
Even to madness: 'tis here, but yet confus'd;
Knavery's plain face is never seen, till us'd.

$$\text{(II.i.281-307)}$$

Spivack's conception of the conventional medieval figure of
the Vice,[5] the devil prankster, overlaid, enriched, and subtil-
ized by Shakespeare in accordance with the naturalistic expectations of his audience, offers the most fruitful account
of this paradigm of "motiveless malignity."[6] And the play's
progression exhibits the character expanding from the original
embryonic troublemaker of I.i; modulating through the cynical destroyer of values, the destroyer of the spirit, first presented in the garden dialogue in I.iii and developed in Act II,
to the culminating vision of the arch-devil taking possession
of his victim's soul in Act III. This vision, terrifying in its
sudden glimpse into the depths, is of a perversion of eros
truly satanic. In the scene where Iago torments Othello almost beyond endurance with the story of Cassio's dream, and,
we are invited to perceive, derives a salacious satisfaction from
the very telling, sexual desire reaches an ultimate point of
desolate self-consumption. It is a diabolic negation of love,
equivalent, it is perhaps not fanciful to note, to the negation
of the tetragrammaton in "I am not what I am."

If the nature of the adversary who opposes Othello is thus

[5] B. Spivack, *Shakespeare and the Allegory of Evil* (New York:
Columbia Univ. Press, 1958).
[6] The phrase is Coleridge's in *Shakespearean Criticism*, ed. T. M.
Raysor, I, 44.

made abundantly clear in the predicament of the play, so is the fact that Othello's personal distinction is rooted in the fact of his soldiership. It is as a practiced commander that he first establishes his ascendancy in the street scene. It is to the Venetian war council that he is imperiously summoned. It is his exotic account of a martial career rich in adventure and fortitude that has caught Desdemona's imagination. It is the great soldier that she loves, and her own testimony to this effect—"And to his honours, and his valiant parts / Did I my soule and Fortunes consecrate"—is inadvertently corroborated by the account her father gives of her: "So opposite to marriage, that she shunn'd / The wealthy curled darlings of our nation" (i.ii.67-68).

Othello's great lament for his lost occupation and his famous final speech also make clear that the primary and overriding devotion of Othello's life has been to soldiership. He is warrior first and lover secondarily. The construction of the Senate scene makes this clear. It is to be observed that the private and the public concerns are very skillfully interwoven —first by Brabantio's seizing of the opportunity to plead his case in the Senate, which is meeting in extraordinary midnight session for reasons of state, and again in his bitter reply to the Duke's perfunctory consolation, "So let the Turk of Cyprus us beguile" (i.iii.210ff.). Brabantio is an extremely important dramatic means for conveying the relation between public and private concerns. And what is conveyed through the impact of his role is the primacy of the public event and of Othello's role as general, and the secondary nature, to the Senate and to Othello himself, of his private affairs. This primacy Othello announces in vehement terms:

> Let housewives make a skillet of my helm,
> And all indign and bare adversities
> Make head against my reputation!
>
> (i.ii.272-274)

while the Duke's relief at an outcome which will not deprive Venice of Othello's services is evident in his speech to Brabantio: "I think this tale would win my daughter too" (1.iii.195). One has only to compare Othello's declaration with Antony's "Let Rome in Tiber melt" and "the nobleness of life / Is to do thus" to perceive that Mars and Venus stand in precisely opposite relationship to each other in the two plays. The comparison is worth pursuing further, but for the moment suffice it to show that though *Othello*, as has often been remarked, is the most domestic of Shakespeare's great tragedies, Othello's downfall is nevertheless placed in a context of issues larger than the merely private and intimate. And though the story is insulated from too close an involvement in state affairs by the wrecking of the Turkish fleet and the receding of the Turkish danger to Cyprus, nevertheless the sense of the dependence of a whole community's welfare upon the outcome of Othello's private affairs is insistently maintained in the plot by rioting soldiers and the exigencies of military government.

Our perception of that axis of the tragic development that concerns the hero's involvement in, defeat by, repudiation of, and final settlement of accounts with his world depends therefore upon the locating of Othello's distinction in the fact that he is the acclaimed great general of Venice. It is worth recalling the opening paragraph of Cinthio's story: "There once lived in Venice a Moor, who was very valiant and of a handsome person; and having given proofs in war of great skill and prudence, he was highly esteemed by the *seniores* of the Republic, who in rewarding deeds of valour advanced the interests of the State."[7]

If Iago's open and palpable villainy makes the answer to the question "Whence evil?" easy to answer, the total predicament presented in Act 1 is anything but simple. It possesses the peculiar complexity that is characteristic of the mature trage-

[7] Trans. J. E. Taylor (1855), *Variorum*, p. 377.

dies: the knotting of past with future, of the fatalities that have already shaped the protagonist's circumstances and character with those on the brink of which he stands. It is, in Auerbach's phrase, "fraught with background."[8] What makes Othello's situation challenging and testing is the fact, salient, specific, and plain for all to see, that Othello is a Moor. This circumstance complicates Othello's role both as soldier and as lover, and is brought into prominence in many ways. The very title of the play points to the focal prominence of Othello's ethnic origin, and it is manifest in the theatrical spectacle itself. He is singled out, this extravagant and wheeling stranger, this erring barbarian, redoubtable soldier-servant of the Venetian state, as physically distinguished from those about him, as alien and unique. This Moor has risen to command the respect of the subtlest and most sophisticated of cities in its most vulnerable point: defense. This erstwhile pagan has transcended his wild Berber ancestry to become the shield of the Venetian city against the menace of the Turkish infidel.[9]

The entire presentation of Othello in the first act is geared to this perception of him, and it is in this light that both Iago's contemptuous references to black rams and Barbary horses and Othello's exotic evocation of antres vast and deserts idle, his free unhoused condition and his descent from men of royal siege, become fully operative in the dramatic scheme. Both sets of associations existed in the Elizabethan imagination: blackamoors, bondslaves, and pagans—barbarians both menacing and repulsive; and the romantic or chivalric wild Berber chiefs. The strategy of the opening raises the highest expectations concerning his entrance, his performance. Iago's coarse denigration; the facts and the mysteries of the elope-

[8] E. Auerbach, *Mimesis*, trans. Willard Trask (Princeton: Princeton Univ. Press, 1953), pp. 9-12.

[9] Upon the geographical symbolism—Cyprus an island outpost between the barbarous Turk and the Venetian city—see Alvin Kernan, *Introduction*, Signet ed. (New York: New American Library, 1963).

ment; Brabantio's distress; the foolish Roderigo, who, as rival suitor to Desdemona, suggests a contrast of some kind; all these intensify expectation for that first sight of Othello himself. Such heightened expectation is in any case inherent in the universal human spectrum of possible responses (from xenophobia to love of the exotic) to the outsider; and this expectation is the source of the breathtaking effectiveness of "Keep up your bright swords, for the dew will rust 'em" when the single commanding figure subdues the excited Venetian burghers with one ineradicable gesture of composed authority. The exhibition of Othello's impressive authority, control, and dignity, his unflinching sense of his own worth, strikes upon the sensibility of the audience in this context of expectation, establishing the image of a figure who is the composed embodiment of a unique triumph.

The contrast between the Moor and Venice works two ways. Venice is pampered, soft, overcivilized by comparison with this rugged stranger. But Venice is sophisticated and worldly-wise, and he "little of this great world can speak, more than pertains to feats of broil, and battle." He is in a very special sense a self-made man, and there is behind him no store of patient wisdom stemming from rootedness in a particular culture, to fall back upon in the face of Iago's subversion. What there is is pride of difference, a self-confidence and self-reliance splendidly delineated in his assertion of royal lineage, his relish of an "unhoused free condition," which he is nevertheless ready to renounce, and in the full acceptance of the responsibility that he takes upon himself concerning his marriage-for-love:

> . . . for know, Iago,
> But that I love the gentle Desdemona,
> I would not my unhoused free condition
> Put into circumscription and confine
> For the sea's worth.　　　(I.ii.24-28)

It is this quality of proud self-determination that provides a clue to a passage which has proved a stumbling block to interpretation and provided the pivot upon which the Othello controversy has hinged. The passage is Othello's appeal to the Senate to accede to Desdemona's wish to travel with him to Cyprus:

> . . . beseech you, let her will
> Have a free way; I therefore beg it not
> To please the palate of my appetite,
> Nor comply with heat, the young affects
> In me defunct, and proper satisfaction,
> But to be free and bounteous to her mind;
> And heaven defend your good souls that you think
> I will your serious and great business scant,
> For she is with me; no, when light-wing'd toys,
> Of feather'd Cupid, foils with wanton dullness
> My speculative and active instruments,
> That my disports corrupt and taint my business,
> Let housewives make a skillet of my helm,
> And all indign and base adversities
> Make head against my estimation!

> (i.iii.260-274)

Following the Eliot-Leavis views of Othello, Kirschbaum has found in this speech a "dangerous disclaimer of sexual feelings,"[10] which, thus repressed, erupt in the violence of the later jealousy. If we are not bent upon explanatory depth psychology, however, the alleged disclaimer of sexual feeling can be otherwise construed. It is the legitimate claim of sexual consummation that is firmly asserted, precisely in order to assert equally firmly the speaker's readiness to set this claim aside, since he is able to control its most peremptory promptings. If we accept, as the Arden editor does, the emendation first proposed by Upton in 1746 to solve the difficulty of the

[10] L. Kirschbaum, "The Modern *Othello*," *ELH*, ii (March 1944).

Folio text, which gives "the young affects in *me* defunct,"[11] it becomes possible to mark the distinction between passion and its *young* affects, that is, the uncontrollability of youth, to which he is no longer subject. The series of negative assertions concerning "appetite" is climaxed, it should be noted, by the insistent "proper satisfaction." What he is saying, then, is "I do not ask this boon because I am unable to control my natural desire for the legitimate consummation of my marriage, but to be free and bountiful to the lady's expressed wishes." "Mind" in the context is not in the least necessarily opposed to "body." Such an opposition would indeed be grossly inappropriate to the decorum of the Senate scene. If "mind" means no more than wishes or desires, it also means no less; and to be free and bountiful to these is at the very least a gracious and chivalrous gesture. It is a courtly, not a quasi-platonic, love which is expressed in these lines, and the continuance beyond courtship into marriage of the courtly attitude is part of the speech's import.

It is the second part of the speech, however, that has most particularly been set down in evidence against Othello, since its vocabulary implies a distinct disparagement of the offices of love in marriage. Wantonness, the dulling of mental perspicuity, mere feathered sport which distracts a man from serious business—such expressions suggest rather a vulgar and trivializing estimation of eros than anything in the nature of a grand passion. I would suggest, however, that the syntax of line 268 gives to the structure of the speech an indication of the direction in which we are expected to take it. The caesura after "For she is with me"—a phrase of simple tenderness, touching in its colloquiality—is followed by the emphatic "no, when light wing'd toys etc.," so that we may conceive of this repudiation as being addressed specifically to the Senators. We may then safely infer that his disclaimer is of any such light

[11] *Variorum*, p. 72ff. See also C. J. Sisson, *New Readings in Shakespeare* (Cambridge: Cambridge Univ. Press, 1956), p. 249.

o' love idea of his relationship with Desdemona as they, in their Venetian sophistication, might hold; as Brabantio in his denunciations has shown that he does hold. The disparagement disparages them, not him. And such an expression of disassociation is perfectly consistent with the characterization of Othello up to this point as proudly distinct from the Venetians.

But in Othello's account of his courtship and in the subsequent Senate scene something is held in reserve. What is left unstated and unexpressed is the quality of the love he does have for Desdemona. He has defined what it is not; he has not yet defined what it is. His reply to the Duke's commission,[12] "With all my heart," very skillfully draws their relationship into the terms of the predicament. We know from his account of their courtship that it is grounded in an imaginative reciprocity; we know that it is honorable; we know that Othello is concerned to consider his wife's feelings, to be free and bounteous to her mind. But we have nowhere heard him express passion for her. His devotion is to the state's service and the flinty and steel couch of war. This, on the one hand, and on the other the fact of the elopement, kept intensely to the fore through the figure of Brabantio, whose bitterness and grief are in striking contrast to the formality of the scene and the measured speech of Othello, make of the love between the Moor and Desdemona an open question. And the question is specific. It is not how nobly or self-centredly he loves her, nor

---

[12] If, as Alice Walker holds, the Quarto interpolation of Desdemona's question "Tonight, my lord?" before Othello's prompt reply to the Duke represents a bookkeeper's memorial reconstruction of the acted version, we have an interesting light on the episode. For if the interpolation "vulgarizes" Desdemona, where its omission in the Folio "strikes the right warrior note," the bookkeeper's *memory* of the scene suggests its power, in the playhouse, to produce wonder and surmise at Othello's readiness thus to leave his newly-wed wife. See the discussion of the textual point in Alice Walker, *Textual Problems of the First Folio* (Cambridge: Cambridge Univ. Press, 1953), p. 140-141.

whether he "really" loves her, but how this love will measure up to the prior claims of the martial life. Once again comparison with *Antony and Cleopatra* makes this clear. Here there is no reckless assertion of love as the nobleness of life. It is precisely this reserve, this latency, that leaves us in suspense concerning the open question of Othello's love for Desdemona. Have we witnessed in Othello control of passion, absence of passion, or repudiation of passion? Is passion to be classified as Iago classifies it, or will it reveal powers and resources of the spirit regarding which he who doubts the power of sanctimony and a frail vow between an erring barbarian and a supersubtle Venetian can have no notion, or to which he can respond only with a spasm of vindictive envy?

Brabantio, as has been noted, plays an extremely important role in the definition of the play's predicament. With regard to the open question he is an anticipatory mirror of Othello —he too is to lose that which is most precious to him— and his bitter parting shaft, "Look to her, Moor, have a quick eye to see: / She has deceiv'd her father, may do thee" (I.iii.202-203), while immediately expressive of the father's grief and pain, is terrifyingly confirmatory to Othello, later, once Iago has poured his pestilence into his ear. But Brabantio's witchcraft speeches fulfill a similar anticipatory function. His reference to witchcraft expresses his shock, outrage, and disbelief, and the natural impulse to mitigate the scandal, if that is still possible—to defend his daughter's honor from the worst aspersions against her virtue—by the imputation of some force over which she had no control.

> She is abus'd, stol'n from me and corrupted,
> By spells and medicines, bought of mountebanks,
> For nature so preposterously to err,
> (Being not deficient, blind, or lame of sense)
> Sans witchcraft could not.
>
> (I.iii.60-64)

What then happens, however, is that Othello takes up the challenge. His self-defense gives the witchcraft a local habitation and a name. He explains it:

> She lov'd me for the dangers I had pass'd,
> And I lov'd her that she did pity them.
> This only is the witchcraft I have us'd.
>
> (I.iii.167-169)

"Witchcraft," thus introduced into the play through Brabantio's anxiety and distress, remains to reverberate with rich suggestiveness as the very symbol of a love which by imaginative sympathy can transform a sexual attraction into a profoundly valuable personal relationship. And it is immediately after this, in the third scene of Act I, that we are introduced to the polar contrary of this "witchcraft,"[13] namely, Iago's "wit"— superbly rational, utterly reductive. Iago, self-styled excoriator of irrationality in all its forms, is capable also of transformations—of the transformation of love into a "sect or scion of our raging motions, our carnal stings or unbitted lusts," and of humanity into a baboon:

> O villainous! I have looked upon the world for four times seven years, and since I could distinguish betwixt a benefit and an injury, I never found man that knew how to love himself. Ere I would say I would drown myself for the love of a guinea hen, I would change my humanity with a baboon.
>
> (I.iii.306-311)

[13] Robert B. Heilman, *Magic in the Web: Language and Action in Othello* (Lexington, Ky.: Univ. of Kentucky Press, 1956), chap. 7, has an excellent account of the thematic implications of the antithesis, though I believe he makes the familiar reductive move of thematic criticism when he says it is what *Othello* is "about": "in this antithesis is the symbolic structure, or the thematic form, of *Othello*," thus transforming a single motif into "the theme" of the play (p. 225).

These transformations give us our bearings upon the terms of the psychomachia as it is shaped and framed in Act II. Iago's first semiruminating, semiconfidential soliloquy to the audience has given the psychomachia its largest dimension: "Hell and night / Must bring this monstrous birth to the world's light" (I.iii.401-402). The contest between Hell and Heaven reveals itself, in Act II, as the contest for the soul of Othello between what Iago represents and what Desdemona represents. And it is precisely the reserve, the latency, the sense of experience as yet not known upon the pulse and felt along the blood, that makes of this conflict an agonizing test for Othello of his faith in Desdemona.

Act II exhibits the contraries between which Othello is caught. What is about to happen is presented symbolically at the outset of Act II when Othello's storm-tossed bark is momentarily expected:

Methinks the wind does speak aloud at land,
A fuller blast ne'er shook our battlements:
If it ha' ruffian'd so upon the sea,
What ribs of oak, when the huge mountains melt,
Can hold the mortise? . . .
The chiding billow seems to pelt the clouds,
The wind-shak'd surge, with high and monstrous main,
Seems to cast water on the burning bear,
And quench the guards of th' ever-fixed pole;
I never did like molestation view
On the enchafed flood.

(II.i.5-9, 12-17)

The description of tempest, metaphor for contraries at war and "traitors ensteeped to clog the guiltless keel," is followed by a second oblique presentation in the form of the word game of the watchers on the shore. Naturalistically motivated as a casual, witty exchange designed to distract their anxious thoughts, the chop-logic definitions of women exhibit a further aspect of Iago's reductive cynicism contrasted with Desdemona's faith—playful in the context but essentially serious—in the possibility of "a deserving woman indeed—one that in the authority of her merit did justly put on the vouch of very malice itself."

> IAGO. If she be fair and wise, fairness and wit;
>   The one's for use, the other using it.
> DESDEMONA. Well prais'd! How if she be black and witty?
> IAGO. If she be black, and thereto have a wit,
>   She'll find a white, that shall her blackness hit.
>   (II.i.129-133)

Iago, who can produce a Character of a Virtuous Woman with no difficulty at all, finds no purpose in existence for such a wight ("if ever such wight were") but such as is indicated by the infinitely contemptuous dismissal: "To suckle fools, and chronicle small beer." Brilliantly disguised as badinage, this actually candid expression of Iago's cynicism concludes a passage in which contraries are presented with the dazzling chiasma which marks the dramaturgy throughout. In Act I old black ram tupped white ewe (in Iago's unappealing phrase) but black and white were reversed on the spiritual or moral level, so that, in the Duke's opinion, Brabantio's son-in-law could be said to be far more fair than black. Events bring about further reversals: Othello's candor, his honesty or simplicity, which thinks men honest that but seem to be so, encounters the Janus-faced Iago, paradigm of black-hearted duplicity. Desdemona's candor, appearing to Othello as dissimulation (she had indeed once innocently dissimulated her desire to be wooed) is her undoing. It is her very virtue that Iago turns to pitch. Symbolic black and white indeed crisscross the play, dissonant chords whose dominant is the skin whiter than snow and smooth as monumental alabaster, the beauty which, despite all the perplexities and dubieties which attempt to engulf and assimilate it, is in fact what it seems.

The question whether beauty is what it seems is the leitmotif of Act II. Cassio joins Roderigo to function as a mirror of Othello from yet another angle. Both are tested by Iago in scenes which are preliminary to the central deception scene, and both repudiate Iago's suggestion of Desdemona's "lechery" in a way that is meant to prepare for and to contrast with Othello's reception of the same insidious message. To the simple Roderigo she is full of the most blessed condition ("Blest fig's-end!" says Iago. "The wine she drinks is made of grapes. . . . Didst thou not see her paddle with the palm of his hand?"); and to Cassio she is perfection indeed, and neither is deflected from his course by Iago's insinuations, which are adapted with exquisite finesse to the nature of his companion and to his particular designs upon each. The act is composed so that Iago's salacious tavern talk concerning Desdemona alternates with such affirmations of her goodness as those of Roderigo and Cassio. The system of antitheses is at its concealed high point when Iago watches Cassio kiss Desdemona's hand and wishes, in a spasm of envy, malice, and foul-mindedness unequaled for sibilant virulence, that "they were clyster-pipes for his sake"; and this is immediately followed by the meeting between Othello and Desdemona at the port of Cyprus.

In a manner reminiscent of Romeo and Juliet's balcony scene following upon Mercutio's medlar joke, Othello steps ashore and gives passionate utterance to his feeling for Desdemona for the first time in the play. And it is worth noticing the terms in which he expresses his soul's joy:

O my fair warrior! . . .
It gives me wonder great as my content

193

To see you here before me: O my soul's joy,
If after every tempest come such calmness,
May the winds blow, till they have waken'd death,
And let the labouring bark climb hills of seas,
Olympus-high, and duck again as low
As hell's from heaven. If it were now to die,
'Twere now to be most happy; for I fear
My soul hath her content so absolute,
That not another comfort, like to this
Succeeds in unknown fate.

(II.i.182-193)

The first words of his greeting to her, "My fair warrior," effectively remind us of the *concordia discors*—Mars and Venus harmonized—which Othello dreamed his marriage might be. It is this background that gives to the later "Excellent wretch . . . and when I love thee not, / Chaos is come again" its expressive power. The wonder and the rapture, that very expression of passionate discovery absent from the first act, acquires a richer resonance by contrast with Iago's world view, which has by now been broadly displayed. The forces in conflict are here fully confronted: Iago will blacken Othello's imagination where Desdemona illuminates it. And it is the cunning of Iago to know that if he undermines Othello's faith in Desdemona—the agent and vessel of Othello's great discovery of love—he will indeed put out the light.

While the terms of the temptation of Othello are thus set out in Act II, the temptation itself is the content of Act III. Through it is exhibited the collapse and disintegration of the splendidly achieved poise of the Moor of Venice. We watch him played upon by Iago, caught in the tormenting vice of a choice the import of which we understand from Act II, the issue of which is the vow of revenge in Act IV—token of Iago's possession of his soul.

At the start Othello is characteristically sure of himself, as he is sure of the nature of the life he will choose to lead:

> Think'st thou I'ld make a life of jealousy?
> To follow still the changes of the moon
> With fresh suspicions? No! To be once in doubt,
> Is to be resolv'd: exchange me for a goat,
> When I shall turn the business of my soul
> To such exsufflicate and blown surmises,
> Matching thy inference: 'tis not to make me jealous,
> To say my wife is fair, feeds well, loves company,
> Is free of speech, sings, plays, and dances well;
> Where virtue is, these are more virtuous:
> Nor from mine own weak merits will I draw
> The smallest fear, or doubt of her revolt,
> For she had eyes, and chose me. No, Iago,
> I'll see before I doubt, when I doubt, prove,
> And on the proof, there is no more but this:
> Away at once with love or jealousy!
>
> (III.iii.181-196)

Sexual jealousy is what Iago induces in Othello. But the means he employs to make Othello amenable to his potent suggestions are calculated upon the premise that Othello's confidence in himself can be undermined. Iago's subtlest stratagem is his enlisting on the devil's side the whole paraphernalia of rationality—the wisdom of the worldly Venetian world—whereby he subverts the instinctive responses Othello becomes afraid to trust. It is to this one breach in Othello's defenses that his shafts, his appeals to man-of-the-world attitudes, are aimed:

> I know our country disposition well;
> In Venice they do let God see the pranks
> They dare not show their husbands: their best conscience
> Is not to leave undone, but keep unknown.
>
> (III.iii.205-208)

> Ay, there's the point: as, to be bold with you,
> Not to affect many proposed matches,
> Of her own clime, complexion, and degree,
> Whereto we see in all things nature tends;
> Fie, we may smell in such, a will most rank,
> Foul disproportions, thoughts unnatural.
> But pardon me: I do not in position
> Distinctly speak of her, though I may fear
> Her will, recoiling to her better judgment,
> May fall to match you with her country forms,
> And haply repent.   (III.iii.232-242)

Iago's insinuation of sexual perversity in Desdemona's choice
follows his profession of worldly knowledge concerning the
proclivities of Venetian wives, of which a stranger cannot be
expected to know. That these barbed shafts strike home is
witnessed by Othello's subsequent soliloquy:

> Haply, for I am black,
> And have not those soft parts of conversation
> That chamberers have, or for I am declin'd
> Into the vale of years—yet that's not much—
> She's gone, I am abus'd, and my relief
> Must be to loathe her: O curse of marriage,
> That we can call these delicate creatures ours,
> And not their appetites!   (III.iii.267-274)

Othello falls back, in his disorientation, confusion, and per-
plexity, upon the clichés of a worldly wisdom not his own:

> . . . yet 'tis the plague of great ones,
> Prerogativ'd are they less than the base,
> 'Tis destiny, unshunnable, like death:
> Even then this forked plague is fated to us
> When we do quicken. . . .   (III.iii.277-281)

196

and Iago, in the scene which concludes with the consummation of the diabolic alliance between them ("I am your own
for ever"), strikes again and again the note of appeal to a
pseudostoical acceptance of what Othello should of course
know is the common lot of husbands:

Would you would bear your fortunes like a man!

> Good, sir, be a man,
> Think every bearded fellow that's but yok'd
> May draw with you; there's millions now alive
> That nightly lies in those unproper beds
> Which they dare swear peculiar. . . .

Whilst you were here erewhile, mad with your grief—
A passion most unsuiting such a man. . . .

> . . . marry, patience,
> Or I shall say you are all in all in spleen,
> And nothing of a man.
>
> (IV.i.61, 65-69, 76-77, 87-89)

In the confident self-reliance of Act I he vowed "My life
upon her faith." The play progresses through its grand peripeteia to an ironic reversal of that proposition, so that it becomes in effect "Her life upon my doubt" by the time his
rejection of her proffered napkin reveals the working of the
poison and delivers him into Iago's hands, and into a torment
such that

> . . . not poppy, nor mandragora,
> Nor all the drowsy syrups of the world,
> Shall ever medicine thee to that sweet sleep
> Which thou owedst yesterday.
>
> (III.iii.335-339)

We are watching the disintegration of a triumphant achievement: a marriage of native instinctive qualities of energy, reso-

lution, courage, and fortitude with the gentleness and *civilità* suggested by Othello's account of his courtship. Desdemona's brave attempt to make allowances, to come to terms with what she persuades herself is no more than a normal state of post-honeymoon matrimony, strikes a melancholy note as of a lost dream:

> . . . nay, we must think
> Men are not gods;
> Nor of them look for such observances
> As fits the bridal: beshrew me much, Emilia,
> I was (unhandsome warrior as I am)
> Arraigning his unkindness with my soul;
> But now I find I had suborn'd the witness,
> And he's indicted falsely.
>
> (III.iv.145-152)

The doubt which Iago, supersubtle Venetian master of dialectic, injects into Othello's mind does more than put him on the rack. It destroys him, it drives him, quite literally, out of his mind. Othello's own perception of this destruction of the self is registered in his speech of farewell to arms:

> What sense had I of her stol'n hours of lust?
> I saw't not, thought it not, it harm'd not me;
> I slept the next night well, was free and merry;
> I found not Cassio's kisses on her lips;
> He that is robb'd, not wanting what is stol'n,
> Let him not know't, and he's not robb'd at all. . . .
> I had been happy if the general camp,
> Pioneers, and all, had tasted her sweet body,
> So I had nothing known: O now for ever
> Farewell the tranquil mind, farewell content:
> Farewell the plumed troop, and the big wars,
> That makes ambition virtue: O farewell,
> Farewell the neighing steed, and the shrill trump,

The spirit-stirring drum, the ear-piercing fife;
The royal banner, and all quality,
Pride, pomp, and circumstance of glorious war!
And, O you mortal engines, whose wide throats
The immortal Jove's great clamor counterfeit;
Farewell, Othello's occupation's gone!

(III.iii.344-363)

The break in the thought at "O now for ever," like all such unbridged transitions in dramatic speech, invites us to infer, by a corresponding leap of the mind, the nature of the connection between the present anguish of his "knowledge" and the martial life. His fantasy of the bliss of ignorance (he takes it now for granted that she is faithless) induces a nostalgia for the blessedness of his state in the previous circumstances of wholeness and integrity. It is in the challenge and achievement of warfare, in that summoning up of the energetic resources of mind and body for an exacting purpose, that Othello, we perceive, had found satisfaction for all the needs of his nature. It is for this reason that the fife and the drum and the neighing steed quicken his pulse with the excitement of anticipation, anticipation of happiness, of fullness and completeness of being. The speech ends with his recognition that that which occupied him, that which fulfilled him, which defined and gave form to the self of the man of action, is gone for ever. For back to the past he can never go. Thus is Othello's own recognition of his disintegrating loss of self given poignant expression.

No longer in command of himself or of others, Othello moves inexorably toward irreversible acceptance of Iago's tale and of Iago's viewpoint. Every instinct tells him that Desdemona is as fair as she appears, but how can he be so foolish as to believe in appearances when all Iago's wisdom, "imputation and strong circumstance," every notion of reason and likelihood, "lead directly to the door of truth." He is without compass in this world in which "I think my wife be honest, and think she is not, / I think that thou art just, and think thou art not" (III.iii.390-391). Only ocular proof, it seems to him in his delusory and frantic need for certainty, will satisfy him; and Iago turns the absurdity of this crazed and self-defeating demand to his own advantage with a stroke which at once makes apparent the masochistic impasse in which he has caught Othello:

> IAGO.   . . . how satisfied, my lord?
>   Would you, the supervisor, grossly gape on,
>   Behold her topp'd?
> OTHELLO.   Death and damnation! O!
>   (III.iii.400-402)

It is with a diabolical virtuosity that Iago conjures with Othello's desperate appeal for "a living reason, that she's disloyal," still further inflaming his poisoned and festering erotic imagination. Cassio's "dream," described with considerable verve, he judiciously dismisses as "but his dream," shrewdly understanding that by now Othello's delusion is all but beyond cure. With the masterstroke of the handkerchief, Iago's overthrow of Othello is complete. The world is Iago's color and nothing less than the surge and power of the Black Sea itself—"the Pontic Sea, / Whose icy current and compulsive course, / Ne'er feels retiring ebb"—can represent the force of Othello's resolution, now that the anguished paralysis of the divided mind has found release in decision.

> O, that the slave had forty thousand lives!
> One is too poor, too weak for my revenge:
> Now do I see 'tis true; look here, Iago,
> All my fond love thus do I blow to heaven. . . .
> 'Tis gone.

Arise, black vengeance, from the hollow cell,
Yield up, O Love, thy crown and hearted throne,
To tyrannous hate, swell, bosom, with thy fraught,
For 'tis of aspics' tongues.

(III.iii.449-457)

In Act IV Iago's victory is consolidated. He can risk any sleight of hand now, and indeed, his delight in "pleasure and action," a sheer superabundance of vitality and ingenuity, induces him to multiply "ocular proofs"—not mere hearsay— for Othello's delectation, when this is by now pretty well supererogatory. Iago stages his ribald conversation with Cassio, which Bianca conveniently caps, in order not only to provide Othello with proof positive of Desdemona's infidelity, but in order to keep him confirmed in his new wisdom, the wisdom which is to drive him mad:

Good sir, be a man,
Think every bearded fellow that's but yok'd
May draw with you; there's millions now alive
That nightly lies in those unproper beds
Which they dare swear peculiar: your case is better:
O, 'tis the spite of hell, the fiend's arch-mock,
To lip a wanton in a secure couch,
And to suppose her chaste.

(IV.i.65-73)

Nevertheless, in the dialogue which follows is exhibited the tenacity of the rival claim upon Othello's imagination.

Othello's replies to Iago's persistent instigations poignantly indicate the inner contest:

OTHELLO. I would have him nine years a-killing; a fine woman, a fair woman, a sweet woman!
IAGO. Nay, you must forget.

OTHELLO. And let her rot, and perish, and be damned to-
   night, for she shall not live; no, my heart is turn'd to
   stone; I strike it, and it hurts my hand: O, the world hath
   not a sweeter creature, she might lie by an emperor's side
   and command him tasks.

IAGO. Nay, that's not your way.

OTHELLO. Hang her, I do but say what she is: so delicate
   with her needle, an admirable musician, O, she will sing
   the savageness out of a bear; of so high and plenteous wit
   and invention!

IAGO. She's the worse for all this.

OTHELLO. A thousand thousand times: and then of so gentle
   a condition!

IAGO. Ay, too gentle.

OTHELLO. Ay, that's certain, but yet the pity of it, Iago! O
   Iago, the pity of it, Iago!

(IV.i.174-192)

Iago's pressure is unremitting, and the diabolical intelligence
wins the day. Othello breaks down with a savage mutter: "I
will chop her into messes"; he will not expostulate with her
lest her body and beauty unprovide his mind again. And the
irony of this reversal of the traditional relationship between
delusory appearance and reality is pointed up by the extremity
of opposition in Othello's reply to Desdemona's "I hope my
noble lord esteems me honest":

O, ay, as summer's flies, are in the shambles,
That quicken even with blowing:
O thou black weed, why art so lovely fair?
Thou smell'st so sweet, that the sense aches at thee,
Would thou hadst ne'er been born!

(IV.ii.67-71)

The fourth act of *Othello*, the phase which articulates the
darkened vision of the protagonist, is superbly conducted. It

is Iago's construction that Othello puts upon the fair paper, the most goodly book of Desdemona's beauty. It is upon Iago that Othello has come to rely for his intelligence. The blackened and distorted vision of Desdemona that Iago has succeeded in inducing in Othello is translated into actions which represent an extremity of repudiation: first in public, when Othello strikes Desdemona in the presence of the Venetian ambassadors, and then in private, when he treats Desdemona as a strumpet and Emilia as the mistress of a brothel. The collapse of Othello under his tormentor's provocations into an incoherent and savage raving suggests a re-emergence of the primitive, savage, and barbarous. The form his frenzy at least sporadically takes—"I see that nose of yours, but I see not the dog I will throw it to"; "I will chop her into messes"; "Goats and monkeys," etc.—when considered *sub specie aeternitatas*, represents no doubt the evil imagination of all mankind, but the degradation is particularly poignant in view of Othello's dignity at the opening. Nevertheless it is from these lowest depths that there emerges, in Othello's great speech of lamentation, his clearest recognition of the magnitude of that which he has lost.

> Had it pleas'd heaven
> To try me with affliction, had they rain'd
> All kinds of sores and shames on my bare head,
> Steep'd me in poverty, to the very lips,
> Given to captivity me and my utmost hopes,
> I should have found in some place of my soul
> A drop of patience; but, alas, to make me
> A fixed figure for the time of scorn
> To point his slow and moving fingers at . . . oh, oh.
> Yet could I bear that too, well, very well:
> But there, where I have garner'd up my heart,
> Where either I must live, or bear no life,

The fountain, from the which my current runs,
Or else dries up, to be discarded thence,
Or keep it as a cistern, for foul toads
To knot and gender in!

(IV.ii.49-63)

It is precisely in his agony of loss that he defines and affirms his knowledge of the good and the desirable; the commitment of his nature to the transcendent values falling in ruin about him. Thus is realized in imagination that which in reality is now unattainable; realized with a greater clarity and a more impassioned insight than ever before. These scenes occur during that phase of the tragic discovery which brings value and loss into tormenting collision in his mind. Thus what is for him menaced, undermined, or already lost is poignantly and powerfully realized; and it is this which, in the midst of loss, conveys and affirms the spiritual stature of the loser.

Shakespeare's fourth-act pathos and irony contribute characteristically to the realizations of this phase. The willow-song scene provides us with a dual perspective upon the events: we become aware at once of the immense distance traveled by the protagonist from the center of his well-being, for the transparent innocence of Desdemona exhibits and makes utterly manifest (as does the reconciliation scene in *Lear*) the happiness of which the hero is presently to be totally bereft; while Emilia's irony understates the issues, mitigates them, accommodates them to a world which refuses to take them with complete seriousness (and renders her passionate outburst against Othello later the more effective). The issue is the question that has constituted Othello's crisis of faith throughout. "Wouldst thou do such a thing for all the world?" Desdemona asks. And Emilia's wordplay transmutes the stark opposition of absolutes into the prevarications, half-shades, and contingencies of the workaday world:

EMILIA. Why, would not you?
DESDEMONA.   No, by this heavenly light!
EMILIA. Nor I neither, by this heavenly light.
I might do it as well in the dark.

(IV.iii.64-68)

Emilia is less absolute than Iago, her husband, in whose posi-
tivistic view all women are a priori motivated by that which
is a mere lust of the blood and permission of the will. She,
Emilia, would contemplate such a deed, for a consideration—
not indeed for a joint-ring, nor for measures of lawn, nor for
gowns, petticoats, or caps, nor any petty exhibition; but for
the whole world? For this she would venture purgatory. But
if Emilia's view of women's faith is less absolute than Iago's it
is also less absolute than Othello's. To her the world's a huge
thing; it is a great price for a small vice. To him, the world
serves merely as a term of comparison for the true Desdemona
he would not have sold for it:

> . . . had she been true,
> If heaven would make me such another world,
> Of one entire and perfect chrysolite,
> I'ld not have sold her for it.

(v.ii.144-147)

Thus is the protagonist's high passion pitched against the
lower viewpoint, and its inalienable specific distinction measured. At this point in the progress of events the pathos and
the irony make a peculiarly effective catalyst of the pity and
terror the catastrophe is to produce.

The catastrophe of Act v, it has been well said, "both in
conception and execution shows a dramatic mastery unexcelled
even in Shakespeare."[14]

There are three great passages of soliloquy within the space
of Act v which articulate what in earlier plays extended over

[14] Jenkins, "The Catastrophe in Shakespearean Tragedy," p. 15.

several acts. The retardation of the fatal act itself from its usual timing in Act III to this late stage gives us the deliberation preceding the act, the horror of the recognition of it, and the final account made with it all within the compass of the catastrophe. Such compression is remarkable indeed. And the dramatic mastery is in no small measure due to Shakespeare's mastery of the expressive possibilities of the self-revelatory monologue. No longer the direct, unself-conscious explanation of role to the audience, as in the naïve Elizabethan drama, the self-revelation may be to any degree self-conscious, whether disingenuous or confessional. The Shakespearean soliloquy contained within itself a spectrum of possibilities of interplay between what the character knows or thinks about himself, what the character inadvertently reveals about himself, and what the audience knows about him from sources outside himself in the play as a whole. It is this margin of speculation, this play of the audience's mind between the ostensible and the inferred, that accounts for the realism of the great characters of realistic drama. And it is this play of the mind that is flattened out of existence by the dogma of self-dramatization propounded by Eliot and Leavis. The absurdity of the position has frequently been pointed out, but it has had a longer life than its twin absurdity—the idea that all the characters who speak poetry are poets. So-called "self-dramatization" is the medium of existence of dramatic characters. They enact themselves, they unfold themselves; they have no *other* mode of being of which the dramatic representation is proxy.

When Othello invokes justice in his "It is the cause" speech, he is ostensibly declaring his reasons for the killing of Desdemona:

> It is the cause, yet I'll not shed her blood,
> Nor scar that whiter skin of hers than snow,
> And smooth, as monumental alabaster,
> Yet she must die, else she'll betray more men.

Put out the light, and then put out the light:
If I quench thee, thou flaming minister,
I can again thy former light restore,
Should I repent me; but once put out thy light,
Thou cunning's pattern of excelling nature,
I know not where is that Promethean heat
That can thy light relume: when I have pluck'd the rose,
I cannot give it vital growth again,
It must needs wither; I'll smell it on the tree,
A balmy breath that does almost persuade
Justice herself to break her sword: once more:
Be thus, when thou art dead, and I will kill thee,
And love thee after: once more, and this the last,
So sweet was ne'er so fatal: I must weep,
But they are cruel tears; this sorrow's heavenly,
It strikes where it doth love.

                                             (v.ii.3-22)

Othello's reasons are immediately presented as being in extreme paradoxical conflict with his agonized reluctance to kill
Desdemona, his poignant awareness of her loveliness, and his
vivid consciousness of the absolute finality of death. The cause
is her blood—Iago's "lust of the blood." And nothing in the
speech is more powerful than the sense of the preciousness
of the life thus about to be utterly and irrevocably quenched.
What the audience then infers is the whole state of mind of
a man who is forcing himself to an appalling and unthinkable
deed—a deed which he can only perform so long as he believes it to be necessitated by an overriding imperative—so
overriding as to have for sanction no less than a divine
analogy: like God himself "it strikes where it doth love."
When the outrageous hyperbole of this *sancta superbia* comes
home to the audience, it is registered as the perception that
Othello is insane, in any common-sense or customary meaning
of sanity, when he kills Desdemona, and this perception is the

more startling since the speech is in the measured accents of
the old Othello, exhibiting none of the incoherence, tumult,
and rage of the preceding "mad" scenes, nor the frenzied
anguish of the subsequent "madness" when he realizes his
error. The imaginative leap of the mind required to make this
inference is a measure of the insight we are afforded into the
extremity of the character's passion at this point.

We are afforded confirmation of the accuracy of the inference suggested above further on in the scene, when what we
have perceived to be Othello's precariously strained resolution
is shattered by Desdemona's denial of what by this time is
gospel truth to him. It is the strain of the mental act that
has forced love and law, as it seems to him, into a single
atoning act which gives way under the provocation of "I never
gave him token," so that rage and resentment, previously
sublimated with an iron hand, overcome him:

> O perjur'd woman, thou dost stone thy heart,
> And makest me call what I intend to do
> A murder, which I thought a sacrifice. . . .
>
> (v.ii.64-66)

Obviously, and with appalling irony, everything that Desdemona says from this point enflames his fury still further, until,
quite beside himself, he smothers the unendurable insolence of
the strumpet he takes her to be. I believe that "I that am
cruel, am yet merciful" should be enunciated with a muttered
grim ferocity at the greatest emotional distance from the tone
of the "It is the cause" speech. There is further support for
this view of the emotional carriage of the scene in what we
are invited to see as the explanation of the episode of the lie
in the subsequent dialogue with Emilia. The shock of what
appears to be a momentary attempt to exonerate himself by
seizing the opportunity of Desdemona's dying words is immediately resolved by his "She's like a liar gone to burning hell, /
'Twas I that killed her" (v.ii.130-131). And we realize with

redoubled force the hallucinatory nature of the obsession under which he labors. For her final pitiful gesture of loving
forgiveness, whereby she attempts to save him from the consequences of his deed, must appear to him, in its implicit denial of her guilt, to be the final insupportable denial of the
justice of his action.

No one could realize more intensely than Othello the
extremity of the issues. If his action is not absolutely justified
then it is absolutely damning:

> O, I were damn'd beneath all depth in hell,
> But that I did proceed, upon just grounds,
> To this extremity. . . .
>
> (v.ii.138-140)

Therefore there is nothing more appalling in Shakespeare than
Othello's discovery of the truth.

It is to be noted that the agony is brought to the intensest
pitch by the onset of grief even before the truth is revealed:

> My wife, my wife, my wife; I ha' no wife;
> O, insupportable! O heavy hour!
> Methinks it should be now a huge eclipse
> Of sun and moon, and that the affrighted globe
> Should yawn at alteration.
>
> (v.ii.98-102)

As the story is unraveled there is a masterly alternation of
modes of expression. On the one hand there is the immense
restraint of lines like:

> Are there no stones in heaven
> But what serves for the thunder?
>
> (v.ii.235-236)

> . . . cold, cold, my girl. . . .
>
> (v.ii.276)

I am not sorry neither, I'ld have thee live,
For in my sense 'tis happiness to die.

(v.ii.290-291)

On the other the violent repetitive rhetoric of:

Whip me, you devils,
From the possession of this heavenly sight,
Blow me about in winds, roast me in sulfur,
Wash me in steep-down gulfs of liquid fire!

(v.ii.278-281)

But both reserve and fullness of expression seem to suggest an infinity of pain that no language can chart or encompass. The effect is intensified by comparison with Emilia's passionate utterance, eloquent in its blunt downright earthiness:

O gull, O dolt,
As ignorant as dirt; thou hast done a deed—
I care not for thy sword, I'll make thee known,
Though I lost twenty lives.

(v.ii.164-167)

Othello, as has been remarked, is noteworthy in that the full burden of knowledge is reserved for the end. Othello knows nothing of his *error*—though he has marvelously articulated his knowledge of what he has already lost—until a hundred lines from the end of the play. This is surely a daunting challenge to the dramatist, who must wind up his plot and allow for the full and culminating force of the protagonist's realization almost at the same moment. In this *Othello* is at an opposite extreme from *Macbeth* and from *Lear*, where knowledge of error begins as early as Act II, or even the end of Act I. And even in *Hamlet* the death of Polonius is, say, two-and-a-third acts from the end of the play. As Granville-Barker put it with sublime understatement: "The ending of the play is technically not a very simple task." Technical solutions, however, are made to serve ends far beyond the technical. It is the very simultaneity of Othello's anagnorisis with the catastrophe of the play that gives the final speech its extraordinary power.

Othello's final confrontation with his fully revealed, self-made destiny is a tour de force of the dramatist's art. And the degree to which sheer theatrical spectacle plays its part in serving the ends of formal development is often insufficiently noticed. The final speech is preceded by the double disarming of Othello, a matter which is heavily emphasized by his warrior's humiliation:

> I am not valiant neither,
> But every puny whipster gets my sword. . . .
>
> (v.ii.244-245)

The reference to the second weapon, "It is a sword of Spain, the ice-brook's temper," catches attention with its suggestion of a steely endurance, the self-command of a poised resolution. The situation must be taken in: Othello, disarmed, disgraced, apparently helpless, broken and in agony of soul, is surrounded by the Venetians, who will now convey him to Venice for trial. It is indeed the end—the very seamark of his utmost sail. And it is at this point that the conduct of this natural conclusion is halted by "Soft you, a word or two." It is an arresting and commanding gesture of native authority like "Keep up your bright swords." They must listen spellbound as to the words of a man at death's door, though they do not yet know that this is what they are attending to.

And thus he distracts their attention for the production, presently, of his third and final weapon. Othello, who has no friend, must be his own Horatio; he must tell his own story, under that impulse of magnanimity which impels the Shakespearean tragic hero to set on record the inner truth of his life as he sees it and as he has lived it. And his words are, in fact, despite the perplexities they have caused to literal-minded critics, the plain and lambent truth.

> . . . then must you speak
> Of one that lov'd not wisely, but too well:
> Of one not easily jealous, but being wrought,
> Perplex'd in the extreme. . . .

$$(\text{v.ii.}343\text{-}347)$$

This is as precise a summary of what the drama has exhibited as could be made—provided only that "too well" is taken not in a narrowly moralistic sense, but in the sense implied by "Excellent wretch, . . . and when I love thee not, / Chaos is come again"—in the sense of the pitch of expectation he had of the transcendent possibilities of love. Not wisely indeed, perhaps with a glance at Iago-wisdom. And not easily jealous, in the sense of jealousy easily entertained and easily endured.[15] The import of the speech's crescendo is significant too. For, as we have seen, the process of tragic discovery in *Othello* began with the predicate of the warrior-servant of the state and moved through the ordeal of love tested and tried to the ultimate recognition of a supreme value self-betrayed by one who "Like the base Judean, threw a pearl away / Richer than all his tribe" (348-349).[16] The final metamorphosis of the figure of the arch-betrayer into the infidel traducing Turk of Aleppo, into himself, sets into perfect relation, in the context of his own role as Moor of Venice, his utterly unexonerating self-judgment. Law unto himself as he has always been, Othello executes sentence upon himself, exacts from himself the ultimate penalty. He will wait upon no court of law to pronounce

---

[15] Coleridge, it will be remembered, was convinced that Othello's jealousy was not that of the innately jealous nature. There is a good comment on the point in M. R. Ridley's Introduction to the New Arden ed., p. ivff.

[16] I have preferred the Folio "Judean" (the reference being to Judas) to the "Indian" of the Quarto not only because "the general superiority of the Folio text has never been seriously in question" (Walker, *Textual Problems*, p. 138), but because the allusion to the arch-betrayal seems more powerfully significant at this point in the play than the allusion to the merely heathen or barbarian.

sentence and determine punishment. No court of law can fathom his case to its depths as he does. No court of law can ever be possessed as he is of the ultimate, authentic knowledge of the goodness of the good which he has thrown away, and of the folly of the evil which possessed him. It is to this that his suicide bears witness, to this recognition that he commits himself, as he reenacts a consummating action of the past in the blinding light of present agony.

CHAPTER VII

MACBETH

Of all Shakespeare's tragedies, *Macbeth* is the most rapid and compressed, and its action the most perspicuous. Since Macbeth's crime itself provides the motive power of the action, the element of intrigue—of plotting and calculation—conspicuously present in *Romeo and Juliet, Hamlet, Othello, Lear*, and even *Antony and Cleopatra* and *Coriolanus*, is absent. For this reason a Chinese mime of the actions and reactions which make up the story of Macbeth would be a less truncated model, would include more of the essential dynamic of the play than such a mime of any of the other tragedies. Though this may be accounted for by the hypothesis of a shortened and incomplete text, it is also undoubtedly because the play is Hamlet's dumb show writ large; it is self-explanatory. The reversal of expectation, which is tragedy's determining formal feature, is inherent in the boomerang consequences of the crime. And because the logic of the tragic form thus coincides with the logic of the fable, the great opportunity and challenge the subject offered the dramatist was to energize and amplify these events, to render them expressive in the highest degree. Hence the prolific opulence of the imagery:[1] crime and consequence are correlated with a veritable multitude of experiences and conceptions of good and evil. Metaphor and metonymy transpose these conceptions through a whole gamut of symbolic and synaesthetic equations for concord and disorder: health, growth, and vitality; disease, arrest, and sterility; peace and strife; sympathy and savagery;

[1] Most notably expounded by Wilson Knight, *The Imperial Theme* (London: Methuen, 1951), L. C. Knights, *Some Shakespearean Themes* (London: Chatto, 1959), and D. A. Traversi, *An Approach to Shakespeare* (New York: Doubleday, 1956).

angel and demon forms; the beautiful and the monstrous; light and darkness; above all, perhaps, fear. The result is an orchestration of themes of exceptional intensity and power.

But if, in respect of plot, *Macbeth* is Hamlet's dumb show writ large, it is also the waking speech of Richard III writ large. The play's inward dimension is its dramatization of self-evasion—of the self-destruction of a soul at war upon itself. And these two aspects of the play, the outer and the inner, the dumb show and the soliloquy, are interlocked by two strategies which are deployed with consummate artistry. One is the intersection of the supernatural with the natural, and the other is the advancing of the fatal error to a point as early as the beginning of Act ii—a matter presently to be considered.

The witches admit us to the presence of a source of evil outside the events and characters themselves. Yet the function of the weird sisters is not to represent an ineluctable fate. As Moulton perceived, "their function is to intensify and illuminate human action, not to determine it."[2]

> . . . the conditions of natural working in the course of events are not in the least degree altered by the revelation of the future. The actor's belief (or disbelief) in the oracle may be one of the circumstances which have influenced his action—as it would have done in the real life of the age— but to the spectator . . . the oracular action is presented not as a force but as a light. . . . this illumination [is] progressive in intelligibility . . . [in] step with the progress of the events themselves . . . until by the end the oracle is at once clear and fulfilled.[3]

What Shakespeare has evidently seized upon, however, in this idea of the witches is something more germane to his development of tragic form than is suggested by Moulton's

---

[2] *Shakespeare as Dramatic Artist* (Oxford: The Clarendon Press, 1893), p. 390.
[3] Ibid., p. 131.

excellent remarks upon oracular action. Macbeth's career is endowed with an excitement of interest over and above the intellectual satisfaction attendant upon the ironic and devious fulfillment of an oracle.

Oracles constitute the greatest of all tests and challenges to the mind and the will of the person to whom they are vouchsafed. They therefore supply fertile ground for tragic development. How the protagonist shall interpret the signs and portents, the shadowy, mysterious, equivocal, or incomprehensible word, becomes the chief source of dramatic interest. His every choice becomes personally crucial, hazardous, momentous. He is, in the older and stricter sense of the word, obnoxious, "exposed or liable to injury, evil or harm," and, in the legal sense, "answerable, responsible." Whether he obeys or defies the warning or tempting oracle may have little effect upon its inexorable fulfillment; but how he obeys, defies, evades, eludes is of the greatest dramatic consequence, for these responses create in their sequence the tragic self-discovery.

Shakespeare's presentation of the supernatural constitutes a subtler achievement than is often recognized. The question which agitated the speculation of the time concerned not the existence of supernatural apparitions—there was far too much testimony for that—but the Devil's damning monopoly over such phenomena. Though few took as radical a Calvinist stand as Reginald Scot[4] (whom Shakespeare, it is generally agreed, had read) upon the immateriality of apparitions, or, as he maintained, devilish hallucinations, the air of the time was heavy with the circular arguments of predestinarianism. Yet, while the witches determine a great deal of our response to Macbeth's crime, they do not determine his crime. He is not, as is sometimes maintained, a damned soul fulfilling the inexorable writ of reprobation. The first witch's account of

[4] Reginald Scot, *The Discoverie of Witchcraft* (London, 1584).

her revenge upon the master of the Tiger serves as an anticipation of the fate in store for the greater victim, but also indicates the limits of her power:

Sleep shall neither night nor day
Hang upon his penthouse lid;
He shall live a man forbid.
Weary sev'n-nights nine times nine,
Shall he dwindle, peak, and pine:
Though his bark cannot be lost,
Yet it shall be tempest-tost.

(I.iii.19-25)

What Shakespeare's dramatization contrives is the measure of free will necessary for tragic development, together with the measure of portentousness appropriate to the awesome reality of the beyond. The Elizabethan consensus was that the devil could fashion spiritual substance, or bodies of air, in order to confuse, tempt, delude, and ensnare the soul. But a sufficient body of Elizabethan opinion held that men in excited states could have hallucinations, ultimately no doubt the response of evil concupiscence to the sinister promptings of Satan but for all practical purposes autonomous projections of their own foul imaginings. It is this margin of doubt concerning the objectivity of apparitions that Shakespeare's dramatization exploits. On the one hand he cuts the ground from the skeptic position by having not only the audience introduced to the witches before Macbeth's first appearance but also Banquo as co-witness of their first encounter with Macbeth and, more important, of their mysterious disappearance. They vanish, melt into thin air, as no corporeal creature, not even a witch in league with the powers of darkness, can do. Banquo's amazement, "The earth hath bubbles as the water has," brings out the point. They are therefore indubitably genuine spirits. But from this point on in the play the "supernatural solicitings" are mediated through a whole series of agencies available to Macbeth alone—the air-drawn dagger, the voice crying "Macbeth hath murdered sleep," the ghost of Banquo and, most crucially problematic of all, Lady Macbeth, who invokes spirits and may or may not be herself possessed by an evil succubus. The effect is analogous to that produced by those ambiguous figurations used in the study of perception: looked at one way they appear concave, another, convex; or, as in a well-known example of visual ambiguity, by the drawing of a duck which transforms itself under the spectator's gaze into the likeness of a hare.[5] Thus, looked at in terms of one predisposition (that of the royal author of *Daemonologie*, for instance), the whole series could be objectively supernatural; looked at in another perspective (Reginald Scot's) the whole series—with the first appearance of the witches as dramatic convention—simply hallucinatory, susceptible of explanation in psychological terms. The key to the switch of perception is the ambiguity of the link which is established between Macbeth and the weird sisters.

The repetition upon his first appearance of their "Fair is foul, and foul is fair" in his "So foul and fair a day I have not seen," is open to a variety of interpretations. The witches' enigmatic saying may be construed either as referring to the deceptiveness of appearances, or as expressing a thoroughgoing satanic perspective upon the world: whatever is fair is to them abomination; whatever is foul is beautiful to them. The syntax of Macbeth's fair-foul day suggests a still further possibility of relation between good and evil: their coexistence, not as appearance versus truth, not as total inversion, but as disjunctive and discordant aspects of reality. And it is in terms of such discords that his nature will presently be at war, that his temptation will present itself to him. But the link that

[5] E. H. Gombrich, *Art and Illusion*, 2nd ed. (Princeton: Princeton Univ. Press, 1961), p. 4.

is established by the echo itself remains obscure, mysterious, unexplained. Have they already worked their charm upon him? Is there a native affinity between Macbeth and the evil spirits? Or is it by a kind of antiphonal contrast that we perceive the future progress: his native power to distinguish between good and evil will in the event be completely perverted. The ambiguity of the relationship between them is further underlined by Macbeth's start at the witches' prophecy, which Banquo notices. "That," he says, "trusted home, / Might yet enkindle you unto the crown." He himself remains unintoxicated, and his sober, prudent, common-sense response to the situation suggests the potency of the thoughts previously entertained by Macbeth which gave rise to the start—the start of a man who recognizes his own mind objectified.

What Shakespeare achieves by his deliberate mystification, and maintains by the graded series of apparitions and invocations, is an internalization or psychologizing of evil without prejudice to the sense of its objective reality. His witches, demons in human form, represent the myth of satanic power in the universe "which ensnares human souls by means of diabolical persuasion, hallucination, internal illusion and possession,"[6] while the measure of psychological naturalism in Macbeth's commerce with these forces makes available to drama an inner dimension, and reveals reaches of the mind's transactions with itself which no earlier dramatist of the supernatural had attained, and few later historians of the psyche were to achieve save at the expense of the animating myth.

Macbeth's power to distinguish between good and evil is the subject of his first monologue.

[6] Walter Clyde Curry, *Shakespeare's Philosophical Patterns* (Baton Rouge, La.: Louisiana State Univ. Press, 1937), p. 92. See also Robert H. West, "Night's Black Agents," *Renaissance Papers* (Columbia, S.C.: Univ. of South Carolina Press, 1956).

Two truths are told,
As happy prologues to the swelling act
Of the imperial theme.—I thank you, gentlemen—
[*Aside*] This supernatural soliciting
Cannot be ill; cannot be good:
If ill, why hath it given me earnest of success,
Commencing in a truth? I am Thane of Cawdor:
If good, why do I yield to that suggestion
Whose horrid image doth unfix my hair,
And make my seated heart knock at my ribs,
Against the use of nature? Present fears
Are less than horrible imaginings.
My thought, whose murder yet is but fantastical,
Shakes so my single state of man,
That function is smother'd in surmise,
And nothing is, but what is not.

(1.iii.127-142)

"Cannot be ill; cannot be good" continues the effect of high tension in the mode of vertiginous poised indecision character-istic of Macbeth in the predicament of the play. How can the prophecy be ill if what it says is the truth, now that the borrowed robes of Cawdor have proved, by Angus' account, to be legitimately his own? How can it be good if its effect upon him—the instantaneous thought of murder—is to unfix his hair and make his seated heart knock at his ribs? It is once again the logic of disjunction as in "so foul and fair a day." It is also the logic of a man possessed of no firm moral principle of conduct, a man who is tossed between the claims of what he takes to be simple empirical facts, and the spon-taneous reactions of an extremely excitable nature. The ques-tion of the role he is called upon to play is the subject of his rapt soliloquy. What is expressed is more than merely his ambition for the crown. The lines are superbly expressive of the excitement of an instantly inflamed imagination. The climactic syntax, the orchestration of vowel and consonant, and the theatrical metaphor all combine to give to the lines the pulse of surging anticipation as the immense possibilities open out before him. Then comes the inhibition and the conversion to immediate horror of the thought of the murder, hardly as yet fully conceived even in imagination.

The predicament of the play thus presents the evil potential in a strong individual will to power, held in precarious check by some inner force the nature and strength of which is what the drama will put to the test. Under the witches' instigation Macbeth is gripped in the violent oscillation of conflicting impulses. The result is a breathless suspense. But the oscillation itself is a source of immense psychic energy. The news of Duncan's choice of Malcolm for the succession sets the pendulum of decision swinging once again.

> The Prince of Cumberland!—That is a step
> On which I must fall down, or else o'erleap,
> For in my way it lies. Stars, hide your fires!
> Let not light see my black and deep desires;
> The eye wink at the hand; yet let that be,
> Which the eye fears, when it is done, to see.
>
> (I.iv.48-53)

At this point, however, the natural momentum of the pendulum's swing is given extra impetus by the encounter with Lady Macbeth. It is powerfully reinforced by the provocations of his "fiend-like queen," now possessed of her fell purpose.

Lady Macbeth's reception of her husband's letter is full of important information about them both. Her sketch of Macbeth's character is admirably concise:

> Yet do I fear thy nature:
> It is too full o'th'milk of human kindness,
> To catch the nearest way. Thou wouldst be great;
> Art not without ambition, but without

The illness should attend it: what thou wouldst highly,
That wouldst thou holily; wouldst not play false,
And yet wouldst wrongly win; Thou'dst have, great Glamis,
That which cries, "Thus thou must do," if thou have it;
And that which rather thou dost fear to do,
Than wishest should be undone.

(I.v.16-25)

This account explicitly summarizes what we have seen exhibited as the nature of the tragic protagonist: one who cannot be said to be a man of conscience, but who is most indubitably a man with a conscience. But what it contributes
to the understanding of Macbeth's temptation is even more important, and has been the subject of much critical controversy.

Even so experienced a critic as Wayne Booth takes Lady
Macbeth's "What thou wouldst highly, / That wouldst thou
holily; wouldst not play false, / And yet wouldst wrongly
win" as "the unimpeachable testimony of a wicked character
deploring goodness."[7] This perversion of the plain sense of
the text arises from Booth's attempt to "save the appearances" for the sentimental doctrine of the exemplary noble
hero. He is forced to do violence not only to the play but
to reason itself in order to convince us of his view that
Shakespeare sets out to keep Macbeth as little to blame as
possible. The murders, he says, are committed offstage, and
not even (except Duncan's—an important exception, one
would think) by Macbeth himself. He has never understood,
accustomed as he is to "bloody execution," to "carving out his
passage" in battle, "what will be the effect on his own character if he tries to carve out his passage in civil life." If he
did understand, Wayne Booth piously assures us, "he could
not, being who he is, do the deed." We thus, it seems, do

---

[7] "Macbeth as Tragic Hero," *Journal of General Education*, VI
(October 1951).

not lose our sympathy for the criminal, though one might make it a question whether the alleged motivation—refraining from the crime of murder in order to preserve one's "character" from harm—is strictly productive of sympathy. "When we do see him" (after Banquo's death) the argument continues, "he is suffering the torments of the banquet scene. Our unconscious inference: the self-torture has already expiated his crime." It is perhaps not by accident that the "inferences" involved in this tissue of special pleading and question-begging are announced to be unconscious. They could hardly, one feels, be otherwise; though the interesting question concerning the sense in which an inference can be said to be unconscious remains. The maudlin conclusion must come as no surprise: "We judge Macbeth, as Shakespeare intends, not merely for his actions but in the light of the total impression of the play. Malcolm and Macduff do not know Macbeth and the forces that have worked on him; the spectator does know him and can feel great pity that a man with so much potentiality for greatness should have fallen so low and should be so thoroughly misjudged. The pity is that everything was not otherwise, when it so easily could have been otherwise." Against this parody of a doctrine of tragic pity one would like to suggest that if Shakespeare "intended" anything by his tragedies beyond the discovery and the shaping of a form for his sense of the tragic in life, it may well have been to present an experience of a kind that would precisely be our protection against sentimental vulgarity of the good guys–bad guys kind, against the deadening habitual formulae with which we organize our practical life, no more seeing that life than we see the objects which surround us in the rooms we inhabit.

I believe, again with Moulton, that the phrase " 'the milk of human kindness,' divorced from its context and become the most familiar of commonplaces, has done more than anything

223

else towards giving a false twist to the general conception of Macbeth's character."[8] It is not an excess of benevolence, loving-kindness, and tenderness that Lady Macbeth is deploring in her husband—albeit, presumably, with grudging admiration —any more than it is in fact an impulse of love, of sympathy, of identification with a fellow human being which, in the imperial theme speech, is shown as deterring him from overstepping the bounds of accepted morality. On the contrary, the violence of his mental withdrawal from the murder he has scarcely begun to contemplate should rather alert us to the features of a phenomenon familiar to any psychology capable of the least sophistication: the strength of the overt repugnance is the index of the strength of the hidden desire. The true import of Lady Macbeth's words, as Moulton saw, lies in the older sense of the word "kind"; the sense of the passage, he says, would be more obvious if the whole phrase were printed as one word, not "human kindness" but "humankindness."

Lady Macbeth's "milk" is impatiently contemptuous;[9] the mild unintoxicating liquid a metonymy for the timid, tame, domestic, cautious, protection-seeking impulses of the human herd; in strongest possible contrast to the "spirits" (like "kind" also in the older sense) which she will pour into his ear. It is indeed worth noticing the series of metaphors derived from the idea of intoxication: "Was the hope drunk, / Wherein you dress'd yourself?" (i.vii.35); "That which hath made them drunk hath made me bold" (ii.ii.1). While Lady Macbeth confidently distinguishes between the spiritual intoxication which will lend greater power to her faculties and the stupor induced

[8] Moulton, *Shakespeare as a Dramatic Artist*, p. 71.

[9] As is Goneril's in her turn (i.iv.351 and iv.ii.50). D. W. Harding, "Women's Fantasy of Manhood: A Shakespearean Theme," *Shakespeare Quarterly*, xx (Summer 1969), has a revealing analysis of Goneril, Lady Macbeth, and Volumnia, each of whom wills to enact, through lover, husband, or son, a fantasy of exaggerated virility.

by hard liquor, one of the most powerful ironies of the Porter is his exposure of her illusion: "much drink may be said to be an equivocator with lechery: it makes him and it mars him; it sets him on, and it takes him off; it persuades him, and it disheartens him; makes him stand to, and not stand to: in conclusion, equivocates him in a sleep, and, giving him the lie, leaves him" (II.ii.33-38). The Macbeths, intoxicated with the witches' brew, which has replaced the milk of human kindness, are indeed "left by it" in the end. In the following speech, when Lady Macbeth invokes the demonic powers, what she asks for is infernal assistance against the compunctious visitings of what she knows to be an inherent part of her physiological nature, her female "humankindness."[10] And it is for this that the milk, to be exchanged for gall, stands.

But it is to be noted that "milk," in whatever other semantic relations it enters, is also, simply and primarily, the original and essential nourisher and preserver of life; that the thoughts upon which the spirits tend are mortal, that is murderous, but also the thoughts of mortals; that when blood is too thick to flow, so that the access and passage to the heart is stopped, mortality indeed results. In this texture of relationships, in the closeness of the poetry to physiology, is powerfully suggested the transaction between the opposing forces of destruction and preservation in human vitality itself. The expressiveness of the language is admirable beyond analysis. Suffice it to note the physical catch in the throat which "thick" creates in the line, and again in "Come, thick Night," and yet again in the antiphonal "Light thickens" of Macbeth, which draws into the metaphor yet another system of correspondences. She is

---

[10] Coleridge was the first to reject the idea of Lady Macbeth as an unfeminine monster: "So far is the woman from being dead within her, that her sex betrays itself in the very moment of dark and bloody imagination." Report of a lecture given in Bristol (1813) in *Four Centuries of Shakespearean Criticism*, ed. Frank Kermode (New York: Avon Books, 1965), p. 538.

bold while he is fearful, but the sensation of a choked utterance gives us the common denominator: horror at the violation of a fundamental nature in both the daring and the dared.

Lady Macbeth's speech registers her full awareness that what could prevent her carrying out her full purpose is her sex, the milk of her woman's breasts, the correlative, so to speak, of an inherent, native tendency in human nature towards tenderness, protectiveness, and pity. The inference we are invited to make is carried alive into the mind: that which is destructive in nature, nature's mischief, she embraces; that which is preservative, the great bond, she cancels and tears to pieces. She is doing far more than asking to be made a man-like virago so that she can commit a murder. She is allying herself with all that is destructive in nature—the cursed thoughts which nature gives way to in repose—and against all that is sustaining and protective. That this is the wider import of the speech is confirmed by what follows.

The dramatic irony of Duncan's entrance has sufficiently been observed; but it is not only what follows it that gives it its ironic effect; it is also what has preceded it. The particularly expressive effect of the speech is a result of its coming so close upon Lady Macbeth's "unsex me here."

> This guest of summer,
> The temple-haunting martlet, does approve,
> By his loved mansionry that the heaven's breath
> Smells wooingly here: no jutty, frieze,
> Buttress, nor coign of vantage, but this bird
> Hath made his pendent bed, and procreant cradle:
> Where they most breed and haunt, I have observ'd
> The air is delicate.
>
> (1.vi.3-10)

The whole cycle of procreation is given its gentlest, most winning aspect in this nesting imagery, where the bird chooses the softest airs, the mellowest summer weather for its habitat.

226

"Wooingly," "procreant," "delicate," glosses what Lady Macbeth has renounced with a poignance of effect which cannot be accounted for save in terms of the immediate alternations of dramatic sequence.

Furthermore, looked at from the point of view of its place in the sequence the speech feeds our understanding of Macbeth's following soliloquy, which, like that of Brutus in the orchard or of Hamlet sparing the King at prayer or of Othello as he stands over the sleeping Desdemona, has produced a spate of controversy. Considered from the point of view of the speaker, such speeches certainly offer us "reasons" for the decision taken. Considered, so to speak, after the event, they offer the critic a mine of "causes" for the decision taken. But the dramatic imagination which renders our reading simultaneous with events as they unfold requires them to be perceived as the dynamic articulations of the very process of decision-making. These speeches are of the essence of Shakespearean drama, catching the very movement of the mind in their expressive net. They do not sum up an argument in retrospect but render reflection itself in the dramatic present, in the form of verbal action. The relation of argument to image, the subtly differentiated syntactic structures, allow us to infer the forces which are at work in the mind of the speaker—give us therefore direct intelligence of the nature of his dilemma. Speeches of this intensely dramatic kind—the basis of Shakespearean realism—occur where there arises an obstacle to the impetus of the will, which is held in agonizing check while the mind seeks its direction.

> If it were done, when 'tis done, then 'twere well
> It were done quickly: if th' assassination
> Could trammel up the consequence, and catch
> With his surcease success; that but this blow
> Might be the be-all and the end-all—here,
> But here, upon this bank and shoal of time,

We'd jump the life to come. But in these cases,
We still have judgment here; that we but teach
Bloody instructions, which, being taught, return
To plague th' inventor: this even-handed Justice
Commends th' ingredience of our poison'd chalice
To our own lips. He's here in double trust:
First, as I am his kinsman and his subject,
Strong both against the deed; then, as his host,
Who should against his murtherer shut the door,
Not bear the knife myself. Besides, this Duncan
Hath borne his faculties so meek, hath been
So clear in his great office, that his virtues
Will plead like angels, trumpet-tongu'd against
The deep damnation of his taking-off;
And Pity, like a naked new-born babe,
Striding the blast, or heaven's Cherubins, hors'd
Upon the sightless couriers of the air,
Shall blow the horrid deed in every eye,
That tears shall drown the wind. I have no spur
To prick the sides of my intent, but only
Vaulting ambition, which o'erleaps itself
And falls on th' other.

(I.vii.1-28)

That Macbeth's whole mind is set upon the committing of the contemplated act is established by the very first lines: their plunge *in media res*, their obsessive syntax and the vertiginous seesaw brought to a climax in "surcease-success." But the whole speech takes its impetus from the conditional "if," and the impossibility of fulfilling the condition of "doneness" floods his mind with consequences to be expected. Ostensibly in the first six lines Macbeth is spurring his intent; actually, as the structure of the speech invites us to perceive, he is under a compulsion to find reasons powerful enough to justify his non-committing of the deed. As Stoll noted, it is the "deterrents that he dwells upon not the incentives."[11]

He begins with a cool and practical prudentialism: the killing of Duncan will expose him to the risk of a similar fate. Significantly, moral sanctions come next, as having more power to deter. The speech throughout adduces consequences, retributive consequences, in a rhetorical climax: an ascending order. First the poisoned chalice of worldly retribution, then the doom of an apocalyptic sentence, and finally the punishment of humanity's rejection: and it is this very sequence which is the clue to our master inference. For this crescendo is a reversal of the normal hierarchy of values: the trump of final doom should surely be the culmination in a rationally ordered argument against the taking of an innocent life. It is to be further observed that this "taking of an innocent life" —the subject of the decision—is variously designated and recurs with obsessive frequency throughout the course of the speech. Nouns, highly abstract and latinate (assassination, surcease) alternate with simpler nouns which have a strong verbal content (deed, blow). The nearest Macbeth comes to a concrete image of the murder—"not bear the knife myself"— is the signal for the transition to the most agitated part of the speech and to the flight into the pictorial fantasy of the angels, whose trumpets, whose flight upon the winds, intervene, so to speak, between his imagination and the act it refuses to contemplate. Even a literal word for the deed is now avoided: it is "his taking off." At the very moment of refusal to entertain the imagination of murder itself there rises before his mind's eye the image of the babe. And surely we must ask, since Duncan was an elderly and venerable sovereign, why such an image should have occurred to Macbeth. True, it is pity, not Duncan, which is like a naked new-

[11] "Source and Motive in Macbeth and Othello," in *From Shakespeare to Joyce* (New York: Doubleday, 1944).

born babe. But pity is "like" a naked newborn babe because that is what Macbeth has thought of at that moment. It is this image that has the final power to express, support, and justify his instinctive, inhibitory revulsion from the deed. What we are to infer, I believe, is that this revulsion, present from the start, grows upon him, insistently, *while he is speaking*, in a way that finds final release not in an image of remote judgment, but in an image that suggests to him the most basic, primary, and fundamental prohibition. Nothing less would represent at once the strength of his inhibition and the strength of that which it inhibits. If this is the expressive effect of the speech and its climactic image, we are enabled to perceive that it is not considered moral principle as such, nor even divine judgment, that holds him back; what holds him back is of the nature of a taboo, as primitive and powerful as his vaulting will itself. Macbeth does not decide not to kill Duncan at this point because he "believes in the holiness of the heart's affections," as Helen Gardner holds.[12] It would be truer to say (and it was the genius of Shakespeare to perceive the general truth of this) that he expresses a "belief" of this nature because it enables him to decide not to kill Duncan. And his will not to kill Duncan expresses itself by the substitution of a babe figure for the father figure of Duncan and so links up with the saving, preserving instinct for life that the whole of the act presents as opposed to the witches', or the devil's, instigation. The insight and consistency with which Shakespeare depicts his natural man, down to the emotionality of the rhetoric, the sentimental working-up of pathos in the tears passage, is superb. Before the sacredness and prohibitedness with which his victim is

---

[12] In "A Reply to Cleanth Brooks," in *The Business of Criticism* (Oxford: The Clarendon Press, 1959), a fine riposte to the latter's famous exercise in the construction of symbolic patterns, "The Naked Babe and the Cloak of Manliness," *The Well Wrought Urn* (London: Methuen, 1947).

now invested he has indeed no spur to prick the sides of his intent. The speech ends with the collapse of Macbeth's will to power.

Lady Macbeth's appeal works upon this momentary emotional vacuum in a way which is peculiarly effective. "Art thou afeared / To be the same in thine own act and valour / As thou art in desire?" and "When you durst do it, then you were a man" are appeals to the primitive courage of an essentially primitive moral nature. The play's first mention of Macbeth presents the heroic image of a man of extreme physical courage and resolution; but it is significant that the situation is one that demands no moral decision. His course is clear, his duty apparent. Unhesitating physical hardihood therefore characterizes his assault upon Macdonwald, and is praised as such:

> For brave Macbeth (well he deserves that name),
> Disdaining Fortune, with his brandish'd steel,
> Which smok'd with bloody execution,
> Like Valour's minion, carv'd out his passage,
> Till he fac'd the slave;
> Which ne'er shook hands, nor bade farewell to him,
> Till he unseam'd him from the have to th' chops,
> And fix'd his head upon our battlements.
>
> (I.ii.16-23)

Faced with a situation which places him in a moral dilemma Macbeth fails, despite his knowledge that "I dare do all that may become a man; / Who dares do more, is none," to transcend a notion of honor grounded upon mere forthright strength of will, and a conception of good and evil derived from calculable prudential considerations. Hence he asks "If we should fail?" before her reply sweeps his trepidation aside in the flood of her own energy.

Her appeal is also overtly a sexual provocation. She is daring his manhood, proposing a test of his virility. This in itself is strong instigation, and that she would, she claims, have dashed

231

out the brains of her unweaned child if she had so sworn chimes with the very terms of his own taboo-inhibition, so that the effect is irresistible. Both the witches and his wife speak his very thoughts. He is swayed as by contagion, energized by the double force she is exerting to overcome both her own and his nature, and the resolution with which he embraces the false face and the false heart he will wear has the elation of a sudden release from shackles. It is perhaps not too fanciful to see in the verbal collocation of his expression of awed admiration, "Bring forth men-children only!" an image, verging on the grotesque, that suggests some monstrous changeling instead of the infant to which such constant reference has been made.

In Shakespeare's regular management of psychomachia, the promptings of conscience are made to seem themselves temptation; the protagonist is blind to his own true good. But what is remarkable in Macbeth is the kind of resolution which marks the acceptance of the fatal choice, the election of self which it implies. And here too the changeling idea may help to organize our responses in a relevant way. The dagger speech registers with great power the nature of Macbeth's conquest of "temptation."

> Art thou not, fatal vision, sensible
> To feeling, as to sight? or art thou but
> A dagger of the mind, a false creation,
> Proceeding from the heat-oppressed brain?
> I see thee yet, in form as palpable
> As this which now I draw.
> Thou marshall'st me the way that I was going;
> And such an instrument I was to use.
> Mine eyes are made the fools o'th' other senses,
> Or else worth all the rest: I see thee still;
> And on thy blade, and dudgeon, gouts of blood,
> Which was not so before. There's no such thing.

It is the bloody business which informs
Thus to mine eyes. Now o'er the one half-world
Nature seems dead, and wicked dreams abuse
The curtain'd sleep: Witchcraft celebrates
Pale Hecate's off'rings; and wither'd murder,
Alarum'd by his sentinel, the wolf,
Whose howl's his watch, thus with his stealthy pace,
With Tarquin's ravishing strides, towards his design
Moves like a ghost. Thou sure and firm-set earth,
Hear not my steps, which way they walk, for fear
Thy very stones prate of my where-about,
And take the present horror from the time,
Which now suits with it.

(II.i.36-60)

His assertion of manhood takes the form of the willed diab-
olism with which he invests his purpose. The dagger itself
is worth a moment's consideration. If we respond to it as to
a natural phallic symbol I believe that this would be consonant with the deep impulse which is shaping the material
of the play at this point. I am not suggesting that the dagger
is a phallic symbol for the reason that such symbolizations are
clearly anachronistic, imported into the play from a system of
thought which it historically antecedes. Yet such symbolizations occur in imaginative literature before they become available for theoretical discussion. Nor would it be possible for a
seventeenth-century mind to be unaware of the sexual analogues immemoriably connected with demonic possession. I
would suggest, at all events, that, in the light of the sexual
loading of language, situation, and image in this part of the
play, a phallic dagger playing its subliminal part in the powerful effect would be perfectly possible. Certainly in the arsenal
of Shakespeare's weapons daggers have proved expressive in
just this way before: Juliet's is a case in point. It is to be
noted moreover that, with nature dead o'er the one half world,

Macbeth's imagination transforms withered murder—figure of the death's head—into lustful Tarquin, so that that which he avoids calling by its name—the "design"—becomes an object of erotic attention. Murder presents itself to him as a rape. The paradox of willed abnegation of will, the ecstasy of horror and fascination that he feels, the fullness of his knowledge of evil are brought here to so fine a point that the impression of demonic possession and of almost ecstatic election are indistinguishable.

Macbeth's choice is thus made, his dilemma resolved. It is of the greatest importance to note that in this play the temptation of the tragic protagonist is immensely advanced. It has been inserted, so to speak, into the very unfolding of the predicament, and made a constitutive part of our understanding of the nature and limitations of his tragic distinction—his possession of a nature in which temperamental high courage and powerful vitality[13] are unenlightened and undisciplined by anything more specifically moral than received convention, though they are held in check by instinctual forces, themselves of great power. This advancing of the temptation issues in the committing of the fatal act as early as Act ii.ii; and the consequence of this acceleration is the provision of time for recognitions and for the extension and development of recognitions. *Lear* is the only other tragedy (if we except the early *Titus*) where a similar advancement of the fatal error occurs, and both *Lear* and *Macbeth* may be compared with *Othello* and *Coriolanus* (where the fatal error is retarded to the catastrophe) in respect of the immensely increased opportunities for the exploration of the operation upon the mind of guilt already incurred. The phase, Act ii, which normally

---

[13] Dorothea Krook, *Elements of Tragedy* (New Haven: Yale Univ. Press, 1969), has an admirable exposition of that particular form of courage or spiritedness that constitutes the tragic hero's distinction (p. 42, and chap. 3, passim).

exhibits psychomachia, is thus conditioned by the presence of guilt consequent upon a deed already committed.

In the logic of his either/or—his eyes either fools or inspired—(ii.44-45) there is no remedy for or amelioration of fear, and no suggestion of an alternative to obedience as a response to the summoning vision. Macbeth is not politic in crime like Claudius; nor cynical like Edmund. He does not believe, like Brutus, that the ethical coloring he projects upon his actions has power to change their nature. He produces no ideology, nor policy, nor high altruistic aim with which to rationalize his deed. It is through this total absence of rationalization *for* the deed (by comparison with his anguished reasoning against it) that the diabolical is suggested. And it is further suggested by a transposition into a diabolic mode of the marriage relationship.

Act II.ii makes Macbeth the creature of the deed. He is now beyond the point of no return, cut off and severed from all channels of piety, of reintegration. He therefore cannot say "amen," and is paralyzed by the terror of his inchoate knowledge of the irrevocable. That the word sticks in his throat, physical manifestation of psychic fact, is in keeping, in this most psychosomatic of plays, with the whole rendering of the Macbeth experience. And in keeping, too, with its naturalization of the demonic, or diabolizing of the natural, is the calling into play of the intimate dynamics of the marriage between the partners in crime. Indeed the marriage relationship itself operates as a metaphor for the stages of their partnership. A demonic parody of courtship precedes its mutual engendering; the crime (the hoped-for kingdom) is the child of the union. From this interinvolvement between them Shakespeare derives continuing and progressive effects of antiphony. The "amen" that sticks in his throat is the literal fulfillment of her prayer, "make thick my blood, / Stop up th' access and passage to remorse," as her sleepless agony, in which she knows that she will never erase the mark of Cain from her hand, reflects his "Will all great Neptune's ocean wash this blood / Clean from my hand?" Together they murder sleep in a monstrous travesty of sexual consummation, and are ridden by nightmare. But through this overall duality are articulated the most subtle effects of mirrored contrast between the two partners and between their beginning and their end. For their lines of development converge and cross during the play. By the time he has supped so full of horrors that he can feel nothing, she, for whose cavalier positivism a little water was enough to clear them of their deed and to whom the sleeping and the dead were but as pictures, cannot efface from her memory the quantity of blood the old man had in him; cannot rid her imagination of the simplest and most stubborn sensations, the smell of blood and the sight of blood. As his conscience falls silent, hers awakes. As he seeks frantic oblivion in deeds—"From this moment, the very firstlings of my heart shall be / The firstlings of my hand" (IV.i.146-148)—she is subject to the ceaseless remembrance her somnambulism reveals. She, to whom at first "what's done is done," learns to understand the great law of human existence in time: "What's done cannot be undone." He, who knew in his heart of hearts that a thing is not done when it is done, finds in the end in the passage of human existence through time a tale told by an idiot signifying nothing.

At the crucial moment of the play, when the murder is committed, when Macbeth's state of mind is the anguish of total awareness, hers takes the form of a blackout of consciousness. Lady Macbeth's fainting is of considerable importance. If we take it as calculated, to distract attention from Macbeth's difficulties in accounting for the murder of the grooms, we miss the finer effect. To interpret her collapse as the shrewd maneuver of a very alert conspirator runs counter first of all to the splendid consistency of the portrayal of her gauche literal-mindedness in her reply to Banquo: "What! in our house?" In fact, when her "spirits" are not with her she is a very mediocre conspirator indeed. Moreover, her faint provides a pause in which Malcolm and Donalbain arrange their flight, and this nemesis-irony can only have a deeper than melo-dramatic effect if a deeper reading of the fainting is sought. If the faint is not stratagem but symptom, this would be pro-foundly consistent with the implicit theme of the psychomachia —that conflict between the diabolic perversion of nature that is life-destroying and the procreative tenderness of nature that is life-sustaining—which, I have suggested, is what the play has developed intensively up to this point. For it is then her own violently repressed womanhood which rises from the inner depths of her emotional nature to overthrow the outer super-rationality in which she has dressed herself. A previous indi-cation that this is indeed the case is given in her "Had he not resembled / My father as he slept." For this suggests more than the survival in her, despite her dedication to ruthlessness, of moral norms. It also, in the whole sexual context that has been so subtly and powerfully evoked, suggests the deepest psychic strata of personality in which taboo is rooted.

If the marriage relationship of the Macbeths serves to rein-force suggestions of infernal possession, the porter scene makes explicit allusion to hell itself. Primarily, however, the porter scene enforces the sense of the fatality of the fatal error. The seven scenes of the first act are symmetrically divided between the supernatural (or Lady Macbeth's invocation of it) and the natural—accounts of the battle and its aftermath, Dun-can's arrival at Macbeth's castle, and so on. The effect is of an interlocking of forces of such energy, impetus, and power that the murder is upon one almost before the drama is felt to be under way. Since, as I have suggested, this advancement of the fatal act is of the utmost importance to the tragic develop-ment, it was necessary to draw attention to it, to underline and emphasize it in every possible way; and this is what the port-er's scene, and the old man's prodigies a little later, in fact do.

That this is the effect of the scene De Quincey's eloquent report confirms. "We feel," he says, "as the goings on of life are suddenly resumed, that human nature, i.e., the divine nature of love and mercy, spread throughout the hearts of all creatures, and seldom utterly withdrawn from man—was gone, banished, extinct; and that the fiendish nature had taken its place."[14]

From the content and mode of the scene, aside from the effect of the knocking itself, further important effects are derived. The drastic shift from the inner to the outer point of view is what gives us pause, creates perspective, and invites the play of mind on and around events just dramatized so that manifold aspects may be taken in. The point of view is that of a drunken common man's macabre joviality. To the porter, speculators, equivocators, and thieves are all on their way to hell-fire, and his descriptions of these characters bear by analogy directly upon Macbeth. But Macbeth, speculator, equivocator, and thief, is not reducible to the terms of the porter's casual familiarity. Thus, while making him one with all common humanity which treads the primrose way to the everlasting bonfire, the porter's words at the same time point up the difference in scale and scope between the passionate suffering mind within the gate and anything this porter, in rough worldly wisdom, could possibly conceive. The porter thus functions as a device for measuring the intensity of inner anguish at the same time as he gives notice that Macbeth's castle is now, in a sense, hell itself. Certainly, in the sense that Marlowe had already made, and Milton was later to make the leitmotif of Satan's experience, to Macbeth from now on "this is Hell, nor is he out of it."

Nevertheless I would venture to suggest that there is an effect of foreshortening, of prematurity, produced by the scene. The farmer who hangs himself in the expectation of

---

[14] "On the Knocking at the Gate in *Macbeth*" (1823).

plenty is at the end of the road. Macbeth has still a long way to go. If the deed of darkness were complete, as De Quincey says, the play would be over. But in fact Banquo is still alive, Lady Macduff and her children are still to be slain; there are depths upon depths of tragic discovery, of anguish and perturbation, still to be undergone by Macbeth.

These are anticipated, by dramatic irony, in Macbeth's dissimulating speech to the thanes:

> Had I but died an hour before this chance,
> I had liv'd a blessed time; for, from this instant,
> There's nothing serious in mortality;
> All is but toys: renown, and grace, is dead:
> The wine of life is drawn, and the mere lees
> Is left this vault to brag of.
>
> (II.iii.91-96)

This of course is the false face which the false heart must wear, but it is himself he is deceiving. He is afraid to think what he has done. It is from himself that he is disguised, and it is this circumstance that characterizes the further stage of Macbeth's progress which is set out in Act III. When Lady Macbeth says, "These deeds must not be thought / After these ways: so, it will make us mad," she too speaks with an irony of which she is unaware. For Macbeth is denied the escape of madness. The breach in his soul, the horror at himself which he expresses by scarcely recognizing his own hands, the self-alienation of "To know my deed, 'twere best not know myself," the restless torment in which he lives—these he attempts to escape by laying hold with increasingly frantic energy upon the deed. From now on recognition will be evaded, self-disguised; yet it insistently betrays its presence through the experience of futility, frustration, anxiety, guilt, and dread which accompanys his every action. The second half of the porter's speech indeed anticipates this continuation of struggle and suggests its nature through the intoxication analogy. The making and marring of a man, the setting of him on, the taking of him off, the persuading and disheartening are a catalogue of the perturbations and the reversals of expectation into which Act III will resolve itself. Thus Macbeth will know his guilt by its effects; but he will not recognize it for what it is.

In Act III we watch a more profound disintegration of the tragic protagonist than in any other of the tragedies. Crime leads to crime in the futile search for security, but each crime leads also to a reflection of itself in tormented consciousness. What we watch is the struggle to subdue that reflection, to conceal the deed from the soul, or the soul from the deed; or to subdue the soul to the deed like the dyer's hand. What we watch is Macbeth's awful success, his habituation to his abandonment; his tranced refusal to allow his inchoate knowledge to take possession of him; and finally the submergence of all that might have saved him from the continuance of the nightmare.

Act III opens with Macbeth's realization that "To be thus is nothing, / But to be safely thus." Banquo is the immediate stumbling block to "safety" on account of his knowledge of the encounter with the witches, and on account of his role in the prophecy—he will be father to a line of kings where Macbeth's scepter is barren.

> If 't be so,
> For Banquo's issue have I fil'd my mind;
> For them the gracious Duncan have I murder'd;
> Put rancors in the vessel of my peace,
> Only for them; and mine eternal jewel
> Given to the common enemy of man,
> To make them kings, the seed of Banquo kings!
> Rather than so, come, fate, into the list,
> And champion me to th' utterance!
>
> (III.i.64-72)

That he has filed his mind and put rancors in the vessel of his peace presents itself to him in connection with Banquo's role in the prophecy. What he does not realize, though it is implicit in the speech, is that Banquo's very character, his immunity to the cursed thoughts nature gives way to in repose, is a perpetual reproach to him. Banquo represents, externalizes, his conscience and his envy; and it is these, even more than the danger to his position, that he must kill. Overtly he admits no such perception. His philosophy is of utilities, as in his speech to the murderers, where the virtues of dogs and men consist in what they are capable of performing. But in the subsequent dialogue with Lady Macbeth the defiled mind becomes the tortured mind and a deeper level of distress is revealed.

> We have scotched the snake, not kill'd it:
> She'll close, and be herself; whilst our poor malice
> Remains in danger of her former tooth.
> But let the frame of things disjoint, both the worlds suffer,
> Ere we will eat our meal in fear, and sleep
> In the affliction of these terrible dreams,
> That shake us nightly. Better be with the dead,
> Whom we, to gain our peace, have sent to peace,
> Than on the torture of the mind to lie
> In restless ecstasy. Duncan is in his grave;
> After life's fitful fever he sleeps well;
> Treason has done his worst: nor steel, nor poison,
> Malice domestic, foreign levy, nothing
> Can touch him further!
>
> (III.ii.13-26)

That Macbeth should envy his victim's peace is a powerful irony. So also is the couple's reversal of role. She is no longer the instigator; she is in retreat, played out by the murder of Duncan. Her "But in them Nature's copy's not eterne" is evidently an appeal to him to let well enough, or ill enough, alone, and leave the future to the course of nature. It is he now who is the initiator of further evil in words that recall her invocation of the spirits which tend on mortal thoughts.

>   Come, seeling Night,
> Scarf up the tender eye of pitiful Day,
> And, with thy bloody and invisible hand,
> Cancel, and tear to pieces, that great bond
> Which keeps me pale! Light thickens; and the crow
> Makes wing to th' rooky wood;
> Good things of day begin to droop and drowse,
> Whiles night's black agents to their preys do rouse.
>
>   (III.ii.46-53)

The bond must be in the first place that between Banquo and his destiny, that is to say, Banquo's life; and therefore Macbeth is telling himself that what keeps him pale is the futility of Duncan's murder so long as Banquo or Fleance live to inherit the crown so dearly bought. What he is expressing despite himself is his knowledge of an inner bondage, of the vanity of the deed when all it purchases is the reverse of what was envisaged. What he sought was power, self-fulfillment, freedom, autonomy, glory. What he experiences is sleepless torment, soul-sickness, and dread. It is this bondage of conscience which he would cancel and tear to pieces, in the interests of a fantasy of perfect self-possession and security.

His reception of the news of Fleance's escape restates the vicious, soul-destroying dialectic of fantasy and reality which engages him:

> Then comes my fit again: I had else been perfect;
> Whole as the marble, founded as the rock,
> As broad and general as the casing air:
> But now, I am cabin'd, cribb'd, confin'd, bound in
> To saucy doubts and fears.
>   (III.iv.20-24)

The dream and the reality, that which he wished to be and that which he is, are placed in extreme opposition; the dream is further off than ever, the present bondage more irksome than ever. Still he will plot Fleance's death too, and it is not until the grand peripeteia—the appearance of Banquo's ghost at the banquet—that Macbeth's state is fully revealed to him. Lady Macbeth, attempting to restore him to himself, cries: "It is the very painting of your fear." It is indeed the very painting of his fear. Banquo exists in his mind. The ghost is a horrible shadow, an unreal mockery, but it cannot be laid for it is Macbeth's haunting knowledge of his guilt. He can kill Banquo only by killing himself.

And in very truth "We are yet but young in deed" is the grim resolution of spiritual suicide, the determination to extinguish the conscience that would compel him to recognize his guilt.

> I will to-morrow
> (And betimes I will) to the Weird Sisters:
> More shall they speak; for now I am bent to know,
> By the worst means, the worst. For mine own good,
> All causes shall give way: I am in blood
> Stepp'd in so far, that, should I wade no more,
> Returning were as tedious as go o'er.
>
> (III.iv.131-137)

But he has given himself away; shame and obloquy replace the golden honors that his banquet was intended to celebrate. The royal ceremony collapses in the unceremonious departure of the guests, and Lennox's heavy sarcasm marks the complete reversal of his status and his situation in the public eye:

> Things have been strangely borne. The gracious Duncan
> Was pitied of Macbeth:—marry, he was dead:—
> And the right-valiant Banquo walk'd too late;
> Whom, you may say (if 't please you) Fleance kill'd,

For Fleance fled . . . . how monstrous
It was for Malcolm, and for Donalbain,
To kill their gracious father? Damned fact!
How it did grieve Macbeth! Did he not straight,
In pious rage, the two delinquents tear,
That were the slaves of drink and thralls of sleep?
Was not that nobly done? Ay, and wisely too;
For 'twould have angered any heart alive
To hear the men deny 't.

(III.vi.3-16)

Hecate's speech in III.v, supposed an interpolation by Middleton or by an anonymous hand,[15] names explicitly the stage in the protagonist's progress which Act IV will exhibit:

He shall spurn fate, scorn death, and bear
His hopes 'bove wisdom, grace, and fear.

(III.v.30-31)

There is no better description of this fourth phase of the play, initiated by the visit to the witches, than Kierkegaard's account of "the sin of despairing over one's sin":

Sin itself is detachment from the good, but despair over sin is a second detachment. This of course tortures out of sin its utmost demoniac powers, bestowing upon it the ungodly hardiness of obduracy which must constantly regard everything which is of the nature of repentance and everything which is of the nature of grace not only as empty and meaningless but as its foe, as the thing which most of all it has to guard against, quite in the same way as the good guards itself against temptation. . . . To indicate the character of this potentiation from sin to despair over sin one might say that the former is the breach with the good, the

15 Upon the Hecate scenes and the possibly corrupt sequence of scenes between III.iv and IV.i, see K. Muir, Introduction, New Arden ed., p. xxxvff.

latter is the breach with repentance. Despair over sin is an attempt to maintain oneself by sinking still deeper. As one who ascends as a balloon rises by casting weights from him, so does the despairing man sink by casting from him the good. . . . he sinks, doubtless he thinks he is rising—he does indeed become lighter. . . . Despair over sin . . . is a step in advance, an ascent in the demoniacal, but of course it means sinking deeper in sin. It is an attempt to impart to sin as a positive power firmness and interest, but the fact is that now it is eternally decided that one will hear nothing about repentance, nothing about grace. Nevertheless despair over sin is conscious of its own emptiness, conscious of the fact that it has nothing whatever to live on, not even a lofty conception of one's own self.[16]

The visions that the witches show Macbeth are of course perfidious oracles, inducing in Macbeth the buoyancy of new hope. The witches' prophecy now serves to support Macbeth's evasion of responsibility by the notion that Fate is on his side, that he will "live the lease of nature" and has nothing to fear. Nevertheless he will make assurance doubly sure

And take a bond of Fate: . . .
That I may tell pale-hearted fear it lies,
And sleep in spite of thunder.
                              (iv.i.82-86)

The buoyancy however is short lived. The nagging question, the nagging knowledge of futility of which Banquo's issue is the symbol, must be answered; and the line of kings which stretches out to the crack of doom confirms the despair with which he curses the pernicious hour. Kierkegaard's "ungodly hardiness or obduracy" is perfectly rendered in the speech in which he determines his course of savagery without one mo-

[16] *Fear and Trembling* and *The Sickness Unto Death*, trans. W. Lowrie (Princeton: Princeton Univ. Press, 1941), pp. 240-241.

ment's compunction, without so much as an oblique and involuntary expression of regret for the lost sphere of his proper valor, such as was wrested from him by Banquo's ghost (". . . be alive again, / And dare me to the desert with thy sword; / If trembling I inhabit then, protest me / The baby of a girl" [III.iv.104-107]).

> From this moment,
> The very firstlings of my heart shall be
> The firstlings of my hand. And even now,
> To crown my thoughts with acts, be it thought and done:
> The castle of Macduff I will surprise;
> Seize upon Fife; give to th' edge o' th' sword
> His wife, his babes, and all unfortunate souls
> That trace him in his line. No boasting like a fool;
> This deed I'll do, before this purpose cool. . . .
>
> (IV.i.144-154)

Macbeth's visit to the witches marks the opening of the slow movement of Act IV, which is divided thereafter between the events which constitute the counteraction in England and the murder of Lady Macduff and her children. It is in accordance with Shakespearean form that Macbeth's total repudiation of moral commitment, his complete quenching of conscience, should occur in this phase of the play. Nor will we be surprised at the placing of the scene between Lady Macduff and her boy; for it is at the very point of repudiation that our imaginative hold upon the good which is repudiated must be vividly enforced. We are to be placed by drastic emotional transition at a point of maximum distance from the negation, the darkness, or the chaos mirrored in the hero's mind. It is by this means that the poignance of loss is realized. In each of the great tragedies the nature of the scenes of pathos is a touchstone of the consistency of the tragic realization. Their content is not arbitrary, they are not a mere expedient (however moving and effective) for arousing "a sense of beauty" or "an outflow of admiration and affection."[17] For in each case the pathos is related specifically to that which constituted the tragic hero's fatal choice. The scenes are a projection of that which is now irrevocably lost to him, that from which he is now utterly separated. The least deviation from this principle would reduce such scenes to melodramatic sentiment, whereas in fact the pathos is chastened and disciplined by one's perception of its intelligibility, its dialectical constitutive function in the total development. These scenes do not evoke pity as an end in itself, nor pity as a relief from more violent emotions, but pity in relation to the whole. The outflow of pity, of compassion, of affection is the measure of the human loss sustained by the hero: the measure of his distance from the center of well-being. Thus, this rendering of the Macduffs, the mother's anxious tenderness, the charming, cheeky, brave child, makes palpable, concrete, and unforgettable the great bond of nature which Macbeth canceled and tore to pieces. The scene is the dramatic equivalent of those verbal images of the newborn babe and the milk of human kindness through denial of which Lady Macbeth unsexed herself, and Macbeth, by daring to do more than doth become a man, became none.

It is in this light that I would interpret Macduff's reply to Malcolm when he receives the news of the murder. "Be comforted," says Malcolm, "Let's make us med'cines of our great revenge, / To cure this deadly grief" (iv.iii.214-215). And Macduff replies:

He has no children.—All my pretty ones?
Did you say all?—O Hell-kite!—All?
What, all my pretty chickens, and their dam,
At one fell swoop?

(iv.iii.216-219)

Nothing, Macduff would seem to be saying, nothing done to

[17] A. C. Bradley, *Shakespearean Tragedy* (Oxford: The Clarendon Press, 1904), p. 57.

Macbeth could ever cause him to suffer the anguish he, Macduff, is suffering. Therefore revenge affords no possibility of consolation, for there is no revenge that would be commensurate with the crime. The compression of the exchange, however, which forces us to infer our meanings, gives yet a further level of significance to the sentence. It epitomizes the total vanity of the career of Macbeth. He has no children, no tie, no root, no line. He is beyond the possibility of Macduff's grief; he is beyond the human pale. The crime which is the unnatural child of Macbeth and Lady Macbeth has now come to monstrous birth. And Banquo's natural children will reign in Scotland.

It remains to examine the puzzling exchange between Malcolm and Macduff before the arrival of Ross. The puzzle is resolved when it is realized that the exchange serves the regular purpose of the fourth phase, namely to establish a perspective upon the hero's progress from other than his own point of view. For what is mirrored in the testing of Macduff and in Malcolm's dissimulations is first of all the state of complete suspicion and mistrust that Macbeth's role of tyrant has brought about. The elaboration of the scene brings this home, since for purposes of plot construction and counteraction it is clearly unnecessary. In the first part Malcolm probes Macduff's motives for contacting him in England. And when Malcolm is finally convinced of Macduff's probity Macduff's loyalty to Malcolm still remains to be tested by the portrait of a tyrant that Malcolm paints for Macduff's delectation. It is only the vehemence of Macduff's final affirmation of loyalty to Scotland and the dead king's memory that enables Malcolm to throw off his mask and make a pact of fellowship with Macduff. Only by indirection, by false seeming, are candid and loyal relationships tested in the predatory world of fear that Macbeth has created. The social order of peace and trust, the disintegration of which was symbolized by the breaking up in disorder of the banquet, are here exhibited at length. Thus the two parts of Act IV in which Macbeth is absent from the stage represent what his actions have brought about. Malcolm's description of a contrary state of affairs, the healing benediction of England's good king, makes the obvious point.

All that is contained in this long scene is thus thematically justifiable. But as one reflects upon the general structural similarities between the tragedies, one becomes aware of a marked deviation here from Shakespeare's own model, his own usual practice. Wherever, in the other tragedies, we are to be given the viewpoint of common humanity in Act IV, it is the common man who gives it to us. Gravediggers, musicians, servants, clowns: these are our commentators. There are none such here. Macduff and Malcolm represent "common humanity" only by virtue of the problems of the public weal with which they concern themselves. Yet there is, in *Macbeth*, the very common man we are looking for; only he has been transferred from his proper place. The porter scene, perfect example of Shakespeare's common-man irony, which places heroic aspirations in a mundane light, occurred in Act II.ii. There, as we have seen, it fulfilled a perspectivist function, which, one remembers, for all the scene's impressive effectiveness and its thematic assimilability, did seem to foreshorten the action, to create a discernible break in the narrative rhythm. One remembers Coleridge's disgust with the scene. And though Coleridge had certain hampering preconceptions concerning decorum and psychological realism, his sensitivity is not in question. De Quincey's eloquent defense, moreover, is directed toward the knocking at the gate as such; he has nothing to say of the comic-ironic mode in which the episode is conducted.

The question tentatively forms itself: is it possible to conceive that the energy and address of his opening rushed Shakespeare on, in the heat of creation, to a point rather further than his developing story was quite ready for; and that, having already employed his devices of common humor

and common humanity to articulate a complex act of imaginative measurement, he refrained from doing so at the later
point where this was customary for him? One is tempted,
indeed, to press the argument still further. Would not the
burden of the porter scene, the suggestion that Macbeth's
castle, Macbeth's mind, is hell, have possessed greater force,
and even greater accuracy, at the point in his fortunes Macbeth has now reached? It is difficult to imagine the familiar
features of a face in a position other than that in which we
have always known them. But I have the stubborn feeling
that, the knocking itself only excepted, the scene might well
have been transposed, virtually in its entirety, to Act IV with
excellent effect, and certainly to the satisfaction of those critics
who have expressed uneasiness over the English scenes in Act
IV, finding them longer than would seem to be strictly necessary, and somewhat cold, remote, or unconvincing. Certainly
the effect of the hell-metaphor and of the irony it produces
upon Lady Macbeth's sleepwalking scene would have been
grim indeed. Since the porter scene where it occurs is anticipatory, some of the effect is achieved in any case. But the nihilism
of Macbeth's final soliloquy might well have been more clearly
understood than it has been in much of the criticism had it
been spoken in the shadow of such a juxtaposition.

The catastrophe of Macbeth presents its tragic discoveries
more fully than in any of the previous tragedies, yet in forms
of extreme disassociation. Actions are punctuated by recognitions but never integrated with them. The terrible fullness of
Lady Macbeth's knowledge that "what's done cannot be undone" is divulged, against her conscious will, in a somnam-
bulist trance. It is the unbearable burden of a soul which can
express itself only when the conscious mind is off its guard.
Where confession heals and eases, in this discharge of the
infected mind there is no expiation; only the torment of conscience for a deed which is beyond atonement because it is

unacknowledged. The whole of the fifth act marvelously exhibits the equivalent fission in Macbeth.

He never heals the breach in the self which was announced as early as ii.ii: "To know my deed, 'twere best not know myself." Evasion, flight, characterize his every response, and the mark of this is his obsessive preoccupation with fear despite his ostensible supreme confidence in his invulnerability. The more he asserts his immunity to fear—"I cannot taint with fear"; "The heart I bear, / Shall never sag with doubt, nor shake with fear"—the more one is led to perceive that what is reflected is the presence in him of an unspeakable dread. His real state of mind is given away by his uncontrollable outburst at the unfortunate boy who announces the approach of the English soldiers: "The devil damn thee black, thou cream-fac'd loon!" He will fight, he says, till from his bones the flesh be hacked. He will hang those that talk of fear. His castle's strength will laugh a siege to scorn. Yet again and again his uncontrollable agitation, his nervous tension, are betrayed by his distracted commands, his insistence upon donning armor before there is any occasion to do so, the violently impulsive oscillation of his responses to each succeeding blow. The grotesque images used to describe him in v.ii, "He cannot buckle his distemper'd cause / Within the belt of rule" and "now does he feel his title / Hang loose about him, like a giant's robe / Upon a dwarfish thief," underline the degree to which Macbeth is no longer a general in command, either of himself or others, but, at the last, a savage brute at bay; by his own choice, even when all is lost, never the Roman fool dying upon his own sword when he would do better inflicting gashes upon all who come his way.

It is from the pressure of this intense oscillation between dread and desperate hope that his recognitions arise, but they float to the surface from a self so deeply submerged as to be beyond reach.

Seyton!—I am sick at heart,
When I behold—Seyton, I say!—This push
Will cheer me ever, or disseat me now.
I have liv'd long enough: my way of life
Is fall'n into the sere, the yellow leaf;
And that which should accompany old age,
As honor, love, obedience, troops of friends,
I must not look to have; but in their stead,
Curses, not loud, but deep, mouth-honor, breath,
Which the poor heart would fain deny, and dare not.

(v.iii.19-28)

What is suppressed at "When I behold . . ."? Whatever thought demands utterance is displaced by the immediate saving concern: "This push / Will cheer me ever, or disseat me now." Yet this is again replaced by the desolate sensation of a withered vitality. His recognition of his situation takes in both the absence of positive goods which should accompany old age, and the hatred in which (successful though he may be) he will be held. But even this recognition is, so to speak, held off, depersonalized, seen as if from an immense distance. The inward mind finds expression in his speech to the doctor—"Canst thou not minister to a mind diseas'd . . . ?"—but indirectly, ostensibly with reference to Lady Macbeth; and the rooted sorrow, which is his own as well as hers, is in effect repudiated by "Throw physic to the dogs; I'll none of it." The insinuation in the doctor's "Therein the patient / Must minister to himself" is cleverly evaded by Macbeth's adoption of the medical metaphor for his own purposes: it is the land that is diseased, not its ruler. He reacts to the "cry of women" like a doomed man who is perpetually taking his own pulse, crowding an inner dread from the forefront of his mind by excessive occupation with a more immediate and manageable anxiety.

I have almost forgot the taste of fears.
The time has been, my senses would have cool'd
To hear a night-shriek; and my fell of hair
Would at a dismal treatise rouse, and stir,
As life were in 't. I have supp'd full with horrors:
Direness, familiar to my slaughterous thoughts,
Cannot once start me.

(v.v.9-15)

The great speech which follows continues in the vein of absorbed self-concentration:

She should have died hereafter:
There would have been a time for such a word.
To-morrow, and to-morrow, and to-morrow,
Creeps in this petty pace from day to day,
To the last syllable of recorded time;
And all our yesterdays have lighted fools
The way to dusty death. Out, out, brief candle!
Life's but a walking shadow; a poor player,
That struts and frets his hour upon the stage,
And then is heard no more: It is a tale
Told by an idiot, full of sound and fury,
Signifying nothing.

(v.v.17-28)

It is essentially a gesture of pushing away. Seen in this light, the vexed question whether Macbeth's words refer to the inevitability of his wife's death (she would have died some time in any case) or its untimeliness (she should have died after the battle, or—still further off—after the promised achievement of our ambitions) can be resolved. I believe that the latter is more consonant with the structure and the rhythm of the inner drama. For thus it is his tranced willed belief in the witches' oracle that first expresses itself. Then the break

253

in the thought between the first two lines and the third can be interpreted as indicating that the shock of the news penetrates through his concentration upon his beleaguered state, so that he catches himself in the very act of anticipation, and so is precipitated the moment of intense reflection and the fine dramatic effect of his sudden realization of time's stop.

The perspectivist trick of the syntax at this point is characteristic of the play. We are momentarily uncertain at what point in time Macbeth conceives himself to be, and whether he is looking forward or back. Time is in effect abrogated by the subjunctives in the first lines and Macbeth could be speaking of his present tomorrows stretching out ahead in meaningless tedium, or reflecting upon all the past tomorrows which, with all their promise, have come to nothing in this moment. The sense of a loop in time produces a finer irony than the sense of mere linear continuance, however melancholy; and is borne out by Macbeth's own switch from "to-morrow" to "yesterday," which identifies, or makes interchangeable, the future and the past. What was once the future slips imperceptibly and irrevocably into the past, what is past can still be seen as it was when it was future, but is now recognized as the *ignis fatuus* it is. For we in our deluded anticipations follow this fool's light to nowhere but the grave. "Out, out brief candle" I take to be expressive of a desire: Macbeth would welcome the finishing of temporal existence itself, since it is but a walking shadow against the fool's light of time, inessential, insignificant, insubstantial, and worthless.

The theatrical metaphor completes the irony of the loop of time by its reference back to the great surge of anticipation so long ago: "Two truths are told, / As happy prologues to the swelling act / Of the imperial theme." That vitality is certainly all but exhausted. But the theatrical metaphor also enlarges the scope of the statement. The world as stage was the Elizabethan commonplace that more than any other articulated the age's reflections upon the nature of reality. The *theatrum mundi* idea, which presents man as actor and life as the soul's drama, provides a metaphor with unlimited possibilities for the exploration of the validity of human knowledge and the autonomy of human will. The speech is more than a lament upon the vanity of human wishes. It is a denial of any value in life as ground for human wishes at all. For life—the strutting and fretting of the actor, the tale told "to the last syllable of recorded time," the script which is set down for existence to enact—is reduced to no more than idiot gesticulation. Macbeth's frustration overflows the whole universe, absorbs the whole universe into itself, in this withering vision of being diminished to zero. That it is his own life which is gibberish—not life itself—is a distinction he cannot make because he cannot face the meaning of his deed, or the fact of his guilt; he cannot face himself. Thus he still lays frantic hold upon the very goals that are emptied of meaning. To the news of the movement of Birnham Wood his response is:

> If thou speaks't false,
> Upon the next tree shalt thou hang alive,
> Till famine cling thee: if thy speech be sooth,
> I care not if thou dost for me as much.
>
> (v.v.39-41)

All seems to him still at stake though "all" was nothing to him a moment before.

Lady Macbeth dies of her deed; whether by her own hand or not is scarcely important. Whereas Macbeth, briefly, lives on. It is a fractured existence, the existence of a bear at the stake. Knowing only a failing vitality—"I 'gin to be aweary of the sun"—he is driven by his animal instinct and his supernatural delusion to the continuance of the mere physical existence he still believes to be charmed. Then comes the final encounter with the man whom of all men else he most wished to avoid, the man who was not of woman born. And the spell is broken.

His first impulse is instinctive flight. That which sustained him, the oracle of the juggling fiends, no longer has power to do so. With "I'll not fight thee" Macbeth gives up. But at this last moment before the end he is saved from utter collapse. Macduff's taunt of cowardice strikes the one note which can save him, lost soul though he be, from total dishonor.

> Then yield thee, coward,
> And live to be the show and gaze o' th' time:
> We'll have thee, as our rarer monsters are,
> Painted upon a pole, and underwrit,
> "Here may you see the tyrant."
>
> (v.viii.23-27)

Now without illusion, without subterfuge and, at last without fear, he faces Macduff, for one brief final moment in command of himself and of his fate:

> I will not yield,
> To kiss the ground before young Malcolm's feet,
> And to be baited with the rabble's curse.
> Though Birnham Wood be come to Dunsinane,
> And thou oppos'd, being of no woman born,
> Yet I will try the last: before my body
> I throw my warlike shield: lay on, Macduff;
> And damn'd be him that first cries, "Hold, enough!"
>
> (v.viii.27-34)

In this reflex of pride and physical hardihood he is clear-eyed, undeluded, without metaphysical aid and without hope; knowing himself damned, yet pronouncing damnation upon surrender; self-identified by his soldier's intrepidity. What Macbeth is, the one inalienable value he has it in him to affirm, is thus granted the final dignity of realization. If, as Holloway has illuminatingly pointed out, the green branches of Birnham Wood signal the defeat of the demon and the

return of nature,[18] that defeat and that return are dramatized
in these last moments of Macbeth himself; while Ross's tribute to Siward's son, mirror-image of Macbeth himself, recalling the play's beginning battle, recalling the very terms
of Macbeth's temptation, provides us with our final bearings
upon that vital energy which is the most precarious, but not
the most negligible, of man's natural endowments.

> He only liv'd but till he was a man;
> The which no sooner had his prowess confirm'd
> In the unshrinking station where he fought,
> But like a man he died.
>
> (v.ix.6-9)

[18] J. Holloway, *The Story of the Night* (Lincoln, Nebr.: Univ. of
Nebraska Press, 1963).

CHAPTER VIII

KING LEAR

The influence of Christian moral doctrine upon the interpretation of *King Lear* has given us the story of a penitent's progress through a school of suffering to the great spiritual discovery of love. One characteristic formulation is: ". . . the declining action which is the dogging of the hero to death is complemented by a rising action which is the hero's regeneration. . . . Its primary story is not the descent of the King into Hell but the ascent of the King as he climbs the mountain of Purgatory and is fulfilled."[1] This view has been presented with varying degrees of subtlety, with varying degrees of allowance for the obdurate residue of pain and loss, with varying degrees of analytical sophistication. And indeed it has much to substantiate it. The highly symmetrical morality play grouping, suggesting Everyman traveling toward Death between false friends and true friends; the plenitude of references to the great topics of Christian reflection—*nosce teipsum*, man and nature, providence, wisdom and folly, deceptive appearances; the powerful polarization of good and evil; the story of the Abasement of the Proud King:[2] all lend themselves to assimilation in the direction of Christian myth, particularly if one is permitted to invoke what Enid Welsford has called "the wilder paradoxes" of the Christian religion.[3] Yet the optimistic Christian reading fails to take adequate account of Lear's state of mind at the close of the play. It imposes upon what is exhibited the idea that Lear, having

[1] Russell Fraser, Introduction, Signet ed. (New York: New American Library, 1963), p. xxii.

[2] M. Mack, *King Lear in our Time* (Berkeley and Los Angeles: Univ. of California Press, 1965), pp. 49-50, makes skillful interpretative use of the parable.

[3] *The Fool* (London: Faber, 1935), p. 271.

passed through the refining fires of affliction and attained humility, patience and self-knowledge, is thereby redeemed: "*King Lear* is, like the *Paradiso*, a vast poem on the victory of true love."[4] Opponents of this view will be quick to point out that what we witness is considerably more in the nature of a defeat than a victory, that love proves to be the ultimate and most bitter mockery of the human condition, and that the unholy *pietà* of the final scene, as Lear enters with Cordelia in his arms, is an appalling parody not less than satanic in its import.

It is my purpose here to argue that love has only obliquely to do with the case, though filial reconciliation has seldom been more movingly portrayed; that it is the inadequacy, if anything, of love to redeem that is the burden of the play, though love is given, in Cordelia, France, the Fool, Kent, Gloucester, Edgar, in the obscure impulse which moves Cornwall's servants to turn against their master and succor a blind old man, and in Lear himself, a rich variety of forms more compelling, persuasive, and ethically appealing than in any other of the great tragedies; that what is enacted is a

---

[4] R. W. Chambers, *King Lear* (Glasgow, 1940), p. 49. The neo-Christian case has been effectively challenged by W. Elton, *King Lear and the Gods* (San Marino, Calif.: Huntington Library, 1966), who has amassed an impressive body of evidence for his contention that Shakespeare has carefully and deliberately dramatized varieties of paganism in the characters of *Lear*, the good and the wicked alike. He invokes the troubled skepticism of the Renaissance as background, and concludes that the optimistic Christian interpretation of the play is invalid since (*a*) no evidence exists to show that Lear arrives finally at "salvation," "regeneration," or "redemption" and (*b*) "the purported benevolent, just or special providence cannot be shown to be operative" (p. 336). Elton's book is a mine of invaluable information about the Renaissance topoi embedded in the play, and of insights into the dramatic deployment of them. I have leaned heavily upon his scholarship at innumerable points, though his thesis, that Lear's pagan progress to despair provided Shakespeare with an analogue for the theological crisis of his day, is at a tangent to my own concerns.

titanic agon rather than a purgatorial progress; and that the death of Cordelia, at which the sensibility of the eighteenth century shuddered, and which the sensibility of the twentieth century shudderingly embraces, is dramatically intelligible. By dramatically intelligible I mean intelligible not in terms either of a providentialist or a nihilist philosophy, but in terms of that tragic movement of the spirit which the play dramatizes, a necessary part of the self-discovery[5] of which the play is a mimesis.

The sins of Lear, for which, it is so often held, he is punished, have been indefatigably catalogued. Wicked pride, self-will, self-love, vanity, choler, egoism, senile puerility, a crass materialism which views love as a commodity to be bartered and traded, tyranny, sloth, and want of courage, which lays down burdens and offers as rationalization the excuse of old age[6]—all have found their place, severally and together, in the indictment of Lear. And as the indictment grows heavier, the punishment becomes more and more deserved, at the very least justifiable upon Regan's pedagogic grounds:

> O! Sir, to willful men,
> The injuries that they themselves procure
> Must be their schoolmasters.
>
> (ii.iv.304-306)

The play makes Regan the spokesman of this cold self-righteousness, rendering further comment unnecessary. But under any guise, the moral sense which can be stilled by the logic of Job's comforters is probably impervious to tragic experience. Bildadism is so prevalent in the criticism of *King*

---

[5] The term forms part of the title of P. Jorgensen's illuminating study, *Lear's Self-Discovery* (Berkeley and Los Angeles: Univ. of California Press, 1967), but the author, basing himself upon Renaissance treatises on *nosce teipsum*, takes self-discovery in a sense somewhat different from and more general than mine.

[6] See Lily B. Campbell, *Shakespeare's Tragic Heroes* (Cambridge: Cambridge Univ. Press, 1930), p. 183.

Lear, I suggest, because the play is a Shakespearean version of the Book of Job, raising the problem of undeserved suffering with a similar insistence, power, and intensity. The Elizabethans saw Job as the pattern of all patience which Lear invokes on the heath; but in the rebellion which is a constitutive part of that ancient contest with God the imagination reared upon the Scriptures could hardly have failed to find the paradigm of what Harbage has so perceptively isolated for comment: "Lear's molten indignation, his huge invective, his capacity for feeling pain."[7]

Like Job, Lear takes his initial prosperity as a sign of heavenly favor; like Job in affliction, he calls the heavens themselves to heavenly account. Like Job, though he die for it, yet will he affirm his own conviction of what injustice is. Like Job, his natural egotism reaches beyond itself to embrace a universe of suffering creatures and returns to the bedrock reality of the suffering creature. Like Job, he refuses to compromise with pain and with evil; refuses to surrender to the plot of optimistic quietism whereby pain and evil are denied, are made into goods, disciplinary or deserved or redemptive; are made nonexistent. Lear, raging in the storm, is no hero of renunciation but of an enormous expostulation; "raging, ravening and uprooting into the desolation of reality."[8] What is dramatized in the action of *Lear* is the opposite of resignation. It is the way in which an erring man's passionate protest against injustice and humiliation affirms human dignity despite the most relentless pressure of cruelty, cynicism, and degradation that can be brought to bear on it.

So much ink has been spilt upon the allegation that Lear's proposed division of the kingdom was in itself in some way

[7] A. Harbage, "King Lear," Introduction, Pelican ed. (1958), p. 27. The Job analogue has also been noticed by J. Holloway, *The Story of the Night* (Lincoln, Nebr.: Univ. of Nebraska Press, 1963), and by John D. Rosenberg, "Lear and his Comforters," *Essays in Criticism* (April 1966).

[8] W. B. Yeats, "Meru."

wrong or morally reprehensible that it is worth pausing for a moment to consider its implications. One eminent scholar has defended it thus:

> . . . to withdraw in one's age from the cares of state has the appearance of wisdom, to dispose of one's goods by gift instead of testament the appearance of generosity. . . . The things Lear wants—fidelity and love—are good things. That he should find them in his servant and his child seems to him an aspect of universal order.[9]

But I believe we can pursue the point even further. Given that Lear wished both to withdraw in his old age from the cares of state and to leave his kingdom in good order, three alternative courses of action were open to him: primogeniture, complete equality of division between his heirs, and that disposition of affairs which would reflect an ideal justice— "honours, rewards and benefits bestowed according to virtue and merit."[10] Cordelia was Lear's favorite daughter not without good reason, as the outcome of events certainly confirms, and if he wished to make sure of her having her share, her deservedly largest share, this can be seen as not only truly just but also sensible. But the justice and reasonableness of the decision require public demonstration, public confirmation. Hence the so-called love-test, conceived as purely formal, a ceremonial which shall reflect and make manifest the self-evident justice of his distribution.

Coleridge long ago noted Shakespeare's antedating of the particulars of the proposed division of the kingdom in the form of the court gossip of the prefatory scene. Coleridge's conclusion, dictated by his bias toward psychological realism ("the trial of love is but a trick; and . . . the grossness of the old king's rage is in part the natural result of a silly trick

[9] Harbage, "King Lear," p. 24-25.
[10] *The Beginning, Continuance and Decay of Estates* (1606).

suddenly and most unexpectedly baffled and disappointed")[11] proved reductive; it fathered a host of later vulgarizations of the tragic predicament which make of Lear at the very beginning of the play a senile, obtuse, or crass materialist, who must be chastized into learning what every Sunday-school child knows by heart.

The technique of juxtaposition in evidence here has been used by Shakespeare before, most notably in *Richard II*, a play anticipatory of *King Lear* in many ways and particularly in its exploration of self-discovery. There, too, in Act 1 formal ritualistic ceremonies are juxtaposed with glimpses behind the scenes which disclose the realities of state politics. There are two languages: the language of chivalric challenge and counterchallenge, and the language of political facts and political accommodations. In the conversation between Kent and Gloucester, which reveals, be it noted, no particular dismay on their part regarding the proposed division, it is the Dukes of Albany or Cornwall whom the King favors or does not favor. Here the two languages—the matter-of-fact language of state gossip and the language of ceremony with its elaborate and symmetrical theatricality—serve notice that the division scene is deliberately staged, a public ceremonial dramatizing and sanctioning a decision which a moment's simple arithmetic shows has in fact already been made. Recent criticism[12] has rightly stressed the ritualistic nature of the scene, and has enabled us thereby to perceive, rather than Coleridge's signs of senility (there are indeed far more signs of "senility" in the recovery scenes than here), the degree to which Lear's first speech is in fact cogent, decisive, and masterful. Lear is impressively in command of the court and his faculties.

We are invited, I suggest, to perceive what Lear's symbolic

[11] *Coleridge's Shakespearean Criticism*, ed. Raysor, I, 50.
[12] W. Frost, "Shakespeare's Rituals and the Opening Scene of *King Lear*," *Hudson Review*, x (Winter 1958).

ceremony was meant by him to represent: the act of a wise, responsible, and careful king, prudent in looking ahead and capable of disciplining himself in his own lifetime to the conferring of power upon younger strengths. It is to be a ritual enactment of wise and just rule (the very opposite of caprice or chance), which distributes rewards and powers where "nature doth with merit challenge." Moreover, Lear's "quantification of love," boldly ritualized, has warrant in the semantics of the concept itself.[13] Anglo-Saxon "lofian" (and one sense of "love" as late as 1596, according to the Oxford English Dictionary) meant to estimate, evaluate, appraise (compare the colloquial "dear" of today). That Regan metaphorically coins herself to metal in her reply while Cordelia in her rejection invokes a "bond" (hardly to be cleared of fiscal associations) is Shakespeare's way of meshing into the language of the play a universal aspect of human evaluations.

But, and this is the crucial point, between Regan's "I am of that selfsame mettle as my sister" and Cordelia's "according to my bond" occurs the play's definitive event. The replies of Goneril and Regan are according to expectation—ours and Lear's. Cordelia's is not. Cordelia refuses to play her ceremonial part. She rejects form in favor of substance and thereby irremediably alters the terms of reference of the entire scene. Lear was on dangerous ground in his identification of the theatre of the world with the theatre in his mind. Like Hamlet in the staging of his Mousetrap, he believes that he can stage-manage nature, master reality, make his will, his "sovereignty, knowledge and reason," transparent in appearances. But, in the autocracy his composite role of king, father, lawgiver, judge, and magistrate has nourished, he has taken insufficient account of the wayward obduracy of needs and desires—his own and others'. The problem of sibling

[13] See T. Hawkes, "Love in *King Lear*," *RES*, x (May, 1959), pp. 178-81.

rivalry, for instance, is evidently not a planet which has swum into his ken (nor into Gloucester's), though Shakespeare's awareness of that dimension of his fable is fully exhibited in Cordelia's replies and in the parting dialogue between the sisters. And yet, it is important to perceive, though he exhibits something less than the wisdom of Solomon in his grand ceremony, he might have got away with it. Three formal declarations of love and loyalty, whatever the details of their expression, would perfectly have served his purposes. But three such formal declarations are precisely what he does not receive. And the nonmaterialization of the third is what shatters his staged demonstration, brutally translates his language of ritual into the language of personal feeling, and causes the wounded rage which leads him to commit his fatal error.

"But goes thy heart with this?" is a crucial moment. It shows Lear to be less naïve, less "puerile" and unsophisticated, than many of his critics (notably Wilson Knight)[14] have made him out. He is perfectly aware of a possible discrepancy between speech and intention. But Cordelia's reply, the cold rationality with which (in mirror-image fashion) she halves love and denies him its mysterious fullness which is beyond mathematics, leaves him no recourse, in his bewildered incredulity, mortification and disappointment, but the punitive passion which presently breaks out in the writ of disinheritance. There is between these two protagonists, both proud, both self-righteously rationalizing their own spontaneous emotions—he, the insult of his repudiated gift, she, her inability to "heave her heart into her mouth"—both at fault, an irreducible clash of will, understanding, and purpose. It is a clash whose terrifying inevitability is grounded in the most familar and universal of circumstances: the parental-filial "knot intrinsicate," which of all other relations is the

---

[14] *The Wheel of Fire* (London: Oxford Univ. Press, 1930), p. 161ff.

most familiar to human beings. His conception of his dignity and her idea of hers are in fatal opposition. His demand for the tenderness she denies him and hers for truth are irreconcilable in the situation created. But if he, in his artist's hubris has created the situation, she, in her moralist's zeal fails to save it. If he imputes to her a gross self-interest in his warning, "Nothing will come of nothing," it is also possible to hear among the many echoes of the word "nothing" an echo from Corinthians 13, to Cordelia's disadvantage: what after all could he have done, with the form of his authority thus repudiated? He is publicly shamed and humiliated by his best-loved daughter, beneficiary of his just affection, argument of his praise and balm of his age. What would Cordelia have had him do? Is not her truth—her "nothing"—too much less than the truth? Is it not also, in its way, a false appearance, well-intentioned (unlike Edmund's "nothing" later) but nevertheless misleading? Is her appeal to reason totally free of Coleridge's "little faulty admixture of pride and sullenness," aroused by her sister's fulsome usurpation (as she sees it) of the truth she cherishes as her own prerogative?

Yet when Lear disinherits Cordelia—"so young and so untender"—invoking the universal laws of nature themselves to abrogate the other natural law of paternal care and propinquity of blood, he is manifestly, violently, unjust, as Kent's interference powerfully conveys. This ferocious plucking out of the eye that has offended is a colossal hubris. Without hesitation he takes upon himself both the knowledge and the execution of a justice of iron symmetry—nothing for nothing —blind to human vulnerability, to the falsity of the position he has placed her in, and to the source of his own passionate violence. As the shrewdest of his daughters notes, he has ever but slenderly known himself, let alone the needs and desires of others. There is no more compelling rendering in literature of what Tyndale, in a strikingly apposite passage, called natural blindness:

The root of all evil and the greatest damnation and most terrible wrath and vengeance of God that we are in, is natural blindness. We are all out of the right way. One judgeth this best, another that to be best. Now is worldly wit nothing else but craft and subtlety to obtain that which we judge falsely to be best. As I err in my wit, so err I in my will. When I judge that to be evil which indeed is good, then hate I that which is good. And when I suppose that good which is evil, indeed then love I evil. And if I be persuaded and borne in hand that my most friend is mine enemy, then hate I my best friend; and if I be brought in belief that my most enemy is my friend, then love I my most enemy.[15]

The chiastic symmetry of Tyndale's syntax delineates with deadly accuracy the mutual blindness from which this tragedy takes its rise.

Our clear perception of the import of this opening sequence is impeded by the attempt to find Lear solely to blame for the assault which is presently to be made upon him. The more culpable Lear is made to appear the more Christlike Cordelia becomes, while the exculpation of Lear involves the incrimination of Cordelia. It is precisely this transvaluation of contraries, this dialectic of guilt, that the predicament dramatizes. As Gloucester observed, "The wisdom of nature can reason it thus and thus, but nature finds itself scourged by the sequent effects." The reasoning of it thus and thus, which takes up so much critical energy, prevents us from properly perceiving the sequent effects, and distracts our attention from the precision of the dramaturgy. Only, I believe, when we perceive the true nature of the predicament, when we fully take in—it is the fool's single and obsessive theme—that it is

---

[15] W. Tyndale, *The Obedience of a Christian Man* (1528), in *The Thought and Culture of the English Renaissance*, ed. E. M. Nugent (Cambridge: Cambridge Univ. Press, 1956), p. 192.

not the original proposed division of the kingdom, nor even the love-test as such, that constitutes Lear's fatal error, but, specifically and precisely, the redistribution which actually takes place, the disinheritance of Cordelia and the giving of entire power into the hands of the wicked sisters, are we enabled to follow the tragic progress which takes shape upon the basis of the folktale.

Lear's fatal error is the occasion for the villainy which waits in ambush to express its evil nature. The error, itself the issue of an impossible choice, creates impossible choices for all about him: choices between virtue and expediency, obedience and conscience, integrity and self-betrayal. Kent's loyal and reckless courage, Burgundy's venality, France's magnanimity, Goneril's calculated opportunism instance the possibilities. But it is to be noted that these possibilities for good and ill precede the initial situation. They represent the perennial stuff of human nature, of human motivations. The King's error exposes, and exposes him to, the plighted cunning of the sisters; but it does not cause it, any more than the good sport that there was at Edmund's illegitimate making causes his doctrine of ruthless self-interest. It is a moment's folly, a breach through which evil rushes, disintegrating his monolithic identity. He becomes, if not a hero with a thousand faces, at least a fractured glass, the shivered fragments of which are reflected separately in each of the figures that surround him, as the division scene is reflected in phantasmagoric parodies.

That both Cordelia on the one hand and Goneril and Regan on the other embody, represent, or reflect aspects of their father has often been observed; Cordelia his pride, Goneril and Regan the retributive calculus which in him appears to be the rational order of justice, in them is the correlative of predatory and self-seeking gain. The fool reflects his folly, Kent his integrity; Gloucester, co-protagonist, his entire tragic role. Yet they are his antitheses as well: the fool wiser than he in his practical wisdom; Kent unchanging, too old at forty-eight for the great excursions into wisdom of the King at eighty; Gloucester submissive, where he is indomitable.

It is not my purpose here to enumerate in detail the multiplicity of effects arising from the contrast in resemblance of the subplot's mirror-image. It constitutes Shakespeare's most sustained and complex system of mirrors; and because it is both complex and systematic, it is the matrix of unlimited interrelated relationships and cross-relationships. The basic equation is that Lear is to Gloucester as Cordelia is to Edgar and Goneril and Regan to Edmund. But Edmund, too, is a mirror-image of Lear, and so is Edgar. Edmund is, at his first appearance in the play, much concerned with distribution and division, in the mode of getting rather than giving, and with argument, derived by way of a perverse skepticism, from the same calculus of merit and desert. Nature is his goddess as she is Lear's, but it is to *natural* law that he gives his allegiance not natural *law*.[16] Again, Edgar, outcast and refugee, despised and rejected of men, mirrors Lear in his aspect of naked man and victim. The subplot is that feature of the play's invention which accounts for the sheer magnitude of *Lear*, for it brings under the aspect of unity a truly awesome multiplicity of parts. The play, on its account, possesses the systematic symmetry of *Julius Caesar* or *Richard II*, the improvising spontaneity of *Hamlet*, which arises from the generation within the scheme of fresh relationships and fresh awarenesses in the process of action, and the dense texture of verbal recurrences of *Macbeth*.

When we next see Lear after the division scene, much has occurred. Edmund's plot has been conceived and initiated, and the orderly disposition of events in the world called into radical question by Gloucester's nervous premonitions. Lear

---

[16] The neat distinction is Elton's, p. 127.

now speaks prose, and the discrepancy between the high style of his announcement of intention to the court—"while we unburdened crawl toward death"—and the colloquialism of "Let me not stay a jot for dinner" generates irony. A lifetime's high living and hearty appetite, so far from preceding a comfortable and enjoyable retirement, is, as the audience anticipates, upon the verge of disastrous deprivation. The first intimation is the insolence of the lackey Oswald; but to Lear's imperious habit the world seems merely asleep, insufficiently alert to his presence. It is not until Lear calls for his fool that we are made aware of a subterranean ferment of consciousness.

The fool, gnomic truthteller, yet another reflection of Lear who has been a fool, serves as a sounding board for the events in Lear's mind. It is significant that the latter demands his presence at the moment when a reluctant admission of the way things are is elicited by his knight's sympathetic anxiety: "Thou but remembr'rest me of mine own conception. I have perceived a most faint neglect of late, which I have rather blamed as mine own jealous curiosity than as a very pretense and purpose of unkindness" (I.iv.70-74). The fool throughout their dialogue mirrors Lear's mind, articulates his foreboding anxiety, and allows him a hidden self-examination, a dialogue between self and soul in which, however, he can still take refuge in the props of his long-established role: "Take heed, sirrah; the whip" (I.iv.116). The echoes—"Nothing can be made out of nothing"; "thou hadst little wit in thy bald crown when thou gav'st thy golden one away"; "thou hast pared thy wit o' both sides, and left nothing i' th' middle"; "now thou art an O without a figure. I am better than thou art now; I am a Fool, thou art nothing"— keep the past simmering in the present and ominously anticipate the arrival of Goneril with her attack upon the knights. Lear's "Are you our daughter?" is another form of the question he asked Oswald: "Who am I sir?" to which he received the reply: "My Lady's father." Therefore when he bursts out with

> Does any here know me? This is not Lear:
> Does Lear walk thus? speak thus? Where are his eyes?
> Either his notion weakens, his discernings
> Are lethargied—Ha! Waking? 'tis not so.
> Who is it that can tell me who I am?
>
> (I.iv.234-238)

the effect is of a disorientation already far advanced.

Lear has given his golden crown away, and with it, he discovers, as every normal expectation is reversed, his identity. He is appalled as only a man who recognizes a terrible truth can be. Yet he thrusts away the knowledge, taking up the fool's "Lear's shadow" in a self-protective sense. This must be a nightmare illusion, else he should be false persuaded he had daughters. With heavy sarcasm he inquires her name. She counters with a plain unvarnished tale indeed: of his "pranks," his debauched and riotous knights, and with the nonnegotiable demand that he disquantity his train and be attended by such men as may besort his age, which know themselves and him. He lashes out in reply:

> Detested kite! thou liest.
> My train are men of choice and rarest parts,
> That all particulars of duty know,
> And in the most exact regard support
> The worships of their name. O most small fault,
> How ugly didst thou in Cordelia show!
> Which, like an engine, wrench'd my frame of nature
> From the fix'd place, drew from my heart all love,
> And added to the gall. O Lear, Lear, Lear!
> Beat at this gate, that let thy folly in,
> And thy dear judgment out! Go, go, my people.
>
> (I.iv.271-281)

What is of supreme importance to notice is that Lear's self-accusation, though he is no further than the very outset of his odyssey, is complete, his recognition of his error as full as it will ever be, though so many discoveries are still before him.

This is the fact that is overlooked in nearly all moralistic and "redemptive" readings of *Lear*, where it is a prime element in the case that Lear's sufferings are justified by the repentance they *finally* produce. The fact of the matter is that Lear has needed no more than two days to know the woe that too late repents. His recognition is expressed with an unexampled completeness and candor within the first eight hundred lines of the play. Therefore he is from now on under attack from two sources. The remorse for what he has done to Cordelia, the gnawing sorrow of the love he has repudiated, is one source. The other is the marble-hearted fiend itself, now, with dreadful irony, emerging in its true location. All the evil that he had indignantly imputed to Cordelia now manifests itself in the daughter who has been the recipient of what should properly have been Cordelia's.

The curse which in violent transport he calls down upon Goneril's head is significantly different from the disinheritance of Cordelia. The magisterial surface of that first speech is now eroded. That was a sentence from the seat of power. This is a petition from one who is without power to a power that is both infinitely remote and infinitely closer to the seat of pain. What is now articulated is overtly in the language of suffering, and the degree and the kind of his suffering is indicated by the reference to all that is desirable and valuable—a babe to honor her, a mother's pains and benefits, which his curse would obliterate. Apollo gives way to the presiding goddess of creatures whose existence is defined by their capacity to feel pain. It is a measure of his own pain, which is almost too much for him. Lest he break down in the indignity of tears at her feet he summons up a fierce pride:

Old fond eyes,
Beweep this cause again, I'll pluck ye out
And cast you, with the waters that you loose,
To temper clay. . . . Thou shalt find
That I'll resume the shape which thou dost think
I have cast off for ever.

(I.iv.310-315)

In *King Lear*, Coleridge observed, old age is itself a character.[17] It is certainly a crucial circumstance in the complex predicament. Old age implies, ideally, expectations of honor and respect deservedly accorded to long experience consummated in rich wisdom. But in old age, as Regan puts it, nature stands on the very verge of her confine. It is a precarious ledge upon the downward slope toward bodily decrepitude and mental vacuity: weakness, dotage, and dependence. An old man is either a figure of veneration or an object of contempt, a nuisance to his family and friends, a babe again to be used with checks and flatteries. Lear's personal, specific plight is that he stands upon just such a precarious verge, is acutely vulnerable on this score; and this is an aspect of his situation which, presented with an insistent iteration in Act I, is intensified throughout the contest of Act II.

Thus the royal pomp and command of the court scene is disrupted with a breathtaking effect of dramatic shock by Kent's blunt and reckless "What woulds't thou do, old man?"; and then refracted and diminished in the domestic tattle between Goneril and Regan which immediately follows it:

GONERIL. . . . he always lov'd our sister most; and with what poor judgment he hath now cast her off appears too grossly.

REGAN. 'Tis the infirmity of his age; yet he hath ever but slenderly known himself.

[17] S. T. Coleridge, *Shakespearean Criticism*, ed. T. M. Raysor (London: J. M. Dernt, 1960), p. 56.

273

GONERIL. The best and soundest of his time hath been but rash; then must we look from his age, to receive not alone the imperfections of long engraffed condition, but therewithal the unruly waywardness that infirm and choleric years bring with them.

(1.i.290-299)

Goneril's account of elderly tantrums,

> Idle old man,
> That still would manage those authorities
> That he hath given away! Now, by my life,
> Old fools are babes again, and must be us'd
> With checks as flatteries, when they are seen abus'd.

(1.iii.17-21)

is indeed countered by Kent's statement of the authority in Lear's countenance which he would fain call master. But this in turn is followed by the fool's parody of parental abdication and the fool's clairvoyance:

I have used it, Nuncle, e'er since thou mad'st thy daughters thy mothers; for when thou gav'st them the rod and put'st down thine own breeches,

> Then they for sudden joy did weep,
> And I for sorrow sung,
> That such a king should play bo-peep
> And go the fools among.

(1.iv.179-185)

In the subplot the theme is repeated in Edmund's vein, "I have heard him oft maintain it to be fit that, sons at perfect age, and fathers declin'd, the father should be as ward to the son, and the son manage his revenue" (1.ii.71-74), and demonstrated in the staging of his imposture. What we are meant to perceive is the nature of Lear's tragic distinction—

the tremendous force, power, and energy of the character (to which Gloucester is the frailer foil) precisely as it is in disproportion to the natural infirmity of his age.

The fourth scene brings to a close a tragic exposition that for immediacy, profundity, and address it is impossible to overpraise. If the fool is meaning to distract Lear's attention from his troubles, he chooses a curious way of doing so, since every word of his crazy common sense harps relentlessly upon the latter's daughters and his folly. Lear is abstracted, intermittently attending, uttering in snatches that which is beating in his mind: "I did her wrong." "I will forget my nature. To take 't again perforce!" "Monster ingratitude!" The strange duet counterpoints the two voices: the voice of worldly wisdom, which knows that a snail has a house to put's head in, and the voice of the soul struggling with its knowledge of guilt and passion, struggling to keep above the water in which it is drowning. "O! let me not be mad, not mad, sweet heaven" registers Lear's desperation before the force of the inner torment that is threatening to destroy him.

The analogical structuring of the scenes in Act II frames and directs our perception of the dilemma Lear now faces, while their extraordinarily dramatic expressiveness resides, as in the last scene of Act I, in the erratic incompleteness of Lear's speech, the shifts and lacunae through which we must infer the inner mind. The spontaneous utterances, half-expressed, half-stated, arise as from immense depths, as if forced to the surface by relentless pressure.

Lear's confrontation with his daughters is presented in II.iv; it is cunningly prefaced, both by the subplot scenes of Edmund's practice upon his father, and by the set-to between Kent and the lackey Oswald. In the former Edmund's evil appears good to Gloucester and is rewarded as "virtue and obedience" by Cornwall, so that a parallel is established with the first act; in the latter faithful Kent, outspoken servant of

his master's true interests, outfaces the superserviceable fini-
cal halcyon rogue who does his mistress doubtful service, and
is recompensed with the stocks for his pains. What we have
then in Act II is the inversion of values which places virtue
and true service in the stocks and rewards villainy and venality with honors. Edgar's flight and disguise as Poor Tom suggests the totality of the regime of deception by the extremity
of the counterdeception taken to escape it. It also, in its deliberate stripping of identity—"Edgar I nothing am"—adum-
brates Lear's later flight. Such is the preparation for the arrival
of Lear at Gloucester's house, where Kent in the stocks provides new confirmation of the abatement of kindness which
he has already perceived.

Lear's attempts to be patient, forbearing, considerate, clash-
ing with those imperious habits of command which express
themselves in his scornful dismissal of Cornwall's excuses as
"mere fetches" and in the incredulity of "They durst not
do't; / They could not, would not do't; 'tis worse than
murther, / To do upon respect such violent outrage" (II.iv.
22-24) are, as Coleridge noted, extremely pathetic. But they
suggest less the mere pathos of a newly chastened spirit than
the tension of a man in the grip of a terrible anxiety. "Thou
shalt have as many dolors for thy daughters as thou cans't tell
in a year" the fool acidly informs him. And Lear's "O! how
this mother swells up toward my heart; / Hysterica passio!
down, thou climbing sorrow!" (II.iv.56-57) renders the chok-
ing fear physically apprehensible. It is surely the panic terror
of the doubt, of the suspicion that the fool speaks truly, the
desperate will to believe well of his one remaining daughter,
that struggles with indignation at the treatment of his servant—a calculated affront to himself as he rightly perceives.

This preliminary trial of strength reaches a preliminary
climax in the peremptory command which the effrontery of
the Duke's "fiery quality" strikes upon the flint of his pride:

> Give me my servant forth.
> Go tell the Duke and's wife I'd speak with them,
> Now, presently: bid them come forth and hear me,
> Or at their chamber-door I'll beat the drum
> Till it cry sleep to death.
> (II.iv.115-119)

But "Oh me, my rising heart" serves as a reminder of the inner turmoil—the pressure of grief, pain, and anxiety which he must subdue, must control, if it is not to break out and render him incapable of maintaining himself at all. He turns to Regan upon her entrance as to the source of all comfort, almost as a child turns to its mother with a tale of injury sustained; and ironically, much in the manner of a hortatory parent, she produces her injunction and her demand:

> O, sir! you are old;
> Nature in you stands on the very verge
> Of her confine: you should be rul'd, and led
> By some discretion that discerns your state
> Better than you yourself. Therefore I pray you
> That to our sister, you do make return;
> Say you have wrong'd her.
> (II.iv.147-153)

This is the first intimation we have of that which constitutes Lear's impossible choice. Return to her? Ask her forgiveness?

> Do you but mark how this becomes the house:
> "Dear daughter, I confess that I am old.
> Age is unnecessary: on my knees I beg
> That you'll vouchsafe me raiment, bed, and food."
> (II.iv.154-157)

The scathing bitter sarcasm of his mock contrition exposes the ignominy of her expectation that he behave like a scolded child; "to be slave and sumpter / To this detested groom" measures the infamy of the demand that he go down upon his knees to beg a pittance and a pension to keep base life afoot. But this pride of Lear's, this stubborn claim to dignity and independence, is to be further tested. At present he still has the hope that Regan's tender-hefted nature will not give her o'er to harshness; that her eyes will comfort and not burn:

> 'Tis not in thee
> To grudge my pleasures, to cut off my train,
> To bandy hasty words, to scant my sizes,
> And, in conclusion to oppose the bolt
> Against my coming in.
>
> (II.iv.175-179)

The further curses that he hurls at Goneril's head ward off the fool's wise knowledge of her identity with her sister in marble-heartedness. That she is different is an illusion presently to be shattered, but his perception of what is at issue is no illusion.

As Goneril enters he prays for the assistance not of Regan but of the heavens themselves; and not as distant symbols of cosmic law but as beings whose sway has become inexplicably questionable:

> O Heavens,
> If you do love old men, if your sweet sway
> Allow obedience, if you yourselves are old,
> Make it your cause; send down and take my part!
>
> (II.iv.191-194)

That he sees himself as thus universally representative, the dignity due to his age a fundamental human claim, is the mark of a largeness of spirit unshared by many of his critics who find his "concern with dignity and authority when out of office" no more than "a testy obsession."[18] His appeal calls

[18] J. Danby, *Shakespeare's Doctrine of Nature* (London: Faber, 1949), p. 176.

forth the brutality of "All's not offense that indiscretion finds / And dotage terms so" (II.iv.198-199) and "I pray you, father, being weak, seem so" (II.iv.203). The infamous pair harp incessantly upon his age, Regan taking courage from her bolder sister; and their nagging rivets attention upon the material fact of Lear's eighty years, unnecessary in their scheme of things but utterly central for the discarded father. Lear is doubly threatened: from without by the ruthless obdurate self-seekers, and from within by the tumult of grief and passion which rises to engulf him, threatens to reduce him to helpless sobbing at their feet, to actual physical break-down. Goneril's entrance revives the *casus belli* of the fifty followers and adds a further twist to the knife at Lear's heart. The contest enters its third round, and the breaking point, signaled by the flight into the storm and the cry "O fool! I shall go mad," concludes it.

The calculated resemblance of this bargaining scene to the first court scene has of course invariably been noted. In the opening scene, it is said, Lear put a kingdom up for auction; now he is being paid in his own coin. As he was then, so he is now: as blind as he ever was to the difference between price and value; as ready as he ever was to measure spirit by matter. And the conclusion often drawn is that his analysis of the economics of conspicuous consumption that follows, in which he acknowledges his great need for a long-suffering patience, represents the humiliation which he deserves and which was necessary to bring him to his senses. That so far from bringing him to his senses it in fact causes him to go out of his mind is a matter for which this view of events offers no explanation save indeed the disciplinary affliction which is regularly invoked by the Bildadian tribe. The power-ful point of the ghastly resemblance between the two scenes is precisely that it is a resemblance and not an identity. The two episodes are mirror-images of division, and as the scene progresses the emerging perception of apparent resemblance, which conceals an utter contradiction, represents the structure of Lear's dawning recognition.

The face that Lear sees in the mirror is indeed his own. When he had power he demanded professions of love and denied Cordelia her dowry when she was too proud to comply. Now that they are in power they demand professions of contrition, demand that he beg for his pittance and when, like his daughter, he is too proud to comply, deny him his servants, emblem, and means of independent subsistence. "I gave you all" he stutters, to be brought up short with the ice of "And in good time you gave it."

As his responses to these assaults change from outrage and incredulity through the recollected anguish of the daughters' lovelessness—a pain as intolerable as an embossed carbuncle in his flesh—through the poignant attempt to abjure magistracy:

> But I'll not chide thee;
> Let shame come when it will, I do not call it;
> I do not bid the thunder-bearer shoot,
> Nor tell tales of thee to high-judging Jove.
> Mend when thou canst; be better at thy leisure. . . .
>
> (II.iv.227-231)

we are enabled to perceive what Lear perceives and more than he perceives. The face that he sees in the mirror is his own, but he watches in mounting horror as his own features are transformed to monstrous caricature before his eyes. For it is a demonic parody that the distorting mirror produces. What was well-intentioned error on his part in the first scene is cunning malice on their part in this. He took words for deeds, forms for substance, appearances for realities, and interest for disinterest. But for all that he acted in good faith and upon the assumption of good faith in others; intended a just distribution of wealth and power and gave without reservation, save the reservation of a hundred knights for his own needs. The daughters' actions are founded upon a lie (just as their

first protestations of love were a lie) since the accusations
against Lear's retainers mask the lust to take and to get; and
their ruthless greed for deprivation and acquisition has no
purpose (since they are already in possession of their portions
of the kingdom) save the untrammeled enjoyment of total
power. What is exhibited now is not an imperfect human love
and an imperfect human justice but a diabolical negation of
love and justice. The human "all" is now the devil's "nothing," the void, the "O" without a figure which punctuates
the play's rhetoric, the fool's emblem of the consequences of
Lear's folly.

But if this is what the mirror structure reveals to the audience, who are in possession of more knowledge than the protagonist, it can only partially and opaquely be perceived by
Lear. For Lear's agon is with his inner anguish as well as
with his outer adversaries. Lear has listened to the worldly
wisdom the fool has dinned into his ears. He is tasting the
bitter reality of the abdication of power. He who so confidently rewarded good (as he believed) with goods, and punished evil with privations, has glimpsed terrible flaws in the
power of his reason, sovereignty, and justice to represent truth
and order reality. Good and evil have terrifyingly changed
places, as in the fool's logic: "Why, this fellow has banish'd
two on's daughters, and did the third a blessing against his
will" (I.iv.107-109). And that third daughter, cast out without
his blessing, is tormentingly present to his memory. The redoubled anguish and horror threaten to overwhelm him: the
pangs of disprized love, so much more cruelly desolating at
eighty than at eighteen, reflect back dizzyingly upon the love
he denied Cordelia; while the sense of an insufferable wrong
done him reflects the dread of a terrible wrong done by him.
With this tumult of emotion within he must contend while
the daughters beat him down with their cross bids. Caught
like a creature at bay he capitulates, in savage irony, turning
to the daughter he has annihilated with curses, with

Those wicked creatures yet do look well-favored
When others are more wicked; not being the worst
Stands in some rank of praise. I'll go with thee.
Thy fifty yet doth double five-and-twenty,
And thou art twice her love.

(II.iv.258-262)

It is, however, a capitulation from which their relentless vindictiveness as much as his own stubborn pride saves him. The logic of measure for measure, which was the pride of his rationality, is shivered into fragments, for now he knows that "twice her love" is twice times nothing. With Regan's "What need one?" he turns upon them with a mighty repudiation of the calculus of material needs when survival is the question:

O! reason not the need; Our basest beggars
Are in the poorest thing superfluous.
Allow not nature more than nature needs,
Man's life is cheap as beast's. Thou art a lady:
If only to go warm were gorgeous,
Why, nature needs not what thou gorgeous wear'st,
Which scarcely keeps thee warm. But for true need. . . .

(II.iv.266-272)

There's beggary, Lear is saying, in the need that can be reckoned. Man's need lies elsewhere. It is a major insight, which the break in the speech indicates he is not yet ready to assimilate. For if he repudiates their style of rationing, he also repudiates his own. And where shall he find a substitute for the quantum—the principle of measure for measure which has been the staff of his mind?

Lear's unfinished sentence allows us to glimpse the chasm in his mind, from which he draws back with his appeal to the heavens for patience. We bridge his incoherence with a flash of insight, become aware of Lear's awareness. What is articulated in this greatly moving speech is the transformation of Lear into a tragic hero of grander dimension than any who have preceded him. He is as full of grief as age, wretched in both, but he will not surrender to what he now repudiates. The patience that is his true need is no pious long-suffering. The patience that he needs to resist and remain master of the rising insanity—and there is no more literal a cry in Shakespeare than "O fool! I shall go mad"—is the patience precisely not to "bear it tamely." For, it is important to remember, that he could do, as he has already done in his brief rehearsal of capitulation. He could indeed confess his helplessness humbly and abjectly (as Danby actually believes he does),[19] choose comfort, and live upon his daughters' cold charity, saying aye and no at their bidding for his bed and board. "Fool me not so much" is his prayer, and the phrase powerfully suggests that he has seen not only the indignity but the plausibility of this course of compromise, accommodation, acceptance as a relative good (since deserved) of what in his soul he knows is an absolute evil.

Thus his temptation is quiet, the temptation of Yeats's old man. But he can purchase quiet only at a price he cannot pay. To justify the doings of these unnatural hags, even as instrumental, is a violation of justice greater than his own, a trading of justice itself for a monstrous lie. Yet, standing his ground, he is helpless and impotent, and this as a consequence of his own fault and folly. Therefore he beseeches the "noble anger" which will give him strength to protest against a travesty of justice, even though his own justice was deeply at fault and he no longer knows how he shall compute just dealing or where in reason it is to be found. His muttered imprecations of revenge are at the edge of breakdown, a lashing-up of energy at the point of extinction. His age and frailty and the weight of sorrow make themselves felt in the tears it is

[19] Ibid., p. 180.

impossible to control. He has indeed good cause for weeping, but it is the passionate pride of his daughter Cordelia, magnified and intensified, that speaks in "this heart shall break into a hundred thousand flaws / Or e'er I'll weep." He will be destitute, defenseless, and wretched to a degree only matched by the poorest and most despised of his subjects; but his rage as he rushes out into the storm, as he wills his exposure to the elements, to wild nature, to the driven beasts, measures both the anguish and the stature of his spirit. For Lear has made the choice that was impossible.

The total reversal of his status and situation, the complete disintegration of his identity, is what the peripeteia of Act III exhibits. Its seven scenes are symmetrically arranged, a scene upon the heath alternating with an episode from the subplot, with the first scene as an overture to the complex orchestration of voices, themes, and encounters. The gentleman's account of the King in the storm announces the themes which are presently to be writ large. He is

> Contending with the fretful elements;
> Bids the wind blow the earth into the sea,
> Or swell the curled waters 'bove the main,
> That things might change or cease; tears his white hair,
> Which the impetuous blasts, with eyeless rage,
> Catch in their fury, and make nothing of;
> Strives in his little world of man to out-storm
> The to-and-fro-conflicting wind and rain.
> This night, wherein the cub-drawn bear would couch,
> The lion and the belly-pinched wolf
> Keep their fur dry, unbonneted he runs,
> And bids what will take all.

(III.i.4-14)

The description establishes the analogy between the storm in Lear's mind and the storm in nature, which attacks him in its blind fury, makes "nothing" of his white hair. The metaphor personifies the storm's impetuous blasts and naturalizes Lear's conflicting passions, so that it is the composite, mythopoeic figure of a titan—as obdurate as the elements themselves—which presently calls down destruction upon the cosmos. Lear is the storm's alter ego and antagonist in the speech that follows, in which he bids what will take all. As Job cursed the day of his birth and the night of his conception, so Lear calls down the curse of barrenness, now universalized and magnified to include the principle and source of generation itself; only so can the child's offense, grown so monstrous and so general, be removed. But the titanic indictment is shot through with suggestions of confusion, of disorientation, expressed by the tonal range of his epithets. The lightning flashes—vaunt couriers of oak-cleaving thunderbolts—are thought-executing, the thunder all-shaking. But these suggestions of an apocalyptic judgment, an omnipotent governing force, are juxtaposed with suggestions of mere malice, of a grotesque and anarchic demonism: "Rumble thy bellyful! Spit, fire! spout rain!" "Blow, winds, and crack your cheeks!" makes the wind-cherubs at the corners of old maps appear imps of mischief. Thus, in Lear's frenzied fantasy, nature and the heavens have turned as inexplicably inimical as his own daughters, like them under the dual aspect of punishment and malevolence. To the fool's plea, "Good nuncle, in, and ask thy daughters blessing," Lear makes no reply, but the interruption clears his mind and enables him to make a crucial distinction:

> I tax not you, you elements, with unkindness.
> I never gave you kingdom, called you children,
> You owe me no subscription.
>
> (III.ii.16-18)

It is at this point that Lear invokes his prototype—the pattern of all patience—and by a natural transition turns to arraign the agents of affliction not as servile ministers, but as the great gods themselves that keep this dreadful pudder o'er our heads. What was inchoate in his previous imagery of world-destruction is now fully divulged. It is doomsday, the day of absolute justice, that he sees figured in these sheets of fire, these bursts of thunder, these groans of roaring wind and rain; and himself that he sees before the seat of judgment.

> Tremble, thou wretch,
> That hast within thee undivulged crimes
> Unwhipp'd of Justice; hide thee, thou bloody hand,
> Thou perjur'd, and thou simular of virtue
> That art incestuous; caitiff, to pieces shake,
> That under covert and convenient seeming
> Has practiced on man's life; close pent-up guilts,
> Rive your concealing continents and cry
> These dreadful summoners grace. I am a man
> More sinn'd against than sinning.
>
> (III.ii.51-59)

He does not curse God and die; he arraigns what is accursed— that which is within and shall be revealed—inner truth, inner guilt. But the great effort to achieve clarity and understanding and a just assessment of himself collapses into the renewed sensation of an unimaginable fracture in nature that he cannot encompass, and his physical plight impinges upon his consciousness. From the vision of judgment Lear descends to his creatural situation: cold, desolation, tenderness for the faithful being at his side, and the great lesson in relativity which the body teaches:

> My wits begin to turn.
> Come on, my boy. How dost, my boy? Art cold?
> I am cold myself. Where is this straw, my fellow?
> The art of our necessities is strange,
> That can make vile things precious.
>
> (III.ii.67-71)

The alternating scenes which follow combine to present the state of division and disintegration to which the customary frame of things is reduced. In the subplot Edmund seizes his opportunities and climbs into Cornwall's favor, making Gloucester co-victim with Lear of a limitless inhumanity, deriding Lear's vision of judgment. The alternating subplot scenes produce such effects of retrospective savage irony throughout Act III, casting upon the scenes of the agony on the heath the hideous mockery of a demon's laughter. Yet there is a principle of progression powerfully at work as well. Evil, it seems, contains its own divisive principle. There is constant rumor of division among the dukes and of the French army approaching the gates of the kingdom. Good, on the other hand, not only remains steadfast, in the dogged faithfulness of Kent and the fool, but proliferates. Both these immanent human possibilities are actualized in the climactic scene of Act III, where Gloucester is blinded and Cornwall's servants rebel against their master.

In the main scenes Lear's progress takes the form of decline, of increasing fragmentation, of nightmarish glimpses into the fractured mirrors which pass before his eyes—the fool, Poor Tom, Gloucester. The whole sequence is a tour de force of montage effects, phantasmagoric in their wildly arbitrary juxtapositions, yet cumulatively unified by the obsessive themes: filial ingratitude, punishment, and sorrow; exposure of the truth, of the flesh; these themes make a surface incoherence yield to the impression of a single powerful undercurrent.

The second storm scene reverses the relation of Lear to the storm. It is no longer an adversary but his friend, distracting his attention from the greater malady, the tempest in his mind. He welcomes it, as he welcomes the physic he can derive from it for pomp. The rhythm of the alternating scenes dilates the play's beat, its systole and diastole of passion and compassion. Just as "Strike her young bones, / You taking airs, with lameness!" expanded till it became "Crack Nature's moulds, all germens spill at once," so "I have one part of my heart / That's sorry yet for thee" becomes "Poor naked wretches, whereso'er you are."

At the very moment when Lear, exposed to feel what wretches feel, is contemplating a justice of distribution that shall be based upon creatural weakness rather than creatural strength, Edmund is contemplating his fair deserving—the betrayal of Gloucester which must draw him that which his father loses—no less than all. And it is at this ironic midpoint of the play that Edgar, Lear's fellow refugee, taking the soundings of the deluge, emerges from his hovel to precipitate in Lear the madness that he has dreaded.

> LEAR. What! has his daughters brought him to this pass?
> Couldst thou save nothing? Woulds't thou give 'em all?
>
> (III.iv.63-64)

Now the universe is entirely demonic, presenting to Lear no intimations of a greater order of justice, but only the crazed fragments of Edgar's devil-lore and his daughters' wolfish features.[20]

> Death, traitor! nothing could have subdu'd nature
> To such a lowness but his unkind daughters.
> Is it the fashion that discarded fathers
> Should have thus little mercy on their flesh?
> Judicious punishment! 'twas this flesh begot
> Those pelican daughters.
>
> (III.iv.69-75)

That which was an aberration of nature, a disease in his flesh which he must needs call his, is now the iron law of a

---

[20] H. Skulsky, in an article full of perceptive commentary, draws attention to this obsessively "provincial sympathy," compared with Lear's larger concern with "poor naked wretches"; "*King Lear* and the Meaning of Chaos," *Shakespeare Quarterly*, XVII (Winter 1966).

nature which generates only depravity, evil, obloquy, and pain; Lear's thirst for truth, the will which drove him into the storm to seek it, will be slaked by nothing less than an enactment of the truth that he has discovered, which has been hidden from him till now by the trappings and the lendings, the masks and appurtenances of civilization. He will embrace it and embody it, he will sophisticate it no longer. He will be what he sees that he is—the naked thing itself, sufferer and generator. Tearing at the button he attempts to strip himself of the garment of falsehood:[21]

> Thou wert better in a grave than to answer with thy un-cover'd body this extremity of the skies. Is man no more than this? Consider him well. Thou ow'st the worm no silk, the beast no hide, the sheep no wool, the cat no per-fume. Ha! here's three on's are sophisticated; thou art the thing itself; unaccommodated man is no more but such a poor, bare, forked animal as thou art. Off, off, you lend-ings! Come, unbutton here.
>
> (III.iv.103-112)

The rhetorical figure, the "distributer," articulates yet another distribution, in justice, of "to each his own"; and to man his naked body which is all in sober truth he can say that he possesses. In his mad joy Lear refuses to be parted from his philosopher, his good Athenian, as he is coaxed into the hovel. Edgar's

> Child Rowland to the dark tower came;
> His word was still: Fie, foh, and fum,
> I smell the blood of a British man.
>
> (III.iv.185-187)

which closes the scene suggests, with its garbled fragments of legend, a perspective of desolate and irreversible collapse.

[21] For a good discussion of the contrary implications of clothing symbolism in the Renaissance, see T. Greenfield, "The Clothing Motif in *King Lear*," *Shakespeare Quarterly*, v (Summer 1954).

In the third heath scene in the hovel, Lear's descent into darkness is completed in the key of grotesque parody. The lunatic cacophany of fragments includes his own voice gloatingly invoking hell fire: "To have a thousand with red burning spits / Come hissing in upon 'em" (III.vi.15-16). Still he does not relinquish his quest for justice. He will arraign Goneril in legal form, have the evidence against her brought before the court. But there is no redress. The court is corrupt, the judge false, and the accused escapes. The vision of a day of judgment has dwindled to this abortive travesty in which the fool and the madman are the learned justicers and a jointstool the daughter who kicked the poor King, her father. Completely enclosed now within his own frenzy, he recognizes no one about him and no object possesses its real identity. The jointstool is Goneril, Poor Tom's rags are a Persian fashion, the bench in an outhouse is a curtained royal bed. Nothing is left of Lear's mind as he is borne away to Dover, not even the consolation Edgar can draw from companionship in adversity.

But Lear is spared what the audience must still witness: another form of travesty, not in crazed fantasy but in the play's evil reality of predatory power. The blinding of Gloucester is a fitting culmination to these scenes of sparagmos in Act III, for *King Lear* is a play that stops at nothing. But Lear is, for the moment, preserved from further suffering by his madness, while Gloucester becomes his proxy.

It is generally held that Gloucester is a replica of Lear upon a lower level. Where Lear's original sin, it is held, was of the spirit, his was of the flesh. He therefore suffers the loss of his sight, Lear the loss of his reason. But the logic of levels breaks down at this point, since the attempt to measure the atrocious suffering he undergoes as "worse" or "less" than that of Lear is surely to winnow the wind and to fall into the very dichotomy of spirit and flesh which Lear's discovery of the whole man transcends. In the episode of his blinding Gloucester becomes the play's paradigmatic heroic figure. Not, I would wish to emphasize, because suffering "ennobles" him, as is often held—Shakespeare knew the great truth that suffering ennobles noble natures and debases base natures—but because in and by suffering the inmost being is tested and revealed. The tragic protagonist discovers under duress that in which he believes, and its furthest cost. What "ennobles" both Lear and Gloucester is the choices they make. Lear chooses the heath ("touch me with noble anger"), Gloucester, with terrible irony, the defense of Lear ("Because I would not see thy cruel nails pluck out his poor old eyes"). But Gloucester, basically submissive, save in this one instance, lacks Lear's spirit—the very "noble anger" which many minds of the period were ready to recognize as heroic virtue.[22] Gloucester is a mirror-image of Lear, blindness, past and present, of the eye or the mind, constituting the identity, and the cruder tragic movement consequent upon his low-spiritedness (in which recognition proceeds from affliction, rather than affliction from recognition) constituting the inversion. It is Regan's ferocious sadism, and no spontaneous insight, which adds to his physical injury the terrible knowledge of his injustice to Edgar. Whereas Lear's recognition of error constitutes a major part of his affliction throughout.

In the agony on the heath, justice has been passionately invoked, questioned, sought, challenged, parodied. In the travesty of Gloucester's trial it is finally derided, trodden underfoot, obliterated. And "Turn out that eyeless villain. Throw this slave upon the dunghill" gathers up in its blunt brutality the whole inventory of evil that the third act, in action and

[22] Elton quotes King James, "I love not one that will never bee angry: For as he that is without *Sorrow*, is without *Gladnesse*: so hee that is without *Anger*, is without *Love*"; Bacon, "To seek to extinguish Anger utterly is but a bravery of the Stoics"; and the author of a commentary on Thessalonians who wonders whether those "whom no crosse from God or men can affect to sorrow . . . their patience is it, or rather their blockish senselessnesse?" (pp. 275-276).

image, has presented: dispossession, degradation, obloquy, and the infliction of pain; hunger, nakedness, poverty; the stocks, the rack, the whip; brute existence, belly-pinched, savage, wretched, and repulsive. It is the triumph of the demon, the utter subversion of that human dignity which Lear fought to maintain until his wits turned, and Gloucester defended at the cost of his sight.

Yet there is a defeat of the demon too. In the very moment of triumph the servant who cannot stand by and watch Gloucester's martyrdom turns upon his master. It is an action that speaks louder and reverberates more potently than any of the play's numerous and contradictory statements of belief in ultimate providence which the course of events turns to irony. To these servants the relation of act and consequence is an open question:

> SECOND SERVANT. I'll never care what wickedness I do
>   If this man come to good.
> THIRD SERVANT.   If she live long,
>   And in the end meet the old course of death,
>   Women will all turn monsters.
>
> (III.vii.98-101)

But the service which they render:

>   Hold your hand, my lord!
> I have served you ever since I was a child;
> But better service have I never done you
> Than now to bid you hold.
>
> (III.vii.73-76)

and the flax and white of egg which they apply to Gloucester's bleeding sockets is the voice which opposes Cornwall's satanism. In them speak all the good and faithful servants of Act III, who act as they do out of the spontaneous impulse of the heart, for the hardness or tenderness of which no cause can be found in nature. Few things in Shakespeare are more significant or more moving than this anonymous servant's disinterested, uncalculating, gratuitous act of faith, and it is the first of the miracles ("nothing almost but misery sees miracles") which lighten the darkness of the second half of the play.

Evil concupiscence breeds further contrivance from every contingency; Goneril finds Cornwall's death will serve her purposes, though a widowed sister is a dangerous rival in the competition for Edmund's favors. Nevertheless, in the outcome it is the death of Cornwall that in fact reverses the play's decline into chaos, and stems the tide of evil. The plot from now until the catastrophe works toward restoration. The King's party finds a new champion in Albany, whose conviction that "You are above, you justicers" lends power to his repudiation of his wife; and a succoring power in the army from France. The incriminating letters fall into Edgar's hands and Cordelia returns to England.

Act IV presents an antiphonal dialectic of comfort and despair, of sympathy and isolation, in which pathos—the "art of known and feeling sorrows"—and the irony of situation combine in complex orchestration. Edgar, *régisseur* of consolations, counterpoints Lear's relentless Jobian progress from bad to worse:

> EDGAR. Yet better thus, and known to be contemn'd,
>   Than still contemn'd and flatter'd, to be worst.
>   The lowest and most dejected thing of Fortune,
>   Stands still in esperance, lives not in fear:
>   The lamentable change is from the best;
>   The worst returns to laughter.
>
> (IV.i.1-6)

But his imagination of options is immediately followed by Gloucester's pitiful entrance; his father's sufferings distract his thoughts from himself and produce his acknowledgment of a further vista, perhaps infinite, of the misfortune that can be sympathetically felt by one who is pregnant to good pity:

EDGAR. O gods! Who is 't can say "I am at the worst"?
I am worse than e'er I was . . . the worst is not
So long as we can say "This is the worst."

(IV.i.25-27)

The dialogue between Cordelia and the doctor provides a further gloss upon the theme of remedy. Nature itself produces from its own resources that which is remedial, sustaining, and restorative. Lear, mad as the vexed sea, is crowned with herbs which, the older pharmacopeia tells us, are of "bitter, biting, poisonous, pungent, livid and distracting properties."[23] Cordelia places these emblems of Lear's agony in a pastoral perspective—"the idle weeds that grow / In our sustaining corn"; and implores "All bless'd secrets, / All you unpublish'd virtues of the earth" to spring with her tears. Tears indeed, both those that scald like molten lead, and those that are in very truth wet and flow for another's distress, symbolize and enact the remedies of Act IV—remedies, however, which do no more than counterpoint and subserve the progress into despair of the protagonists.

Gloucester's despair—"As flies to wanton boys, are we to th' gods, / They kill us for their sport" (IV.i.36-37)—issues in the attempt at suicide upon the cliffs of Dover. The episode is anticipatory of Lear's experience in Act IV, and it gives us our bearings upon that experience. Gloucester can be saved by the fabricated miracle which Edgar stages upon the cliffs of Dover: naturalistically, because his recent blindness has led to sensory disorder; figuratively, because his despair is a form of resignation. It is significant that his compassion for poor naked wretches, the concomitant of suffering in the good nature, is an echo of Lear's, but finely distinguished from it not only by the absence of the latter's expressive, vivid imagery, but in that it takes the form of a prayer to the powers that be

---

[23] *Variorum*, p. 257.

for a more righteous distribution, where Lear waited upon no power but his own to show the heavens more just. Gloucester has from the beginning believed in the great opposeless wills, which he is content to think tyrannical, determining men's fortunes in arbitrary mystery. He has never felt Lear's need nor made Lear's imperious demand for an absolute justice made manifest and intelligible. He has never required Lear's God. Therefore he is not compelled to Lear's promethean agon, and his salvation is irremediably undignified. His renunciation of the world is a submission of the will, an escape from that before which his intellect stands defeated. Lear's denunciation of the world is the fearlessly radical and unmitigated conclusion he draws from experience fully faced. Conversely, for Lear is reserved the genuine miracle.

A further reach of Edgar's "worst" is exhibited in the encounter between mad Lear and blind Gloucester. Lear is at first completely withdrawn in the inaccessible fastness of his madness, his lunatic mutterings the broken fragments of memory loosed from its moorings. Recollections of the royal professions of soldiering and hunting mingle with the weird incongruity of a mouse and a piece of toasted cheese. As he dimly recognizes Gloucester—Goneril with a white beard, Goneril who escaped his learned justicers in the previous scene—the past pain throbs like the ache in an amputated limb. What is suggested by the disassociated lucidity which replaces his incoherence has the effect of a pure distillation of experience so tempestuous and profound as to have exhausted all but its simplest and most fundamental elements:

They flattered me like a dog, and told me I had the white hairs in my beard ere the black ones were there. To say "ay" and "no" to everything that I said! "Ay" and "no" too was no good divinity. When the rain came to wet me once and the wind to make me chatter, when the thunder would

not peace at my bidding; there I found 'em, there I smelt
'em out. Go to, they are not men o' their words: they told
me I was everything; 'tis a lie, I am not ague-proof.

(iv.vi.96-108)

All rhetoric is spent; all the grander conceptions drained and
extinguished. Lear's very speech is stripped, so to speak, to
the bone, to the rhythms, idioms, and usages of common
speech, his metaphors, scarcely seeming such, composed of
those elements of bodily experience most universally and immediately available.[24] "The trick of that voice I do well remember," says Gloucester. And it is perhaps not fanciful to
suppose him to be calling attention to the great stylistic
achievement "the trick of that voice" represents. "Ay, every
inch a king," in its inimitable irony and limitless pathos, is
representative of the stylistic device which marks the remainder of the play: all experience presents itself to Lear
under the aspect of the simplest physical sensations, qualities,
and dimensions: "Let me wipe it first; it smells of mortality"
(iv.vi.135). In his bewildered return to sanity he seeks assurance of his condition in a pinprick. Later with Cordelia,
unsure of time, place, or identity, he will ask "Be these tears
wet?" finding in unmediated sensory reality the only assurance and guarantee of authentic truth. This simplicity plays a
subtle role in the articulation of the tragic experience of self-
discovery, but it is so incomparably moving in itself that one
is led to speculate whether this is not Shakespeare's master
stroke in the mode of encounter between high and low that
is so marked a feature of his fourth acts. He has absorbed
into the figure of his great King himself the perspective of
common humanity, which in other tragedies is given its
separate personae.

[24] The best account of the way the expressiveness of common speech
is exploited in *King Lear* is in W. Nowottny, "Some Aspects of the
Style of *King Lear*," *Shakespeare Studies*, xiii (1960), and "Lear's
Questions," *Shakespeare Studies*, x (1957).

"Every inch a king" restores to Lear's mind a further measure of lucidity. He will enact again a king's prerogative to pardon and condemn, and so he launches into yet another of the parodies in the play's rich gamut of such parodies:

When I do stare, see how the subject quakes.
I pardon that man's life. What was thy cause?
Adultery?
Thou shalt not die: die for adultery! No:
The wren goes to 't and the small gilded fly
Does lecher in my sight.
Let copulation thrive; for Gloucester's bastard son
Was kinder to his father than my daughters
Got 'tween the lawful sheets. To 't, luxury pell-mell!
For I lack soldiers. Behold yond simp'ring dame,
Whose face between her forks presages snow;
That minces virtue, and does shake the head
To hear of pleasure's name;
The fitchew nor the soil'd horse, goes to 't
With a more riotous appetite.
Down from the waist they are Centaurs,
Though women all above:
But to the girdle do the Gods inherit,
Beneath is all the fiend's: there's hell, there's darkness,
There is the sulphurous pit-burning, scalding,
Stench, consumption; fie, fie, fie! pah, pah!
Give me an ounce of civet; good apothecary,
To sweeten my imagination.
There's money for thee.

(IV.vi.111-134)

Lear has sought love and he has sought justice with all the energy and passion of his nature. Now he abandons the enterprise, for he can discover no transcendent value in the name of which to pardon or condemn. Once the wolf, the tiger, the kite were metaphors for aberration. Now Lear's view is larger. Now man's animal nature is all his nature and no man shall die for the coital function he shares with the fly, the fitchew, and the horse. Love is copulation; justice a dog in office; measure for measure handy-dandy. Robes and furred gowns hide all, and all is vice, interchangeably venal and vene-real, the bribe and the brothel; the obscene concupiscence masked by the mincing virtue of women; the lust which wields the beadle's whip. Still obsessively tearing off his clothes, he prefers, like Diogenes, the minimal dignity of nakedness to the fulsome lie with which accommodated man covers and compounds the lechery and savagery of the in-nocent contemptible beasts. All that is left of the old passion, the old indignation, is the repulsion aroused by the thought of the face between the forks of the simp'ring dame (the fig-ure of woman which has taken the place of the lost Cordelia in his imagination), nausea at the universal stench and cor-ruption, and the harsh sardonic mirth with which he bids Gloucester get him glass eyes like a scurvy politician and seems to see the things he does not.

It is all, indubitably, true enough. But it is not the whole truth. It is not even the limited local truth, for Gloucester's bastard son was not kinder to his father than Lear's lawfully begotten daughters. But the fool is gone, Kent is hidden in his disguise, Cordelia lost; nowhere in life is there a source of sweetness, enchantment, or pleasure. He has been cut to the brains. "I'll not love" is an abdication made out of despair —perfect antithesis to his original abdication made in confi-dent expectation of continued order. "None does offend, none I say, none" is forbearance founded upon an abyss. If this black despondency were all that these speeches express, they would still shake our hearts with the silent compassion that is their due. It is an old man's bitter cynicism that we hear, but it is phrased with splendor; with the fearless energy, rigor, and candor of an intellect which will not merely sub-mit to the way the world goes, content with agnosticism. His nihilism is invested with a transcendent courage, an indomitable will to face realities, to have no truck with the admirable evasions of whoremaster man, who lays his goatish disposition on the charge of a star. It is this that measures the stature of the figure of Lear, and it is this largeness of spirit which, by a superlative stroke, is contrasted and mingled with the simplicity and humility of the unadorned anagnorisis he has of himself. Lear needs no wry fool's wisdom to inform him of the impotence, the finitude, and the physical bondage of human existence; he is himself the vessel of all ironic knowledge of the great stage of fools to which mankind is born. The scene ends with the collapse again of Lear's lucidity into shattered fragments of impulse: he will kill these sons-in-law; he will die bravely like a smug bridegroom; if he is a king commanding obedience, then there's life in't; they shall get him, if at all, by running.

In the greatest of all Shakespeare's scenes of fourth-act pathos —Lear's awakening in the presence of Cordelia—Lear is granted recovery. No longer distracted, his "ingenious feeling of his huge sorrows" is articulated in an image which catches in its net of associations the entirety of his situation. The wheel of fire is a rack, an inferno, a timeless fixation of anguish in the passage of time. Sun king and promethean Ixion (rebellious father of centaurs) and majesty fallen to be fortune's fool are contained in it; the wheel is laden with connotations from Renaissance iconology,[25] but the scalding tears are Lear's own: a final distillation of his odyssey of suffering, passion, and guilt. Nowhere (save in the very last scene) is Shakespeare's mixture of styles more effective than in the superimposition upon this figure of crucifixion of the frail senex pathos, the touch of irrelevant garrulity in "fourscore and upwards, not an hour more nor less." Lear, thus transfixed in the searing knowledge of his irremediable pain, uncertain of his own condition or even of his own identity, perceives self and

[25] For documentation see Elton, *King Lear*, p. 369, index entry.

other in a single act of compassion: "I should e'en die with pity / To see another thus." And to Lear, thus transfixed, is granted the miracle, the genuine irreducible miracle that Gloucester's factitious salvation foreshadowed: all that has been restorative, healing, and serviceable to man in the second half of the play is summed up and contained in this reconciliation. It is a cancellation of all debt; an atonement and an absolution, freeing the soul from its intolerable burden of guilt.

> Had you not been their father, these white flakes
> Did challenge pity of them. Was this a face
> To be oppos'd against the warring winds?
> To stand against the deep dread-bolted thunder?
> In the most terrible and nimble stroke
> Of quick, cross lightning? to watch—poor perdu!—
> With this thin helm? Mine enemy's dog,
> Though he had bit me, should have stood that night
> Against my fire.
>   (IV.vii.30-38)

The speech articulates that which renders their reunion so dramatically compelling. Its expressive shifts encompass the whole range of feelings which constitute fullness of love between father and daughter. "Poor perdu" marvelously suggests a tenderness more than half maternal in its loving protectiveness, its recognition of Lear's dauntlessness, for the "enfans perdus" to which the phrase refers were the most reckless and intrepid volunteers for military exploits regarded as desperate ventures.[26] And this transcendence of the merely filial (one remembers "according to my bond; no more nor less") is answered by a transcendence of the solely patriarchal (one remembers "Better thou / Hadst not been born than not t' have pleased me better") in Lear's admixture of chivalric deference to a father's possessiveness: "For, as I am a man, I think this lady to be my child Cordelia." All the abused and

[26] *Variorum*, p. 300.

disrupted parental relationships of the play, all the displaced and substituted filial ones (Edmund's relationship to Cornwall, for instance, and the fool's to Lear) here fly together, so to speak, in a scene which affirms the possibility of freedom, harmony, and reciprocity between parent and child. The exchange between them is a reciprocal confession in which both declare themselves in ways which are characteristic of their essential natures: Cordelia's "No cause, no cause," expressive of unspoken inner depths in its very inarticulateness and reticence; and Lear's

> If you have poison for me, I will drink it.
> I know you do not love me; for your sisters
> Have, as I do remember, done me wrong.
> You have some cause, they have not.
>
> (IV.vii.72-75)

expressive of a characteristic resolute candor.

Though momentarily and immediately the pathos of the scene functions to bring sweetness from strength, to affirm not loss but gain, beyond price and beyond computation, nevertheless, since all is lost, in the outcome this unlooked-for and inordinate joy becomes the measure of the gratuitous and inordinate pain which is its obverse. Had Lear died in the despair of his darkened vision, his self-knowledge would have been incomplete. With no more to lose than is already lost, he would have been released from a vision of hell; not bereft of the actuality of a soul in bliss. "You do me wrong," he says, "to take me out of the grave." But he is taken out of the grave to suffer the agony of the loss of that which is of infinite and transcendent value. It is this that makes of the catastrophe of Act v Shakespeare's most unmitigated and quintessential tragic outcome, pitched as it is against an opposing pull toward restoration in the plot itself.

Cordelia's French army is defeated, but the savage intrigue between the sisters has issued in Regan's poisoning; the vigilant Edgar is armed with the incriminating letters. The exposure of the wicked is a matter of time. And it is just this matter of time which provides the catastrophe of the play with its thematic leitmotif. Men are as the time is, says Edmund, as he persuades the Captain to undertake the "man's work" of the hanging. When, wounded to death, with the dead bodies of Regan and Goneril before him, he acknowledges the wheel of nemesis and would reverse what he has set afoot, it is too late. Edgar's stoic naturalism, "Ripeness is all," whereby he rationalizes fortitude, gives way to the realization that he did wrong to withhold from his father the healing joy it was his to confer. Commentators have wrongly, I believe, read Edgar's "ripeness" as referring to the character of the steadfast man to whom increase of spirituality accrues from his capacity patiently to endure.[27] The topos is as stoic as it is Christian in the Renaissance, and its nonprovidential connotations have been fully exploited by Shakespeare's own Jaques, in a play which is in many ways a comic obverse of *Lear*. It is time itself, I believe, that is the referent in Edgar's exhortation. His judgment of the fullness and ripeness of time determines his actions, his disguises, his emergence from concealment, even his view of the poetic justice of the gods: "the dark and vicious place where thee he got / Cost him his eyes." But the repeated blows the catastrophe deals to the optimistic conviction that there is a time for everything culminate in a plethora of special ironies: the entrance of Lear with Cordelia immediately after the prayer to the gods to protect her; "And my poor fool is hang'd" immediately after Albany has announced a providential scheme of retributions and rewards. Edgar is saved just in time by time's vicissitudes from the burden his conscience would have had to bear if Gloucester had died before he revealed himself to him. But an unexpiated guilt for the

[27] Conflicting interpretations of the topic are to be found in E. Wind, *Pagan Mysteries of the Renaissance* (New Haven: Yale Univ. Press, 1958); J. V. Cunningham, *Woe or Wonder* (Denver, Colo.: A. Swallow, 1951), pp. 9-15; and Elton, *King Lear*, pp. 99-106.

fault of unnecessarily drawing out Gloucester's pain, committed in the name of a ripeness he presumed to judge, is expressed, it may be, in the last words of the play: "The weight of this sad time we must obey; / Speak what we feel, not what we ought to say."

Nevertheless Gloucester does die in joy at the miraculous preservation of Edgar. For him, in that moment, all losses are restored and sorrows end. For Lear is reserved the ultimate tragic recognition of his nature as man. Nothing could more intensify the obdurate fact of tragic existence than the tension between the inevitable and the merely untimely in the final outcome. Shakespeare must be supposed with perfect deliberation to have so framed this greatest, because most universal, of his tragic experiments. Suppose, we may imagine him saying, suppose the very worst is to happen after all; the very worst that can be conceived by human terror, after such contest, after such affliction, after such restoration: what then?

Lear expresses his complete conviction of the power of love renewed in reconciliation to redeem all sorrow, to compensate for all loss, to sweeten all adversity, and to confer blessedness upon the most meager and wretched of material conditions. For Lear the fullness of time is identical with the fullness of the spirit:

> Come, let's away to prison:
> We two alone will sing like birds i' th' cage:
> When thou dost ask me blessing, I'll kneel down
> And ask of thee forgiveness: so we'll live,
> And pray, and sing, and tell old tales, and laugh
> At gilded butterflies, and hear poor rogues
> Talk of court news; and we'll talk with them too,
> Who loses and who wins, who's in, who's out;
> And take upon's the mystery of things,
> As if we were God's spies: and we'll wear out,
> In a walled prison, packs and sects of great ones
> That ebb and flow by th' moon. (v.iii.8-19)

But there is a powerful irony in the very conception of the speech. For if birds singing in a cage represent a canonization of love in a hermitage of the blessed, they are nonetheless helpless and captive creatures. Lear's Olympian indifference to the ebb and flow of the power-seekers and the time-servers is an ironic image of the indifference to remote, frail, and petty life of the heavenly powers to whom Lear had thundered his demand for care, concern, and justice. For himself, he possesses all that his soul desires, therefore he has become godlike; Cordelia's sacrifice is the object of the obeissance of the gods themselves; and they, God's spies, are within ecstatic sight of the very mystery of things. So he consigns the world to the devil and embraces eternity. The unreconstructed hubris of the speech, the unextinguishable vitality of the spirit, is the most necessary prelude to the death blow to follow. It is his heroic distinction, this resilience, this capacity for renewal, which has survived unheard-of trials, and risen triumphant like the phoenix from the ash heap of affliction.

But if it is in Lear's imaginative compass to be king of infinite space in an eternity of blessedness, it is Lear's irreversible tragic destiny to suffer the loss of the life upon which that blessedness solely depends, to suffer the finitude of the human condition in the bitterest and highest degree. It is unaccommodated man who enters with his beloved child dead in his arms. In the play's final mirror-image Lear hangs upon Cordelia's lips in death as he did once in life, but all that was concealed from him then has emerged into the clearest light. Cordelia's death hurls Lear back into his Jobian posture of irreconcilable, inconsolable protest against the arbitrary and inexplicable slaughter of innocence.

O! you are men of stones: . . .
Why should a dog, a horse, a rat, have life,
And thou no breath at all? Thou'lt come no more,
Never, never, never, never, never.   (v.iii.257-308)

But for him there is no voice from the whirlwind, no conviction of a Being or a realm of being beyond the absolute temporality of life. Lear's gods are dead, as dead as earth, and Lear is one who knows when one is dead and when one lives. Kent's question "Is this the promised end?" suggests apocalypse but leaves the question ironically open. For the play's last scene is an image, perfect and undeviating, of anguish at the finitude of an existence infinitely desired.

CHAPTER IX

ANTONY AND CLEOPATRA

Antony and Cleopatra, like *Romeo and Juliet*, presents a tragic experience shared by two protagonists; but in *Antony and Cleopatra* the distribution of the experience is asymmetrical, with the entire fifth act devoted to Cleopatra after Antony's death. From the turning point of the play at Actium, Cleopatra is not exhibited, as before, as an opposing principle to Caesar in the struggle for Antony's allegiance, but as Antony's coeval and proxy. She takes over the tragic role after his death and carries the burden of the final phase of catastrophe, with its accompanying recognitions, alone. The two protagonists are throughout notably more distinguished and opposed, more separate, than were Romeo and Juliet; yet neither is instrumental and subordinate to the other, as in the case of the other great tragic pairs: Hamlet and Ophelia, Othello and Desdemona, Macbeth and Lady Macbeth. This mutual pair is composed of individuals differentiated in their entire rhythm of experience: Antony vacillates between Rome and Egypt but he does not change; he becomes more and more what he was. Cleopatra is marble constant, we discover, from the beginning, however devious she appears, but she develops at the end in unexpected and unimagined ways. The synchronization of these two differing velocities within the context of the tragic progress posed an unconscionably exacting problem. One may doubt whether even Shakespeare could have solved it at an earlier stage, for it demands a perfection of control over pace, balance, relative intensities, and the artifices of counterpoint.

Philo's disapprobation of his General's dotage establishes the masculine Roman point of view upon the regrettable affair. The triple pillar of the world has become a strumpet's fool; his Captain's heart the bellows and the fan to cool a gypsy's lust. And indeed for the Roman spectators the lovers' frivolity is immediately displayed. Antony's utter indifference to the ambassadors from Rome evinces his infatuation. But the Roman view is challenged by Antony's defiant assertion of the peerless pleasure, the *summum bonum* in which alone is to be found the nobleness of life. Upon the great stage of Rome and Egypt—his moiety of the world—Antony exhibits his grand passion for all to see, striking the highest of notes with his reduction of outer kingdoms to clay and his announcement of his possession of a kingdom of infinite space.

Though the wit-combat which is initiated by her challenge "If it be love indeed, tell me how much" is given the effect of a lyrical reciprocity by the shared progression from beggarly boundaries to a new heaven and a new earth, it is his passion, it is to be noted, not hers, that is articulated by this grand abolition of reckoning. Cleopatra is cool, elusive, and reserved. Antony's headlong declaration of love is met by her taunting provocation:

> Nay, hear them, Antony:
> Fulvia perchance is angry; or who knows
> If the scarce-bearded Caesar have not sent
> His powerful mandate to you; "Do this, or this;
> Take in that Kingdom, and enfranchise that;
> Perform 't, or else we damn thee."
>
> (I.i.19-24)

and followed by a realistic and self-tormenting aside:

> Excellent falsehood!
> Why did he marry Fulvia, and not love her?
> I'll seem the fool I am not.
>
> (I.i.40-42)

This first encounter reveals them, in a brilliant extension of the dramaturgy of the play within the play, in the posture which contains their entire inner drama. For it is immediately apparent that their public performance, the very zest of the display, masks a covert struggle, an intensely serious hide-and-seek. We are to perceive that Cleopatra's taunts disguise anxiety as much as they flaunt power. Her final ploy— "Antony / Will be himself"—is suavely diplomatic and impenetrably opaque; his reply evades the irony but leaves the unasked question of what Antony will be unanswered. It is the question, however, which closes the scene. He peremptorily dismisses the ambassador and carries off his wrangling Queen, completely absorbed in his anticipation of the pleasures of her company; his Roman friends perceive in this a lapse from an ideal self:

> Sir, sometimes, when he is not Antony,
> He comes too short of that great property
> Which still should go with Antony.
>
> (1.i.57-59)

And the audience has become aware of the predicament that each of the pair poses for the other.

Antony's tragic distinction is his capacity to serve as the repository of both Rome's and Egypt's values. He is as preeminent in the man's world of contest as he is in the woman's world of love. He is a universal cynosure: a glass of fashion and a mold of form—observed of all observers—upon a scale so cosmopolitan as to reduce the court of Denmark to a province in the realm of values. The legend of Rome's grandeur rests upon him, not upon Octavius, for its authentication; and by the same token the enkindling vision of "the nobleness of life" requires his validation of the value claimed for it. In association with Antony both Rome and Egypt partake of the heroic, both are enhanced by his commitment to them.

If Scene i exhibits his commitment to Egypt, it is no later than Scene ii that we hear of the Roman thought that has struck him, and hear the Roman thought itself, in Philo's own idiom:

> O then we bring forth weeds,
> When our quick minds lie still, and our ills told us
> Is as our earing. . . .
> These strong Egyptian fetters I must break,
> Or lose myself in dotage.
>
> (I.ii.106-108, 113-114)

The defiant and unrepentant defection from empire, the grand assertion of the value of passion are, it seems, more precarious than we could have suspected. If Cleopatra is enigmatic, he is divided. The play's predicament thus presents a situation fraught with multiple uncertainties, and therefore entailing multiple expectations. What Cleopatra means, and means to him, is Antony's problem; what he will do, which Antony is his true self, which of his legends becomes him, and which he will become, is hers. And whether Rome is to be preferred to Egypt or Egypt to Rome is the question that will become, during the course of the play, as much an impossible choice for the audience as it is for Antony himself.

The fluctuating shifts of scene which are so marked a feature of the play turn out upon inspection to conform to a very carefully planned design. Act I takes place in Egypt with one Roman scene; Act II in Rome, with one Egyptian scene; Act III is symmetrically divided between Rome and Egypt (if we are willing to regard the Ventidius episode as "Roman"), with one Egyptian scene in the Roman part and one Roman scene in the Egyptian part. Acts IV and V are Egyptian, but the battle scenes bring the Romans to Egypt, and Enobarbus, inwardly divided, shuttles us between the two camps, as did the unfortunate pawn Octavia in the first part of the play, and Dolabella with his proposal from Caesar to Cleopatra in

Act v. This perpetual oscillation of the play between its two milieus provides for continual shifts in point of view and gives rise to the "differing and apparently irreconcilable evaluations of the central experience"[1] which the play embodies. It would appear to be supererogatory to require (as a recent study does)[2] the special category of "problem play" to account for this feature, since it is no more than the most immediate and thoroughly dramatic way of representing Antony's predicament and the psychomachia that Shakespeare has chosen to dramatize. If Antony could reconcile himself to one or other of the irreconcilable evaluations of life that make their claim upon him, he would solve his conflict and cease to be dramatizable as a man played upon by conflicting impulses, tempted in opposite directions. If he could either let Rome in Tiber melt, or break his strong Egyptian fetters, he would presumably be saved either from the ruin, defeat, and disgrace which attend his political collapse, or the blunders and losses which attend his pursuit of his love. But, as has been frequently noted, Antony is no more a candidate for idyllic retirement to a cottage in the country than he is capable of subduing his dolphin nature entirely to the stony exigencies of *Realpolitik*. The very dramaturgy is thus expressive of his conflict.

And it is expressive in a very particular way. If we are offered the "alternative heroisms of stone and water," in the words of a perceptive recent critic,[3] we are offered them not simply

[1] L. C. Knights, *Some Shakespearean Themes* (London: Chatto, 1959), p. 144. Cf. "the balancing of points of view in the challenge and response of argument is the inner logic or dialectic of the tragic form as it appears in fully developed drama"; R. B. Sewall, *The Vision of Tragedy* (New Haven: Yale Univ. Press, 1959), p. 14.

[2] E. Schanzer, *The Problem Plays of Shakespeare* (London: Routledge, 1963).

[3] G. K. Hunter, "The Last Tragic Heroes," in *Later Shakespeare*, ed. J. R. Brown and B. Harris, Stratford-upon-Avon Studies, VIII (London: Edward Arnold, 1966), 25. See also R. Ornstein's admirable

but dialectically contrasted, each alternately enhanced and degraded. The opposing principles of monumentality and life-flow, of stone and blood or tears, which organized so much of the imagery of *Julius Caesar*, are here developed to their furthest reach through a marvelous opulence and fertility of metaphorical invention. The monumental pillars and arches of empire, when seen heroically, are set against the dissipation and deliquescence of Old Nile; the latter, romantically enhanced, suggests a beneficent and fertile life, as opposed to the cold petrifaction that Cleopatra envisages in her avowal of constancy in III.xiii. Antony's decision to fight at sea delivers him to the mutable feminine element itself, but the marble constancy of the Egyptian Queen emerges to confound the fluent Roman faithlessness. It is for this reason that no interpretation or judgment of the play based upon a moral position, whether condemnatory or exonerating of the grand passion it portrays, will fail to find sufficient evidence in the text. But the effect of the chiastic interchange of these infinitely varied metaphors for life and death, flux and permanence, reality and unreality (which articulate the most complex acts of evaluation) is to keep the mind in a state of acute and sustained suspense while the tragic actualization takes place upon the stage. Antony, Bradley says, "breaks away from Cleopatra without any strenuous conflict," though Shakespeare possesses a "matchless power of depicting an inward struggle."[4] There are indeed virtually no soliloquies (until the third act) to focus and channel our perceptions through the point of view of a single psyche. But what in fact happens is that the impossible choice from which the tragedy springs is reproduced, upon a higher level of generality and in the imagination of the audience, by the expressive structure of oscillation with its

---

"The Ethic of the Imagination: Love and Art in *Antony and Cleopatra*" in the same volume.

[4] *Oxford Lectures on Poetry* (London: Macmillan, 1965), p. 286.

dialectic of contraries. It is this that creates the play's special effect of distance and perspective.

The first dialogue with Enobarbus mirrors the predicament of Antony. Enobarbus, who has just been tumbling upon the beds of Ptolemy (at least conversationally), is in as mocking a vein with Antony as he was when, deliberately mistaking Cleopatra for Antony, he implied the latter's total loss of manhood. To Antony's announcement that they must leave Egypt, he responds, "Why, then we kill all our women"; certainly Cleopatra, "catching but the least noise of this, dies instantly. I have seen her die twenty times upon far poorer moment: I do think there is mettle in death, which commits some loving act upon her, she hath such a celerity in dying" (I.ii.137-142). His irony is transparent, making the burlesque *Liebestod* convey the idea that her excessive "dying" (in all the Elizabethan senses) is thoroughly calculated. Antony concurs with the tenor of the irony—"She is cunning past man's thought"—and at this point Enobarbus appears to reverse his previous position entirely. "Alack, sir, no, her passions are made of nothing but the finest part of pure love. We cannot call her winds and waters sighs and tears; they are greater storms and tempests than almanacs can report. This cannot be cunning in her; if it be, she makes a shower of rain as well as Jove" (I.ii.144-149). If Cleopatra's sighs and tears mean not cunning but true love—intensity of feeling, depth of devotion, a sovereign commitment of the whole soul—then there is good reason for his "alack." For if this is what she is, and no mere scheming courtesan, then Antony's danger is formidable indeed. Enobarbus does not relinquish the mode of comic hyperbole, and therefore we are free to interpret his "pure love" also as ironical. He is saying so much more than can reasonably be affirmed that he must mean less. And less than "the finest part of pure love" is no other than a not so fine part of a not so pure love. Again, his reply to Antony's "Would I had never seen her!" is impenetrably ambiguous.

What he says is: "Oh sir, you had then left unseen a wonderful piece of work, which not to have been blest withal, would have discredited your travel" (I.ii.151-153). His comment mocks Antony as naïve, a wide-eyed Sir Peregrine gaping at the Taj Mahal. But it is also a subtle offer to Antony of an escape-hatch against passion through the cynicism of a man of the world.

What then does Enobarbus mean? Is he another Philo, subtler, more sophisticated, dissimulating his pain at Antony's decline by an exaggerated quasi-recognition of the great attractions of the Egyptian harlot? Is he himself, against his will perhaps, bewitched by her sensual magic? Could he possibly be resorting to sheer brutal flat irony, asserting in order to deny? What is professed and what is held in reservation is precisely what Enobarbus' irony conceals, so that speculation is carried into the participating mind of the audience, where the rival possibilities continue to reverberate. Whether Antony has sold and continues to sell his birthright for a mess of pottage, whether Cleopatra is Circe or Isis, whether his grand asseverations of value are a vanity of vanities, are questions the audience is forced to ask with the intensity of a participant in the immediate action.

The scene which exhibits Cleopatra's predicament can be compared only with the quarrel scene between Brutus and Cassius for the spontaneity of action and reaction and for its mastery of the interplay between surface and depth. Cleopatra's predicament is of an entirely different order from Antony's. She is faced with his decision to return to Rome; she must accommodate to her possibilities, plan her course, reveal or not reveal her feelings. Plans of campaign, in advance, she does not lack:

> If you find him sad,
> Say I am dancing; if in mirth, report
> That I am sudden sick. (I.iii.3-5)

313

Like Falstaff she is "the impresario of her own performance," guileful with unabashed zest. Her exchange with Charmian upon the subject of lovers, and her curt dismissal of Charmian's caveat against caprice, "Thou teachest like a fool: the way to lose him," place Cleopatra's "becomings" squarely where they belong—among the tricky stratagems of coquetry played for the effect they can produce. But in the manner of the antic disposition of yet another, more complex impresario of his own performance, Cleopatra's performance indirectly discloses the inner truth that gives rise to the artifice.

Her first (apparent) victory is immediate. Antony, who has come to break the news to her, is put on the defensive before he has time to broach the matter of Fulvia's death, and rendered speechless by her scornful tirade against the power of the wife and his faithlessness to her. What she is up to is obvious. She is afraid of his leaving and is therefore making every effort to hold him, both by the contempt she pours upon his marital fidelity and by her appeal to the power of the love they have shared and the pledges he has made. And her speech is hauntingly expressive of the emotions she is thus hoping to exploit:

> ... when you sued staying,
> Then was the time for words: no going then;
> Eternity was in our lips, and eyes,
> Bliss in our brows' bent; none our parts so poor,
> But was a race of heaven. They are so still,
> Or thou, the greatest soldier of the world,
> Art turn'd the greatest liar.
>
> (I.iii.33-39)

The crux of the scene occurs when Antony finally manages to break his news and ends his explanation of the broils in Rome with the conciliatory "And that which most with you should safe my going, / Is Fulvia's death" (I.iii.55-56). Up to this point the scene has exploited the effect of dramatic irony:

the audience, aware of Fulvia's death, has been in possession of more knowledge than Cleopatra. With her reply, however, "Though age from folly could not give me freedom, / It does from childishness. Can Fulvia die?" (1.iii.57-58) the enigmatic ellipsis in the speech inverts the dramatic irony and puts the audience at a disadvantage. The audience is forced to interpret, to plunge below the superficial feigning in order to infer what is submerged—what is partly hidden and partly revealed by the abrupt transitions.

The two main alternatives that have been proposed as explanations of these puzzling lines are these: the shock of the news has sobered her, and what she wishes to express is simply a decent regret; "folly" describes her love for Antony and the excesses she recognizes its having brought her to, and "Can Fulvia die?" is an expression of incredulous shock and distress. A second explanation is that she contemptuously refuses to believe him, dismissing as "childishness" the folly of believing yet another excuse. But this would make nonsense of the question "Can Fulvia die?" since Cleopatra could hardly profess astonishment or incredulity at the fact that Fulvia shares the fate of common mortality. What follows is consonant with neither of these readings unless we regard the scene as an entirely capricious zigzag of feline pouncings and pettings—in which case either reading would serve and the choice between them would be a matter of indifference, though it remains hardly reasonable to suppose that Cleopatra would seriously believe Antony to have intended so gross a lie. If, however, we are alert to the emotional rhythm of the scene running beneath and giving rise to its surface moves, we will be enabled to perceive the way in which the playacting both expresses and masks the emotion which induces it. The desperate hope that he may after all stay is checked by the news of Fulvia's death. I would interpret the puzzling lines as a response to a blunder on Antony's part. In his delivery of this news he has been guilty of a piece of masculine clumsi-

ness. For "that which most with you should safe my going"
must surely act as a powerful irritant upon Cleopatra's already
exacerbated pride. That she should be "safe" only because
Fulvia is dead—Fulvia the married woman—goes against the
whole thrust of her accusation, which has presented his defection as high treason against the grandest and most commanding of passions, against the lovers' eternity in which all
comings and goings are consumed. Her first reaction then is
sheer irritation at his obtuseness, at his getting the pitch and
level of their relationship so wrong and so placing her under
the imputation of being a rival to the despised Fulvia for his
favors. It is this umbrage which expresses itself in an im-
pulsively contemptuous hauteur. This impulse once expressed
and therefore spent, however, she then, and only then, fully
takes in the import of what he has told her. "Can Fulvia
die?" with, I take it, the emphasis almost equally on each
of the words, registers her absorption of so radical a change
in his and her circumstances, a change which, while it clearly
necessitates a revision of her whole strategy, also produces a
new set of feelings with which she must herself contend.

Antony's position is extremely awkward. He has come after
all to part from her, and she is not making it easy. He
blunders again with the supererogatory "at the last, best, /
See when and where she died." In his anxiety to appease her he is
guilty of gross callousness, and thus initiates a new arc of
feeling in Cleopatra. His callousness wounds her, particularly
since she has now no further hope that he will not return
to Rome. She exploits his blunder to wound him, but her
self-identification with Fulvia makes clear the nature of her
own very real pain:

> O most false love!
> Where be the sacred vials thou should'st fill
> With sorrowful water? Now I see, I see,
> In Fulvia's death, how mine receiv'd shall be.
>
> (1.iii.62-65)

And this pain increases in proportion as Antony remains reserved, distant, and formal. Now the great need of her nature is to provoke an emotional response from him; any emotional response. She is suffering, he is remote and formal, speaking of being her soldier, her servant, of making peace and war at her behest. So she taunts him, going to ever further lengths as her shafts fail in their effect.

On this view of the scene, Cleopatra's "Cut my lace, Charmian, come, / But let it be, I am quickly ill, and well, / So Antony loves" (I.iii.71-73) is not conciliatory ("as long as, or if, Antony loves") but bitterly accusatory ("thus Antony loves"). And her reply to his "My precious queen, forbear, / And give true evidence to his love, which stands / An honourable trial" (I.iii.73-75) brings provocation to danger point:

> So Fulvia told me.
> I prithee turn aside and weep for her,
> Then bid adieu to me, and say the tears
> Belong to Egypt. Good now, play one scene
> Of excellent dissembling, and let it look
> Life perfect honour.   (I.iii.75-79)

His "You'll heat my blood: no more" heats her to still more outrageous mockery, "You can do better yet" and "Still he mends," until she realizes with exhilarated triumph that she has broken through his defenses with her derision of his honor, has caused him, quite simply, to lose his temper. And now that her own chagrin, anger, and pain have found relief, reaction sets in. Now she can allow herself to appease him, to pacify him, to expose her vulnerability in the faltering sincerity of her gesture of submission: "Courteous lord, one word." He remains unappeased, on his dignity, self-righteous against "idleness"; and his reproof draws a magnificent rejoinder, a last word whereby she reestablishes her command over herself and him with a grand and regal gesture of dignified renunciation:

317

> This sweating labour,
> To bear such idleness so near the heart
> As Cleopatra this. But sir, forgive me,
> Since my becomings kill me, when they do not
> Eye well to you. Your honour calls you hence,
> Therefore be deaf to my unpitied folly,
> And all the Gods go with you! Upon your sword
> Sit laurel victory and smooth success
> Be strew'd before your feet!
>
> (1.iii.93-101)

In Cleopatra candor and calculation, the heart's truth and its mask, merge in a dazzling display of agility. And it is this indistinguishability of candor and calculation which is the source of her fascination for Antony, her infinite variety, her immunity to the staling of custom and the withering of age. It is also the source of our understanding of the love of these not young lovers, who are worldly in a unique and special sense. They will not yield to the demand that the world be counted well lost for love because they know that love is the highest pleasure the world itself can offer. Their love is not opposed to the world; on the contrary, the world is their love's royal footstool. It is in the world that they desire to enjoy their love, not in retreat from it. This, I believe, is the deep reason for the preponderance of comedy (genial comedy being essentially an expression of an at-home-ness in the world) in the first part of *Antony and Cleopatra*, as it is the reason for the same preponderance in *Romeo and Juliet*. For they too, honeymoon couple that they were, had not the slightest desire to die to the world, but only to live in it and have "all these woes . . . serve / For sweet discourses in our time to come." The course of the tragedy forces love and the world into irreconcilable opposition, and so puts to the test each partner's inmost allegiance. But even when circumstances make finally clear the impossibility of their earthly Eden, the unfolding progress of the play keeps the issue in suspense to the very end.

The whole of Act I is devoted to setting out the terms of this dilemma. In particular, Scenes iv and v catch in their expressive texture the play's incessant seesaw, its ebb and flow of attraction and repulsion. Caesar's censure of Antony stresses the time's need of him and presents his Alexandrian revels as lascivious wassailing:

> If he fill'd
> His vacancy with his voluptuousness,
> Full surfeits, and the dryness of his bones
> Call on him for 't. But to confound such time,
> That drums him from his sport, and speaks as loud
> As his own state, and ours,—'tis to be chid. . . .
>
> (1.iv.25-30)

But for Cleopatra his absence in Rome is a great gap of time which only mandragora can help her to sleep out.

The transaction of contraries is subtly and ceaselessly maintained. Caesar's

> Let's grant it is not
> Amiss to tumble on the bed of Ptolemy,
> To give a kingdom for a mirth, to sit
> And keep the turn of tippling with a slave,
> To reel the streets at noon, and stand the buffet
> With knaves that smell of sweat. . . .
>
> (1.iv.16-21)

is counterpointed by Cleopatra's "delicious poison," as the pain of parting yields to the compensating joys of reminiscence— her delectable recollections of the greater Caesar, and of Pompey who

Would stand and make his eyes grow in my brow,
There would he anchor his aspect, and die
With looking on his life.

(I.v.32-34)

Mardian's "fierce affection," his "unseminared" thoughts of "what Venus did with Mars," are counterpointed in their turn by Caesar's account of Antony's stoic fortitude:

Thou didst drink
The stale of horses, and the gilded puddle
Which beasts would cough at: thy palate then did deign
The roughest berry, on the rudest hedge;
Yea, like the stag, when snow the pasture sheets,
The barks of trees thou browsed. On the Alps
It is reported thou didst eat strange flesh,
Which some did die to look on. . . .

(I.iv.63-70)

Caesar's disparagement and the horse happy "to bear the weight of Antony" in the thought of which Cleopatra luxuriates by the "arm-gaunt steed" upon which the firm Roman "soberly did mount" in Alexas' sternly martial report.

. . . he fishes, drinks, and wastes
The lamps of night in revel; is not more manlike
Than Cleopatra; nor the queen of Ptolemy
More womanly than he. . . .

(I.iv.4-7)

by Cleopatra's panegyric:

. . . demi-Atlas of this earth, the arm
And burgonet of men.

(I.v.23-24)

The contest between stoic and epicurean, *virtus* and *voluptas*, world mastery and women's maistry, Mars and Venus which is Antony's predicament is set out in Act I so that the current flows toward Rome; while Act II, still by means of

320

subtly related contraries, sets the current of attraction and repulsion, of enhancement and disparagement, flowing in the opposite direction. The seven scenes which culminate with the feast upon Pompey's galley are punctuated by constant thoughts of Egypt, by a turning of all eyes to Egypt, as if Egypt were a loadstone exerting its silent pull through all the flurry of diplomacy, pacts, and political marriages.

The peace which is patched up between Caesar and Antony with Octavia as pledge is an exchange in which Antony is masterful, frank, and disarming. But he has mortgaged his freedom and the scene is immediately followed by the gossip between Enobarbus, Maecenas, and Agrippa in which the latter's avid curiosity concerning the goings-on in Alexandria is more than satisfied by Enobarbus' account of Cleopatra at Cydnus. Enobarbus' account draws expressions of wondering admiration from Agrippa, who significantly fails to reply to Maecenas' highly conditional assessment of the present situation:

> If beauty, wisdom, modesty, can settle
> The heart of Antony, Octavia is
> A blessed lottery to him.
>
> (II.ii.241-243)

The soothsayer who tells Antony's fortune, "If thou dost play with [Caesar] at any game, / Thou art sure to lose," has a juster view of that lottery. His prophecy precipitates in Antony neither alarm nor a defiance of augury nor an attempt to evade the truth which he at once recognizes, but a revulsion of his whole spirit from his Roman enterprise. It is himself that the soothsayer reveals, just as the prophecy of the Egyptian soothsayer in I.ii, submerged in the bawdy hilarity of the harem chatter, revealed the deepest preoccupations, concerns, and needs of Cleopatra's retinue, and so, by indirection, of Cleopatra herself. Antony's soothsayer reveals to him, by revealing Caesar's superior fortune, the real bent and pull of his nature: "I' the east my pleasure lies." Before the act is completed with the finality of "He will to his Egyptian dish again," the progression of scenes effects a further modulation of the Roman perspective, and a subtle transvaluation of values.

Where in Act I Roman duty was presented as sternly splendid and imperial, Egyptian seduction as decadent and effeminate, now the cynical show of camaraderie on Pompey's galley contrasts retrospectively, to its disadvantage, with the sumptuous magnificence of Cleopatra's barge. Of the tawdry bacchanals that celebrate the treaty Caesar himself says "the wild disguise hath almost / Antick'd us all." And indeed the tissue of duplicity, the baiting of the drunken fool Lepidus, the faithless and politic calculations of the world-sharers, the barroom gossip of the lieutenants, all provide a sardonic antimasque to the marvelous spectacle of pleasure and desire composed by Cleopatra at Cydnus. The traps of political alliance are thus opposed to the web of delight which made great Caesar also lay his sword to bed:

> The barge she sat in, like a burnish'd throne
> Burn'd on the water: the poop was beaten gold;
> Purple the sails, and so perfumed that
> The winds were love-sick with them; the oars were silver,
> Which to the tune of flutes kept stroke, and made
> The water which they beat to follow faster,
> As amorous of their strokes. For her own person,
> It beggar'd all description: she did lie
> In her pavilion—cloth of gold, of tissue—
> O'er-picturing that Venus where we see
> The fancy outwork nature. On each side her,
> Stood pretty dimpled boys, like smiling Cupids,
> With divers colour'd fans, whose wind did seem
> To glow the delicate cheeks which they did cool,
> And what they undid did.
>
> (II.ii.191-204)

322

It is a masque of beauty to whose high artifice animated nature itself, its amorous waters and love-sick winds, pays homage. Pompey's galley is a cacophonous exposure of the man's world Antony has set himself to choose; Cleopatra's barge a mythopoeic fantasy of a woman's world in which Eros presides over the delicate harmonies of a marriage of Mars and Venus.

The one Egyptian scene in Act II—the arrival of the messenger at Cleopatra's court with the news of Antony's marriage—provides the subtlest of comments upon the disposition of events. There is irony enough in Cleopatra's thoughts of a caught Antony, a tawny fine fish, pierced by a bended hook; of an Antony whose sword Philippan is flaunted by a woman who has drunk him to bed and put her tires and mantles on him, since the cool expediency of those that trade in war has proved in fact stronger than the moody food of those that trade in love. Cleopatra's confidence in her powers is rudely shocked by the messenger's tidings, as the violence of her attack on him, beyond all bounds of dignity and decorum, shows. But she rallies; she is far indeed from surrender. And by the end of the scene the masculine and feminine experience, Cleopatra's mockery of a pompous masculinity and Caesar's exploitation of his sister's docility, are left in exquisitely ironic balance.

In Act III the Ventidius episode alerts us to a further unromantic aspect of the trade of war, and Enobarbus' sardonic exchanges with Agrippa cast doubt upon all professions of feeling:

AGRIPPA. 'Tis a noble Lepidus.
ENOBARBUS. A very fine one: O, how he loves Caesar!
AGRIPPA. Nay, but how dearly he adores Mark Antony!
ENOBARBUS. Caesar? Why he's the Jupiter of men.
AGRIPPA. What's Antony? The god of Jupiter.
ENOBARBUS. Spake you of Caesar? How, the nonpareil?

AGRIPPA. Oh Antony, O thou Arabian bird!
ENOBARBUS. Would you praise Caesar, say "Caesar," go no
further.
(III.ii.6-13)

AGRIPPA. Why, Enobarbus?
When Antony found Julius Caesar dead,
He cried almost to roaring; and he wept,
When at Philippi he found Brutus slain.
ENOBARBUS. That year, indeed, he was troubled with a rheum;
What willingly he did confound, he wail'd,
Believe 't, till I weep too.
(III.ii.53-59)

Antony is not the initiator of events, but respondent to them.
Offstage he defiantly crowns himself and Cleopatra in response to Pompey's murder, and is a pawn in the Roman
garboils which govern the intrigues of the plot. He is present
only for the brief scene in which, provoked by Cleopatra
("Celerity is never more admir'd, / Than by the negligent")
and dissuaded by his more level-headed officers, he determines
to fight at sea. And this, though it is in fact a crucial decision,
is not expanded or given any weight of detail or presented as
absorbing Antony's attention. Where Shakespeare in previous
tragedies presented both decisions and consequences through
the prism of the protagonist's mind, here the inner drama
remains submerged; the play's sequence of scenes by creating
an ambivalence in the mind of the audience suggests the protagonist's impossible choice.

The peripeteia of Act III, which articulates the reversal of
the lovers' fortunes at the very moment when they are together again, also brings about, for the first time, the direct
utterance of the inner experience which has thus, in subterranean fashion, been gathering to a head. It is the indirections
of Acts I and II that give to Antony's soliloquies in Act III the
effect of an accumulated charge of emotion. The flight from
Actium irrevocably reverses Antony's fortune, giving Caesar

the upper hand in the struggle between them. And the primary recognition to which his reversal of fortune gives rise is indeed the bitter shame of defeated generalship and self-betrayal:

> Hark, the land bids me tread no more upon 't,
> It is asham'd to bear me. Friends, come hither:
> I am so lated in the world that I
> Have lost my way for ever. I have a ship,
> Laden with gold, take that, divide it; fly,
> And make your peace with Caesar.
>
> (III.xi.1-6)

What is impressive about this speech is the absence of blame for Cleopatra, in contrast with the anguish of Antony's lieutenants in the previous scene. In the humiliation of a defeat so shameful they heap abuse upon the ribaudred nag of Egypt; they can hardly find language derogatory enough to express their rage and contempt. She is a cow in June, he a doting mallard, whereas Antony sees himself alone as having "offended reputation, / A most unnoble swerving." He is unqualitied with very shame, so lated in the world that he has lost his way for ever, his very hairs mutinying in the knowledge that he must now, with all his memories of prowess at Philippi

> To the young man send humble treaties, dodge
> And palter in the shifts of lowness, who
> With half the bulk o' the world play'd as I pleas'd,
> Making and marring fortunes.
>
> (III.xi.62-65)

Yet his single intimation of reproach to Cleopatra is

> Egypt, thou knew'st too well,
> My heart was to thy rudder tied by the strings,
> And thou shouldst tow me after.
>
> (III.xi.56-58)

325

And his response to her contrition is the breathtakingly un-conditional

> Fall not a tear, I say, one of them rates
> All that is won and lost: give me a kiss,
> Even this repays me.
> (III.xi.69-71)

Thus what Antony expresses and affirms, despite the shame of the abortive sea fight, is the supremacy of love, cost what it may. In his moment of most acute humiliation, he remains true to his assertion of "the nobleness of life." But the world of power, of command, and of responsibility is paradoxically enhanced by loss. It is not Pompey's galley, but kingdoms and provinces that he has kissed away. It is with half the bulk of the world that he sees himself as having played as he pleased before his captainship was nicked. If he rises superior to his disgrace, both in the transcendence of his renunciation and in the generosity of his command to his followers to leave him and take their better fortunes, the audience, caught in the play's contraries, is nevertheless compelled to wonder whether the scene it is witnessing is an instance of the sublime or of the ridiculous, a thing of beauty or an exhibition of the besotted dotage of which Philo originally spoke. And Caesar's cool dispatch of his ambassador to win Cleopatra from Antony—women being in their best fortunes not strong, and want able to perjure even the ne'er touched vestal (which she certainly is not)—casts a further shadow of doubt over the issue.

It is with immense cunning that Shakespeare has managed the Thidias episode so that it intensifies this corrosive doubt. Thidias' mission is carefully introduced before he delivers his message personally to Cleopatra:

> ANTONY. The Queen shall then have courtesy, so she
> Will yield us up.
> AMBASSADOR.   He says so.

ANTONY.   Let her know't.
To the boy Caesar send this grizzled head,
And he will fill thy wishes to the brim,
With principalities.
CLEOPATRA. That head my lord?

(III.xiii.15-19)

There is nothing to prevent us from responding to Cleopatra's rhetorical question as Antony does, as intimating a depth of tenderness which is inexpressible and which indeed needs no expression since it rests upon the understanding of lovers. His response, the issue of the challenge to single combat, indicates an elated upsurge of confidence in his old powers, induced by the reassurance of Cleopatra's love for his "grizzled head." But, as Enobarbus' acidly worldly-wise comment shows, there is little, if anything, to prevent us taking the opposite view. For Enobarbus implies that Antony is deluded as much in the matter of the love as in the matter of the old powers:

            Yes, like enough! High-battled Caesar will
Unstate his happiness, and be stag'd to th' show
Against a sworder! I see men's judgments are
A parcel of their fortunes, and things outward
Do draw the inward quality after them,
To suffer all alike, that he should dream,
Knowing all measures, the full Caesar will
Answer his emptiness; Caesar thou has subdued
His judgment too.

(III.xiii.29-37)

Enobarbus is clearly predisposed to take the cynical worldly view of the likely effect of Thidias' proposal. He falls into the trap of Caesar—Caesar, who believes neither in vestal virgins nor in the nobleness of life—and interprets the bottomless irony with which Cleopatra parries the ambassador's ploy as confirmation of his worst suspicions:

THIDIAS. He knows that you embrac'd not Antony
   As you did love, but as you fear'd him.
CLEOPATRA.   O!
THIDIAS. The scars upon your honour, therefore he
   Does pity, as constrained blemishes,
   Not as deserv'd.
CLEOPATRA.   He is a god, and knows
   What is most right. Mine honour was not yielded,
   But conquer'd merely.

                                (III.xiii.56-62)

Who indeed can blame Enobarbus for smelling treachery in

   I kiss his conquering hand: tell him, I am prompt
   To lay my crown at 's feet, and there to kneel:
   Tell him, from his all-obeying breath I hear
   The doom of Egypt.

                                  (III.xiii.75-78)

Enobarbus, the spectator at this little play within the play, infers that Cleopatra is already calculating the main chance, preparing to cut her losses, and is not averse to recalling the lover she has previously compared unfavorably to Antony, her man of men, when it is most likely to serve her turn with that lover's nephew. If this were the case, it would make of Antony's subsequent outburst a piece of gross self-delusion and folly, presenting him as concerned over niceties of ceremony and slights to his sensitive honor when in reality he is being thrown over and basely betrayed at this first invitation of the newest master of Rome. Nothing, however, that Antony says indicates that his outburst against Thidias, and against Cleopatra herself, is a consequence of a simple belief that Cleopatra is paltering with Caesar's messenger in order to betray him. It is solely as an intolerable affront to his dignity and their mutual royalty that he chooses to take the incident. But the nature of his ferocious and disproportionate outburst, his violent repudiation of their love as a viciousness and a filth, enables us to perceive with a flash of insight the nature of the pent-up feelings which have created such pressure as to require so extreme a release and relief.

What we perceive is that, despite the grand assertion that one tear "rates / All that is won and lost," the dialectic of contraries which the play has presented has entered corrosively and destructively into Antony's own experience, has set up a counteraction as violent as the initial action of renunciation was intense. If she, his Queen, can so lower herself, what is, after all, the value of this love for which he has sacrificed so much? The pressure of violent, frustrated, pent-up feelings can be measured by the vindictive sadism with which he orders Thidias whipped and rejoices in his power to inflict pain. It is a dismal overthrow of magnanimity, this loss of every vestige of self-command. The oscillation of his tirade between savage self-hatred ("When we in our viciousness grow hard . . . the wise gods seel our eyes, in our own filth drop our clear judgments") and exorbitant self-aggrandizement indicates the degree of his disorientation:

> Moon and stars,
> Whip him. Were 't twenty of the greatest tributaries
> That do acknowledge Caesar, should I find them
> So saucy with the hand of she here,—what's her name
> Since she was Cleopatra? Whip him, fellows,
> Till like a boy you see him cringe his face,
> And whine aloud for mercy. . . .
>
> (III.xiii.95-101)

The strength of the Roman allegiance against which he has struggled reasserts and expresses itself in this conscience-stricken fury, in which he perfectly utters the Roman viewpoint, and savagely punishes himself and her.

If Antony loses his head at this point, however, Cleopatra keeps hers. That she understands him we infer from her "I must stay his time." And when his fury has spent itself, their lovers' pact is reestablished, even before the declaration of her oath of allegiance, in a dialogue which for its pregnant brevity is perhaps unmatched in the play:

> ANTONY. To flatter Caesar, would you mingle eyes
>   With one that ties his points?
> CLEOPATRA.   Not know me yet?
> ANTONY. Cold-hearted toward me?
> CLEOPATRA.   Ah, dear, if it be so,
>   From my cold heart let heaven engender hail,
>   And poison it in the source, and the first stone
>   Drop in my neck: as it determines, so
>   Dissolve my life; the next Caesarion smite,
>   Till by degrees the memory of my womb,
>   Together with my brave Egyptians all,
>   By the discandying of this pelleted storm,
>   Lie graveless, till the flies and gnats of Nile
>   Have buried them for prey!
>
> (III.xiii.156-167)

What Cleopatra is presenting as the consequence of what is to her an inconceivable condition of coldheartedness, to Antony is a complex summation of all that the play's poetry has set in opposition. The poisoned hailstones, dissolving and dissolving life, their dissolution transforming the prolific continuity of the royal line into the rot and decay that will feed only the basest creatures of the teeming Nile, suggests with the vehement force of contradiction the reality of the sensuous, vivid, animating warmth to which she lays claim. Antony is satisfied, and the pendulum-swing of his emotion sets once more toward the feverish elation of one more gaudy night. But the audience is returned to the ambivalence of its own pendulum experience by the ironic echo in "since my lord / Is Antony again, I will be Cleopatra." The words refer to his renewed courage, but they also echo Philo's at the beginning of the play. The questions—what Antony is and what Cleopatra is—which were posed then are temporarily resolved. But the nature of the claims upon Antony's spirit have been immensely amplified and intensified. The stakes are higher than they were, and the struggle has taken dire toll in defeat, disgrace, and suffering. The final comment upon Antony's "There's sap in 't yet" is Enobarbus' wry assessment of the situation, and the forming of *his* tragic decision:

Now he'll outstare the lightning; to be furious
Is to be frighted out of fear, and in that mood
The dove will peck the estridge; and I see still,
A diminution in our captain's brain
Restores his heart; when valour preys on reason,
It eats the sword it fights with: I will seek
Some way to leave him.

(III.xiii.195-201)

At the still center of the perturbations and oscillations of Act III stands Enobarbus, Shakespeare's most complex and independent reflector. Enobarbus, like Lear's fool, is truthteller, and, though higher in the social hierarchy, he too is snubbed (in II.ii) for his pains. Again, like the fool, he accompanies his master's travail with the observant eye of a worldly wisdom the latter lacks. Yet he too loves where his master loves, is capable of articulating the enchanted vision of Cleopatra at Cydnus which makes a mockery of Antony's good intentions toward Octavia. He too, therefore, is both sympathetically involved and ironically detached, an alter ego who voices what his master knows but will not or cannot admit. Like the fool, too, he is drawn into the drama's vortex, so that he both figures and suffers from his master's collapse and disintegration; and when he has fulfilled his antiphonal function he ceases to exist. The fool follows his heart, Enobarbus his head, but the departure from life of both has the same nameless cause. In *Antony and Cleopatra*, Enobarbus, thus peculiarly adapted to the task, is also the fulcrum of its pendulum swing, which veers between the Roman and the Egyptian, the masculine and the feminine points of view, in an unceasing fluctuation. But unlike the fool Enobarbus is himself independently a tragic figure and his tragedy is the mirror-image of Antony's, originating in the same predicament ("Alack sir no . . ."), reflecting the same conflict of divided inclination, and passing, contrapuntally, through the same phases of dilemma, fateful decision, betrayal, and remorseful recognition.

Enobarbus' fatal error succeeds his master's and is both a consequence of and a commentary upon it. As he watches the encounter between Thidias and Cleopatra, his urbanity deserts him. Master ironist himself, he fails to interpret Cleopatra's magnificently noncommittal diplomacy as itself deeply ironic, and puts that construction upon her reaction which leads, as a most direct consequence, to his desertion of Antony, his remorse, and his death. It is not a wrong decision in itself. His construction is plausible enough, in all conscience. Cleopatra is impenetrable, and who can tell what possibilities flicker in her mind behind the mask of her irony. But for Enobarbus, who is capable of perceiving what the world calls folly in a quixotic light, it proves in the event to be disastrously wrong. For

> The loyalty well held to fools does make
> Our faith mere folly: yet he that can endure
> To follow with allegiance a fall'n lord,
> Does conquer him that did his master conquer,
> And earns a place i' the story.
>
> (III.xiii.42-46)

Therefore when he knows himself to have lost more even than his place in the story, his death in wretchedness, grief, and self-contempt serves to reaffirm that truth of his nature of which, till definitely repudiated, he was never sure:

O Antony,
Nobler than my revolt is infamous,
Forgive me in thine own particular,
But let the world rank me in register
A master-leaver, and a fugitive.
(IV.ix.18-22)

The longer and fuller process of the testing of Antony's inmost allegiance is the substance of Act IV, where the dramaturgy of oscillation is taken up into the three-day battle sequence and the fluctuation in Antony's fortunes, while the principle of tragic progression brings Antony to experience and articulate the darkest view of his life which he is to have before the catastrophe which ends his long day's task.

Upon the high crest of his decision to be absolute for Egypt Antony determines to retrieve his losses; vows to "live, / Or bathe my dying honour in the blood / Shall make it live again" (IV.ii.5-7) and fetes his followers with a gesture of frank self-effacing magnanimity:

Perchance to-morrow
You'll serve another master. I look on you,
As one that takes his leave. Mine honest friends,
I turn you not away, but like a master
Married to your good service, stay till death:
Tend me to-night two hours, I ask no more,
And the gods yield you for 't!
(IV.ii.27-33)

Antony's winning charm, his power over men's loyalties, his sense of the fellowship of warriors, is here splendidly exhibited, as is the generous responsiveness of his heartening reply to Enobarbus' protest:

ENOBARBUS.   What mean you, sir,
   To give them this discomfort? Look, they weep,

And I, an ass, am onion-ey'd; for shame,
Transform us not to women.

ANTONY.   Ho, ho, ho!
Now the witch take me, if I meant it thus!
Grace grow where those drops fall, my hearty friends;
You take me in too dolorous a sense,
For I spake to you for your comfort, did desire you
To burn this night with torches: know, my hearts,
I hope well of to-morrow, and will lead you,
Where rather I'll expect victorious life,
Than death, and honour.

(iv.ii.33-44)

Yet Enobarbus, reserved and alert, perceives the hidden cause
of Antony's compensatory sentiment, the erosion of loss and
anxiety which it conceals. It is one of those odd tricks which
sorrow shoots out of the mind. And what Antony means, he
says, is to make his followers weep. To construct a world of
sentiment and sympathy—Enobarbus, refusing to be carried
away, judges this a poor bulwark against the might of Caesar's
battalions. That that world of sentiment and sympathy has
more power over him, in the event, than the conquering and
unsentimental battalions is, as we have seen, his own tragic
realization. But the soldiers on guard concur with him in
their intuition of the meaning of the mysterious music: " 'Tis
the god Hercules, whom Antony lov'd, / Now leaves him."
The scene of the arming of Antony is thus framed by suggestions of the ominous, the sorrowful, and the heartsick
which gloss with the nuance of pathos the high hopes the
scene expresses.

Antony is indeed himself again, putting aside Cleopatra's
appeal to "sleep a little," demanding his armor, and finding
his Queen, the armorer of his heart, now serviceable and not
subversive to the tasks of manhood: "Thou fumblest, Eros,
and my queen's a squire / More tight at this than thou" (iv.iv.

14-15). The tenderness, the elation, the marriage harmony of this scene and of the scene of their greeting after the triumph of the second day's battle recalls the joy of Othello greeting his fair warrior at Cyprus. Antony has come smiling from the world's great snare uncaught, but the omens and the forebodings which have been built into the scenes stress the delusion. These scenes catch in their harmonies the dream of Antony, the lovers' victory, their mutual triumph. But, as we know, swallows have built their nests in Cleopatra's sails. The dream is short-lived, but it provides a measure for the pain of the subsequent blow, and the steep descent into despair.

Antony's speech "All is lost" poignantly registers the despair. He knows himself "beguiled to the very heart of loss": deprived both of his good fortune in the world and of the "chief end" for which he knows himself to have sought it.

> O sun, thy uprise shall I see no more,
> Fortune and Antony part here, even here
> Do we shake hands. All come to this? The hearts
> That spaniel'd me at heels, to whom I gave
> Their wishes, do discandy, melt their sweets
> On blossoming Caesar: and this pine is bark'd,
> That overtopp'd them all. Betray'd I am.
> O this false soul of Egypt! this grave charm,
> Whose eye beck'd forth my wars, and call'd them home;
> Whose bosom was my crownet, my chief end,
> Like a right gipsy, hath at fast and loose
> Beguil'd me, to the very heart of loss.
>
> (IV.xii.18-29)

It is an abyss which he faces; and it is in total repudiation of her that he consigns Cleopatra to the mockery and derision of Caesar's triumph. The shirt of Nessus is upon him, and in the anguish of betrayal, defeat, and ignominy he turns upon her with a vengeful imprecation:

> Ah, thou spell! Avaunt! . . .
> Vanish or I shall give thee thy deserving,
> And blemish Caesar's triumph. Let him take thee,
> And hoist thee up to the shouting plebeians,
> Follow his chariot, like the greatest spot
> Of all thy sex. Most monster-like be shown
> For poor'st diminutives, for dolts, and let
> Patient Octavia plough thy visage up
> With her prepared nails.
>
> (IV.xii.33-39)

The rage which issues in the determination that the witch shall die then gives way to the languor, the lassitude, of the cloud scene with Eros. As a drowning man is said to do, he reviews as from an immense distance the scenes of a dissolving pageant, and knows his life to have been an illusion and his goals a mockery of appearances. The insubstantiality and mutability of these dissolving shapes reflect his sense of a total disintegration. He has no will to live and even the impulse to revenge vanishes. This is the nadir of his realization of the collapse of all possible ends. There is no longer any choice to be made, for love and glory are both emptied of meaning of any kind.

> . . . here I am Antony,
> Yet cannot hold this visible shape, my knave.
> I made these wars for Egypt, and the queen,
> Whose heart I thought I had, for she had mine:
> Which whilst it was mine, had annex'd unto 't
> A million more, now lost: she, Eros, has
> Pack'd cards with Caesar, and false-play'd my glory
> Unto an enemy's triumph.
> Nay, weep not, gentle Eros, there is left us
> Ourselves to end ourselves.
>
> (IV.xiv.13-22)

In order to savor the full effect of the play as it now proceeds it is necessary only to reflect for a moment upon the effect Antony's death at this point would have had. Defeated, humiliated, and betrayed, his suicide at this point could only have registered the total failure of a life and the recognition that Philo's words at the beginning of the play were strictly true and his love for Cleopatra a snare and a delusion. What saves Antony from this consummation of his story is (*feliciter audax!*) Cleopatra's lie. For the fact (as he believes it to be) that she has killed herself reverses the situation entirely. His faith in her and in himself is restored, and with it his resolution to kill himself, not in a despairing apathy, but in the saving anguish of grief. Hope for this world there is indeed none. The torch is out and all length is torture. But the dream of harmony, of reconciliation between love and martial dedication, is retrospectively validated:

> I come, my queen. . . . Stay for me,
> Where souls do couch on flowers, we'll hand in hand,
> And with our sprightly port make the ghosts gaze:
> Dido and her Aeneas shall want troops,
> And all the haunt be ours.
>
> (IV.xiv.50-54)

Together with the renewal of love, comes the return of glory's value:

> Since Cleopatra died,
> I have lived in such dishonour that the gods
> Detest my baseness. I, that with my sword
> Quarter'd the world, and o'er green Neptune's back
> With ships made cities, condemn myself, to lack
> The courage of a woman, less noble mind
> Than she which by her death, our Caesar tells
> "I am conqueror of myself."
>
> (IV.xiv.55-62)

This, however, is still not the last of the vicissitudes which mark Antony's death as they marked his life. There is a further bitter shame to be drained from the cup by the Roman Antony, and further knowledge of irreparable yet not inevitable loss to be realized by that part of his soul which is given to Egypt. Eros, thrice nobler than himself, forestalls him, his own suicide wretchedly fails, and Diomed brings the news, too late, of Cleopatra's stratagem.

She has, then, caused everything; nodded him to her, towed his heart after her rudder, governed his every action. But when he discovers that Cleopatra has thus fatally deceived him at the last, he has no single word of repudiation, anger, or contempt. On the contrary they are never more perfectly, candidly, even serenely at one than in this moment of irrevocable loss. It is truly as if the spirit of Eros presides over the play when Enobarbus' spirit of skepticism dies. There is moreover an extraordinarily moving and reassuring realism about this part of the catastrophe of Shakespeare's most romantic tragedy—Cleopatra's caution about appearing outside the monument lest she be taken, Antony's final instruction to her to seek her safety and to trust none but Proculeius. It is not by chance that Cleopatra refers to "the false housewife Fortune," for the scene possesses a curiously domestic, marital intimacy, that of grown-up lovers in a real world, which does not admit the desires of the mind as the sole arbiter of the falling out of things:

> Here's sport indeed! How heavy weighs my lord!
> Our strength is all gone into heaviness,
> That makes the weight. Had I great Juno's power,
> The strong wing'd Mercury should fetch thee up,
> And set thee by Jove's side. Yet come a little,
> Wishers were ever fools. . . .
>
> (IV.xv.32-37)

And the effect of homeliness in Cleopatra's distracted chatter

338

combines inimitably with the festive sobriety of Antony's
farewell:

I am dying Egypt, dying; only
I here importune death awhile, until
Of many thousand kisses, the poor last
I lay upon thy lips.

(IV.xv.18-21)

But if the breach in Antony's spirit is thus healed, his death
opens a great breach in hers. It is for this reason—the intricate
interlocking of the two tragedies—that there is none of Shakespeare's customary fourth-act irony in *Antony and Cleopatra*.
We cannot pause here to survey events from a viewpoint distant and external to the protagonists, for we are to be propelled into another parabola of anguish and despair arising
out of the first before the latter has had time to subside. And
a compromising, accommodating, common man's view of passion is, as we shall see, precisely the adversary against which
Cleopatra struggles and against which she tests herself.

She recoils in desolate misery from her bereavement and
from the dull world, which to her in Antony's absence is no
better than a sty, with nothing left remarkable beneath the
visiting moon. "The odds is gone," leaving a desolating bore-
dom; but, though the savor of life has departed, she is still
bound to the world by a thousand threads.

In Act v will be exhibited the working of Cleopatra's imagination as she realizes her alternatives and moves toward the
fulfillment of her resolve. It is of the most absorbing interest,
this exhibition not only of what Cleopatra will do, but of how
she will do it; and it will affect retrospectively our entire
view of the play. With a subtlety of insight and a richness of
suggestion unsurpassed perhaps even in his own work, Shakespeare exhibits the growth, the expansion, and the completion
of her great idea, its taking possession of her to the point
where she will be marble-constant in its service, and her final

enacting of it, with a grand, triumphant, histrionic audacity. What Shakespeare dramatizes in Act v is Cleopatra's realization of fidelity, a fidelity that must rise above and conquer both her natural fear of death and her superabundant vitality, and which, in doing so, redeems Antony's blunders and fulfills —in a degree far beyond anything he could have imagined— his own desire for a high Roman fashion in death.

As Antony dies, she faints, and Iras and Charmian attempt to rouse her, calling her "our Sovereign," "Royal Egypt," "Empress," to which she responds in evident repudiation of her royal titles, or at least, as the Arden editor suggests, as "the outcome of a train of thought" suggested by them:

No more but e'en a woman, and commanded
By such poor passion as the maid that milks,
And does the meanest chares. It were for me
To throw my sceptre at the injurious gods,
To tell them that this world did equal theirs,
Till they had stol'n our jewel. All's but naught:
Patience is sottish, and impatience does
Become a dog that's mad: then is it sin,
To rush into the secret house of death.
Ere death dare come to us? How do you, women?
What, what, good cheer! Why, how now, Charmian?
My noble girls! Ah, women, women. Look,
Our lamp is spent, it's out. Good sirs, take heart,
We'll bury him: and then, what's brave, what's noble,
Let's do it after the high Roman fashion.
And make death proud to take us. Come, away,
This case of that huge spirit now is cold.
Ah, women, women! come, we have no friend
But resolution, and the briefest end.

(IV.xv.73-91)

It is important to follow closely the movement of this speech, for it is the brief chronicle of what is to come: the outline of what in Act v is writ large. It is often taken as perhaps Cleopatra's single motion of humility, and thus regarded as the basis for her "regeneration" to the better life: great grief breaks the proud spirit and she bows her head in an acknowledgment of "the common humanity that binds her to those who have loved her."[5] But the speech invites a radically different interpretation if it is not forced into the service of a pious morality. It is a revulsion against the universal commonplace anonymity of mere grief that she surely expresses, and "No more but e'en a woman" refers not to her love but to the fainting spell, a mark of physical or emotional weakness appropriate in a kitchen wench but unworthy of a Queen for whom the demi-Atlas of the earth kissed away kingdoms and provinces. The connotations of "poor" in "poor passion" are the crux of the matter. Poor as "pitiful" could express the humility of great grief; poor as "mean" could not. It is in the latter sense that it occurs again and again in *Antony and Cleopatra*, registering powerfully, in one instance in particular, the idea of a transcendent excellence: "none our parts so poor / But was a race of heaven" (i.iii.36-37).

The speech represents a reflex of rebellion, a reaction against this great leveling power of woman's sorrow; and it is her sense of her grief's incommensurability that prompts her to the assertion of a mightily wounded greatness, a mighty deprivation. It is from the high pride of this refusal to be humbled by the injurious gods that courage comes. The acting out of defiance, the expression of a profound scorn for her condition, for the world reduced to worthlessness by the theft of its jewel, and for all forms of behavior—patience or impatience, acquiescence or frenzy—which would be considered appropriate to an ordi-

---

[5] See D. A. Traversi, *Shakespeare: The Roman Plays* (London: Hollis and Carter, 1963), p. 185. For the opposite view see D. Krook, *Elements of Tragedy* (New Haven: Yale Univ. Press, 1969), chap. 8, passim. To her brilliant insight into the heroic aspects of the play I am indebted for the interpretation given above, though her conclusions regarding the drama's tragic effect differ from mine.

nary grief, produces the strength and the brave show of will of "What, what, good cheer! . . . Good sirs, take heart" and so on—the repudiation of a world which has lost that which alone made it worth living in. The speech is profoundly moving precisely because of the stamp upon it of a proud self-conscious encounter with sorrow. It is precisely the nonuniversal quality of the grief that is stressed, a grief unshared and unmeasured (because excessive and exceptional) for a being so uniquely valuable that only the final and greatest possible self-assertion is commensurate with his loss: the self-assertion which chooses so to die as to "make death proud to take us."

This is her motive; this her need: not for fortitude or endurance, but for some gesture, some manifest demonstration of an unvanquished spirit. Such a quest for greatness is, of course, within the convention of the heroic death: a leave-taking from life which shall "become it," which shall make its mark upon the brute event. But here, it is important to notice, it is not a motive opposed to her love for Antony, but on the contrary derived from it, supported by it, and vindicating of it; the love and the pride are mutually sustaining and mutually dependent.

Caesar's reception of the news of Antony's death confirms the value of stoic self-conquest, and hence of Cleopatra's idea. Caesar is profoundly moved; Maecenas' flattery ("When such a spacious mirror's set before him / He needs must see himself") serves to point up the degree of Caesar's genuine self-transcendence under the impact of the breaking of so great a thing:

> Oh Antony!
> . . . I must perforce
> Have shown to thee such a declining day,
> Or look on thine: we could not stall together,
> In the whole world. But yet let me lament
> With tears as sovereign as the blood of hearts,

That thou my brother, my competitor,
In top of all design; my mate in empire,
Friend and companion in the front of war,
The arm of mine own body, and the heart
Where mine his thoughts did kindle;—that our stars,
Unreconcilable, should divide
Our equalness to this.

(v.i.35-48)

It also serves to point up the formidable odds Cleopatra will
have to face to earn her part in the story. For Caesar is bent
upon the final crowning of his triumph over his great competitor: "her life in Rome / Would be eternal in our triumph."
Her own reflections follow with the affect of antiphony:

My desolation does begin to make
A better life: 'tis paltry to be Caesar:
Not being Fortune, he's but Fortune's knave,
A minister of her will: and it is great
To do that thing that ends all other deeds,
Which shackles accidents, and bolts up change;
Which sleeps, and never palates more the dung,
The beggar's nurse, and Caesar's.

(v.ii.1-8)

That the "better life" which her desolation begins to make
can in no wise be taken in a Christian or quasi-Christian
sense would, on the reading of the drama suggested here, be
self-evident. Shakespeare is consistently Roman in the Roman
plays and the "better life" can only mean the growing ability
to look upon life with the detachment and dispassion which
gives a stoic his single recourse against Fortune, the strength
to "bid that welcome / Which comes to punish us, and we
punish it / Seeming to bear it lightly" (iv.xiv.136-138). Hence
the astringent tone of *contemptus mundi* in "never palates
more the dung." Moreover, "dung" echoes Antony's defiant

343

claim for their "nobility of life," their peerlessness, and places Caesar (with audacious scorn) into the category of mere beggar, inasmuch as he too is a slave to Fortune, all his power being nought by comparison with the better life of the only and truly great who attain power over mutability itself. This sense of the speech is what creates the possibility of Cleopatra's magnificent loftiness in the scene with Proculeius immediately following:

> Antony
> Did tell me of you, bade me trust you, but
> I do not greatly care to be deceiv'd
> That have no use for trusting. If your master
> Would have a queen his beggar, you must tell him,
> That majesty, to keep decorum, must
> No less beg than a kingdom: if he please
> To give me conquer'd Egypt for my son,
> He gives me so much of mine own, as I
> Will kneel to him with thanks.
>
> (v.ii.12-21)

And the same attitude reveals itself when, startled, caught off her guard by her capture, she again uses images of the poor, the powerless, or the inconsiderable to define her self-assertion:

> Where art thou, death?
> Come hither, come; come, come, and take a queen
> Worth many babes and beggars!
>
> (v.ii.46-48)

Though Cleopatra broods unceasingly upon death, though in her bereavement life and death are equally contemptible, death being merely that which "rids our dogs of languish," though she proclaims "resolution, and the briefest end" over Antony's body not yet cold, nonetheless an entire act goes by before the words are put into effect. It is this delay that enables Shakespeare to internalize, intensify, and expand Cleopatra's recognition of what is now at stake. And this he achieves by means of what Middleton Murry has called "triumphs of imagery [which] are to be conceived as swift and continuous acts of exploration of the world of imagination."[6] It is such acts of exploration, of imaginative rehearsal, that fill the strange delay of Act v. They turn upon Caesar's Roman triumph, and it is the theme of the triumph that meaningfully relates both Cleopatra's dream-vision of Antony and her own final speech.

The passages on the triumph recur five times, but there is nothing mechanical about their repetition. They operate as a kind of incremental refrain, and they mark the stages of Cleopatra's resolution. Their placing is always significant. The first, it will be remembered, occurs in Act iv after the second sea battle and the flight of the Egyptian ships, upon the occasion of Antony's most violent repudiation of Cleopatra:

> Let him take thee,
> And hoist thee up to the shouting plebeians,
> Follow his chariot, like the greatest spot
> Of all thy sex. Most monster-like be shown
> For poor'st diminutives, for dolts, and let
> Patient Octavia plough thy visage up
> With her prepared nails.
>
> (iv.xii.30-39)

In his persuasion of Eros to save him, by death, from a similar fate, the tone is less violent but sufficiently emphatic in its insistence upon the humiliation, the unbearable dishonor, of the triumphal procession:

> Eros,
> Wouldst thou be window'd in great Rome and see
> Thy master thus with pleach'd arms, bending down
> His corrigible neck, his face subdued

[6] *Countries of the Mind* (London: Humphrey Milford, 1937), p. 10.

345

To penetrative shame; whilst the wheel'd seat
Of fortunate Caesar, drawn before him, branded
His baseness that ensued?

(IV.xiv.72-77)

Cleopatra does not hear Antony's persuasion of Eros, but she remembers his previous words and echoes them as she pleads the necessity of remaining within the monument:

> I dare not, dear,
> Dear my lord, pardon: I dare not,
> Lest I be taken: not the imperious show
> Of the full-fortune'd Caesar ever shall
> Be brooch'd with me, if knife, drugs, serpents, have
> Edge, sting, or operation. I am safe:
> Your wife Octavia, with her modest eyes,
> And still conclusion, shall acquire no honour
> Demuring upon me.

(IV.xv.21-29)

This speech modulates from the extreme agitation of the refusal to descend to the note of regal self-possession, not unmixed with the smaller pride of her rivalry with Octavia. The words follow Antony's, both those she heard and those which were addressed to Eros, with the echoing reciprocity of speech and idea between them which significantly marks the last two acts. A single continuity of image is thus established: the chariot of the full-fortuned victor, the led captives, the watching wife, the whole imperious show. But when one compares Antony's speech in IV.xii.30-39 with this speech of Cleopatra's, it becomes clear that she has not taken in to the full the degradation he depicts. The show is imperious, which is sufficiently galling, but she is not shown "monster-like . . . / For poor'st diminutives, for dolts." In her imagination of the scene she is a brooch, an adornment, which, in her pride, she will deny to Caesar. Octavia does no more than to "demure"[7] upon her, which again sufficiently indicates the sense of an affront to her own pride of amorous conquest, but suggests nothing like the pitch of revulsion with which she later repudiates Proculeius' proposal.

Proculeius, Caesar's spokesman, proposes his master's view:

> . . . let the world see
> His nobleness well acted, which your death
> Will never let come forth.
>
> (v.ii.44-46)

And it is to this that she replies with an accumulated charge of passion:

> Sir, I will eat no meat, I'll not drink, sir,—
> If idle talk will once be necessary,—
> I'll not sleep neither. This mortal house I'll ruin,
> Do Caesar what he can. Know, sir, that I
> Will not wait pinion'd at your master's court,
> Nor once be chastis'd with the sober eye
> Of dull Octavia. Shall they hoist me up,
> And show me to the shouting varletry
> Of censuring Rome? Rather a ditch in Egypt
> Be gentle grave unto me, rather on Nilus' mud
> Lay me stark-nak'd, and let the water-flies
> Blow me into abhorring; rather make
> My country's high pyramides my gibbet,
> And hang me up in chains.
>
> (v.ii.49-62)

Octavia is demolished with a superbly vindictive adjective; but the brooch with which she would not adorn Caesar's triumph

---

[7] C. J. Sisson, in *New Readings in Shakespeare*, vol. II (Cambridge: Cambridge Univ. Press, 1956), confirms Ridley's choice, in the New Arden ed., of "demure" rather than "demurr."

has been replaced by an image of desecration—the ultimate indecency of exposure: "rather on Nilus' mud lay me stark nak'd and let the waterflies / Blow me into abhorring." This hyperbolic exposure is a measure of the horror of other—the being made a motley to the view, hoisted up to the sound of the lewd jeering of the despised populace; and the lines contain a most significant verbal echo:

> Let him take thee,
> And hoist thee up to the shouting plebeians. . . .

> Shall they hoist me up,
> And show me to the shouting varletry
> of censuring Rome?

The heroic view of life, the aspiration toward superior prowess or rare excellence, rests upon an aristocratic disdain for the common or mean. This disdain is exacerbated to an extreme scorn in the above passages, for it is for the delectation of the despised rabble that the show is to be put on. It will be noticed that members of the multitude, the many-headed monster, increasingly figure in Act v: the Roman mechanics, the saucy lictors, the mere boys and girls who are level now with men, the beggar, the maid that does the meanest chores. These figures punctuate the long reverie of Cleopatra like the tolling of a bell, for they are the petty contemptible life from which either she and Antony will be marvelously distinguished, or by whom they will be mocked, derided, and debased.

To Proculeius' attempt to reassure her and to his offer to bear a message to Caesar, her response is the obdurate "Say, I would die," a cry of mingled despair and defiance which is the aftermath of the passionate abhorrence expressed before. Then follows the rapt, abstracted dialogue with Dolabella and the dream of "an Emperor Antony." The nightmare of humiliation with which she has tormented her imagination vanishes, and in its place is conjured up the dream of lost grandeur, of sovereign prodigality and colossal stature.

> His face was as the heavens, and therein stuck
> A sun and moon, which kept their course, and lighted
> The little O, the earth.
>
> . . . .
>
> His legs bestrid the ocean, his rear'd arm
> Crested the world: his voice was propertied
> As all the tuned spheres, and that to friends:
> But when he meant to quail, and shake the orb,
> He was as rattling thunder. For his bounty,
> There was no winter in't: an autumn 'twas
> That grew the more by reaping: his delights
> Were dolphin-like, they show'd his back above
> The element they lived in: in his livery
> Walk'd crowns and crownets: realms and islands were
> As plates dropp'd from his pocket.
>
> (v.ii.79-92)

As we take in the extraordinary gigantism of the images, the distance from which they seem to be seen, the spectacular hyperbole, the processional, emblematic quality, the sense of the cosmic, indeed, but a cosmic which is somehow contrived— a ritual autumn which never becomes winter—we realize with a shock of recognition that it is precisely as a king in a pageant that she is envisaging him: the pageant of ignominy is exorcised in her imagination by the pageant of majesty. Cleopatra's intense reverie in Act v—the forming and maturing of her heroic resolution—is projected through the double images of the magnificence of Antony and the rival would-be magnificence of Caesar. The whole series of images of masque and pageant provide the metaphor for Cleopatra's state of

349

mind and thereby convey the essence of the drama that Shake-speare is exhibiting.[8] Not only is Cleopatra's vision of the Antony who "condemns shadows quite" formed in the image of the masque; so also is her imagination of what she will do. And this in its turn arises from the connection the context establishes between the masque-like vision which expresses Antony's magnificence and the indignity of Caesar's triumph which is its obverse, and as we have seen, its prelude in the play.

The connection is obliquely enforced by the Seleucus epi-sode. Seleucus' exposure to Caesar of Cleopatra's reservation of her treasure shames her. She does not lose her composure for a moment—her "immoment toys" is superb—but the ex-change makes manifest in the most concrete manner the humiliation implicit in her situation. Caesar's disavowal of petty materialism in his dealings with her is significantly phrased:

> Feed, and sleep:
> Our care and pity is so much upon you,
> That we remain your friend, and so adieu.
>
> (v.ii.186-188)

"Feed and sleep" catches in its net of echoes both "our dungy earth alike / Feeds beast as man" and "Which sleeps, and never palates more the dung, / The beggar's nurse, and Caesar's," itself an echo of Antony's "the long day's task is done, / And we must sleep." Cleopatra's "He words me, girls, he words me, that I should not / Be noble to myself" (v.ii.

---

[8] In an essay entitled "The Masque of Greatness," *Shakespeare Studies*, III (1967), I have set out in detail the evidence for Shakes-speare's having in mind the splendid court masques as the basis for his imagination of the final phase of the play. The connection between Cleopatra's dream of Antony and the "imagery" of masques and pageants was first observed by Walter Whiter in his fascinating early examination of image clusters, *A Specimen of a Commentary on Shakespeare* (London, 1794), cited in *Variorum*, pp. 343 and 347, and recently edited by A. Over and M. Bell (London: Methuen, 1967).

190-191) indicates her perception of what is at issue and registers the final strengthening of the resolution which, the reservation of the treasure suggests, has not until this moment been entirely consolidated.

She will outdo Caesar, out-triumph Caesar, leave him indeed "ass unpolicied," not merely by removing herself physically from the possibility of being exhibited in his triumph, but by a grand and queenly spectacle of her own. What she has realized while weighing her possibilities, enacting in imagination her alternatives, is that it lies within her power to vindicate the passion that has ruined the triple pillar of the world: that it rests with her either heroically to affirm the rare quality of their love, its possession of heroic stature and value, of a supreme excellence among human things, or to leave it upon the pages of history as a royal strumpet's lust for an infatuated libertine.

Her final evocation of the triumph Dolabella has assured her Caesar intends epitomizes this decisive insight:

> Now, Iras, what think'st thou?
> Thou, an Egyptian puppet shall be shown
> In Rome as well as I: mechanic slaves
> With greasy aprons, rules, and hammers shall
> Uplift us to the view. In their thick breaths,
> Rank of gross diet, shall we be enclouded.
> And forced to drink their vapour.
> IRAS.   The gods forbid!
> CLEOPATRA. Nay, 'tis most certain, Iras: saucy lictors
> Will catch at us like strumpets, and scald rhymers
> Ballad us out of tune. The quick comedians
> Extemporally will stage us, and present
> Our Alexandrian revels: Antony
> Shall be brought drunken forth, and I shall see
> Some squeaking Cleopatra boy my greatness
> I' the posture of a whore.   (v.ii.206-219)

351

The horror of exposure to the leering, jeering, alien faces of the rabble and the cold contempt of the Roman matron had come home to her before. But now the horror of exposure is transformed by her lordly scorn for the base, the vulgar, the gross, the low; that which produced a paroxysm of revulsion and abhorrence is now described with sovereign contempt. The last lines in particular measure the great distance she has come from that which will now never be, because now she knows what she will do to "fool their preparation, and to conquer / Their most absurd intents." She has conceived of her own spectacle, her own triumph, her own way of affirming the truth that she was Antony's lass unparalleled and not Antony's whore: a grand affirmation of his manhood, his valor, his virtue, and their greatness. Caesar's triumph functions now, imaginatively, as an antimasque: that part of the spectacle which represents the obscene or antic grimaces of the ignoble and unworthy, prelude to the magnificence and dignity soon to follow in a pride and splendor enhanced by contrast. The linked sequences of images—queen, woman, greatness, beggary; triumphal masque and antimasque—have converged in an intimation of the means she will take in order to be noble unto herself, and so to give the world to know "We stand up peerless."

She is drawing upon the power to affirm of the grand style. Their Alexandrian revels can be debased by scurrilous burlesque, or honored by what Dryden called the "fine majesty of the heroic." Cleopatra has perceived that in her very renunciation of life, her farewell to the bright day, she can strike again the high sumptuous note of the meeting at Cydnus: "Show me, my women, like a queen: go fetch / My best attires" (v.ii.226-227). For the equivalent of such a "discovery," Allardyce Nicoll tells us, "The entire masque was conceived; all the rest—the changing prospects, the descents of deities, the eccentric measures of the antimasque—was merely a framework and a preparation for the true masquing display when the noble courtiers, suddenly revealed in their glory, doffed their vizards and descended in solemn state from their thrones or triumphal chariots."[9]

And it is at this penultimate moment that Shakespeare introduces perhaps the most daring of all his clowns, displaced from the usual penultimate phase of Act IV by the elongation of the double catastrophe. Indeed nothing could more effectively dramatize Cleopatra's magnificent composure than her capping of the clown's malapropism concerning the immortal worm: "those that do die of it, do seldom or never recover," with her own "immortal longings." The whole proud, defiant *sprezzatura* of her conception is contained in the wordplay.

But if the clown's presence renders almost palpable her transcendence of "the baser life," his fool's patter also casts a final ironic and pitiful light upon Cleopatra's self-created situation. She is marble-constant from head to foot, the fleeting moon no longer her planet; she exults that there is nothing of woman in her now. But the clown's inconsequential absurdities articulate a common sense which embraces even such a woman as Cleopatra: "I heard of one of them no longer than yesterday, a very honest woman, but something given to lie, as a woman should not do, but in the way of honesty, how she died of the biting of it, what pain she felt: truly, she makes a very good report o' the worm" (V.ii.249-254).

As for the final speech itself, nothing brings out with greater force the element of deliberately conceived performance in it than a comparison with the factual description of Cleopatra's end given in North's Plutarch:

Cleopatra being layed upon a little low bed in poor estate, when she sawe Caesar come in to her chamber, she sodainly rose up, naked in her smocke, and fell downe at his feete

[9] Allardyce Nicoll, *Stuart Masques and the Renaissance Stage* (London: Harrap, 1937), p. 214.

marvellously disfigured: both for that she had plucked her hair from her head, as also for that she had martired all her face with her nailes, and besides, her voyce was small and trembling, her eyes sonke into her head with continual blubbering: and the most part of her stomake torn in sunder. To be short, her bodie was not much better than her minde: yet her good grace and comelyness, and the force of her bewtie was not altogether defaced.[10]

This description points up the fact that the question at issue for Cleopatra is a question of style, entirely outside the realm of morality. North's Cleopatra, in "oughly and pitiefull state" is no doubt considerably less reprehensible than Shakespeare's vessel of pride. But she is an object of commiseration, not a figure of heroic grandeur.

It is not perhaps the least of this triumph of the high Roman fashion that it is the triumph of her own voluptuous Egyptian woman's nature that is displayed. She is another Venus, in her self-created spectacle, or Isis, goddess of love and the fertile Nile: her sign is the asp upon her arm, or upon her breast, the asp of the easy death, "As sweet as balm, as soft as air, as gentle." It is a superb performance in which she enacts not the poor woman's passion of the milkmaid, nor the atoning virtue which could make a woman "a dish for the gods, if the devil dress her not," but the *feliciter audax* which transforms death itself into a metaphor for love, an apotheosis of sensuality. In this, as in so much else, she echoes Antony's will to be a bridegroom in his death, and run into 't as to a lover's bed. The kiss that is her heaven to have, the lover's pinch, the babe that sucks the nurse asleep, in these garnerings of the heart the great contraries, valor and *voluptas*, the royal and the riggish, are resolved, and in their wake the antinomy between hero and fool is obliterated. No wonder she is exultant, seeing

[10] North's Plutarch, in *Narrative and Dramatic Sources of Shakespeare*, ed. G. Bullough (New York: Columbia Univ. Press and London: Routledge and Kegan Paul, 1964), p. 313-314.

354

Antony "rouse himself / To praise [her] noble act," mocking the luck of Caesar, claiming her title of mate and match to the greatest soldier of the world. For by her own inspired identification with Antony she demonstrates as true what she herself once challenged provocatively as "excellent falsehood," and defended, later, against Dolabella's skepticism:

> You lie up to the hearing of the gods.
> But if there be, or ever were one such,
> It's past the size of dreaming: nature wants stuff
> To vie strange forms with fancy, yet to imagine
> An Antony were nature's piece, 'gainst fancy,
> Condemning shadows quite.
>
> (v.ii.95-100)

What her great act of faith in the life of the imagination puts to the test is the power of love over death: of that love between man and woman whose mark is mutuality, a consonance of pulse, imagination, and sense; and of the power of such love, such pleasure of life, to neutralize the terror, the pain and the shame of loss and defeat.

CHAPTER X

CORIOLANUS

The salient feature of *Coriolanus* is, as Bradley noted, the absence in it of "the exhibition of inward conflict, or of the outburst of one or another passion, terrible, heartrending or glorious to witness."[1] Bradley is careful to stress that it is the "exhibition" of inner conflict that is absent, not the conflict itself, which, he says, is "veiled from us." That it is so veiled is undoubtedly the reason for the impression of harshness and coldness, about which there is universal agreement. If Coriolanus is Shakespeare's most unpopular tragic hero, it is without doubt less on account of his possession of unsympathetic qualities of character, however conspicuous, than on account of his nonpossession of the resonance of inner experience. Yet to conclude from this circumstance that the play is no tragedy, or that it is a tragedy in which "failing powers" are evident, as is common in the criticism, is a misapprehension, springing ultimately from a sentimentalized notion of the "noble" hero. Campbell's view that the play is entirely derisive and "can be understood only if it be recognized as perhaps the most successful of Shakespeare's satiric plays,"[2] is perhaps particularly perverse; but his contention that "neither in his presentation of the central figure nor in his construction of the plot does [Shakespeare] follow orthodox tragic principles"[3] is found in one form or another even in criticism which is otherwise perceptive and illuminating of many facets of the play. "The

[1] British Academy Shakespeare Lecture (1912), in A. C. Bradley, *A Miscellany* (London: Macmillan, 1929), p. 77.
[2] O. J. Campbell, *Shakespeare's Satire* (Oxford: The Clarendon Press, 1943), p. 199.
[3] Ibid., p. 198.

theme," we are told, "is not pursued to the point at which a truly tragic conflict occurs."[4]

But in fact the play follows Shakespeare's regular tragic structure, with, as in *Othello*, the fatal error and the recognitions attendant upon it delayed to the last act. As in *Othello*, therefore, the motive power of the action does not originate with the protagonist; it is not self-generated. It is the tribunes and later Aufidius who manipulate both the people and Coriolanus, just as Iago manipulates both Desdemona and Othello. There is of course in this Roman play no metaphysic of evil to render the manipulators diabolical or to give them a diabolical zest; it is Coriolanus himself who supplies them with their irresistible occasions. The tribunes and Aufidius are able to predict his reactions to certain kinds of incitement with a deadly accuracy. Again and again, in a marked pattern of recurrences, he is played upon, propelled into action, or deflected from his course of action against his will or without the consent of his will; yet, paradoxically, it is his self-consistency that these reversals serve to exhibit. The recurrences are not identical; they function incrementally, and our awareness of that which differentiates them marks what we perceive of the tragic progress. The boldly repetitive composition is thus the determining formal feature of the tragedy.

The retardation of recognition till the very end entails a protagonist who shall be in error, or ignorance, or blind to himself and others for the greater part of the play. Othello's error of judgment regarding Iago breeds further error in which he remains until after the committing of the fatal act itself. But in Coriolanus ignorance is more radical. He is not only the most lacking in self-awareness of all Shakespeare's heroes but the most naïve in his knowledge of the world. He is the least self-expressive and the least reflective of them all, at

[4] D. J. Enwright, "*Coriolanus*: Tragedy or Debate?" *Essays in Criticism*, IV (January 1954).

an opposite pole from Hamlet, Lear, and Macbeth. The formal correlative of this quality of character is of course the absence (until, briefly, in Act IV) of the soliloquy—the complex and versatile Shakespearean monologue, itself in varying degrees disingenuous or candid. In *Hamlet, Lear,* and *Macbeth* outer action is constantly reflected upon an inner screen, given an inner dimension. In *Coriolanus,* where inner experience is not uttered, the material for the inferences we are required to make comes almost entirely from cross-observation made by others of Coriolanus in a montage of "shots" taken of him from various angles. And this feature, too, is a constituent of the root mode of the play's dramaturgy, which is the propelling or maneuvering of its hero into contradictory actions by the volition of others. What we watch for the most part is not an overt struggle with inner experience as in *Lear* or *Macbeth,* nor the imaginative projection of roles as in *Hamlet,* but a series of compulsive responses determined by inner needs, the significance of which is progressively revealed to us.

In the first instance this significance is revealed through the provision of more intimate domestic information about him than we have of any other of the tragic protagonists. Psycho-analysts should—indeed do—find a richer field for their in-vestigations in Coriolanus than in Hamlet, who has proved so irresistibly tempting to them. For the absence of introspection we are more than compensated by the colloquy upon him of the ladies of his household, who provide us with a mine of insights. But it is the dramatic juxtaposition of these insights with the outward events that is peculiarly effective in generat-ing our understanding.

In no other first act, indeed, does Shakespeare pack so much outward event. Disaffection is aroused and diverted in Rome, victory nearly lost and barely won in the campaign against Corioli. By spotlighting Coriolanus in certain highly significant postures during these events, and by the inserted scene at his home, Shakespeare most deftly contrives to suggest the complex of need and motive from which Coriolanus' tragedy will be wrought. The complexity is so deeply "internalized" as to be concealed from the protagonist himself; and it is this that constitutes the dramatist's challenge—the challenge the artist seeks, or creates, that will stretch his powers. For the paucity of utterance relating self and world leaves form alone to symbolize the tragic movement and mediate our perception of it. This last of Shakespeare's tragedies thus exhibits the most sophisticated deployment of the art whose manifold possibilities he ceaselessly explored.

The circumstances which the first act presents center upon the famine in Rome and the consequent danger of insurrection. Rome and her rats, as Menenius so elegantly puts it, are at the point of battle, and it is—there being nothing new under the sun—only the threat of a foreign attack (itself provoked by Rome's internal weakness) that can divert the danger. Caius Marcius, strong man of Rome, stands at the very point of convergence of these threats to the city, the focus of the people's anger for his intransigence to their demands, and chief shield of the city against the Volscian foe by virtue of his supremacy in warfare. Hence the citizens' ambivalence toward him. "Consider you what services he has done for his country?" The first citizen's shrewd reply places in the forefront of attention that attribute of Coriolanus' upon which all will turn: "Very well; and could be content to give him good report for't, but that he pays himself with being proud" (1.i.31-33). It is a key sentence, for it states the dialectic of desert and reward, of individual self-assertion and social acceptance, which the tragedy will explore.

The plebeians are Coriolanus' contrary and mirror-image, menial, suggestible, and pliant where he is arrogant, implacable, and "constant." They are, in his view, despicably cowardly in their craven flight from the enemy, where he is valorous to the point of foolhardiness, in their view, in his singlehanded entry into the stoutly defended city of Corioli;

they keep a base weather eye on the possibility of loot, he is nobly disinterested in material gain of any kind; they are tolerant even in hostility, he is inflammably choleric at all times. He is a very dog to the commonalty, they a common cry of curs to him. They are many where he is one; hungry where he is full. They do not deserve the corn in the city's granaries, Coriolanus maintains, because they "ne'er did service for it." He, on the other hand, has deserved immeasurably of his city. Their price for the consulship, they tell him, is that he should ask it kindly, that he should acknowledge a shared humanity; his definition of himself is founded upon a transcendence of common humanity. Coriolanus' heroic valor, his singlehanded prowess in battle, is unmitigated self-assertion. He is no general as is Cominius, marshaling his forces, encouraging them, rallying them, aware of the natural fluctuation of fear and courage. Alone he takes Corioli from within the walls. Yet his action is not self-sustaining. His "painful service" he lays on the altar of his homeland, and for it he expects the humble gratitude of its population and fame in its annals. It is the mirror-image relationship between these contenders which shows that the political theme is subsumed in the tragic. Hazlitt maintained that anyone who studies *Coriolanus* may "save himself the trouble of reading Burke's Reflections, or Paine's Rights of Man, or the debates in both Houses of Parliament since the French Revolution or our own,"[5] while the Marxists of a later period have found in the play a proof text for their major premises. Yet I venture to suggest that the politics of poverty and privilege serve as the marvelously observed occasion for a deeper antagonism of contraries. What is pressed to a tragic issue through this story of class conflict in ancient Rome is the question of human self-sufficiency. The plebs are human weakness and Coriolanus is human strength, but he is overthrown less by their para-

[5] W. Hazlitt, *Characters of Shakespeare's Plays* (London: J. M. Dent, 1906), p. 53.

doxical strength-in-weakness, or his paradoxical weakness-in-strength, than by the dichotomy within him between these two aspects of human experience and his denial of their interdependence.

Throughout these first scenes we become aware of an extraordinary degree of personal animus in Coriolanus' relation to the people. It is indeed our perception of this animus which it is the function of the Menenius scene—preceding our first view of Coriolanus—to mediate. Menenius' sly fable of the belly is a skilful diversion which succeeds in its aim of confusing the citizens and distracting their attention. That the fable operates by reducing sentient suffering human beings to the instrumentality of organs and limbs is a matter without doubt beyond their powers of analysis. Nor, as Menenius well knows, would they press his own analogy to a conclusion less favorable to his argument: limbs deprived of their blood supply become infected with gangrene, as soldiers were likely to know. If the tricky devices of rhetoric are beyond them, however, the realities of their situation are very much within their grasp:

> FIRST CITIZEN. Care for us! True, indeed! They ne'er cared for us yet: suffer us to famish, and their storehouses crammed with grain; make edicts for usury, to support usurers; repeal daily any wholesome act established against the rich, and provide more piercing statutes daily, to chain up and restrain the poor. If the wars eat us not up, they will; and there's all the love they bear us.
>
> (1.i.78-85)

It is not by the specious logic of the parable of privilege that they are taken in. What they respond to is Menenius' apparent bonhomie, the blunt man-to-man guise he employs to mask his own relatively good-humored patrician contempt for the populace. He has always loved the people, they say; he's one honest enough, would all the rest were so. The dramatic irony is

deftly underlined by Menenius' clear-eyed brief assessment of
the situation: "Rome and her rats are at the point of battle; /
The one side must have bale" (1.i.162-163). It is hardly "love"
for the people, we perceive, that expresses itself in the opposition between Rome and her rats. But Menenius' combination
of soft soap and bland superciliousness is precisely what provides for the shock of contrast when Coriolanus appears. For
such tactics of persuasive demagoguery he has nothing but the
purest contempt. It is to him flattery beneath abhorring, an
intolerable degradation. And his own address to the people
leaves us in no doubt of his unmitigated frankness:

> What would you have, you curs,
> That like nor peace nor war? the one affrights you,
> The other makes you proud. He that trusts to you,
> Where he should find you lions, finds you hares;
> Where foxes, geese: you are no surer, no,
> Than is the coal of fire upon the ice,
> Or hailstone in the sun. Your virtue is
> To make him worthy whose offense subdues him
> And curse that justice did it. Who deserves greatness
> Deserves your hate; and your affections are
> A sick man's appetite, who desires most that
> Which would increase his evil. He that depends
> Upon your favors swims with fins of lead,
> And hews down oaks with rushes. Hang ye! Trust ye?
> With every minute you do change a mind,
> And call him noble that was now your hate,
> Him vile that was your garland.

(1.i.167-183)

What finds ostensible expression in this tirade is the ethos
of an aristocratic warrior class, which bases its hierarchy of
values upon fortitude and the pursuit of martial prowess. But
if their nonparticipation in the code of martial honor renders
them utterly base and contemptible in his eyes, why should

he care what they call him, or how they esteem him? The opinions of this despised rabble should not be worth a moment's attention to him; his high-pitched truculence betrays that it is. Coriolanus' pride is a complex of many factors; the one factor it does not include is the self-reliant composure of a nature at peace with itself.

His compulsion to speak his mind is what is most immediately impressive and demanding of interpretation. The images through which he articulates his contempt for that which is extinguishable or deliquescent, unable to keep its form—the coal of fire upon the ice, and the hailstone in the sun—duplicated in contrasting modes of heat and cold—parallel the double images of frustrated force: the fins of lead and the rush axes, again in a chiasma of heavy and light. What is implied by this quadruple emphasis is the supreme value to him of implacable resistance to pressure, and of unimpeded energy. The degree of spleen which is then expressed in the culminating image of ruthless force:

> Would the nobility lay aside their ruth,
> And let me use my sword, I'd make a quarry
> With thousands of these quartered slaves, as high
> As I could pick my lance. . . .
>
> (1.i.196-199)

surely adverts us to the presence of a powerful inner unrest rather than merely an inherited attitude.

The commons clearly are not to him as they are to Menenius the practical politician simply the stuff of state, the menial, often obstreperous mechanics managed and manipulated by their patrician masters, who, in their unassailable conviction of superiority, can afford to unbend to them. They are to him an object of implacable hostility by virtue of the fact that they represent an opposing and threatening principle, which he will not or dare not admit. His choleric sincerity strikes us as the kind of aggression that springs from a precarious structure of personality where what is feared within is outwardly projected. We perceive, as yet dimly, the pressure of an unresolved contradiction: his self-esteem cannot maintain itself. It requires acclamation, adulation even, yet rejects with a supercilious disdain the need he cannot allow himself to recognize. It is to support this perception that we are shown the welcome he accords to a relationship of open rivalry in arms. For his sworn foe Aufidius he professes an ardent admiration. He is a lion that he is proud to hunt, a warrior of such nobility that "were I anything but what I am, / I would wish me only he." Only in a relationship of legitimized enmity, the antithesis of mutual dependence, does Coriolanus, it seems, feel free and untrammeled, for in such a relationship the overcoming of resistance by force is self-evidently justified and vindicated.

Clearly he is no man for politics, for tempered and measured maneuvers, for adaptations of means to ends, for the tactical overcoming of opposition. Such a man in such a situation promises ample dramatic conflict. Thus we keenly perceive in what way he is set apart from his fellows, with what distinctive energy he pursues aims that are not consonant with theirs. We are to receive further intimations of that which renders him deeply vulnerable to the dangers inherent in his circumstances.

To the tribunes Coriolanus' pride is the irksome and overbearing conceit of a power-seeker whose success threatens their own position:

> BRUTUS. Fame, at the which he aims,
> In whom already he's well grac'd, can not
> Better be held nor more attained than by
> A place below the first; for what miscarries
> Shall be the general's fault, though he perform
> To the utmost of a man; and giddy censure

Will then cry out of Marcius, "O! if he
Had borne the business."
SICINIUS.   Besides, if things go well,
Opinion, that so sticks on Marcius, shall
Of his demerits rob Cominius.

(i.i.263-271)

They can conceive of fame only as an adjunct and a means to
power. But power is, to Coriolanus, his by natural right; and
we have perceived the degree to which expediency is in fact
foreign to his nature. The question of what motivates him is
therefore deepened by the discrepancy between the tribunes'
assessment and ours. And it is at this point that we make the
acquaintance of that formidable matriarch, Coriolanus' mother,
and are invited to make further and more complex inferences concerning the nature of the pride about which there
is so much conjecture.

To Volumnia her son's martial fame is not a trump card
in the power struggle but the object of an all-absorbing and
deeply perverted passion:

I pray you, daughter, sing; or express yourself in a more
comfortable sort. If my son were my husband, I should
freelier rejoice in that absence wherein he won honor
than in the embracements of his bed where he would
show most love. When yet he was but tender-bodied, and
the only son of my womb, when youth with comeliness
plucked all gaze his way, when, for a day of kings' entreaties a mother should not sell him an hour from her
beholding, I, considering how honor would become such
a person, that it was no better than picture-like to hand
by the wall, if renown made it not stir, was pleased to
let him seek danger where he was like to find fame. To
a cruel war I sent him; from whence he returned, his

365

brows bound with oak. I tell thee, daughter, I sprang not
in joy at first hearing he was a man-child than now in
first seeing he had proved himself a man.

VIRGILIA. But had he died in the business, madam; how
then?

VOLUMNIA. Then his good report should have been my son;
I therein would have found issue. Hear me profess sincerely: had I a dozen sons, each in my love alike, and
none less dear than thine and my good Marcius, I had
rather had eleven die nobly for their country than one
voluptuously surfeit out of action.

(I.iii.1-25)

What Volumnia rejoices in in this exhortation to Virgilia is
her own power to rise above her feminine sensibility, to conquer the needs and the claims of her woman's nature. The
phrase that is most revealing is that which recalls his fair
youth, "when, for a day of kings' entreaties a mother should
not sell him an hour from her beholding." It is no absence of
maternal feeling that is expressed here. On the contrary. What
we are invited to perceive is that the whole current of a
powerful love has been deflected, and with an uncompromising absoluteness. What we infer, therefore, is the force of
energy that was required to divert the mother's love, the
mother's instinct to cherish and protect and enjoy her child,
into the unflinching and inflexible pursuit of martial renown.
And what we may further infer is the corresponding power
of the control thus exerted over the child. The self-imposed
"taboo on tenderness"[6] has made love, approval, praise entirely dependent upon feats of arms, upon undaunted and
unswerving valor. He who "did it to please his mother," we
remember, has had unceasingly to prove himself a man by
this single uncompromising standard of manliness. And man-

[6] This useful phrase is I. D. Suttie's, *The Origins of Love and Hate*
(London: Kegan Paul, 1939), chap. 6.

liness, in Volumnia's scheme of things, can admit no natural need, frailty, or vulnerability. To her all loveliness is transferred from the breasts of Hecuba when she did suckle Hector to the bleeding forehead of Hector dead by a Grecian sword. Virgilia's solicitude fills her with contempt; Valeria's account of the young Marcius savaging his butterfly with complacency.

Coriolanus is a play in which Shakespeare has chosen the method of economy rather than that of plenitude. He does not here expansively deploy his prodigious powers of image-making upon the life-sustaining and life-destroying properties of nature. The butterfly (escaped perhaps from Lear's prison?) which is "mammocked" by Coriolanus' fierce little son is therefore the more prominently, and ironically symbolic, its frail impotence a silent protest and a silent plea, akin to Virgilia's own. Coriolanus' mother has made her son in the image of a ruthless ferocity which she has conceived as manliness. But his own independent manhood she has usurped. Even his household is under her roof. If he believes that it is a disinterested and magnanimous love of honor which impels him upon his bellicose career, we are invited to perceive that it is in reality a role which she has constrained him to live. He is less a self-determining being, truly in command of his choices, than he appears. His compulsive arrogance, his constantly exacerbated sensitivity, his defensive-aggressive mask express what we see to be a passionate craving for independence, for autonomy, for self-determination, that no large patrician freedom, no feats of battle, however awesome, can still. In his inmost being he knows himself enslaved by his dependence upon her approval; and therefore the contempt in his unbridled abuse of his inferiors—shames of Rome, base slaves, souls of geese that bear the shapes of men—we can understand as a repudiation of all that is menial, slavish, and dependent by one who senses that his own independence is founded upon quicksand. Volumnia's own vision of her warrior is unwittingly ironic:

367

His bloody brow
With his mail'd hand then wiping, forth he goes,
Like to a harvest-man that's task'd to mow
Or all or lose his hire.

(1.iii.34-37)

The monstrous figure of blood and iron is an icon of death—
the universal harvest man, himself constrained to "mow all or
lose his hire." Unawares she betrays the deadly transvaluation her assumption of a grotesque masculinity has imposed
upon herself and her family. Lady Macbeth's feverish transcendence over her sex is womanly compared with this
ferocious transvestism.

Shakespeare has taken Plutarch's account of the "discom-
modities of orphanage" far further than was within the
power or the interest of the Roman historian to do. The only
thing, Plutarch says, that made Coriolanus love honor was the
"joy he saw his mother did take of him"; and he approvingly
quotes the similar piety of Epaminondas.[7] That he was,
though possessed of both natural wit and great heart, "so
chollericke and impacient, that he would yeld to no living
creature"[8] Plutarch ascribes to the lack of paternal discipline—
a defect of his virtues.[9] Shakespeare's shaping of the story
uncovers the very springs of a tragic dialectic in a nature

[7] "For he thought nothing made him so happie and honorable, as
that his mother might heare everybodie praise and commend him,
that she might allwayes see him returne with a crown upon his head,
and that she might still embrace him with teares ronning downe her
cheekes for joye. Which desire they saye Epaminondas dyd avowe
and confesse to have bene in him: as to think him selfe a most happie
and blessed man, that his father and mother in their life time had
seene the victorie he wanne in the plaine of Leuctres"; G. Bullough,
Narrative and Dramatic Sources (New York: Columbia Univ. Press
and London: Routledge and Kegan Paul, 1964), p. 508.

[8] Ibid., p. 506.

[9] H. Heuer, "From Plutarch to Shakespeare," *Shakespeare Studies*,
x (1957), claims that something of Shakespeare's sense of Coriolanus'
radically defective humanity is already to be found in North's translation of Plutarch.

368

constrained to isolation and a self-frustrating self-assertion through loss of the intrinsic autonomy it craves to realize. Coriolanus' is the tragic progress that consists of the passionate pursuit of ends—of autonomy—in circumstances that present him with dilemmas impossible to resolve. His choices bring about reversals of fortune which involve him in progressively greater losses, and force him, in effect, to define his freedom with ever-increasing rigor, until the final downfall through which he realizes the cruelly narrow circumscription of those powers of human achievement he has attempted to surpass.

In the scene of general acclamation in the Roman camp after the defeat of Corioli is exhibited at large the rigid constraint in which Coriolanus lives, moves, and has his being. Coriolanus shuns praise like the plague. Significantly,

> . . . my mother,
> Who has a charter to extol her blood,
> When she does praise me grieves me.
>
> (i.ix.13-15)

"When seeking or avoiding riches, advantages and honours," Milton said, "we are actuated by our own dignity rightly understood." As Coriolanus understands his dignity, it is to have his deeds a free gift of his own donation, "bought" by no external inducement. He therefore refuses reward—a tenth of all the war booty—as "a bribe to pay [his] sword," and repudiates the fanfare in his honor with belittlement so surly as to draw a reproof from Cominius:

> Too modest are you;
> More cruel to your good report than grateful
> To us that give you truly. By your patience,
> If 'gainst yourself you be incens'd, we'll put you,
> Like one that means his proper harm, in manacles,
> Then reason safely with you.
>
> (i.ix.53-58)

Cominius' insight is impressive. Acceptance, give and take, reciprocity is the mark of the free nature. But Coriolanus, as we increasingly observe, is not a free being. He must therefore perpetually assert himself, flaunt an independence of megalo-maniac proportions. Rather than be obliged to gratitude he will disparage every kind of recompense. His is not the false modesty which courts acclaim under the mask of self-depreca-tion. For it is acclaim itself—his deepest unacknowledged need —that Coriolanus cannot stand. To be praised is to be ap-praised, an implicit limitation upon self. All forms of reward therefore present themselves to him as payment, intrinsically humiliating, reducing to the limits of beggarly dependence the act that was to define him as free and untrammeled, superior even to his peers, master of destinies. The episode of the poor man of Corioli exhibits with the ironic detachment char-acteristic of the play at once the grand scope and the pitiable reach of his aspiration. What will Coriolanus beg who proudly refuses princely gifts? What he begs indicates the magna-nimity to which he aspires—the greatness of soul, the super-generosity which will surpass their horses and spoils and trumpet calls, and even the glory of the name of Coriolanus, and restore to him the role of supreme giver. His one request —the acme of disinterestedness—is freedom for the poor man who sheltered him and is now his country's prisoner. Co-minius responds with a salute to magnanimity:

> O, well begg'd.
> Were he the butcher of my son, he should
> Be free as is the wind.

> (1.ix.87-89)

But alas, the conception is more impressive than the perform-ance. So self-enclosed, so self-regarding, so truly disinterested is this fantasy of magnanimity that Coriolanus has failed to take note of the man's name. The juxtaposition in this episode of a name received and a name forgotten[10] throws its own ironic light upon the problem which Coriolanus' career will relentlessly explore—the problem of the man within the name. Upon his return to Rome we have one of our rare glimpses of the man within the name of Coriolanus. Much has been made of Coriolanus' greeting to his wife upon his triumphant return to Rome. The mother of course is all to the fore, rejoicing less at her son's return than at the addition to the wounds—cicatrices to show the people—that she and Menenius have exultantly catalogued in anticipation of his arrival. It is in contrast both to the maternal unction with which Volumnia makes a show of not remembering the new name she must call him, and to Menenius' affection and jubilation in response to Coriolanus' teasing ("And live you yet?"),

> A hundred thousand welcomes: I could weep,
> And I could laugh; I am light, and heavy. Welcome!
> A curse begin at very root on's heart,
> That is not glad to see thee!
>
> (II.i.180-183)

that Coriolanus' greeting of his reticent and withdrawn wife makes its effect.

> My gracious silence, hail!
> Wouldst thou have laugh'd had I come coffin'd home,
> That weep'st to see me triumph? Ah! my dear,
> Such eyes the widows in Corioles wear,
> And mothers that lack sons.
>
> (II.i.172-176)

It is a complex impression. Had Coriolanus any sympathetic comprehension of his wife's tears he could hardly have drawn

---

[10] There is a different emphasis in the interpretation of this episode by James L. Calderwood, "Coriolanus: Wordless Meanings and Meaningless Words," *Studies in English Literature*, VI (Spring 1966).

her attention precisely to the widows and orphans of Corioli. What we are therefore to hear in the lines is surely a touch of reproof, springing evidently from disappointment in the one person whom it seems he cannot please by his triumphs.[11] The desire to please is salient, it constitutes the spring of tenderness in his nature, the affection which his mother has exploited and rigidly constrained within the dichotomy of values she has established—the fissure between Mars and Venus, masculine and feminine, force and yielding.

The psychomachia of Act II places squarely before us the first of Coriolanus' dilemmas. He must choose integrity or mastery, since he cannot have them both. Our understanding of this phase of his progress is fed by the impression we have already received concerning the peculiar intensity and stress of his fanatical sincerity and by the impression we currently receive of the massive welcome, both popular and patrician, which is accorded the conquering hero. Our sense of his dilemma is mediated by no extended utterance of his own. What is exhibited is his reluctance to undergo the ordeal of election in the marketplace against the background of the general enthusiasm, itself refracted through the envious account of the tribunes and the panegyric of Cominius, and so allowing for a further play of suggestion and assessment.

As Brutus' sour description indicates, all complaints against him on the part of the populace have been swept out of mind:

> All tongues speak of him, and the bleared sights
> Are spectacled to see him: your prattling nurse
> Into a rapture lets her baby cry
> While she chats him: the kitchen malkin pins

[11] Cf. the view taken by Una Ellis Fermor, *Shakespeare the Dramatist* (London: Methuen, 1961), of a Coriolanus dedicated to an ideal Rome which in reality is everywhere brazen and corrupt and in which only Virgilia preserves for him "some source of peace, silence, and wonder from which the thirst of his spirit can be assuaged" (p. 77).

Her richest lockram 'bout her reechy neck,
Clambering the walls to eye him: stalls, bulks, windows,
Are smother'd up, leads fill'd, and ridges hors'd
With variable complexions, all agreeing
In earnestness to see him: self-shown flamens
Do press among the popular throngs, and puff
To win a vulgar station: our veil'd dames
Commit the war of white and damask in
Their nicely-gawded cheeks to the wanton spoil
Of Phoebus' burning kisses: such a pother,
As if that whatsoever god who leads him
Were slyly crept into his human powers,
And gave him graceful posture.

(ii.i.201-217)

Cominius' encomium to the Senate, during which Coriolanus
is absent, preferring, rudely, to have his head scratched in the
sun when the alarm is struck than idly sit to hear his nothings
monstered (ii.iii.76-78), records the patrician salute to his
abundant possession of that valor which is the chiefest virtue
and deserves the chief office in the state. Cominius' famous
description of the implacable Juggernaut repays close attention for the subtlety with which its suggestion of a godlike
machine advance our emergent perception of Coriolanus.

At sixteen years,
When Tarquin made a head for Rome, he fought
Beyond the mark of others; our then dictator,
Whom with all praise I point at, saw him fight,
When with his Amazonian chin he drove
The bristled lips before him. He bestrid
An o'erpress'd Roman, and i' the consul's view
Slew three opposers: Tarquin's self he met,
And struck him on his knee: in that day's feats,
When he might act the woman in the scene,
He prov'd best man i' the field, and for his meed

Was brow-bound with the oak. His pupil age
Man-enter'd thus, he waxed like a sea,
And in the brunt of seventeen battles since,
He lurch'd all swords of the garland. For this last,
Before and in Corioles, let me say,
I cannot speak him home: he stopp'd the fliers,
And by his rare example made the coward
Turn terror into sport: as weeds before
A vessel under sail, so men obey'd,
And fell below his stem: his sword, death's stamp,
Where it did mark, it took; from face to foot
He was a thing of blood, whose every motion
Was tim'd with dying cries: alone he enter'd
The mortal gate of the city, which he painted
With shunless destiny; aidless came off,
And with a sudden reinforcement struck
Corioles like a planet.

(II.ii.87-114)

The control of connotation in this speech is remarkable. The impression is of a force as terrible as it is irresistible and as inhuman as it is superhuman. The transformation of the beardless boy of sixteen (the Amazonian chin suggestively identifying him with his mother) into the thing of blood, whose every motion is timed with dying cries, obliterates the sentient in the mechanical.[12] This entrance into manhood suggests not a rich maturation of relationship with the world, but the insensate automatism of a robot. The speech thus at once supports and reinforces our evaluation of the deadly mechanism that Volumnia has set in motion, and suggests, by its mesmeric quality, by its larger-than-life images of mass and velocity—of swelling seas, a vessel mowing down weeds, a striking planet—a more than human, a remorseless mo-

[12] Wilson Knight, *The Imperial Theme* (London: Methuen, 1951), was the first to introduce into the criticism of *Coriolanus* the idea that "he is a blind mechanic, metallic thing of pride" (p. 161).

mentum. Heroic supremacy is the natural end to which this monstrous will-in-action strives. But the energy that powers the dynamo meets a counterforce within, another facet of the complex phenomenon which is Coriolanus' pride.

If Coriolanus could take no reward from Cominius and the senators, how much more is it a part that he shall blush in acting

> To brag unto (the commons),—"Thus I did, and thus";—
> Shew them the unaching scars which I should hide,
> As if I had receiv'd them for the hire
> Of their breath only! (II.ii.147-150)

The officers, laying cushions in the Capitol for the conference of senators, reiterate common knowledge concerning Coriolanus' hostility to the people. The second officer, who is a partisan of Coriolanus, defends him against the first officer's reservations; to be refuted by an insight the truth of which we have already observed:

FIRST OFFICER. That's a brave fellow; but he's vengeance proud, and loves not the common people.

SECOND OFFICER. Faith, there hath been many great men that have flattered the people, who ne'er loved them; and there be many that they have loved, they know not wherefore: so that, if they love they know not why, they hate upon no better a ground. Therefore, for Coriolanus neither to care whether they love or hate him manifests the true knowledge he has in their disposition; and out of his noble carelessness lets them plainly see't.

FIRST OFFICER. If he did not care whether he had their love or no, he waved indifferently 'twixt doing them neither good nor harm; but he seeks their hate with greater devotion than they can render it him, and leaves nothing undone that may fully discover him their opposite. Now, to seem to affect the malice and displeasure of the people is as bad as that which he dislikes, to flatter them for their love.

(II.ii.5-23)

That Coriolanus leaves nothing undone that may fully discover him their opposite is, as we have discovered, a strategy of self-preservation. Now he faces a situation in which he must impossibly demean himself, stoop to kowtow to the despised rats of Rome, don the napless vesture of humility, suffer the indignity of begging the people's consent, for his wounds' sake, to the high office which is his natural right. It is to this that his mother wills him:

> I have liv'd
> To see inherited my very wishes,
> And the buildings of my fancy: only
> There's one thing wanting, which I doubt not but
> Our Rome will cast upon thee.
>
> (II.i.194-198)

and against which he demurs:

> Know, good mother,
> I had rather be their servants in my way
> Than sway with them in theirs.
>
> (II.i.198-200)

And in a bitter aside he voices his sense of the impossible choice his situation represents:

> Most sweet voices!
> Better it is to die, better to starve,
> Than crave the hire which first we do deserve.
>
> . . . .
>
> Rather than fool it so,
> Let the high office and the honor go
> To one that would do thus.
>
> (II.iii.111-122)

Yet to let the high office and the honor go is more than his will can encompass: "I am half through: / The one part suffer'd, the other will I do" (ii.iii.122-123).

He cannot renounce the consulship; cannot die, or starve rather, as he momentarily supposes, for he cannot renounce the ambition of greatness. He is caught in a situation which resembles the meeting of irresistible force and immovable object. He must violate himself, betray himself, either way. In the forum scene he contrives to save his face—or his soul— despite the gown of humility, by his open flouting of Hob and Dick in the very act of begging their stinking breath:

> You know the cause, sir, of my standing here.
> THIRD CITIZEN. We do, sir; tell us what hath brought you to't.
> CORIOLANUS. Mine own desert.
> SECOND CITIZEN. Your own desert!
> CORIOLANUS. Ay, not mine own desire.
> THIRD CITIZEN. How! not your own desire!
> CORIOLANUS. No, sir; 'twas never my desire yet to trouble the poor with begging.
> THIRD CITIZEN. You must think, if we give you anything, we hope to gain by you.
> CORIOLANUS. Well then, I pray, your price o' the consulship?
> FIRST CITIZEN. The price is, to ask it kindly.
> CORIOLANUS. Kindly! Sir, I pray, let me ha't: I have wounds to show you, which shall be yours in private. Your good voice, sir; what say you?
> SECOND CITIZEN. You shall ha't, worthy sir.
> CORIOLANUS. A match, sir. There's in all two worthy voices begged. I have your alms: adieu.
>
> (ii.iii.64-81)

The undisguised scorn preserves his self-respect; for the moment he appears to have had his own way. But he has provided the tribunes with their chance to sway the populace against him. In Act III, in the major encounter between these adversaries, their advantage is driven home.

Significantly, the tribunes' challenge of Coriolanus with the announcement of the people's retraction of their vote is prefaced by a brief moment of nostalgia for the battlefield. Lartius brings word of Aufidius brooding in defeat and Coriolanus wishes he had "a cause to seek him there, / To oppose his hatred fully" (III.i.19-20).

This bodes ill for the impending combat with his countrymen, and indeed he is up in arms from the moment Brutus announces that "it will be dangerous to go on." "Have I had children's voices?" he menacingly demands, and in the preliminary clash with the tribunes he gives as good as he gets:

> BRUTUS. The people cry you mock'd them; and of late,
>   When corn was given them gratis, you repin'd;
>   Scandal'd the suppliants for the people, call'd them
>   Time-pleasers, flatterers, foes to nobleness.
> CORIOLANUS. Why, this was known before.
> BRUTUS.   Not to them all.
> CORIOLANUS. Have you inform'd them sithence?
> BRUTUS.   How! I inform them!
> CORIOLANUS. You are like to do such business.
> BRUTUS.   Not unlike,
>   Each way, to better yours.
> CORIOLANUS. Why then should I be consul? By yond clouds,
>   Let me deserve so ill as you, and make me
>   Your fellow tribune.

> (III.i.41-51)

Despite Menenius' attempts to allay the approaching storm, he launches into an impassioned harangue of the patricians for allowing the abrogation of their power to "the mutable rank-scented meynie":

378

> I say again,
> In soothing them we nourish 'gainst our senate
> The cockle of rebellion, insolence, sedition,
> Which we ourselves have plough'd for, sow'd, and scatter'd,
> By mingling them with us, the honour'd number;
> Who lack not virtue, no, nor power, but that
> Which they have given to beggars. (III.i.67-73)

With a certain recovery of dignity Brutus says, "You speak o'
the people / As if you were a god to punish, not / A man
of their infirmity," and Sicinius adds his terrier yapping:
" 'Twere well / We let the people know 't." It is Menenius'
well-meant attempt at palliation, "What, what? his choler?"
repudiated in turn by the headstrong Coriolanus, "Choler! /
Were I as patient as the midnight sleep, / By Jove, 'twould
be my mind," which provokes Sicinius' "It is a mind / That
shall remain a poison where it is, / Not poison any further,"
and so looses the full torrent of Coriolanus' indignation.

> Shall remain!
> Hear you this Triton of the minnows? mark you
> His absolute "shall"? . . .
>   "Shall!"
> O good, but most unwise patricians! why,
> You grave but reckless senators, have you thus
> Given Hydra here to choose an officer,
> That with his peremptory "shall," being but
> The horn and noise o' the monster's, wants not spirit
> To say he'll turn your current in a ditch,
> And make your channel his? If he have power,
> Then vail your ignorance; if none, awake
> Your dangerous lenity. If you are learn'd,
> Be not as common fools; if you are not,
> Let them have cushions by you. You are plebeians
> If they be senators; . . . By Jove himself,

379

> It makes the consuls base; and my soul aches
> To know, when two authorities are up,
> Neither supreme, how soon confusion
> May enter 'twixt the gap of both and take
> The one by th' other.
>
> (III.i.87-111)

The thrust and counterthrust of crescendo with which the conflict is built up produces the inimitable impression of a spontaneous force. Coriolanus' outspoken authoritarianism is political folly, but its vehement eloquence carries conviction as the expression of the whole man, feeling, creed, and conduct running powerfully in a single current. Here is no tongue-tied embarrassment, no gauche incivility, but the unimpeded rhythm and the incisive phrase of an absolute and unreserved commitment.

Coriolanus' rhetoric recalls Menenius' parable of the body politic. But Coriolanus is fearlessly radical. He will not grant the populace even the functionality of limbs and organs. They are a disease, a monstrous excrescence. To him the city is not the populace but its warrior elite alone; these are not Romans though calved in the porch of the Capitol. They are beyond the pale. Therefore he beseeches his fellow patricians to remake the state in his image, and returns to the organic metaphor for the purpose of a ruthless dismembering:

> You . . . that prefer
> A noble life before a long, and wish
> To jump a body with a dangerous physic
> That's sure of death without it,—at once pluck out
> The multitudinous tongue; let them not lick
> The sweet which is their poison. Your dishonour
> Mangles true judgement, and bereaves the state
> Of that integrity which should become 't,
> Not having the power to do the good it would,
> For the'ill which doth control 't.
>
> (III.i.151-160)

Thus, with what is virtually a denial of the statutes of Rome, he renders both the tribunes' accusation of treason and his own single-handed defiance inevitable.

As the people rise against him to seize him and bear him to the Tarpeian rock, he draws the formidable sword with which on fair ground he could beat forty of them, against the whole mutinous rabble; and determines with a fierce elation to die fighting. The state is indeed created in his image at that moment, and it is as much as the senators can do to prevent the outcome they foresee: "to unbuild the city and to lay all flat." Though chaos has been averted by a hair's breadth, Menenius experiences a momentary compunction at his mediating role of go-between and conciliator, and affirms the heroic quality of this uncompromising, unyielding integrity:

His nature is too noble for the world:
He would not flatter Neptune for his trident,
Or Jove for's power to thunder. His heart's his mouth:
What his breast forges, that his tongue must vent;
And, being angry, does forget that ever
He heard the name of death.

(III.i.253-258)

The tribute is the more impressive for his rueful man-of-the-world disapprobation of the inopportune sincerity which has marred Coriolanus' fortunes: "I would they were in Tiber! What the vengeance! / Could he not speak 'em fair?" (III.i. 260-261).

This first stage of the crisis of Act III is followed by the encounter with Volumnia. Still raging, still determined upon a martyr's death if need be:

Let them pull all about mine ears; present me
Death on the wheel, or at wild horses' heels;
Or pile ten hills on the Tarpeian rock,

That the precipitation might down stretch
Below the beam of sight; yet will I still
Be thus to them.

(III.ii.1-6)

he is struck by his mother's divergent view of events.

I muse my mother
Does not approve me further, who was wont
To call them woollen vassals, things created
To buy and sell with groats, to shew bare heads
In congregations, to yawn, be still, and wonder,
When one but of my ordinance stood up
To speak of peace or war.

(III.ii.7-13)

The cross-purposes between them become painfully evident. Volumnia is a practical politician, finding no discrepancy between her pursuit of the glory of Spartan hardihood and the natural prerogatives of power. Whatever tactics will gain the consulship are to her justified precisely on account of her patrician scorn for the multitude, her participation in the very sentiments he has expressed.

Cunningly she appeals to him through the logic of warfare. The principle of justifiable stratagem in war she turns to her own purposes, annulling all distinction between "honor" and "policy":

Because that now it lies you on to speak
To the people; not by your own instruction,
Nor by the matter which your heart prompts you,
But with such words that are but roted in
Your tongue, though but bastards and syllables
Of no allowance to your bosom's truth.
Now, this no more dishonours you at all
Than to take in a town with gentle words,

Which else would put you to your fortune and
The hazard of much blood.
I would dissemble with my nature where
My fortunes and my friends at stake requir'd
I should do so in honour.

(III.ii.52-64)

The political doctrine here expressed is in extreme contradiction to Coriolanus' passion for utter candor, but he is clearly not possessed of the intellectual agility which could counter the specious logic of her "honorable" dissembling.

Volumnia's mind is marvelously portrayed. She is so invincibly justified in her own eyes, so unassailably confident, that she can allow herself to be carried away in an imaginative enactment of what she quite blandly acknowledges as "fawning":

I prithee now, my son,
Go to them, with this bonnet in thy hand;
And thus far having stretch'd it, here be with them,
Thy knee bussing the stones, for in such business
Action is eloquence, and the eyes of th' ignorant
More learned than the ears, waving thy head,
Which often, thus, correcting thy stout heart,
Now humble as the ripest mulberry
That will not hold the handling: or say to them,
Thou art their soldier, and being bred in broils
Hast not the soft way which, thou dost confess,
Were fit for thee to use as they to claim,
In asking their good loves; but thou wilt frame
Thyself, forsooth, hereafter theirs, so far
As thou hast power and person.

(III.ii.72-86)

The unconsciously comic image of the mulberry strikes wonderfully upon a sensibility attuned to the imagery of hard,

383

metallic, rigid resistance, and renders wryly ironic Coriolanus'
helplessness to resist, though his own inherent honesty is in
deep rebellion:

> Must I go shew them my unbarb'd sconce? must I
> With my base tongue give to my noble heart
> A lie that it must bear? Well, I will do't:
> Yet were there but this single plot to lose,
> This mold of Marcius, they to dust should grind it
> And throw't against the wind. To the marketplace!
> You have put me now to such a part which never
> I shall discharge to the life.
>
> (III.ii.99-106)

Yet he cannot do it. He envisages the part he must perform
in an imaginative rehearsal of his own so vivid as to be physically apprehended:

> Away, my disposition, and possess me
> Some harlot's spirit! My throat of war be turn'd,
> Which quired with my drum, into a pipe
> Small as an eunuch, or the virgin voice
> That babies lulls asleep! the smiles of knaves
> Tent in my cheeks, and school-boys' tears take up
> The glasses of my sight! a beggar's tongue
> Make motion through my lips, and my arm'd knees,
> Who bow'd but in my stirrup, bend like his
> That hath receiv'd an alms!
>
> (III.ii.111-120)

And from the vision his soul revolts. He cannot, as she so
easily can, dissever his inmost commitment from his conduct,
and play the fraud and hypocrite,

> Lest I surcease to honor mine own truth,
> And by my body's action teach my mind
> A most inherent baseness.
>
> (III.ii.121-123)

384

But Volumnia defeats him. She is "mankind," as the tribune says, but she knows the time-honored woman's method of getting her way: the pretense of permission which masks an ultimatum. She has as high a sense of dignity as he has, she claims, and is as unafraid of consequences. His pride, which she now calls vice, she disowns. "Do as thou list," she says; "Thy valiantness was mine, thou suck'dst it from me, / But owe thy pride thyself" (III.ii.129-130).

His surrender is acutely, intimately humiliating. His mother's ambition for him is that he take the high office she believes is his due. Her methods are those of the nursery. Though reason and order support the action itself, the self-prostitution we perceive that it entails for Coriolanus sways our sympathy in the direction of unreason—of the passion which is the mainspring of Coriolanus' integrity. Therefore it is with something of Coriolanus' own relief that we witness his response to the trap Sicinius has laid for him.

Sicinius has shrewdly judged the accusation of treason to be calculated to put Coriolanus beside himself—and being chafed he cannot be reined again to temperance. And indeed, to be accused by these insolent wretches of treason, he whose service to Rome is immeasurable, who has even been prepared against every instinct and inclination to speak them fair, is the proverbial red rag to a bull:

> The fires i' the lowest hell fold-in the people!
> Call me their traitor! Thou injurious tribune!
> Within thine eyes sat twenty thousand deaths,
> In thy hands clutch'd as many millions, in
> Thy lying tongue both numbers, I would say
> "Thou liest" unto thee with a voice as free
> As I do pray the gods.
>
> (III.iii.68-74)

The fulsome pair ("since he hath / Serv'd well for Rome") reduce Coriolanus to spluttering fury, but we cannot but perceive the measure of his release, of the relief of a restoration to himself with which, now the die is cast, he resumes his embattled defiance:

> Let them pronounce the steep Tarpeian death,
> Vagabond exile, flaying, pent to linger
> But with a grain a day, I would not buy
> Their mercy at the price of one fair word,
> Nor check my courage for what they can give,
> To have't with saying, "Good morrow."
>
> (III.iii.88-93)

Paradoxically, with his fortune in ruins, banished from his native country, in the total failure of his enterprise, he is liberated. In the passionate vehemence of his final vituperation is freely expressed the deepest need of his being:

> You common cry of curs! whose breath I hate
> As reek o' the rotten fens, whose loves I prize
> As the dead carcasses of unburied men
> That do corrupt my air, I banish you;
> And here remain with your uncertainty!
> Let every feeble rumor shake your hearts!
> Your enemies, with nodding of their plumes,
> Fan you into despair! Have the power still
> To banish your defenders; till at length
> Your ignorance, which finds not till it feels,
> Making but reservation of yourselves,
> Still your own foes, deliver you as most
> Abated captives to some nation
> That won you without blows! Despising
> For you the city, thus I turn my back:
> There is a world elsewhere.
>
> (III.iii.120-135)

The glow of a liberation from an intolerable constraint is still upon him when he bids farewell to his wife, mother, and friends at the gates of Rome at the beginning of Act IV. It is a new man who is suddenly divulged to us, a Coriolanus who is self-possessed, composed, ready in his sympathies, resolute in adversity. He has a good word for each, encouraging Volumnia with her own stoic precepts and a reminder of her old indomitability, which strikes a perfect balance between deference and authority; acknowledging with affection the friendship of Menenius; confidently assuring them that he'll "do well yet." It is a revelation. Our impression that the role of solitary and formidable wanderer is peculiarly welcome to him is overwhelming. "Tell these sad women," he tells Cominius,

> 'Tis fond to wail inevitable strokes
> As 'tis to laugh at 'em. My mother, you wot well
> My hazards still have been your solace; and
> Believ't no lightly, though I go alone,
> Like to a lonely dragon, that his fen
> Makes fear'd and talk'd of more than seen, your son
> Will or exceed the common or be caught
> With cautelous baits and practice.
>
> (IV.i.25-33)

We note, however, the admission—fruit of bitter experience not yet completely assimilated—that trickery is one form of vicissitude which *can* overcome him. And the elated current of feeling meets a check in Volumnia's response:

> My first son,
> Whither wilt thou go? Take good Cominius
> With thee awhile: determine on some course,
> More than a wild exposure to each chance
> That starts i' the way before thee.
>
> (IV.i.34-37)

More than cross-purposes or a discrepancy of view is revealed by this subtly conceived dialogue. His inarticulate cry "O the gods!" suggests that her maternal protectiveness wounds an unassuaged sensitivity to tutelage which is entangled in the fabric of their relationship and which recent events, despite his daring defiance, have done little to dispel. His very inarticulateness suggests the presence of a frustration the more thwarting as it is inexpressible, perhaps inadmissible. Nevertheless he rallies, rejects Cominius' companionship and with it the idea of possible repeal, and leaves them with a final assurance of resolute constancy:

> I pray you, come.
> While I remain above the ground you shall
> Hear from me still; and never of me aught
> But what is like me formerly.
>
> (IV.i.50-53)

This reading of the parting scene is able to account for the placing of what follows. Volumnia returns to Rome to engage in bitter recriminations with the tribunes. To Menenius' invitation to sup with her she replies:

> Anger's my meat; I sup upon myself,
> And so shall starve with feeding. Come, let's go.
> Leave this faint puling and lament as I do,
> In anger, Juno-like.
>
> (IV.ii.50-53)

She is, as we have more than once had occasion to notice, a formidable lady, and her influence upon her son is profound. Since the relationship of mother to son is at the heart of Shakespeare's fable, her every appearance reflects in some way upon Coriolanus. It is at this point no more than an anticipatory suggestion, but the sequel will confirm that he too, supping with no one, sups upon himself, in a long slow anger which nothing but Rome afire will appease. It is a similar preparatory function that the scene between the Roman turncoat and the Volscian fulfills, reminding us that "the fittest time to corrupt a man's wife is when she's fallen out with her husband." These indirections take the place of any direct utterance on the part of Coriolanus, thus playing their part in the structuring of our response to the profound change which his soliloquy before Antium registers.

Gone is the near-gaiety of his fortitude at parting. Gone is the elation with which he embraced his outlaw fortune and sought a world elsewhere. The speech is curiously flat, passionless, as if passion had died with his departure from his birthplace, source of the love-hate ambivalence which kept him in unceasing tension, through which he strove to find himself and from which he strove to free himself.

It is constancy, self-consistency itself, which he now rejects. No one has been true to him; it is a question whether he has even been true to himself. The very principle of such truth now appears to him delusory, of less moment than "some trick not worth an egg":

> O world, thy slippery turns! Friends now fast sworn,
> Whose double bosoms seems to wear one heart,
> Whose hours, whose bed, whose meal and exercise,
> Are still together, who twin, as 'twere, in love
> Inseparable, shall within this hour,
> On a dissension of a doit, break out
> To betterest enmity: so, fellest foes,
> Whose passions and whose plots have broke their sleep
> To take the one the other, by some chance,
> Some trick not worth an egg, shall grow dear friends
> And interjoin their issues. So with me:
> My birth-place hate I, and my love's upon
> This enemy town.[13]

(iv.iv.12-24)

---

[13] It is interesting to compare Hamlet's "even for an eggshell" in the "How all occasions" soliloquy, which occurs at the exactly equivalent point in the tragic progress.

He is lost indeed, with no inner resources to sustain him in his solitary state. Lacking the opposition within Rome against which to define himself, he lacks all power of self-definition. Hollow and adrift he seeks out his ancient enemy, to place in his hands, in effect, the determination of his fate: "if he slay me, / He does fair justice; if he give me way, / I'll do his country service" (iv.iv.24-26).

Nowhere in the tragedies is the defeat of the protagonist, his retreat from his former values, which he has been unable to sustain or which have proved unable to sustain him, more concisely rendered. The darkness of his spirit is given in one striking metaphor, in which he sees all of nature under the aspect of his own bleak, withering experience. He has been, he tells the Antium servants, in "the city of kites and crows," thus assimilating the natural world to the predatory and carrion body of Rome that corrupted his air. So, homeless, he sells his services to the highest bidder, to a city not his own, seeking recognition denied him by his countrymen.

Once again, in this paradoxical play in which losses appear as gains, all appears to go extraordinarily well with him. From the moment he turns his back upon Rome honors are once again showered upon him. The scene with the servants at Aufidius' house enacts the transformation of the ragged stranger once more into a "son and heir to Mars; set at upper end o' the table; no question asked him by any of the senators, but they stand bald before him" (iv.v.197-199). Turned mercenary and renegade,

> He is their god: he leads them like a thing
> Made by some other deity than Nature,
> That shapes man better; and they follow him,
> Against us brats, with no less confidence
> Than boys pursuing summer butterflies,
> Or butchers killing flies.
>
> (iv.vi.91-96)

Even eros, still appropriately transvestite, dances attendance upon him; he is made a mistress of by the general himself:

> . . . here I clip
> The anvil of my sword, and do contest
> As hotly and as nobly with thy love
> As ever in ambitious strength I did
> Contend against thy valour. Know thou first,
> I lov'd the maid I married; never man
> Sigh'd truer breath; but that I see thee here,
> Thou noble thing, more dances my rapt heart
> Than when I first my wedded mistress saw
> Bestride my threshold.
>
> (IV.V.III-II9)

Coriolanus' course appears to be triumphantly vindicated. Yet there are ominous signs. The fickle favor of the servants of Antium, persuading themselves that they knew at once there was something special about the poorly clad stranger they were abusing a moment before, serves the familiar purpose of fourth-act irony, reminding us how easily hide-and-seek can be played by a man within a name, and requiring of us a complex assessment:

SECOND SERVINGMAN. Nay, I knew by his face that there was something in him: he had, sir, a kind of face, methought, —I cannot tell how to term it.

FIRST SERVINGMAN. He had so; looking as it were,—would I were hanged but I thought there was more in him than I could think.

SECOND SERVINGMAN. So did I, I'll be sworn. He is simply the rarest man i' the world.

FIRST SERVINGMAN. I think he is; but a greater soldier than he, you wot one.

SECOND SERVINGMAN. Who? my master?

FIRST SERVINGMAN. Nay, it's no matter for that.

SECOND SERVINGMAN. Worth six on him.

FIRST SERVINGMAN. Nay, not so neither, but I take him to be the greater soldier.

SECOND SERVINGMAN. Faith, look you, one cannot tell how to say that: for the defense of a town our general is excellent.

(IV.v.157-174)

Coriolanus' very success, we perceive, is the petard with which he will be hoist. The charisma which is carrying Coriolanus to supremacy in Antium, which will make him to Rome, Aufidius thinks, like the osprey to the fish, who takes it by sovereignty of nature, arouses in Aufidius a corrosive jealousy:

AUFIDIUS. Do they still fly to th' Roman?
LIEUTENANT. I do not know what witchcraft's in him; but
  Your soldiers use him as the grace 'fore meat,
  Their talk at table, and their thanks at end;
  And you are darken'd in this action, sir,
  Even by your own.

(IV.vii.1-5)

Coriolanus' unawareness embraces more than the mines beneath the surface of success. He knows nothing, as indeed he has never known, of give and take, of the realities of need and power, the knowledge of which is available to the wry wisdom of the common man. Peace, says the First Servingman, makes men hate one another. And his companion assents:

THIRD SERVINGMAN. Reason: because they then less need one another. The wars for my money. I hope to see Romans as cheap as Volscians. They are rising, they are rising.

(IV.v.236-239)

Aufidius, reviewing Coriolanus' strange career, wonders what made so noble a servant of Rome feared, hated, and banished. Whether it was pride, or defect of judgment, or a nature

Not to be other than one thing, not moving
From the casque to the cushion, but commanding peace
Even with the same austerity and garb
As he controll'd the war. . . .

(IV.vii.42-45)

Aufidius does not know. But he knows, as do his servants, that "our virtues lie in the interpretation of the times." It is the lack of this practical, adaptable, worldly knowledge that delivers Coriolanus into the hands of his treacherous lover-like foe; but the recognitions which his downfall will produce for him are upon a plane of conception far beyond the reach of any of his lovers or his foes.

What is first of all exhibited in Act v is the new face of Coriolanus toward the Rome from which he has severed himself. Cominius, once his friend of noble touch, he refuses to receive, repudiating the honorific title received at his hand:

Coriolanus

He would not answer to; forbad all names;
He was a kind of nothing, titleless,
Till he had forg'd himself a name o' the fire
Of burning Rome.

(V.i.11-15)

The new name which he will forge in the fire of burning Rome is aptly symbolic of the phoenix destruction and renewal Coriolanus wills for himself. Nothing, no tie, is to stand in his way. His personal friends are now the recipients of the vengeful, wounding arrogance he once vented upon such as Sicinius and Brutus:

. . . his answer to me was,

He could not stay to pick them in a pile
Of noisome musty chaff: he said 'twas folly
For one poor grain or two, to leave unburnt
And still to nose the offense.

(V.i.24-28)

393

Begged by the cowed and apologetic tribunes to intervene, Menenius hopes, from his own experience as *bon vivant*, that a good dinner might set all right and put his sometime friend and adoptive son into warmer humor. But Cominius warns him in a significant image: Coriolanus' chagrin, his sense of injured merit, is "gaoler to his pity." He sits in gold, resistant glittering metal, his eye "red as 'twould burn Rome." Irony thickens as Menenius goes on his fruitless errand:

> I tell thee, fellow,
> Thy general is my lover: I have been
> The book of his good acts, whence men have read
> His fame unparallel'd, haply amplified.
>
> (v.ii.13-16)

He has indeed been Coriolanus' friend, faithful and just to him, the sounding-board of his praises. But the general has a new lover and knows not wife, mother, child. To Aufidius he takes pride in his adamantine temper while Menenius is sent packing, to the jeers of the watch.

We realize what Coriolanus is doing when we hear him confess to Aufidius the feeling that he concealed from Menenius:

> This last old man,
> Whom with a crack'd heart I have sent to Rome,
> Lov'd me above the measure of a father;
> Nay, godded me indeed. Their latest refuge
> Was to send him. . . .
>
> (v.iii.8-11)

He is proving himself to himself as much as to the Volscians. Disavowing his inheritance as native Roman patrician and patriot, he will remake himself as conqueror, self-created, self-determined. He is trying his utmost strength in this duel with the motherland, matrix of his being. And he is tense. The shout within which heralds the family embassage finds him flexing his resolution: "Shall I be tempted to infringe my vow / In the same time 'tis made? I will not" (v.iii.20-21). And then he faces Rome's deputation.

> My wife comes foremost; then the honour'd mold
> Wherein this trunk was fram'd, and in her hand
> The grandchild to her blood. But out, affection!
> All bond and privilege of nature break!
> Let it be virtuous to be obstinate.
> What is that curt'sy worth? or those doves' eyes,
> Which can make gods forsworn? I melt, and am not
> Of stronger earth than others. My mother bows;
> As if Olympus to a molehill should
> In supplication nod; and my young boy
> Hath an aspect of intercession, which
> Great Nature cries, "Deny not." Let the Volsces
> Plough Rome, and harrow Italy; I'll never
> Be such a gosling to obey instinct, but stand,
> As if a man were author of himself
> And knew no other kin.
>
> (v.iii.22-37)

The drama of the encounter is intensified in the highest degree by the thrice-repeated situation. Twice before his mother has prevailed upon him and bent his will to hers. But now the stakes are higher and his commitment graver and deeper. Then he was caught in the countercompulsions of his mother's domination over him and his festering, frustrated integrity. It is still pride of consistency and natural affection which struggle within him, but now his revenge represents a perversity of megalomaniac proportions, and surrender of it will cost him no less than everything. He will know himself totally defeated, bereft of any shred of autonomy, broken in spirit, if he yields. Yet for a moment, reckless of consequences, he yields, lets love and the sweetness of reunion have their way:

> Like a dull actor now,
> I have forgot my part and I am out,
> Even to a full disgrace. Best of my flesh,
> Forgive my tyranny; but do not say
> For that "Forgive our Romans." O, a kiss
> Long as my exile, sweet as my revenge!
> Now, by the jealous queen of heaven, that kiss
> I carried from thee, dear, and my true lip
> Hath virgin'd it e'er since.
>
> (v.iii.40-48)

Though instinct is a gosling and revenge is sweet, neverthe-less in ritual succession he kisses his wife, kneels to his mother, greets graciously the noble sister of Publicola and prays the god of soldiers, in poignant self-projection, to inform his son with nobleness that he may prove

> To shame unvulnerable, and stick i' the wars
> Like a great sea-mark, standing every flaw,
> And saving those that eye thee!
>
> (v.iii.73-75)

He is the image of a Roman paterfamilias at the very moment when he has renounced great Nature and determined to stand as if a man were author of himself and knew no other kin. He warns them that he has sworn, that he is firm, that it will be useless to attempt to allay his rages and revenges with their colder reasons. Volumnia's reasons, however, are not cold.

It is in the name of the "instinct" that melts him that she puts her case and assures him of her own intrepid purpose should he march to assault his country. It is the bond of kin, the center and the nucleus of his and of any man's emotional nature, that she invokes:

> . . . since that thy sight, which should
> Make our eyes flow with joy, hearts dance with comforts,
> Constrains them to weep, and shake with fear and sorrow;

Making the mother, wife, and child to see
The son, the husband, and the father, tearing
His country's bowels out.

(v.iii.98-103)

Virgilia seconds her with the boy, his name living to time; but it is the boy himself, his father's image and here his greatest adversary, most diabolical of Shakespeare's innocents, who delivers the *coup de grâce*: "A' shall not tread on me: / I'll run away till I am bigger, but then I'll fight."

It is with consummate judgment that Shakespeare, in this stiffly monolithic play, has reserved his characteristic pathos for this crucial meeting. The pathos regularly mediates our awareness of that norm of human happiness or well-being which the inexorable tragic progress has rendered forfeit. Here, concentrated at this moment and operating directly upon Coriolanus himself, the pathos of these encounters effects the recognitions he is incapable of uttering. The boy, in his childish defiance a naïve replica of his father, channels our compassion for both father and son. The effect upon Coriolanus himself is to wrest from him the bitter admission of the mastery over him of that gosling instinct he has so long denied, and would still escape if he could:

Not of a woman's tenderness to be,
Requires not child nor woman's face to see.
I have sat too long.

(v.iii.129-131)

These are the last words he speaks till the end of the episode.

She is a clever woman, Volumnia, and the situation as she perceives him silent and adamant brings out her shrewdest resources of argument. It is not his dishonor that she requests, but the greater honor that will accrue to a great name through a political solution—a reconciliation of Roman and Volsci. He has affected the fine strains of honor; does he think it honorable for a noble man still to remember wrongs? She tries recriminations: "There's no man in the world more bound to's mother, yet here he lets me prate like one i' th' stocks." She presents herself, perhaps sees herself—with her flair for being carried away by an image—as the motherly hen, touching in her self-effacing anxiety for her single chick, and recipient of nothing but ingratitude for her pains. We blink at the astounding accusation:

> Thou hast never in thy life
> Shew'd thy dear mother any courtesy;
> When she, poor hen, fond of no second brood,
> Has clock'd thee to the wars, and safely home
> Loaden with honour.
>
> (v.iii.160-164)

She shames him with her knees; she excoriates his pride; she flourishes the child; and finally, still unable to wrest a response from him, she resorts to the weapon that has never failed, and the scathing lash of her displeasure draws blood:

> Come, let us go:
> This fellow had a Volscian to his mother:
> His wife is in Corioles, and his child
> Like him by chance. Yet give us our dispatch:
> I am hush't until our city be a-fire,
> And then I'll speak a little.
>
> (v.iii.177-182)

The Folio's stage direction tells us that Coriolanus "holds her by the hand, silent" before he at last speaks. Throughout the scene it is the pattern of speech and silence, utterance and the suppression of utterance—the ritual greetings whose very restraining formality is expressive of intensely heightened emotions, the forensic display of Volumnia's rhetoric, the hiatus of Coriolanus' withdrawal into himself—which establishes the profound difference between this encounter and its predecessors, superficially so similar. Coriolanus' silence concentrates within the depths of its reticence the entire intense inner drama. It is our cue to the perception that Volumnia's persuasions miss the mark, but that the mark has been struck for her in a way that she does not comprehend. It is not by her authority, nor by her appeals to virtue, honor and filial duty that Coriolanus has been moved. He is moved by what his honesty compels him to recognize as none of these things. His entire relationship with his mother is under agonizing review in these tense moments. Between them now, like a two-edged sword to save or to destroy, is that woman's tenderness which Volumnia's domination and his own martial creed have repressed and repudiated, and which he knows himself unable to deny.

He is defeated in his march upon Rome, and more gravely and intrinsically defeated in his aspiration to stand alone, free, above humanity. Coriolanus resigns his passion for revenge but he does not speak. He is silent, we must infer, because there is no way he can validate his action or make himself intelligible even to himself. Therefore it is in incommunicable anguish that he finally speaks, renounces "true wars" for "convenient peace," and appeals in fumbling uncertainty to Aufidius for moral confirmation:

> O mother, mother!
> What have you done? Behold, the heavens do ope,
> The gods look down, and this unnatural scene
> They laugh at. O my mother, mother! O!
> You have won a happy victory to Rome;
> But, for your son, believe it, O, believe it,
> Most dangerously you have with him prevail'd,
> If not most mortal to him. But let it come.
> Aufidius, though I cannot make true wars,
> I'll frame convenient peace. Now, good Aufidius,
> Were you in my stead, would you have heard
> A mother less, or granted less, Aufidius?
>
> (v.iv.182-193)

In a situation thus fraught with ruinous paradox (to which the multiple ironies of "unnatural" alert us), every course of action represents a contrary temptation to self-betrayal. He determines, fighting to keep his head above water, to return to Corioli with Aufidius, and not to Rome with the triumphant ladies. This decision requires more than a moment's consideration, for it is by no means simply necessitated by the action. As the scenes in Rome have made us amply aware, he could have returned to Rome, her deliverer rather than her conqueror, and reaped the benefits of power manifested at its most magnanimous.[14] But being what he is he cannot barter his integrity, his sense of his own inner consistency, however desperately undermined and invaded, for what would be to him spurious honor, a false acclaim, since in his inmost being he would know it to be undeserved. He cannot accept mercy as a supreme value and ultimate sanction, for no such possibility exists within his fanatic's ethic of self-assertive force; nor pity, for pity he knows only as a milder form of contempt. Aufidius, watching, understands, and he understands his opportunity:

AUFIDIUS. [*Aside.*] I am glad thou hast set thy mercy and
thy honour
At difference in thee: out of that I'll work
Myself a former fortune.

(v.iv.200-202)

Coriolanus chooses Corioli, chooses exile as the seal and guarantee of his proud, hard, solitary independence, a "subsistence"

[14] D. A. Traversi, *Shakespeare: The Roman Plays* (London: Hollis Carter, 1963), takes a completely opposing view, which blunts the tragic point and which, I believe, is in any case untenable in view of the scenes in Rome: "Having agreed to make peace with Rome, his recent past prevents him from returning there; and so he must back with an Aufidius who is now ready to discard him" (p. 282).

which is uninfected by the bonds and ties and affections of
his nature:

No more infected with my country's love
Than when I parted hence; but still subsisting
Under your great command.

(v.vi.71-73)

The decision costs him all that has been so impressively represented as most dear to him—his mother, wife, and child. It
also costs him, in the event, his life, for it is his fatal error,[15]
the more powerfully ironic in that the intention it represents,
the idea it embodies, is the most painful and the most arduous
bid for freedom Coriolanus has ever made.

We are invited to contemplate what is at stake through the
ironic juxtaposition of two opposing perspectives. Menenius,
ignorant as yet of the turn taken, expresses his bitter conviction that Volumnia's mission will prove fruitless. "Is't possible," asks Sicinius, "that so short a time can alter the condition of a man?" Menenius replies:

> There is a differency between a grub and a butterfly; yet
> your butterfly was a grub. This Marcius is grown from
> man to dragon: he has wings; he's more than a creeping
> thing.
>
> SICINIUS. He loved his mother dearly.
> MENENIUS. So did he me; and he no more remembers his
> mother now than an eight-year-old horse. The tartness of
> his face sours ripe grapes: when he walks, he moves like
> an engine, and the ground shrinks before his treading: he
> is able to pierce a corslet with his eye; talks like a knell,
> and his hum is a battery. He sits in his state, as a thing
> made for Alexander. What he bids be done is finished

---

[15] I am indebted to a colleague, Mrs. Efrat Ben-Menachem, whose
insight into this final phase of the play enabled me thus to identify
the definitive fatal error of Coriolanus.

with his bidding. He wants nothing of a god but eternity
and a heaven to throne in. . . . there is no more mercy in
him than there is milk in a male tiger; that shall our
poor city find.

(v.iv.11-30)

The sun dances in Rome when Menenius' estimate is proved
wrong. But in Corioli the mercy of the male tiger takes on a
different complexion in the mirror of Aufidius' jealous envy,
and becomes that from which he will manufacture his enemy's
overthrow:

At a few drops of women's rheum, which are
As cheap as lies, he sold the blood and labour
Of our great action.

(v.vi.45-47)

The dramaturgy here is reminiscent of the flanking of
Hamlet by his fellow avengers Laertes and Fortinbras in the
final stages of the play, and the flanking of Lear by his fellows
in adversity, Edgar and Gloucester. The contrasting juxtapositions serve to bring out and define the specifically tragic
experience of the protagonist. Here the contradictory bias of
both Menenius' prediction and Aufidius' condemnation of
Coriolanus' action underlines the absolute individuality of the
protagonist, dramatizes the inviolable, unencompassable reality of a single, complex, sentient individual, doomed, by a
process of tragedy beyond Polonius' ken, if true to himself,
to be false to other men.

The final turns of the catastrophe therefore possess an extraordinary pure tragic poignance, reversal and anagnorisis
producing in their simultaneity, as Aristotle knew, the greatest degree of pity and terror.

Coriolanus returns at the head of the Volscian soldiers to
offer their city peace with honor, and to offer them his own
soldier's service. He is met yet again by the blunt accusation of

treason. The cruelly calculated insult of Aufidius' taunt, "Name not the god, thou boy of tears" (v.vi.100), exposes the pity in the name of which he sacrificed his revenge and the compassion which moved him as contemptible effeminacy—a twist of rotten silk; and it turns to mockery and derision the hard-won, incommunicable self-emancipation of his choice of Corioli.

Coriolanus is shocked beyond words, thrown back into his characteristic posture of defiant, excessive self-assertion. Called "Marcius," he claims again the name which honored and shackled him, which twice he attempted to forget, to cast like a snake's skin. Forced to scold, as he puts it, for the first time in Corioli, for the first time ever, it seems to him, so new a person has he felt himself to be, he flings his proud, solitary exploit in their faces:

> Cut me to pieces, Volsces; men and lads,
> Stain all your edges on me. "Boy! false hound!
> If you have writ your annals true, 'tis there,
> That like an eagle in a dove-coat, I
> Flutter'd your Volscians in Corioles:
> Alone I did it. Boy!
>
> (v.vi.110-115)

And Aufidius springs his trap.

>   Why, noble lords,
> Will you be put in mind of his blind fortune,
> Which was your shame, by this unholy braggart,
> 'Fore your own eyes and ears?
>
> (v.vi.115-118)

Despite the attempted intervention of one fair-minded Volscian lord, he is lynched by the mob which a moment before had enthusiastically acclaimed him. It is an unimagined and atrocious culmination of a long agon between self and world, the unremitting struggle for integrity of being. Its horror articulates what is perhaps the bleakest reach of Shakespeare's tragic conception: the pursuit of truth to the self—the heroic attribute—is treason to the world, and the world will exact its inexorable penalties. Therefore, though he is given no dying speech in which to move us with the making-up of his accounts, the fall of this harsh, unyielding, unenlightened man is as searing in the end as is the tragedy of any of Shakespeare's larger spirits.

INDEX